An Introduction to Bilir

The study of bilingualism and all of its aspects—from theory and models to social approaches and their practical applications—form the cornerstone of the second edition of this work. The chapters cover the latest advancements in the domains of psycholinguistics, neuroscience, creativity, and executive functioning. Contributions, new to this edition, offer the reader the most up-to-date research on lifespan and developmental issues. The work also provides insights into how human language is processed by all, not just by bilingual and multilingual speakers. This text is ideal for senior undergraduate and graduate courses in psycholinguistics and the psychology of language, especially those with an emphasis on bilingualism or second language learning.

Jeanette Altarriba is Professor of Psychology and Collins Fellow at the University at Albany, State University of New York, where she directs the Cognition and Language Laboratory. She earned her MA and PhD in cognitive psychology from Vanderbilt University and has published extensively in the fields of bilingualism, language, memory, and emotion. She also serves as Vice Provost and Dean for Undergraduate Education.

Roberto R. Heredia is Regents Professor at Texas A&M International University where he directs the Cognitive Neuroscience Laboratory. He earned his PhD in experimental psychology from the University of California, Santa Cruz, and has published in the fields of bilingualism, figurative language processing, and evolutionary psychology.

An Introduction to Bilingualism
Principles and Processes

Second Edition

**Edited by Jeanette Altarriba
and Roberto R. Heredia**

NEW YORK AND LONDON

Second edition published 2018
by Routledge
711 Third Avenue, New York, NY 10017

and by Routledge
2 Park Square, Milton Park, Abingdon, Oxon, OX14 4RN

Routledge is an imprint of the Taylor & Francis Group, an informa business

First edition published by Routledge 2008

Library of Congress Cataloging-in-Publication Data
Names: Altarriba, Jeanette, 1964- editor. | Heredia, Roberto R., 1964- editor.
Title: An introduction to bilingualism: principles and processes / [edited by] Jeanette Altarriba and Roberto R. Heredia.
Description: Second edition. | New York, NY: Routledge, [2017] | Originally published as An Introduction to bilingualism, 2008.
Identifiers: LCCN 2017016941| ISBN 9781848725850 (hard back: alk. paper) | ISBN 9781848725867 (paper back: alk. paper) | ISBN 9781315101682 (ebook)
Classification: LCC P115 .A46 2017 | DDC 404/.2–dc23
LC record available at https://lccn.loc.gov/2017016941

ISBN: 978-1-84872-585-0 (hbk)
ISBN: 978-1-84872-586-7 (pbk)
ISBN: 978-1-315-10168-2 (ebk)

Typeset in Times New Roman
by Deanta Global Publishing Services, Chennai, India

In memory of Mercedes Arsenia Tutusaus
de Altarriba – Jeanette Altarriba

For Andrea and Michelle – Roberto R. Heredia

Contents

Contributors

Ashley Adams (Ch. 17), *Doctoral Candidate*, Department of Speech and Hearing Science, Arizona State University

Jeanette Altarriba (Chs. 1, 4), *Professor of Psychology and Vice Provost and Dean for Undergraduate Education*, University at Albany, State University of New York

Beatriz Barragan (Ch. 17), *Doctoral Candidate*, Department of Speech and Hearing Science, Arizona State University

Angélique M. Blackburn (Ch. 6), *Assistant Professor of Psychology*, Texas A&M International University

Barbara E. Bullock (Ch. 13), *Professor of French Linguistics*, University of Texas

Anna B. Cieślicka (Ch. 3), *Associate Professor of Psychology*, Texas A&M International University

Cynthia García Coll (Ch. 12), *Associate Director of Institutional Center of Scientific Research*, Carlos Albizu University

Vivian Cook (Ch. 15), *Emeritus Professor of Applied Linguistics*, Newcastle University

Kees de Bot (Ch. 5), *Chair of Applied Linguistics*, Faculteit der Letteren, Rijksniversiteit Groningen

Susan Gass (Ch. 16), *University Distinguished Professor*, Michigan State University

Margo Glew (Ch. 16), *Coordinator of Global Initiatives and Global Educators Cohort Program*, Michigan State University

Roberto R. Heredia (Chs. 1, 3), *Regents Professor*, Department of Psychology and Communication, Texas A&M International University

Nienke Houtzager (Ch. 5), *Lecturer*, Department of Applied Linguistics, Rijksuniversiteit Groningen

Anatoliy V. Kharkhurin (Ch. 8), *Professor of Psychology*, American University of Sharjah

Dalia Magaña (Ch. 14), *Assistant Professor*, School of Social Sciences, Humanities & Arts, University of California-Merced

Viorica Marian (Ch. 2), *Ralph and Jean Sundin Endowed Professor of Communication Sciences and Disorders*, Northwestern University

Elena Nicoladis (Ch. 10), *Professor of Psychology*, University of Alberta

Kenneth R. Paap (Ch. 9), *Professor of Psychology*, San Francisco State University

Viviana Padilla-Martínez (Ch. 12), *Staff Psychologist*, Lee County Health Care Centre, Bay Pines VA Healthcare System

Flavia C. Peréa (Ch. 12), *Director*, Mindich Program for Engaged Scholarship, Harvard University

M. Adelaida Restrepo (Ch. 17), *Professor*, Department of Speech and Hearing Science, Arizona State University

Crystal J. Robinson (Ch. 4), *Master's Degree Recipient*, Department of Psychology, University at Albany, State University of New York

Lisa Smithson (Ch. 10), *Doctoral Candidate*, Department of Psychology, University of Alberta

Almeida Jacqueline Toribio (Ch. 13), *Professor of Linguistics*, University of Texas

Jyotsna Vaid (Ch. 7), *Professor of Psychology*, Texas A&M University

Luis A. Vega (Ch. 11), *Professor of Psychology*, California State University

Preface to the First Edition

We take great joy and honor in presenting *An Introduction to Bilingualism: Principles and Processes* to students, teachers of bilingualism, and the scientific community. This volume is intended for use in undergraduate courses and undergraduate seminars such as *The Psychology of Bilingualism* and *Second Language Acquisition*, as well as graduate courses in psycholinguistics with an emphasis on bilingualism or second language learning. It is our hope that this volume provides the undergraduate and graduate student with a general overview of the methods and theories used in the broad domain of bilingualism. Indeed, this interdisciplinary approach is reflected in the various topics covered in this book, ranging from early childhood intellectual development to the educational and social-cognitive challenges, if any, faced by the "normal" and aging bilingual, as well as the maturing bilingual brain. Although other excellent and seminal introductory textbooks (e.g., Grosjean, 1982) are available, these books were in need of updating and the inclusion of new developing areas of bilingual inquiry that comprise cognitive aging (Schrauf, Chapter 5, current volume), creativity (Simonton, Chapter 7), the social and cultural context perspective (Peréa & García Coll, Chapter 10), communication disorders (Kohnert, Chapter 13), and sentence processing (Gianico & Altarriba, Chapter 4). We would be remiss, however, if we did not cite Grosjean's (1982) classic text, and Romaine's (1995) volume that we have been using in our Psychology of Bilingualism classes for the last seven years, and Hamers and Blanc's (2000) excellent book that triggered and shaped the direction and focus of the current volume. Finally, it is hoped that we succeed in providing the bilingual student, teacher, and researcher with an updated and interdisciplinary perspective about the intricacies of the bilingual mind.

Roberto R. Heredia and Jeanette Altarriba

References

Grosjean, F. (1982). *Life with two languages: An introduction to bilingualism*. Cambridge, MA: Harvard University Press.

Hamers, J. F., & Blanc, M. H. A. (2000). *Bilinguality and bilingualism* (2nd ed.). Cambridge, MA: Cambridge Press.

Romaine, S. (1995). *Bilingualism*. Cambridge: Blackwell.

Preface to the Second Edition

We were happy with the positive reception of the first edition of *An Introduction to Bilingualism: Principles and Processes*; it was a humbling experience as students and colleagues from China, Taiwan, and Europe approached us at conferences or wrote to us to remark about the impact of *An Introduction to Bilingualism: Principles and Processes* as a textbook for their teaching, and as an empirical and theoretical reference guide for their research. Although by 2011 other equally good books about the psycholinguistics of bilingual cognition started to appear, our volume "stood its ground" and remained highly visible, and emails from our colleagues from all over the world kept flowing, underscoring the usefulness of our book. Oxford Bibliographies Online recommended our volume as *a must-read resource on psycholinguistics*. We are grateful to the late Cathleen Petree whose enthusiasm and vision made the first edition possible. As we considered a second edition and proceeded with the proposal, we were extremely pleased with Paul Dukes' enthusiasm and willingness to go forward with this second edition.

We are here, again, introducing the second edition of *An Introduction to Bilingualism: Principles and Processes*. It has been said that second editions are the best, and so far it looks that way. This second edition is truly an updated and expanded version. This edition adds four chapters to reflect the *state-of-the-art* of bilingual research. *The Bilingual Brain* (Chapter 6) incorporates and expands on the latest neuropsychological techniques and findings from the neuroimaging field investigating the interface between the bilingual brain and mind. *Bilingualism and Executive Functioning* (Chapter 9) provides critical insights into the "hot issues" of the benefits of bilingualism and the ongoing methodological assessment of replication and the interpretation of statistically equivalent findings. *The Sociolinguistics of Bilingualism* (Chapter 13) provides a much-needed perspective on *linguistic variation* or the means by which bilinguals construct or use diverse forms for expressing meanings as a function of gender, race and ethnicity, and language mode. *Code-Switching* (Chapter 14), for the first time, provides a general overview of why bilinguals might mix their languages from an interdisciplinary perspective grounded in qualitative methodology. Indeed, the research domain of bilingualism has expanded so much that the inclusion of these four chapters was simply a "must have." Although the good-old days of "one versus two memory systems" are long gone, we do address and update these issues to reflect the current thinking.

The chapters on aging (Chapter 5), creativity (Chapter 8), and communication disorders (Chapter 17) were re-written by new authors. We are grateful to Robert Schrauf, Dean K. Simonton, and Kathryn Kohnert for their contribution and making our book worthy of a second edition.

Back then, during the publication of the first edition, we cited three books that are now classics (see Preface to the first edition) as competitors. Now, the bilingual literature is so extensive and highly specialized—on topics that 15 to 20 years ago were purely wishful thinking!—that citing some of these books would take pages and pages. Despite the numerous books and book series (e.g., *Springer's Bilingual Brain and Mind, Routledge's Cognitive Science and Second Language Acquisition,* and *John Benjamins' Bilingual Processing and Acquisition*), *An Introduction to Bilingualism: Principles and Processes* is distinctive and provides a unique perspective on "pressing issues" being debated in the bilingual literature and in the general domain of experimental psychology.

Twelve years ago, as we considered the possibility of authoring a book on bilingualism, we wanted our final product to be published by Erlbaum, simply because this was the place we were most familiar with, and the place where all the "big shots" would publish. We made the right choice, and again, we are grateful to Paul Dukes, Senior Publisher for Taylor & Francis Group, for his flexibility and everlasting support, and to Talia Graff for the never-ending cascade of electronic emails with all kinds of requests, and her willingness to always provide us with the best editorial advice. Finally, it is our hope that we deliver what instructors and students of bilingualism have characterized as a *state-of-the-art* textbook of an introduction to bilingualism, and to researchers "a guiding" empirical and theoretical reference tool.

Roberto R. Heredia and Jeanette Altarriba

Acknowledgments

We would like to thank the many people who helped us directly and indirectly in the completion of this book. First, we thank Paul Dukes of Taylor & Francis for catching the vision of this unique work for a second edition. Also, we would like to express our gratitude to the contributors themselves who were cooperative in meeting our deadlines and graciously accepting our editorial suggestions. We thank the anonymous reviewers whose comments and suggestions made our book worthy of a second edition. Finally, we thank Allison M. Wilck for assisting us with the editing process.

I, Roberto, dedicate this volume to my beloved mother (Esperanza) who spoiled me so much, and in a kind of interesting way, sheltered me from dropping out of high school when my father was laid off due to his rheumatism that he could no longer hide. She is an exceptional woman with zero formal education, but with a clear understanding of the power of education. She never wanted her children to be farmworkers or laborers like her beloved husband. To my beloved father (Eliseo), who worked from dawn to dusk in the tomato fields of the Sacramento Valley whose only task in life, as he sometimes puts it, was to care and provide for his family. He tried to show me the tools of his trade; I was never good at that. I almost got him fired when I refused to work for about $3.15 per hour and walked over 10 miles to get back home. As always, I sought the protection of my savior (my mother) who was always there for me!

I am grateful to my undergraduate and graduate students who have indirectly contributed to this volume, and who are always ready to work diligently and enthusiastically. To my beloved Michelle for her love, patience, and support, and my daughter Andrea who has taught me to appreciate and love my parents even more. I thank my family (6 sisters, 1 brother, 14 nieces, 9 nephews), particularly my sisters Erika, Yolanda, and Juane who always wonder *wassup* as the *señales de humo* fail to materialize in the skies of the California Central Valley!

I, Jeanette, feel grateful that the colleagues who contributed to this book acknowledge the importance of the topic in all its variations and continue to serve as role models for other scientists in this area. In particular, I thank my close colleagues (and you all know who you are) for providing, as Norman Segalowitz researcher and scholar would say, an "academic family" affording guidance and friendship and a constant source of stimulation to create new knowledge and to share that knowledge all around the globe. I join Roberto in thanking our students for motivating us, making us think, and providing those wonderful "Ah-ha!" experiences in the laboratory. We do, indeed, live for those moments of discovery, and we're happy we can share the wealth of our knowledge with you, as inspired by our mentors and our colleagues. This book was truly something that Roberto and I did to bring together the many worlds of bilingualism in one place, and we are grateful that Taylor & Francis sought to further our journey through to the completion of this book.

My family is a constant source of guidance and inspiration, and their pride in my work and accomplishments shall far outlast the writings in this book. It is to them that I dedicate the realization of this volume.

Finally, we wish to acknowledge our friends who are too numerous to name and our wonderful families—related, extended, and adopted throughout the world. It is their *cariño* and support that always motivates and encourages us.

Roberto R. Heredia and Jeanette Altarriba

Section I

Introduction

Methodological and Theoretical Background

1 Introduction

Jeanette Altarriba and Roberto R. Heredia

The Study of Bilingualism

There is no doubting the notion that interest in bilingual and multilingual studies has increased since the publication of the first edition of the current volume, *An Introduction to Bilingualism: Principles and Processes*. The field has seen a steady increase in submissions of quality articles on this topic to such venues as the *International Journal of Bilingualism*, *Multilingual and Multicultural Development*, and *Bilingualism: Language and Cognition*. Further, participation in scholarly venues that include research in this field such as the International Symposium on Bilingualism (ISB; now in its 11th year, meeting biennially), the American Association for Applied Linguistics (AAAL), International Association of Applied Linguistics (AILA), and The Mental Lexicon conference, just to name a few, has increased in recent years. Thus, the motivation to learn more and write more about how bilingual speakers encode, store, and retrieve information has increased over the past 10 years. For this reason, the present volume attempts to present an update of research in the field and a review of some of the newer aspects of the field both from a theoretical perspective and from an applied or practical perspective, as well.

In addition to basic research that has been produced by those who examine language in the laboratory domain, those who seek to understand how languages can best be learned and used in more applied domains have asked interesting questions regarding the most effective methods of second language acquisition. Updated volumes, such as *Theories in Second Language Acquisition* (Van Patten & Williams, 2014) and *Introducing Second Language Acquisition* (Saville-Troike, 2012), and newer volumes, such as *Bilingualism and Multilingualism* (Bhatia, 2013), underscore the notion that individuals, researchers, and interested readers are seeking the newest or latest information on how best to teach a second language (L2) and how best to fashion a set of "best practices" in this field of endeavor. The more we know about the nuances of word types (e.g., concrete vs. abstract vs. emotion) within and across languages (Altarriba, 2003) and the more we know about the relationship between language and culture in the acquisition of new languages (e.g., Robinson & Altarriba, 2015), the better equipped we are in understanding just what mechanisms might underlie the notion of being a practiced, expert user of a new language. It is clear that this endeavor has continued to gain momentum and garner great interest from the science and public communities at large. Thus, the crafting of this second edition of the current text is meant to further the discussion on these topics with new and interesting data that should pique the interest of those who enjoyed the first edition and those who are delving into these areas and issues for the first time. In this introduction, we hope to address a few avenues of research endeavors that have been delineated more thoroughly over the past decade or so, and to introduce the reader to new areas of bilingual inquiry that have come forth based on the earlier work. A discussion of newer contributions appears below, as well as an overview and outline of the current set of works.

Informing the Study of Bilingualism (and Monolingualism)

What has prompted the field of bilingual research to move forward has been the ever-expanding globalization of language and communication in recent years. Though English is a predominant language and *lingua franca* throughout the world, we know that other languages come close to English as firmly representing a large proportion of the world's inhabitants (see Figure 1.1).

Moreover, by some estimates, over half of the world's population is at least bilingual, and fluently so, and still another strong proportion of speakers is well-versed in more than two languages as a natural course of the learning and mastery of linguistic skills. As the expansion in technologies and new medias has given rise to ever more efficient ways of using language to convey meaning across the globe, so too has an interest arisen in knowing how to communicate effectively across languages, as well as across variants of the same language. Indeed, one of the primary uses of language has been to communicate thoughts, facts, feelings, and beliefs. Additionally, we have known for quite some time that when language is impoverished or otherwise hampered in any way, a clear knowledge of the relationship between the brain and language can provide solutions to those situations in which production is less than desirable. The current volume continues to seek to

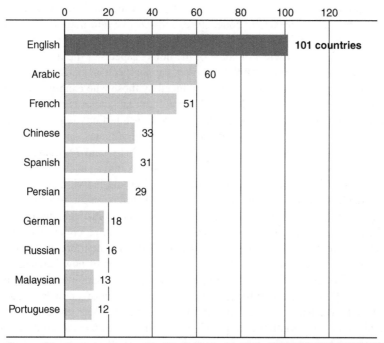

Sources: Ethnologue: Languages of the World, Eighteenth Edition THE WASHINGTON POST

Figure 1.1   The world's predominant languages and the number of countries in which they are most widely spoken (adapted from https://www.washingtonpost.com/news/world views/wp/2015/04/23/the-worlds-languages-in-7-maps-and-charts/?utm_term=. 74a29fe6cde7).

include the extant neuroscience data in order to inform future research on the connection between the brain and communication. It is also the case that methodologies that have been used in the past to uncover the ways in which bilingual speakers encode and store language information (and multilingual speakers, as well) have improved, and their use has been expanded over the past decade to encompass other ways of examining the brain, the automaticity of language processing, and the elements of retrieval of information from memory. The current text, therefore, includes discussions of the new and existing methodologies that inform the hypotheses and research questions that have been pursued in this field, and the interpretation of the data that has resulted from experimentation.

As the fields of cognitive, linguistic, and psycholinguistic sciences often dictate, reasoned investigations of language processing should extend from the careful formation of testable hypotheses and theories and from thoughtful considerations regarding the development of the proper methods so as to produce the data that inform the theory—the scientific method. Many of the works included herein focus on this approach to adding to the fundamental knowledge regarding bilingual research, and do so in expert ways that leave little to consider in terms of confounds or alternative interpretations. The aim with the current edition is that works that review experimental theory and data, and the original data sets that are included among the current chapters, emphasize the link between theory and data in their focus on advancing the field of bilingual research.

Currently, the fields of bilingualism and multilingualism have taken on a greater interdisciplinary or multidisciplinary approach. That is, one sees in the field that beyond the areas of psycholinguistics and language processing are the contributions of bilingual approaches to areas such as social psychology, creativity and problem-solving, speech and communication disorders, and developmental aspects of aging. Indeed, it has become quite clear, and researchers have known for a short time, that bilingual approaches to questions of interest across a broad range of topics can actually illuminate issues and concerns that were previously addressed using only monolingual models and samples. More and more the question has become: How can a bilingual or multilingual approach answer question X or Y? Capitalizing on the fact that words in two languages might overlap in meaning but diverge in form has been one tool that cognitive scientists, for example, have used to understand the relative impact of the use of bilingualism as a tool to understand the relationship between semantics (e.g., meaning) and lexical (e.g., word) representations (e.g., Altarriba & Soltano, 1996; Heredia & Blumentritt, 2002; Heredia & Cieślicka, 2016).

Theories that explore the relationship between the mind and the brain might also be interested in the theory and data that surround bilingual research, as some accounts would suggest that bilingualism poses certain cognitive benefits (see de Bot & Houtzager; Paap, current volume). Some of the work in the pages that follow will allude to these discussions, but we do know that there have been accounts of bilingual speakers showing greater flexibility retrieving items or engaging in problem-solving and turn-taking exercises. They may show benefits in terms of creativity and divergent thinking, reading, and concept formation, and certain metalinguistic abilities may be enhanced due to managing and knowing more than one symbol-sct for language. While the nuances of these notions have been challenged and contested in some regards, before this newer area of studying *bilingual advantages* was brought to the foray in the language sciences, it was already documented some time ago that there were enhancements in thinking and language use that bilinguals could accumulate over time, by virtue of knowing how to manipulate an L2 and subsequent languages. Thus, as applied to theory development overall, in terms of the cognitive underpinning of what makes us human—language—the study of bilingual speakers' abilities continues to be extremely important to furthering our overall knowledge of how we continue to evolve as a species in an ever-changing industrial world.

Overview and New Content

With the aforementioned background as a type of *backdrop* for this second edition of the current work, we would now like to introduce the reader to an overview of the contents that are to be explored in the next several chapters that await a closer look. The present volume retains the original number of primary Sections:

Section I: Introduction: Methodological and Theoretical Background
Section II: Cognitive and Neurological Mechanisms
Section III: Creativity and Developmental Principles
Section IV: Social and Sociocultural Processes
Section V: Linguistics, Second Language Acquisition, and Communication Disorders

Section V has been expanded from the prior section heading in the first edition, *Linguistic Principles and Applied Perspectives*. Principally, the emphasis in the newer derivation of this section is to include an update on work specifically in the domain of Second Language Acquisition and to also make Communication Disorders a more salient part of the chapters included within this final section. An attempt was made at recruiting many of the original authors from the first edition, with a few notable changes, detailed below. Overall, the balance remains in covering a rich and dense (though highly readable) set of chapters that focus on basic research and theory, and including areas that would be thought of as more applied in nature, but still with a rigorous eye towards making sure that the works are comprehensive and stem from an empirical and scientifically driven approach.

Section I includes an overview of basic and expanded methods in use in the area of bilingual research by Marian, who describes a variety of tools and techniques that uncover the processing of language inputs across a bilingual's languages and focuses both on online and offline methodologies to help the field at large derive a *composite* picture of what we currently know, via these methodologies. The focus of this first section continues to be on laying the groundwork or basic background of work upon which readers can continue to build with knowledge from subsequent sections and chapters. Heredia and Cieślicka present the reader with an update on the actual *models* or theories upon which most of our bilingual research to date has been built, underscoring the ways in which one should compare and contrast those models to produce newer research questions, furthering the field of bilingual research. Together, the two chapters that start off this newer edition of the current work set the stage for readers at any level to more smoothly and seamlessly integrate the chapters that follow into their new network of knowledge in this overall domain.

While the volume itself is comprised roughly of the same five sections as the prior edition, the total number of chapters has increased by three to a total of 17 (four brand-new topic areas are included, while one chapter was not carried over into this new edition). It is in Section II that we have included a new chapter on a related and very prominent theme, the *Bilingual Brain*. Before, this topic was included within a single chapter; in the current text, we have expanded the treatment of this area into two distinct chapters covering both what we know about the mechanisms that help to regulate the uses of multiple languages (Blackburn), and what we now know about the actual representation of languages across the hemispheres of the brain (Vaid). As noted earlier, this is perhaps one of those areas for which the research has expanded quite rapidly over the past decade, due to the development and availability of newer technologies and methods that allow us to ask more interesting questions regarding the relationship between language and brain, in general. Additionally, the topic of multilingualism and aging is covered quite well in the chapter by new contributors to this volume (de Bot & Houtzager), as they present theories of cognitive aging in a well-written listing of the current, extant knowledge on what we know about the aging process and its effects on cognitive functioning. To round out the chapters in Section II, Robinson and Altarriba update and expand upon the theme of psycholinguistics in a bilingual context by reviewing the ways in which the study of semantic and lexical processing, couched in a multilingual and cultural vein, has continued to grow over the past decade to examine issues of word choice, word representation, and the features that underlie the use of the multiple, known languages of a speaker to produce and analyze features of discourse. Each chapter in the current section informs the connection between mind, language, and the brain and updates the reader on what is known about that connection since the publication of the first edition of the present work.

Section III focuses on creativity and the cognitive/developmental aspects of being and becoming a bilingual speaker and thinker. Kharkhurin is a new author to the current volume, and his comprehensive treatment of the relationship between bilingualism and creativity informs the reader of practically all of the extant areas of endeavor that have been explored within this relatively new topic in this genre of research. Issues related to divergent and convergent thinking, such as the use of tests that elucidate the underpinnings of reasoning and problem-solving for complex and often novel situations, are all aptly explored in a context that, by its very nature, takes into account both language and culture in the definitions of what constitutes the creative, bilingual mind. Another new addition to the present text (the second of the four new contributions) focuses on executive functioning and the newer research that has evolved with great prominence in the area of cognitive control and bilingualism (Paap). While, as alluded to earlier, there have been reports of arenas in which those who possess knowledge of more than one language have shown fluidity in role-taking, problem-solving, and other related tasks, Paap critically examines literature in this area with an eye towards the ways in which populations, tasks, and methodological controls have been used in examining the reported benefits of bilingualism across a multitude of studies. Rounding out this section is an update of a chapter in the earlier edition on bilingualism and cognitive development (Nicoladis & Smithson). The focus on communicative competence in the developing bilingual speaker is examined by recounting the research on theory of mind, strategic processing, and attentional control from both a monolingual and a bilingual perspective. At times and in differing contexts, the emerging bilingual is immersed in one or the other language environment, but still must maintain the language that is not currently in use. The duality of switching between languages in early language development and how that ability relates to further language development on the whole for a bilingual speaker are reviewed in full and interesting detail within this updated chapter.

Section IV focuses on the social and sociocultural aspects of bilingualism and the pragmatics of bilingual language usage. A comprehensive overview of the influence of social contexts on being bilingual, as well as the accompanying attitudes, stereotypes, social expectations, and group norms that impinge on the culture of bilingualism, is presented with an update on how social constructs such as *identity* are informed by knowing multiple languages (Vega). Additionally, a second chapter within this section also updates the earlier volume with a focus on the social and cultural contexts of bilingualism (Peréa, Padilla-Martínez, & Coll). One of the areas of interest focused on within this chapter is the role of the larger, national context and language policies that affect the ways in which bilingual speakers are viewed, stemming from immigration and historical views. A third chapter that is new to the current edition focuses on the sociolinguistics of bilingualism and the linguistic variation in the expression of meanings within and across linguistic groups (Bullock & Toribio). Questions as to how linguistic variation came about, the factors that have influenced and continue to influence diversity across languages, and the ideologies of groups that shape the standard language practices of groups are explored in a comprehensive framework that is interdisciplinary in nature. This approach makes for a very integrated review of the extant literature and the applications of various published works in this domain. The fourth new chapter to the current volume resides within Section IV and focuses on code-switching (Magaña). While code-switching in and of itself has been explored for several decades, a comprehensive overview of the research and empirical approaches to this topic might not have led to the ability to provide a complete chapter on this area when the first edition of this work was created. Rather, the current moment is a propitious time to gather together the research, theory, and data that pertains to this area of investigation and represents this topic in the current edition of this work. Within this chapter, code-switching is examined within the vein of how it serves to facilitate the socio-pragmatic functions of language, the development of bilingual competence, the formation of identity roles for the bilingual speaker, and psycholinguistic studies in the domain of bilingualism. This chapter ends with an interdisciplinary overview of how code-switching informs communication on the whole and narrates or directs written and face-to-face interactions within a larger communicative context.

Rounding out the slate of contributions for this second edition are linguistic contributions to the study of bilingualism, an overview of second language acquisition, and communication disorders in the realm of bilingual studies. All three of these areas were aptly represented in the first edition of the current volume, but have now been expanded and updated to include new and interesting data that have furthered the field in the past decade or so. The chapter on linguistic contributions to bilingualism by returning author Cook focuses on the role of linguistics and linguistic description in understanding how features such as syntax figure prominently in the ways in which new languages are acquired in terms of grammatical structure. While quite a bit of work has focused on the acquisition of concepts or semantics for a new or emerging L2, overviews have sometimes overlooked the notion that other levels of language representation are being developed as well—those considered more within the realm of language description, such as phonetics, phonology, and morphology. Thus, this chapter serves as a primer for the basic definitions of *grammar*, while also interweaving aspects of emerging bilingualism within its review of the extant literature in this field. Gass and Glew updated their work, as well, providing a chapter for the current work based on that produced for the first edition of the current volume. The focus is squarely on second language acquisition and the attributes of native and near-native speakers in the acquisition of a new language. They focus on the distinctions between early and advanced language learners, the latter often used as a synonym for near-native when describing language abilities. How can one hope to achieve near-native-like fluency? What are the features that distinguish levels of ability both within and across a bilingual's languages? These and other related questions are aptly explored within this updated chapter. Finally, a set of new authors has tackled the theme of a chapter from the earlier edition that focused on language impairments in bilingual speakers. This updated chapter focuses on communication disorders and how they are represented among this group of speakers (Restrepo, Adams, & Barragan). In this comprehensive overview, deficits in the use of language and the corresponding areas that are affected in the brain are reviewed for new and developing bilingual speakers. Language impairment in both children and adults and the ways in which language use is impacted by various deficiencies are discussed with reference to the research that explores how the brain processes language under conditions that affect typical cognitive and physical development. This chapter underscores the need to understand the fully functioning bilingual speaker so that when impairments occur, we are able to establish best practices for treatment so as to result in positive outcomes in terms of rehabilitation and overall health and wellbeing. Clearly, due to advances in methodological approaches and technology, we are better equipped to understand how the bilingual brain may recover from aphasia, anomia, and other language-related impairments through the careful and concerted efforts made in this domain of bilingual science exploration.

Summary and Conclusions

The study of bilingualism and all of its aspects—theory and models, psycholinguistic/ sociocultural/linguistic and social approaches, developmental and neuroscience applications, creativity, executive functioning, pragmatic and communicative approaches, and theories of acquisition—formulate the cornerstone of the second edition of an *Introduction to Bilingualism: Principles and Processes*. The current volume contains areas of investigation that have been updated from the earlier edition, plus a number of new contributions that highlight new and expanding areas of interest in the field—most notably those focusing on the brain, executive functioning, and cognitive control. An area of pragmatic use—code-switching—came into its own in the current volume as a formidable body of research, and exploration has emerged in recent years focusing in this area of language usage. Additionally, newer contributions that focus on the lifespan and developmental issues broaden those areas of inquiry and bring the reader into alignment with current thoughts regarding theories and models in those particular areas of research endeavor. The hope is that the current edition motivates and inspires new areas of research investigation and that those who are interested in these areas of work recognize the importance of examining the cognitive processing of bilinguals—our previously coined term in an earlier volume by these same editors (Heredia & Altarriba, 2014), *bilingual cognitive psychology*—for what this line of research might tell us, not only about bilingual and multilingual speakers, but for what it might tell us about human language processing overall.

List of Key Words and Concepts

Anomia, Aphasia, Bilingual advantages, Bilingual brain, Bilingual cognitive psychology, Bilingual models, Code-switching, Cognitive control, Executive functioning, Grammar, Identity, Language impairment, Language variation, Lexical representations, Morphology, Multidisciplinary approach, Multilingualism, Near-native, Phonetics, Phonology, Pragmatics, Scientific method, Scientifically driven approach, Sociocultural aspects, Sociolinguistics

Internet Sites Related to the Study of Bilingualism

Developmental Aspects of Bilingualism: http://www.hanen.org/Helpful-Info/Articles/Biling ualism-in-Young-Children--Separating-Fact-fr.aspx

Questioning the *Bilingual Advantage*: http://www.newyorker.com/science/maria-konnikova/
    bilingual-advantage-aging-brain
The Benefits of Being Bilingual: http://www.nytimes.com/2012/03/18/opinion/sunday/the-
    benefits-of-bilingualism.html

Discussion Questions

(1) Summarize the information on the number of countries where there are the largest groups
    of speakers of a given language, as per Figure 1.1. Which is the most widely spoken
    language depicted in the graph, and which is the least-spoken language in the graph?
(2) Summarize the importance of using empirical approaches—the scientific method,
    experimentation, etc.—on advancing our knowledge of bilingual language process-
    ing. Why is it important to continue to conduct research on this topic area?
(3) Has interest in the study of bilingualism increased or decreased in recent years? What
    is noted in support of your answer to this question, within the current chapter?
(4) What areas of emphasis or topic areas are cited as new or current areas in the study of
    bilingualism, in relation to the contents of the current volume as a whole? Why do you
    believe that these are new areas of interest in the field?

Suggested Research Projects

(1) *Experimental Study: Code-Switching*. With permission, record a conversation between
    two bilingual speakers and examine the ways in which they switch between their two
    languages. Document the frequency of occurrence of those switches and examine the
    situations for which speakers decide to switch or not to switch between languages.
(2) *Literature Search:* Use a database such as PsychInfo (http://www.apa.org/psycinfo)
    for recent literature on bilingualism and the brain, with a focus on bilingual aphasia.
    Examine the different ways that language abilities are affected in the two languages of
    a bilingual who experiences aphasia early in life and late in life. Compare and contrast
    the outcomes of these two situations.
(3) *Research Paper:* Examine the historical background of investigations of bilingual
    language processing by selecting a research article on bilingual memory. Write a
    three-page summary of a given experimental article that focuses on how language and
    memory were examined in the early 1970s in this area of investigation.

Suggested Readings

Altarriba, J., & Isurin, L. (Eds.). (2012). *Memory, language, and bilingualism: Theoretical and
    applied approaches.* Cambridge, UK: Cambridge University Press.
Bhatia, T. K., & Ritchie, W. C. (Eds.). (2004). *The handbook of bilingualism.* Malden, MA:
    Blackwell.
Heredia, R. R., Altarriba, J., & Cieślicka, A. (Eds.). (2015). *Methods in bilingual reading
    comprehension research.* New York: Springer Science+Business.

References

Altarriba, J. (2003). Does *cariño* equal "liking"? A theoretical approach to conceptual nonequivalence
    between languages. *International Journal of Bilingualism, 7*, 305–322.
Altarriba, J., & Soltano, E. G. (1996). Repetition blindness and bilingual memory: Token
    individuation for translation equivalents. *Memory & Cognition, 24*, 700–711.

Bhatia, T. K. (2013). *Bilingualism and multilingualism*. Oxford, UK: Oxford University Press.

Heredia, R. R., & Altarriba, J. (Eds.). (2014). *Foundations of bilingual memory*. New York: Springer Science+Business.

Heredia, R. R., & Blumentritt, L. T. (2002). On-line processing of social stereotypes during spoken language comprehension. *Experimental Psychology, 49*, 208–221.

Heredia, R. R., & Cieślicka, A. B. (2016). Metaphoric reference: An eye movement analysis of Spanish–English and English–Spanish bilingual readers. *Frontiers in Psychology, 7*, 1–10.

Robinson, C. J., & Altarriba, J. (2015). Culture and language processing. In F. Sharifian (Ed.), *The Routledge handbook of language and culture* (pp. 240–252). New York: Routledge.

Saville-Troike, M. (2012). *Introducing second language acquisition* (2nd ed.). Cambridge: Cambridge University Press.

Van Patten, B., & Williams, J. (2014). *Theories in second language acquisition: An introduction* (2nd ed.). New York: Routledge.

2   Bilingual Research Methods

Viorica Marian

Introduction

In 1924, the US Congress passed what became known as the *Immigration Restriction Act*, a law that regulated immigration to the US for many years and served as the basis for discriminatory immigration policies favoring immigrants from Western and Northern Europe over those from Southern and Eastern Europe. The law had a eugenic (i.e., *improvement of the gene pool*) intent designed to halt the immigration of supposedly *dysgenic* groups, groups that purportedly contributed to a decline of the gene pool. The Immigration Restriction Act relied in part on data from seemingly scientific studies (Brigham, 1923; Goddard, 1914), as well as a Public Health Service project that tested the intelligence of different groups and found that some immigrant groups—for example, Italians and Eastern European Jews—scored lower, often below average, and sometimes even in the *feebleminded* range, compared to other groups. Herrnstein and Murray (1994, p. 5), in their much-publicized book, *The Bell Curve*, described these events as follows: *In the early 1920s, the chairman of the House Committee on Immigration and Naturalization appointed an "Expert Eugenical Agent" for his committee's work, a biologist who was especially concerned about keeping up the American level of intelligence by suitable immigration policies.*

One can just imagine how, in the years that followed, streams of immigrants lined up at Ellis Island to undergo comprehensive medical examinations, coupled with psychometric tests to assess their intellectual abilities. Never mind that many of these immigrants spoke not a word of English, while their testers did not know many of the languages that were represented among those fresh off the boats. Imagine yourself as a Ukrainian farmer, illiterate, never having taken a paper-and-pencil test in your life and speaking no English, after a long and stressful journey to a country at the other side of the world, having to take an IQ test. Is it any wonder then that some groups—e.g., British, Dutch, German (whose languages were from the same Germanic family group as English and shared many common words and word roots)—had fewer problems understanding their testers and tests than other groups—e.g., Russian, Polish, Italian (whose languages belonged to other language families and were more different from English)? Is there any doubt that some groups did better than others for reasons that had nothing to do with intelligence?

The Immigration Restriction Act of 1924 was later repealed, and looking back, we can safely say that those mental tests were biased, that they did not take into account the linguistic and cultural background of the test-takers. Mental tests have come a long way since then and test makers are acutely aware of the need to create assessment tools that are linguistically and culturally sensitive. Yet, accomplishing such goals is not an easy task. To this day, mental tests seem to yield higher scores in some groups than in others (e.g., Herrnstein & Murray, 1994), and arguments for the lack of cultural and linguistic/dialectal fairness of these tests abound. Some of this is due to the fact that those who conduct research with linguistically and culturally diverse populations continue to be trained primarily in a context that focuses on middle-class, English-speaking white populations and have a limited understanding and knowledge of what studying cognitive abilities of other groups entails (Henrich, Heine, & Norenzayan, 2010). Studies focusing on linguistically and culturally diverse groups frequently yield seemingly contradictory findings, and conclusive answers to research questions remain elusive. The dearth of training on issues related to cognitive performance in linguistic and cultural minorities, coupled with the failure to take into account relevant experimental variables, continue to pose a challenge in obtaining a clear picture of cognitive abilities in diverse populations. There is also the risk of inappropriately driving public policy, for instance, on issues related to raising bilingual children or to bilingualism in the classroom.

In this chapter, we take you through the steps necessary to conduct a research project with bilinguals, multilinguals, or second and foreign language learners. We talk about designing a study, selecting participants, putting together materials, collecting and analyzing data, and then disseminating the findings among an audience of peers. We consider strengths and weaknesses of different approaches, and discuss how to avoid the most common pitfalls in conducting bilingualism research and in interpreting the findings of already existing studies. The first part of the chapter introduces key terminology and concepts necessary to embark upon a research project. The second part of the chapter samples research areas that fall under the umbrella of bilingualism and illustrates how methodological differences and limitations can influence findings. The final part of the chapter considers specific methodological aspects in conducting a study with bilinguals. Sample questions and research projects, as well as resources for further information, are included at the end.

This chapter is intended for graduate and advanced undergraduate students, and for anyone new to research with linguistically diverse populations. Most frequently, these researchers find themselves in the fields of psychology, linguistics, communication sciences and disorders, or education, but can also work in other disciplines (e.g., anthropology, neuroscience, etc.). Though one chapter alone is not sufficient to provide comprehensive training in such a complex area, it can serve as a starting point for those who are interested in bilingualism and want to ensure that they avoid the most common mistakes along the way. Being aware of some of the most important variables to consider and knowing some of the things that could go wrong if not properly thought through constitute the first steps in conducting a successful research project.

Designing a Research Project with Bilinguals

In this part of the chapter, we introduce some of the key concepts designed to familiarize you with both the vocabulary used in research and the basic procedures in running a study. If you have never taken a research methods course before, much of this information will be new; if you are already familiar with the basics of research design, this will serve as a refresher tailored specifically toward research with bilinguals and multilinguals.

Observational and Experimental Studies

Research with bilinguals usually relies on measuring cognitive and behavioral performance. There are a number of ways in which one may go about doing that. One may, for instance, observe human cognitive and behavioral performance in natural settings, record such performance, and describe it for scientific understanding. This is usually known as *naturalistic observation* and is also referred to as *descriptive research* because it describes naturally observed phenomena instead of experimentally controlled or manipulated ones. An example of observational research with bilinguals may be observing a bilingual child on a playground and writing down the words the child uses in each language.

Alternatively, one may design an experiment and look at how changing variables influences cognitive and behavioral performance. This is referred to as *experimental research*. An example of experimental research with bilinguals may consist of asking bilinguals to label pictures in either their first or their second language and comparing *reaction times* in the *picture naming task* across the two languages. Experimental research makes it possible to control variables (such as language of the task) and in general provides greater control over the behavioral and cognitive processes of interest. It makes *hypothesis testing* easier and allows one to draw causative inferences. However, experimental research is not always feasible, practical, or ethical. For example, if one were interested in studying bilinguals' *flashbulb memories*—memories of dramatic events, such as a presidential assassination or a great disaster—across the two languages, one could not create such memories experimentally and would have to use the naturalistic approach by conducting first and second language interviews about, for example, bilinguals' memory for the 9/11 attacks on the World Trade Center towers and the Pentagon.

In addition to observational and experimental research, some studies can also be qualified as *correlational research*. Correlational studies measure the relationship between two or more variables. These designs are useful when the manipulation of variables is not possible due to ethical constraints or when the behavior of interest does not lend itself to experimentation. For example, one may find that the larger the vocabulary in a bilingual's second language, the higher his/her score on an intelligence test. You may have already heard the statement *correlation does not imply causation*. In correlational studies, one is unable to make causal judgments about the effect of one variable on the other. In the case of the relationship between *vocabulary size* and intelligence, the only conclusion that can be reached is that the two variables are related.

Longitudinal and Cross-Sectional Research

Longitudinal studies are studies that follow experimental participants over a period of time, be it months, years, or decades. In longitudinal studies, performance at Time 1 is usually compared to performance of the same individual or group of individuals at Time 2. This is different from *cross-sectional* research, in which different individuals or groups of individuals are compared to each other at the same point in time. For example, if one was interested in measuring first language (L1) and second language (L2) vocabulary in children at ages 1, 2, and 3 years, one could go about collecting data in two ways. The first, a longitudinal approach, would be to measure vocabulary size in the same group of twenty children over time, testing them at age 12 months, 24 months, and 36 months. The second, a cross-sectional approach, would be to measure vocabulary size of three different groups of children, one group of twenty 12-month-olds, one group of twenty 24-month-olds, and one group of twenty 36-month-olds at about the same point in time. The advantage of longitudinal research is that it follows the same group under different conditions, thereby minimizing between-group differences (such as socioeconomic status, for example) that may influence the findings. Another advantage is that it allows for a smaller sample size of participants and is therefore usually the preferred choice when studying rare groups, such as speakers of an endangered language or bilingual children with *specific language impairment*. The disadvantage of longitudinal research is that it usually has higher attrition rates, with more participants dropping out of the study, moving away, or undergoing a life change that makes it impossible to continue with the experiment. Moreover, longitudinal research can take a long time, making it less-than-ideal for those researchers who have to work within time constraints, such as graduate and undergraduate students who tend to want to graduate before their infant participants enter college. The advantages and disadvantages of cross-sectional research are precisely the opposite to those of longitudinal research. On the up-side, cross-sectional studies take less time to run, and in that way are the more practical choice. On the down-side, there are more differences between the various groups of participants, making it difficult to control for extraneous factors.

While some research questions can be answered with either of the two approaches, other hypotheses are better tested with one of these types of research only. In *intervention studies*, the method of choice is usually the longitudinal approach, so that the same group of participants is tested before and after an intervention takes place. Also known as *pre-test/post-test studies*, these studies can focus on a clinical, educational, behavioral, or cognitive intervention. For example, an intervention study in bilingualism may be a study in which the effect of language therapy on linguistic performance is studied by having a bilingual child with language impairment take a battery of language tests before and after undergoing language therapy, to observe the change in performance as a result of therapy. Another example is measuring test performance before and after enrollment in a dual-language immersion classroom. In both of these cases, taking a longitudinal approach and comparing performance of the same group before and after *treatment* is preferable to comparing performance of two different groups.

Finally, it is also possible to combine both approaches, if the research questions warrant doing so and if sufficient resources (e.g., time, participants, money) are available. In the language therapy example above, the design could be altered from longitudinal to a combined longitudinal and cross-sectional design by having two groups of bilingual children with similar language impairments and providing language therapy in the first language to one group of bilinguals and language therapy in the second language in the other group of bilinguals. Pre- and post-intervention measures collected for both groups allow cross-group comparisons that can indicate (1) whether language therapy is effective for this particular language disorder in bilinguals, and (2) whether language therapy in one of the bilinguals' languages is more effective than language therapy in their other language.

Independent, Dependent, and Confounding Variables

In an experiment in which you study how a change in a certain variable influences performance, the variable that is being manipulated is called the *independent variable* and the variable that is being measured is called the *dependent variable*. For example, if you were interested in how *language proficiency* influences reading speed, you may want to design an experiment in which bilinguals with varying proficiency levels are asked to read text passages. In this case, language proficiency is the independent variable and reading speed is the dependent variable. For example, reading time or how fast the text passage is being read (the dependent variable) would decrease (will be fast) for high proficiency bilinguals and increase (will be slow) for low proficiency bilinguals. The same variable can be either an independent variable or a dependent variable, depending on the design of the study. In another study focusing on the effect of *age of acquisition* of a second language on proficiency in that language, age of acquisition would be the independent variable and language proficiency would become the dependent variable.

The independent variable is usually varied across groups. That can be accomplished by either having different groups receive different conditions of the independent variable, or by having one group in which the independent variable is being manipulated (called the *experimental group*) and one group in which the independent variable is not being manipulated (called the *control group*). Experimental and control groups should be identical on all variables except the variable of interest, in order to ensure that whatever differences are observed between groups are genuine differences due to the independent variable and not due to other differences between groups or to placebo effects. *Placebo effects* (the term originates from medical studies that found that patients who were given a sugar pill, called a placebo, showed some clinical improvement in medical symptoms similar to those patients who received a real pill containing medication) in bilingualism research can arise from participants simply knowing that they are participating in a research study. Whenever possible, including control groups in your study is a good way to ensure its validity.

In the example considering language therapy for bilingual children with language impairment, performance on a language assessment scale is the dependent variable. The independent variable is language therapy. This independent variable could include multiple conditions, depending upon the design of the study. It could, for instance, have two conditions—treatment and no treatment—in which two groups of bilinguals are tested, one that receives language therapy and one that does not. Using a control group that does not undergo language therapy ensures that passage of time alone, without any treatment, is not responsible for improvements in performance. Alternatively, language therapy could vary across three conditions—treatment in the first language, treatment in the second language, and no treatment—to compare the benefits of treatment in each of a bilingual's languages. Another condition that could be added to this study is a combination of first and second language use in treatment. In general, an independent variable can vary across multiple conditions, but whenever possible, the most efficient and simplest design that will answer the target question should be chosen.

In addition to independent and dependent variables, researchers are often faced with confounding variables. *Confounding variables* are variables that the experimenter did not plan to alter in the study design, but that nevertheless influenced participants' performance on the dependent variables *in addition* to the stated independent variables. Possible experimental confounds include *participant characteristics*, such as socioeconomic status, gender, and language proficiency, as well as experimental variables, such as linguistic background of the experimenter, experimental setting, and stimuli selection. For example, participants may switch back and forth across languages more if the experimenter is bilingual than if the experimenter is monolingual. Therefore, a study that looks at code-switches (overt verbal switches between a bilingual's two languages) should take into account the linguistic status of the experimenter.

At the same time, it is not possible to control for every single potentially confounding variable. When designing a study, consider the factors that are most likely to pose a problem for that particular research question and focus on those. A study is at greater risk for invalid and unreliable results if it does not take into account the relevant confounding variables in the design. Consider as example the studies reporting findings that bilinguals in the US score lower than monolinguals on intelligence tests. Before you run forward with the conclusion that bilingualism is bad for you and that monolinguals are smarter than bilinguals, consider the fact that bilingualism studies from outside the US, such as the Quebec area of Canada (a bilingual French–English community), have failed to find differences in performance on IQ tests between bilinguals and monolinguals (Pearl & Lambert, 1962). Consider also that the studies reporting lower IQ scores for bilinguals did not take into account socioeconomic factors, such as family income and education. That, combined with the facts that the majority of bilinguals in the US are Hispanic immigrants from Central and South America and that these groups are also frequently of lower socioeconomic status, changes the interpretation of that research entirely. What it really tells us is that *poverty* (not bilingualism) is bad for you and that linguistically diverse groups are disproportionately represented in the lower socioeconomic brackets. Armed with a critical eye and a basic understanding of research, one can easily identify weak experimental designs and poor control over confounding variables.

Operational Definitions, Reliability, and Validity

For a variable to be valid and reliable, it needs to be appropriately operationally defined. *Operational definition* refers to the exact measure that is used to assess a particular construct. For example, if an experiment uses vocabulary size as its dependent variable, the operational definition has to indicate whether vocabulary size is defined as production vocabulary or comprehension vocabulary and what assessment tool or scale is used to measure it. One study may operationally define vocabulary size as a child's performance on the *Peabody Picture Vocabulary Test* (PPVT) as a measure of comprehension. A different study may operationally define vocabulary size as all the words a child is producing, as reported by the parent. Of the two operational definitions, the latter would work better for a 13-*month*-old, while the former would work better for a 13-*year*-old. Note, however, that both measures assess the same variable—vocabulary size. Because different studies may use different operational definitions to measure the same dependent variable, it is important to pay careful attention to the operational definitions of both the dependent and the independent variables when designing or interpreting a study. In the case of vocabulary, for instance, one would have to specify that the variable of interest was vocabulary size, defined as comprehension vocabulary, operationally defined as performance on the PPVT, and measured by administering the PPVT test in English by a licensed *speech-language pathologist*.

Operational definitions are used to define constructs (such as vocabulary, or bilingualism, or creativity) in ways that are clearly measurable and that refer to observable behaviors, rather than abstract concepts. For example, one may want to study the effects of bilingualism on creativity. But what is creativity? A good operational definition and a way to reliably measure the behavior of choice are necessary in order for the study to be valid. Obviously, if one defines creativity as the ability to maintain focus on a given task and then operationalizes it as the time one remains awake while reading and measures it as the length of time it takes a reader to doze off while reading a scientific paper, then the definition of creativity in that particular study is not a valid one. A better way to test creativity may be to administer the verbal *Torrance Test of Creative Thinking* or one of the more recent tests designed to measure creativity (see Chapter 8, this volume). The length of time it takes to doze off while reading a paper may be more indicative of the author's writing prowess, the reader's knowledge about and interest in the topic, as well as extraneous variables such as how much sleep the reader got the night before, how much coffee was consumed that day, and whether there will be a test on the material later, lending this particular measurement of creativity both invalid and unreliable.

A *valid* operational definition is one that measures precisely what it set out to measure. *Reliability* refers to the likelihood that the same finding will be obtained if the study is repeated, either by the same or by a different researcher. If the construct of creativity *and* the construct of bilingualism are carefully operationally defined, then any researcher who uses the same operational definitions, the same criteria, and the same tools, should be able to replicate the original experiment and obtain the same set of findings.

Note that, in the example above, bilingualism is a construct that requires operational definition as well. In fact, one of the most critical problems with bilingualism research is the lack of clarity in defining bilinguals and lack of consistency in classifying different bilingual populations. Many new to bilingualism research tend to group everyone who has any number of vocabulary words in another language as *bilingual*. As a result, research results often appear contradictory when reporting experimental findings with bilinguals. The bilinguals under study may be sometimes foreign language learners who have never used their non-native language outside the classroom; other times, they are fluent, equally *balanced bilinguals* who use both languages frequently in their everyday life; and yet other times, they fall somewhere in between the two extremes, perhaps using both languages frequently, yet being more proficient in one than the other. Additionally, while attempts to define the different types of bilinguals by age of acquisition and language proficiency are not new (Ervin & Osgood, 1954, 1965; Weinreich, 1974), a consistent and universally agreed-upon classification of bilinguals is lacking in empirical reports. You may think that it is only a matter of labels, but consider the shortcut and clarity afforded to a researcher studying *aphasia* (loss of language resulting from damage to the brain caused by injury or disease) by universally agreed upon terminology to describe the aphasic population under study. Referring to participants as having Broca's or *Wernicke's aphasia* makes many of the characteristics of the population in question evident, including affected areas of the brain and characteristic language deficits. Similarly, using a universal language to describe bilingual populations would increase the reliability and validity of empirical studies. Until consensus is reached on which labels to affix to bilingual groups that share certain characteristics, it is best to include any language history variables that describe the group under study when reporting a finding. This way, future replications of the findings are more likely since similar bilingual groups will be targeted for testing. In addition, by knowing what groups have already been tested, it becomes possible to extend a finding to other groups of bilinguals or second language learners that were not included in the population of the original study.

Between-Group, Within-Group, and Mixed Designs

Between-group (also called between-subject) studies are studies in which the independent variable varies across groups. Whenever more than one group of participants is tested and performance across groups is compared, the design of the study includes a between-group component. For example, whenever bilinguals are compared to monolinguals, or different groups of bilinguals are compared to each other, the design of the study is a between-group design. If there are only two groups tested, for example a bilingual experimental group and a monolingual control group, then the study is said to have one independent variable, *group*, with two conditions (also called levels), experimental and control. If four groups are tested and compared to each other (say, an English–Japanese group with English as the native language, a Japanese–English group with Japanese as the native language, a monolingual English group, and a monolingual Japanese group) the study is said to follow a between-group design with an independent variable that has four conditions/levels.

Within-group studies (also called within-subject and repeated-measure designs) are studies in which the independent variable varies within the same group of participants. Pre-test/post-test studies are one example of a within-group design. In within-group studies, performance of a group of participants is compared to performance of the *same group* of participants under different conditions or at different points in time. For example, when the same group of bilinguals is tested in their first language and then tested again in their second language, the design of the study is said to be a within-group design. The number of times a measurement is made determines the number of levels a within-group independent variable has. So, if measurements are made twice, once in the first language and once in the second language, the study is said to follow a within-group design with an independent variable that has two levels. A study can have multiple independent variables at the same time. For example, in addition to first and second language, a study may include treatment status as another within-group independent variable. If a bilingual's performance is measured before, during, and after language therapy, for example, then the study is said to have a within-group design with an independent variable, treatment, that has three levels. A study that would combine both language (first or second) and treatment (before, during, and after) into the same design is said to have two independent variables. The first independent variable, language, has two levels, and the second independent variable, treatment, has three levels, resulting in six conditions—$2 \times 3 = 6$: (1) tested in the first language before treatment, (2) tested in the first language during treatment, (3) tested in the first language after treatment, (4) tested in the second language before treatment, (5) tested in the second language during treatment, and (6) tested in the second language after treatment. This study is referred to as a 2×3 (or two-by-three) within-group or within-subjects design.

Studies that incorporate both between- and within-group variables are referred to as *mixed-design studies*. Mixed-design studies include independent variables that vary both across the different groups tested and within each group. For example, if the four groups mentioned earlier (an English–Japanese group with English as the native language, a Japanese–English group with Japanese as the native language, a monolingual English group, and a monolingual Japanese group) were tested each in different conditions (for example, before, during, and after a language intervention), the study would be described as a 4×3 (four-by-three) mixed design, with two independent variables, where the first independent variable is group and is a between-subject variable with four levels, and the second independent variable is treatment and is a within-subject variable with three levels.

Any empirical study in the literature can be classified as between-, within-, or mixed-design. It is not unusual for those new to research to have difficulties identifying independent and dependent variables, their levels, and the study design. With enough practice reading research papers and designing experiments, this understanding quickly falls into place. Once internalized, the notions make it very easy to understand and process research. So that, for example, if you read a study that describes itself as a 2×2 mixed design with group (bilingual, monolingual) as a between-group variable and condition (picture prime, word prime) as a within-group variable, you can quickly use the learned heuristics to conjure up the specifics of that particular study. Thinking of your own experiment in these terms aids both you and your audience in clarity and precision.

Keep in mind that the more complex the design, the more difficult it becomes to control for confounding factors and interpret the results, making it challenging to conduct well-controlled empirical studies and limiting the reliability and validity of a study. Oftentimes, carving a bigger question into its smaller components and designing simple, elegant experiments that test individual predictions is the optimal choice. More often than not, the simpler the experiment, the more *elegant*, and the easier it is to interpret.

How Methodology Can Drive Outcomes in Bilingualism Research

The topics of study under the bilingualism umbrella are as diverse and the methodologies as numerous as those with monolinguals and include research in social science, biological science, and humanities. Around the world, scientists are studying bilingualism from developmental, cognitive, linguistic, neurological, psycholinguistic, and sociolinguistic perspectives. Researchers are focusing on topics such as cortical organization and neural processing of the two languages in bilinguals, acquisition of the two languages in bilingual children, second (and subsequent) language learning in adults, bilinguals' lexico-semantic representation and processing, language and memory in bilinguals, *language loss*/attrition and language interaction, communication disorders in bilinguals, and numerous others. In this section, we consider some of the most common difficulties and oversights that those new to bilingualism research face.

Representation and Processing of Languages in Bilinguals

The first aspect to underscore when studying representation and processing of the two languages in bilinguals is that the terms *representation* and *processing* are not interchangeable; rather, they refer to different phenomena and should not be confused. Representation refers to the structure and organization of the different language components in bilinguals, while processing refers to activation of these components and their interaction within and between languages. Studies that focus on representation of the two languages usually focus on identifying, locating, and representing the organization of the two languages in the bilingual cognitive architecture. Studies of bilingual language processing usually focus on activation of the two languages (e.g., parallel or *sequential*), examining variables that influence the levels of activation of each language at each processing level, and the interactions within and between the two languages. For purposes of heuristics, it may be helpful to think of representation as a static phenomenon and of processing as an active one.

Second, when considering language representation and processing, it is important to distinguish between different levels of representation and processing. Higher levels of processing, such as mappings to the semantic level from the *lexical level*, may differ from lower levels of processing, such as mappings to the lexical level from orthographic/phonetic levels. Consider, for instance, Weinreich's model of *lexico-semantic organization* in bilinguals (see Figure 2.1).

Weinreich's discussion is written in terms of *signifieds* (conceptual structure/meaning at the semantic level) and *signifiers* (labels/words at the lexical level). According to his model, bilinguals' lexico-semantic system can be organized in three ways, depending on how the languages were acquired. *Coordinative* bilinguals learn the two languages in separate environments and have one signified for every signifier. *Compound* bilinguals learn their two languages in the same context concurrently and have only one set of signifieds, with two signifiers for each signified. *Sub-coordinative* bilinguals interpret words of their weaker language through the words of their stronger language, and the

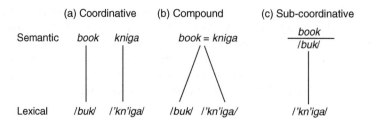

Figure 2.1   Classification of bilinguals by mode of acquisition (adapted from Weinreich, 1974, pp. 9–19).

signifier in the first language becomes a signified for the second language. Multiple theories and models have been proposed to capture the nature of bilingual representation and processing, including such recent theories of language organization and processing in bilinguals as Kroll's (1993, 1994) *revised hierarchical model* and de Groot's (1992) *distributed feature representation model*, both focused on higher levels of processing in bilinguals. In contrast, models like the *bilingual interaction activation model* (Dijkstra, Van Heuven, & Grainger, 1998) and the *self-organizing model of bilingual processing* (Li & Farkas, 2002) focus more on orthographic and phonological processing, respectively. Consequently, experimental paradigms that probe different levels of processing can lead to seemingly contradictory results. When designing or interpreting bilingual research, it is important to be aware of the levels of processing that the experiment taps into.

Third, bilingualism is not a static phenomenon; it is a dynamic process that undergoes continuous change. As the level of proficiency and/or the manner of acquisition change, so do language processing and representation. Models that adjust representations based on new language experience capture the dynamic nature of bilingualism better than models where representations are pre-set and cannot be changed. Moreover, it is possible that within a bilingual person, different representational systems coexist. Some words may be stored coordinatively; others, compoundly; yet others, subordinatively, depending upon the manner in which the words were acquired and/or upon specific characteristics of the words. Individual studies and general theories of bilingual language acquisition, representation, and processing must take into account the complex and fluid nature of the bilingual cognitive architecture when designing and interpreting studies.

Modern models of language representation and processing in bilinguals aim to take into account all of the above considerations in order to render the most accurate understanding of the bilingual cognitive architecture. For example, the *bilingual language interaction network for comprehension of speech* (BLINCS; Shook & Marian, 2013) is a computational model of bilingualism that reflects the interactive nature of bilingual *spoken language processing* (see Figure 2.2). The model adapts the architecture of the monolingual *TRACE* model of language processing (McClelland & Elman, 1986) to two languages, and combines it with the dynamic development of self-organized maps (e.g., Li & Farkas, 2002; Zhao & Li, 2007). BLINCS represents a functional architecture in which the acoustic signal perceived by bilinguals travels to a *feature level*, then to a phonemic level, then to the lexical level, and further to the semantic level. The interaction between levels is bi-directional, allowing for both feed-forward and *back-propagation*. Within levels, language-specific and language-shared representations are included, with bi-directional connections between languages allowing for competition within and across languages. Each processing level contains a self-organizing map organized automatically based on the amount and type of dual-language input. Between levels, the system creates bi-directional excitatory and inhibitory connections via *Hebbian learning*, where connections between items that occur together are strengthened through self-updating algorithms. Single items can have multiple inter-level connections and provide spreading activation during language processing. Within levels, lexical items are mapped based on location in the *neural network* so that structurally related items map together. The physical organization in the neural net allows for words that are structurally similar across languages to map closely together. The BLINCS model illustrates both the complexity of the bilingual system and the advances in research methodology that allow researchers to mathematically model sophisticated human behavior, such as spoken language processing.

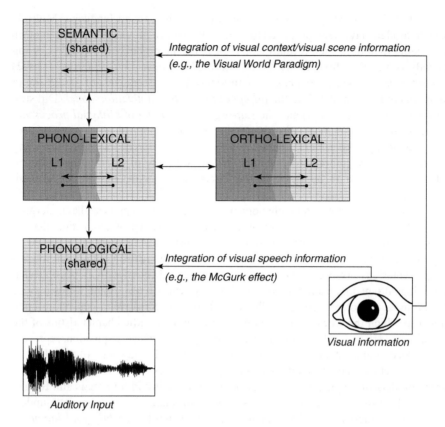

Figure 2.2   The bilingual language interaction network for comprehension of speech (BLINCS) model (adapted from Shook & Marian, 2013, Figure 1).

Cortical Organization of Languages in Bilinguals

Another area of bilingualism research that frequently yields what appear to be contradictory findings is neurolinguistics. Neurolinguistic research with bilinguals usually focuses on *hemispheric organization* of the two languages and on location, size, and spread of activation associated with the two languages. The paradigms used include *event-related potentials* (ERPs), *positron emission tomography* (PET), *functional magnetic resonance imaging* (fMRI), cognitive-behavioral studies with bilingual and multilingual individuals who have aphasia, and others. A topic that has received the most attention in neurolinguistic research with bilinguals is that of organization of the two languages in the brain.

On the one hand, many studies have supported the position that the two languages are associated with different cortical structures. For example, selective disruption of first and second language naming has been reported in cortical stimulation studies (e.g., Ojemann & Whitaker, 1978). Selective language loss and/or differential language recovery in multilingual aphasic patients have also been interpreted as evidence for distinct cortical representations for each language (e.g., Gomez-Tortosa, Martin, Gaviria, Charbel, & Ausman, 1995; Nilipour & Ashayeri, 1989; Paradis, 1995; Paradis & Goldblum, 1989). Using functional neuroimaging in studies with bilinguals who acquired their second language postpuberty, Kim, Relkin, Lee, and Hirsch (1997) and Marian, Spivey, and Hirsch (2003) found that the two languages were associated with activations whose centers differed across the two languages within some cortical areas (e.g., the *inferior frontal gyrus*), but not others (e.g., the *superior temporal gyrus*).

On the other hand, a number of other studies have found evidence for overlapping cortical representations in bilinguals. Overlapping regions of activation in the left inferior frontal gyrus were found in French–English bilinguals using PET (Klein, Milner, Zatorre, Meyer, & Evans, 1995). Chee, Tan, and Thiel (1999) found that *late bilinguals* activated the same regions for both languages in frontal, temporal, and parietal lobes. Additionally, Illes et al. (1999) reported identical frontal lobe activations for both languages in Spanish–English bilinguals.

These differences are due in part to differences in methodologies and/or participant populations. For example, studies with early bilinguals (bilinguals who acquired both languages in early childhood) have found mostly the same cortical areas activated for both L1 and L2 (Chee et al., 1999; Illes et al., 1999; Kim et al., 1997; Perani et al., 1998). Studies with late bilinguals (bilinguals who acquired their second language later in life) produced mixed results, ranging from reports that the two languages are processed similarly (Chee et al., 1999; Illes et al., 1999; Perani et al., 1998) to reports that the two languages are processed differently (Dehaene et al., 1997; Kim et al., 1997). The variability is sometimes accounted for by taking into account language proficiency (Abutalebi, Cappa, & Perani, 2001). But even the distinctions in language proficiency and age of acquisition are rather global. In part, the differences in findings are also due to failure to distinguish between distinct activation patterns for different types of information, for example, orthographic, phonological, lexical, and semantic. Studies that focus on monolingual language processing have long been differentiating between different types and modalities of processing (Binder et al., 1994; Fujimaki et al., 1999; Nobre, Allison, & McCarthy, 1994; Petersen, Fox, Snyder, & Raichle, 1990; Price & Giraud, 2001; Shaywitz et al., 1995), and similar distinctions should be considered when studying bilingual processing.

In bilinguals, a global L1 versus L2 approach—one that poses the general question of whether the same or different areas in the brain are associated with the first and second languages—is misleading because language processing and the associated neural correlates are influenced by the type of processing involved, by the tasks and stimuli used, by experimental methodology, and by participant language history. Moreover, because there is not one area of the brain alone that is devoted to language processing, but rather a network of areas that work together, the question of same or different cortical activation in bilinguals is fundamentally misguided and needs to be reframed in more appropriate terms that reflect the network processing approach.

Indeed, recent research on the bilingual brain provides a more nuanced approach by examining activation in a network of brain areas depending on differences between tasks, stimuli, and participants. Findings suggest that bilingualism changes gray matter density in the inferior parietal cortex (Mechelli et al., 2004), influences recruitment of the inferior frontal cortex during language processing (Kovelman, Baker, & Petitto, 2008; Marian, Spivey, & Hirsch, 2003), and impacts how the bilingual brain processes math (Salillas & Wicha, 2012). Bilingualism can also influence the neural underpinnings of attention processes (Bialystok, Martin, & Viswanathan, 2005; Luk, Anderson, Craik, Grady, & Bialystok, 2010; Naylor, Stanley, & Wicha, 2012) and the processing of competing words (Marian, Chabal, Bartolotti, Bradley, & Hernandez, 2014). While research has shown that bilingual experience is associated with changes in cortical activity (Kroll & Bialystok, 2013), the neural bases of bilingual language processing are not yet well understood, and this is one area that will likely see extensive growth in the next few decades.

Language Development in Bilingual Children

Developmental research on bilingualism tends to generate broad public interest. From issues that affect bilingual children directly, such as educational placement of bilingual children, to issues that have the potential to influence the entire population, such as the requirement (or lack of requirement) of a foreign language in schools, research on bilingual children can impact educators, parents, funding agencies, and government policies. To illustrate the broad range of findings, consider the following two opposite scenarios that happen every day in almost every school district in the US. Every year, thousands of middle-class and upper-class American children take a foreign language for purposes of enrichment. These children, their parents, and teachers function under the assumption that knowing another language *is good for you*. At the same time and sometimes in the same school, countless other children, usually of lower-class and, sometimes, middle-class backgrounds, usually immigrant, often Hispanic or Asian, are discouraged from and sometimes forbidden to speak a native language, under the assumption that that will prevent them from mastering English and that, in general, raising children with more than one language *will confuse them* and will have long-lasting detrimental effects.

If pressed, both sides can provide what appears as convincing evidence supporting their position. There are, for instance, studies on the impact of bilingualism on *cognitive development* that point out that bilingualism in children is associated with increased metacognitive skills and superior divergent thinking ability (a type of *cognitive flexibility*) and with better performance on some *perceptual tasks* (such as recognizing a perceptual object *embedded* in a visual background) and classification tasks (see Bialystok, 2001; Cummins, 1976; Diaz, 1983, 1985, for review). There are also studies that suggest that bilingualism has a negative impact on language development and is associated with delay in lexical acquisition (e.g., Pearson, Fernández, & Oller, 1993; Umbel & Oller, 1995) and a smaller vocabulary than that of monolingual children (Verhallen & Schoonen, 1993; Vermeer, 2001). Both arguments are right in a sense, but before going on to discuss the methodological aspects behind such findings, let's digress here to provide assurance that, by all accounts, bilingual children catch up with their monolingual counterparts on tests of verbal ability by the time they are in middle school, and well-controlled studies provide no evidence for lower intellectual abilities of bilingual children compared to monolinguals. The early differences in linguistic performance of bilingual children can be attributed to a language development pattern that is somewhat different from that of a monolingual. Bilingual children learn earlier than their monolingual counterparts that objects and their names are not one and the same, that these are two separate entities, and that one object can have more than one name. However, whereas understanding that language is a symbolic reference system is advantageous for metacognitive development, it does not necessarily translate to superior vocabulary development early in life.

Consider, for instance, how *language assessment* usually takes place. If a monolingual child has three lexical labels for three semantic items, say *milk*, *grandma*, and *dog*, and a bilingual child has two lexical labels in English (say *milk* and *grandma*) and two in Spanish (say *leche* and *abuela*, the Spanish words for *milk* and *grandma*), the monolingual child's vocabulary will be counted as consisting of three words and the bilingual child's vocabulary will be counted as consisting of two words. That is the case because vocabulary size is counted not as the number of lexical items known, but as the number of conceptual representations that have lexical labels. In this way, even though the bilingual child has four words in his/her vocabulary, the lexical labels map onto two conceptual representations only, compared to the three conceptual representations in the monolingual child.

This technique of assessment frequently places bilingual children at a disadvantage. Even worse, sometimes bilinguals are assessed in only one of their two languages, therefore providing an inaccurate assessment of the child's actual level of linguistic and cognitive development. For example, if the bilingual child in the example above knew four words in Spanish and four words in English, two of which in each language were *translation equivalents*, the child should be assessed as having a vocabulary of six words total (two concepts that had labels in Spanish only, two concepts that had labels in English only, and two concepts that had labels in both English and Spanish). Too often, however, children are assessed in only one of their languages, typically the language of the country in which they are being tested (e.g., English, often their second and less proficient language), therefore resulting in assessments that erroneously place the bilingual child at a lower level of cognitive development than his or her true level. The problem, although clearly disturbing, is not an easy one to fix. Most school districts and speech-language pathology clinics are physically and financially unable to test children in Polish, Romanian, Kirghis, Urdu, Quechua, or any number of languages that may serve as a child's native language. As a result, children may be subject to academic placement below their appropriate level, handicapping their later academic advancement (for more comprehensive discussions of first/second language knowledge and cognitive processing in bilingual children, see work by Cummins, e.g., Cummins, 1984, Chapter 2).

To this day, the majority of clinical and experimental studies focusing on cognitive development in bilingual children assess participants in one language only. However, when *best performance* across the two languages is considered, thus assessing the highest level of cognitive development attained by a bilingual child (as opposed to the level reflected in one language), bilinguals do not appear to be at a disadvantage (e.g., Sheng, McGregor, & Marian, 2006), and in fact may show some advantages. Measures of best performance are measures of cognitive development that are not limited by the constraints of one language. For example, in a recent study comparing semantic organization in elementary school-age bilingual Mandarin–English children and monolingual English children, Sheng, McGregor, and Marian (2006) compared the number of syntagmatic and paradigmatic responses in a *word association task*. *Paradigmatic* responses (i.e., responses that are from the same grammatical class, such as *dog-pet, dog-cat, dog-collie*) are indicative of a more mature semantic system organized around category relationships, whereas *syntagmatic* responses (i.e., responses that are from different grammatical classes, such as *dog-bark, dog-good*) are experience-based and characteristic of a less developed system (Nelson, 1977). Comparisons among children's performance in the first language, second language, and best performances indicated that performance in one language, even when that was the dominant language, was not an accurate reflection of the child's level of semantic development, reinforcing the argument that assessment of bilingual individuals was most accurate when combining best performance across both languages.

Methodological Considerations

Now that the basics of research design and the necessary research vocabulary are in place, the next section will serve as a primer on what variables to consider when studying bilingualism, multilingualism, and second/foreign language learning. The focus is primarily on selection of languages, selection of participants, selections of tasks and stimuli, and data coding and analyses. Failure to take these into account when designing, conducting, or interpreting bilingualism research can yield debates and even heated arguments between scientists who find seemingly contradictory results (as the field of inhibitory control advantages in bilinguals has recently witnessed), where the contradictions can in fact be explained by methodological differences, which then tap different linguistic and cognitive processes.

Selection of Languages

Before deciding on the characteristics of the bilinguals to be tested in any given study, a more basic decision to make is what languages the bilingual participants should be speakers of. Aside from obvious practical considerations, such as access to a subject pool and ability of the experimenter or research assistant to test in that language, another concern is proper choice of languages from a theoretical standpoint. The answer to some research questions may be directly influenced by the choice of languages that the bilingual group speaks. Languages of the world differ in their auditory qualities, written form, and *cross-linguistic similarity*. Not only do languages that are closer in a language family tree share origins, but they are also more likely to share vocabulary, phonological qualities, and alphabets. Bilingual speakers of two languages that are similar (i.e., from the Indo-European language family), such as Spanish and Portuguese, for example, or Dutch and Afrikaans, may yield dramatically different results in a study of spoken or written language processing, for instance, than speakers of two languages that belong to different language families, such as English and Mandarin, or Russian and Japanese.

Because languages vary in how similar they are to each other, the relationship between the letters, sounds, words, and grammars of the two languages differ depending upon the languages studied. To conduct well-controlled research, scientists must take into account similarities and differences between words in different languages. For example, the cross-linguistic easy access resource for phonological and orthographic neighborhood densities, or CLEARPOND (Marian, Bartolotti, Chabal, & Shook, 2012) allows scientists who study performance in different languages to examine how similar or different words are phonologically and orthographically across languages (as well as within languages) by providing detailed information about the *phonological* and *orthographic neighborhoods* of any word in English, French, Dutch, German, or Spanish (phonological and orthographic neighborhoods refer to the density of words that are similar to the target word and differs from it in only one sound or letter). This way, when designing a study, care should be taken that the words selected for that study do not bias performance in a way that would invalidate the results. For example, the number of words that sound or are spelled similarly to the target word influences how fast a participant responds to that word; therefore, if the sets of words in each language are not controlled for *neighborhood density*, then any differences in reaction times between the two languages can be mistakenly attributed to language proficiency or age of acquisition or other participant characteristics as opposed to the confounding variable of phonological or orthographic neighborhood density, thereby invalidating the conclusions.

Moreover, some questions can only be answered with bilingual speakers of some, but not other, languages. If one were interested in studying how different alphabets influence processing of the same language, for instance, one would have to select a language that can be transcribed using more than one alphabet, such as Serbo-Croatian, which can rely on either the Latin or the Cyrillic alphabets. Some questions can only be answered by studying bilinguals whose two languages share alphabets (such as German–English bilinguals), other questions can only be answered by studying bilinguals whose two languages use different alphabets (such as Korean–English bilinguals), yet other questions can only be answered by studying bilinguals whose two written systems share some, but not all written symbols (such as Russian–English bilinguals). In studies of bilingual reading, for example, taking into account ease of *grapheme-to-phoneme mapping* is particularly important, because languages with *shallow orthographies* (consistent *letter-to-sound mapping*, like Spanish) are processed differently in some aspects than languages with *deep orthographies* (inconsistent letter-to-sound mapping, like English). When selecting the languages for a study, understanding the constraints that each language places on the research at hand and taking these constraints into account when interpreting findings is essential.

Selection of Participants

In general, research in psychology, communication sciences and disorders, education, and linguistics is not representative of individuals with a diverse linguistic and cultural background, despite the fact that, when the world as a whole is considered, bilingualism is the norm, rather than the exception (Grosjean, 1997; Harris & Nelson, 1992; Kroll & de Groot, 1997; Romaine, 1995) and that the proportion of bilinguals in the US is rapidly growing (Marian & Shook, 2012). It is estimated that there are about thirty times as many languages in the world as there are countries and that at least half of the world population is bilingual (Romaine, 1995). In the US, the results of the 2000 Census indicate that, due to changes in ethnic, linguistic, and racial composition, the minority population (Spanish-speaking, in particular) is growing 12 times faster than the majority population and that the foreign-born population grew from 19.8 million to 30.5 million between 1990 and 2000. By the year 2000, 18% of American households spoke a language other than English at home, a proportion that is steadily increasing, and yet, the vast majority of experimental populations under study are monolingual. Linguistically diverse populations remain severely under-studied, under-served, and under-represented.

We have already mentioned that selection of target languages can influence the outcomes of a study and may lead to apparently contradictory results. But even in speakers of the same languages, a number of variables other than the language *per se* can and will influence research outcomes. For example, factors such as age of acquisition may influence cortical organization of a bilingual's two languages, with bilinguals who learned both languages in parallel from early in life showing more overlap in cortical areas associated with first and second language activation, compared to bilinguals who learned a second language later in life (e.g., Kim et al., 1997). *Manner of acquisition* is another factor that has been found to influence results of bilingualism studies. For example, bilinguals who learn their second language by rote memorization of translation equivalents in a classroom setting show a lexico-semantic organization consistent with the *word association model* (in which the meaning of a word in L2 is accessed via its translation equivalent in L1), while bilinguals who learn their second language via everyday use in a second-language-speaking environment show a lexico-semantic organization consistent with the *concept mediation model* (in which access to word meaning is by direct route from lexical label to concept in both the first and second languages). Moreover, the actual conceptual representation of a word is more likely to differ in these two groups of bilinguals, with representation being more similar for those bilinguals who learned their second languages in a classroom setting via translation of L1 lexical labels, and representations being more different across the two languages for bilinguals who learned both languages via everyday use in environments in which those languages were spoken (de Groot, 1992).

In addition to age of acquisition and manner of acquisition, another crucially important factor to consider is *proficiency*. How well do these bilinguals know their first and second languages? How well can they speak, understand, read, and write in their two languages?

In addition to absolute proficiency in each of the two languages, what is the *relative* proficiency of one language with respect to the other—are these balanced bilinguals or is one language stronger than the other? In balanced and non-balanced bilinguals, relative activation of the two languages may differ, thus leading to different results in studies that compare activation and *interference* of the two languages in bilingual language processing. Relative activation of the two languages is likely to also be influenced by current use of and recent exposure to the two languages.

Psycholinguistic studies with bilinguals may require the researcher to also control for differences on such variables as working memory capacity, vocabulary size, verbal/non-verbal IQ scores, and/or other cognitive attributes of the bilingual participants. Sociolinguistic studies with bilinguals may require the researcher to control for such differences as socioeconomic status, level of education, gender, or birth order. When more than one group of participants is tested, control for potentially problematic confounding variables can be accomplished by *matching* participants in the two groups on relevant variables (e.g., non-verbal IQ scores) or by *random assignment* of participants to groups.

Selection of Tasks and Stimuli

There are a number of classic tasks in bilingualism research that have been shown to be valid and reliable measures of cognitive performance in bilingual studies. For example, picture naming, *word translation*, *word recognition*, passage reading, *cross-linguistic priming*, and *Stroop tasks* have all been used to study bilingual language representation and processing (see for example, Heredia, Altarriba, & Cieślicka, 2015). Variations on classic monolingual tasks are frequently used. For example, priming tasks are frequently used with monolinguals to study lexical and *semantic activation*. A simple example would be presenting a participant with the prime *dog* and examining speed-of-recognition in a *lexical decision task* (is this a word or a nonword?) for targets such as *cat* and *cloud*. Because *cat* is semantically related to *dog*, it is usually recognized faster than *cloud*, a semantically unrelated item. In bilinguals, priming tasks are frequently used to establish whether semantic representations are shared between languages. For example, in a Spanish–English bilingual, would the prime *dog* activate the target *gato* (Spanish for *cat*) in the same way that it activates the target *cat* and/or in the same way that the prime *perro* (Spanish word for *dog*) does? Similarities and differences in priming across languages and within languages provide insights into the extent to which the two semantic networks are integrated in a bilingual. Variations in the priming paradigm include presenting bilinguals with a prime that is either in the visual modality and can be a written word, syllable, letter, symbol, a feature such as a line; or in the auditory modality and can be a spoken word, syllable, phoneme, linguistic or non-linguistic sound such as tone or music. Similarly, the target can also vary within and across modalities, languages, and levels of processing that it taps into.

New tasks and methodologies are continually emerging. These, coupled with novel approaches or technologies, make it possible to study questions that were previously impossible to answer. For instance, in studies of bilingual spoken language processing, it has proved difficult to reliably measure activation of a non-target language without overtly using that language in a task. Recent developments in *eye tracking* methodology made it possible to use bilinguals' eye movements as an index of language activation, allowing to behaviorally test activation of a language that is not overtly used by recording bilinguals' eye movements to objects whose names in the non-target language overlapped at onset with the name of another object in the target languages (Marian & Spivey, 2003; Spivey &

Marian, 1999). This use of eye tracking technology to study non-target language activation in bilinguals provided the strongest support to date for parallel activation of both languages in bilingual spoken language processing. However, it is not the task's novelty that is important, but its ability to validly and reliably answer the questions at hand.

Virtually every task used to study monolinguals and virtually every approach in cognitive, behavioral, and neural sciences can be successfully applied with bilingual populations. Methodologies such as fMRI, PET, or ERPs have all been successfully used with bilinguals. Challenges arise not because different tasks are used, but because the different tasks often probe different phenomena, and that is not always taken into account when interpreting the findings. For instance, a priming paradigm can be used to study phonological, lexical, or semantic processing and can show facilitation in one case and inhibition in another. Taking into account the tasks that were used and the types of processing that were tapped into when obtaining a particular result is very important.

In addition, careful consideration should be given to all stimulus characteristics that may bear on the outcome of the study. For example, most experiments with bilingual participants use linguistic stimuli, such as sentences, words, and phonemes. If the stimuli are words, for instance, factors such as word frequencies in the two languages may influence outcome. Regardless of what languages or bilingual populations one uses, *high-frequency words* are likely to be recognized faster than *low-frequency words*, and this effect may influence research results. On top of considering frequencies within a language, as is also recommended in research with monolinguals, in bilingualism research it is often necessary to also control for word frequencies *across* languages, to ensure that word frequency differences across languages are not driving the results. Even when the actual stimuli used are not words, for example, when pictures are used, the label of the picture may continue to be important, and factors such as word frequencies for the labels that the pictures represent should still be taken into account. Further, variables such as *bigram frequency* (the likelihood of two graphemes co-occurring together in a language) or consistency of letter-to-sound mappings in stimuli can become important as well, depending upon the question under investigation (Marian et al., 2012).

Data Collection and Analyses

Before a researcher can begin running a study and collecting actual data, any research project with human participants must be approved by an *Institutional Review Board* (IRB), and all researchers must undergo training to comply with the Health Insurance Portability and Accountability Act (HIPAA). When testing participants, it is important to follow ethical guidelines and considerations, protecting participants' rights to privacy and confidentiality. Participants must provide informed consent, and care should be taken so that no physical or psychological harm is inflicted upon them. When testing bilinguals, consideration should be given to which of the two languages should be used when obtaining informed consent.

Actual data collection can take place in many ways, including face-to-face format, computer-collected format, paper-and-pencil format, recordings of brain activity, etc. During experimental procedures, the guidelines set for language use throughout the experiment should be consistent with the purposes of the study. In some studies, language switches may be discouraged or even prohibited, while in other studies they may be acceptable or even encouraged.

When analyzing data, some may work with videotaped or audiotaped recordings, written transcriptions, or digital files. In many cases, the raw data need to be transcribed and coded first. When transcribing and coding data, it is important to ensure that a coder is consistent within her/his own coding from time A to time B and that multiple coders are consistent across each other, something that can be accomplished by having more than one coder for any given data set, and by computing intra- and inter-coder reliability.

When testing a research hypothesis, most studies will rely on statistical analyses to ensure that their effects did not emerge by chance and are reliable (i.e., statistically significant). *Statistical significance* refers to the likelihood of a particular set of results to have happened by chance. For example, when reporting analyses that have a *probability level* less than 0.05 (reported as $p < 0.05$), what the researcher is saying is that the likelihood of those results to have happened by chance is less than 5 in 100 times. In behavioral research, probability levels of 0.05 and 0.01 (one in a hundred) are typically used, while in medical research, more stringent criteria are usually used, with probability levels of 0.001 (one in a thousand) and 0.005 (five in a thousand) more common. For strong data analysis skills, there is no substitution for a good statistics course and good statistical analysis resources, such as software and textbooks.

Summary and Conclusions: The Journey to Scientific Paper

If you've ever stayed up all night reading a book because you could not wait to find out how it ended, or if you've been excited by the prospect of discovering or learning something new, your intellectual curiosity may make you a prime candidate for a research career, one marked by many hours at the library, in the lab, in front of the computer, and in the classroom. But there is a long way between that initial intellectual curiosity and a completed scientific endeavor. Although the exact quest will differ in its content, with questions asked and specific studies varying widely, the path from the original idea to a shared scientific truth is very similar, at least for those working with bilinguals. It includes familiarizing oneself with the literature, defining a research question, considering relevant variables, running the experiment, analyzing data, and reporting the results.

This chapter covered some of the key aspects of doing research with bilinguals. Once the data are collected and analyzed, you begin to approach the end of the journey when you sit down to write up a report of the findings. You may think that the stack of papers reporting the outcomes of statistical analyses symbolizes the grand finale, but no research project is truly complete until its findings are written up and disseminated among the community of scholars working in that area. And whether it is a doctoral dissertation, a conference paper, or a journal article, writing up the research project and transforming it into a scientific paper is for many the most challenging part of the research journey. Writing can be a difficult process; it requires discipline and organization. Writing is also the process that reveals any weaknesses of ideas and execution that may have not been obvious at the start of the project, another anxiety-inducer for many. Some have a difficult time because they expect perfection and fear anything less. Others will say that, once they know the results of the study, once they know how it all turns out, they are no longer interested in the project. Whatever the reason, absence of a written report makes it difficult for findings to reach an audience, and without shared scientific knowledge, a project that has not been written up is about as good as one that has never been run.

If you find that the writing stage does not come as easily as you would have liked, try to come up with a few things that can help you accomplish your goals of a well-written, fine research paper. Figure out what works best for you as far as effective approaches to writing. Though the techniques that are successful vary from person to person, there are a couple of things that seem to work consistently. One is perseverance: not giving up, staying on course, working on the project until it is completed. You may write more on some days, less on others, but be sure to write consistently. Make goals that are not overwhelming to start with. If it is going well, keep at it; if you are not particularly productive on a given day, work on the *busy work*, things that take time and effort but do not require as much creativity. The second thing that many find helpful in early stages of their writing careers is having someone to turn to for support. Be it a mentor, an adviser, a significant other, a parent, a student, a colleague, a friend, a former teacher, a therapist, a writing coach— anyone who will be there for you when you need a word of encouragement and support. Eventually, as you become a more experienced writer, internalize the techniques that work for you, and learn the ebb and flow of your particular writing style. You may no longer need a touchstone person to turn to, but in those early stages, seeking out an environment that is supportive and encouraging may make the difference between a completed dissertation and an eternal ABD (all-but-dissertation) status. Finding out what and who motivates you to be a better writer and researcher can open the secret to a successful research career for many years to come. And, as you benefit from the support and encouragement of others, remember to be that supportive and encouraging person to someone else in turn.

You will most likely go through numerous drafts before the final paper is published in a peer-reviewed scientific journal. The first completed draft will be revised and polished many times before it is ready to be submitted to a journal or turned in to your advising committee. And the work does not end there. Advising committees often require revisions. Scientific journals follow a peer-review process and also, more often than not, require revisions. It is not unusual for an author to have to go through more than one round of revisions. Ultimately, the goal of that process is to produce an informative, well-written, and high-impact study, expanding scientific understanding.

Indeed, this chapter was written in a similar way, and was guided by the goal of serving as a foundation for future researchers interested in contributing to the understanding of the human linguistic capacity and the ability to accommodate more than one language simultaneously. In very broad strokes, this chapter provided an introductory overview to bilingual research methods.

List of Key Words and Concepts

Age of acquisition, Aphasia, Back-propagation, Balanced bilinguals, Between-group, Bigram frequency, Bilingual interaction activation model, Bilingual language interaction network for comprehension of speech, Cognitive development, Cognitive flexibility, Compound, Concept mediation model, Confounding variables, Control group, Coordinative, Correlational research, Cross-linguistic priming, Cross-linguistic similarity, Cross-sectional, Deep orthographies, Dependent variables, Descriptive research, Distributed feature representation model, Event-related potentials (ERPs), Experimental group, Experimental research, Eye tracking, Feature level, Flashbulb memories, Functional magnetic resonance imaging (fMRI), Grapheme-to-phoneme mapping, Hebbian learning, Hemispheric organization, High-frequency words, Hypothesis testing, Immigration Restriction Act, Independent variables, Institutional review board (IRB), Interference, Language assessment, Language loss, Language proficiency, Late bilinguals, Letter-to-sound mappings, Lexical decision task, Lexical level, Lexico-semantic organization, Longitudinal studies, Low-frequency words, Manner of acquisition, Mixed-design, Naturalistic observation, Neighborhood density, Neural network, Operational definitions, Orthographic neighborhood, Paradigmatic, Participant characteristics, Peabody Picture Vocabulary Test (PPVT), Perceptual tasks, Phonological neighborhood, Picture naming task, Placebo effects, Positron emission tomography (PET), Post-test, Pre-test, Probability level, Proficiency, Random assignment, Reaction time, Reliability, Representation, Revised hierarchical model, Self-organizing model of bilingual processing, Semantic activation, Sequential, Shallow orthographies, Signifieds, Signifiers, Specific language impairment, Speech-language pathologist, Spoken language processing, Statistical significance, Stroop tasks, Sub-coordinative, Syntagmatic, Torrance Test of Creative Thinking, TRACE, Translation equivalents, Treatment, Validity, Vocabulary size, Wernicke's aphasia, Within-group, Word association model, Word association task, Word recognition, Word translation

Internet Sites Related to Bilingualism Research

Bilingual Children: http://www.linguisticsociety.org/resource/faq-raising-bilingual-children
Bilingualism and Psycholinguistics: http://www.bilingualism.northwestern.edu/
CLEARPOND Database of Word Properties: http://clearpond.northwestern.edu/
Life as a Bilingual: https://www.psychologytoday.com/blog/life-bilingual
Linguistic Society of America: http://www.lsadc.org/
Multilingual Children's Association: http://www.multilingualchildren.org/faq.html

Discussion Questions

Choose two of the examples used in text and answer the three questions below for those sample experiments:

(1) Identify the design, the independent variables, and the dependent variables.
(2) When conducting these studies, what confounds would you attempt to avoid and how?
(3) How may the outcome of these studies vary between bilinguals who are highly proficient in both languages and bilinguals with different proficiency levels in the two languages?

Suggested Research Projects

(1) *Experimental Study: The Stroop Effect with Bilinguals and Monolinguals.* Write color words using different color ink; for example, write the word *black* in either black or red ink. For half of the words the color of the ink and the color word should match, for the other half the color of the ink should be different from the color spelled by the word. Now ask your classmates to name the color of the ink for each word, ignoring the words themselves. Time the responses. Compare response times for items in which the color of the ink and the word match to items where the two do not match. How do you explain the results? Now ask those classmates who speak more than one language to name the color of the ink in the other language they know (not the language that the words are written in). Again, time their responses. Compare response times for trials in which the language used to name pictures is the same as the language of the written words to trials in which the language used to name pictures is different from the language of the written words. How do you explain these results? Did it make a difference whether the bilingual subjects were speaking their first or second language? Their stronger or weaker language? For more about the bilingual Stroop task, read Preston and Lambert (1969) and Tzelgov, Henik, and Leisner (1990).

(2) *Observational Study: Bilingual Narrative Analysis.* Interview a bilingual speaker about a salient childhood event (e.g., a memorable birthday, a visit to the doctor, a move, a vacation trip, etc.) in each of the two languages s/he speaks (if you are not bilingual yourself, ask a bilingual classmate to conduct the interview). Tape the narratives. Does the bilingual switch to the other language during a narrative? Do the switches appear random or do they occur in a systematic fashion (e.g., at the same point in a sentence, or related to the same topic, or in one language more than in the other)? How do you explain these results? Are there other differences across the two languages (e.g., emotional content and intensity, self-construal)?

Suggested Readings

Baker, C., & Jones, S. P. (1998). *Encyclopedia of bilingualism and bilingual education.* Clevedon, UK: Multilingual Matters.

Bialystok E., Martin M. M., & Viswanathan M. (2005). Bilingualism across the lifespan: The rise and fall of inhibitory control. *International Journal of Bilingualism, 9,* 103–119.

Grosjean, F. (1998). Studying bilinguals: Methodological and conceptual issues. *Bilingualism: Language and Cognition, 1,* 131–149.

Pavlenko, A. (2009). *The bilingual mental lexicon.* Clevedon, UK: Multilingual Matters.

Ray, W. J. (1993). *Methods: Towards a science of behavior and experience.* Pacific Grove, CA: Brooks/Cole.

Shook, A., & Marian, V. (2012). The cognitive benefits of being bilingual. *Cerebrum.* Retrieved from www.dana.org/news/cerebrum/detail.aspx?id=39638.

Author Notes

Preparation of this chapter was supported in part by grants NICHDR01HD059858 from the National Institutes of Health and BCS0418495 from the National Science Foundation.

References

Abutalebi, J., Cappa, S. F., & Perani, D. (2001). The bilingual brain as revealed by functional neuroimaging. *Bilingualism: Language and Cognition, 4*(2), 179–190.

Bialystok, E. (2001). *Bilingualism in development: Language, literacy, and cognition.* New York: Cambridge University Press.

Bialystok, E., Martin, M. M., & Viswanathan, M. (2005). Bilingualism across the lifespan: The rise and fall of inhibitory control. *International Journal of Bilingualism, 9*(1), 103–119.

Binder, J. R., Rao, S. M., Hammeke, T. A., Yetkin, F. Z., Jesmanowicz, A., Bandertini, T. A., Wong, E. C., Estkowski, L. B., Goldstein, M. D., Haughton, V. M., & Hyde, J. S. (1994). Functional magnetic resonance imaging of human auditory cortex. *Annals of Neurology, 35,* 662–672.

Brigham, C. C. (1923). *A study of American intelligence.* Princeton, NJ: Princeton University Press.

Chee, M. W. L., Tan, E. W. L., & Thiel, T. (1999). Mandarin and English single word processing studied with functional magnetic resonance imaging. *Journal of Neuroscience, 19,* 3050–3056.

Cummins, J. (1976). The influence of bilingualism on cognitive growth: A synthesis of research findings and explanatory hypotheses. *Working Papers on Bilingualism, 9,* 1–43.

Cummins, J. (1984). *Bilingualism and special education: Issues in assessment and pedagogy.* San Diego, CA: College-Hill Press.

de Groot, A. M. B. (1992). Bilingual lexical representation: A closer look at conceptual representations. In R. Frost & L. Katz (Eds.), *Orthography, phonology, morphology, and meaning* (pp. 389–412). Amsterdam: Elsevier.

Dehaene, S., Dupoux, E., Mehler, J., Cohen, L., Paulesu, E., Perani, D., van de Moortele, P. F., Lehéricy, S., & Le Bihan, D. (1997). Anatomical variability in the cortical representation of first and second language. *Neuroreport, 8*(17), 3809–3815.

Diaz, R. M. (1983). The impact of bilingualism on cognitive development. In E. W. Gordon (Ed.), *Review of research in education* (Vol. 10, pp. 23–54). Washington, DC: American Educational Research Association.

Diaz, R. M. (1985). Bilingual cognitive development: Addressing three gaps in current research. *Child Development, 56*, 1376–1388.

Dijkstra, A., van Heuven, W. J. B., & Grainger, J. (1998). Simulating cross-language competition with the Bilingual Interactive Activation model. *Psychologica Belgica, 38*, 177–196.

Ervin, S. M., & Osgood, C. E. (1954). Second language learning and bilingualism. *Journal of Abnormal and Social Psychology, 49*, 139–146.

Ervin, S. M., & Osgood, C. E. (1965). Second language learning and bilingualism. In C. Osgood & T. Sebeok (Eds.), *Psycholinguistics: A survey of theory and research problems with a survey of psycholinguistic research* (pp. 139–146). Bloomington, IN: Indiana University Press.

Fujimaki, N., Miyauchi, S., Puetz, B., Sasaki, Y., Takino, R., Saakai, K., & Takada, T. (1999). Functional magnetic resonance imaging of neural activity related to orthographic, phonological and lexicosemantic judgements of visually presented characters and words. *Human Brain Mapping, 8*, 44–59.

Goddard, H. H. (1914). *Feeble-mindedness. Its causes and consequences.* New York: Macmillan.

Gomez-Tortosa, E., Martin, E. M., Gaviria, M., Charbel, F., & Ausman, J. I. (1995). Selective deficit of one language in a bilingual patient following surgery in the left perisylvian area. *Brain and Language, 48*, 320–325.

Grosjean, F. (1997). Processing mixed language: Issues, findings, and models. In A. M. B. de Groot & J. Kroll (Eds.), *Tutorials in bilingualism: Psycholinguistic perspectives* (pp. 225–254). Hillsdale, NJ: Lawrence Erlbaum.

Harris, R. J., & Nelson, E. M. M. (1992). Bilingualism: Not the exception any more. *Advances in Psychology, 83*, 3–14.

Henrich, J., Heine, S. J., & Norenzayan, A. (2010). The weirdest people in the world? *Behavioral and Brain Sciences, 33*, 61–83.

Heredia, R. R., Altarriba, J., & Cieślicka, A. B. (Eds.). (2015). *Methods in bilingual reading research comprehension research: The bilingual mind and brain series* (Vol. 1). New York: Springer.

Herrnstein, R. J., & Murray, C. (1994). *The bell curve.* New York: Simon & Schuster.

Illes, J., Francis, W. S., Desmond, J. E., Gabrieli, J. D. E., Glover, G. H., Poldrack, R., Lee, C. J., & Wagner, A. D. (1999). Convergent cortical representation of semantic processing in bilinguals. *Brain and Language, 70*, 347–363.

Kim, K. H. S., Relkin, N. R., Lee, K. M., & Hirsch, J. (1997). Distinct cortical areas associated with native and second languages. *Nature, 388*, 171–174.

Klein, D., Milner, B., Zatorre, R., Meyer, E., & Evans, A. (1995). The neural substrates underlying word generation: A bilingual functional-imaging study. In *Proceedings of the National Academy of Science, USA, 92*, 2899–2903.

Kovelman, I., Baker, S. A., & Petitto, L. A. (2008). Bilingual and monolingual brains compared: A functional magnetic resonance imaging investigation of syntactic processing and a possible "neural signature" of bilingualism. *Journal of Cognitive Neuroscience, 20*(1), 153–169.

Kroll, J. F. (1993). Accessing conceptual representations for words in a second language. In R. Schreuder & B. Weltens (Eds.), *The bilingual lexicon* (pp. 53–82). Amsterdam: John Benjamins.

Kroll, J. F., & Bialystok, E. (2013). Understanding the consequences of bilingualism for language processing and cognition. *Journal of Cognitive Psychology, 25*(5), 497–514.

Kroll, J. F., & de Groot, A. M. B. (1997). Lexical and conceptual memory in the bilingual: Mapping form to meaning in two languages. In A. M. B. de Groot & J. F. Kroll (Eds.), *Tutorials in bilingualism: Psycholinguistic perspectives* (pp. 169–199). Mahwah, NJ: Lawrence Erlbaum.

Kroll, J. F., & Stewart, E. (1994). Category interference in translation and picture naming: Evidence for asymmetric connections between bilingual memory representations. *Journal of Memory and Language, 33*(2), 149–174.

Li, P., & Farkas, I. (2002). A self-organized connectionist model of bilingual processing. In R. R. Heredia & J. Altarriba (Eds.), *Bilingual sentence processing* (pp. 59–85). North Holland: Elsevier.

Luk, G., Anderson, J. A., Craik, F. I., Grady, C., & Bialystok, E. (2010). Distinct neural correlates for two types of inhibition in bilinguals: Response inhibition versus interference suppression. *Brain and Cognition, 74*(3), 347–357.

McClelland, J. L., & Elman, J. L. (1986). The TRACE model of speech perception. *Cognitive Psychology, 18*, 1–86.

Marian, V., Bartolotti, J., Chabal, S., & Shook, A. (2012). CLEARPOND: Cross-linguistic easy access resource for phonological and orthographic neighborhood densities. *PloS One, 7*(8), 1–11.

Marian, V., Chabal, S., Bartolotti, J., Bradley, K., & Hernandez, A. E. (2014). Differential recruitment of executive control regions during phonological competition in monolinguals and bilinguals. *Brain and Language, 139*(717), 108–117.

Marian, V., & Shook, A. (2012). The cognitive benefits of being bilingual. *Cerebrum.* http://dana.org/news/cerebrum/detail.aspx?id=39638.

Marian, V., & Spivey, M. (2003). Competing activation in bilingual language processing: Within- and between-language competition. *Bilingualism: Language and Cognition, 6*, 1–19.

Marian, V., Spivey, M., & Hirsch, J. (2003). Shared and separate systems in bilingual language processing: Converging evidence from eyetracking and brain imaging. *Brain and Language, 86*, 70–82.

Mechelli, A., Crinion, J. T., Noppeney, U., O'Doherty, J., Ashburner, J., Frackowiak, R. S., & Price, C. J. (2004). Neurolinguistics: structural plasticity in the bilingual brain. *Nature, 431*(7010), 757–757.

Naylor, L. J., Stanley, E. M., & Wicha, N. Y. (2012). Cognitive and electrophysiological correlates of the bilingual Stroop effect. *Frontiers in Psychology, 3*(81), 1–18. doi:10.3389/fpsyg.2012.00081.

Nelson, K. (1977). The syntagmatic-paradigmatic shift revisited: A review of research and theory. *Psychological Bulletin, 84*, 93–116.

Nilipour, R., & Ashayeri, H. (1989). Alternating antagonism between two languages with successive recovery of a third in a trilingual aphasic patient. *Brain and Language, 36*, 23–48.

Nobre, A. C., Allison, T., & McCarthy, G. (1994). Word recognition in the human inferior temporal lobe. *Nature, 372*, 260–263.

Ojemann, G. A., & Whitaker, H. A. (1978). The bilingual brain. *Archives of Neurology, 35*, 409–412.

Paradis, M. (Ed.). (1995). *Aspects of bilingual aphasia.* Oxford, UK: Tarrytown.

Paradis, M., & Goldblum, M. C. (1989). Selective crossed aphasia in a trilingual aphasic patient followed by reciprocal antagonism. *Brain and Language, 36*, 62–75.

Pearl, E., & Lambert, W. E. (1962). Relation of bilingualism to intelligence. *Psychological Monographs, 76*, 1–23.

Pearson, B. Z., Fernández, S. C., & Oller, D. K. (1993). Lexical development in bilingual infants and toddlers: Comparison to monolingual norms. *Language Learning, 43*(1), 93–120.

Perani, D., Paulesu, E., Galles, N. S., Dupoux, E., Dehaene, S., Bettinardi, V., Cappa, S. F., Fazio, F., & Mehler, J. (1998). The bilingual brain: Proficiency and age of acquisition of the second language. *Brain, 121*, 1841–1852.

Petersen, S. E., Fox, P. T., Snyder, A. Z., & Raichle, M. E. (1990). Activation of extrastriate and frontal cortical areas by visual words and word-like stimuli. *Science, 249*, 1041–1044.

Preston, M., & Lambert, W. (1969). Interlingual interference in a bilingual version of the Stroop Color-Word Task. *Journal of Verbal Learning and Verbal Behavior, 8*, 295–301.

Price, C., & Giraud, A. L. (2001). The constraints functional neuroimaging places on classical models of auditory word processing. *Journal of Cognitive Neuroscience, 13*, 754–765.

Romaine, S. (1995). *Bilingualism.* Oxford, UK: Blackwell.

Salilas, E., & Wicha, N. Y. (2012). Early learning shapes the memory networks for arithmetic: Evidence from brain potentials in bilinguals. *Psychological Science, 23*(7), 745–755.

Shaywitz, B. A., Pugh, K. R., Constable, R. T., Shaywitz, S. E., Bronen, R. T., Fulbright, R. K., Shankweiler, D. P., Katz, L., Fletcher, J. M., & Skudlardki, P. (1995). Localization of semantic processing using functional magnetic resonance imaging. *Human Brain Mapping, 2*, 149–158.

Sheng, L., McGregor, K., & Marian, V. (2006). Lexical-semantic organization in bilingual children: Evidence from a repeated word association task. *Journal of Speech, Language, and Hearing Research, 49*(3), 572–587.

Spivey, M., & Marian, V. (1999). Cross talk between native and second languages: Partial activation of an irrelevant lexicon. *Psychological Science, 10,* 281–284.

Shook, A., & Marian, V. (2013). The bilingual language interaction network for comprehension of speech. *Bilingualism: Language and Cognition, 16,* 304–324.

Tzelgov, J., Henik, A., & Leisner, D. (1990). Controlling Stroop interference: Evidence from a bilingual task. *Journal of Experimental Psychology: Learning, Memory, and Cognition, 16,* 760–771.

Umbel, V. M., & Oller, D. K. (1995). Developmental changes in receptive vocabulary in Hispanic bilingual school children. In B. Harley (Ed.), *Lexical issues in language learning* (pp. 59–80). Amsterdam: John Benjamins.

Verhallen, M., & R. Schoonen (1993). Lexical knowledge of monolingual and bilingual children. *Applied Linguistics, 14*(4), 344–363.

Vermeer, A. (2001). Breadth and depth of vocabulary in relation to L1/L2 acquisition and frequency of input. *Applied Psycholinguistics, 22,* 217–234.

Weinreich, U. (1974). *Languages in contact: Findings and problems.* Paris: Mouton.

Zhao, X., & Li, P. (2007). Bilingual lexical representation in a self-organizing neural network model. In *Proceedings of the 29th Annual Conference of the Cognitive Science Society* (pp. 755–760).

3   Bilingual Mental Models

Roberto R. Heredia and Anna B. Cieślicka

Introduction

As a way to introduce this chapter, consider sentences 1a-b uttered by a Spanish–English bilingual child.

(1a)   *Papi quelo bailal* (Translation: *Daddy I want to dance*).
(1b)   *Yo quelo candy* (Translation: *I want candy*).

Besides the obvious phonological variants of the Spanish verb conjugations (e.g., *quelo* for *quiero* and *bailal* for *bailar*), these sentences illustrate the bilingual's ability to function in a monolingual (sentence 1a) or a bilingual (sentence 1b) language mode. This ability of bilinguals to function independently in one language or in both languages simultaneously has led bilingual researchers to hypothesize about how bilinguals might represent their two languages in memory. This chapter provides an overview of some of the most influential and current models of how bilinguals represent their languages in memory. The discussion starts by providing a general overview of the different types of memories that have been identified in the bilingual cognitive literature, followed by an evaluation of the one- versus two-memory hypotheses, as well as the view that proposes a bilingual memory representation based on how the bilingual's languages are learned. Next, models that assume a memory structure composed of language-specific mental lexicons and a shared general memory store are evaluated. The discussion continues with bilingual models that focus primarily on the different types of words (e.g., abstract vs. concrete), and how these words interact across the bilingual's two languages. The chapter concludes with a brief introduction to the *bilingual interactive activation plus model* (BIA+) that assumes activation of multiple levels during bilingual word recognition.

Memory or Multiple Memories

The issue of bilingual memory storage has been the primary focus of bilingual research for the past five decades. Bilingual research has sought to discover the manner in which the bilingual's two languages are stored under the assumption that a memory trace must be kept in some type of memory store or structure. However, the issue of memory storage is a complex one because memory researchers have identified different types of memories that serve highly specialized purposes (cf. Roediger, 1991, 2008). That is, the human memory system is not unitary, and it would be difficult to talk about memory or memories without specifying the particular type of memory that is being addressed.

Figure 3.1 shows a possible theoretical human memory structure. This model underscores the traditional distinction between *working* and *long-term memory* (LTM). Working memory is the temporary memory store where incoming and ongoing information is being processed before being lost or transferred to LTM. LTM, on the other hand, is the permanent memory store that contains all of the information an individual knows about the world in general. Unlike the LTM, whose capacity is conceived as unlimited, working memory capacity is limited (see Repovš & Baddeley, 2006, for a thorough discussion of working memory). It should be acknowledged, however, that the distinction between working memory and LTM is not as clear cut as suggested in this discussion. In fact, some researchers are not convinced that working memory and LTM are different memories (see for example, Radvansky, 2017). Also, it should be noted that working memory and LTM are interactive, in the sense that information stored in LTM could be accessed by working memory as needed.

Figure 3.1 shows the complexity of LTM. For example, this memory store is subdivided into various highly specialized subsystems or submemories. In general, *declarative memory* is typically described as the store involved in knowing factual information or "knowing that" about information. This store is further divided into two highly specialized memories. *Episodic memory* is involved with specific time-related memory for events and personal experiences. For some of us, 9/11 was an event that had so much impact on our lives that it has become part of our personal memories or episodic memory. This is why we are able to remember specific details about this event. However, 911 is also part of our world knowledge or *semantic memory*. It represents the telephone number that must be dialed for an emergency. Information about world knowledge or encyclopedic knowledge is maintained in semantic memory. *Nondeclarative* or *procedural memory*, on the other hand, is concerned with information about "knowing how" to do things. This memory is directly involved with our knowledge concerning how to ride a bicycle or how to type on a keyboard, for example. How do bilinguals organize their two languages within this rich and complex memory system? The next section proposes two alternatives to the issue of bilingual memory storage. For the present purposes and in reference to the memory model described in Figure 3.1, the focus of the following discussions is on semantic memory. Thus, the hypotheses detailed below describe the possibility that bilinguals might possess one or two semantic memories.

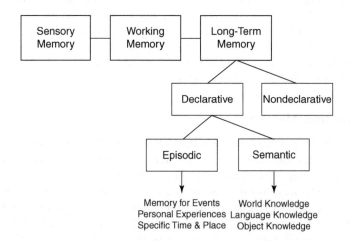

Figure 3.1   A possible structure of the human memory system (adapted from Atkinson & Shiffrin, 1968; Roediger, 1991).

Bilingual Memory: One or Two Memory Systems

Two hypotheses have dominated the field of bilingual memory. The *shared* or *interdependence memory* proposed a bilingual structure in which the bilingual's two languages were organized in one memory store. Words from the bilingual's two languages were stored in memory in the form of language-free concepts (or abstractions) with a single meaning underlying both words or labels (e.g., Caramazza & Brones, 1980). This model proposed that for translation equivalents (e.g., *HOUSE* in English and *CASA* in Spanish), only their meaning was coded or stored in memory and that the same meaning is applied to both labels of the translation equivalents. How are the two languages identified in this memory store? Accordingly, there is some type of "tagging" mechanism that identifies words with the proper language at the time of retrieval (López & Young, 1974). The *separate* or *independence memory hypothesis*, on the other hand, posited a memory organization in which the bilingual's two languages were organized in two separate independent memory stores; one memory store for each language, with information from one language not readily available to the other (cf. Heredia & McLaughlin, 1992). In addition, it is assumed that the only interaction between the two memories is through translation processes (McCormack, 1977). It is important to underscore that these two hypotheses were mainly concerned with meaning and concepts, and not so much with other linguistic aspects, such as phonemic (e.g., sound) or orthographic (e.g., spelling) representational properties.

These hypotheses make the following general predictions. The *shared memory hypothesis* predicts that because both languages share the same underlying code or meaning, both languages would show similar patterns or behave in the same way. This is to say that material or information that is learned in one language should be transferred to the other language. For example, if it is learned in English that 3 + 4 = 7, this information should also be available to Spanish, and the bilingual should not have to relearn the same information in Spanish. Under the assumptions of this hypothesis, concepts across languages are identical. Moreover, in bilingual research, it is customary to distinguish between monolingual and bilingual modes as a way to describe whether a bilingual speaker is using one language (monolingual mode) or two languages (bilingual mode). In experimentation, this is referred to as *within-language* or *between-language* conditions, respectively. In the typical bilingual experiment, word pairs such as *casa-hogar* or *house-home* are described as within-language synonyms. On the other hand, word pairs such as *casa-house* and *hogar-home* are considered between-language or *cross-language* synonyms or translations. As predicted by the shared memory hypothesis, a comparison between within- and between-language conditions would yield similar or identical results.

In relation to the separate memory or *interdependence hypothesis*, the predictions are opposite to those of the shared memory hypothesis. Because the bilingual's two languages are organized in *separate* stores, both languages should exhibit different patterns and behave differently. Thus, a comparison between within- and between-language conditions would result in differences. Typically, percentage of recall is greater for the between- than the within-language conditions. In memory research, this is attributed to the possibility that during the learning or encoding process, bilinguals might encode the to-be-learned information in multiple ways, thus increasing the likelihood that the memory trace is strengthened and therefore remembered better at a later time (see for example, Heredia & García, 2017). Which hypothesis does a better job of explaining bilingual memory? As it will become apparent from the discussion below, the evidence supports both hypotheses. In the following discussion, representative studies supporting both hypotheses are reviewed.

Evidence for the Interdependence Memory

In one experiment, López and Young (1974) asked whether information learned in one language would facilitate or transfer to another language, as measured by a free recall task. To test this possibility, López and Young had Spanish–English bilinguals read a series of adjectives in English (e.g., *angry, tired, smart*) or Spanish (e.g., *verde* [*green*], *hinchado* [*swollen*], *pelón* [*bald*]). Phase one of the experiment was designed to familiarize participants with the materials and have bilinguals learn the list of Spanish and English words. Participants were given no information about the purpose of this list. In the second testing phase, bilinguals listened to another list of words. However, depending on the experimental condition, words in this second list were either direct translations or exactly the same words as the ones from the original list. To assess language transfer and to serve as experimental controls, words that never appeared in the original list were included as well (see Figure 3.2b). To summarize, if a participant in phase one read the adjectives, *angry, tired, smart*, the list in phase two might contain the Spanish translations *enojado, cansado, listo*, or the same English words as the original list, but in different random order. Participants were then asked to recall as many words as possible. Figure 3.2 summarizes the results.

Figure 3.2a shows that, in comparison to Figure 3.2b (the control condition), virtually all language conditions showed language facilitation or language transfer. Specifically, if during the learning phase, the language of familiarization was English and the language of testing was a Spanish translation (i.e., English–Spanish), the mean percentage of words recalled was 10.25 from Figure 3.2a, relative to 9.16 for the control condition from Figure 3.2b, for example. The same pattern is observed for Spanish–English (11.91) in Figure 3.2a, and English–Spanish (11.35) in Figure 3.2b. Likewise, both Spanish–Spanish and English–English within-language repetitions followed similar patterns. The finding that language transfer was possible demonstrated, as predicted by the shared memory hypothesis, that both languages shared the same underlying code. Otherwise, language transfer would not have occurred. Moreover, the fact that both between- and within-language conditions followed the same basic patterns further supported the shared memory model.

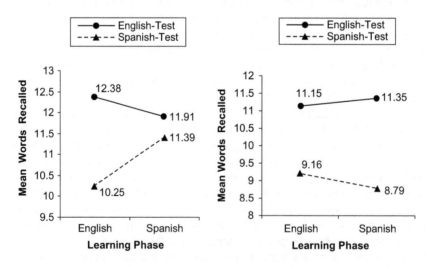

Figure 3.2a–b   Mean of words recalled as a function of language of original learning (learning phase), and language of testing for the experimental condition in Figure 3.2a, left side, and the control condition depicted in Figure 3.2b, right side (figures adapted from López & Young, 1974, p. 982, Figure 1).

In another highly cited study, Glanzer and Duarte (1971) investigated the *repetition effect* and the *spacing effect,* also known as the *distance, lag effect*, and *distributed-practice effect* in bilingual memory (see Heredia & García, 2017). Briefly, the repetition effect refers to the general finding that words that are repeated more than once are remembered better, relative to a word that is non-repeated. In the spacing effect, words are repeated; however, the repetitions are spread out or separated by one or more items over time, rather than presented all at once (e.g., Cepeda, Pashler, Vul, Wixted, & Rohrer, 2006).

The purpose of this study was to test the generalizability of these memory effects to bilingual speakers. Of particular interest was the comparison among the between- and within-language conditions. In this experiment, Spanish–English bilinguals studied a series of word lists containing between- and within-language word repetitions systematically divided into four distances of 0, 1, 2, and 5 intervening words. (A distance of zero would be equivalent to cramming for a test the night before.) To illustrate, consider the following list of words: *store, casa [house], house, grass, pez [fish], grass, zapato [shoe], dog, tree, zapato, wheel, mono [ape], rice, perro [dog]*. From this list, notice that the words *store, pez, tree, wheel, mono,* and *rice* appear only once. These are the non-repeated items. Further, note that *casa* is immediately followed by its translation *house*. This between-language word pair would correspond to a distance or lag of zero because there are no items in between the translation equivalents. The corresponding distances for the English–English word pair (*grass-grass*), the Spanish–Spanish (*zapato-zapato*), and the between-language word pair (*dog-perro*) are 1, 2, and 5, respectively. Note that in designing an experiment of this kind, the investigator must ensure that the same number of language repetitions includes all possible distances. Memory retention was assessed by a free recall test given after list presentation. Figure 3.3 summarizes the results.

Figure 3.3 summarizes the results for the between- and within-language repetitions at distances 0, 1, 2, and 5. The between-language condition was created by combining the Spanish–English and English–Spanish word repetitions. Similarly, the within-language condition was created by combining the English–English and the Spanish–Spanish word repetitions. The open circle above C in Figure 3.3 represents the Spanish and English non-repeated words combined. In general, the percentage of recall for both between- and within-language conditions was much higher than the non-repeated condition. Moreover, note that although the between-language repetitions provided a higher percentage of recall

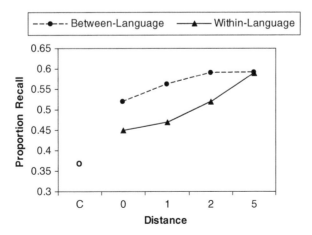

Figure 3.3   Proportion of words recalled as a function of between- and within-language conditions and distance (adapted from Glanzer & Duarte, 1971, p. 628, Figure 1).

at shorter distances, at distance 5, recall was identical to that of the within-language repetitions. Also, in relation to the predictions of the shared memory hypothesis, notice that both language repetitions exhibited the same patterns. That is, as distance increased from 0 to 5, the percentage of recall increased for both language conditions (see Heredia & McLaughlin, 1992; Paivio, Clark, & Lambert, 1988, for similar results).

Other studies involving more direct measures of semantic memory have arrived at similar conclusions. Typically, studies of semantic memory utilize reaction time (RT) as a measure of retrieval or search time. RT is typically measured in milliseconds (ms), and one second is equivalent to 1000 ms. RT measures the time taken to retrieve or to search semantic memory for a particular word. Thus, according to the shared memory hypothesis, because both languages are represented in one memory, retrieval or search of words from the bilingual's two languages should take similar amounts of time. A comparison between monolingual and bilingual conditions should exhibit similar RTs. To test this possibility, Caramazza and Brones (1980) utilized a semantic classification task. In this task, participants were first shown a Spanish or English word representing a category (e.g., *furniture* or *muebles*). Each category word was immediately followed by an instance or a member of that category (e.g., *bed* or *cama*). The participant's task was to determine if the particular instance presented was a member of the previously specified category. For example, given the category *furniture*, participants were required to decide, as fast as possible, if the word *bed* was or was not a member of the category furniture. This was done by pressing one of two computer response keys labeled TRUE or FALSE. RTs represented the amount of time taken to decide whether the critical word was or was not a member of the specified category. Of special interest in this experiment was a comparison of the between-language conditions (e.g., *furniture-cama* and *muebles-bed*) versus within-language conditions (*furniture-bed* and *muebles-cama*). In general, results revealed virtually no differences in RTs for the between- and within-language conditions (for similar findings see Schwanenflugel & Rey, 1986), thus supporting the interdependence hypothesis. Moreover, McCormack's (1977) survey of the bilingual memory literature indicated that the bulk of the research evidence supported the bilingual shared memory hypothesis. However, this conclusion may have been too premature given the support for the independence hypothesis, to which we now turn.

Evidence for the Independence Memory Hypothesis

A recurring issue in the bilingual memory literature is whether words or concepts in the bilingual's two languages are qualitatively different. One possibility is that words or concepts in bilingual memory are identical because both share the same code, as posed by the shared memory hypothesis. For example, Kolers and González (1980) demonstrated that bilingual synonym repetitions (e.g., *house-casa*) were no different than monolingual repetitions (e.g., *house-house*) as aids to retrieval, even if these repetitions required more mental elaboration (Slamecka & Katsaiti, 1978). However, other findings (e.g., Basi, Thomas, & Wang, 1997; Goggin & Wickens, 1971) suggested qualitative differences across the two concepts. Accordingly, this distinctiveness may be due to the manner in which the material was originally learned. It may very well be the case that during the learning process, concepts are coded into LTM in more than one way, with rich linguistic associations specifically related or "coded" to each particular language (see also Heredia & García, 2017).

In a classic study, Goggin and Wickens (1971) effectively demonstrated qualitative and structural differences between the bilingual's two languages. To do this, Goggin and Wickens utilized the *proactive interference paradigm* (PI). This paradigm produces a very well-known and robust finding in the monolingual literature. In demonstrations of PI, older or already-learned material interferes forward in time with the learning of new material. As a consequence, the learning of the to-be-learned material is greatly diminished as measured by a free recall task. To demonstrate, consider Lists 1–4 in the "fruits" category condition in Table 3.1. Each list is composed of two members of the category "fruit." In the typical PI experiment, participants study each list, and after each list a free recall test assesses learning.

As shown by Figure 3.4, under the control condition, proportion of recall drops sharply from List 1 (65%) to List 4 (25%). PI, as pointed out by Goggin and Wickens, is partly due to item similarity (for the latest on PI and item similarity, see Hinson & Whitney, 2006). Therefore, PI could be prevented by changing the category or type of code in the studied lists. Table 3.1 shows that Lists 1–3 are made up of instances of body parts for the category shift condition. However, a category shift occurs in List 4, as it is made up of members of the category "fruit." Indeed, this category shift produces what is called *release from proactive interference*, and the proportion of recall increases as a consequence. For the category shift condition, Figure 3.4 shows a sharp decline of recall from Lists 1–3, as all the words are from the same category. However, notice how the category shift in List 4 triggers a release from PI and the proportion of recall increases significantly. Given that a change of category or a change of code induced release from PI, Goggin and Wickens asked whether the bilinguals' two linguistic codes were distinct enough to produce a release from PI.

To investigate this issue, in addition to the English control and category shift conditions described above, Spanish–English bilinguals were given lists in which a language and a language + category shift occurred for both languages. From Table 3.1, notice that for the language shift condition, all four lists are composed of body parts. Notice that for List 4, *hígado* and *boca* (Translations: *kidney* and *mouth*) are in Spanish. In the language + category shift condition, both the language (from English to Spanish) and category are altered (from body parts to fruits). Figure 3.4 summarizes the findings.

To summarize, tests 1–3 show the traditional buildup of PI, wherein previously learned material interferes with the learning of new (related material). No release of PI is evident for the control condition because all lists were from the same language and same category.

However, the change of category and language shift in the remaining conditions produced release from PI. More impressive was the finding that, if both language and category shifts were combined, release from PI produced much higher recall rates than language or category shifts independently. These results led Goggin and Wickens (1971) to conclude that highly fluent bilinguals were capable of encoding information in more than one dimension or using two distinctive codes. Although these researchers did not take sides on

Table 3.1 Example of an Experiment on Release from Proactive Interference

Condition	List 1	List 2	List 3	List 4
Fruits				
I. **English**	apple	grape	orange	apricot
(Control)	peach	cherry	plum	pineapple
Body Parts				
II. **English**	arm	eye	finger	apricot
(Category Shift)	head	nose	hand	pineapple
III. **English–Spanish**	arm	eye	finger	hígado
(Language Shift)	head	nose	hand	boca
IV. **English–Spanish**	arm	eye	finger	durazno
(Language + Category Shift)	head	nose	hand	piña

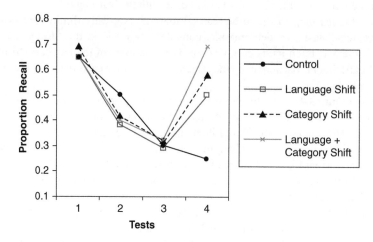

Figure 3.4   Proportion of words recalled as a function of language and concept shifts (adapted from Goggin & Wickens, 1971, p. 455, Figure 1).

the issue of one or two memory systems, their results are clearly consistent with the general idea that the bilingual's two linguistic codes are distinct and that the bilingual's two languages are represented in memory by two distinctive memory systems (see also Dillon, McCormack, Petrusic, Cook, & Lafleur, 1973; Heredia & García, 2017).

In a study similar to that of López and Young (1974), Scarborough, Gerard, and Cortese (1984) asked whether Spanish–English bilinguals would show automatic transfer of word recognition experiences across their two languages. Language transfer in the RT literature is referred to as *priming*. In priming, response to a particular word is faster if a preceding or antecedent word is related, relative to an unrelated word. For example, response to *butter* would be faster if preceded by a related (e.g., *bread*) rather than an unrelated word (*desk*). Depending on the experiment, the priming could involve exact within-language (*war-war*) or between-language (e.g., *war-guerra*) repetitions. Scarborough et al. utilized a lexical decision task to measure priming. In the lexical decision task, participants may be presented with an actual word in English (e.g., *bread*) or a nonword (e.g., *knote*) that is not found in the language. The participant's objective is to decide if a presented item is an actual word, then press a key or button labeled YES if it is an actual word or NO if it is not an actual or legal word in English. More often, however, real words are of more theoretical value than nonwords (see Altarriba & Basnight-Brown, 2007, for a review of the cross-language priming literature).

In summary, Scarborough et al.'s (1984, Experiment 1) study involved two parts. In the first part, bilinguals made lexical decisions on a series of Spanish and English words. The results for the first part of the experiment showed that bilinguals were faster to respond to English words than to Spanish words. Accordingly, bilinguals were slower to respond to Spanish words simply because they were dominant in their English language. For the second part of the experiment, bilinguals were asked to respond to the same English word previously seen. This English–English experimental condition is essentially the same as a within-language condition. However, for the between-language condition (Spanish–English), bilinguals made lexical decisions to the English translations of the previously seen Spanish word. The general findings showed language priming, but only for the within-language conditions. In other words, bilinguals were faster to respond to *war* the second time around, relative to the first exposure, but only if they had seen *war* before in the monolingual condition. However, the between-language condition failed to show priming or language transfer. Previous exposure to *guerra* did not facilitate response to its English translation *war* (see also Gerard & Scarborough, 1989; Kirsner, Smith, Lockhart, & King, 1984; cf. Zeelenberg & Pecher, 2003).

Other studies employing RT techniques and sentence comprehension have found that bilinguals are usually faster to process or comprehend monolingual than bilingual sentences (Cieślicka & Heredia, 2016; Heredia & Altarriba, 2001). In the typical experiment, bilinguals are presented with monolingual (i.e., within-language) and bilingual (i.e., between-language) sentences of the type described in the introduction (1a-b), and 2a-2b below.

(2a) *After LUNCH, the children asked for a piece of CAKE for DESSERT.*
(2b) *Depois do LUNCH os miudos pediram uma fatia de CAKE para DESSERT.*

Sentence 2a is a monolingual sentence. Sentence 2b is a code-switched or mixed-language sentence because it contains words from English and Portuguese. One important aspect to underscore is that code-switching has its own grammatical rules and does not occur randomly (Lederberg & Morales, 1985; see also Bullock & Toribio; Magaña, this volume). Soares and Grosjean (1984) had Portuguese–English bilinguals listen to monolingual and bilingual sentences similar to 2a-b. Of special interest was the comparison between a monolingual word target in sentence 2a (e.g., *CAKE*) and the same word in the code-switched sentence 2b. At the beginning of each sentence, participants were provided with a phonemic cue that directed them to the critical word. For sentence 2b, if the critical target was *CAKE*, the initial phonemes of the word (e.g., [kej]) were provided. The bilinguals' objective was to use the phonemic information as they listened to the sentences to identify the appropriate critical word. This experimental technique is known as the *phonemic monitoring task*. Upon the identification of the critical target, bilinguals performed lexical decisions on these words. The findings showed that Portuguese–English bilinguals were much faster responding to the monolingual critical words from sentence (2a) than to the code-switched words in sentence (2b). These patterns of results are robust and have been replicated using different experimental techniques (e.g., Altarriba, Kroll, Sholl, & Rayner, 1996; see also Cieślicka & Heredia, 2016) and with children as well (see Li, 1996).

The finding that the comprehension of code-switched information takes significantly more time than monolingual material has been taken to support independence of the bilingual's two languages. Moreover, the differences in time between the monolingual and code-switched words have been interpreted as the time required for a cognitive *input switch* to "turn off" (i.e., inhibit) one language while the other is "turned on," or activated (MacNamara & Kushnir, 1971). Although this proposed cognitive input switch is intuitively appealing and accounts for the findings, at issue is whether this linguistic switch is psychologically real (for a review see Green, 1998; see also Li, 1996). Some researchers have proposed that these time differences may also reflect the possibility that, during word retrieval, the bilingual's first language (L1) memory is searched first and only after that is the second language (L2) searched (Soares & Grosjean, 1984). Other proposals view this time issue as representing a competition between the bilinguals' two systems to determine which language (i.e., L1 or L2) is more highly activated and most likely to win the competition (cf. Dijkstra & Van Heuven, 2002).

One major drawback stemming from the research described above concerning both hypotheses is that some of the research findings were open to interpretation. That is, depending on the investigator's theoretical preference, the same results could be used to support one or the other opposing hypothesis (cf. de Bruin, Treccani, & Della Sala, 2015). As an example, consider López and Young's (1974) results shown in Figures 3.2a-b. Pairing each language familiarization condition with its corresponding language at test shows that recall differences were larger for the bilingual (English–Spanish vs. Spanish–English) than the monolingual (Spanish–Spanish vs. English–English) language conditions. The opposite holds true for the language control conditions for Figure 3.2b. Indeed, these differences are consistent and would be generally predicted by the language independence hypothesis that predicts language differences. In addition, Glanzer and Duarte's (1971) findings (see Figure 3.3) are also open to interpretation, especially at distances 0, 1, and 2, where free recall for the between-language repetitions is greater than for the within-language repetitions (see also Paivio, Clark, & Lambert, 1988). In short, the independence and interdependence hypotheses were accurate in describing and proposing solutions to the theoretical issues of bilingual memory; yet, their formulations and descriptions were too general, thus preventing the generation of clear and testable predictions. This limitation, as argued in the following sections, is overcome by current bilingual models that generate clear, distinct, and testable predictions.

Given that the research findings described above support both hypotheses, what can we conclude about bilingual memory, and how can these results be reconciled in a plausible theory of bilingual memory representation? Durgunoğlu and Roediger (1987, 2008) effectively demonstrated that the mixed results in the bilingual memory literature were due primarily to the fact that previous research failed to consider *task demands* (see also Cieślicka, Heredia, & García, 2017; Heredia & McLaughlin, 1992; Zeelenberg & Pecher, 2003). The general argument was that the evidence for the one- or two-memory hypotheses depended upon the processing demands of the retrieval tasks used. In other words, free recall and recognitions tasks that were sensitive to semantic and conceptual processes yielded results consistent with the shared memory model (e.g., Glanzer & Duarte, 1971; Kolers & González, 1980; López & Young, 1974; Slamecka & Katsaiti, 1978). On the other hand, tasks that were sensitive to perceptual or lexical processes (i.e., the similarity between the surface features of the study and test stimulus) generally produced language-specific results, consistent with the two-memory model. Among some of the tasks identified as producing language-specific results were lexical decision tasks, word-fragment completion, and lexical naming (e.g., Gerard & Scarborough, 1989; Kirsner, Smith, Lockhart, & King, 1984). As an interesting contrast, recall that the language transfer issue was addressed by López and Young (1974) using a recall task, and by Gerard and Scarborough (1989) using a lexical decision task. What is noteworthy is that the different tasks produced different results. The free recall task produced language transfer and the lexical decision task did not. This pattern of results is consistent with the tasks demands account, and leads to the conclusion that in studying bilingual memory, task requirements should be considered. *Conceptually driven tasks*, such as free recall, measure the bilingual's semantic and conceptual word representations, thus supporting a one-memory system view. Moreover, these tasks can be seen as measuring the processes required to access the overall general knowledge store of the two languages, or the general conceptual system. In contrast, *data-driven tasks* (e.g., lexical decision, word-fragment completion, and naming) that involve perceptual processing support the independent memory hypothesis. As such, these tasks can be seen as measuring the processes required to access the bilingual lexical system.

To summarize, Durgunoğlu and Roediger's (1987) findings lead to the general conclusion that both the independence and interdependence hypotheses were correct, and that both accounts were actually describing bilingual storage at different levels. The shared memory store hypothesis was seen as accurately describing bilingual memory representation at the semantic or meaning level, where information was readily available to the bilingual's two languages. In contrast, the separate memory store hypothesis was seen as describing a bilingual memory structure in which the bilingual's two languages were stored in separate mental dictionaries or lexicons that were specific to each language. What is the relationship between the semantic memory store and the bilingual lexicons, and how are these two systems interrelated? Indeed, this is the focus of the *hierarchical models* described shortly. However, before discussing these models, let us address briefly the recurrent and popular issue of the compound versus coordinate bilingual distinction, and Paivio and Desrochers' (1980) *dual coding theory* that bears on the issue of multiple memory storage for bilinguals.

Compound versus Coordinate Bilingualism

Is the context in which the L1 and L2 were learned likely to influence how bilinguals represent their languages in memory? Ervin and Osgood (1954), based on the seminal paper by Weinreich (1953), proposed a bilingual memory structure that depended largely on the context in which it was learned (see also Marian, this volume). The proposal was that, if a bilingual learned both languages simultaneously or through a teaching method that involved associating or translating the to-be-learned material in the L2 to the L1, this bilingual would be a *compound bilingual*. This bilingual, in turn, would develop a linguistic representation in which corresponding words from the two languages underlie one conceptual or meaning-based representation. Thus, according to this system, the words *love* and *amor* (its Spanish translation), although having different labels, would share the same meaning. In contrast, a *coordinate bilingual* would arise from a situation in which the bilingual's two languages were learned in different places (e.g., home vs. school), taught by different people and under different situations. Thus, a coordinate bilingual would develop a linguistic system in which words from each language are directly associated to a distinct and separate conceptual or meaning-based representation (e.g., Gekoski, 1980). Thus, for a coordinate bilingual, the words *love* and *amor* would have different meanings.

In general, the compound-coordinate distinction is highly intuitive and easily understood. However, the evidence for this theoretical distinction is quite mixed (see, for example, Guttfreund, 1990; Heredia & Cieślicka, 2014; Kolers, 1963). The conceptual difficulties encountered by the shared memory and the independent memory hypotheses apply to this proposed memory organization as well. To make the bilingual compound-coordinate systems more testable and open to experimentation, the compound system was reformulated as the shared memory hypothesis; whereas the coordinate system became the memory independence hypothesis.

Is the compound-coordinate bilingual distinction useful? While this concept remains popular in some areas of education and psychology, as pointed out by Heredia and Cieślicka, (2014), this theory implies that, during language learning, bilinguals must code linguistic information in a context-specific manner and that this information remains somewhat unaltered over time. Indeed, this line of reasoning is consistent with Koler's (1963, p. 299) original argument:

> One can also take issue with the assumption in the [compound-coordinate] dichotomy that linguistic performance is forever determined by the way the bilingual learned [the L2] initially, an assumption which suggests that experience obtained living in a culture after its language was learned will not affect usage. This does not seem to be a reasonable way to describe an adult capable of assimilating new experiences.

Moreover, any differences or similarities that might arise during language learning may be due to the nature of the words or concepts themselves (Heredia & Brown, 2004). For example, some researchers (e.g., de Groot, 1992; de Groot, Dannenburg, & Van Hell, 1994; see also Brysbaert, Ameel, & Storms, 2014) have convincingly argued that certain words (e.g., abstract words) are more likely to exhibit language-specific meanings. *Love* and *amor*, for example, are similar in some general aspects; however, their usages are quite distinct. In English, for instance, it would be quite acceptable *to love a rock* but in Spanish, the verb would have to be substituted by *gustar* as in *to like a rock*. Failure to know this distinction would simply suggest that the particular individual lacks understanding in the particular language. In contrast, concrete words (or translations) and cognates (words that share meaning and orthographic representation) are likely to show higher levels of associations across languages. Indeed, the theoretical compound-coordinate distinction as a general model of bilingualism, and a model of how the L2 is learned and organized would be difficult to defend, especially when bilinguals achieve higher levels of proficiency in the L2, or when the L2 becomes the dominant language (e.g., Heredia & Brown, 2004; Heredia & Cieślicka, 2014; Kolers, 1963; see also Sebastían-Gallés, Echeverría, & Bosch, 2005).

Bilingual Dual Coding Theory

Paivio's *bilingual dual coding theory* (e.g., Paivio, 2014; Paivio & Desrochers, 1980; Pritchett, Vaid, & Tosun, 2016), like the independence hypothesis, poses separate but interconnected bilingual memory stores. However, unlike any of the bilingual proposals discussed so far, this model is formulated well enough so as to generate specific predictions about bilingual memory. Figure 3.5 illustrates the bilingual dual coding theory. The model assumes one verbal system (V1) for the L1 and a second verbal system (V2) for the L2. Accordingly, the verbal systems are highly specialized in linguistic processing and speech production. Although the verbal systems are separate and able to function independently, both systems are linked by V1-V2 connections. The connections between translation equivalents (e.g., *boy-niño*) appear to be stronger and more readily accessible than bilingual paired associates (e.g., *girl-niño*). It follows then that during retrieval, bilingual translations should provide better recall than bilingual paired associates. As argued by Paivio (2014) and Paivio and Desrochers (1980), research findings in which bilinguals generate associations seem to follow this pattern.

Additionally, the model poses an image system (I). The image system appears to be highly specialized in the processing of perceptual or visual information that involves non-verbal information and events, and for generating images of such events (Paivio, 1991, 2014; Paivio & Desrochers, 1980).

It is also assumed that pictures in this system are stored as true copies, analogs, or templates of the original representation (Jared, Poh, & Paivio, 2013; Paivio, 1991). This assumption is a controversial one because the opposing view suggests that pictures are stored as general verbal descriptions. Although this system is capable of functioning separately, it is connected to both verbal systems via links from the verbal system for the L1 to the image system (depicted in Figure 3.5 as V1-I) and from the verbal system for the L2 to the image system (depicted as I-V2 in Figure 3.5). As a consequence of this interconnectivity, the verbal and image systems are mutually influenced.

For instance, a concrete word such as *table*, from V2 may trigger a referent or a picture of a *table* in the imagery system. Likewise, a picture of a *table* may activate its equivalent label in V1, or V2, or in both. Indeed, this interconnectivity assumption leads to the prediction that during learning or encoding processes, words or stimuli that have access to the

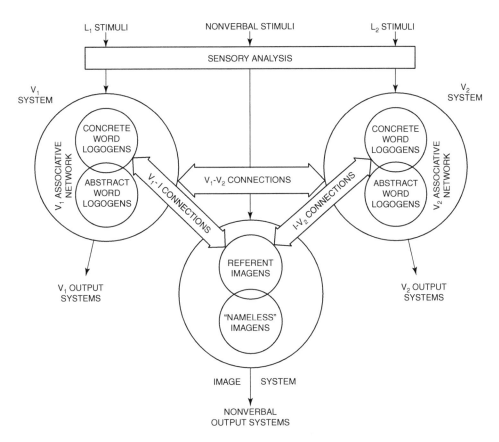

Figure 3.5   The bilingual dual coding theory (adapted from Paivio & Desrochers, 1980, p. 391, Figure 1).

two systems or codes (verbal + nonverbal) would exhibit higher retrieval than stimuli that have access to only one code (verbal or nonverbal).

In general, the strength of the bilingual dual coding theory is its ability to explain the *bilingual concreteness effect* (e.g., de Groot, 1992; de Groot, Dannenburg, & Van Hell, 1994). This highly replicated effect in the monolingual and bilingual research demonstrates that words that represent tangible objects (e.g., *table*) are recalled better than abstract words that typically represent intangible ideas or concepts (see also Altarriba & Bauer, 2004). Figure 3.6a-b is a replication of Glanzer and Duarte's (1971) shown in Figure 3.3, but in this case, carefully separating concrete and abstract words. Inspection of these results shows that, as expected, the proportion of recalled words is higher for concrete (Figure 3.6a) than for abstract words (Figure 3.6b). Notice that the two language conditions exhibit virtually the same pattern in both the concrete and abstract conditions. Why are concrete words remembered better? Concrete words, because of the virtue of their inherent high imagery, can be coded using the verbal and image system, for a total of two codes (see Figure 3.5). Abstract words, on the other hand, can only be coded using the verbal system.

Another bilingual effect supported by the dual coding theory is the finding that retrieval for between-language conditions is typically higher than for within-language conditions, as summarized in Figures 3.6a-b, and reported by other researchers (e.g., Basi et al., 1997;

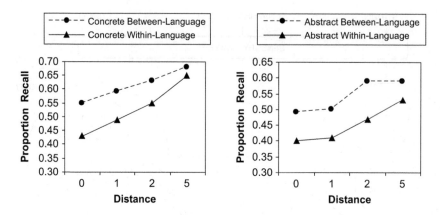

Figure 3.6a-b   Proportion of words recalled as a function of between- and within-language conditions, concrete (Figure 3.6a, left) versus abstract (Figure 3.6b, right) and distance (adapted from Paivio, Clark, & Lambert, 1988, Figure 2, p. 168).

Glanzer & Duarte, 1971; Vaid, 1988; but see Kolers & González, 1980; Slamecka & Katsaiti, 1978). Retrieval for the between-language condition (e.g., Spanish–English), at least at short distances, has benefited from a verbal code from L1 and another verbal code from the L2. In contrast, the within-language condition (e.g., English–English) can only benefit from one verbal code. An in-depth analysis for concrete words in the between-language condition in Figure 3.6a suggests that the between-language conditions may possibly have access to three codes, one for each verbal system and the other from the image system (V1 + V2 + I), whereas concrete words in the within-language condition may have access to only two codes, one from one verbal system and another from the image system (V1 or V2 + I).

Bilingual dual coding theory also accounts for the general finding that pictures are remembered better than words, as measured by free recall. This robust finding is known as the *picture superiority effect*. This effect is not unique to bilingualism because most of its evidence comes from monolingual studies. However, this effect has been replicated with bilinguals as well (e.g., Paivio & Lambert, 1981; Vaid, 1988; see also Jared et al., 2013). Why are pictures better remembered than words? According to the theory, a picture in the image system may be able to elicit its label from V1 or V2. In any case, access to the image system appears to be much superior to the language code because it profits from the mnemonic superiority of the image code (Paivio & Lambert, 1981).

In short, bilingual dual coding theory's proposal was that bilinguals organized their languages into separate but interconnected verbal systems, and one language-free image system interrelated to the verbal systems as well. In general, this theory is perhaps one of the first theories to provide a clear and concise comprehensible explanation of a possible bilingual memory structure and the first one capable of generating clear and testable predictions. It is not clear as to the reasons why bilingual dual coding theory did not generate as much research as its monolingual predecessor. However, its influence on current models of bilingual memory that assume separate verbal systems and shared conceptual representations is unquestionable. The following section focuses on these types of models collectively known as hierarchical models.

Hierarchical Models

Word Association and Concept Mediation Models

Hierarchical models start with the assumption that bilinguals organize their languages into one general conceptual level that is shared by the two languages, and a lexical level that is particular to each language. This conjecture is illustrated in Figures 3.7a-b below. The conceptual system is represented by the rectangles labeled "concepts," and the lexical level is depicted by the squares labeled "L1" and "L2" for first and second language lexicons, respectively. The shared conceptual system is said to contain general abstract information that is language free; the lexical level represents a bilingual's two languages in separate mental lexicons or dictionaries, with information specific to each language (Potter, So, Eckardt, & Feldman, 1984; for similar proposals see Paradis, 1980; Weinreich, 1953; see also Marian, this volume). These models are hierarchical because they distinguish between a general level (i.e., the conceptual system) and language-specific mental lexicons. Another important assumption of these models, as shown in Figures 3.7a-b, is that the L1 lexicon is larger than the L2 lexicon. This difference in lexicon size, as argued by Kroll and Stewart (1994), reflects the notion that bilinguals know more words in their L1 than their L2.

Two hierarchical models were proposed to explain bilingual memory. In the word association model (Figure 3.7a) Potter et al. proposed a bilingual memory structure in which the bilingual's two languages interact at the lexical level or word level, based on translation equivalents. Thus, according to this model, words from the bilingual's L2 are directly associated with words from the L1. Access to the general conceptual store (i.e., "concepts" in Figure 3.7a) from the L2 is not possible, unless the L2 word is translated into the L1, as shown by the directional solid arrow from the L2 to the L1 lexicon. In contrast, the L1 is hypothesized to have direct access to the conceptual store. This link is represented by the bi-directional solid arrow from the L1 to the conceptual system. Thus, to know the meaning of an English word (e.g., *house*), a Spanish–English bilingual would have to translate it into Spanish (e.g., *casa*), the L1.

The *concept mediation model* (Figure 3.7b), on the other hand, assumed that the bilingual's two languages operated independently of each other. As proposed by Potter et al., both lexicons were independently capable of accessing the conceptual system. According to this model, a bilingual speaker was able to access the meaning of a particular concept regardless of the language and, unlike the word association model, without having to translate from the L2 to the L1. As argued by Potter et al., the native and non-native languages of a bilingual operate independently so that words are not associated interlingually, but instead associated with the non-linguistic conceptual system common to both languages.

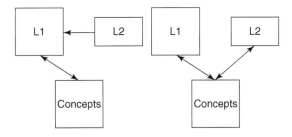

Figure 3.7a-b   The word association model (Figure 3.7a, left) and the concept mediation model (Figure 3.7b, right) (adapted from Potter et al., 1984, p. 25).

To test these models, Potter et al. (1984) used a picture naming and a translation task. In the picture naming task, Chinese–English bilinguals were presented with a picture, and the objective was to name the picture in their L2, English. For the translation task, they translated a word from their L1 (Chinese) to their L2 (English).

The two models make specific predictions regarding picture naming and translation. For picture naming, the word association model (Figure 3.7a) predicts the following steps: (1) recognize the picture, (2) retrieve the concept of the picture—actually going into the conceptual system, (3) retrieve the name or label of the picture in the L1—going from the conceptual system to the L1 lexicon, (4) translate word into the L2, and (5) say the name of the picture in the L2. Note that in step (1), during the recognition of the picture, recognition is assumed to be language free. In other words, at this level, the picture has not yet been labeled. In fact, hierarchical models assume that, in addition to the general conceptual system and the lexicons, there is an additional image store that is specifically involved with pictures (Paivio & Desrochers, 1980; Potter et al., 1984). On the other hand, translating from L1 to L2, the word association model predicts the following steps: (1) recognize the word in the L1—going directly into the L1 lexicon, (2) translate the L1 word into the L2, and (3) say the word in the L2. These three steps, as opposed to the five steps for picture naming, translate into less response time. Thus, according to the word association model, translating an L1 word into L2 takes significantly less time than naming a picture in the L2.

In contrast, the concept mediation model (Figure 3.7b) predicts no differences between picture naming and translating into the L2. Specifically, picture naming requires the following steps: (1) recognize the picture, (2) retrieve the concept of the picture, (3) retrieve the name or the label of the picture in the L2—the L2 lexicon can be accessed directly from the conceptual system, and (4) say the name of the picture in the L2. Likewise, translating into L2 would require: (1) recognize the L1 word, (2) retrieve the concept of the word, (3) retrieve the name of the word in the L2, and (4) say the name of the picture in the L2.

Potter et al.'s (1984) results showed that their Chinese–English bilinguals showed no differences in naming or translating into the L2, as predicted by the conceptual mediation model, regardless of the participant's L2 proficiency. These results led Potter et al. to conclude that words of a second language were associated with corresponding words in the L1 via a common conceptual store, and not by direct associations between vocabulary items, as predicted by the word association model, even for non-fluent bilinguals. However, other evidence (see for example, Kroll & Sholl, 1992; Kroll & Stewart, 1994) suggested that the word association model described a bilingual structure corresponding to bilinguals at early stages of L2 learning, associating every new L2 word learned with the L1 translation equivalent. In contrast, the concept mediation model described a bilingual structure corresponding to bilinguals with high proficiency levels in their L2. More important were the findings showing that bilinguals translated faster from their L2 to L1 than their L1 to L2. This translation asymmetry held for early and advanced bilinguals (Kroll & Sholl, 1992). Neither the word association nor the concept mediation model could account for this pattern of results. To account for these findings, Kroll and Sholl (1992) and Kroll and Stewart (1994) proposed a revised version in which the word association and concept mediation models were incorporated into the revised hierarchical model, shown in Figure 3.8.

The Revised Hierarchical Model

According to the *revised hierarchical model* (RHM) depicted in Figure 3.8, the bilingual lexicons are bi-directionally interconnected via *lexical links*. The lexical link (represented by the solid arrow) from the L2 lexicon to the L1 lexicon is stronger than the L1 to L2 link, to reflect the way the L2 was learned. Accordingly, during L2 acquisition, bilinguals learn to associate every L2 word with its L1 equivalent (e.g., learn *house* and associate it with *casa*), thus forming a lexical-level association that remains active and strong (Kroll & Stewart, 1994). Furthermore, this link is assumed to be sensitive to processes that require physical or perceptual characteristics of word translation equivalents. Stronger lexical links from L2 to L1 than in the reverse direction, also reflect the bilingual's ease of translation. Thus, for a native Spanish speaker, it would be easier to translate *house* to *casa* than *casa* to *house* because every L2 word is mapped onto its L1 equivalent, but not every L1 word is mapped onto its L2 equivalent (Kroll & Sholl, 1992; Kroll & Stewart, 1994). Moreover, the connection from the L1 to L2 language lexicon (depicted by a broken line) is assumed to be weaker because of a lack of translation practice. However, this link is hypothesized to be sensitive to semantic factors or semantic (meaning) processing.

The conceptual store and the lexicons are connected via *conceptual links*. The conceptual link from the L1 (depicted by a solid line) is stronger than the link from the L2 (represented by a broken line). This difference in strength reflects the fact that L1 is the native language, and bilinguals are more familiar with word meanings in their L1 (Kroll & Sholl, 1992; Kroll & Stewart, 1994). Although it is theoretically possible that the link from L2 to the conceptual store may develop strong connections, Kroll and Stewart argue that this link remains relatively weaker, even for bilinguals with high L2 proficiency levels.

Support for the RHM is obtained from experiments that involve translations from L1 to L2 and from L2 to L1. In the typical experiment, bilinguals are presented with an L1 word (e.g., *casa*) and asked to generate a translation in their L2 (e.g., *house*), and vice versa. The general finding, as predicted by the RHM, is the translation asymmetry where translating from L2 to L1 is faster than translating from L1 to L2. Translating from L1 to L2 takes significantly more time than from L2 to L1 because the former is achieved through concept mediated and the latter through word-word (translation) associations. Thus, concept mediated retrieval tasks take significantly more time than lexically mediated or word-word association tasks (La Heij, Hooglander, Kerling, & Van Der Velden, 1996; Potter et al., 1984).

Evidence supporting the assumption that the bilingual's two lexicons are sensitive to semantic (meaning) and lexically based information comes from Kroll and Stewart (1994). Kroll and Stewart utilized a translation task and manipulated the semantic context in which translations were performed. Participants in this task translated L1 to L2 or L2 to L1 in randomized or categorized (e.g., *dress*, *suit*, and *pants* belong to the category *clothes*) lists of words. The question of interest was whether L1 to L2 translations would be affected more by the change of semantic context (i.e., categorized vs. randomized lists) when compared to L2 to L1 translations, which were assumed to be lexically mediated. Because of the finding

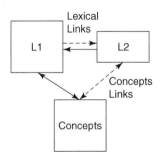

Figure 3.8   The revised hierarchical model (adapted from Kroll & Stewart, 1994, p. 158).

that L1 picture naming—which requires conceptual-semantic processing—produced *category interference* with categorized lists and not randomized lists (Experiments 1 and 2) and that translations are similar to L1 picture naming (Potter et al., 1984), Kroll and Stewart predicted that if L1 to L2 translations were indeed conceptually mediated, then L1 to L2 translation would also exhibit category interference.

In short, Kroll and Stewart (1994) found, as predicted by the RHM, that L1 to L2 translations were indeed influenced by the change in semantic context of the lists. It took more time to translate categorized lists of words from L1 to L2 than to translate randomized lists from L1 to L2. In contrast, semantic context did not affect L2 to L1 translations. More interestingly, L2 to L1 translations behaved similarly in both the naming and translation tasks. In a more recent study, Bowers and Kennison (2011) replicated Kroll and Stewart's category interference effect for forward translation, but only in conditions in which critical words were learned early in life or had an early age of acquisition. When critical words had a late age of acquisition, the category interference effect disappeared. However, backward translations were faster than forward translations, as originally reported by Kroll and Stewart.

Additional support for this model comes from experiments reporting asymmetrical cross-language *priming effects*. Priming is the phenomenon in which a word (e.g., *war*) is responded to faster when preceded by a related word (e.g., *peace*) than when preceded by a nonrelated word (e.g., *cat*). In the bilingual version, participants are presented with a bilingual word pair that is either related (*peace-guerra: war*) or unrelated (*peace-gato: cat*). In one language condition, the prime may be in L1 (*paz*) and the target in L2 (*war*) or vice versa.

In general, cross-language priming is obtained, but only if an L2 target is preceded by a related rather than an unrelated L1 prime (e.g., Davis et al., 2010; Dimitropoulou, Duñabeitia, & Carreiras, 2011; but see, Fox, 1996; Keatley & De Gelder, 1992). In contrast, regardless of the relatedness between the target and prime, no cross-language priming is obtained if the critical prime is in the L2 (e.g., Grainger & Frenck-Mestre, 1998; Jiang & Forster, 2001). That is, cross-language facilitation is obtained only if the prime is in L1 and the target is in L2. Consistent with the RHM, the results suggest that accessing L2 from L1 is conceptual because it is achieved via the conceptual store or through concept mediation, which is the locus of the semantic priming effect (Keatley, Spinks, & Gelder, 1994, p. 77). On the other hand, accessing L1 from L2 takes place only at the lexical level, thus producing no semantic priming (see Tytus & Rundblad, 2016, for similar findings involving the visual and auditory modalities).

However, experimental findings call into question some of the RHM's main assumptions (e.g., Brysbaert & Duyck, 2010; Jared et al., 2013; Schoonbaert, Duyck, Brysbaert, & Hartsuiker, 2009; but see Kroll, Van Hell, Tokowicz, & Green, 2010). For example, some studies have suggested that contrary to the claims of RHM, both L1 to L2 and L2 to L1 translation directions may be sensitive to meaning-based processing (e.g., Basnight-Brown & Altarriba, 2007; de Groot et al., 1994; Duñabeitia, Perea, & Carreiras, 2010; Duyck & Brysbaert, 2004; Heredia, 1995, 1997; La Heij et al., 1996; see also Altarriba & Mathis, 1997; Finkbeiner, Forster, Nicol, & Nakamura, 2004; see also Perea, Duñabeitia, & Carreiras, 2008). For example, Heredia (1995) had Spanish–English bilinguals translate concrete and abstract words in both language directions. Heredia's results revealed no translation time differences for concrete words in both language directions, suggesting that both translation directions were sensitive to the semantic factors provided by the concrete words (see also de Groot, 1992; de Groot et al., 1994). More inconsistent with the predictions of the RHM was the finding that in the abstract condition, translating from

L1 to L2 was actually faster than translating from L2 to L1. At least in the abstract condition, it appeared that the bilingual's L1 had actually become the L2 (see also Altarriba, 1992; Altarriba, 2001; Basnight-Brown & Altarriba, 2007; Kroll et al., 2010; cf. Jiang & Forster, 2001).

Indeed, these results led Heredia (1997; Heredia & Altarriba, 2001; Heredia & Brown, 2004) to conclude that the RHM did not allow for the possibility that the effects of translation direction and strength of word translations, and to some extent priming, were not fixed characteristics in bilingualism. Thus, unlike the predictions of the formulation of the RHM, the L1 can fall in strength while the L2 can become the dominant language. As pointed out by Heredia and colleagues, bilingual memory representation is not a static but rather a dynamic system that can be influenced by language usage.

Thus, to account for the bilingual translation reversal described above, Heredia (1997) and Heredia and Brown (2004) proposed that in studying bilingual memory representations, *language dominance*, or which language is used more frequently, should be considered. Words in the language that is used more frequently will be responded to more quickly. In contrast, words in the language that is used less frequently will be responded to slower. Thus, according to the language dominance argument (see for example, Dunn & Fox Tree, 2009), regardless of which language was learned first, the more active (dominant) language would determine which lexicon would be retrieved faster. According to this view, the bilinguals in Heredia's (1995, 1997) experiment were faster in accessing their L2 lexicon simply because it was the language they used more frequently or their most dominant language. Thus, it would be theoretically possible for the bilingual's L2 to become the dominant language and the L1 to become the least dominant language. Therefore, it would be safe to suggest that, regardless of which language was learned first, the more frequently used language will most likely subordinate the other (Heredia & Brown, 2004, p. 239). Basnight-Brown and Altarriba (2007) also reported a similar reversal in language dominance in participants who demonstrated significant priming for word translations across languages, but less priming for semantically related word pairs under the strictest of testing conditions.

As pointed out by Heredia and Cieślicka (2014), the RHM provides an intuitive account of how bilinguals might organize their languages in relation to lexical and conceptual structural representations. How these structures evolve over time and the mechanisms leading to the strengthening of the lexical and conceptual links, however, are unspecified. Unlike other bilingual models (e.g., bilingual dual coding theory) that emphasized the interaction of L2 learning and contextual effects, the RHM is not equipped with the learning mechanisms to predict how the lexical or conceptual systems develop as a result of learning. The model does a good job in explaining the mechanisms of conceptual and lexical activation during translation between languages; however, there is no unanimous support of its conceptualization of the relationship between the lexicons and the conceptual system.

Distributed Conceptual Feature Model

Representations at the Word Type Level

The next model discussed is de Groot's *distributed conceptual feature model of bilingual memory*. This model, unlike the other models discussed in this section, allows for the possibility that bilingual memory may be represented at the word level (e.g., de Groot, 1992, 1993; de Groot et al., 1994; Kroll & de Groot, 1997; van Hell & de Groot, 1998). This model, like hierarchical models, distinguishes between the lexical level, represented by the open circles labeled "L1" and "L2" for first and second language lexicons, and the conceptual level depicted by small solid and open circles in Figure 3.9a-b. In direct contrast to the RHM described before, one important aspect of the distributed conceptual feature model is that it elaborates on how the conceptual store may be represented at the word level for different word types.

As can be seen in Figure 3.9, this model postulates connections from the lexicons to the conceptual nodes or features which represent each word meaning. The number of conceptual features or elements in these memory structures may determine their activation or translation performance. The more similar two concepts are, the more "meaning elements" they would have in common. It follows then that the more feature or meaning elements overlap between words across languages, the more the concepts would be alike. Likewise, the less feature overlap across languages, the more different or dissimilar the concepts would be. For example, it has been argued by de Groot and colleagues that concrete words (Figure 3.9a, left) are more likely than abstract words (Figure 3.9b, middle) to share a number of semantic features across languages, or Spanish and English in this particular case. Figure 3.9a depicts an example of concrete words across languages in which the feature overlap at the conceptual level for Spanish *casa* and its English translation *home* is complete. The same argument would apply to cognates, or words that are spelled similarly and have similar meanings across (e.g., *hospital* in Spanish vs. *hospital* in English). Figure 3.9b, in contrast, depicts a configuration for *amor* and its translation equivalent *love* with very little feature overlap. Therefore, concrete and cognate words are more likely to be very similar in meaning across languages, whereas abstract words are more likely to exhibit language specific information (e.g., de Groot, 1992, 1993; de Groot et al., 1994; van Hell & de Groot, 1998). Such is the case with abstract words such as *amor* and its English translation equivalent *love*. Although both words are roughly similar in both languages, *love* in English is less constrained and could be used for animate (living things) and inanimate (non-living things). Spanish, on the other hand, more frequently constrains the usage of *amor* to living things and more specifically to some form of human relationships such as *amo a mi esposa* (Translation: *I love my wife*), but not *amo a mi padre* (Translation: *I love my father*); in which case, *I love my father* would become *quiero a mi padre*. However, it would be permissible to talk about *amor de padre o hijo* (Translation: *father's love, children's love*) or *cuidar el jardín con amor* (Translation: *to take care of the garden with love*).

In general, evidence for this model comes from experiments revealing the *concreteness effect*, in which concrete words are recognized and translated faster than abstract words (de Groot, 1992; Heredia, 1995; van Hell & de Groot, 1998). The concreteness effect has been attributed to the possibility that concrete words provide more imagery and have access to multiple codes (e.g., Paivio et al., 1988), are more frequently used and acquired earlier than abstract words (Schwanenflugel, Akin, & Luh, 1992), and are easier to retrieve and more accessible. Other studies (e.g., van Hell & de Groot, 1998) suggest a distinction between the grammatical status of a word; nouns are more likely to behave similar to concrete words, and verbs are more likely to behave similar to abstract words.

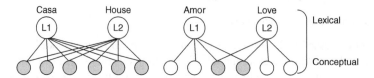

Figure 3.9a-b   The distributed conceptual feature model of bilingual memory for concrete (left) and abstract words (right) (adapted from de Groot, 1992, p. 1016, Figure 2).

However, as pointed out by Heredia and Brown (2004), there are certain situations in which even concrete words maintain some level of language specificity. Such is the case with the English word *ball* that exhibits a high degree of overlap with one of its translation equivalents (*pelota*), but less overlap with (*balón*), an alternative translation. It could be argued that all *balls* are *pelotas*, but not all *balls* can be translated into *balones*. A *balón* is typically a heavier, larger, and specialized ball used in soccer, American football, or basketball. It would be inaccurate, for example, to translate *tennis ball* as *balón de tenis* or *baseball ball* as *balón de beisbol*; instead, *pelota* would be the appropriate translation equivalent. Moreover, *ball* in English would also maintain some of its various possible meanings such as gatherings for social dancing, describing a pleasant experience, and showing competence (e.g., *to be on the ball*). In other words, it is possible for concrete words across languages to share some overlapping features, while other features may or may not overlap. In any case, the usefulness of this model is its explanatory power to capture our intuitions about similarities and differences between words across languages (Heredia & Brown, 2004). This model does an excellent job of describing some differences and similarities between words across languages. However, it is limited in the sense that it can only explain some of the findings—mainly those at the word level—and not other general findings, such as the ones described in relation to the hierarchical models (Finkbeiner et al., 2004; but see Kroll & de Groot, 1997).

More recently however, Finkbeiner et al. (2004, p. 8) have proposed interesting modifications to de Groot's distributed conceptual feature model. The most significant change is that semantic features, as described in Figure 3.9a-b at the conceptual level, become *senses*. Senses in this case correspond to "*bundles of features corresponding to distinct usages*" referred to as "*semantic senses.*" Senses could be conceived of as the number of meanings or ways in which a word could be used. For example, *house* in English is polysemous, or a word with multiple meanings, with up to 14 senses (WordNet 2.1, 2005). Some of its senses include: *A dwelling that serves as living quarters for one or more families* (e.g., "*she felt she had to get out of the house*"); *an official assembly having legislative powers* (e.g., "*a bicameral legislature has two houses*"); and *a building in which something is located*, just to name a few. Thus, according to the *sense model*, this word would be composed of 14 senses or *bundles of features*. In contrast, its Spanish translation may or may not have the same number of senses; how many senses are represented at the conceptual level by a given word would vary from language to language. Inspection of *El Diccionario de la Real Academia Española* (1992) suggests that, like its counterpart in English, *casa* is equally polysemous. Thus, the more semantic senses shared between words across languages, the more identical the concepts are shared as well.

What is significant about this proposal is that it is intuitive and able to operationalize the contents of the conceptual system from abstract conceptual features to semantic senses that are tangible and somewhat easier to bring under experimental control. Although this model has the potential to account for the translation and priming asymmetries reported earlier (see discussion of the RHM), more research is needed to determine its usefulness in describing bilingual memory representations (see for example, Basnight-Brown, 2014; Wang & Forster, 2010; see also Brysbaert et al., 2014).

Bilingual Interactive Activation Model

The last model to be discussed is the *bilingual interactive activation model* (BIA; Dijkstra & Van Heuven, 2002). The BIA is a network model in which different levels (e.g., features, letter, word, and language) interact and are activated in parallel or simultaneously (see Figure 3.10). Models of this sort are referred to as *connectionist* or *parallel distributed processing* (PDP) models. Although other interactive models such as the *bilingual model of lexical access* (BIMOLA; Grosjean, 2008; Léwy & Grosjean, 2001), the *self-organizing model of bilingual processing* (Li & Farkas, 2002), and the *competition model* (MacWhinney & Bates, 1989) have been proposed to explain the bilingual linguistic system, the focus of this brief introduction is on the BIA, mainly because it has received the most attention in the bilingual literature.

The BIA is a word recognition model and its purpose is to explain how bilinguals retrieve orthographical representations from the mental lexicon that correspond to a word (Dijkstra & Van Heuven, 2002). As can be seen from Figure 3.10, the BIA is divided into the *feature level* (e.g., the letter *A* could be decomposed into a forward diagonal '/', a horizontal line '-', and a backward diagonal '\'), the letter, the word, and the language levels. Activation for this model is said to be *bottom-up*. This means that activation (depicted as solid arrows) for the BIA starts from the lowest level (the feature) to the highest level (the language).

Thus, according to the BIA, when a string of letters (word or nonword) is presented (i.e., *visual input*), features represented by the letters in the different positions (*pos 1–4* in Figure 3.10) are activated. These features, in turn, excite letters that contain such features and, at the same time, inhibit or deactivate (depicted by lines with solid circles) other letters that do not share such features.

For example, the features in the second letter *A* (/ - \) of the letter string *PAN* would inhibit letters such as *O* or *C*. Moreover, letters excite words in both languages that contain the letters in the correct position and inhibit words that have letters in the wrong position. At the word level, the BIA assumes two lexicons, one for each language. However, the lexicons (depicted as broken circles in Figure 3.10) are integrated across the two languages, as posed by the interdependence or shared memory hypothesis discussed earlier. Next, words activate the language nodes (Dutch or English, in Figure 3.10). At the same time, words send activation back to the letter level (depicted by bi-directional solid arrows). These active words inhibit other words that should not be active (depicted by the loop with the solid circle). Simultaneously, the language node (e.g., Dutch) inhibits competing words from the other language lexicon (e.g., English; shown as diagonal lines crossing over with solid circles). According to the BIA, word recognition occurs when a word's activation level surpasses a recognition threshold that depends on such factors as *word frequency* (how frequent a word occurs in the respective language) and how similar the words are across the two languages (Dijkstra & Van Heuven, 2002). Unlike the bottom-up driven word activation, selection is implemented in the model in a top-down fashion, via inhibitory control from language nodes to word-level representations, so as to ensure that only the word nodes associated with the language currently being processed remain highly activated.

In general, the BIA is a connectionist model that attempts to explain bilingual word recognition effects by simulations. For example, this model has been able to account for the finding that during the recognition or word retrieval of ambiguous words, bilinguals engage in *multiple activation*. Ambiguous words, such as cross-language homographs, are words that are spelled similar across languages but have different meanings (e.g., *PAN* in English refers to a *cooking utensil*, and *PAN* in Spanish refers to *bread*). During bilingual lexical access, the two meanings of the homograph are activated simultaneously (see Robinson & Altarriba, this volume, for specific examples of lexical ambiguity). This of course is due to the BIA's inherent assumption that bilingual lexical access is non-selective in nature (Dijkstra & Van Heuven, 2002).

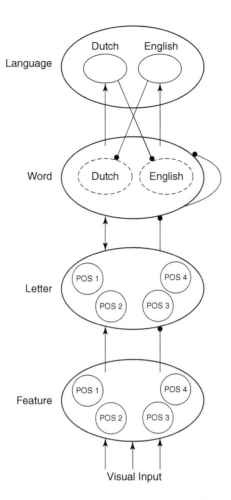

Figure 3.10   The bilingual interactive activation model (adapted from Dijkstra & Van Heuven, 2002, p. 177, Figure 1).

Based on criticisms that concerned how the BIA did not propose a mechanism that accounted for phonological and semantic representations, it has been updated, and it is now called the bilingual interactive activation plus model (BIA+). This new modification of the model has been applied to account for language switching effects (Chauncey, Grainger, & Holcomb, 2008) and L2 vocabulary acquisition (Grainger, Midgley, & Holcomb, 2010). BIA+ incorporates the principle of Hebbian learning and envisages the lexicon as a dynamic network, where connections between L2 and L1 lexical representations become gradually strengthened simultaneously with the strengthening of the links between L2 lexical nodes and semantics. This strengthening of lexical and semantic connections is simultaneous with the modification of L2 lexical representations, which are gradually integrated into a unified, lateral inhibitory network, storing words from both languages. This framework is compatible with the RHM, but differs from its static modeling in that it employs the dynamic principles of Hebbian learning. Accordingly, the increased connectivity between word form representations is accompanied by the improved inhibitory control capable of globally inhibiting L1 lexical representations while processing L2.

Summary and Conclusion

How do bilinguals organize their two languages in memory? The purpose of this chapter was to provide an overview of the different models that have been proposed in the bilingual memory literature and describe some of the classic studies in bilingualism. As we have seen, bilingual memory research has come a long way, from general and at times underspecified theoretical accounts, such as the shared versus the separate memory hypotheses and the equally problematic but attractive notion of compound versus coordinate bilingualism, to clear and well-formulated models such as bilingual dual code theory and hierarchical models. More important, however, has been the further development and the revision of classic bilingual models, such as de Groot's bilingual distributed conceptual feature model into the sense model, which generates interesting and testable hypotheses. And finally, the updated BIA+ provides a general theoretical framework that could be used to generate research and to relate research findings to the predictions and assumptions of the BIA. Again, bilingual memory has come a long way, but much more work is needed to refine existing models even more, in order to arrive at a fuller understanding of how bilinguals organize their two languages. At the present time, it seems that the hierarchical models, including de Groot's conceptual feature model, probably provide the clearest and most elegant solution to the bilingual storage issue.

List of Key Words and Concepts

Between-language, Bilingual concreteness effect, Bilingual dual coding theory, Bilingual interactive activation model (BIA), Bilingual interactive activation plus model (BIA+), Category interference, Compound bilingualism, Concept mediation model, Conceptually driven tasks, Concreteness effect, Connectionist, Coordinate bilingualism, Data-driven tasks, Declarative memory, Distance effect, Distributed conceptual feature model, Distributed-practice effect, Episodic memory, Hierarchical models, Input switch, Interdependence memory, Lag effect, Language dominance, Long-term memory (LTM), Nondeclarative memory, Parallel distributed processing (PDP), Phonemic monitoring task, Picture superiority effect, Polysemy, Priming effects, Proactive interference paradigm (PI), Procedural memory, Release from proactive interference, Repetition effect, Revised hierarchical model, Sense model, Shared memory hypothesis, Spacing effect, Within-language, Working memory, Word association model

Internet Sites Related to Bilingual Memory

Bilingual Language Acquisition: https://hablalab.wordpress.com
Heritage Language Journal: http://www.heritagelanguages.org
Idiom Translation: http://blog.ted.com/40-idioms-that-cant-be-translated-literally/
Lexical Test for Learners of English: http://www.lextale.com
Research Materials for L2: http://www.iris-database.org/iris/app/home/index
Resources for Experimentation: http://www.tamiu.edu/~rheredia/materials.html

Discussion Questions

(1) Are there any similarities between the *compound-coordinate* bilingual distinction and current *hierarchical models* of bilingual memory?
(2) What is the main difference between Paivio's *bilingual dual coding theory* and the *hierarchical models*? Are there any similarities?

(3) Compare and contrast the *independent* and *interdependent hypotheses* of bilingual memory, and discuss some of the evidence supporting each. What is your opinion regarding these two hypotheses? Which one makes the most sense to you and why?

(4) Compare and contrast the *word association* and the *concept mediation models*. Make sure that you describe each model and its specific assumptions. What are the specific predictions regarding picture naming in L2 and translating into L2, according to these models? What can we conclude about these two models?

(5) Describe the RHM and suggest how this model can be tested. What are some possible problems with this model and how would you modify this model to account for its weaknesses?

(6) In relation to the *sense model* and the *distributed conceptual feature model*, what makes the *sense model* a potentially better proposal than the *distributed conceptual feature model*?

(7) What makes the BIA a much different model than the other models described in this chapter?

(8) Why are pictures remembered better than words? What model makes this prediction?

(9) What is the *bilingual concreteness effect*, and how would you obtain this effect?

(10) Do you have your own theory of bilingualism? If you do, state your theory in detail and suggest some ways to test it.

Suggested Research Projects

(1) Choose three related articles on bilingual memory from the *Journal of Memory and Language* or from another psychological journal. Choose the article that you like the most and try to see if you can replicate its results by carefully following instructions from the methods section. After you finish your experiment, discuss it with your professor and present your findings to your class.

(2) Visit http://www.math.yorku.ca/SCS/Online/paivio/ and select 20 high-frequency words. Choose 10 of these words, at random, and translate them into Spanish or any other language. You should have 10 words in English and 10 in Spanish. Mix the 20 words and have your classmates study these words for about 40 seconds. Make sure that you present one word at a time. To do this, use available visual presentation software such as *OpenOffice* (download it free of charge from: www.openoffice.org) or other specialized experimental software such as *PsyScope* or other programs that can be obtained free of charge from http://www.tamiu.edu/~rheredia/materials.html. After studying the 20 words, have your classmates try to remember as many words as possible in any order. In what language were your classmates able to remember the most words? Can you explain why? What are some possible explanations? Can you explain your results in terms of some of the models described in this chapter?

(3) In relation to the *sense model*, visit https://wordnet.princeton.edu/ and download the program for your particular computer platform free or charge. After you install *WordNet*, find out how many senses are associated with the concept of *love*. Now, consult *El Diccionario de la Real Academia Española* or visit http://www.wordreference.com/definicion/, enter *amor*, and estimate the various meanings or different usages of *amor*. Do you see any differences and similarities between the usage of this concept between English and Spanish? Are there any language-specific aspects of this concept for Spanish and English?

(4) For this project, you can use the 20 high-frequency words (10 English and 10 Spanish) from project 2. First, randomize the 20 words and use a different group of participants.

This experiment should be performed in a secluded place with one participant at a time. For this experiment, have participants translate the English words into Spanish and vice versa. Do this one word at a time, and note the time taken to translate each word. You can keep track of the time by using a stop-watch or by using one of the specialized programs mentioned in project 2. Compute the average time taken to translate from English to Spanish and Spanish to English. Did you obtain the predicted translation asymmetries? Do you notice any differences? Which direction was faster to translate? How would you explain these results?

(5) For this next project, follow the same procedure as project 1, but this time choose the *concreteness ratings* to obtain concrete and abstract words. The concreteness ratings provided by the norms in the website range from 1–7. After the selection of 20 to 30 words, go to a psychological data base (e.g., *PsychINFO or Google Scholar*) and search for articles related to the *concreteness effect* to find out the criteria used to define *concrete* and *abstract* words. What did you find out? How are concrete words defined? In other words, what is the criterion used to define abstract and concrete words?

Author Notes

This chapter is dedicated to the memory of Elizabeth Bates and David Swinney, whose work and love for psychology continue to inspire us.

References

Altarriba, J. (1992). The representation of translation equivalents in bilingual memory. In R. J. Harris (Ed.), *Cognitive processing in bilinguals* (pp. 157–174). Amsterdam: Elsevier Science B.V.

Altarriba, J. (2001). Language processing and memory retrieval in Spanish–English bilinguals. *Spanish Applied Linguistics, 4*, 215–245.

Altarriba, J., & Basnight-Brown, D. M. (2007). Methodological considerations in performing semantic and translation priming experiments across languages. *Behavior Research Methods, Instruments, & Computers, 39*(1), 1–18.

Altarriba, J., & Bauer, L. M. (2004). The distinctiveness of emotion concepts: A comparison between emotion, abstract, and concrete words. *American Journal of Psychology, 117*, 389–410.

Altarriba, J., Kroll, J. F., Sholl, A., & Rayner, K. (1996). The influence of lexical and conceptual constraints on reading mixed-language sentences: Evidence from eye fixations and naming times. *Memory & Cognition, 24*, 477–492.

Altarriba, J., & Mathis, K. M. (1997). Conceptual and lexical development in second language acquisition. *Journal of Memory and Language, 36*, 550–568.

Atkinson, R. C., & Shiffrin, R. M. (1968). Human memory: A proposed system and its control processes. In K. W. Spence & J. T. Spence (Eds.), *The psychology of learning and motivation: Advances in research in theory* (Vol. 2, pp. 89–105). New York: Academic Press.

Basi, R. K., Thomas, M. H., & Wang, A. Y. (1997). Bilingual generation effect: Variations in participant bilingual type and list type. *The Journal of General Psychology, 124*, 216–222.

Basnight-Brown, D. M. (2014). Models of lexical access and bilingualism. In R. R. Heredia & J. Altarriba (Eds.), *Foundations of bilingual memory* (pp. 85–107). New York: Springer.

Basnight-Brown, D. M., & Altarriba, J. (2007). Differences in semantic and translation priming across languages: The role of language direction and language dominance. *Memory & Cognition, 35*, 953–965.

Bowers, J. M., & Kennison, S. M. (2011). The role of age of acquisition in bilingual word translation: Evidence from Spanish–English bilinguals. *Journal of Psycholinguistic Research, 40*, 275–289.

Brysbaert, M., Ameel, E., & Storms, G. (2014). Bilingual semantic memory. A new hypothesis. In R. R. Heredia & J. Altarriba (Eds.), *Foundations of bilingual memory* (pp. 133–146). New York: Springer.

Brysbaert, M., & Duyck, W. (2010). Is it time to leave behind the revised hierarchical model of bilingual language processing after fifteen years of service? *Bilingualism: Language and Cognition, 13*, 359–371.

Caramazza, A., & Brones, I. (1980). Semantic classification by bilinguals. *Canadian Journal of Psychology, 34*, 77–81.

Cepeda, N. J., Pashler, H., Vul, E., Wixted, J. T., & Rohrer, D. (2006). Distributed practice in verbal recall tasks: A review and quantitative synthesis. *Psychological Bulletin, 132*, 354–380.

Chauncey, K., Grainger, J., & Holcomb, P. J. (2008). Code-switching effects in bilingual word recognition: A masked priming study with event-related potentials. *Brain and Language, 105*(3), 161–174.

Cieślicka, A. B., & Heredia, R. R. (2016). Priming and online multiple language activation. In R. R. Heredia, J., Altarriba, & A. B. Cieślicka (Eds.), *The bilingual mind and brain series: Vol. 1. Methods in bilingual comprehension research* (pp. 123–156). New York: Springer.

Cieślicka, A. B., Heredia, R. R., & García, T. (2017). Task effects in idiom comprehension. *Poznań Studies in Contemporary Linguistics, 53*(1), 95–118. doi:10.1515/psicl-2017-0001.

Davis, C., Sánchez-Casas, R., García-Albea, J. E., Guasch, M., Molero, M., & Ferré, P. (2010). Masked translation priming: Varying language experience and word type with Spanish–English bilinguals. *Bilingualism: Language and Cognition, 13*, 137–155.

de Bruin, A., Treccani, B., & Della Sala, S. (2015). The connection is in the data: We should consider them all. *Psychological Science, 26*(6), 947–949. doi:10.1177/0956797615583443.

de Groot, A. M. B. (1992). Determinants of word translation. *Journal of Experimental Psychology: Learning, Memory, and Cognition, 18*, 1001–1018.

de Groot, A. M. B. (1993). Word-type effects in bilingual processing tasks. In R. Schreuder & B. Weltons (Eds.), *The bilingual lexicon* (pp. 27–51). Amsterdam: John Benjamins.

de Groot, A. M. B., Dannenburg, L., & Van Hell, J. G. (1994). Forward and backward word translation by bilinguals. *Journal of Memory and Language, 33*, 600–629.

Diccionario de la Real Academia Española (1992). (21st ed.). Madrid, Spain: Real Academia Española.

Dijkstra, T., & Van Heuven, W. J. B. (2002). The architecture of the bilingual word recognition system: From identification to decision. *Bilingualism: Language and Cognition, 5*, 175–197.

Dillon, R. F., McCormack, P. D., Petrusic, W. M., Cook, G. M., & Lafleur, L. (1973). Release from proactive interference in compound and coordinate bilinguals. *Bulletin of the Psychonomic Society, 2*, 293–294.

Dimitropoulou, M., Duñabeitia, J. A., & Carreiras, M. (2011). Masked translation priming effects with low proficient bilinguals. *Memory & Cognition, 39*, 260–275.

Dunn, A. L., & Fox Tree, J. E. (2009). A quick, gradient bilingual dominance scale. *Bilingualism: Language and Cognition, 12*, 273–289. doi:10.1017/S1366728909990113.

Duñabeitia, J. A., Perea, M., & Carreiras, M. (2010). Masked translation priming effects with high proficient simultaneous bilinguals. *Experimental Psychology, 57*, 98–107.

Durgunoğlu, A. Y., & Roediger, H. L. (1987). Test differences in accessing bilingual memory. *Journal of Memory and Language, 26*, 377–391.

Duyck, W., & Brysbaert, M. (2004). Forward and backward number translation requires conceptual mediation in both balanced and unbalanced bilinguals. *Journal of Experimental Psychology: Human Perception and Performance, 30*, 889–906.

Ervin, S. M., & Osgood, C. E. (1954). Second language learning and bilingualism. *Journal of Personality and Social Psychology, 58*, 139–145.

Finkbeiner, M., Forster, K., Nicol, J., & Nakamura, K. (2004) The role of polysemy in masked semantic and translation priming. *Journal of Memory and Language, 51*, 1–22.

Fox, E. (1996). Cross-language priming from ignored words: Evidence for a common representational system in bilinguals. *Journal of Memory and Language, 35*, 353–370.

Gekoski, W. (1980). Language acquisition context and language organization in bilinguals. *Journal of Psycholinguistic Research, 9*, 429–449.

Gerard, L., & Scarborough, D. L. (1989). Language-specific lexical access of homographs by bilinguals. *Journal of Experimental Psychology: Learning, Memory, and Cognition, 15*, 305–315.

Glanzer, M., & Duarte, A. (1971). Repetition between and within language in free recall. *Journal of Verbal Learning and Verbal Behavior, 10,* 625–630.

Goggin, J., & Wickens, D. D. (1971). Proactive interference and language change in short-term memory. *Journal of Verbal Learning and Verbal Behavior, 10,* 453–458.

Grainger, J., & Frenck-Mestre, C. (1998). Masked priming by translation equivalents in proficient bilinguals. *Language & Cognitive Processes, 13,* 601–623.

Grainger, J., Midgley, K., & Holcomb, P. J. (2010). Re-thinking the bilingual interactive-activation model from a developmental perspective (BIA-d). *Language Acquisition across Linguistic and Cognitive Systems, 52,* 267–283.

Green, D. W. (1998). Mental control of the lexico-semantic system. *Bilingualism: Language and Cognition, 1,* 67–81.

Grosjean, F. (2008). *Studying bilinguals.* Oxford: Oxford University Press.

Guttfreund, D. G. (1990). Effects of language usage on the emotional experience of Spanish–English and English–Spanish bilinguals. *Journal of Counseling and Clinical Psychology, 58,* 604–607.

Heredia, R. R. (1995). *Concreteness effects in high frequency words: A test of the revised hierarchical and the mixed models of bilingual memory representations* (Unpublished doctoral dissertation). University of California, Santa Cruz.

Heredia, R. R. (1997). Bilingual memory and hierarchical models: A case for language dominance. *Current Directions in Psychological Science, 6,* 34–39.

Heredia, R. R., & Altarriba, J. (2001). Bilingual language mixing: Why do bilinguals code-switch? *Current Directions in Psychological Science, 10,* 164–168.

Heredia, R. R., & Brown, J. M. (2004). Bilingual memory. In T. K. Bhatia, & W. C. Ritchie (Eds.), *Handbook of bilingualism* (pp. 225–249). Malden, MA: Blackwell.

Heredia, R. R., & Cieślicka, A. B. (2014). Bilingual storage: Compound-coordinate and derivates. In R. R. Heredia & J. Altarriba (Eds.), *Foundations of bilingual memory* (pp. 11–40). New York: Springer.

Heredia, R. R., & García, E. A. (2017). Bilingual episodic memory. In A. Ardila, A. B. Cieślicka, R. R. Heredia, & M. Rosselli, (Eds.), *The bilingual mind and brain series: Vol. 5. The psychology of bilingualism: The cognitive world of bilinguals.* New York: Springer.

Heredia, R. R., & McLaughlin, B. (1992). Bilingual memory revisited. In R. J. Harris (Ed.), *Cognitive processing in bilinguals* (pp. 91–103). Amsterdam: Elsevier.

Hinson, J. M., & Whitney, P. (2006). Proactive interference and item similarity in working memory. *Journal of Experimental Psychology: Learning, Memory, and Cognition, 32,* 183–196.

Jared, D., Poh, R. P. Y., & Paivio, A. (2013). L1 and L2 picture naming in Mandarin-English bilinguals: A test of Bilingual Dual Coding Theory. *Bilingualism: Language and Cognition, 16,* 383–396.

Jiang, N., & Forster, K. I. (2001). Cross-language priming asymmetries in lexical decision and episodic recognition. *Journal of Memory and Language, 44,* 32–51.

Keatley, C. W., Spinks, J. A., & De Gelder, B. (1994). Asymmetrical cross-language priming effects. *Memory & Cognition, 22,* 70–84.

Keatley, C., & De Gelder, B. (1992). The bilingual primed lexical decision task: Cross-language priming disappears with speeded responses. *European Journal of Cognitive Psychology, 4,* 273–292.

Kirsner, K., Smith, M. C., Lockhart, R. S., & King, M. L. (1984). The bilingual lexicon: Language-specific units in an integrated network. *Journal of Verbal Learning and Verbal Behavior, 23,* 519–539.

Kolers, P. A. (1963). Interlingual associations. *Journal of Verbal Learning and Verbal Behavior, 2,* 291–300.

Kolers, P. A., & González, E. (1980). Memory for words, synonyms, and translations. *Journal of Experimental Psychology: Human Learning and Memory, 6,* 53–65.

Kroll, J. F., & de Groot, A. M. B. (1997). Lexical and conceptual memory in the bilingual: Mapping form to meaning in two languages. In A. M. B. de Groot & J. F. Kroll (Eds.), *Tutorials in bilingualism: Psycholinguistic perspectives* (pp. 169–199). Mahwah, NJ: Erlbaum.

Kroll, J. F., & Sholl, A., (1992). Lexical and conceptual memory in fluent and nonfluent bilinguals. In R. Harris (Ed.), *Cognitive processing in bilinguals* (pp. 157–174). New York: Elsevier Science Publishers.

Kroll, J. F., & Stewart, E. (1994). Category interference in translation and picture naming: Evidence for asymmetric connections between bilingual memory representations. *Journal of Memory and Language, 33*, 149–174.

Kroll, J. F., Van Hell, J. G., Tokowicz, N., & Green, D. (2010). The revised hierarchical model: A critical review and assessment. *Bilingualism: Language and Cognition, 13*, 373–381.

La Heij, W., Hooglander, A., Kerling, R., & Van Der Velden, E. (1996). Nonverbal context effects in forward and backward translation: Evidence for concept mediation. *Journal of Memory and Language, 35*, 648–665.

Lederberg, A. R., & Morales, C. (1985). Code-switching by bilinguals: Evidence against a third grammar. *Journal of Psycholinguistic Research, 14*, 113–136.

Léwy, N., & Grosjean, F. (2001). The computerized version of BIMOLA: A bilingual model of lexical access. *Manuscript, University of Neuchâtel, Switzerland.*

Li, P. (1996). Spoken word recognition of code-switched words by Chinese-English bilinguals. *Journal of Memory and Language, 35*, 757–774.

Li, P., & Farkas, I. (2002). A self-organizing connectionist model of bilingual processing. In R. Heredia & J. Altarriba (Eds.), *Bilingual sentence processing* (pp. 59–85). North Holland: Elsevier Science Publisher.

López, M., & Young, R. K. (1974). The linguistic interdependence of bilinguals. *Journal of Experimental Psychology, 102*, 981–983.

MacNamara, J., & Kushnir, S. L. (1971). Linguistic independence of bilinguals: The input switch. *Journal of Verbal Learning and Verbal Behavior, 10*, 480–487.

MacWhinney, B., & Bates, E. (1989). *The crosslinguistic study of sentence processing*. New York: Cambridge University Press.

McCormack, P. D. (1977). Bilingual linguistic memory: The independence-interdependence issue revisited. In P. A. Hornby (Ed.), *Bilingualism* (pp. 57–67). New York: Academic Press.

Paivio, A. (1991). Dual coding theory: Retrospect and current status. *Canadian Journal of Psychology: Outstanding Contributions Series, 45*, 255–287.

Paivio, A. (2014). Bilingual dual coding theory and memory. In R. R. Heredia & J. Altarriba (Eds.), *Foundations of bilingual memory* (pp. 41–62). New York: Springer.

Paivio, A., & Desrochers, A. (1980). A dual-coding approach to bilingual memory. *Canadian Journal of Psychology, 34*, 388–399.

Paivio, A., & Lambert, W. E. (1981). Dual coding and bilingual memory. *Journal of Verbal Behavior and Verbal Learning, 20*, 532–539.

Paivio, A., Clark, J., & Lambert, W. E. (1988). Bilingual dual-coding theory and semantic repetition effects on recall. *Journal of Experimental Psychology: Learning, Memory, and Cognition, 14*, 163–172.

Paradis, M. (1980). Language and thought in bilinguals. In W. C. McCormack & H. J. Izzo (Eds.), *The sixth LACUS forum 1979* (pp. 420–431). Columbia, SC: Hornbeam Press.

Perea, M., Duñabeitia, J. A., & Carreiras, M. (2008). Masked associative/semantic priming effects across languages with highly proficient bilinguals. *Journal of Memory and Language, 58*, 916–930.

Potter, M. C., So, K., Eckardt, V., & Feldman, L. (1984). Lexical and conceptual representation in beginning and proficient bilinguals. *Journal of Verbal Learning and Verbal Behavior, 23*, 23–38.

Pritchett, L. K., Vaid, J., & Tosun, S. (2016). Of black sheep and white crows: Extending bilingual dual coding theory to memory for idioms. *Cogent Psychology, 3*, 1–18. doi:10.1080/23311908. 2015.1135512.

Radvansky, G. A. (2017). *Human memory* (3rd ed.). New York: Routledge.

Repovš, G., & Baddeley, A. (2006). The multi-component model of working memory: Explorations in experimental cognitive psychology. *Neuroscience, 139*, 5–21.

Roediger, H. L. (1991). Implicit memory: Retention without remembering. *American Psychologist, 45*, 1043–1056.

Roediger, H. L. (2008). Relativity of remembering: Why the laws of memory vanished. *Annual Review of Psychology*, *59*(22), 225–254.

Scarborough, D. L., Gerard, L., & Cortese, C. (1984). Independence in bilingual word recognition. *Journal of Verbal Learning and Verbal Behavior*, *23*, 84–99.

Schoonbaert, S., Duyck, W., Brysbaert, M., & Hartsuiker, R., J. (2009). Semantic and translation priming from a first language to a second language and back: Making sense of findings. *Memory & Cognition*, *37*, 569–586.

Schwanenflugel, P. J., Akin, C., & Luh, W. M. (1992). Context availability and the recall of abstract and concrete words. *Memory & Cognition*, *20*(1), 96–104.

Schwanenflugel, P. J., & Rey, M. (1986). Interlingual semantic facilitation: Evidence for a common representational system in the bilingual lexicon. *Journal of Memory and Language*, *25*, 605–618.

Sebastían-Gallés, N., Echeverría, S., & Bosch, L. (2005). The influence of initial exposure on lexical representation: Comparing early and simultaneous bilinguals. *Journal of Memory and Language*, *52*, 420–255.

Slamecka, N. J., & Katsaiti, L. T. (1978). The generation effect as an artifact of selective displaced rehearsal. *Journal of Memory and Language*, *26*, 589–607.

Soares, C., & Grosjean, F. (1984). Bilinguals in a monolingual and a bilingual speech mode: The effect on lexical access. *Memory & Cognition*, *12*, 380–386.

Tytus, A. E., & Rundblad, G. (2016). Cross-language priming as a means of investigating bilingual conceptual representations: A comparison of visual and auditory modality. *Linguistic Approaches to Bilingualism*, *6*(4), 440–466.

Vaid, J. (1988). Bilingual memory representation: A further test of dual coding theory. *Canadian Journal of Psychology*, *42*, 84–90.

van Hell, J. G., & de Groot, A. M. B. (1998). Disentangling context availability and concreteness in lexical decision and word translation. *The Quarterly Journal of Experimental Psychology: Section A*, *51*(1), 41–63.

Wang, X., & Forster, K. I. (2010). Masked translation priming with semantic categorization: testing the sense model. *Bilingualism: Language and Cognition*, *13*, 327–340. doi:10.1017/ S1366728909990502.

Weinreich, U. (1953). *Languages in contact*. New York: The Linguistic Circle of New York.

WordNet 2.1 (2005). Princeton University Press. Retrieved from http://wordnet.princeton.edu/

Zeelenberg, R., & Pecher, D. (2003). Evidence for long-term cross-language repetition priming in conceptual implicit memory tasks. *Journal of Memory and Language*, *49*, 80–94.

Section II

Cognitive and Neurological Mechanisms

4 The Psycholinguistics of Bilingualism

Crystal J. Robinson and Jeanette Altarriba

Introduction

As humans, we have the innate ability to communicate in a complex, creative, and meaningful fashion. Human language, in its productive nature, is unique from all other forms of animal communication. How is it that we process, comprehend, and produce such a complex communication system? It is this question that is central to the study of psycholinguistics. This question becomes even more elaborate when we consider that many individuals are able to functionally communicate across more than one language, as is the case for bilinguals. A bilingual speaker can be defined in a variety of ways. An individual who is equally proficient in both their first (L1) and second (L2) language would be considered a balanced bilingual, whereas, in many other cases, a bilingual is either more proficient in their L1 or their L2. Is it the case that bilingual speakers process language in the same manner as monolingual speakers? What factors influence the way bilinguals process and comprehend language? The current chapter aims to provide an overview of the research attempting to answer these questions. This overview will include the current debates and theoretical oppositions within the realm of bilingual language processing.

Levels of Analysis

Psycholinguists, in general, can examine the processing of human language from a variety of approaches or levels. The convergence of evidence from research focusing on these different levels of language processing can ultimately help to form coherent and holistic theories within the field. These levels can be conceptualized as different aspects of language processing. For example, phonology, semantics, morphology, syntax, and pragmatics work together to make up the whole of our linguistic system. For the bilingual, these levels not only interact with each other within a single language, but also interact with each other cross-linguistically; it is this cross-linguistic interaction that will be discussed throughout the following sections.

Before discussing research findings relevant to each level of analysis, it is first important to define each level, as it relates to the study of psycholinguistics and bilingualism. *Phonology* is the study of sounds associated with language. For example, in English, it is possible to study the processing differences between the pronunciation of the "c" sound as in *cake* (which requires a hard /k/ sound) and the "c" as in *cellar* (which requires a soft /s/ sound). From the bilingual perspective, a psycholinguist would be interested in exploring the degree to which a bilingual speaker processes the sounds in his or her two languages differently, and what specific factors may be contributing to these differences.

Additionally, it may be theoretically beneficial to know the degree to which, if any, a bilingual's two phonological systems interact with one another, altering the processing of speech sounds in each of the two languages.

Semantics is concerned with how meaning is processed. More specifically, a psycholinguist might be interested in the mental processing that occurs whenever an English speaker encounters the word *cake*, as in the baked dessert that is often served at a birthday or graduation celebration, versus the word *brownie*, or the baked chocolate dessert that differs in consistency from cake. Additionally, from the bilingual perspective, a psycholinguist would be interested in any processing differences between the words *cake* and *torta/pastel* for a Spanish–English bilingual.

Morphology refers to the study of the smallest meaningful until of language, a *morpheme*. These units do not necessarily have to be complete words on their own. One such example is the word ending, *-ing*. This morpheme cannot be used independently. However, when this unit is added to the end of a verb, as in *I am eating*, the morpheme is indicative of the present progressive tense. A psycholinguist would be interested in what factors contribute to processing differences across a variety of morphemes. One such factor of interest is the presence of two or more morphological systems, as is the case for a bilingual speaker. It is important to know how the two morphological systems interact and impact individual language processing.

Syntax refers to the underlying grammatical structure of a given language. Psycholinguists are interested in research questions concerning how different grammatical structures are processed and the difference in processing between correct and incorrect grammatical structures. In the case of the bilingual, the underlying grammatical structures of the speaker's two languages could be vastly different from one another. Researchers are interested in the impact of these differences on overall language use and processing.

Pragmatics refers to the set of social and contextual rules a speaker uses to communicate more effectively. As an example, consider the following ambiguous sentences:

(1a)   *The missionaries are ready to eat.*
(1b)   *Flying planes can be dangerous.*

In sentence (1a), the missionaries could either be interpreted as *the eaters* or the *to-be-eaten*. However, most readers will automatically assume the first interpretation, as the cannibalism suggested by the second interpretation would be, in most cases, socially inappropriate. In sentence (1b), it is more likely that the sentence will be interpreted as, *the act of piloting a plane is dangerous*, and not, *planes that fly are dangerous*. The reason for this is that, as English speakers who are familiar with the purpose of planes, we understand that all planes are built to fly, rendering the second interpretation illogical. For a bilingual, the social meanings of words may not be identical across their two languages. In this case, if the speaker is either not aware of the varying social meanings, or is unable to disentangle these meanings, communication can become difficult and confusing.

Language Selective versus Language Non-Selective Views

Researchers interested in studying bilingualism from the psycholinguistic perspective are often concerned with the overarching theoretical question of how bilinguals mentally organize their two linguistic systems. To address this question, two competing theories were originally posited, the *language selective* and the *language non-selective view* (see Figure 4.1). The language selective view asserts that a bilingual works in only one

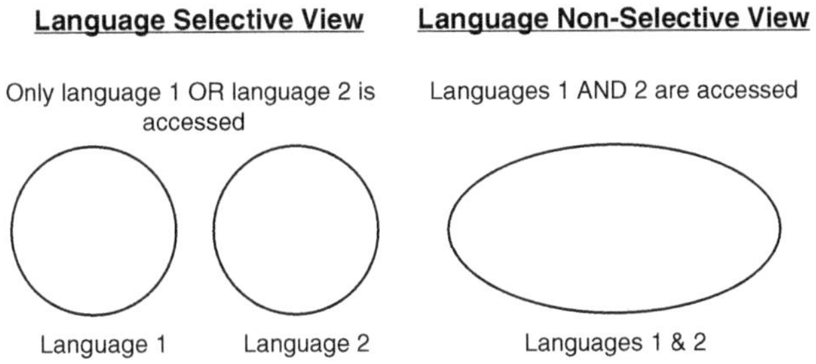

Language Selective View **Language Non-Selective View**

Only language 1 OR language 2 is accessed

Languages 1 AND 2 are accessed

Language 1   Language 2

Languages 1 & 2

Figure 4.1   Illustrations of the language selective and language non-selective views of bilingual language access.

language at a time, and thus, the two languages do not interact with one another during language processing (Gerard & Scarborough, 1989; Macnamara & Kushnir, 1971). The language non-selective view, alternatively, states that both a bilingual's two languages are continuously active during linguistic processing. Thus, this theory would predict that the two languages interact and interfere with each other on a consistent basis (Altenberg & Cairns, 1983; Beauvillain & Grainger, 1987; Dijkstra & Van Heuven, 1998). The following sections will address the two competing theories from each of the five aforementioned levels of analysis (phonology, semantics, morphology, syntax, and pragmatics).

Phonology

In a classic study of bilingual word recognition, Spivey and Marian (1999) presented Russian–English bilingual adults with groups of objects where the label for one of the objects presented (the target object) overlapped phonologically with the participants' L2 label of a presented distracter object. For instance, the Russian label for the target object *marka* (*stamp*) overlapped phonologically with the English label for the presented distracter object, *marker*. The authors found that the presence of the other-language distracter interfered with target recognition; participants looked more toward the distracter object, *marker*, on hearing the similar-sounding Russian word, *marka*, relative to a phonologically unrelated distracter object (e.g., *ruler*). These results suggested that participants coactivated the English label for the depicted object, *marker*, which caused the participants to look toward this object upon hearing the target label, *marka*. This study was the first to show language non-selective access in bilingual auditory processing.

In a follow-up study, Marian and Spivey (2003) used a similar paradigm, exploring the degree to which the phonology of each of their participants' two languages (Russian and English) interfered with processing in the other. In their first experiment, the authors found that participants experienced significant phonological interference from their L1 (Russian) on processing in their L2 (English). However, in their second experiment, the authors found that participants did not experience significant phonological interference from their L2 (English) on processing in their L1 (Russian). In general, the results from this study supported the language non-selective view. However, the degree to which a bilingual's second, or perhaps less fluent, language is active may be dampened relative to their L1. Similarly, Jared and Kroll (2001) found that French–English bilinguals were slower in naming English words after being presented with a French word. These results suggested that French phonology was being accessed during English word naming, slowing down the processing speed.

In studies that use a lexical decision task, as opposed to a pronunciation task, to determine the degree of phonological activation across both of a bilingual's languages, there is rarely an effect of language dominance or proficiency. That is, the L1 and L2 tend to interfere with each other to a similar degree (Von Holzen & Mani, 2012). Duyck (2005) reported effects of *translation priming* through phonology. In the critical condition, Dutch–English bilingual adults were visually presented with pseudohomophones, that is, nonwords such as *roap* whose phonological counterparts sounded similar to real English words (e.g., *rope*). The pseudohomophones served as primes in this study, such that the participants were not expected to make a response to these nonwords. Following the presentation of the primes, participants were asked to determine whether the presented target (a string of pronounceable letters) was a word or a nonword. Participants showed faster recognition of the Dutch translation of the English phonological counterparts to the presented nonword primes. For example, in the case where the presented prime was *roap*, participants were faster to recognize *touw* (Dutch for *rope*) as compared to when the presented prime was a nonhomophonic nonword such as *joll*. This result was consistent regardless of language dominance or proficiency across participants (Lagrou, Hartsuiker, & Duyck, 2011).

Taken together, the research to date supports the language non-selective view of phonological activation. There remains debate concerning the conditions in which the phonological codes for both of a bilingual's languages are activated to the same degree. Additionally, many of the above studies do not consider the role of semantics in causing the observed cross-language interference. Specifically, it could be the case that the phonological activation in one language is leading to an activation of meaning in that language, which in turn, causes activation of meaning in the L2.

Semantics

The psycholinguistic study of semantics is concerned with the *mental lexicon* (i.e., mental dictionary), or the collection of words associated with a given language. The bilingual speaker could either have one lexicon comprised of information from both languages (the language non-selective view), or the speaker could have two independent lexicons, one for L1, and another for L2 (the language selective view). In addition to the mental lexicon(s), a bilingual's semantic knowledge is comprised of information from the *conceptual store*, or the map of concepts that are held together in memory. Thus, the mental lexicon includes all relevant labels for a given concept, while the conceptual store includes properties of that concept. For example, the word and its label "dog" would be stored in the lexicon, while the concept's properties (e.g., *has four legs*, *has fur*, *barks*) would be located in the conceptual store.

The *bilingual interactive activation model* (BIA) is a model of bilingual visual word recognition. This model is structured by four levels of different linguistic representations: letter features, letters, words, and language tags (or language nodes). The model suggests that when a word is presented, the features of its letters are first activated. Then, these letter features work together and activate the letters as a whole. In turn, these letters activate the words of that language. The word candidates activate the language nodes that are connected. They simultaneously send feedback activation to the letter level. Language nodes can also inhibit the activation of word candidates from other languages (e.g., the English language node reduces the activation of Dutch word candidates). After this interactive process of activation and inhibition, the lexical candidate corresponding to the presented word becomes the most active word unit (Dijkstra, Van Heuven, & Grainger, 1998). The *BIA+* model is an extension and adaptation of the BIA model. The BIA+ model includes not only orthographic representation and language nodes, but also phonological and semantic representations. All these representations are assumed to be part of a word identification system that provides output to a task/decision system (Dijkstra & Van Heuven, 2002). Both the BIA and the BIA+ models represent word activation as a language non-selective process. Specifically, the competing or interfering language must be inhibited throughout the process of word identification and recognition.

Kroll and Stewart (1994) devised the *revised hierarchical model* of bilingual lexical access. This model suggests that there are two distinct lexicons for the L1 and the L2, and that these two lexicons are connected to a singular conceptual store. Additionally, this model states that the L1 lexicon is larger than the L2 lexicon, due to the fact that, as the L1, it is more likely to contain more lexical entries. Furthermore, this model includes *lexical links* and *conceptual links.* One conceptual link connects the L1 lexicon to the conceptual store, and another conceptual link connects the L2 lexicon to the conceptual store. According to this model, the L1 conceptual link is stronger than the L2 link, due to the assumed strength of L1 relative to L2 (but see Altarriba & Mathis, 1997 for a competing view). These L1 and L2 conceptual links are bi-directional, such that a concept can activate the lexical entry and a lexical entry can activate a concept.

With regards to the lexical links, there is one link that connects the L1 lexicon to the L2 lexicon, and one link that connects the L2 lexicon to the L1 lexicon. Unlike the conceptual links, these lexical links are unidirectional. Specifically, there is a strong link from the L2 lexicon to the L1 lexicon, due to the L2 learning process. Generally, when learning an L2, the speaker forms a connection between the newly learned L2 lexical entries and the equivalent, but stronger, L1 lexical entries. It is important to note that this model does not map on well to the lexical processes of *simultaneous bilinguals*, or bilinguals who acquired both of their languages at the same time. Additionally, this model makes no predictions about bilinguals who are more fluent in their L2, rather than their L1.

Since the introduction of the revised hierarchical model, updates have been made to account for further research on the bilingual lexical and conceptual systems. Pavlenko's (2009) *modified hierarchical model* is one such example. This model assumes that the conceptual representations do not have to be fully shared between a bilingual's two languages. Specifically, conceptual representations may be partially shared between the L1 and L2, or they could be specific to either L1 or L2, with no overlap. This lack of overlap is due to the occasional lack of translation equivalents across L1 and L2. For example, words like *frustration* and *privacy* do not have an appropriate Russian translation, and thus there would be no possible link between the Russian lexicon and the conceptual entries for *frustration* or *privacy*. Additionally, this modified model accounts for what is referred to as *conceptual transfer*, or the phenomenon where the complete conceptual content associated with an L1 word is assigned to a near translation equivalent in the L2. For example, an English–Russian bilingual may call a paper cup without a handle a *chaska*, even though the appropriate Russian term would actually be *stakanchiki*. What this model does not consider is that this same conceptual transfer could theoretically occur in the opposite direction for bilinguals who are more fluent in and spend more time communicating in their L2.

Morphology

When morphology is explored from the bilingual perspective, it is necessary to consider it from three separate aspects across languages. First, this section will discuss the impact of overlap, or lack thereof, in word frequency and number of morphemes per word across a bilingual's L1 and L2. Second, differences in word tense formation across L1 and L2 will be explored. Lastly, L1 and L2 differences with regards to morphological gender will be discussed.

With regards to word frequency, Lehtonen and Laine (2003) investigated morphological processing across monolingual Finnish speakers and bilingual Finnish–Swedish speakers. Participants in this study were asked to determine whether or not a variety of presented items were words or nonwords. The presented items were either real Finnish words, or pronounceable nonwords. The Finnish words were of varying frequencies within the language. The authors were interested in whether participants would recognize the presented words holistically, or based upon the individual morphemes that make up the whole word. In order to test this, the researchers presented words containing either one or multiple morphemes. Words that contained multiple morphemes included *inflections*, or additions to the word stem that do not change the meaning of the word. For example, in English, a single morpheme word would be *car*, and a multiple morpheme word would be *cars*. The added inflection, *-s*, does not change the meaning of the stem, *car*, but rather indicates the plural form of the stem. The authors found that the bilinguals were using the added inflections to aid in word recognition. However, the monolinguals were recognizing the words holistically. This is likely due to bilinguals having less exposure to each of the words than their monolingual counterparts.

De Diego Balaguer, Costa, Sebastián-Gallés, Juncadella, and Caramazza (2004) were interested in differences between irregular and regular morpheme processing in bilingual speakers. In order to investigate these differences, the researchers tested Spanish–Catalan bilinguals suffering from *Broca's aphasia*, brain damage resulting in non-fluent speech patterns. Participants were asked to produce both regular and irregular word forms across both Spanish and Catalan. The researchers found that aphasic participants had greater difficulty producing irregular word forms than regular word forms. This was true across both Spanish and Catalan. These results support the language non-selective view of bilingualism. Specifically, since damage to one area of the brain affected processing across both languages, this suggests that both languages are processed in the same location.

Finally, researchers investigating the processing of morphological gender in bilingual speakers are interested in effects of grammatical gender on various cognitive processes. Languages with grammatical gender systems (e.g., German, Spanish, Russian, Italian, French, etc.) typically contain masculine, feminine, and occasionally neuter genders. In most cases, specific word endings, or morphemes, are mapped onto a particular gender. For example, in Spanish, words that end in *–a* are typically feminine, while words that end in *–o* are typically masculine.

Scheutz and Eberhard (2004) were interested in the role of gender agreement in sentence processing for German–English bilinguals as compared to English monolinguals. Participants in this study were presented with various English sentences (note that, unlike German, English does not have specific morphemic markers of gender. However, in German, the ending *–er* is the masculine gender marker.) Each of the presented sentences contained a noun, ending in *–er*, that referred to a person, as well as the word *himself* or *herself*, in order to indicate the gender of the person being referred to (see Sentence 2a; Scheutz & Eberhard, 2004, p. 567).

(2a)   *The hunter hurt herself after falling out of a tree.*

After the presentation of the sentence, participants rated each of the presented nouns based upon how masculine or feminine each noun seemed to them. There was a tendency for the German–English bilinguals to rate the nouns as more masculine as compared to the English monolinguals, even if they had "herself." It is likely that the *–er* ending of the nouns prompted bilingual participants to be biased towards a masculine perspective. This research clearly demonstrates how morphological processing in one language (German) can impact interpretation in another (English).

Taken together, the morphological research supports a language non-selective view of bilingual processing. It is the case that morphological features of one language can impact processing in another language, even when that language does not contain the same features. Additionally, deficits to morphological processing tend to occur across both L1 and L2, indicating a similar localization of processing across languages.

Syntax

Syntax, or sentence structure, can vary across languages. In many cases, the sentence structure of a bilingual's L1 may not map directly onto the sentence structure of the bilingual's L2. For example, the syntactic structure for English is quite strict, dictating the following pattern: subject + verb + object (SVO). However, in languages such as Spanish, the subject is optional unless it is needed for emphasis (e.g., *quiero* vs. *yo quiero*: I want.). Researchers are interested in determining whether the syntactic systems for L1 and L2 are stored separately, with limited interaction, or connected, allowing for interaction between the L1 and L2 syntax.

Hoover and Dwivedi (1998) compared syntactic processing across slow-reading and fast-reading English–French bilinguals and French monolinguals. Participants were given sentence pairs to read, followed by a comprehension question. The first sentence always contained contextual information (3a), and the second sentence was the critical, or target sentence. This second sentence was one of four types of sentences: causative with clitic (3b), causative without clitic (3c), non-causative with clitic (3d), non-causative without clitic (3e). A causative sentence is one in which the subject of the sentence is performing the action of the sentence. Clitics are pronouns that precede the verb within a sentence. Clitic-type sentences are not syntactically appropriate in English, but are quite common in French. Below is an example of each type of sentence and its English translation (Hoover & Dwivedi, 1998, p. 9).

Context sentence:
(3a) *Serge s'achetait fréquemment un bon vin rouge* (Translation: Serge would often buy a good red wine).

Causative with clitic:
(3b) *Il le faisait tranquillement gouter avec son fromage doux préféré* (Translation: He had it be tasted quietly with his favorite mild cheese).

Causative without clitic:
(3c) *Il faisait tranquillement gouter le vin avec son fromage préféré* (Translation: He had the wine be tasted quietly with his favorite cheese).

Non-causative with clitic:
(3d) *Il aimait tranquillement le gouter avec son fromage doux préféré* (Translation: He loved to taste it quietly with his favorite mild cheese).

Non-causative without clitic:
(3e) *Il aimait tranquillement gouter le vin avec son fromage préféré* (Translation: He loved to taste the wine quietly with his favorite cheese).

The researchers found that the slow-reading, English–French bilinguals had more difficulty processing the sentences, both causative and non-causative, containing clitics. This difficulty was likely due to the influence of English syntax on the processing of French syntax. Specifically, the lack of syntactic constructions containing clitics in English made it more difficult for less-practiced bilinguals to process these constructions in French.

In many cases, syntactic constructions could be interpreted in multiple ways. When this is the case, a sentence is said to be syntactically ambiguous. Dussias (2003) was interested in differences between monolinguals and bilinguals with regards to processing this type of ambiguity. Participants in this study were presented with a series of ambiguous sentences, such as (Dussias, 2003, p. 541):

(4a)   *Peter fell in love with the daughter of the psychologist who studied in California.*

In the above sentence (4a), there are two possible interpretations. It could either be the case that the daughter studied in California *or* the psychologist studied in California. There were three groups of participants in the Dussias (2003) study: Spanish monolinguals, Spanish–English bilinguals (L1 Spanish), and English–Spanish bilinguals (L1 English). All sentences were presented in Spanish. Additionally, sentences were either easy or difficult to disambiguate. If the sentences were difficult to disambiguate, the necessary context for appropriate interpretation was not made explicitly clear. Conversely, in the easy condition, this context was clearly provided in the sentence. In general, the bilingual speakers, in particular the L1 Spanish bilingual speakers, were faster at reading the difficult-to-disambiguate sentences. The opposite pattern of results was present for the Spanish monolinguals.

Pragmatics and Figurative Language

Pragmatics refers to the way language is used, rather than its individual components. For bilingual speakers, language use is very much tied to a given social context. Silva (2000) studied the pragmatic differences between English and Spanish, with particular interest in how these differences affected bilingual processing. The specific exemplar used in the study was the English term, *Why don't you?* This term is generally used to make a polite suggestion. However, when translated into Portuguese, the term does not maintain the polite connotation.

In order to examine the effects of this difference, Silva (2000) asked Portuguese-dominant and English-dominant bilinguals to judge the correctness of various scenarios. Participants were read a description of a social situation and then asked to decide whether the request or suggestion in the situation was appropriate or not. Silva suggested that participants' judgments would be based upon the amount of time spent in either the American or the Brazilian context. Indeed, Americans who had spent more time in Brazil rated the phrase as less appropriate than Americans who had not spent much time in Brazil. Thus, they were not fully aware of the appropriate social use of Portuguese. This same pattern was apparent for Brazilians. It is clear from this research that both linguistic as well as social context impact the use and processing of language for bilingual speakers. It is rarely the case that bilingualism occurs within a single social or cultural context. This aspect of bilingualism makes it difficult to investigate linguistic variables without considering social and cultural variables as well. This notion will be discussed in greater detail in following sections.

An additional aspect of processing pragmatic information is the ability to process ambiguous language that requires the appropriate social knowledge for interpretation. One example of this is *figurative language*. If you are a native English speaker, you are likely familiar with the phrase, *she let the cat out of the bag*. You are aware that this phrase does not indicate that a literal cat has been released from a bag, but rather that a secret has just been revealed. However, without this prior knowledge, a non-native speaker would likely be questioning why a cat has suddenly been introduced into the conversation. It is rarely the case that figurative language can be directly translated from one language to another, creating difficulties for bilingual speakers.

With regards to figurative language processing, the *graded salience model* suggests that the salient meaning of a word is always activated and cannot be bypassed, and that the most salient meaning is always activated first, before the less salient meanings of any given word (Giora, 1997). Additionally, there are two models informed by bilingual processing. The first of these two models is the *constraint-based processing model of L2*. This model suggests that during figurative language comprehension, bilinguals, like monolinguals, simultaneously make use of all the available information, resulting both from direct retrieval and knowledge of figurative language structure. The second model, the *literal salience model*, further elaborates on bilingual figurative language comprehension, accounting for the acquisition and processing of figurative expressions by foreign language learners.

Using event-related potentials (ERPs), Paulmann, Ghareeb-Ali, and Felser (2015) investigated phrasal verbs in monolinguals and bilinguals. Phrasal verbs (e.g., *run into*), are ambiguous and can be understood literally (e.g., "to go inside": *He ran into the building*) or figuratively (e.g., "to meet someone": *He ran into his old friend*). Paulmann et al.'s results indicate that comprehension of phrasal verbs is not necessarily problematic for proficient L2 learners of English. Thus, the researchers concluded that non-native but proficient speakers of English use processing strategies similar to those of native speakers when comprehending phrasal verbs (see also Matlock & Heredia, 2002). For example, Cieślicka (2013) found that a number of linguistic factors, such as language status, salience, and context influenced the processing of idiomatic phrases. In the study, native language (Polish) and foreign language (English) idioms were embedded in an ambiguous (biasing neither a figurative nor a literal meaning) and an unambiguous (biasing figurative meaning) context. They were then followed by target words related to the figurative meaning of the idiom or literal meaning of the last word of the idiom.

Vaid and Martinez (2001) investigated figurative language processing in Spanish–English bilinguals. The authors were interested in how bilingual speakers processed proverbs. Proverbs are culturally significant sayings that illustrate social mores and beliefs. In this study, participants were presented with familiar and unfamiliar proverbs across English and Spanish. Participants were then asked to either paraphrase the proverb in the same language, or to translate the proverb into the alternate language. Finally, participants were asked to recognize which proverbs they had previously translated or paraphrased. The results indicated that participants were able to retain the original language of the proverb in memory. Specifically, they were more likely to correctly recognize the proverb when it was shown in the language of its original presentation. Proverbs were not remembered as a conceptual whole, but rather they were stored as literal translations.

To examine metaphor processing, Arzouan, Goldstein, and Faust (2007) used two-word expressions conveying literal, conventional metaphoric, novel metaphoric, or no meaning (unrelated). Participants performed a semantic judgment task in which they decided whether a two-word expression was meaningful. Literal expressions were found to be the least demanding in terms of processing, followed by conventional metaphors, novel metaphors, and unrelated two-word expressions. Thus, the retrieval of the stored conceptual knowledge related to novel metaphors is more demanding than the retrieval of knowledge related to literal expressions or conventional metaphors.

As far as bilingual speakers are concerned, Johnson and Rosano (1993) concluded that there was no difference between L1 and L2 speakers in the interpretation of metaphors. That is, L2 learners were able to interpret metaphors as good as native speakers. Early Electroencephalogram (EEG) research about L2 learners, in contrast, stated a difference between L1 and L2. Here, however, the attention was directed to the neuronal processing of metaphors instead of their interpretation. Perani et al. (1996) indicated that low-proficient L2 speakers used different brain areas to process L1 or L2, but high-proficient L2 learners used the same region for both languages. Chen, Peng, and Zhao (2013) investigated the neural mechanism underlying the comprehension of Chinese and English metaphors by Chinese–English bilinguals. ERP data indicated that processing metaphors in the L2 (English) was more difficult than processing metaphors in the L1 (Chinese). In addition, both hemispheres were more activated in processing L2 metaphors as compared to L1 metaphors.

Language in Context

Most current studies of bilingual lexical access are based on the comprehension of iso-lated words without considering whether contextual information affects lexical access in bilinguals. However, in everyday communication, words are most often encountered in a meaningful context and not in isolation (e.g., in a newspaper article). Researchers have begun to investigate the cognitive nature of bilingual lexical access in context by examin-ing word recognition in sentences (see e.g., Heredia & Altarriba, 2002).

In sentence processing, a number of online measuring techniques are helpful in detecting the cognitive activity at the very moment it takes place or only slightly after. The cognate or interlingual homograph words are often used as a marker inserted in test sentences with the following tasks (Heredia, Altarriba, & Cieślicka, 2015).

Self-Paced Reading. In this reading task, participants face a screen, on which a text appears in successive segments. They are asked to process each sequential segment by pressing a key. A trial starts with the presentation of groups of dashes separated by spaces. Each group serves as a placeholder for a word in the text, which is to be presented on that trial, and each dash represents a letter. When the participant subsequently presses the key, the first segment appears (e.g., the first two words) replacing the corresponding placehold-ers for the right words, while the placeholders for the left words remain on the screen. Once pressing the key again, the two words from the first segment are replaced by their placeholders again and the next segment appears, taking the position of the corresponding placeholders. This continues until the whole text has been read. A follow-up comprehen-sion question is presented to ensure that participants indeed pay attention to the meaning of the sentences. The interval between the two successive key presses is measured and registered as the response time.

Rapid Serial Visual Presentation. In this task, participants are presented with suc-cessive segments/words, one by one, at a fixed rate in the same location on the screen. Participants in this task cannot control the speed of reading, while the experimenter deter-mines the presentation speed. Participants are required to read the words aloud and their reaction time of each segment is registered. Again, a follow-up comprehension question is presented to ensure that participants indeed pay attention to the meaning of the sentences. A pictured object can be readily detected in a rapid serial visual presentation sequence when the target is specified by a superordinate category name, such as animal or vehicle.

Eye Tracking. This is a more natural and more sensitive online technique, which records the participants' eye movements and eye fixations while they read a text presented on a computer screen. It documents what the participants are looking at and how long it takes for them to read a particular region of interest or a target. Experimental eye tracking data are obtained to investigate topics such as language comprehension, cognitive processes related to both written and spoken language, body language, lip reading, etc.

Functional Magnetic Resonance Imaging (fMRI) and ERPs. These two additional methods can be used to explore the neurological basis of sentence processing across languages. fMRI measures brain activity by detecting associated changes in blood flow. This technique relies on the fact that cerebral blood flow and neuronal activation are coupled. When an area of the brain is in use, blood flow to that region also increases. An ERP, on the other hand, is the measured brain response that is the direct result of a specific sensory, cognitive, or motor event. More formally, it is any stereotyped electrophysiological response to a stimulus.

The question as to whether the presentation of words in a sentence context restricts lexical access only to words of the target language is most often studied in bilinguals' L2 processing. This sentence context effect might be an efficient strategy to speed up lexical search because it reduces the number of lexical candidates. For example, Elston-Güttler, Gunter, and Kotz (2005) showed that cross-lingual activation is very sensitive to the influence of a sentence context and previous activation state of the two languages in a semantic priming study. In their study, German–English bilinguals were presented with relatively low-constraint sentences in which a homograph (e.g., *the woman gave her friend a pretty GIFT*; "gift" means poison in German) or a control word was presented at the end (e.g., *the woman gave her friend a pretty SHELL*). "Constraint" here is defined as the degree to which the sentence frame preceding the target biased that particular target word. The sentence was then replaced by a target word (*poison*) for a lexical decision. They found that participants were able to recognize the target word faster after being primed with the related homograph sentence as compared to a control sentence. However, this was only true for participants who saw a German film prior to the experiment. Additionally, this priming effect was only present in the first block of the experiment. These results suggest that bilinguals can quickly *zoom into* the L2 processing situation even after the L1 activation was boosted.

In other work, Schwartz and Kroll (2006) used cognates and homographs as target words presented in low- and high-constraint sentences to Spanish–English bilinguals. They investigated how word presentation and semantic constraint modulated lexical access in bilinguals. Schwartz and Kroll used a rapid serial visual presentation, and the target word had to be named. No homograph effects were found, but less proficient bilinguals made more naming errors, especially in low-constraint sentences. They observed cognate facilitation (non-selective bilingual lexical access) in low-constraint sentences, but not in high-constraint ones. The results suggest that the semantic constraint of a sentence may restrict cross-lingual activation effects. Similar results on cognate effects were obtained by Van Hell and de Groot (2008) in their study of Dutch–English bilinguals in an L2 lexical decision task and a translation task in forward (from L1 to L2) and in backward directions (from L2 to L1). Libben and Titone (2009) used eye tracking methodology and found that the cognate facilitation in semantically constrained sentences only happened at early stages of comprehension and rapidly resolved at later stages of comprehension.

Although the majority of studies on bilingual sentence processing are focused on L2 processing, there are still a few studies that have investigated cross-language activation during native language (L1) reading. For example, Van Assche, Duyck, Hartsuiker, and

Diependaele (2009) replicated the cognate effect in L1 with Dutch–English bilinguals, and found that a non-dominant language may affect native language sentence reading, both at early and at late reading stages. Titone, Libben, Mercier, Whitford, and Pivneva (2011) observed this cross-language activation in English–French bilinguals at early reading stages only when the L2 was acquired early in life. They also concluded that the semantic constraint provided by a sentence could attenuate cross-language activation at later stages in reading.

Comprehension of Mixed Passages

In earlier studies, researchers found that bilinguals can comprehend passages composed of words entirely from only one language more quickly than passages composed of words from both languages (Kolers, 1966). According to the language selective view, when comprehension in one language falls short due to switching into an L2, attention must be directed towards the L2 system. Therefore, bilinguals are slower at reading mixed-language passages than reading single language passages because they must spend time on switching languages. However, if the two languages are activated simultaneously, there could be lexical competition in choosing which language information to use, explaining why bilinguals spend more time understanding passages in mixed languages (Moon & Jiang, 2012). Other studies have found that there is no significant cost incurred by inter-sentential language switching and mixing. Ibáñez, Macizo, and Bajo (2010) showed that there was no cost to switching between languages when bilinguals read sentences for comprehension. Additionally, Tamargo (2012) found that when making metalinguistic judgments and performing non-comprehension-based tasks, switch costs were evident, but there was no evidence to support the hypothesis that there is a cost at the switch site when bilinguals read a mixed sentence. This indicates that under normal circumstances and given sufficient linguistic context, language switching does not necessarily incur a cost (Gullifer, Kroll, & Dussias, 2013).

The Production of Language

There are four necessary processes involved in speech production: conceptualizing a thought to be expressed, formulating a linguistic plan, articulating the plan, and monitoring the output (Carroll, 2004). At various points within each of these processes, there is the possibility of error. This error could be due to a lapse in memory or a lack of fluency within the target language. One such error is the *tip-of-the-tongue* (TOT) phenomenon. A TOT occurs when information (e.g., a particular word or fact) becomes temporarily unavailable, despite the speaker's knowledge of the unavailable information. Gollan, Bonanni, and Montoya (2005) investigated the TOT experience from the bilingual perspective using a name elicitation task and a picture naming task. Specifically, Spanish–English bilinguals and English monolinguals were asked to answer questions in English about famous figures and former instructors. The researchers found that TOT rates were greatest (approximately 36%) for famous names, but did not differ for former teachers and objects (approximately 30%). Overall, TOT rates did not differ between the bilingual and the monolingual participants. However, bilinguals did show increased TOT rates for objects as compared to their monolingual counterparts. It is the case that individuals (both famous and not) have only one associated label, whereas, objects have both a Spanish and an English label. Thus, as the language non-selective view would predict, the Spanish labels could have been interfering with the production of the English labels.

The TOT phenomenon has been found to be dampened when an object's labels across the L1 and L2 are cognates (Costa, Santesteban, & Caño, 2005). *Cognates* are words that overlap in spelling across languages and typically share the same meaning. For example, the English word *trophy* and the Spanish word *trofeo* are cognates that share the same meaning. The authors argue that this reduction in TOTs for cognates is due to the inter-action between the lexical and phonological representations of the cognates. However, phonological overlap between L1 and L2 can also be a source of interference in online speech production (Costa, Colomé, Gómez, & Sebastián-Gallés, 2003).

Code-Switching and Its Implications

Code-Switching occurs when a bilingual speaker switches from one language to another when speaking. The following is an example of code-switching taken from Heredia and Altarriba (2001, p. 164):

(5a) *Dame una hamburguesa sin LETTUCE por favor* (Translation: Give me a ham-burger without lettuce please).

Heredia and Altarriba (2001) examined some of the causes of code-switching. Specifically, the authors explored the limited proficiency account of code-switching. According to this account, if a bilingual is weaker in one language, he or she may need to switch between languages in order to compensate and continue with the dialogue. This lack of proficiency view runs into problems when considering the structural aspects of code-switching. It is the case that when code-switching, speakers continue to follow the appropriate grammar of the initial language within the dialogue. Thus, the sentence structure does not change. The limited proficiency account cannot explain why the initial grammatical structure does not change throughout the mixed utterance. The authors pointed out that bilinguals likely use code-switching as a means of improving communication with other bilinguals. For example, a word might be a better fit in one language than another. When this is the case, a bilingual speaker may choose to insert a word from the alternate language, knowing that the audience will be better able to arrive at the intended meaning. Similarly, Chan (2004) argued that code-switching is a *textualization cue* that signals parts of an utterance that ought to be interpreted differently from the rest of the conversation.

The next question to ask concerning code-switching is whether or not it is costly to the speaker (i.e., does it take longer to produce a mixed utterance than a single-language utter-ance?). Macnamara and Kushnir (1971) developed the idea of the *two-switch mechanism*, reliant on two separate lexicons for each language. This mechanism determines which of the two lexicons is "on" and which is "off." Thus, according to this early view, both lexicons could not be active simultaneously. This language selective view of processing would support the idea that code-switching is more time consuming than producing a single-language utterance.

Meuter and Allport (1999) suggested that the cost associated with code-switching was dependent upon the relative strength of each of the two languages. According to this *relative strength hypothesis,* if a bilingual switches from the stronger to the weaker lan-guage, the stronger language needs to be suppressed in order to produce an utterance in the weaker language. When switching back to the stronger language, the suppression still persists, resulting in a cost to processing time. However, when a bilingual switches from the weaker language to the stronger language, less suppression is needed to produce the desired utterance in the stronger language. As a result, there is less of a cost when switching back to the weaker language.

In order to test this hypothesis, Meuter and Allport (1999) presented participants with a number naming task (see Figure 4.2). Participants were asked to respond in either their stronger or weaker language. At various intervals, the required response language would switch from one language to another. The researchers found that language switch trials took longer than non-switch trials. More specifically, this difference was due to the fact that participants were slower when switching back from their weaker language to their stronger language. These results support the relative strength hypothesis. However, this asymmetrical switch cost is not consistently found across studies. This is particularly the case when bilingual speakers are highly proficient in both their L1 and L2 (Costa & Santesteban, 2004).

The Case of Sign Language

It is important to note that producing language goes beyond verbal production and also applies to non-verbal communication such as Sign Language. Thus, individuals who are fluent in both spoken and Sign Language are also classified as bilinguals (Kuntze, 2000; Most, 2003). Additionally, a deaf individual may be fluent in multiple varieties of Sign Language, also classifying this individual as a bilingual. With regards to this first type of bilingual (Sign Language–spoken language), Kuntze (2000) examined code-switching between written English and American Sign Language (ASL). The code-switching of interest in this particular study was that of an ASL history teacher at a deaf school. An instance of code-switching occurred whenever the teacher would switch to finger spelling of the English letters within a particular word. Certain proper names and nouns that do not exist in ASL require the use of finger spelling. Kuntze noted that the instructor also used this type of code-switching to help emphasize certain aspects of the material and to aid the students' understanding.

Concerning the second type of bilingual mentioned (fluent in two or more varieties of Sign Language), a great deal of research has examined the cross-linguistic and cross-cultural influence of a bilingual signer. Pizzuto and Volterra (2000) were interested in the processing of opaque and transparent signs across varieties of Sign Language. *Transparent signs* are those that can usually be correctly guessed by non-signers and signers of a different variety. *Opaque signs*, on the other hand, are those that cannot usually be guessed by individuals who are not familiar with that particular variety of Sign Language. The researchers found that culturally related transparent signs in Italian (e.g., the sign for good/well)

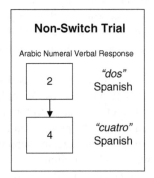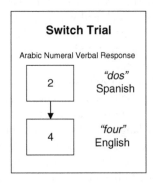

Figure 4.2   Switch trails and non-switch trials (adapted from Meuter & Allport, 1999).

were guessed above chance by both signing and non-signing Italians. Additionally, non-Italian signers performed better on the guessing task than non-signing Italians. However, the meaning of these signs was not accurately guessed above chance by non-Italian non-signers. These results suggest that although culture can aid in the understanding of Sign Language for non-signers, fluency in another variety of Sign Language can aid understanding in the unfamiliar variety.

Language Acquisition and Bilingualism

Bilingual speakers can come from a variety of language learning environments. Specifically, both languages could be acquired during childhood, resulting in a simultaneous learning environment. Conversely, the L2 could be acquired at various points in time after the acquisition of the L1. The following sections will review different aspects of language processing for bilinguals at different stages in the learning process.

Language Non-Selective Lexical Access in Bilingual Development

In recent years, some studies have investigated L2 processing and production in bilingual school-aged children. For instance, Brenders, van Hell, and Dijkstra (2011) showed faster processing of English–Dutch cognates, or words that share similarity in form across the two languages, in the children's L2 (English) relative to non-cognate control English words. These findings were interpreted as providing evidence for language non-selective lexical access in school-aged bilingual children. However, it is important to note that these results may be specific to the processing of cognate words alone. In particular, children may have increased exposure to cognate words simply because they are present in both of their languages (Sherkina-Lieber, 2004). Therefore, although these findings suggest language non-selective access in bilingual school-aged children, the use of cognates may limit the generalizability of this conclusion.

Phono-Lexical Processing During Development

Research has shown that by 10 to 12 months, both monolingual and bilingual infants successfully discriminate speech sound contrasts that occur in their native language (Albareda-Castellot, Pons, & Sebastián-Gallés, 2011; Burns, Yoshida, Hill, & Werker, 2007). Additionally, monolingual infants appear to detect small mispronunciations of words at a much earlier age (e.g., 12 months) compared to bilingual infants (Mani & Plunkett, 2010). For example, bilingual Spanish–Catalan infants display sensitivity to mispronunciations of Catalan words starting at around 24 months of age (Ramon-Casas, Swingley, Sebastián-Gallés, & Bosch, 2009). These findings suggest that bilingual toddlers might not access the phonological detail associated with words in some tasks and might not display phonological priming effects to the same extent as monolingual toddlers. However, Mattock, Polka, Rvachew, and Krehm (2010) suggest that bilingual infants are sensitive to the internal phonological structure of a word to the same degree as monolingual infants. Therefore, developing bilinguals may display sensitivity to phonological priming to the same extent as monolingual toddlers.

Von Holzen and Mani (2012) examined how words from bilingual toddlers' L2 (English) primed recognition of related target words in their L1 (German). On critical trials, prime-target word pairs were either phonologically related, with second language primes overlapping phonologically with L1 target word (e.g., if the second language prime were *slide*, then the first language target could be *kleid*, or "dress"), or they were phonologically related through translation, with first language translations of second language primes that rhymed with the first language target words (e.g., if the second language prime were *leg* "bein," the first language target could be *stein* "stone"). The authors found facilitation in target recognition in the phonological priming condition, suggesting language non-selective access but not necessarily lexical access in developing bilinguals. Additionally, there was a late interference effect on target recognition in the phonological priming through translation condition, providing evidence for language non-selective lexical access in developing bilinguals. Specifically, since the second language prime (*leg*) influenced the first language target recognition (*stein*), both the prime (*leg*) and its translation (*bein*) must have been concurrently activated. Furthermore, age and gender-matched monolingual toddlers showed no difference between conditions, providing further evidence that the results with bilingual toddlers were driven by cross-language activation.

Learning an L2

According to the *critical period hypothesis,* it is more difficult to acquire any language, let alone an L2, after a certain stage in development. Specifically, Hakuta, Bialystok, and Wiley (2003) used archival data to determine whether or not there was an optimal age for L2 acquisition. The authors examined data from a variety of US emigrants. They hypothesized that if there were a true critical period, the number of emigrants who were able to fully acquire an L2 would drop substantially after a given age. They found that L2 acquisition was not strictly dependent upon age, but that L2 proficiency did drop as age increased. This hypothesis was examined experimentally by Birdsong and Molis (2001). Participants in this study were Spanish–English bilinguals of varying ages of English acquisition. Participants were asked to determine whether the presented English sentence was grammatical or non-grammatical. The researchers found that there was a consistent pattern such that performance declined with age of the participants. However, there was no strict age of English acquisition at which point performance across the board dropped significantly. These data suggest that a strict critical period hypothesis may not be very representative of reality.

Lexical and Conceptual Representations for L2 Learners

Altarriba and Mathis (1997) investigated the conceptual representations across novice and experienced bilinguals. The researchers aimed to test the hypotheses set forth by Kroll and Stewart's (1994) revised hierarchical model, specifically the idea that bilinguals have two separate, but linked, lexical stores and a shared conceptual store. English monolingual speakers were given a series of Spanish training tasks. After training, these English monolinguals were considered novice bilinguals, given their limited knowledge of the Spanish language. These novice bilinguals were compared to experienced bilinguals. The participants were provided with a set of Spanish–English word pairs. The presented English word was either a translation equivalent to the Spanish word, orthographically similar to the Spanish word, or entirely unrelated to the Spanish word. Participants were asked to determine whether or not the English word was an appropriate translation of the Spanish word. The results showed that both novice and experienced bilinguals were slower at responding when an orthographically similar English word was presented than when an unrelated

English word was presented. Thus, orthography was interfering for both groups of participants, indicating that orthographic information is stored in memory even after only one training session.

In a second experiment, semantically similar English words were presented in place of the orthographically similar English words. As in the first experiment, both novice and experienced bilinguals demonstrated interference. Specifically, both sets of participants took longer to respond in the semantically similar condition than the unrelated condition. Thus, not only are L2 learners storing lexical information about newly acquired items, but they are also storing the corresponding conceptual information at a very early stage in language acquisition.

Factors Influencing the Rate of L2 Acquisition

In general, it is thought that the degree of overlap between the L1 and the L2 will impact the ease with which the L2 can be acquired. This overlap can occur semantically, orthographically, phonologically, morphologically, or syntactically. With regards to semantics, it has been found that L2 words that exhibit translation ambiguity, such that the given words correspond to two or more words in the L1, are more difficult to learn (Degani, Tseng, & Tokowicz, 2014). Additionally, such words are also produced and recognized more slowly than unambiguous words (Tokowicz & Kroll, 2007).

With regards to syntactic processing, the *competition model* suggests that the degree of morphosyntactic similarity between the L1 and L2 differentially impacts the rate of L2 acquisition. Specifically, similar structures are learned more easily in an L2 than dissimilar ones (Tokowicz & MacWhinney, 2005). However, certain grammatical aspects, such as gender, do not exhibit this similarity benefit. The benefits that are present across semantic and syntactic processing are thought to be due to automatic transfer from the L1 to L2 (Tolentino & Tokowicz, 2014).

Language and Culture

The *linguistic relativity hypothesis* (*Sapir–Whorf Hypothesis*) attempts to connect various aspects of language to the way we process information. The principle of linguistic relativity assumes that the structure of language affects the ways in which speakers perceive and conceptualize their world (Carroll, 1956; Casasanto, 2008; Lucy & Gaskins, 2003). The goal of researchers who ascribe to this hypothesis is to determine how we interpret and classify reality depending upon the language(s) we speak. Several scholars have worked on operationalizing the hypothesis, keeping empiricism central to the question. In the strictest sense, this hypothesis suggests that language has a direct influence on thought, but makes very little mention of culture.

With regards to bilinguals, Athanasopoulos and Aveledo (2012) pointed out that linguistic relativity manifests itself differently in bilinguals than in monolinguals. Most of the research has, thus far, focused on grammatical number and color categorization. Bilingualism appears to affect these cognitive domains in a varying and disparate manner. The main purpose of the studies within this domain is to question the degree to which bilingual mental representations depend upon the linguistic and cultural context of the speaker, and whether these representations are based upon L1, L2, or a unique synthesis of the two. Green (1998) argued that the process of conceptualization must be language specific, and that bilinguals' conceptualization is dependent upon proficiency in each of the two languages. Green (1998) also suggested that bilinguals use languages differen-tially, depending upon occasion and purpose, placing an emphasis on the cultural impact of the linguistic setting. The majority of the empirical findings up to this point suggest that transfer occurs at the conceptual level. However, this transfer may be due to a result of both linguistic and cultural shift.

Grammatical Number

When studies regarding grammatical number were extended to Japanese–English bilin-guals, the bilinguals were not as efficient at attending to changes in number of countable objects as were English monolinguals. Also they did not perform as poorly as the Japanese monolinguals (Athanasopoulos, 2006). These same results were extended to classifying objects based upon shape and material properties. Imai and Gentner (1997) found that speakers of English were more likely to classify objects based upon common shape rather than common material. Speakers of languages such as Yucatec and Japanese exhibited the reverse pattern of results. This is thought to be due to the lack of grammatical differ-ence between mass (e.g., water) and count nouns (e.g., one tree, two trees, three trees ...) in these languages. It can also be noted that Japanese–English bilinguals who had lived within an English-speaking country for a longer period of time tended to categorize objects more similarly to English monolinguals. This finding could be due to either increased English proficiency or cultural immersion.

Athanasopoulos (2007) attempted to disambiguate linguistic and cultural effects by extending his original study on Japanese–English bilinguals to account for length of stay in the L2 country and proficiency within the two languages. This researcher wanted to determine if Japanese–English bilinguals were working with two separate cognitive repre-sentations, each being used in accordance with the language of the task, or if the linguistic effects on cognition were deeper and could withstand task instruction in either language. He found that L2 proficiency was the best predictor of naming responses regardless of length of stay and task language. This result seems to suggest that language is playing a predominant role over culture in cognitive processing, and that linguistic category shifts occur at the conceptual level. However, these results do not account for the possibility that culture may be encoded within language.

Color Categorization

Research on color categorization in bilinguals also supports this language-dominant, conceptual transfer view of processing. Athanasopoulos (2009) studied the differences between color similarity judgments in Greek–English bilinguals and English monolin-guals. He was interested in the distinction between light and dark blue, as two distinct terms exist for the two shades in the Greek language. He asked all participants to deter-mine how far apart they thought the two color spaces were from each other, as well as to make a list of all of the color terms they could think of. He found that length of stay in an English-speaking country was highly predictive of the amount of space participants per-ceived between light and dark blue, such that bilinguals would judge less perceptual space between the two shades if they had been living in an English-speaking country for two or more years, approximating the English monolingual response pattern. However, it was also evident that participants' similarity judgments were dependent upon the availability of the two separate color terms. If participants placed the light/dark blue terms high on the list, they maintained the perceptual space between the two shades.

Temporal Metaphors

It is important to mention that findings from Tse and Altarriba (2008) were unable to identify differences between monolinguals and bilinguals in the way they process temporal metaphors, or the way in which they express temporal ordering. Based on the findings from Boroditsky (2001), Tse and Altarriba studied the processing of temporal and spatiotemporal metaphors in Chinese and English. Horizontal spatiotemporal metaphors conceptualize time in a before/after fashion (e.g., June comes before August), while vertical spatiotemporal metaphors conceptualize time in an up-down fashion, where up refers to the earlier event, and down the later. A purely temporal description of time would simply label events as early/late or first, second, third, and so on. This description is void of any particular spatial orientation. It is the case that Chinese speakers tend to label events in both a horizontal and a vertical fashion, with a preference for vertical labels, whereas English speakers prefer horizontal labeling. However, when both Chinese–English bilinguals and English monolinguals were asked to determine whether a temporal or spatiotemporal metaphor was either true or false, Tse and Altarriba found no differences in reaction times between the two language groups. This occurred regardless of whether the participants had been shown a vertical or horizontal spatial prime prior to reading the metaphors, indicating that neither Chinese–English bilinguals nor English monolinguals process temporal and spatiotemporal metaphors in a linguistically constrained fashion. The similarity between the two groups argues specifically against linguistic relativity in bilinguals, supporting the idea that experience within the two languages, as well as cultural factors, such as the pervasiveness of a vertical calendar system in both eastern and western cultures, could be playing a role in cognitive processing.

Summary and Conclusion

The purpose of this chapter was to provide an overview of the general areas of psycholinguistic research as it pertains to bilingualism. Specifically, the processing of phonology, semantics, morphology, syntax, and pragmatics was discussed from the bilingual perspective (i.e., how do bilinguals process these aspects of language differently from monolinguals?). These processes were examined from the perspective of what they can tell us about the organization and structure of the bilingual linguistic system. Two opposing views were introduced: the language selective view of lexical access and the language non-selective view of lexical access. Research exploring the underlying assumptions and predictions of the two views were introduced. Taken together, the majority of the current literature supports a language non-selective view of lexical access. Thus, for the bilingual speaker, aspects of both the L1 and L2 are simultaneously active, causing either interference or facilitation, depending upon the context. Additionally, bilingual processing was addressed from the perspective of comprehension and production within a linguistic context. As was seen when exploring each individual aspect of linguistic processing, when these aspects interact, the language non-selective view of bilingual access can account for the majority of the findings presented. It is quite rare to find evidence for no interaction between a bilingual's two languages.

Finally, bilingual development was explored from the perspective of L2 acquisition as well as the development of linguistic systems for simultaneous or early bilinguals. In cases of both early and late L2 learners, the phonological, semantic, syntactic, and morphological aspects of both the L1 and L2 interact to determine the ease and/or speed at which bilingual development occurs. This aspect of bilingual development further suggests that the bilingual linguistic environment is both interactive and dynamic.

List of Key Words and Concepts

American Sign Language (ASL), Bilingual interactive activation (BIA), Broca's aphasia, Cognate facilitation, Competition model, Conceptual links, Conceptual store, Conceptual transfer, Constraint-based processing model, Critical period hypothesis, Cross-language activation, Event-related potential (ERP), Eye tracking, Figurative language, Functional magnetic resonance (fMRI), Graded salience model, Homograph, Horizontal spatiotemporal, Idiomatic phrases, Inter-sentential, Interference effect, Interlingual homograph, Language nodes, Language switching, Language-dominant, Language non-selective view, Language selective view, Lexical decision task, Lexical links, Limited Proficiency Account, Literal meaning, Literal salience model, Low-constraint, Mental lexicon, Metalinguistic judgments, Modified hierarchical model, Morpheme, Morphology, Name elicitation task, Non-causative, Opaque signs, Orthographic representation, Phonological interference, Phonological systems, Phonology, Picture naming task, Pragmatics, Prime, Pronunciation task, Proverbs, Rapid serial visual presentation, Relative strength hypothesis, Revised hierarchical model, Sapir–Whorf Hypothesis, Self-paced reading, Semantic judgment task, Semantic priming, Semantics, Sign Language, Simultaneous bilinguals, Social context, Sound contrasts, Spatiotemporal, Syntax, Task/decision system, Temporal metaphors, The linguistic relativity hypothesis, Tip-of-the tongue (TOT), Translation priming, Transparent signs, Two-switch mechanism, Vertical spatiotemporal, Word frequency

Internet Sites Related to the Psycholinguistics of Bilingualism

Bilingualism and Language Processing: http://www.tamiu.edu/~rheredia/bilingualism.html
San Diego State University Laboratory for Language and Cognitive Neuroscience: https://slhs.sdsu.edu/llcn/
Second Language Research Materials: https://www.iris-database.org/iris/app/home/index

Discussion Questions

(1) Compare and contrast morphemes and phonemes.
(2) Briefly explain the asymmetrical code-switching cost.
(3) Does language influence thought? Use two examples to illustrate your point.
(4) Discuss the critical period hypothesis for language learning; do you think one exists? Explain.
(5) Explain the difference between a language specific view and a language non-specific view of bilingualism.
(6) What is figurative language? Explain why it is important for translators to understand figurative language while translating from one language to another.
(7) What are homographs? Give one example in English. What are interlingual homographs? Provide at least one example.
(8) What is the difference between a balanced bilingual and an L1 dominant bilingual? How would this difference affect people's performance on bilingual tasks?
(9) Identify and explain three levels of language analysis discussed in the beginning of the chapter.
(10) What is the difference between opaque and transparent signs in Sign Language?

Suggested Research Projects

(1) *Experimental Study: Language and Culture:* Replicate an experiment that was discussed in this chapter across two culturally distinct groups of bilinguals (i.e., Chinese–English bilinguals born in the US versus Chinese–English bilinguals living in rural China). Collect data to evaluate. Explain how cultural variance impacts your results.

(2) *Literature Search:* Search a database such as PsycInfo (http://www.apa.org/psycinfo) or Google Scholar (http://scholar.google.com) for a recent selection of articles on the psycholinguistics of bilingualism. Identify the languages of the participants in the experiment, the hypotheses, and the methods used for collecting data. Identify the pros and cons of the methods used. How would a different method provide additional insight?

(3) *Research Paper: Choose an area of the psycholinguists of bilingualism.* Write a five-page research paper using at least three references from academic journals.

Suggested Readings

Heredia, R. R., & Altarriba, J. (Eds.). (2002). *Bilingual sentence processing.* Amsterdam: Elsevier.

Heredia, R. R., & Cieślicka, A. B. (Eds.). (2015). *Bilingual figurative language processing.* Cambridge, UK: Cambridge University Press.

Jegerski, J., & Van Patten, B. (Eds.). (2013). *Research methods in second language psycholinguistics.* New York: Routledge.

References

Albareda-Castellot, B., Pons, F., & Sebastián-Gallés, N. (2011). The acquisition of phonetic categories in bilingual infants: New data from an anticipatory eye movement paradigm. *Developmental Science, 14*(2), 395–401.

Altarriba, J., & Mathis, K. M. (1997). Conceptual and lexical development in second language acquisition. *Journal of Memory and Language, 36*, 550–568.

Altenberg, E. P., & Cairns, H. S. (1983). The effects of phonotactic constraints on lexical processing in bilingual and monolingual subjects. *Journal of Verbal Learning and Verbal Behavior, 22*(2), 174–188.

Arzouan Y., Goldstein A., & Faust M. (2007). Dynamics of hemispheric activity during metaphor comprehension: Electrophysiological measures. *Neuroimage, 36*, 222–231.

Athanasopoulos, P. (2006). Effects of the grammatical representation of number on cognition in bilinguals. *Bilingualism: Language and Cognition, 9*, 89–96.

Athanasopoulos, P. (2007). Interaction between grammatical categories and cognition in bilinguals: The role of proficiency, cultural immersion, and language of instruction. *Language and Cognitive Processes, 22*, 689–699.

Athanasopoulos, P. (2009). Cognitive representation of color in bilinguals: The case of Greek blues. *Bilingualism: Language and Cognition, 12*, 83–95.

Athanasopoulos, P., & Aveledo, F. (2012). Linguistic relativity and bilingualism. In J. Altarriba & L. Isurin (Eds.), *Memory, language, and bilingualism: Theoretical and applied approaches* (pp. 236–255). Cambridge, UK: Cambridge University Press.

Beauvillain, C., & Grainger, J. (1987). Accessing interlexical homographs: Some limitations of a language-selective access. *Journal of Memory and Language, 26*(6), 658–672.

Birdsong, D., & Molis, M. (2001). On the evidence for maturational constraints in second language acquisition. *Journal of Memory and Language, 44*, 235–249.

Boroditsky, L. (2001). Does language shape thought: Mandarin and English speakers' concepts of time. *Cognitive Psychology, 43*, 1–22.

Brenders, P., Van Hell, J. G., & Dijkstra, T. (2011). Word recognition in child second language learners: Evidence from cognates and false friends. *Journal of Experimental Child Psychology, 109*(4), 383–396.

Burns, T. C., Yoshida, K. A., Hill, K., & Werker, J. F. (2007). Bilingual and monolingual infant phonetic development. *Applied Psycholinguistics*, *28*(3), 455–474.

Carroll, D. W. (2004). *Psychology of language*. Belmont, CA: Wadsworth.

Carroll, J. B. (Ed.). (1956). *Language, thought, and reality: Selected writings of Benjamin Lee Whorf*. Cambridge, MA: MIT Press.

Casasanto, D. (2008). Who's afraid of the Big Bad Whorf? Cross-linguistic differences in temporal language and thought. *Language Learning*, *58*, 63–79.

Chan, B. H. S. (2004). Beyond "contextualization": Code-switching as a "textualization cue." *Journal of Language and Social Psychology*, *23*, 7–27.

Chen, H., Peng, X., & Zhao, Y. (2013). An ERP study on metaphor comprehension in the bilingual brain. *Chinese Journal of Applied Linguistics*, *36*(4), 505–517.

Cieślicka, A. B. (2013). Do nonnative language speakers chew the fat and spill the beans with different brain hemispheres? Investigating idiom decomposability with the divided visual field paradigm. *Journal of Psycholinguistic Research*, *42*(6), 475–503.

Costa, A., Colomé, Á., Gómez, O., & Sebastián-Gallés, N. (2003). Another look at cross-language competition in bilingual speech production: Lexical and phonological factors. *Bilingualism: Language and Cognition*, *6*, 167–179.

Costa, A., & Santesteban, M. (2004). Lexical access in bilingual speech production: Evidence from language switching in highly proficient bilinguals and L2 learners. *Journal of Memory and Language*, *50*, 491–511.

Costa, A., Santesteban, M., & Caño, A. (2005). On the facilitatory effects of cognate words in bilingual speech production. *Brain and Language*, *94*, 94–103.

de Diego Balaguer, R., Costa, A., Sebastián-Gallés, N., Juncadella, M., & Caramazza, A. (2004). Regular and irregular morphology and its relationship with agrammatism: Evidence from two Spanish–Catalan bilinguals. *Brain and Language*, *91*, 212–222.

Degani, T., Tseng, A. M., & Tokowicz, N. (2014). Together or apart: Learning of translation-ambiguous words. *Bilingualism: Language and Cognition*, *17*(4), 1–17.

Dijkstra, T., & Van Heuven, W. J. (1998). The BIA model and bilingual word recognition. In J. Grainger & A. M. Jacobs (Eds.), *Localist connectionist approaches to human cognition* (pp. 189–225). New York: Psychology Press.

Dijkstra, T., & Van Heuven, W. J. (2002). The architecture of the bilingual word recognition system: From identification to decision. *Bilingualism: Language and Cognition*, *5*(3), 175–197.

Dijkstra, T., Van Heuven, W. J., & Grainger, J. (1998). Simulating cross-language competition with the bilingual interactive activation model. *Psychologica Belgica*, *38*(4), 177–196.

Dussias, P. E. (2003). Syntactic ambiguity resolution in L2 learners. *Studies in Second Language Acquisition*, *25*, 529–557.

Duyck, W. (2005). Translation and associative priming with cross-lingual pseudohomophones: Evidence for nonselective phonological activation in bilinguals. *Journal of Experimental Psychology: Learning, Memory, and Cognition*, *31*, 1340–1359.

Elston-Güttler, K. E., Gunter, T. C., & Kotz, S. A. (2005). Zooming into L2: Global language context and adjustment affect processing of interlingual homographs in sentences. *Cognitive Brain Research*, *25*(1), 57–70.

Gerard, L. D., & Scarborough, D. L. (1989). Language-specific lexical access of homographs by bilinguals. *Journal of Experimental Psychology: Learning, Memory, and Cognition*, *15*(2), 305–315.

Giora, R. (1997). Understanding figurative and literal language: The graded salience hypothesis. *Cognitive Linguistics*, *8*, 183–206.

Gollan, T. H., Bonanni, M. P., & Montoya, R. I. (2005). Proper names get stuck on bilingual and monolingual speakers' tip of the tongue equally often. *Neuropsychology*, *19*, 278–287.

Green, D. (1998). Bilingualism and thought. *Psychologica Belgica*, *38*, 253–278.

Gullifer, J. W., Kroll, J. F., & Dussias, P. E. (2013). When language switching has no apparent cost: Lexical access in sentence context. *Frontiers in Psychology*, *4*, 1–13.

Hakuta, K., Bialystok, E., & Wiley, E. (2003). Critical evidence: A test of the critical-period hypothesis for second-language acquisition. *Psychological Science*, *14*, 31–38.

Heredia, R. R., & Altarriba, J. (2001). Bilingual language mixing: Why do bilinguals code-switch? *Current Directions in Psychological Science*, *10*(5), 164–168.

Heredia, R. R., & Altarriba, J. (Eds.). (2002). *Bilingual sentence processing*. Amsterdam: Elsevier.

Heredia, R. R., Altarriba, J., & Cieślicka, A. (Eds.). (2015). *Methods in bilingual reading comprehension research*. New York: Springer Science+Business Media, LLC.

Hoover, M. L., & Dwivedi, V. D. (1998). Syntactic processing by skilled bilinguals. *Language Learning*, *48*(1), 1–29.

Ibáñez, A. J., Macizo, P., & Bajo, M. T. (2010). Language access and language selection in professional translators. *Acta Psychologica*, *135*(2), 257–266.

Imai, M., & Gentner, D. (1997). A cross-linguistic study of early word meaning: Universal ontology and linguistic influence. *Cognition*, *62*(2), 169–200.

Jared, D., & Kroll, J. F. (2001). Do bilinguals activate phonological representations in one or both of their languages when naming words? *Journal of Memory and Language*, *44*(1), 2–31.

Johnson, J., & Rosano, T. (1993). Relation of cognitive style to metaphor interpretation and second language proficiency. *Applied Psycholinguistics*, *14*(2), 159–175.

Kolers, P. A. (1966). Reading and talking bilingually. *The American Journal of Psychology*, *79*(3), 357–376.

Kroll, J. F., & Stewart, E. (1994). Category interference in translation and picture naming: Evidence for asymmetric connections between bilingual memory representations. *Journal of Memory and Language*, *33*(2), 149–174.

Kuntze, M. (2000). Codeswitching in ASL and written English language contact. In K. Emmorey & H. L. Lane (Eds.), *The signs of language revisited: An anthology to honor Ursula Bellugi and Edward Klima* (pp. 287–302). New York: Psychology Press.

Lagrou, E., Hartsuiker, R. J., & Duyck, W. (2011). Knowledge of a second language influences auditory word recognition in the native language. *Journal of Experimental Psychology: Learning, Memory, and Cognition*, *37*(4), 952–965.

Lehtonen, M., & Laine, M. (2003). How word frequency affects morphological processing in monolinguals and bilinguals. *Bilingualism: Language and Cognition*, *6*(3), 213–225.

Libben, M. R., & Titone, D. A. (2009). Bilingual lexical access in context: Evidence from eye movements during reading. *Journal of Experimental Psychology: Learning, Memory, and Cognition*, *35*(2), 381–390.

Lucy, J. A., & Gaskins, S. (2003). Interaction of language type and referent type in the development of nonverbal classification preferences. In D. Gentner & S. Goldin-Meadow (Eds.), *Language in mind: Advances in the study of language and thought* (pp. 465–492). Cambridge, MA: MIT Press.

Macnamara, J., & Kushnir, S. L. (1971). Linguistic independence of bilinguals: The input switch. *Journal of Verbal Learning and Verbal Behavior*, *10*(5), 480–487.

Mani, N., & Plunkett, K. (2010). In the infant's mind's ear evidence for implicit naming in 18-month-olds. *Psychological Science*, *21*(7), 908–913.

Marian, V., & Spivey, M. (2003). Competing activation in bilingual language processing: Within- and between-language competition. *Bilingualism: Language and Cognition*, *6*(2), 97–115.

Matlock, T., & Heredia, R. R. (2002). Understanding phrasal verbs in monolinguals and bilinguals. In R. R. Heredia & J. Altarriba (Eds.), *Bilingual sentence processing* (pp. 251–274). North Holland: Elsevier.

Mattock, K., Polka, L., Rvachew, S., & Krehm, M. (2010). The first steps in word learning are easier when the shoes fit: Comparing monolingual and bilingual infants. *Developmental Science*, *13*(1), 229–243.

Meuter, R. F., & Allport, A. (1999). Bilingual language switching in naming: Asymmetrical costs of language selection. *Journal of Memory and Language*, *40*(1), 25–40.

Moon, J., & Jiang, N. (2012). Non-selective lexical access in different-script bilinguals. *Bilingualism: Language and Cognition*, *15*(1), 173–180.

Most, T. (2003). The use of repair strategies: Bilingual deaf children using sign language and spoken language. *American Annals of the Deaf*, *148*(4), 308–314.

Paulmann, S., Ghareeb-Ali, Z., & Felser, C. (2015). Neurophysiological markers of phrasal verb processing. In R. Heredia & A. B. Cieślicka (Eds.), *Bilingual figurative language processing* (pp. 245–267). New York: Cambridge University Press.

Pavlenko, A. (Ed.). (2009). *The bilingual mental lexicon: Interdisciplinary approaches* (Vol. 70). Bristol, UK: Multilingual Matters.

Perani, D., Dehaene, S., Grassi, F., Cohen, L., Cappa, S. F., Dupoux, E., Fazio, F., & Mehler, J. (1996). Brain processing on native and foreign languages. *Nueroreport, 7*(15–17), 2439–2444.

Pizzuto, E., & Volterra, V. (2000). Iconicity and transparency in sign languages: A cross-linguistic cross-cultural view. In K. Emmorey & H. L. Lane (Eds.), *The signs of language revisited: An anthology to honor Ursula Bellugi and Edward Klima* (pp. 261–286). New York: Psychology Press.

Ramon-Casas, M., Swingley, D., Sebastián-Gallés, N., & Bosch, L. (2009). Vowel categorization during word recognition in bilingual toddlers. *Cognitive Psychology, 59*(1), 96–121.

Scheutz, M. J., & Eberhard, K. M. (2004). Effects of morphosyntactic gender features in bilingual language processing. *Cognitive Science, 28*(4), 559–588.

Schwartz, A. I., & Kroll, J. F. (2006). Bilingual lexical activation in sentence context. *Journal of Memory and Language, 55*(2), 197–212.

Sherkina-Lieber, M. (2004). The cognate facilitation effect in bilingual speech production: The case of Russian–English bilingualism. *Cahiers Linguistiques d'Ottawa, 32,* 108–121.

Silva, R. S. (2000). Pragmatics, bilingualism, and the native speaker. *Language & Communication, 20*(2), 161–178.

Spivey, M. J., & Marian, V. (1999). Cross talk between native and second languages: Partial activation of an irrelevant lexicon. *Psychological Science, 10*(3), 281–284.

Tamargo, R. E. G. (2012). *Linking comprehension costs to production patterns during the processing of mixed language* (Doctoral dissertation). Pennsylvania State University.

Titone, D., Libben, M., Mercier, J., Whitford, V., & Pivneva, I. (2011). Bilingual lexical access during L1 sentence reading: The effects of L2 knowledge, semantic constraint, and L1–L2 intermixing. *Journal of Experimental Psychology: Learning, Memory, and Cognition, 37*(6), 1412–1431.

Tokowicz, N., & Kroll, J. F. (2007). Number of meanings and concreteness: Consequences of ambiguity within and across languages. *Language and Cognitive Processes, 22*(5), 727–779.

Tokowicz, N., & MacWhinney, B. (2005). Implicit and explicit measures of sensitivity to violations in second language grammar: An event-related potential investigation. *Studies in Second Language Acquisition, 27*(2), 173–204.

Tolentino, L. C., & Tokowicz, N. (2014). Cross-language similarity modulates effectiveness of second language grammar instruction. *Language Learning, 64*(2), 279–309.

Tse, C.-S., & Altarriba, J. (2008). Evidence against linguistic relativity in Chinese and English: A case study of spatial and temporal metaphors. *Journal of Cognition and Culture, 8,* 335–357.

Vaid, J., & Martinez, F. (2001, April). *Figurative language and thought across languages: What transfers.* Poster presented at the 3rd International Symposium on Bilingualism, Bristol, UK.

Van Assche, E., Duyck, W., Hartsuiker, R. J., & Diependaele, K. (2009). Does bilingualism change native-language reading? Cognate effects in a sentence context. *Psychological Science, 20*(8), 923–927.

Van Hell, J. G., & de Groot, A. M. B. (2008). Sentence context modulates visual word recognition and translation in bilinguals. *Acta Psychologica, 128*(3), 431–451.

Von Holzen, K., & Mani, N. (2012). Language nonselective lexical access in bilingual toddlers. *Journal of Experimental Child Psychology, 113*(4), 569–586.

5 Multilingualism Processing and Aging

Kees de Bot and Nienke Houtzager

Introduction

The definition of what constitutes bilingualism or *multilingualism*, is notoriously difficult (see for example, Aronin & Singleton, 2012). There are two extremes: the first one is linked to Bloomfield's (1933, p. 115) definition of bilingualism as *native-like control of two or more languages*. The other extreme is what Edwards (1994, p. 55) calls the *c'est la vie* perspective, implying that any Englishman who can say this short phrase in French can call himself a bilingual. There is a multitude of definitions between this very narrow one and this very wide one, with onset of acquisition (i.e., when the languages were learned), frequency of use, and level of proficiency as the main defining factors. Partly due to the growing impact of *complex dynamic systems theory* (CDST; de Bot, Lowie, & Verspoor, 2007; Herdina & Jessner, 2002; Larsen-Freeman & Cameron, 2008), nowadays bilingualism is seen more as a process than as a state. Complex Dynamic Systems are sets of variables that interact over time. The study of CDSTs focuses on variation over time and the role of external input and internal reorganization. Languages are dynamic systems, and language development is a dynamic process. Languages, both as tools of communication and as parts of the cognitive system, are constantly changing, due to interaction with the larger environment and self-organization. This type of development does not stop at puberty or the end of formal education, but continues over the life span. As a result of all sorts of changes, such as new jobs, divorces, children, stays abroad, retirement, and so on, the linguistic needs change incessantly. A new job may require proficiency in a new language, and likewise buying a second home abroad may encourage individuals to learn the local language. Traditionally, instructed language learning is seen as the major process of development: many people take languages in primary or secondary education or in college. But it is not always clear to what extent the current proficiency is dependent on the levels reached through instruction. In an informal survey among Dutch students at our university on how they acquired their English proficiency, the students indicated that in their estimation, they learned about 40% in school, 30% through the media, and 30% through using the language with other speakers. So, some 60% of development takes place after leaving school. In addition, not all the instruction-based linguistic knowledge will be maintained over the life span. Though there is probably more retention than attrition of non-used languages (Bahrick, 1984; de Bot, 2007; Schmid, 2010), part of the language skills learned at school will merge with later language use and development. This means that bilingual development is a highly individual and generally non-linear process: phases of regular use and increase of skills will be followed by periods of non-use and decline. Each speaker has her own needs and follows her own path due to individual differences over the life span. The same experience, such as a study abroad for a period of six months, will have a differential effect: for some it may be an intense immersion experience, for others a pleasant stay away from home with compatriots, with little contact with the local language.

There are also marked differences between individuals in the timing of their language learning experiences. Some are born in a bilingual family and have, as Merrill Swain (1972) described it, *bilingualism as their first language*. They may continue using their multiple languages, or stop using one or more and acquire additional ones. Other people start late, that is after the age of 12 or even later, and learn the language during a certain period in their lives, but hardly ever use it later in life. Still others learn a language at school, do not use it for a long time, then at some point need it and will relearn and use it extensively. So, distinctions can be made between early and late start and continuous or discontinuous use, but these are continua rather than dichotomies. Bialystok, Craik, Klein, and Viswanathan (2004, p. 301) suggest that an early start by itself may lead to cognitive advantages: *If the boost given by childhood bilingualism is sufficiently strong, bilingualism may continue to influence certain control processes throughout the life span.* Empirical support for this position is still lacking.

A rare case occurs when the language is learned in early adulthood, used intensively, and then not used at all for the rest of their lives. This is what happens, for instance, with missionaries from The Church of Jesus Christ of Latter-day Saints. These missionaries are sent to different countries in the world to proselyte after an intense language training program (Hansen, 2012).

Defining Aging

Throughout the world, new departments and programs are mushrooming that claim to be looking at language and bilingualism over the life span, but in fact the focus is on the first two decades of life and the last two decades, the *third age*. The concept of aging assumes that there is something that a group of people have in common. There are wine lovers, hooligans, party animals, and elderly people. What the latter group has in common is that they were born 60, 70 or 80 years ago, and that they are seen and treated as being old. People born in the other decades are rarely treated as a group, apart from possible advertising purposes. No one will propose to study language development in 40–50-year-olds, since there is nothing interesting going on. Elderly people are assumed to have common traits, like gray hair, arthritis, bad memory, and hearing problems. No such common traits are to be expected with 30-year-olds. This tendency of lumping individuals together on the basis of age is referred to as *ageism*, and is seen as a form of age discrimination. Still, what happens in all these decades leaves its mark on language in the later part of life. One of the findings in research on language and aging is that elderly people have larger vocabularies than younger adults, due to their long existence as a language user and learner.

From a research perspective, age is just an index variable without any explanatory power. Still, it is not uncommon to find research in which age is used as a variable in a correlational approach, suggesting that age may actually explain something.

Theories on Cognitive Aging

Burke and Shafto (2008), in their comprehensive review of the literature, present six more or less complementary theories on cognitive aging:

(1) *Resource Theory*: This assumes that resources, such as memory capacity, attention, and inhibition, are limited and that an exhaustion of resources affects many aspects of cognition and language accordingly.

(2) *General Slowing Theories*: There is substantial evidence for a slowing down of cognitive processing with aging. One issue is that different components of tasks or processes may have different rates of decline in speed, which may be detrimental for language processing. For example, when syntactic processing is too slow, the listener will be constantly lagging behind and miss the next chunk. Processing may be too slow for some operations to be completed, such as finding the right word in time (Levelt, 1989). Another aspect of speed of processing is that when speech rates go up, speech perception in older adults goes down.

(3) *Inhibition Deficit Theory*: States that older adults have problems in the selection and inhibition of information. This implies that they are more easily distracted by irrelevant details. This phenomenon may also explain why older adults' conversation goes off topic more easily. Related to this may be the fact that older adults have more words but also more trouble retrieving them and have more *tip-of-the-tongue* (TOTs) experiences. TOTs can be caused by other words coming to mind and blocking access to the target. Interestingly, this effect is found in controlled laboratory conditions, but in normal lexical production, there is no evidence to support it.

(4) *Working Memory Theories*: Reduced working memory capacity leads to comprehension and production problems in processing longer sentences and dealing with complex conversational settings. These theories assume limited capacity for memory and a separate working memory component.

(5) *Transmission Deficit Theory*: This is a set of theories based on connectionist approaches which focus on activation and strengthening of connections and decay with non-use. As Burke and Shafto (2008, p. 382) argue: *Aging weakens connection strength, causing general processing deficits, rather than deficits limited to a single process such as working memory or inhibition.* This theory is consistent with neurobiological accounts of aging. *Speech error* data show that there is an increase in lexical and *phonological retrieval* deficits, which is in line with age-related transmission deficits.

(6) *Degraded Signal Account*: Many studies on aging have shown declines in sensory and perceptual processes, which impact language processing. Schneider, Daneman, Murphy, and Kwong (2000) show that by equating perceptibility of stimuli across ages, age differences in language processing in various tasks (e.g., word recognition and recall of dialogues) were eliminated. There is discussion on the relative contributions of *sensory* versus *cognitive decline*: is cognitive decline the result or the cause of *sensory decline*? It is most likely that these two processes interact (de Bot & Makoni, 2005). In view of the above, it could be argued that sensory acuity (vision and hearing) has to be checked as a basic component in any research project on language and aging. Baltes and Lindenberger (1997) showed that controlling for sensory decline led to a 20-fold decrease of age-related variance in language measures, and that often eliminated effects of age.

As pointed out earlier, aging is typically associated with improved vocabulary during adulthood to very old age, but there is a need to control for education, since knowledge from earlier phases in life will continue to play a role later on. Semantic processing is at least as strong in older as in young adults, though there are indications of decline of semantic processing with age that may be related to general slowing down. *Syntactic processing* remains stable with age, which may support Caplan and Waters' (1999) model of a dedicated working memory component for syntactic processing.

It is remarkable that even in fairly recent overviews of the research on language and aging, like the one by Burke and Shafto (2008), there is no reference in any sense to the role of multiple languages. A brief check of studies shows that they do not even consider the possibility of the existence of more than one language: for instance, they do not contain questions in background questionnaires on knowledge or use of multiple languages. Language and aging, and multilingualism and aging have been *promising developments in the field* for quite some time now, but research on it has not seriously taken off (de Bot & Makoni, 2005). It is only when the discussion on the *bilingual advantage* started that the topic generated a wave of research and publications.

Language and Aging in Monolinguals and Bilinguals

Schrauf (2008, p. 111) presents a very useful way to organize his overview of the literature on language and aging. He based this overview on the following three hypotheses:

(1) *Age-related patterns of decline and preservation will be seen in bilinguals just as they are seen in monolinguals.*
(2) *Age-related patterns of decline and/or preservation will be the same in both languages for older bilinguals.*
(3) *The unique language switching ability of bilinguals plays a special role in bilingual aging.*

For the first hypothesis, he concludes that when the bilingual elderly person is equally proficient in both languages, then few age-related differential effects on the use of L1 and L2 have been found. No publications of more recent date have refuted this point.

For the second hypothesis, the findings are that with equal proficiency in the two languages, no differences in the development/decline of the two languages have been found. There is some evidence of what has been called *language reversion* (de Bot & Clyne, 1994; Schmid & Keijzer, 2009), but the data on this are not very clear. For Dutch migrants in Australia, it is found that, with aging, the second language (L2) seems to retreat while the first language becomes more prominent. There are indications, however, that some of these immigrants developed only a very elementary command of English, just enough to get by at work and in the community, but that there was actually very little language proficiency to lose. The de Bot and Clyne study is one of the few in which, in addition to standard tests, spontaneous speech was the main source of information. As Schrauf (2008) points out, the majority of work has been done using clinical instruments like the Bilingual Aphasia Test, Mini Mental State Questionnaire and parts of standard aphasia tests. There is, in fact, hardly any research taking spontaneous speech as the main data. As far as we know, apart from the above-mentioned study, no longitudinal studies on language in aging have been carried out so far.

As Schrauf (2008, p. 118) points out, models of cognitive aging are themselves largely naïve about bilingualism, while, on the other hand, models of bilingual processing are largely naïve about aging. Only in recent years, connections between the two have been developed to test the impact of bilingualism on cognitive functioning.

While Schrauf discusses the factors affecting bilingual aging as more or less static, de Bot and Makoni (2005) argue that aging is a complex process in which physical, social, and psychological changes interact. Though physical changes are the most apparent and recognizable ones, for cognitive functioning perceptions of change, both by elderly people themselves and their peers are at least as important. Among the physical changes relevant for cognitive functioning, combinations of four mechanisms play a role: (1) slowed processing speed, (2) shrinking working memory, (3) inhibitory deficits, and (4) declining sensory functions (Burke & Shafto, 2008). Obviously, changes in these mechanisms also have an impact on language use. But not all mechanisms age at the same rate, and there is growing evidence that multilingualism has an impact on various cognitive processes. So following Cook's (1995) views on *multicompetence*, an elderly bilingual is not an elderly monolingual with an additional language, but a language user with a specific set of skills and knowledge that change due to internal reorganization and input from the environment.

There are few studies on multilingualism and aging. Goral (2004) reports a decline in speed of lexical production in L1 and L2 with aging. Rosselli et al. (2000) looked at an English monolingual group and a Spanish–English bilingual group on a number of tests, including *verbal fluency*, sentence repetition, and picture description. In both groups, subjects' ages ranged from 55–84. The monolinguals showed higher scores on *semantic verbal fluency* (*name as many fruits and vegetables as you can in one minute*) than the bilinguals, while the bilinguals had a higher number of connected words in spontaneous speech. For the bilingual subjects, a higher number of words in the English picture description test were found. Since the groups were very small (seven and eight subjects), no effects of age could be measured. Also, the range of the subjects' ages was large, making it difficult to see such results as giving useful information about the elderly in different age ranges. In a follow-up study, Rosselli et al. (2000) looked at verbal fluency and sentence repetition in a group of English–Spanish bilinguals and monolingual controls for the two languages. In this task participants were tested on attention, verbal and non-verbal memory intelligence and language proficiency. Mean age was 61.8. Overall, bilinguals showed lower scores in the two languages than monolinguals. Only for the semantic verbal fluency was an effect of age of acquisition found: early bilinguals (i.e., those who learned the L2 before the age of five years old) had a similar score as the monolinguals, while the late bilinguals (those who learned the L2 after ten years old) had a lower score. A much larger study is the one by Acevedo et al. (2000) on verbal fluency norms in Spanish and English speakers over 50 years of age. The results show that age, education, and gender are the most important factors predicting scores for both groups, regardless of the primary language.

So far, the effects of structural and conceptual differences between languages have not been studied much. Kempler et al. (1998) compared performance on a semantic verbal fluency task in a group of elderly subjects, including Chinese, Hispanic, and Vietnamese immigrants as well as white and Afro-American English speakers. In this study, there were differences for age and education, but here we want to focus on the differences between ethnic groups. Language differences appear to play a major role: the Vietnamese subjects produced many more animal names than the Spanish subjects. This is attributed to the fact that in Vietnamese, animal names are short (mostly one syllable) while in Spanish animal names are longer. This points to one of the problems in comparing data between languages: the same test may lead to different scores, due to differences between the linguistic systems.

As mentioned earlier, another aspect of language proficiency that has recently attracted researchers' attention is the so-called TOT phenomenon: the inability to find the word form for a word one knows. TOTs are typically elicited by giving a definition (*someone who collects stamps*) for the word to be given (*philatelist*). Gollan and Brown (2006) present an overview of research on TOTs in bilingualism and aging. They found opposite trends for the two groups: increased age seems to lead to more TOTs for difficult but not for easy targets, while bilinguals show more TOTs for easy targets than monolinguals, but fewer for difficult targets. One of the problems with studying TOTs in bilinguals is that this group generally has smaller lexicons for a specific language than monolingual speakers of that language, so they may have fewer TOTs because they simply do not know the word required. Gollan and Brown suggest a two-step approach to TOTs to deal with this type of problem in studying lexical access through the study of TOTs. The first step is the activation of meaning-based representation, and the second step is the activation of *form-based* representations. The most widely accepted explanation for an increase in TOTs with aging is that the connections between elements in the lexicon decreases in strength, probably caused by a reduction in use of those words due to a change in social settings.

The Bilingual Advantage in Aging

The interest in the bilingual advantage in aging was sparked by a number of influential publications by Ellen Bialystok and her colleagues in Canada. In her earlier work, Bialystok (2004) reported that children who are bilingual from birth show certain advantages in cognitive processing, in particular, better *inhibitory control*. This line of research was extended to the aging population, and similar positive effects were found. But the findings have been challenged by recent studies. Probably the most sensational findings were those on the impact of bilingualism on the onset of dementia. We will come back to this later.

Components of the Bilingual Advantage

In their *meta-analysis* on the advantages of bilingualism, Adesope, Lavin, Thomson, and Ungerleider (2010) analyzed the literature on this topic and list a number of advantages that have been found for bilinguals:

(1) Greater metalinguistic awareness
(2) Enhanced metacognitive skills
(3) Stronger symbolic representation and abstract reasoning skills
(4) Better learning strategies
(5) Enhanced problem-solving skills
(6) Ability to selectively attend to relevant information and disregard misleading information
(7) Ability to succeed at theory-of-mind tasks, which require the ability to attribute the behavior of others to their own distinct beliefs, desires, and intentions
(8) Enhanced creative and divergent thinking skills
(9) Greater cognitive flexibility

Adesope et al. (2010, p. 218) conclude: *All the outcome measures produced statistically detectable mean effect sizes in favor of bilingualism. Attentional control produced the largest effect with a weighted mean effect size of .96 across 14 studies.* Though they found some stable effects, they also point out that there was significant variability among studies, with some yielding a positive cognitive effect of bilingualism and others a negative cognitive effect. As we will see, such contradictory findings are not uncommon in this field of research. There are many sources of variation, such as *social economic status* (SES), education, criteria for inclusion in the meta-analysis, instruments used, and individual differences within groups. As far as this can be seen in the article, there is no specific attention for elderly adults and bilingual advantages in this overview. Articles reporting potential effects of bilingualism on dementia are not included in the study either.

These results suggest that the process of acquiring two languages and simultaneously managing the use of both of them (i.e., inhibiting the non-target language so that the target language can be used without effects of interference) allows bilinguals to develop skills that extend into other domains. These skills appear to give bilingual speakers insight into the abstract features of language and into their own learning processes. They also appear to give bilingual speakers an enhanced capacity to appropriately control and distribute their *attentional resources*, to develop abstract and symbolic representations, and to solve problems. For their meta-analysis, Adesope et al. (2010, p. 210) distinguish between bilinguals and L2 learners: *Thus, participants who were learning second languages were not regarded as bilinguals but rather as second language learners. Studies with such second language learners were excluded from this meta-analysis.* In our view, this is a questionable perspective, when we consider bilingualism not as a state, but a process. A distinction between (balanced) bilinguals and L2 learners is problematic, because it cannot be ruled out that the latter may well be balanced, and the bilinguals are by definition continuously developing their languages, be it in terms of acquisition or attrition.

One of the core points of the discussion of whether bilingualism can be reliably associated with enhanced cognitive functioning is the extent to which specific linguistic activities, such as using multiple languages and *code-switching* (CS; the ability of bilinguals to mix their two languages during the communicative process), have an impact on general cognitive functions. In the recent literature on bilingual processing this is referred to as *domain-specific* (i.e., used for specific domains of skills, like language production) versus *domain-general* effects (i.e., also relevant for non-linguistic cognitive functioning; Kaushanskaya & Marian, 2009). CS is mentioned often as an activity that is not domain-specific and therefore may transfer to general skills. Some switches may be effortless, and others costly. Even if some or most language switches are costly, it is not clear if "switching" is a domain-general function with enough stages that are truly shared between language control and non-linguistic control in which case it is not clear that there should be transfer. A relevant point here is that aging bilinguals with severe deficits in executive control were largely able to maintain production in a single language. In other words, you basically do not need much executive control to do what bilinguals do.

The Bilingual Advantage in Elderly Adults

In the remainder of this chapter, we will focus on the bilingual advantage. First we will try to define it and show how it has been assessed, then we discuss the evidence supporting the existence of such advantage or not, and finally, we deal with the issue of what might cause a potential bilingual cognitive advantage.

In one of the first times a bilingual advantage is mentioned, it is defined as the enhancement of *executive functions* as a result of *the constant management of two competing languages* (Bialystok et al., p. 290). According to Bialystok et al., this constant management of two languages implies selecting the right language(s) for a given communicative setting, inhibiting the non-target language, and switching between languages.

The idea is that domain-specific activities transfer to more general skills, such as *task switching*, inhibitory control and working memory, following the definition by Miyake et al. (2000) of executive function in terms of three separate, but correlating functions: updating of information, shifting between mental sets, and inhibition. As mentioned above, these executive functions are assumed to be domain-general. In other words, code-switching languages should make non-linguistic task switching more effortless. But this assumption is not without problems. If bilinguals switch all the time and there is effort involved, then the assumption appears to be that effort reflects activation of functions. But does more effort (switching costs) lead to more enhanced executive functions?

In the literature on multilingualism and aging, there are two issues with respect to the Bilingual advantage: the first deals with the extent to which bilingualism leads to a delay in the onset of symptoms of dementia, and the second to the extent to which bilingualism modulates age-related cognitive decline.

A Delay in Onset of Symptoms of Dementia in Bilinguals?

A study by Bialystok, Craik, and Freedman (2007) was the first of a number of retrospective studies which found that groups of bilinguals were diagnosed with dementia significantly later than monolinguals. This study was replicated several times, with the majority of studies reporting the same 4–7 years delay in the onset of symptoms for bilinguals (cf. Bak, Nissan, Allerhand, & Deary, 2014; Bialystok, Craik, Binns, Ossher, & Freedman, 2014; Chertkow, Whitehead, Phillips, Wolfson, Atherton, & Bergman, 2010; Craik, Bialystok, & Freedman, 2010; Woumans, Santen, Siebens, Versijpt, Stevens, & Duyck, 2015; for an overview, see Freedman et al., 2014). The first problem regarding the interpretation of these findings, however, is the possible effect of confounding variables. In particular, immigration status is a factor that may play an important role, since many of the bilinguals involved in these studies had immigrant backgrounds (cf. Fuller-Thomson & Kuh, 2014, for evidence on the healthy migrant effect). Some studies did not control for immigrant status (e.g., Chertkow et al., 2010), but other studies did (e.g., Craik, Bialystok, & Freedman, 2010). A number of studies reportedly controlled for immigration status and a host of other confounding variables as well (Alladi et al., 2013; Bialystok et al., 2014; Woumans et al., 2015). Mortimer (2014) pointed out that, in the study by Alladi et al. (2013), the difference in the age of onset could also be caused by a difference in age distributions between the two language groups, an objection that might apply to other retrospective studies too. This confirms that it is hard to rule out the possibility that effects should at least be partly attributed to hidden differences between the different populations. In that respect, the study by Gollan, Salmon, Montoya, and Galasko (2011) throws an interesting light on this issue, because they looked at the effect of degree of bilingualism on rate of cognitive decline within a group of Spanish–English bilinguals and found a significant correlation only within the group with a low-educational level. In spite of a number of inconsistencies across these studies, however, the above evidence seems to point consistently at a delay in dementia symptoms of 4–7 years for bilinguals.

However, prospective studies that investigated this issue contradict the suggestion that bilingualism would be related to a delay in the onset age of dementia (Crane et al., 2009; Crane et al., 2010; Sanders, Hall, Katz, & Lipton, 2012; Yeung, St John, Menec, & Tyas, 2014; Zahodne et al., 2014). The only exception is a study by Kavé, Eyal, Shorek, and Cohen-Mansfield (2008). In a large group of Jewish–Israeli elderly (above age 75), they found that the number of languages spoken correlated significantly with performance on three subsequent cognitive tests performed over the course of 12 years, beyond all other demographic variables. However, it is doubtful whether this correlation between the number of languages spoken and cognitive performance in later life also implies that this cognitive advantage is a result of the language experience. The majority of prospective studies show no evidence for a bilingual effect on the onset age of dementia-related symptoms, which undermines the results from the retrospective studies. This may be explained by the fact that retrospective studies do not draw their data from a representative part of the population, but only from patients who visited a memory clinic. They also did not draw the data from those who did not visit a memory clinic, nor from individuals who never developed signs of Alzheimer's disease (cf. Valian, 2015). We therefore propose that the studies presented do not provide conclusive evidence for an association of bilingualism with cognitive reserve (i.e., as a factor offering potential protection from dementia-related diseases).

Does Bilingualism Modulate Age-Related Cognitive Decline?

Houtzager, Lowie, Sprenger, and de Bot (2015) report a bilingual advantage effect for switching costs in bilingual middle-aged and older adults (Dutch–Frisian) in the form of modulation of aging effects on language processing. In this study they controlled for various relevant variables, such as education, SES, and migrant status.

One of the problems of the research on cognitive effects in aging is the role of intelligence: is the bilingual advantage caused by differences in intelligence? Bak et al. (2014) carried out a unique experiment by testing a large group of elderly adults that had been tested for intelligence in 1947 and were tested again in 2008–2010. In the analysis, they included age of acquisition of L2 (never/early/late), number of languages (monolingual/bilingual/multilingual), and the frequency of L2 usage. Positive effects of bilingualism on cognition were found for all tasks, independent of intelligence. In contrast to the Alladi et al. (2013) study, proficiency in three rather than two languages had no additional effect.

In her review of the literature on bilingualism and cognition, Valian (2015, p. 3) carefully analyzes the different components of the *bilingual benefit*. She starts by pointing out two possible positions with respect to the bilingual benefit:

(1) *There is a benefit of bilingualism for executive functions, but that benefit competes with other benefits that both mono- and bilinguals have to varying degrees. Depending on the composition of each group in any given experiment, the other benefits may be more plentiful in the monolingual than bilingual group (or sufficiently plentiful in both groups), so that the benefits of bilingualism are invisible. This is the possibility that I favor.*

(2) *There is no cognitive benefit of bilingualism. In experiments that have found a benefit, the effect is either due to the accidentally larger number of other positive factors, such as high SES, that bilinguals have in that particular sample, or due to the correlation of bilingualism with some other active property that is difficult to separate from bilingualism.*

What Causes the Bilingual Advantage?

In essence, the bilingual advantage is based on the idea of language-use-as-exercise. In language use, executive functions, such as updating, inhibition, and task switching, are crucial. Language use implies applying these executive functions simultaneously, which could result in strengthening them. Task-specific activities would then be effective for the enhancement of task-general functions.

Why would bilingualism add to this experience, and how do we define executive functions enhancing activities? The idea is that bilinguals have to manage more than one language, since they have to suppress other languages while speaking one, code-switch when needed, and constantly select the right words and patterns for the language-in-use. As mentioned earlier, there is an enormous variety of bilingual developmental paths and experiences, and we simply do not know what matters most: early or late bilingualism, amount of use in bilingual settings, recent use, or type of use. Current methods of measuring language contact do not provide us with all the relevant information. Informants are typically asked the percentages of use of both languages, levels of education, sometimes amount of CS, and self-reported level of proficiency in their languages. Recently there has been some research looking at the effect of amount of CS over the life span on language processing in later life. Prior and Gollan (2011) present data suggesting that the bilingual advantage is related to reported amount of CS. Similarly, Verreyt et al. (2016) had their subjects rate the amount of CS on a 7-point scale and found a positive correlation between CS behavior and bilingual advantage as measured by executive function tasks. The problem is, as sociolinguistic studies (Dewaele & Li, 2014; Genesee & Bourhis, 1982) have shown, that self-reports on amount and type of CS are notoriously unreliable.

There is another problem with the *language as exercise hypothesis* that lies behind assumptions on the bilingual advantage: If bilinguals have to switch and suppress languages all the time, they should be used to it, and every next switch has a reduced added value.

In addition, it is not clear whether *pure* monolingualism actually exists. Monolinguals have and use more than one register and style of speaking, and the differences between languages/dialects/registers/styles are gradual rather than categorical. In all of them, the selection of the right words and patterns for a given situation have to be selected and maintained. On this account, inhibition of words (e.g., from less formal register in a formal setting) is not different from inhibiting words from another language. So the contribution of bilingualism can only be substantiated when it can be shown that processing two different languages calls on other or more cognitive activity than processing two different dialects or registers. There is hardly any research on this. In an older study, Woutersen, Cox, Weltens, and de Bot (1994) showed that the processing of words from different dialects in terms of reaction times in a lexical decision priming experiment was similar to findings from different languages. So similar results were found for the processing of two dialects as for the processing of two languages. This means that, in the study of monolinguals and bilinguals, speaking a dialect should be taken into account. Bidialectal speakers are not different from bilingual speakers in terms of cognitive processing. This type of argumentation is in line with the growing doubts about the unique effect of multilingualism on cognitive processing (e.g., Valian, 2015). The idea of an impact of forced choices on general executive abilities is not without problems either. People who work at conveyer belts and have to select the right size of vegetables or specific types of bolts are also constantly inhibiting competing choices. As for language, it could be argued that this type of switching and inhibition is not restricted to languages, but also applies to dialects and possibly styles and registers within a language. That makes the distinction between monolinguals (who inevitably have different styles and registers) and bilinguals and multilinguals less strict than what is commonly assumed. Monolinguals are faced with similar choices all the time, but maybe to a lesser degree. Paap and Greenberg (2013, p. 255) conclude: *In summary, fluent bilinguals have additional needs for monitoring, switching, and inhibitory control, but these unique requirements may not be substantial enough to generate group differences in cognitive control.* In their view, bilinguals are faced with additional cognitive challenges, but because there are many other challenges posed by other experiences, this is not enough to have an effect. The question is whether these additional challenges accumulate over time. Do the results of those actions add up and keep their *volume*, or is there a natural draining of the accumulated effort? If the former were true, then elderly adults may show effects that younger adults do not show (yet).

Conclusion

In this contribution an overview is presented of recent research on multilingualism and aging. It is concluded that rather little has been done on this topic over the last few years, apart from the large set of studies that have looked at the bilingual advantage in aging. These studies focus either on a delay of onset of dementia symptoms or on the modulating effect of multilingualism on age-related cognitive decline.

Ever since the first findings on the benefits of multilingualism in aging were published, many research groups have done work on various aspects of executive functions, multilingualism, and aging. It has also led to a narrowing down of the research. For many aspects of bilingualism and aging, such as CS, the learning of new languages or even the loss of languages learned in the past, hardly any research has been carried out so far.

List of Key Words and Concepts

Ageism, Attentional resources, Bilingual advantage, Code-switching (CS), Cognitive decline, Complex dynamic systems theory, Degraded signal account, Domain-general, Domain-specific, Executive function, Form-based, General slowing theories, Inhibition deficit theory, Inhibitory control, Inhibitory deficits, Language reversion, Meta-analysis, Multicompetence, Multilingualism, Phonological retrieval, Resource theory, Semantic verbal fluency, Sensory decline, Social economic status (SES), Speech error, Syntactic processing, Task switching, Third age, Tip-of-the-tongue (TOT), Transmission deficit theory, Verbal fluency, Working memory

Internet Sites Related to the Psycholinguistics of Bilingualism

François Grosjean, Myths about Bilingualism: http://www.francoisgrosjean.ch/myths_en.html

Center for Multilingualism in Society across the Lifespan, University of Oslo: http://www.hf.uio.no/multiling/english/

Discussion Questions

(1) Why would language skills change with age?
(2) What factors could play a role in research on the bilingual advantage in aging?
(3) To what extent are there differences in processing of different languages, dialects, styles, and registers?
(4) Are there actually any real monolinguals?

Suggested Research Projects

(1) Is learning an additional language more difficult for elderly learners? What methods could be used to teach them?
(2) Are bilinguals with dementia equally affected in both their languages?
(3) Will learning an additional language after age 70 be effective as protection against dementia?

Suggested Readings

Bialystok, E., Craik, F. I. M., Klein, R., & Viswanathan, M. (2004). Bilingualism, aging, and cognitive control: Evidence from the Simon task. *Psychology and Aging*, *19*, 290–303.

Burke, D., & Shafto, M. (2008). Language and aging. In F. Craik & T. A. Salthouse (Eds.), *The handbook of aging and cognition* (pp. 373–444). New York: Psychology Press.

Valian, V. (2015). Bilingualism and cognition. *Bilingualism: Language and Cognition*, *18*(1), 3–24.

References

Acevedo, A., Loewenstein, D., Barker, W., Harwood, D., Luis, C., Bravo, M., Hurwitz, D. A., Aguero, H., Greenfield, L., & Duara. R. (2000). Category fluency test: Normative data for English and Spanish speaking elderly. *Journal of the International Neuropsychological Society*, *6*(7), 760–769.

Adesope, O. O., Lavin, T., Thompson, T., & Ungerleider, C. (2010). A systematic review and meta-analysis of the cognitive correlates of bilingualism. *Review of Educational Research*, *80*(2), 207–245.

Alladi, S., Bak, T. H., Duggirala, V., Surampudi, B., Shailaja, M., Shukla, A. K., Chaudhuri, J. R., & Kaul, S. (2013). Bilingualism delays age at onset of dementia, independent of education and immigration status. *Neurology*, *81*(22), 1938–1944.

Aronin, L., & Singleton, D. (2010). *Multilingualism*. Amsterdam: John Benjamins.

Bahrick, H. (1984). Fifty years of second language attrition: Implications for programmatic research. *Modern Language Journal*, *68*, 105–118.

Bak, T. H., Nissan, J. J., Allerhand, M. M., & Deary, I. J. (2014). Does bilingualism influence cognitive aging? *Annals of Neurology*, *75*(6), 959–963.

Baltes, P., & Lindenberger, U. (1997). Emergence of a powerful connection between sensory and cognitive functions accross the life span: A new window to the study of cognitive aging? *Psychology and Aging*, *12*, 12–21.

Bialystok, E., Craik, F. I. M., Binns, M. A., Ossher, L., & Freedman, M. (2014). Effects of bilingualism on the age of onset and progression of MCI and AD: Evidence from executive function tests. *Neuropsychology*, *28*(2), 290–304.

Bialystok, E., Craik, F. I., & Freedman, M. (2007). Bilingualism as a protection against the onset of symptoms of dementia. *Neuropsychologia*, *45*(2), 459–464.

Bialystok, E., Craik, F. I. M., Klein, R., & Viswanathan, M. (2004). Bilingualism, aging, and cognitive control: Evidence from the Simon task. *Psychology and Aging*, *19*, 290–303.

Bloomfield, L. (1933). *Language*. New York: Henry Holt.

Burke, D., & Shafto, M. (2008). Language and aging. In F. Craik & T. A. Salthouse (Eds.), *The handbook of aging and cognition* (pp. 373–444). New York: Psychology Press.

Caplan, D., & Waters, G. (1999). Verbal working memory and sentence comprehension. *Behavioral and Brain Sciences*, *22*(1), 77–110.

Chertkow, H., Whitehead, V., Phillips, N., Wolfson, C., Atherton, J., & Bergman, H. (2010). Multilingualism (but not always bilingualism) delays the onset of Alzheimer disease: Evidence from a bilingual community. *Alzheimer Disease & Associated Disorders*, *24*(2), 118–125.

Cook, V. (1995). Multi-competence and the learning of many languages. *Language, Culture and Curriculum*, *8*(2), 93–98.

Craik, F. I. M., Bialystok, E., & Freedman, M. (2010). Delaying the onset of Alzheimer disease: Bilingualism as a form of cognitive reserve. *Neurology*, *75*(19), 1726–1729.

Crane, P., Gibbons, L., Arani, K., Nguyen, V., Rhoads, K., McCurry, S., Launer, L., Masaki, K., & White, L. (2009). Midlife use of written Japanese and protection from late life dementia. *Epidemiology*, *20*, 766–774.

Crane, P., Gruhl, J., Erosheva, E., Gibbons, L., McCurry, S., Rhoads, K., Nguyen, V., Arani, K., Masaki, K., & White, L. (2010). Use of spoken and written Japanese did not protect Japanese-American men from cognitive decline in late life. *Journals of Gerontology Series B: Psychological Sciences*, *65*(6), 654–666.

de Bot, K. (2007). Dynamic systems theory, life span development and language attrition. In S. Dostert (Ed.), *Language attrition: Theoretical perspectives* (pp. 53–68). Amsterdam: John Benjamins.

de Bot, K., & Clyne, M. (1994). A 16-year longitudinal study of language attrition in Dutch immigrants in Australia. *Journal of Multilingual and Multicultural Development*, *15*(1), 17–28.

de Bot, K., Lowie, W., & Verspoor, M. (2007). A dynamic view as a complementary perspective. *Bilingualism: Language and Cognition*, *10*(1), 51–55.

de Bot, K., & Makoni, S. (2005). *Language and aging in multilingual societies: A dynamic approach*. Clevedon: Multilingual Matters.

Dewaele, J. M., & Wei, L. (2014). Intra- and inter-individual variation in self-reported code-switching patterns of adult multilinguals. *International Journal of Multilingualism, 11*(2), 225–246.

Edwards, J. (1994). *Multilingualism.* London: Routledge.

Freedman, M., Alladi, S., Chertkow, H., Bialystok, E., Craik, F. I. M., Phillips, N. A., Duggirala, V., Bapi Raju, S., & Bak, T. H. (2014). Delaying onset of dementia: Are two languages enough? *Behavioural Neurology, 2014*(Article ID 808137), 1–8.

Fuller-Thomson, E., & Kuh, D. (2014). The healthy migrant effect may confound the link between bilingualism and delayed onset of Alzheimer's disease. *Cortex, 52,* 128–130.

Genesee, F., & Bourhis, R. (1982). The social significance of code switching in cross-cultural communication. *Journal of Language and Social Psychology, 1982*(1), 1–27.

Gollan, T. H., & Brown, A. S. (2006). From tip-of-the-tongue (TOT) data to theoretical implications in two steps: When more TOTs means better retrieval. *Journal of Experimental Psychology: General, 135*(3), 462–483.

Gollan, T. H., Salmon, D. P., Montoya, R. I., & Galasko, D. R. (2011). Degree of bilingualism predicts age of diagnosis of Alzheimer's disease in low-education but not in highly-educated Hispanics. *Neuropsychologia, 49,* 3826–3830.

Goral, M. (2004). First-language decline in healthy aging: Implications for attrition in bilingualism. *Journal of Neurolinguistics, 17*(1), 31–52.

Hansen, L. (2012). *Second language acquisition abroad: The LDS missionary experience.* Amsterdam: John Benjamins.

Herdina, P., & Jessner, U. (2002). *A dynamic model of multilingualism: Perspective of change in psycholinguistics.* Clevedon: Multilingual Matters.

Houtzager, N., Lowie, W., Sprenger, S., & de Bot, K. (2015, April 19). A bilingual advantage in task switching? Age-related differences between German monolinguals and Dutch/Frisian bilinguals. *Bilingualism: Language and Cognition.* doi: http://dx.doi.org/10.1017/S1366728915000498.

Kaushanskaya, M., & Marian, V. (2009). The bilingual advantage in novel word learning. *Psychonomic Bulletin & Review, 16*(4), 705–710.

Kavé, G., Eyal, N., Shorek, A., Cohen-Mansfield, J. (2008). Multilingualism and cognitive state in the oldest old. *Psychology and Aging, 23*(1), 70–78.

Kempler, D., Teng, E., Dick, M., Taussig, I., & Davis, D. (1998). The effects of age, education and ethnicity on verbal fluency. *Journal of the International Neuropsychological Society, 4*(6), 531–538.

Larsen-Freeman, D., & Cameron, L. (2008). *Complex systems and applied linguistics.* Oxford: Oxford University Press.

Levelt, W. J. M. (1989). *Speaking. from intention to articulation.* Cambridge, MA: MIT Press.

Miyake, A., Friedman, P., Emerson, M., Witzki, A., & Howerter, A. (2000). The unity and diversity of executive functions and their contributions to complex "Frontal lobe" tasks: A latent variable analysis. *Cognitive Psychology, 41,* 49–100.

Mortimer, J. A. (2014). Comment on: Alladi et al. (2013), Bilingualism delays age at onset of dementia, independent of education and immigration status. *Neurology, 81*(22), 1938–1944. doi: 10.1212/WNL.0000000000000400.

Paap, K. R., & Greenberg, Z. (2013). There is no coherent evidence for a bilingual advantage in executive processing. *Cognitive Psychology, 66*(2), 232–258.

Prior, A., & Gollan, T. H. (2011). Good language-switchers are good task-switchers: Evidence from Spanish–English and Mandarin–English bilinguals. *Journal of the International Neuropsychological Society, 17*(4), 682–691.

Rosselli, M., Ardila, A., Araujo, K., Weekes, V., Caracciolo, V., Padilla, M., & Ostrosky-Solis, F. (2000). Verbal fluency and repetition skills in healthy older Spanish–English bilinguals. *Applied Neuropsychology, 7*(1), 17–24.

Sanders, A., Hall, C., Katz, M., & Lipton, R. (2012). Non-native language use and risk of incident dementia in the elderly. *Journal of Alzheimer's Disease, 29*(1), 99–108.

Schmid, M. (2010). *Language attrition.* Cambridge: Cambridge University Press.

Schmid, M. S., & Keijzer, M. (2009). First language attrition and reversion among older migrants. *International Journal of the Sociology of Language, 200,* 83–101.

Schneider, B., Daneman, M., Murphy, D., & Kwong See, S. (2000). Listening to discourse in distracting settings: The effect of aging. *Psychology and Aging, 15*, 110–125.

Schrauf, R. W. (2008). Bilingualism and aging. In R. R. Heredia & J. Altarriba (Eds.), *An introduction to bilingualism: Principles and processes* (pp. 105–127). New York: Lawrence Erlbaum.

Swain, M. (1972). *Bilingualism as a first language* (Unpublished doctoral dissertation). University of California, Irvine.

Valian, V. (2015). Bilingualism and cognition. *Bilingualism: Language and Cognition, 18*(1), 3–24.

Verreyt, N., Woumans, E., Vandelanotte, D., Szmalec, A., & Duyck, W. (2016). The influence of language-switching experience on the bilingual executive control advantage. *Bilingualism: Language and Cognition, 19*(1), 181–190. doi: 10.1017/S1366728914000352.

Woumans, E., Santens, P., Sieben, P., Versijpt, J., Stevens, M., & Duyck, W. (2015). Bilingualism delays clinical manifestation of Alzheimer's disease. *Bilingualism: Language and Cognition, 18*(3), 568–574.

Woutersen, M., Cox, A., Weltens, B., & de Bot, K. (1994). Lexical aspects of standard-dialect bilingualism. *Applied Psycholinguistics, 15*(4), 447–473.

Yeung, C., St John, P., Menec, V., & Tyas, S. (2014). Is bilingualism associated with a lower risk of dementia in community-living older adults? Cross-sectional and prospective analyses. *Alzheimer's Disease and Associated Disorders, 28*(4), 326–332.

Zahodne, L., Schofield, P., Farrell, M., Stern, Y., & Manly, J. (2014). Bilingualism does not alter cognitive decline or dementia risk among Spanish-speaking immigrants. *Neuropsychology, 28*(2), 238–246.

6   The Bilingual Brain

Angélique M. Blackburn

Introduction

The brain is a dynamic system—it is shaped by everything we do, perceive, or otherwise experience. In particular, brain structure and function are heavily affected by acquiring a skill through frequent practice and feedback. Neurobiologists have documented changes in the brain that result from skill acquisition such as the ability to play an instrument, chess, and video games. Managing two languages, a skill often acquired early during development, is arguably one of the most frequently engaged skills in daily life and over a lifetime. As such, bilingualism is a well-studied skill that is known to affect both brain structure and function.

The way in which a skill is developed and used can impact not only the neural systems engaged specifically for that skill, but also organization and cooperation with other neural systems that may support use of that skill. Take, for instance, the basic skill of walking. Everyone uses a motor system when they are walking. But we may observe differences between regular students and tightrope walkers in the cooperation between motor systems and those responsible for balance and spatial perception. Likewise, bilingualism is thought to rely on the cooperation of multiple systems. In particular, language systems and other cognitive control systems work together to ensure words are spoken in the appropriate language.

Bilingualism is a complex skill engaged in different ways based on individual preference, learning environment, and cultural norms. Bilinguals may speak both languages daily, speak only one language for years, or even switch rapidly between languages within a conversation—a process known as *code-switching*. Using languages in different ways requires different types of control and may have different long-term consequences for both the language system and control systems. We will see how the way in which bilinguals use their languages affects cooperation between language and other control systems in the brain.

The Language System

Historically, models of the language system were constructed by attributing language functions lost after trauma to damaged brain areas. While brain regions are certainly specialized to handle specific functions, we now know that many regions have more general roles in both language and non-language processes. A discussion of language systems is complicated by the recent understanding that language functions do not simply occur in highly specialized regions of the brain, but rather encompass widely distributed neural networks that are engaged differently for different tasks. Modeling the language system is further complicated by complex interactions between language and other neural systems (e.g., memory and *cognitive control*). The advent of *neuroimaging* has allowed us to view the living brain, observe areas that are connected and/or work together (i.e., structural and functional connectivity), determine the *language-specific* and more *general* functions of cortical areas, and investigate interactions between language and other cognitive systems.

A model of the language networks in the brain has been proposed based on compilation of hundreds of neuroimaging studies. The brain is composed of cell bodies, or gray matter, and white matter tracks connecting these bodies. We can non-invasively look at brain structure using *magnetic resonance imaging* (MRI) and map white matter networks structurally connecting sometimes distant regions of the brain using *diffusion tensor imaging* (DTI). We can also investigate areas of the brain that are functionally connected by using *positron emission tomography* (PET) and functional MRI (fMRI) to track cerebral blood flow and metabolic activity, respectively. Any areas engaged during a task (e.g., the visual cortex) exhibit increased flow and activity while the participant performs that task (e.g., reading). Conversely, we can determine brain regions necessary for a task by evaluating permanent or temporary loss of function occurring either after brain trauma or through *transcranial magnetic stimulation* (TMS). Finally, we can monitor the time-course of activity across a network using *event-related potentials* (ERPs) and *magnetoencephalography* (MEG), in which we observe voltages or magnetic fields passing through the scalp as large populations of neurons become active.

Using a combination of these methods, researchers have been able to form a basic model of language networks—one that is constantly growing in complexity as the field evolves (Friederici & Gierhan, 2013; Poeppel, Emmorey, Hickok, & Pylkkänen, 2012). The brain is divided into four lobes: the frontal, parietal, temporal, and occipital cortices (see Figure 6.1). During comprehension, sensory processing streams originate in the visual cortex of the *occipital lobe* and primary auditory cortex of the *superior temporal gyrus* (STG). These streams compile aspects of the visual or auditory signal and send this information anteriorly to higher processing streams. The inferior frontal and temporal cortices are known to play significant roles in higher language functions. These regions are highly

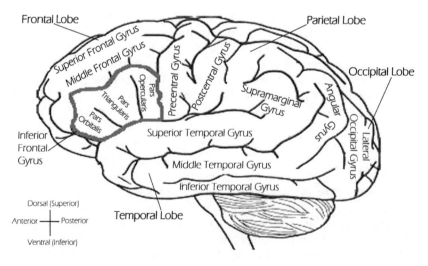

Figure 6.1   Left lateral view of the brain (adapted from Hwozdek & Blackburn, "Labeled Brain" derivative of "Brain in Profile" by Pearish, 2016, openclipart.org, licensed under CC0 1.0: https://creativecommons.org/publicdomain/zero/1.0/legalcode).

connected by multiple bilateral and left-dominant processing streams, and information flows in both directions between these regions.

Specifically, separate pathways between the frontal and temporal cortices are thought to be responsible for three language functions: *input-to-motor mapping*, semantic (*input-to-meaning*) mapping, and syntactic (grammatical) processing (for an in-depth review, see Blackburn, 2016). Input-to-motor mapping involves dorsal auditory streams from the temporal cortex and visual streams from the occipital cortex to the premotor cortex. *Semantic* processing occurs via ventral streams from the temporal and occipital cortices to the anterior portions of the *inferior frontal gyrus* (IFG), including the pars triangularis and pars orbitalis, which are regions associated with semantic processing. The anterior IFG is also thought to mediate *top-down lexical-semantic* access to the *middle temporal gyrus* (MTG) via a ventral projection from the frontal cortex back to the temporal cortex. *Syntactic* processing occurs primarily in the pars opercularis via both a ventral phrase structure processing path from the anterior temporal cortex (particularly the anterior STG) and a dorsal processing path for complex syntactic structures from the posterior temporal cortex. The pars opercularis in the posterior IFG then sends syntactic predictions back to the posterior superior temporal sulcus and gyrus (STS/STG). Finally, semantic information from the anterior IFG, the MTG, and the angular gyrus (which plays a role in sentence level semantics) and syntactic information from the posterior IFG are thought to be sent to the posterior STS/STG for integration of semantic and syntactic information (Friederici, 2009; Friederici, 2012; Friederici & Gierhan, 2013; Hickok & Poeppel, 2007). During production, similar higher-level regions are engaged, followed by substantial engagement of premotor and motor cortices to produce speech.

This is a simplified model of language networks. It is important to realize that language also engages other cognitive functions, such as memory and cognitive control. Researchers typically agree that the regions mentioned above are involved in language, but these cortical areas may be specialized for language or have more general functions.

Bilingualism and Language Networks in the Brain

This basic model of the neurobiology of language is fairly consistent across bilinguals and monolinguals, speakers of different languages (Meschyan & Hernandez, 2006; Paulesu et al., 2000), and even across language modalities such as signed languages versus spoken languages (Hickok, Bellugi, & Klima, 1998; Poeppel et al., 2012). There is overwhelming evidence that this same language network subserves both of a bilingual's languages irrespective of individual differences in *age of acquisition* (AOA) and proficiency, although these factors may influence the structural and/or functional connectivity within the networks and the way these networks are controlled (for a review, see Abutalebi & Green, 2007). Of course, specific properties of the language itself may affect some aspects of production or processing. For instance, the language network engaged during reading in Chinese heavily overlaps with that engaged during English reading, with recruitment of additional areas thought to handle the visual–spatial complexity of the characters (Tan et al., 2001, 2003; Tan, Spinks, Eden, Perfetti, & Siok, 2005). Differences between languages at the perceptual level tend to affect early levels of sensory processing, but higher-language functions in bilinguals are governed by the universal *fronto-temporal network* described above (Crinion et al., 2006).

Despite similarity in bilingual and monolingual language systems, behavioral differences are frequently observed in bilingual and monolingual language performance.

Bilinguals are able to produce and/or comprehend more than one language and demonstrate better understanding of the formal properties of language (i.e., *metalinguistic awareness*) than monolinguals (Adesope, Lavin, Thompson, & Ungerleider, 2010; Bialystok, 1988). But these advantages come at a linguistic cost in each language. Bilinguals tend to have smaller vocabularies in each language (Bialystok, Craik, & Luk, 2008; Bialystok, Luk, Peets, & Yang, 2010; Oller & Eilers, 2002), exhibit reduced fluency (Gollan, Montoya, & Werner, 2002; Rosselli et al., 2000), and have slower lexical access than monolinguals (Gollan, Montoya, Fennema-Notestine, & Morris, 2005), even when tested in their first and *dominant language* (Ivanova & Costa, 2008). Bilinguals also have more experiences when a word is on the *tip-of-the-tongue* (TOT), but they are unable to fully retrieve it (Gollan & Silverberg, 2001). Many of these disadvantages are thought to stem from competition between languages, which is discussed below.

The Language Control System

While subtle differences have been observed between bilingual and monolingual language systems, the largest neural differences which have received much attention in recent years are in the control systems used by bilinguals to manage their languages. As mentioned above, bilinguals are slower than monolinguals to retrieve words in each of their languages. This disadvantage is attributed in part to a bilingual's need to resolve *language conflict*, interference resulting from competition between languages (Green, 1998). We sometimes refer to interference between languages as *cross-language interference*.

There is strong evidence that even when only one language is being used, words and features of the language not in use (i.e., non-target language) are active and interfere with the other language (Costa, 2005; Kroll, Bobb, Misra, & Guo, 2008; Kroll, Bobb, & Wodniekca, 2006; Spivey & Marian, 1999). For instance, eye tracking (Marian & Spivey, 2003) and ERP experiments (Thierry & Wu, 2007) have shown that when bilinguals perform a semantic task in only one language, they are sensitive to features of the word's translation in the other language. Because both languages are active, words from the non-target language interfere and compete for selection. Bilinguals must deal with competition between two active languages using cognitive control functions to select and attend to the appropriate language, inhibit interference from the language not currently in use, and switch between languages (e.g., Green, 1998; Meuter & Allport, 1999).

Cognitive control, also known as *executive function*, is the ability to flexibly guide behavior towards a goal while managing interference and competition (Banich, 2009; Festman, Rodriguez-Fornells, & Münte, 2010). For instance, you are using cognitive control right now to attend to and keep track of task demands (e.g., read this book), and perhaps to switch between tasks (e.g., multitask by reading and watching TV) or inhibit inappropriate responses (e.g., exerting impulse control not to go for a walk). Cognitive control encompasses many different functions, including maintaining goals in memory, directing attention, monitoring for conflicting information, inhibiting irrelevant information, resolving conflict to make a decision, and switching between task goals (Banich, 2009). These different aspects of cognitive control are managed by cortical-subcortical neural circuits. Importantly, different control functions, such as inhibition and attention, are served by largely overlapping, but distinct, neural networks. The prefrontal cortex, *inferior parietal cortex* (IPC), *anterior cingulate cortex* (ACC), and the subcortical basal ganglia are the major players in the *cognitive control networks* (e.g., Botvinick, Nystrom, Fissell, Carter, & Cohen, 1999). However, the involvement of these regions and functional connectivity between them and other control regions, depends on the type of control required for the task being performed. The cognitive control networks involved in non-language tasks are largely overlapping with those employed to maintain attention to the language in use, inhibit interference from the other language, and switch between languages. We will examine in detail the thriving area of research into the interaction of language and cognitive control.

Bilingual language use involves multiple aspects of cognitive control, which are applied at different stages of language production and comprehension. Bilinguals need to attend to linguistic cues to decide which language is appropriate for a given context, monitor and detect conflict between their two languages, and suppress interference from the inappropriate language. Using language in different ways may differentially tap into these aspects of cognitive control. For instance, it has been proposed that there are multiple kinds of *inhibition*, which are supported by distinct but overlapping control networks. *Interference suppression* is the inhibition of information that is irrelevant to the task being performed. Bilinguals suppress interference from one language to *stay* in the other. *Backwards inhibition* refers to inhibition applied in order to disengage from one task and switch into another. Bilinguals use backwards inhibition of one language to *switch* into the other. The language context and current task demands may influence how much or what aspect of control is needed. This is known as the *adaptive control hypothesis* (Green & Abutalebi, 2013). When a bilingual is using only one language for an extended period of time, top-down control may be exerted to proactively and globally inhibit the other language entirely (de Groot & Christoffels, 2006). In situations when global inhibition fails (e.g., interference from highly active words such as translation equivalents) or both languages are needed, local inhibition of specific words might be employed. Inhibition may not be as important when it is appropriate to speak in either language and voluntarily switch between languages (code-switch) within a conversation (Green, 2011).

To isolate the aspects of bilingual language control and map its neural correlates, researchers have manipulated the language context (i.e., one or more languages are necessary), the degree of language conflict while using only one language, the task demands (e.g., translation, *picture naming*, repetition), and types of switching (e.g., within-language and between-language). Many of these studies have focused on language production where control is thought to be more essential, but control has also been observed during comprehension. A few of these studies have been highlighted below to compare and contrast neural regions involved when different aspects of control are engaged to stay or switch between languages.

Controlling Language Interference

A few studies have directly compared bilinguals and monolinguals on single language tasks. These studies aim to determine if competition between languages results in recruitment of additional brain regions or increased activation within language areas. ERP and fMRI studies have shown that when only using one language, bilinguals use the same neural networks as monolinguals, but exhibit more neural activity in areas associated with monolingual language conflict, articulation, and non-language interference. In particular, the left IFG in the prefrontal cortex may be the seat of bilingual interference suppression, as it is active both when monolinguals need to resolve competition between two words (e.g., couch vs. sofa; Thompson-Schill, d'Esposito, Aguirre, & Farah, 1997; Thompson-Schill, d'Esposito, & Kan, 1999) and when bilinguals speak in only one language. In some tasks, additional areas are recruited to manage articulatory and interference demands of bilingualism.

To isolate interference suppression, a type of *go/nogo task* is often used in which participants are asked to respond to a word or picture ("go") only if it matches a criterion, such as belonging to a language or starting with a vowel. When responses are withheld ("nogo"), a frontal negativity in the ERP waveform is observed around 200 ms after the stimulus (Nieuwenhuis, Yeung, Van den Wildenberg, & Ridderinkhof, 2003; Pfefferbaum, Ford, Weller, & Kopell, 1985). This is known as the *nogo N2 effect* and is thought to reflect the detection of conflict between the "go" and "nogo" response, and subsequent inhibition of the "go" response. N2 effects are observed during many tasks that require cognitive control and are characterized as ERP negativities elicited 200–350 ms after stimuli that evoke conflict detection and/or inhibition. These effects have been localized to the ACC when conflict is detected and the dorsolateral part of the prefrontal cortex when inhibition is engaged (Lavric, Pizzagalli, & Forstmeier, 2004).

Importantly, only one language is necessary to perform go/nogo *lexical decision tasks* in which participants are instructed to respond only to real words in a given language. Presenting stimuli in multiple languages is a way to cause potential interference for bilinguals but not monolinguals. For instance, Rodriguez-Fornells and colleagues instructed Spanish–Catalan bilinguals and Spanish monolinguals to respond only to Spanish words and withhold responses to Catalan and pseudowords (Rodriguez-Fornells, Rotte, Heinze, Noesselt, & Münte, 2002). In this case, it would be beneficial for bilinguals to restrict or inhibit access to Catalan, as only Spanish was relevant for the task. Bilinguals appeared to effectively suppress access to Catalan, as no N2 effect was observed in the ERPs elicited in response to Catalan and pseudowords for either bilinguals or monolinguals. Using fMRI, the authors showed that the ability of bilinguals to inhibit interference from Catalan was reflected in increased activation of the left IFG for bilinguals compared to monolinguals. In another study, bilinguals also showed more activity in the left pre-frontal IFG than monolinguals when they were instructed to respond to words in any language ("go") and withhold responses to nonwords ("nogo"; Van Heuven, Schriefers, Dijkstra, & Hagoort, 2008). All of the real words were English, but some were *inter-lingual homographs*, words with the same written form but different meanings in each of the bilinguals' languages. Because interlingual homographs are words in both lan-guages, they are direct sources of language conflict for bilinguals but not monolinguals. In both of these studies, non-target language interference was linked to activity in the left IFG. This region has been associated with interference resolution by selecting rel-evant information over competing but irrelevant information (Bunge, Ochsner, Desmond, Glover, & Gabrieli, 2001; Thompson-Schill et al., 1997; Thompson-Schill et al., 1999), a necessary component of a go/nogo task. It has also been associated with phonological retrieval and controlled semantic retrieval (Gold & Buckner, 2002; Peterson, Fox, Posner, Mintun, & Raichle, 1989), both of which may have occurred during these lexical decision tasks. Importantly, the left IFG is a part of the monolingual language network, but activa-tion in this area during language tasks is often greater for bilinguals than monolinguals, even when performing tasks in only one language (Kovelman, Baker, & Petitto, 2008; Kovelman, Shalinsky, Berens, & Petitto, 2008). This suggests that to suppress language conflict, bilinguals recruit a part of the monolingual language network that is already specialized for suppressing irrelevant information during controlled word retrieval. One effective strategy would be global inhibition of the entire non-target language. In fact, the left frontal cortex has been identified as part of a network that globally inhibits an entire language (Guo, Misra, & Kroll, 2011). It has been suggested that the left IFG may serve to actively inhibit the non-target language when only one language is needed (Rodriguez-Fornells et al., 2002).

In both of the above studies, language conflict only occurred at the stimulus level—while the Catalan words and interlingual homographs induced non-target language interference, only one response ("go" or "nogo") was linked to each word. The go/nogo task has also been adapted to manipulate the degree of response-based language conflict caused by interference of the non-target language. For instance, bilinguals and monolinguals were asked to name pictures when the name began with a vowel, but withhold responses when the word began with a consonant. Again, only one language was necessary to make the go/nogo decision and name the pictures. When both languages evoked the same response, language conflict was low. However, on "go" trials in which the non-target language necessitated a "nogo" response, an N2 was observed for bilinguals but not monolinguals. This N2 was interpreted as partial inhibition of the "go" response by the interfering "nogo" response elicited by the non-target language. The inhibition observed in the N2 response was accompanied in bilinguals by increased activity in the left middle prefrontal cortex and ACC (potential sources of the N2) and the *supplementary motor area* (SMA), a region involved in articulation. No other differences were observed in the language systems of bilinguals and monolinguals (Rodriguez-Fornells et al., 2005). In an extension of the interlingual homograph study mentioned above, Van Heuven and colleagues (2008) induced response conflict for the homographs by restricting the "go" criterion to one target-language only. Now, a "go" response to interlingual homographs would be necessitated by the target language, but a "nogo" response would be evoked by the non-target language. Again, increased response conflict for bilinguals compared to monolinguals activated the *pre-supplementary motor area* (pre-SMA) and ACC, as well as the basal ganglia. Interestingly, the pre-SMA and ACC have been identified in a *local inhibition network* that suppresses specific words during tasks with a high degree of conflict (Guo et al., 2011). Van Heuven et al. (2008) suggest that local inhibitory control networks may reflect the detection of conflict (ACC) and solving of this conflict during the motor response (pre-SMA/SMA). Contrasting these go/nogo tasks with stimulus- and response-level conflict suggests that modifying the task demands and level of conflict alters the control networks engaged, a recurring finding in many language studies (see Moss, Schunn, Schneider, McNamara, & VanLehn, 2010; Nakamura et al., 2006 for more examples).

Even though the tasks in these studies required the use of only one language at a time, in each study, bilinguals were required to perform the task in each of their languages. Recently, a direct comparison was made between monolinguals and highly proficient bilinguals using only their first language. Naming pictures and reading aloud in only the first language recruited similar networks in both groups (Parker Jones et al., 2012). Consistent with the findings above, greater activation for bilinguals compared to monolinguals was found in the pars opercularis and pars triangularis of the IFG. These areas were found to control for interference during word selection in monolinguals and are proposed to be enhanced in bilinguals due to heightened interference from the non-target language. Bilingual enhancement was also observed in the precentral gyrus, a region associated with articulation, and the planum temporale and superior temporal gyrus, areas associated with post-articulatory feedback. Thus, articulation may be more effortful and be monitored to a greater degree in bilinguals, for whom two articulatory systems must be managed. Of particular interest is that these results were found when bilinguals only used their first language, showing that knowledge of a second language alters production in the native language at the neural level.

In summary, to suppress interference from one language to use the other, bilinguals appear to engage more extensive language control than monolinguals, even when operating solely in their first language. This occurs in two ways. First, the same network is used by bilinguals and monolinguals, but the degree of activation is greater when bilingualism necessitates greater control or monitoring. In particular, the left IFG is consistently identified as a source of non-target language interference suppression when bilinguals perform tasks in only one language at a time. This same activation is not observed in monolinguals except in situations with high within-language conflict (e.g., selecting between competing lexical items such as "couch" and "sofa"; Thompson-Schill et al., 1997; Thompson-Schill et al., 1999). Second, additional brain areas are recruited in some tasks to handle articulatory demands (precentral gyrus, planum temporale, and STG) and interference demands (pre-SMA/SMA, ACC, and basal ganglia) at the response level. Therefore, *suppressing interference* to stay in one language is managed by increasing activity in an existing system that includes the left IFG and recruiting additional areas when necessitated by the *task demands*.

Language Context and Switching

The studies above attempted to isolate the effects of bilingualism when only one language was necessary for the task. Sometimes bilinguals only need to use one language at a time like they did during the above tasks or when speaking to a monolingual. But sometimes they spend time with other bilinguals who may change the language at any time or even switch between languages within the conversation (Grosjean, 1982). The needs for language control in bilinguals may fluctuate across a continuum as they move in and out of single-language contexts, *mixed-language contexts* with other bilinguals, and even perhaps highly mixed contexts in which they code-switch rapidly within a conversation (Green & Abutalebi, 2013; Grosjean, 1985). A major focus of bilingual brain research is to determine if the degree of control necessary to manage languages differs when a bilingual is in a single-language context or a mixed-language context. More language conflict is thought to occur in a mixed-language context because both languages need to be active and accessible (Green & Abutalebi, 2013).

Researchers have manipulated language context using *cross-language priming* in which words in one language are briefly presented before a task is performed in the other language (Chauncey, Holcomb, & Grainger, 2009), comparing language tasks such as translation and switching (Price, Green, & Studnitz, 1999), and setting the context before the task by playing videos in one or both of the languages (Elston-Güttler, Gunter, & Kotz, 2005). The majority of context studies have used *language switching* to put bilinguals in a mixed-language context and increase language conflict (Meuter & Allport, 1999). This has generated a rich dataset which enables us to unravel the control mechanisms involved in managing high levels of language conflict and the neural correlates of language and non-language switching. In addition to context effects of being in a *mixed-language environment*, language switching engrosses multiple aspects of cognitive control, including attention, inhibition of the active language, shifting to the new language, and updating working memory resources regarding the new language-relevant goals (Friedman & Miyake, 2004; Miyake et al., 2000; Philipp & Koch, 2009).

In language switching studies, bilinguals typically complete a *single-language* block of trials in which they name pictures in only one language and a *mixed-language* block of trials in which they are cued to switch between languages. Differences between mixed and single-language blocks reveal *mix effects*, the contextual effects of needing to have both languages active. A separate comparison within the mixed block can be made between *non-switch* trials, which are named in the same language as the previous trial, and *switch* trials, which are named in a different language. Differences between switch and non-switch trials reveal *switch effects*, the effects specific to switching between languages (see Figure 6.2).

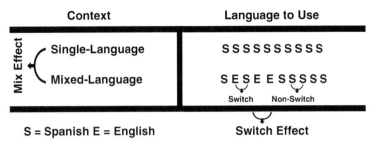

Figure 6.2   Language switching paradigm (adapted from Meuter & Allport, 1999).

Language Switching

ERP studies have found evidence that cognitive control is exerted during language switching. In a *bilingual digit naming task*, predictable language switches induced a sustained left frontal negativity peaking at 320 ms after stimulus presentation relative to non-switch trials. Critically, this *N2 switch effect* resembles the nogo N2 component obtained during *non-language inhibition* and language interference suppression (Jackson, Swainson, Cunnington, & Jackson, 2001; cf. Rodriguez-Fornells et al., 2005). The resemblance in timing and frontal scalp distribution of the nogo N2 and N2 switch effect, and fMRI studies demonstrating overlapping regions of activity during switching and *response inhibition* (Konishi et al., 1999), led Jackson et al. (2001) to conclude that response inhibition and language switching share a common neural substrate. They proposed that the N2 switch effect is a language switching version of the inhibitory nogo N2, and that inhibition is used to switch between languages. It is important to note that while the N2 may reflect inhibition, this component could arguably also indicate conflict detection during *language mixing* and on switch trials, because the previously active language interferes with the new target language (Nieuwenhuis et al., 2003; Yeung, Botvinick, & Cohen, 2004). However, many authors of ERP language switching studies contend that this component reflects inhibition (e.g., Verhoef, Roelofs, & Chwilla, 2009; for a detailed discussion, see Blackburn, 2013).

Both ERP and fMRI researchers have substantiated this claim by arguing that more inhibition should be necessary to disengage from a stronger language in order to switch into a weaker language. Indeed, Jackson et al. (2001) found that the degree of inhibition, reflected in the amplitude of the N2 switch effect, was larger when inhibiting the stronger language to switch into the weaker language. Consistent with these results, switching out of a stronger language increases activation of brain regions associated with inhibition. De Bruin and colleagues reported language dominance effects in two regions of interest specifically selected for their role in non-language inhibition: the right IFG and pre-SMA (de Bruin, Roelofs, Dijkstra, & FitzPatrick, 2014). They found that only switching out of the stronger language resulted in activation of these inhibition areas, providing strong evidence for selective inhibition of the stronger language. Thus, the degree of inhibition, reflected in the amplitude of the N2 switch effect and greater activation of control regions, is larger when inhibiting the stronger language to switch into the weaker language.

Inhibition is one aspect of cognitive control, but language switching also recruits regions involved in other aspects of cognitive control. Language switching has been shown to involve a number of frontal, parietal, and subcortical structures, including but not limited to the prefrontal cortex (Hernandez, Martinez, & Kohnert, 2000), left inferior and superior parietal cortices, SMA, cerebellum, precentral gyrus (Wang, Kuhl, Chen, & Dong, 2009), caudate (Abutalebi et al., 2013; Crinion et al., 2006; Garbin et al., 2011;

Zou, Ding, Abutalebi, Shu, & Peng, 2012), ACC and pre-SMA (Garbin et al., 2011). These control structures are differentially engaged for switching into a stronger or weaker language. Typically, disengaging the stronger language increases activation in the ACC (de Bruin et al., 2014; Wang, Xue, Chen, Xue, & Dong, 2007), caudate (Abutalebi et al., 2013; Garbin et al., 2011), and sometimes the frontal cortices (Wang et al., 2007). In sum, comparison of fMRI responses to switch and non-switch trials within a mixed-language block has revealed an extensive and widely distributed language switching network. This network heavily overlaps with a general cognitive control network which is engaged for non-language inhibition and *task switching* (Abutalebi, 2008; Abutalebi & Green, 2008).

It is noteworthy that, while it may seem obvious that switching between languages during naming requires cognitive control, an exciting finding is that simply comprehending language switches engages neural correlates of cognitive control. An fMRI study using auditory language switches showed that the bilateral prefrontal and temporal regions were engaged when language switches were encountered by highly proficient, *early bilinguals* (who acquired their second language in the first few years of life, as opposed to later in life; Abutalebi et al., 2007). Switches into the less-exposed language required more controlled processing with more subcortical and ACC involvement than switches into the more-exposed language. These findings are paralleled in ERP studies showing that reading language switches evokes an ERP component associated with switching into a new task (Blackburn, 2013; Moreno, Federmeier, & Kutas, 2002; Van Der Meij, Cuetos, Carreiras, & Barber, 2011). These findings are consistent with controlled processing of language switches.

Contextual Effects and Language Mixing

The aforementioned switching studies have shown that language switching requires inhibition and other aspects of cognitive control. We have also seen evidence of inhibition when bilinguals use only one language at a time. But does simply being in a bilingual context where both languages may be needed increase the demand for language control?

Very similar patterns of activation are observed during language switching and during bilingual language tasks with high degrees of conflict, such as when bilinguals operate in a mixed-language environment. To test interference arising as a result of being in a mixed-language environment, Christoffels and colleagues compared picture naming in only one language for an extended period of time to the non-switch trials in the mixed-language picture naming block (Christoffels, Firk, & Schiller, 2007). This comparison revealed that simply being in a mixed-language context evoked an ERP *N2 mix effect* with the same time course and scalp distribution as the N2 switch effect. Again, the N2 was taken to reflect inhibition of interference from the language not in use. This finding substantiates the claim that when bilinguals are in a mixed-language environment, both languages are highly active and compete for selection. Moreover, the N2 mix effect was larger when inhibiting the stronger language than the weaker language, indicating that the stronger language interferes more with the weaker language and is inhibited to a greater degree (see also Verhoef et al., 2009, for evidence supporting the lack of interference from the weaker language and selective inhibition of the stronger language). A similar trend was found in an fMRI comparison of mixed-language versus single-language contexts. Only speaking in the weaker language engaged inhibition centers in the right IFG and pre-SMA (de Bruin et al., 2014). Together these findings suggest that in a mixed language context, the stronger language is selectively inhibited to equalize availability of both languages.

Prefrontal and frontal regions, including the *dorsolateral prefrontal cortex* (DLPFC), are also consistently activated in mixed-language contexts compared to single-language contexts (Hernandez, 2009; Hernandez, Dapretto, Mazziotta, & Bookheimer, 2001; Hernandez et al., 2000; Wang et al., 2009). If you recall, the prefrontal region plays a role in managing interference during the go/nogo task in a single-language context (Rodriguez-Fornells et al., 2002). Thus, the prefrontal and frontal areas may function to attenuate conflict between languages arising from having both languages active (Hernandez, 2009; Hernandez et al., 2000, 2001; Wang et al., 2009). In general, mixed contexts also activate the caudate, ACC, and left IFG (Green, 2011).

It is now generally accepted that a mixed-language environment increases language conflict. But is a special neural system required to control competition from the other language? In theory, bilingual language conflict could be resolved using mechanisms external to the language networks or by using language networks already in place to manage within-language competition. Within-language competition arises during word selection (e.g., "couch" and "sofa") and when switching between different linguistic registers or styles (e.g., for formal scientific work, for legal proceedings, for informal speech with friends). Researchers have contrasted switching within one language and switching between languages to determine if a different neural system is needed to use both languages (Abutalebi et al., 2008; Hernandez et al., 2001). For instance, bilinguals either switched between languages while naming objects in pictures, or they switched between naming the object (e.g., "pencil") or action (e.g., "write") depicted in the picture using only one language at a time. In the former, words were selected in the face of competition from both languages; in the latter, only within-language competition was present. Both within- and between-language switching were contrasted with naming only objects in one language—a situation with little competition. Selecting a word among competitors in both contexts activated traditional language areas in the anterior frontal lobe, including the IFG. However, the presence of cross-language conflict when switching between languages also activated the left caudate and ACC. These results support the idea that when bilinguals are placed in a mixed-language context, cognitive control networks external to the language system are engaged to manage the cross-language conflict (Abutalebi et al., 2008).

Together, these language switching and context studies suggest that a similar cognitive control circuit is exerted both during language switching and when the context necessitates equal access to both languages. The staying and switching studies described above highlight the role of the left IFG in managing conflict that arises as a result of switching within one language and managing cross-language interference to stay in one language. In contrast, the ACC and areas associated with motor planning (caudate, pre-SMA/SMA) play a role in both response-driven conflict when using only one language and cross-language competition in a mixed context. Thus distinct, but overlapping circuits control these different kinds of bilingual language conflict. The prefrontal cortex plays a role in inhibiting cross-language interference in a single-language context. The ACC and motor planning areas play a larger role when the task demands induce higher levels of conflict at the response level, such as during rapid language switching and speeded go/nogo tasks with competing response mappings for each language.

Model of Language Control Networks

It may appear that a vast number of brain areas are involved in language control—and there are! Language control does not occur in only one part of the brain, but rather emerges from the integration of separable neural systems. Distinct, but often overlapping networks may be engaged depending on the task at hand. Abutalebi and Green (2007, 2008) reviewed a number of fMRI experiments on language selection and switching and proposed a left-lateralized *frontal-subcortical network* for language control (see Figure 6.3). The model assumes language control occurs via a general cognitive control network that works with language systems to guide language selection. A critical aspect of the model is that this general cognitive control system is already in place for non-language tasks (or develops in parallel for simultaneous bilinguals who learn both languages from a very young age).

As you can see from Figure 6.3 and the studies discussed above, the major players in this network are the prefrontal cortex, ACC, caudate nucleus (part of the basal ganglia), and the supramarginal gyrus (SMG) of the IPC. According to the model, the ACC detects conflict and modulates cognitive control by alerting the prefrontal cortex. The prefrontal cortex, which maintains task representations, guides response selection by exerting a top-down bias towards task-relevant representations to the basal ganglia and IPC. The IPC aids in the selection of competing responses; the left SMG biases selection away from the previous task and the right SMG biases towards the current task. The basal ganglia are a group of interconnected subcortical nuclei that are well connected to cortical areas and influence inputs to the frontal lobe. The caudate and the putamen make up the striatum—the input center of the basal ganglia—which receives projections from cortical regions including the prefrontal cortex. The basal ganglia subserve language planning by aiding in the selection of responses and words, and in bilinguals, supervise selection of the appropriate language. The caudate, in particular, serves to prioritize selection of the appropriate language, especially during language switching. These regions then project back to the cortex and

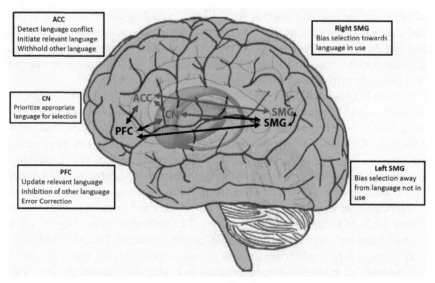

Figure 6.3   Abutalebi and Green's neural model of bilingual language control (2008). Critical players in this network include the ACC, prefrontal cortex (PFC), caudate nucleus (CN) of the basal ganglia, and supramarginal gyrus (SMG) in the inferior parietal lobe. Regions on the lateral surface of the brain are depicted in black; medial regions, subcortical structures, and the right SMG are in gray-scale to illustrate the three-dimensional brain (adapted from Blackburn & Hwozdek, "Language Control Model," 2016, openclipart. org, licensed under CCO 1.0: https://creativecommons.org/publicdomain/zero/1.0/ legalcode).

mediate activation in the ACC and prefrontal cortex to switch attentional focus (Hedden & Gabrieli, 2010; Luk, Green, Abutalebi, & Grady, 2012).

In a subsequent meta-analysis of language switching studies, Luk et al. (2012) found support for this model and identified additional regions that were not included in the original model. They did not find convergence in the ACC, but noted that the variable location and high-level baseline tasks may have obscured activity in this area (see Ma et al., 2014 for evidence of differential activation in language switching based on baseline naming tasks). However, the pre-SMA, a region often co-activated with the ACC, was identified. Together these areas play a role in error detection, *conflict monitoring*, and response control (Bush, Luu, & Posner, 2000; Nachev, Kennard, & Husain, 2008; Yeung et al., 2004). Luk et al. (2012) argue the pre-SMA initiates and executes speech production, especially when language conflict is high (Liu, Hu, Guo, & Peng, 2010). Areas not in the model that were identified in the meta-analysis included the right precentral gyrus and bilateral temporal gyri. The authors tentatively suggest that the former plays a role in motor preparation and the latter relates to general language processing and attention.

Another similar model of language switching has received some attention and is supported by fMRI studies of language switching (Lei, Akama, & Murphy, 2014). The *hodological model* is based on using electrostimulation to map the connections between language and cognitive control, in an attempt to identify widely distributed networks (Moritz-Gasser & Duffau, 2009). Unsurprisingly, the hodological model is quite similar to Abutalebi and Green's model described above (2008). According to this model, a widespread cortical-subcortical cognitive control network governs a language-specific subcircuit. Essentially the same regions described above have been identified for the control network (prefrontal cortex, anterior cingulum, and caudate nucleus) and language subcircuit (posterior temporal areas, supramarginal and angular gyri, the left IFG, and the superior longitudinal fasciculus).

Crucially, all of these models suggest that bilingual language control relies on a general cognitive control network which guides the language system. These networks are composed of distinct control circuits that are engaged differently depending on the aspects of cognitive control required to complete the task at hand. This control network is used by both bilinguals and monolinguals, but the increased demands of bilingualism increase activity in the language control network and recruit additional cognitive control areas.

Bilingualism and General Cognitive Control Networks in the Brain

Shared Networks for Language and Non-Language Control

I alluded above to the fact that language control relies on a general cognitive control network. This cognitive control system is used by bilinguals and monolinguals alike during non-language tasks that require control, such as multitasking and impulse control. There is considerable evidence that the same networks are used both for language and non-language functions. As mentioned above, the left IFG is involved both when bilinguals inhibit interference from the non-target language and when suppressing irrelevant information during a non-language task (Bunge et al., 2001). We also saw that the nogo N2 effect occurs both when inhibiting "go" responses on non-language tasks and when inhibiting responses evoked by the non-target language (Rodriguez-Fornells et al., 2005). We see evidence of overlap between language and non-language switching as well. A variant of the language switching paradigm is often applied in non-language tasks, such as switching between identifying the shape or color of geometrical designs (e.g., Monsell, 2003). Using PET and fMRI, strong overlap has been observed in language and non-language switching activation patterns, including activation in the DLPFC (e.g., Berman et al., 1995; Hernandez et al., 2000, 2001), caudate nucleus (e.g., Monchi, Petrides, Petre, Worsley, & Dagher, 2001; Zou et al., 2012), *premotor areas* (e.g., Allen & Yen, 1979; Wager, Jonides, & Reading, 2004; Wang et al., 2009), and the ACC (e.g., Abutalebi et al., 2011; Abutalebi & Green, 2007, 2008). In addition to anatomical overlap, similar ERP components have been observed in separate studies for task and language switching, referred to as the *differential negativity* (D-Neg) and the N2 switch effect, respectively. Both D-Neg (Karayanidis, Coltheart, Michie, & Murphy, 2003; Nicholson, Karayanidis, Poboka, Heathcote, & Michie, 2005) and the N2 switch effect (Jackson et al., 2001) are sustained frontal negativities with an onset approximately 310–320 ms after a switch stimulus. Like the N2 switch effect, D-Neg has been localized to the DLPFC (Jamadar, Provost, Fulham, Michie, & Karayanidis, 2009). Finally, when the same bilinguals performed a language switching and non-language switching task, the N2 switch effect and D-Neg were modulated by individual differences in the same way (Hwozdek, Blackburn, & Wicha, 2014). This suggests that D-Neg and the N2 switch effect are functionally similar and rely on shared networks. Thus, there is substantial evidence that control networks are partially shared between language and non-language systems.

Because language control relies on cognitive control networks, we might expect bilinguals with stronger cognitive control to have stronger language control. In a series of studies, Festman and colleagues tested this hypothesis by comparing bilinguals who demonstrated strong language control to bilinguals who demonstrated weak control over cross-language interference. They measured language control during a language switching task, in which inadvertently naming pictures in the wrong language was taken to reflect susceptibility to cross-language interference. Bilinguals with strong language control outperformed the other group on a range of tasks designed to measure aspects of non-language cognitive control, including inhibition and monitoring (Festman et al., 2010). In addition to being better at these tasks, bilinguals with strong language control also exhibited a smaller *error related negativity* (ERN), an ERP component linked to monitoring and response conflict (Festman & Münte, 2012). The authors suggested that bilinguals with stronger cognitive control are more efficient at monitoring, discriminating between relevant and irrelevant information (conflict resolution), and inhibiting interference (Festman, 2012). Therefore, they experience a smaller degree of conflict and exhibit a smaller ERN. Better cognitive control abilities translate to more efficient inhibition of cross-language interference. In line with this hypothesis, individuals with worse inhibitory control scores report more unintentional switching in daily life (Rodriguez-Fornells, Krämer, Lorenzo-Seva, Festman, & Münte, 2012). These studies show a strong correlation between language control and non-language cognitive control.

Likewise, there is some evidence that cognitive control used during task switching translates to language switching ability. Bilinguals who are efficient at switching between non-language tasks are also efficient at switching between languages (Prior & Gollan, 2011). In addition, bilinguals who exhibit greater inhibitory ability on non-language tasks also efficiently inhibit their stronger language during language switching (cf. de Bruin et al., 2014; Linck, Schwieter, & Sunderman, 2012). They also show more activation during language switching in brain areas associated with general inhibitory control (de Bruin et al., 2014). However, before we conclude that language switching relies completely on general cognitive control networks, we must consider that the behavioral performance is not always correlated between language and non-language tasks (Calabria, Hernández, Branzi, & Costa, 2012; Klecha, 2013). Researchers more frequently conclude that language control relies on a network that is largely overlapping with general cognitive control networks, but there are some components that are specific to language and others that are specific for each aspect of cognition (e.g., inhibition vs. attention).

In summary, language control appears to rely in part on a general cognitive control system, with recruitment of additional language-specific control areas. There is some evidence that bilinguals with enhanced control abilities are better able to suppress cross-language interference and, in some cases, are better able to inhibit the active language to switch into the other language.

It is important to realize that much of this work is correlational. Although there is evidence that some aspects of cognitive control are mediated by genetic factors (Cirulli et al., 2010), we do not know if cognitive control enhances language control or if practice using language control in turn improves cognitive control. However, as early life bilingualism is generally determined by environmental factors rather than self-selection, we can compare monolinguals and bilinguals to see how using language control shapes cognitive control networks.

Bilingualism Affects Cognitive Control

Recall from the introduction of this chapter, practice of a skill often causes neural changes. Just like practice of any other skill, we would expect bilingual language use to shape the brain. In particular, we have seen that bilingual brains differ from those of monolinguals mainly in the use of cognitive control mechanisms needed to stay and switch between languages. Bilinguals also need to attend to linguistic cues, monitor and detect language conflict, and resolve this conflict. We might expect to find differences between bilinguals and monolinguals in some or all of these aspects of cognitive control.

Indeed, an overwhelming number of studies have shown that bilingualism yields advantages in various aspects of cognitive control. Bilinguals have demonstrated advantages over monolinguals in inhibition (Martin-Rhee & Bialystok, 2008), goal-maintenance (Colzato et al., 2008), switching (Prior & MacWhinney, 2009), conflict monitoring (Costa, Hernández, Costa-Faidella, & Sebastián-Gallés, 2009), attention and conflict resolution (Carlson & Meltzoff, 2008; Costa, Hernandez, & Sebastián-Gallés, 2008), and managing distracting information (see Bialystok, Craik, Green, & Gollan, 2009, for a review).

Interestingly, the bilingual cognitive advantages are most apparent in childhood when cognitive control networks are still developing, and in older age, when they have started to degrade (Bialystok, Craik, Klein, & Viswanathan, 2004; Bialystok, Martin, & Viswanathan, 2005). A particularly relevant finding is that bilingualism delays the onset of neurodegenerative symptoms by up to 4–5 years (Bialystok, Craik, & Freedman, 2007; Craik, Bialystok, & Freedman, 2010). A comparison of bilinguals and monolinguals with equivalent Alzheimer's disease symptoms revealed greater brain atrophy in bilinguals than monolinguals (Schweizer, Ware, Fischer, Craik, & Bialystok, 2012). This suggests that lifelong bilingual language control alters cognitive control patterns in a way that allows older bilinguals to compensate for age-related cognitive decline (Craik & Bialystok, 2006; Craik et al., 2010). In fact, elderly bilinguals have different neural patterns than monolinguals when they demonstrate equivalent or better performance on interference suppression (Ansaldo, Ghazi-Saidi, & Adrover-Roig, submitted; Ghazi-Saidi, Roig, & Ansaldo, 2013) and switching tasks (Gold, Kim, Johnson, Kryscio, & Smith, 2013). Their brain patterns are more indicative of normal young adults. For instance, they do not demonstrate the typical shifts in activation patterns (Ghazi-Saidi et al., 2013) and loss of efficiency associated with normal cognitive aging (Gold et al., 2013). Finally, white matter and functional connectivity of language control networks are preserved in older bilinguals compared to monolinguals (Luk, Bialystok, Craik, & Grady, 2011). These exciting findings have generated interest in bilingual advantages and instigated a number of studies in this area.

While many of these studies have demonstrated that bilingualism enhances cognitive control, we do not always observe bilingual advantages (e.g., Costa et al., 2009; Hernández, Martin, Barceló, & Costa, 2013; Hilchey & Klein, 2011; Kousaie & Phillips, 2012). One interpretation is that we only observe advantages when cognitive control systems are highly taxed (e.g., during a difficult task; Bialystok, 2006) or not performing at their peak (e.g., in elderly adults; Bialystok, Martin et al., 2005). Another possibility is that the different tasks used across studies capture different aspects of cognitive control (see Paap & Greenberg, 2013, for one example of uncorrelated task effects in the same population; see also Paap, this volume). Both of these explanations are probable causes of somewhat inconsistent results.

Another strong possibility, and one that is relevant to the influence of bilingualism on the brain, is that the bilingual advantages that will be conferred over time are specific to ways in which bilinguals use their languages (Blackburn, 2013; Green, 2011; Green & Abutalebi, 2013). Not all bilinguals use their languages the same way or even use both languages regularly. Would we expect bilinguals to exhibit benefits in task switching if they use one language all year and only use the other during vacations? This is, of course, an extreme example, as most studies screen participants to ensure that they do, in fact, use both of their languages in a way that is relevant to the study. But we must consider whether the way in which bilinguals use their languages differentially taps into the various aspects of cognitive control.

Cognitive Advantages and Language Usage

We see evidence of cognitive specialization based on language use in *bimodal bilinguals* who produce language in both a spoken and *signed modality* (e.g., English speakers of *American Sign Language*). Bimodal bilinguals demonstrate advantages in aspects of cognition that are specific to Sign Language, but lack advantages specific to speaking two languages in the same modality (i.e., unimodal bilingualism). For instance, bimodal bilinguals are advantaged in spatial working memory, mental imagery, and face processing—aspects of general cognition that are essential to Sign Language (see Emmorey, 2002, for a review). On the other hand, because bimodal bilinguals can simultaneously produce words in both languages, they have less need to inhibit language interference than *unimodal bilinguals* (e.g., Spanish–English bilinguals). As a result, bimodal bilinguals show no advantage over monolinguals in tasks that measure interference suppression (Emmorey, Luk, Pyers, & Bialystok, 2008) and do not exhibit the increase in DLPFC activation that is associated with this aspect of cognitive control and typically observed in a mixed-language context (Kovelman et al., 2009).

Likewise, the type of advantages we observe in unimodal bilinguals are specific to the aspects of cognition used in unimodal language control. Bilinguals are not advantaged on all aspects of cognitive control, or even all types of inhibition. For instance, cognitive scientists make a distinction between interference suppression (i.e., inhibition of competitors to select one response), and response inhibition (i.e., inhibition of a habitual response in the absence of competitors; Barkley, 1997; Nigg, 2000). The non-language go/nogo task and *stop-signal task* are often used to measure response inhibition because both tasks require participants to inhibit a "go" response (Bunge, Dudukovic, Thomason,

Vaidya, & Gabrieli, 2002). In the former, participants must withhold a response when a "nogo" stimulus is given; in the latter, they are given a signal to stop a response that is already being planned. Interference suppression can be measured on a *Simon* or *flanker task*, in which participants must respond to one of two competing cues and inhibit the other (Bunge, Hazeltine, Scanlon, Rosen, & Gabrieli, 2002; Eriksen & Eriksen, 1974; Simon & Rudell, 1967). Interference suppression can also be measured using variants of the go/nogo task that include conflict, as was the case with the lexical decision tasks mentioned above (Rodriguez-Fornells et al., 2005; Van Heuven et al., 2008). The experimenters introduced interference by incorporating stimuli that evoked two different responses based on the bilinguals' two languages.

The studies described above showed that bilinguals employ interference suppression to inhibit interference from one language to stay in the other (e.g., Rodriguez-Fornells et al., 2005). They do not, however, differ from monolinguals in how often they use response inhibition. For example, they do not stop themselves from speaking altogether any more often than monolinguals do. If these different aspects of cognitive control involve special-ized *neural networks* and bilingual language use selectively engages an interference sup-pression network, we would expect a bilingual advantage specifically on tasks that measure interference suppression. We would also expect bilingualism to modify the neural corre-lates of interference suppression, but not response inhibition. Comparisons of bilinguals and monolinguals on the Simon/flanker and stop-signal/go-nogo tasks have revealed that bilinguals are specifically advantaged at interference suppression, but not simple response inhibition (Colzato et al., 2008; de Bruin et al., 2014; Martin-Rhee & Bialystok, 2008). More efficient interference suppression in bilinguals was associated with a widely distrib-uted network that included the left superior and inferior frontal cortices, the left cingulate, and the right superior and middle temporal regions—regions implicated in language and in Abutalebi and Green's *language control model* (Bialystok, Craik et al., 2005). In contrast, efficient interference suppression in monolinguals was associated with activity only in the middle frontal region. A subsequent study showed that bilinguals activate a more distrib-uted frontal, temporal, and subcortical control network during interference suppression than monolinguals, but that the two groups recruit the same network for response inhibi-tion (Luk, Anderson, Craik, Grady, & Bialystok, 2010). Together, these results suggest that bilingualism specifically modifies the general cognitive control networks engaged during language control.

An extension of this conclusion is that bilinguals who regularly engage certain control networks will specifically modify those networks. Some bilinguals actively refrain from switching between languages within a conversation, thus effectively suppressing cross-language interference on a daily basis. We can contrast these bilingual "*non-switchers*" with bilingual "*switchers*" who freely code-switch when speaking with other bilinguals. The inhibitory N2 ERP response for these non-switchers is different from that of both monolinguals and bilingual switchers, but only on tasks that require interference suppres-sion (Blackburn, 2013; but see Moreno, Wodniekca, Tays, Alain, & Bialystok, 2013, for bilingual N2 effects on a go/nogo task). Like in the studies above, the neural signature of response inhibition is unchanged in all three groups (Blackburn, 2013). Given the poten-tial sources of the N2 in the DLPFC and ACC, the increased N2 amplitude during interfer-ence suppression is consistent with the bilingual pattern of increased activation reported in the aforementioned fMRI study. Similarly, switchers show an advantage over non-switchers that is specific to task switching (Prior & Gollan, 2011) and the ability to per-form two tasks within a mixed block (Soveri, Rodriguez-Fornells, & Laine, 2011). This suggests that using languages in different ways relies on different aspects of cognitive control. Bilingualism selectively modifies the neural circuitry for the aspects of control used by each bilingual.

Effects of Bilingualism on Neural Structure and Function

We have seen that how bilinguals apply cognitive control to language modifies different aspects of shared control systems. One important point is that the language and general cognitive control systems are highly interconnected and, at least in early bilinguals, develop simultaneously. Because of this strong connectivity between systems, not only do bilinguals use cognitive control mechanisms to manage their languages, but they sometimes recruit language control mechanisms to improve general cognitive control. For example, during non-language switching, bilinguals use language control areas, including the left IFG and striatum (i.e., location of the caudate), more than monolinguals (Garbin et al., 2010; Rodríguez-Pujadas et al., 2013). This additional recruitment of language control areas is associated with better task switching performance in bilinguals (Garbin et al., 2010). This may be one way bilinguals are able to compensate for age-related neural decay in cognitive control systems—by using language systems to compensate for degradation of cognitive networks.

One of the most amazing findings is that bilingualism impacts not only the functional organization of the language and cognitive systems, but also changes the very structure of the brain. For instance, we have recently learned that language networks are more connected by white matter tracts in bilinguals than monolinguals (García-Pentón, Pérez Fernández, Iturria-Medina, Gillon-Dowens, & Carreiras, 2014; Pliatsikas, Moschopoulou & Saddy, 2015). These structural adjustments often are accompanied by behavioral or functional changes (Cummine & Boliek, 2013). We mentioned above that the white matter tracts of the language network, which typically degrade with age, maintain greater integrity in older bilinguals than monolinguals. This structural effect of bilingualism is accompanied by greater functional connectivity between the left IFG and more posterior regions of the language network (Luk et al., 2011). Structural brain scans have also revealed more gray matter in the left IPC of bilinguals than monolinguals (Mechelli et al., 2004), a region which becomes more dense with vocabulary growth (Lee et al., 2007) and is part of Abutalebi and Green's language control model (Abutalebi & Green, 2007). Like many effects of bilingualism on the language system, this effect is modulated by individual differences in proficiency and age of second language acquisition.

Bilingualism also incurs structural and functional changes in early sensory processing networks. *Heschl's gyrus*, the primary auditory area, is larger and has larger gray and white matter volumes in early, highly proficient bilinguals than in monolinguals (Ressel et al., 2012). This may be related to functional changes in selective attention and encoding during listening. Compared to monolinguals, bilinguals are better able to selectively attend to and encode a sound embedded in multi-talker babble. Specifically, bilinguals have enhanced subcortical processing of sound features related to grouping auditory objects and pitch perception, which the authors suggest is a result of more experience with novel or challenging sounds (Krizman, Marian, Shook, Skoe, & Kraus, 2012). ERP studies have also indicated that bilinguals may have increased selective attention during early stages of processing (Massa, Kopke, & El Yagoubi, 2013; Moreno et al., 2013). Thus bilingualism alters auditory sensory regions during development and also improves selective attention during listening, possibly by increasing the amount of top-down control to auditory sensory regions.

Bilingualism also incurs structural changes and functional reorganization in the general cognitive control networks. Recall that the ACC and caudate often increase in activation during language switching. A group of bilinguals showing this functional effect in the caudate also had greater gray matter density in the left caudate than monolinguals, and these structural and functional effects were correlated (Zou et al., 2012). Structural effects of bilingualism are also correlated with functional effects in the ACC and behavior. Gray matter density in the ACC is correlated with both the ability to manage conflict and the functional efficiency of the ACC during a non-language conflict task (Abutalebi et al., 2011). Importantly, bilinguals showed less activation in the ACC while outperforming monolinguals on the flanker task, demonstrating more efficient resolution of conflict as a result of bilingualism. Finally, gray matter in the left putamen, a region in the basal ganglia that is involved in articulation, is also denser in multilinguals than monolinguals, but increased activation in this region is only found for their non-native language when they are not highly proficient in that language (Abutalebi et al., 2013). A major focus in bilingual language organization is how these factors influence representation and access to a bilingual's two languages. We will return to this topic at the end of the chapter.

Potential Mechanisms of Bilingual Cognitive Advantages

We can conclude that bilingualism confers cognitive advantages, in part, by strengthening the functional and structural connectivity across widely distributed networks (cf. Paap, this volume). But how exactly does greater connectivity enhance cognitive control? It was previously mentioned that bilinguals rely on language control areas, such as the left caudate in the striatum of the basal ganglia, to switch between tasks, even when the tasks do not involve language (Garbin et al., 2010; Rodríguez-Pujadas et al., 2013). Based on the role of the basal ganglia in switching and skill acquisition (Knowlton, Mangels, & Squire, 1996), Stocco, Lebiere, and Anderson (2010) proposed the *conditional routing model*. According to this model, bilingualism improves cognitive control by "training" the *fronto-striatal control* circuits. The basal ganglia receive a large number of cortical inputs and are thought to act as a "gate" that selects inputs of interest to send back to the prefrontal cortex. In the absence of the basal ganglia, the strongest cortical inputs, such as those from the language currently in use or the more frequently used language, would "win." The basal ganglia serve to override the strongest existing connections by prioritizing relevant inputs, such as new goals and rules during task switching. The prioritized inputs that pass through the "gate" now are more likely to "win." The basal ganglia accomplish prioritization through a set of *IF/THEN rules* (e.g., IF English, THEN pluralize by adding an "s").

Bilingualism trains the system by the engaging the fronto-striatal networks to select appropriate rules for each language and switch between them. Stocco and colleagues propose this practice increases the ability of the basal ganglia to override existing cortical connections and flexibly modify behavior (Stocco, Yamasaki, Natalenko, & Prat, 2014). This model is in line with existing theories that certain bilingual advantages are conferred by practice managing two languages (e.g., Bialystok et al., 2004; Green, 1998). It has also been supported by studies showing that bilinguals are faster than monolinguals to learn novel rules (i.e., flexibly adapt behavior; Stocco & Prat, 2014). Because bilingualism and dopamine deficiencies have opposing effects on electrophysiological correlates of cognitive control, it has been proposed that bilingualism strengthens this system via a dopaminergic pathway (Blackburn, 2013). It is important to keep in mind, however, that there are multiple bilingual advantages. While some advantages can be explained by this model, others, such as bimodal bilinguals' advantage in spatial processing, are better explained by other mechanisms.

In summary, language control and general cognitive control rely on shared networks, but aspects of these networks are specific to language or the aspect of cognitive control engaged by the task. Because they share neural resources, cognitive control ability is often correlated with the ability to control languages, either by inhibiting interference to stay in one language or by switching between them. By using general cognitive control networks to manage languages, bilinguals are thought to strengthen the functional and structural connectivity between networks. This leads to advantages in aspects of non-language cognitive control that overlap with language. For instance, bilinguals most often show advantages in the ability to inhibit interference and switch between tasks. The types of advantages each bilingual will experience would depend on how they use their languages. The advantages are also most observable during periods of life when cognitive control is underdeveloped or declining with age.

Factors Affecting the Bilingual Brain

It is important to realize that individual differences in bilinguals influence the organization of the bilingual brain. An entire literature is focused on factors that affect bilingual language organization, but we will only touch on the major points here. The three major factors known to affect bilingual language systems are behavioral ecology, proficiency, and AOA.

Behavioral ecology refers to the way in which bilinguals use their languages within their community (Green, 2011). According to the adaptive control hypothesis, cognitive control demands differ based on the bilingual environment (Green & Abutalebi, 2013). This hypothesis predicts that spending time in a non-switching environment will compel bilinguals to use their languages competitively and strengthen general interference suppression abilities. On the other hand, it is more acceptable to speak in either language in code-switching communities. Bilinguals spending time in code-switching environments will have less need to inhibit interference. These bilinguals may use languages in a more cooperative manner that will not strengthen cognitive control networks related to inhibition. The adaptive control hypothesis is supported by a series of studies showing that bilinguals who very frequently code-switch exhibit reduced indices of inhibition on a number of tasks, even including switching (Blackburn, 2013; Hwozdek et al., 2014).

An entire sub-field is dedicated to the effects of AOA and proficiency. Briefly, to understand how AOA affects language and cognition, it is important to realize that the brain is a dynamic system in which every experience influences the state of the brain for the next experience. Cognitive control networks do not fully mature until young adulthood (Gogtay et al., 2004; Sowell et al., 2004). Therefore, learning a second language early in life will shape the still-developing control networks more than learning a second language later in life. We see evidence of this in early bilinguals who use language control systems for non-language switching (Garbin et al., 2010; Rodríguez-Pujadas et al., 2013). Early bilinguals likely develop language control in tandem with cognitive control (or even earlier), leading cognitive control functions to utilize networks that are already in place for language. In contrast, monolinguals develop cognitive control without having developed language control networks to the same degree as bilinguals. Therefore, language networks are less involved in the general cognitive control of monolinguals (Garbin et al., 2010). By the same token, learning a new skill, such as bilingualism, will map onto existing brain networks (Green, 2003). Learning a second language later in life will allow the use of existing cognitive control resources. This will affect both the neurostructural changes necessary to accommodate the new language

(Berken, Gracco, Chen, & Klein, 2015) and the way the new language is learned (e.g., explicitly) and accessed (see Hernandez, 2013, for an extensive discussion on the neural impact of AOA).

Finally, large effects in the bilingual brain have been attributed to *proficiency*, the linguistic competence and fluency in each language. The most commonly observed neural effect of language proficiency is that compared to the stronger language, using the weaker language increases activation in language control networks and recruits additional cognitive control resources (see Abutalebi, 2008, for a review). Three reasons for this neural increase have been proposed. First, driving language areas more may compensate for lower efficiency in the weaker language (Indefrey, 2006). Second, because the weaker language is generally less practiced, neural organization for this system may be less efficient and require more neurons to perform tasks (Indefrey, 2006). Third, the increased activation in general control areas may reflect the need to inhibit the stronger language in order to access the weaker language (Abutalebi, 2008). If increased activation reflects the need for more controlled processing of the weaker language, we would expect neural differences between languages to decrease with increases in proficiency (Green, 2003). Indeed, highly proficient bilinguals activate the same brain regions for both languages (e.g., Chee, Tan, & Thiel, 1999; Ding et al., 2003; Perani & Abutalebi, 2005).

This is a brief introduction into the rich literature investigating the effects of AOA and proficiency on bilingual language organization. The impact of behavioral ecology is a newly emerging area that is gaining momentum. We have discussed each of these factors independently. However, it is important to realize that because the brain is a dynamic system, these factors interact with each other and with cognitive control more generally.

Summary and Conclusion

We have seen in this chapter how bilingualism shapes the brain. Bilingualism is a complex skill that requires the brain to select between competing languages, inhibit interference from the language not in use, and switch between them. Neural systems compensate for the additional demands of bilingualism by driving the language system more and recruiting additional brain regions. These additional recruited regions are part of a multifaceted general cognitive control system. The cognitive control system is composed of cortical-subcortical loops which serve to guide behavior toward a goal while managing interference and competition. The major players in this system include cortical regions in the prefrontal cortex, ACC, and IPC, and the subcortical basal ganglia. The control network employed for language and non-language tasks is largely overlapping, but some components are specific to different aspects of cognitive control or to language.

The way that bilinguals use language taps into different aspects of the cognitive control system. When bilinguals are using one language at a time, the left IFG plays a major role in suppressing interference from the other language. The ACC and areas involved in motor planning (the caudate and pre-SMA/SMA) are recruited during language switching and in situations with language conflict at the response level. Even being in a context where either language might be needed increases language conflict and activates cognitive control areas in the prefrontal cortex, ACC, and pre-SMA. This substantiates the adaptive control hypothesis—that the language context influences how much or what aspect of control is needed.

Using these control networks for language strengthens them, perhaps by training fronto-striatal loops to flexibly control behavior. As a result of this strengthening during language use, advantages are conferred to non-language tasks that rely on overlapping control circuits. In some cases, these advantages help bilinguals compensate for degradation of cognitive systems that occur with aging. The advantages conferred appear to be specific to the networks used. During interference suppression, bilinguals recruit more cognitive control areas and show behavioral advantages over monolinguals. However, they do not differ from monolinguals on aspects of inhibition that are not used to manage language.

The way bilinguals use language, proficiency, and age of second language acquisition impacts how the language system is controlled. Importantly, bilingualism appears to selectively modify the neural circuitry for aspects of control used by each bilingual. For instance, bimodal bilinguals are advantaged at face processing, language switchers are advantaged at task switching, and non-switchers have a different neural signature of interference suppression than other bilinguals. Bilinguals with low proficiency in one language recruit more neural resources to use that language. Bilinguals who learned both languages early in life employ language control regions during non-language tasks, presumably because these systems developed simultaneously. The interactions of language and control and the ways that bilingualism modifies the brain depend on the experience of each bilingual.

Finally, bilingualism alters not only brain function, but also structure. Bilingual language networks are more connected by white matter than those of monolinguals, and these white matter tracts are more resistant to age-related degradation. There is also more gray matter in regions of the brain implicated in language and cognitive control, including the IPC, the ACC, and the caudate.

In summary, like any other skill, bilingualism shapes the brain. Because bilingualism is a highly practiced skill that incorporates multiple cognitive systems, its impact on the brain is substantial. In this chapter, we have discussed the impact of bilingualism on the language and cognitive control networks. We have seen that bilingual language use strengthens general cognitive control networks, yielding behavioral advantages in cognitive control and changes to the neural system.

List of Key Words and Concepts

Adaptive control hypothesis, Age of acquisition (AOA), American Sign Language, Anterior cingulate cortex (ACC), Backwards inhibition, Bilingual digit naming task, Bimodal bilinguals, Code-switching, Cognitive control, Cognitive control networks, Conditional routing model, Conflict monitoring, Cross-language interference, Cross-language priming, Differential negativity (D-Neg), Diffusion tensor imaging (DTI), Dominant language, Dorsolateral prefrontal cortex (DLPFC), Early bilinguals, Error related negativity (ERN), Event-related potentials (ERPs), Executive function, Flanker task, Frontal-subcortical network, Fronto-striatal control, Fronto-temporal network, Go/nogo task, Heschl's gyrus, IF/THEN rules, Inferior frontal gyrus (IFG), Inferior parietal cortex (IPC), Inhibition, Input-to-meaning, Input-to-motor mapping, Interference demands, Interference suppression, Interlingual homographs, Language conflict, Language control model, Language interference, Language mixing, Language switching, Lexical decision task, Lexical-semantic, Local inhibition network, Magnetic resonance imaging (MRI), Magnetoencephalography (MEG), Metalinguistic awareness, Middle temporal gyrus (MTG), Mixed-language block, Mixed-language context, Mixed-language environment, Monitoring, N2 effect, N2 mix effect, N2 switch effect, Neural networks, Neuroimaging, Nogo N2 effect, Non-language inhibition, Non-switchers, Occipital lobe, Picture naming, Positron emission tomography (PET), Prefrontal cortex, Premotor areas, Pre-supplementary motor area (pre-SMA), Response inhibition, Signed modality, Single-language block, Stop-signal task, Superior temporal gyrus (STG), Supplementary motor area (SMA), Suppressing interference,

Suppression, Switchers, Task demands, Task switching, Tip-of-the-tongue (TOT), Top-down, Transcranial magnetic stimulation (TMS), Unimodal bilinguals

Internet Sites Related to the Bilingual Brain

Being Bilingual: http://dana.org/Cerebrum/2012/The_Cognitive_Benefits_of_Being_Bilingual/

Brain Builders: https://www.livescience.com/48721-bilingual-brain-bodybuilders.html

My Bilingual Brain: https://info.moravia.com/blog/bid/250314/My-Bilingual-Brain-is-Bigger-than-your-Monolingual-Brain

The Bilingual Brain: http://www.brainfacts.org/sensing-thinking-behaving/language/articles/2008/the-bilingual-brain/

Discussion Questions

(1) What are the major players in the language control networks? How does Abutalebi and Green's model describe the flow of information in this system?

(2) What is cognitive control? Name at least three aspects of cognitive control that bilinguals use during language production.

(3) How does the way in which we use language affect cognitive control systems? Give specific examples of neural modifications that result from using language in different ways.

(4) How do behavioral ecology, age of language acquisition, and proficiency impact language control?

(5) How does interference suppression differ from response inhibition? What tasks can we use to measure these different types of inhibition?

(6) What brain region is typically recruited when bilinguals use only one language? What additional regions are recruited during language switching?

(7) Why do we think bilinguals exhibit bilingual advantages? How might these advantages be conferred at the neural level?

(8) What are the electrophysiological indices of inhibitory control (found using ERPs)? What types of non-language and language tasks elicit these effects?

(9) What are some bilingual advantages? Name three possibilities for why these advantages are not always observed.

(10) What impact does bilingualism have on the structure and function of the brain?

Suggested Research Projects

(1) Using the image of the brain in Figure 6.1, trace the language pathways involved in three types of language processing: input-to-motor mapping, semantic, and syntactic processing.

(2) Download a picture of the brain from the internet. See if you can trace the cortical-subcortical loops involved in language control.

(3) Go to the International Picture Naming Project Database: http://crl.ucsd.edu/experiments/ipnp/method/getpics/getpics.html. Download the file of pictures that are available for free. Select 20 pictures that a bilingual classmate can name in both of their languages and put them all on the screen at the same time. Time your classmate as they name all of the pictures only in one language. Then have them switch between languages so that they name every other picture in the same language. Which method

of naming was faster? Why? What parts of your classmate's brain were probably more active during switching than when naming in only one language? What part of your classmate's brain was probably more active than a monolingual when they were naming in only one language?

(4) Using the same pictures from the last project, have your bilingual classmate only name pictures in one language. First, have them name pictures at the end of class, in the same language used in the classroom. Try to put them in as much of a single-language context as possible by not speaking their other language(s) at all. Time them while they name all 20 pictures. Then ask them to have a conversation with another bilingual (a classmate or a family member), or be creative to induce a mixed-language context. Time them as they name the pictures again. In which context was naming faster? What parts of your classmate's brain were probably more active during the mixed-language context than during the single-language context?

(5) Using these same pictures, see if you can increase *cross-language interference* while your bilingual classmate names pictures in only one language. To do this, ask another bilingual to name the pictures at the same time as your classmate—first in the same language your classmate is using, then in your classmate's other language. Was your classmate slower to name pictures when the other bilingual was naming them in a different language? How would this increase cross-language interference? What brain regions were most likely active when you increased cross-language interference? What other experimental designs could you use to manipulate cross-language interference? Design a new experiment to observe the effects of cross-language interference.

Suggested Readings

Astheimer, L. B., Berkes, M., & Bialystok, E. (2016). Differential allocation of attention during speech perception in monolingual and bilingual listeners. *Language, Cognition and Neuroscience, 31*(2), 196–205.

Buchweitz, A., & Prat, C. (2013). The bilingual brain: Flexibility and control in the human cortex. *Physics of Life Reviews, 10*(4), 428–443.

Costa, A., & Sebastián-Gallés, N. (2014). How does the bilingual experience sculpt the brain? *Nature Reviews Neuroscience, 15*(5), 336–345.

Ferjan Ramírez, N., Ramírez, R. R., Clarke, M., Taulu, S., & Kuhl, P. K. (2016). Speech discrimination in 11-month-old bilingual and monolingual infants: A magnetoencephalography study. *Developmental Science, 20*(1), 1–16. doi: 10.1111/desc.12427.

Li, L., Abutalebi, J., Zou, L., Yan, X., Liu, L., Feng, X., Guo, T., & Ding, G. (2015). Bilingualism alters brain functional connectivity between "control" regions and "language" regions: Evidence from bimodal bilinguals. *Neuropsychologia, 71*, 236–247.

References

Abutalebi, J. (2008). Neural aspects of second language representation and language control. *Acta Psychologica, 128*(3), 466–478.

Abutalebi, J., Annoni, J.-M., Zimine, I., Pegna, A. J., Seghier, M. L., Lee-Jahnke, H., Lazeyras, F., Cappa, S. F., & Khateb, A. (2008). Language control and lexical competition in bilinguals: An event-related fMRI study. *Cerebral Cortex, 18*, 1496–1505.

Abutalebi, J., Brambati, S. M., Annoni J.-M., Moro A., Cappa, S. F., & Perani, D. (2007). The neural cost of the auditory perception of language switches: An event-related functional magnetic resonance imaging study in bilinguals. *The Journal of Neuroscience, 27*(50), 13762–13769.

Abutalebi, J., Della Rosa, P. A., Gonzaga, A. K. C., Keim, R., Costa, A., & Perani, D. (2013). The role of the left putamen in multilingual language production. *Brain and Language, 125*, 307–315.

Abutalebi, J., Della Rosa, P. A., Green, D. W., Hernandez, M., Scifo, P., Keim, R., Cappa, S. F., & Costa, A. (2011). Bilingualism tunes the anterior cingulate cortex for conflict monitoring. *Cerebral Cortex, 22*, 2076–2086.

Abutalebi, J., & Green, D. W. (2007). Bilingual language production: The neurocognition of language representation and control. *Journal of Neurolinguistics, 20*, 242–275.

Abutalebi, J., & Green, D. W. (2008). Control mechanisms in bilingual language production: Neural evidence from language switching studies. *Language and Cognitive Processes, 23*(4), 557–582.

Adesope, O. O., Lavin, T., Thompson, T., & Ungerleider, C. (2010). A systematic review and meta-analysis of the cognitive correlates of bilingualism. *Review of Educational Research, 82*(2), 207–245.

Allen, M. J., & Yen, W. M. (1979). *Introduction to measurement theory.* Long Grove: Waveland Press.

Ansaldo, A.-I., Ghazi-Saidi, L., & Adrover-Roig, D. (submitted). It is never too late to learn: The neural substrate of interference control in elderly late bilinguals. *Brain and Language.*

Banich, M. T. (2009). Executive function: The search for an integrated account. *Science, 18*(2), 89–94.

Barkley, R. A. (1997). *ADHD and the nature of self-control.* New York: Guilford Press.

Berken, J. A., Gracco, V. L., Chen, J.-K., & Klein, D. (2015). The timing of language learning shapes brain structure associated with articulation. *Brain Structure and Function, 221*(7), 1–10.

Berman, K. F., Ostrem, J. L., Randolph, C., Gold, J., Goldberg, T. E., Coppola, R., Carson, R. E., Herscovitch, P., & Weinberger, D. R. (1995). Physiological activation of a cortical network during performance of the Wisconsin Card Sorting Test: A positron emission tomography study. *Neuropsychologia, 33*(8), 1027–1046.

Bialystok, E. (1988). Levels of bilingualism and levels of linguistic awareness. *Developmental Psychology, 24*, 560–567.

Bialystok, E. (2006). Effect of bilingualism and computer video game experience on the Simon task. *Canadian Journal of Psychology/Revue Canadienne de Psychologie, 60*, 68–79.

Bialystok, E., Craik, F. I., & Freedman, M. (2007). Bilingualism as a protection against the onset of symptoms of dementia. *Neuropsychologia, 45*, 459–464.

Bialystok, E., Craik, F. I., Grady, C., Chau, W., Ishii, Y., Gunji, A., & Pantev, C. (2005). Effect of bilingualism on cognitive control in the Simon task: Evidence from MEG. *NeuroImage, 24*, 40–49.

Bialystok, E., Craik, F. I., Green, D. W., & Gollan, T. H. (2009). Bilingual minds. *Psychological Science Public Interest, 10*, 89–129.

Bialystok, E., Craik, F. I., Klein, R., & Viswanathan, M. (2004). Bilingualism, aging, and cognitive control: Evidence from the Simon task. *Psychology and Aging, 19*(2), 290–303.

Bialystok, E., Craik, F. I., & Luk, G. (2008). Cognitive control and lexical access in younger and older bilinguals. *Journal of Experimental Psychology: Learning, Memory, and Cognition, 34*(4), 859–873.

Bialystok, E., Luk, G., Peets, K. F., & Yang, S. (2010). Receptive vocabulary differences in monolingual and bilingual children. *Bilingualism: Language and Cognition, 13*, 525–531.

Bialystok, E., Martin, M. M., & Viswanathan, M. (2005). Bilingualism across the lifespan: The rise and fall of inhibitory control. *International Journal of Bilingualism, 9*, 103–119.

Blackburn, A. M. (2013). *A study of the relationship between code switching and the bilingual advantage: Evidence that language use modulates neural indices of language processing and cognitive control* (Doctoral dissertation). University of Texas at San Antonio, San Antonio.

Blackburn, A. M. (2016). MRI methods in bilingual reading comprehension. In R. R. Heredia, J. Altarriba, & A. B. Cieślicka (Eds.), *Methods in bilingual reading comprehension research* (pp. 313–352). New York: Springer.

Blackburn, A. M., & Hwozdek, C. (2016). Language Control Model. Retrieved from https://openclipart.org/detail/254917/language-control-model

Botvinick, M. M., Nystrom, L. E., Fissell, K., Carter, C. S., & Cohen, J. D. (1999). Conflict monitoring versus selection-for-action in anterior cingulate cortex. *Nature, 402*, 179–181.

Bunge, S. A., Dudukovic, N. M., Thomason, M. E., Vaidya, C. J., & Gabrieli, J. D. E. (2002). Immature frontal lobe contributions to cognitive control in children: Evidence from fMRI. *Neuron, 33*(2), 301–311.

Bunge, S. A., Hazeltine, E., Scanlon, M. D., Rosen, A. C., & Gabrieli, J. D. E. (2002). Dissociable contributions of prefrontal and parietal cortices to response selection. *NeuroImage, 17*, 1562–1571.

Bunge, S. A., Ochsner, K. N., Desmond, J. E., Glover, G. H., & Gabrieli, J. D. E. (2001). Prefrontal regions involved in keeping information in and out of mind. *Brain, 124*, 2074–2086.

Bush, G., Luu, P., & Posner, M. I. (2000). Cognitive and emotional influences in anterior cingulate cortex. *Trends in Cognitive Sciences, 4*, 215–222.

Calabria, M., Hernández, M., Branzi, F. M., & Costa, A. (2012). Qualitative differences between bilingual language control and executive control: Evidence from task-switching. *Frontiers in Psychology, 2*, 1–10.

Carlson, S. M., & Meltzoff, A. N. (2008). Bilingual experience and executive functioning in young children. *Developmental Science, 11*(2), 282–298.

Chauncey, K., Holcomb, P. J., & Grainger, J. (2009). Primed picture naming within and across languages: An ERP investigation. *Cognitive, Affective, & Behavioral Neuroscience, 9*, 286–303.

Chee, M. W. L., Tan, E. W. L., & Thiel, T. (1999). Mandarin and English single word processing studied with functional magnetic resonance imaging. *Journal of Neuroscience, 19*(8), 3050–3056.

Christoffels, I. K., Firk, C., & Schiller, N. O. (2007). Bilingual language control: An event-related brain potential study. *Brain Research, 1147*, 192–208.

Cirulli, E. T., Kasperaviciute, D., Attix, D. K., Need, A. C., Ge, D., Gibson, G., & Goldstein, D. B. (2010). Common genetic variation and performance on standardized cognitive tests. *European Journal of Human Genetics, 18*(7), 815–820.

Colzato, L. S., Bajo, M. T., van den Wildenberg, W., Paolieri, D., Nieuwenhuis, S., La Heij, W., & Hommel, B. (2008). How does bilingualism improve executive control? A comparison of active and reactive inhibition mechanisms. *Journal of Experimental Psychology: Learning, Memory, and Cognition, 34*(2), 302–312.

Costa, A. (2005). Lexical access in bilingual production. In J. F. Kroll & A. M. B. de Groot (Eds.), *Handbook of bilingualism: Psycholinguistic approaches* (pp. 308–325). New York: Oxford University Press.

Costa, A., Hernández, M., Costa-Faidella, J., & Sebastián-Gallés, N. (2009). On the bilingual advantage in conflict processing: Now you see it, now you don't. *Cognition, 113*, 135–149.

Costa, A., Hernandez, M., & Sebastián-Gallés, N. (2008). Bilingualism aids conflict resolution: Evidence from the ANT task. *Cognition, 106*, 59–86.

Craik, F. I., & Bialystok, E. (2006). Planning and task management in older adults: Cooking breakfast. *Memory & Cognition, 34*, 1236–1249.

Craik, F. I., Bialystok, E., & Freedman, M. (2010). Delaying the onset of Alzheimer disease: Bilingualism as a form of cognitive reserve. *Neurology, 75*, 1726–1729.

Crinion, J., Turner, R., Grogan, A., Hanakawa, T., Noppeney, U., Devlin, J. T., Aso, T., Urayama, S., Fukuyama, H., Stockton, K., Usui, K., Green, D. W., & Price, C. J. (2006). Language control in the bilingual brain. *Science, 312*, 1537–1540.

Cummine, J., & Boliek, C. A. (2013). Understanding white matter integrity stability for bilinguals on language status and reading performance. *Brain Structure and Function, 218*(2), 595–601.

de Bruin, A., Roelofs, A., Dijkstra, T., & FitzPatrick, I. (2014). Domain-general inhibition areas of the brain are involved in language switching: FMRI evidence from trilingual speakers. *NeuroImage, 90*, 348–359.

de Groot, A. M. B., & Christoffels, I. K. (2006). Language control in bilinguals: Monolingual tasks and simultaneous interpreting. *Bilingualism: Language and Cognition, 9*(2), 189–201.

Ding, G., Perry, C., Peng, D., Ma, L., Li, D., Xu, S., Luo, Q., Xu, D., & Yang, J. (2003). Neural mechanisms underlying semantic and orthographic processing in Chinese-English bilinguals. *NeuroReport, 14*(12), 1557–1562.

Elston-Güttler, K. E., Gunter, T. C., & Kotz, S. A. (2005). Zooming into L2: global language context and adjustment affect processing of interlingual homographs in sentences. *Cognitive Brain Research, 25*, 57–70.

Emmorey, K. (2002). *Language, cognition, and the brain: Insights from sign language research.* Mahwah, NJ: Erlbaum.

Emmorey, K., Luk, G., Pyers, J. E., & Bialystok, E. (2008). The source of enhanced cognitive control in bilinguals. *Psychological Science, 19*(12), 1201–1206.

Eriksen, B. A., & Eriksen, C. W. (1974). Effects of noise letters upon the identification of a target letter in a nonsearch task. *Perception & Psychophysics, 16,* 143–149.

Festman, J. (2012). Language control abilities of late bilinguals. *Bilingualism: Language and Cognition, 15*(3), 580–593.

Festman, J., & Münte, T. F. (2012). Cognitive control in Russian-German bilinguals. *Frontiers in Psychology, 3,* 1–7.

Festman, J., Rodriguez-Fornells, A., & Münte, T. F. (2010). Individual differences in control of language interference in late bilinguals are mainly related to general executive abilities. *Behavioral and Brain Functions, 6*(5), 1–12. doi: https://doi.org/10.1186/1744-9081-6-5.

Friederici, A. D. (2009). Pathways to language: Fiber tracts in the human brain. *Trends in Cognitive Sciences, 13*(4), 175–181.

Friederici, A. D. (2012). The cortical language circuit: From auditory perception to sentence comprehension. *Trends in Cognitive Sciences, 16*(5), 262–268.

Friederici, A. D., & Gierhan, S. M. E. (2013). The language network. *Current Opinion in Neurobiology, 23,* 250–254.

Friedman, N. P., & Miyake, A. (2004). The relations among inhibition and interference control functions: A latent-variable analysis. *Journal of Experimental Psychology, 133*(1), 101–135.

Garbin, G., Costa, A., Sanjuan, A., Forn, C., Rodríguez-Pujadas, A., Ventura, N., Belloch, V., Hernandez, M., & Ávila, C. (2011). Neural basis of language switching in high and early proficient bilinguals. *Brain and Language, 119,* 129–135.

Garbin, G., Sanjuan, A., Forn, C., Bustamante, J. C., Rodríguez-Pujadas, A., Belloch, V., Hernandez, M., Costa, A., & Ávila, C. (2010). Bridging language and attention: Brain basis of the impact of bilingualism on cognitive control. *NeuroImage, 53*(4), 1272–1278.

García-Pentón, L., Pérez Fernández, A., Iturria-Medina, Y., Gillon-Dowens, M., & Carreiras, M. (2014). Anatomical connectivity changes in the bilingual brain. *NeuroImage, 84,* 495–504.

Ghazi-Saidi, L., Roig, D. A., & Ansaldo, A.-I. (2013). *E3 it is never too late: The neural substrate of interference control in elderly late bilinguals.* Paper presented at the Neurobiology of Language, San Diego, CA.

Gogtay, N., Giedd, J. N., Lusk, L., Hayashi, K. M., Greenstein, D., Vaituzis, A. C., Nugent, 3rd, T. F., Herman, D. H., Clasen, L. S., Toga, A. W., Rapoport, J. L., & Thompson, P. M. (2004). Dynamic mapping of human cortical development during childhood through early adulthood. In *Proceedings of the National Academy of Sciences of the United States of America, 101*(21), 8174–8179.

Gold, B. T., & Buckner, R. L. (2002). Common prefrontal regions coactivate with dissociable posterior regions during controlled semantic and phonological tasks. *Neuron, 35*(4), 803–812.

Gold, B. T., Kim, C., Johnson, N. F., Kryscio, R. J., & Smith, C. D. (2013). Lifelong bilingualism maintains neural efficiency for cognitive control in aging. *The Journal of Neuroscience, 33*(2), 387–396.

Gollan, T. H., Montoya, R. I., Fennema-Notestine, C., & Morris, S. K. (2005). Bilingualism affects picture naming but not picture classification. *Memory & Cognition, 33*(7), 1220–1234.

Gollan, T. H., Montoya, R. I., & Werner, G. A. (2002). Semantic and letter fluency in Spanish–English bilinguals. *Neuropsychology, 16*(4), 562–576.

Gollan, T. H., & Silverberg, N. B. (2001). Tip-of-the-tongue states in Hebrew-English bilinguals. *Bilingualism: Language and Cognition, 4,* 63–83.

Green, D. W. (1998). Mental control of the bilingual lexico-semantic system. *Bilingualism: Language and Cognition, 1,* 67–81.

Green, D. W. (2003). Neural basis of lexicon and grammar in L2 acquisition: The convergence hypothesis. In R. van Hout, A. Hulk, F. Kuiken, & R. Towell (Eds.), *The lexicon-syntax interface in second language acquisition* (pp. 197–218). Amsterdam: John Benjamins.

Green, D. W. (2011). Language control in different contexts: The behavioral ecology of bilingual speakers. *Frontiers in Psychology, 2,* 1–4.

Green, D. W., & Abutalebi, J. (2013). Language control in bilinguals: The adaptive control hypothesis. *Journal of Cognitive Psychology, 25*(5), 515–530.

Grosjean, F. (1982). *Life with two languages: An introduction to bilingualism.* Cambridge: Harvard University Press.

Grosjean, F. (1985). The bilingual as a competent but specific speaker-hearer. *Journal of Multilingual and Multicultural Development, 6,* 467–477.

Guo, T., Misra, M., & Kroll, J. F. (2011). Local and global inhibition in bilingual word production: fMRI evidence from Chinese-English bilinguals. *NeuroImage, 56*(4), 2300–2309.

Hedden, T., & Gabrieli, J. D. E. (2010). Shared and selective neural correlates of inhibition, facilitation, and shifting processes during executive control. *NeuroImage, 51,* 421–431.

Hernandez, A. (2009). Language switching in the bilingual brain: What's next? *Brain and Language, 109,* 133–140.

Hernandez, A. (2013). *The bilingual brain.* New York: Oxford University Press.

Hernandez, A., Dapretto, M., Mazziotta, J., & Bookheimer, S. (2001). Language switching and language representation in Spanish–English bilinguals: An fMRI study. *NeuroImage, 14,* 510–520.

Hernandez, A., Martinez, A., & Kohnert, K. (2000). In search of the language switch: An fMRI study of picture naming in Spanish–English bilinguals. *Brain and Language, 73,* 421–431.

Hernández, M., Martin, C. D., Barceló, F., & Costa, A. (2013). Where is the bilingual advantage in task-switching? *Journal of Memory and Language, 69*(3), 257–276.

Hickok, G., Bellugi, U., & Klima, E. S. (1998). The neural organization of language: evidence from sign language aphasia. *Trends in Cognitive Sciences, 2*(4), 129–136.

Hickok, G., & Poeppel, D. (2007). The cortical organization of speech processing. *Nature Reviews/ Neuroscience, 8,* 393–402.

Hilchey, M. D., & Klein, R. M. (2011). Are there bilingual advantages on nonlinguistic interference tasks? Implications for the plasticity of executive control processes. *Psychonomic Bulletin & Review, 18,* 625–657.

Hwozdek, C., & Blackburn, A. M. (2016). Labeled brain. Retrieved from https://openclipart.org/detail/254918/labeled-brain.

Hwozdek, C., Blackburn, A. M., & Wicha, N. (2014, February 15). *Survey says: Response conflict is easier to resolve with practice from language use.* Paper presented at the 16th Annual Texas National McNair Scholars Research Post-Baccalaureate Conference, Denton, TX.

Indefrey, P. (2006). A meta-analysis of hemodynamic studies on first and second language processing: Which suggested differences can we trust and what do they mean? *Language Learning, 56,* 279–304.

Ivanova, I., & Costa, A. (2008). Does bilingualism hamper lexical access in speech production? *Acta Psychologica, 127*(2), 277–288.

Jackson, G. M., Swainson, R., Cunnington, R., & Jackson, S. R. (2001). ERP correlates of executive control during repeated language switching. *Bilingualism: Language and Cognition, 4*(2), 169–178.

Jamadar, S., Provost, A., Fulham, W. R., Michie, P. T., & Karayanidis, F. (2009). Multiple sources underlie ERP indices of task-switching. In W. Christensen, E. Schier, & J. Sutton (Eds.), *ASCS09: Proceedings of the 9th Conference of the Australasian Society for Cognitive Science* (pp. 154–161). Sydney, Australia: Macquarie Centre for Cognitive Science.

Karayanidis, F., Coltheart, M., Michie, P. T., & Murphy, K. (2003). Electrophysiological correlates of anticipatory and poststimulus components of task switching. *Psychophysiology, 40,* 329–348.

Klecha, A. (2013). Language and task switching in Polish-English bilinguals. *Psychology of Language and Communication, 17*(1), 17–36.

Knowlton, B. J., Mangels, J. A., & Squire, L. R. (1996). A neostriatal habit learning system in humans. *Science, 273,* 1399–1402.

Konishi, S., Nakajim, K., Uchida, I., Kiyo, H., Kameyama, M., & Miyashita, Y. (1999). Common inhibitory mechanism in human inferior prefrontal cortex revealed by event-related functional MRI. *Brain, 122,* 981–991.

Kousaie, S., & Phillips, N. (2012). Conflict monitoring and resolution: Are two languages better than one? Evidence from reaction time and event-related brain potentials. *Brain Research, 1446,* 71–90.

Kovelman, I., Baker, S. A., & Petitto, L.-A. (2008). Bilingual and monlingual brains compared: A functional magnetic resonance imaging investigation of syntactic processing and a possible "neural signature" of bilingualism. *Journal of Cognitive Neuroscience*, *20*(1), 153–169.

Kovelman, I., Shalinsky, M. H., Berens, M. S., & Petitto, L.-A. (2008). Shining new light on the brain's "bilingual signature": A functional near infrared spectroscopy investigation of semantic processing. *NeuroImage*, *39*, 1457–1471.

Kovelman, I., Shalinsky, M. H., White, K. S., Schmitt, S. N., Berens, M. S., Paymer, N., & Petitto, L.-A. (2009). Dual language use in sign-speech bimodal bilinguals: fNIRS brain-imaging evidence. *Brain and Language*, *109*(2–3), 112–123.

Krizman, J., Marian, V., Shook, A., Skoe, E., & Kraus, N. (2012). Subcortical encoding of sound is enhanced in bilinguals and relates to executive function advantages. In *Proceedings of the National Academy of Sciences*, *109*(20), 7877–7881.

Kroll, J. F., Bobb, S. C., Misra, M., & Guo, T. (2008). Language selection in bilingual speech: Evidence for inhibitory processes. *Acta Psychologica*, *128*(3), 416–430.

Kroll, J. F., Bobb, S. C., & Wodniekca, Z. (2006). Language selectivity is the exception, not the rule: Arguments against a fixed locus of language selection in bilingual speech. *Bilingualism: Language and Cognition*, *9*, 119–135.

Lavric, A., Pizzagalli, D. A., & Forstmeier, S. (2004). When "go" and "nogo" are equally frequent: ERP components and cortical tomography. *European Journal of Neuroscience*, *20*, 2483–2488.

Lee, H. L., Devlin, J. T., Shakeshaft, C., Stewart, L. H., Brennan, A., Glensman, J., Pitcher, K., Crinion, J., Mechelli, A., Frackowiak, R. S., Green, D. W., & Price, C. (2007). Anatomical traces of vocabulary acquisition in the adolescent brain. *The Journal of Neuroscience*, *27*(5), 1184–1189.

Lei, M., Akama, H., & Murphy, B. (2014). Neural basis of language switching in the brain: fMRI evidence from Korean–Chinese early bilinguals. *Brain and Language*, *138*, 12–18.

Linck, J. A., Schwieter, J. W., & Sunderman, G. (2012). Inhibitory control predicts language switching performance in trilingual speech production. *Bilingualism: Language and Cognition*, *15*(3), 651–662.

Liu, H., Hu, Z., Guo, T., & Peng, D. (2010). Speaking words in two languages with one brain: Neural overlap and dissociation. *Brain Research*, *1316*, 75–82.

Luk, G., Anderson, J. A. E., Craik, F. I., Grady, C., & Bialystok, E. (2010). Distinct neural correlates for two types of inhibition in bilinguals: Response inhibition versus interference suppression. *Brain and Cognition*, *74*, 347–357.

Luk, G., Bialystok, E., Craik, F. I., & Grady, C. (2011). Lifelong bilingualism maintains white matter integrity in older adults. *The Journal of Neuroscience*, *31*(46), 16808–16813.

Luk, G., Green, D. W., Abutalebi, J., & Grady, C. (2012). Cognitive control for language switching in bilinguals: A quantitative meta-analysis of functional neuroimaging studies. *Language and Cognitive Processes*, *27*(10), 1479–1488.

Ma, H., Hu, J., Xi, J., Shen, W., Ge, J., Geng, F., Wu, Y., Guo, J., & Yao, D. (2014). Bilingual cognitive control in language switching: An fMRI study of English–Chinese late bilinguals. *PLoS ONE*, *9*(9), 1–8.

Marian, V., & Spivey, M. (2003). Competing activation in bilingual language processing: Within- and between-language competition. *Bilingualism: Language and Cognition*, *6*(2), 97–115.

Martin-Rhee, M. M., & Bialystok, E. (2008). The development of two types of inhibitory control in monolingual and bilingual children. *Bilingualism: Language and Cognition*, *11*(1), 81–93.

Massa, E., Kopke, B., & El Yagoubi, R. (2013, May). *Bilingual speaker's executive control enhancement: Event related potentials and behaviourial data during overt picture naming tasks.* Paper presented at the first International Workshop on Bilingualism and Cognitive Control, Jagiellonian University, Krakow, Poland.

Mechelli, A., Crinion, J. T., Noppeney, U., O'Doherty, J., Ashburner, J., Frackowiak, R. S., & Price, C. J. (2004). Neurolinguistics: Structural plasticity in the bilingual brain. *Nature*, *431*(7010), 757–757.

Meschyan, G., & Hernandez, A. (2006). Impact of language proficiency and orthographic transparency on bilingual word reading: An fMRI investigation. *NeuroImage*, *29*, 1135–1140.

Meuter, R. F. I., & Allport, A. (1999). Bilingual language switching in naming: Asymmetrical costs of language selection. *Journal of Memory and Language*, *40*, 25–40.

Miyake, A., Friedman, N. P., Emerson, M. J., Witzki, A. H., Howerter, A., & Wagner, T. D. (2000). The unity and diversity of executive functions and their contributions to complex 'frontal lobe' tasks: A latent variable analysis. *Cognitive Psychology*, *41*(1), 49–100.

Monchi, O., Petrides, M., Petre, V., Worsley, K., & Dagher, A. (2001). Wisconsin card sorting revisited: Distinct neural circuits participating in different stages of the task identified by event-related functional magnetic resonance imaging. *The Journal of Neuroscience*, *21*(19), 7733–7741.

Monsell, S. (2003). Task switching. *Trends in Cognitive Sciences*, *7*(3), 134–140.

Moreno, E., Federmeier, K., & Kutas, M. (2002). Switching languages, switching palabras (words): An electrophysiological study of code switching. *Brain and Language*, *80*, 188–207.

Moreno, S., Wodniecka, Z., Tays, W., Alain, C., & Bialystok, E. (2013). Inhibitory control in bilinguals and musicians: Event related potential (ERP) evidence for experience-specific effects. *PLoS ONE*, *9*(4), 1–8.

Moritz-Gasser, S., & Duffau, H. (2009). Cognitive processes and neural basis of language switching: Proposal of a new model *NeuroReport*, *20*(18), 1577–1658.

Moss, J., Schunn, C. D., Schneider, W., McNamara, D. S., & VanLehn, K. (2010). *An fMRI study of strategic reading comprehension.* Paper presented at the Proceedings of the 32nd Conference of the Cognitive Science Society, Portland, OR.

Nachev, P., Kennard, C., & Husain, M. (2008). Functional role of the supplementary and pre-supplementary motor areas. *Nature Reviews/Neuroscience*, *9*, 856–869.

Nakamura, K., Hara, N., Kouider, S., Takayama, Y., Hanajima, R., Sakai, K. L., & Ugawa, Y. (2006). Task-guided selection of the dual neural pathways for reading. *Neuron*, *52*, 557–564.

Nicholson, R., Karayanidis, F., Poboka, D., Heathcote, A., & Michie, P. T. (2005). Electrophysiological correlates of anticipatory task-switching processes. *Psychophysiology*, *42*, 540–554.

Nieuwenhuis, S., Yeung, N., Van den Wildenberg, W., & Ridderinkhof, K. R. (2003). Electrophysiological correlates of anterior cingulate function in a go/nogo task: Effects of response conflict and trial type frequency. *Cognitive, Affective, & Behavioral Neuroscience*, *3*(1), 17–26.

Nigg, J. T. (2000). On inhibition/disinhibition in developmental psychopathology: Views from cognitive and personality psychology and a working inhibition taxonomy. *Psychological Bulletin*, *126*(2), 220–246.

Oller, D. K., & Eilers, R. E. (Eds.). (2002). *Language and literacy in bilingual children*. Clevedon: Multilingual Matters.

Paap, K. R., & Greenberg, Z. I. (2013). There is no coherent evidence for a bilingual advantage in executive processing. *Cognitive Psychology*, *66*, 232–258.

Parker Jones, O., Green, D. W., Grogan, A., Pliatsikas, C., Filippopolitis, K., Ali, N., Lee, H. L., Ramsden, S., Prejawa, S., Seghier, M. L., & Price, C. (2012). Where, when and why brain activation differs for bilinguals and monolinguals during picture naming and reading aloud. *Cerebral Cortex*, *22*(4), 892–902.

Paulesu, E., McCrory, E., Fazio, F., Menoncello, L., Brunswick, N., Cappa, S. F., Cotelli, F., Cossu, G., Corte, F., Lorusso, M., Pesenti, S., Gallagher, A., Perani, D., Price, C., Frith. C. D., & Frith, U. (2000). A cultural effect on brain function. *Nature Neuroscience*, *3*(1), 91–96.

Perani, D., & Abutalebi, J. (2005). The neural basis of first and second language processing. *Current Opinion in Neurobiology*, *15*(2), 202–206.

Peterson, S. E., Fox, P. T., Posner, M. I., Mintun, M., & Raichle, M. E. (1989). Positron emission tomographic studies of the processing of single words. *Journal of Cognitive Neuroscience*, *1*, 153–170.

Pfefferbaum, A., Ford, J. M., Weller, B. J., & Kopell, B. S. (1985). ERPs to response production and inhibition. *Electroencephalography and Clinical Neurophysiology*, *60*, 423–434.

Philipp, A. M., & Koch, I. (2009). Inhibition in language switching: What is inhibited when switching among languages in naming tasks? *Journal of Experimental Psychology: Learning, Memory, and Cognition*, *35*(5), 1187–1195.

Pliatsikas, C., Moschopoulou, E., & Saddy, J. D. (2015). The effects of bilingualism on the white matter structure of the brain. In *Proceedings of the National Academy of Sciences*, *112*(5), 1334–1337.

Poeppel, D., Emmorey, K., Hickok, G., & Pylkkänen, L. (2012). Towards a new neurobiology of language. *Journal of Neuroscience*, *32*(41), 14125–14131.

Price, C. J., Green, D. W., & Studnitz, R. V. (1999). A functional imaging study of translation and language switching. *Brain*, *122*, 2221–2235.

Prior, A., & Gollan, T. H. (2011). Good language-switchers are good task switchers: Evidence from Spanish–English and Mandarin–English bilinguals. *Journal of the International Neuropsychological Society*, *17*, 1–10.

Prior, A., & MacWhinney, B. (2009). A bilingual advantage in task switching. *Bilingualism: Language and Cognition*, *13*(2), 253–362.

Ressel, V., Pallier, C., Ventura-Campos, N., Díaz, B., Roessler, A., Ávila, C., & Sebastián-Gallés, N. (2012). An effect of bilingualism on the auditory cortex. *The Journal of Neuroscience*, *32*(47), 16597–16601.

Rodriguez-Fornells, A., Krämer, U. M., Lorenzo-Seva, U., Festman, J., & Münte, T. F. (2012). Self-assessment of individual differences in language switching. *Frontiers in Psychology*, *2*, 1–15.

Rodriguez-Fornells, A., Rotte, M., Heinze, H. J., Noesselt, T., & Münte, T. F. (2002). Brain potential and functional MRI evidence for how to handle two languages with one brain. *Nature*, *415*, 1026–1029.

Rodriguez-Fornells, A., van der Lugt, A., Rotte, M., Britti, B., Heinze, H. J., & Münte, T. F. (2005). Second language interferes with word production in fluent bilinguals: Brain potential and functional imaging evidence. *Journal of Cognitive Neuroscience*, *17*, 422–433.

Rodríguez-Pujadas, A., Sanjuán, A., Ventura-Campos, N., Román, P., Martin, C., Barceló, F., Costa, A., & Ávila, C. (2013). Bilinguals use language-control brain areas more than monolinguals to perform non-linguistic switching tasks. *PLoS ONE*, *8*(9), 1–8.

Rosselli, M., Ardila, A., Araujo, K., Weekes, V. A., Caracciolo, V., & Padilla, M. (2000). Verbal Fluency and repetition skills in healthy older Spanish–English Bilinguals. *Applied Neuropsychology*, *7*(1), 17–24.

Schweizer, T. A., Ware, J., Fischer, C. E., Craik, F. I., & Bialystok, E. (2012). Bilingualism as a contributor to cognitive reserve: Evidence from brain atrophy in Alzheimer's disease. *Cortex*, *48*(8), 991–996.

Simon, J. R., & Rudell, A. P. (1967). Auditory S-R compatibility: The effect of an irrelevant cue on information processing. *Journal of Applied Psychology*, *51*, 300–304.

Soveri, A., Rodriguez-Fornells, A., & Laine, M. (2011). Is there a relationship between language switching and executive functions in bilingualism? Introducing a within-group analysis approach. *Frontiers in Psychology*, *2*, 1–8.

Sowell, E. R., Thompson, P. M., Leonard, C. M., Welcome, S. E., Kan, E., & Toga, A. W. (2004). Longitudinal mapping of cortical thickness and brain growth in normal children. *The Journal of Neuroscience*, *24*(38), 8223–8231.

Spivey, M., & Marian, V. (1999). Cross talk between native and second languages: Partial activation of an irrelevant lexicon. *Psychological Science*, *10*, 281–284.

Stocco, A., Lebiere, C., & Anderson, J. R. (2010). Conditional routing of information to the cortex: A model of the basal ganglia's role in cognitive coordination. *Psychol Rev*, *117*(2), 541–574.

Stocco, A., & Prat, C. S. (2014). Bilingualism trains specific brain circuits involved in flexible rule selection and application. *Brain and Language*, *137*, 50–61.

Stocco, A., Yamasaki, B., Natalenko, R., & Prat, C. S. (2014). Bilingual brain training: A neurobiological framework of how bilingual experience improves executive function. *International Journal of Bilingualism*, *18*(1), 67–92.

Tan, L. H., Liu, H.-L., Perfetti, C. A., Spinks, J. A., Fox, P. T., & Gao, J.-H. (2001). The neural system underlying Chinese logograph reading. *NeuroImage*, *13*(5), 836–846.

Tan, L. H., Spinks, J. A., Eden, G. F., Perfetti, C. A., & Siok, W. T. (2005). Reading depends on writing, in Chinese. In *Proceedings of the National Academy of Sciences*, *102*(24), 8781–8785.

Tan, L. H., Spinks, J. A., Feng, C. M., Siok, W. T., Perfetti, C. A., Xiong, J., Fox, P. T., & Gao, J. H. (2003). Neural systems of second language reading are shaped by native language. *Human Brain Mapping*, *18*(3), 158–166.

138 *Angélique M. Blackburn*

Thierry, G., & Wu, Y. J. (2007). Brain potentials reveal unconscious translation during foreign-language comprehension. In *Proceedings of the National Academy of Sciences*, *104*, 12530–12535.

Thompson-Schill, S. L., d'Esposito, M., Aguirre, G. K., & Farah, M. J. (1997). Role of the left inferior prefrontal cortex in retrieval of semantic knowledge: A reevaluation. In *Proceedings of the National Academy of Sciences*, *94*, 14792–14797.

Thompson-Schill, S. L., d'Esposito, M., & Kan, I., P. (1999). Effects of repetition and competition on activity in left prefrontal cortex during word generation. *Neuron*, *23*, 513–522.

Van Der Meij, M., Cuetos, F., Carreiras, M., & Barber, H. A. (2011). Electrophysiological correlates of language switching in second language learners. *Psychophysiology*, *48*, 44–54.

Van Heuven, W. J. B., Schriefers, H., Dijkstra, T., & Hagoort, P. (2008). Language conflict in the bilingual brain. *Cerebral Cortex*, *18*, 2706–2716.

Verhoef, K. M. W., Roelofs, A., & Chwilla, D. J. (2009). Role of inhibition in language switching: Evidence from event-related brain potentials in overt picture naming. *Cognition*, *110*, 84–99.

Wager, T. D., Jonides, J., & Reading, S. (2004). Neuroimaging studies of shifting attention: A meta-analysis. *NeuroImage*, *22*, 1679–1693.

Wang, Y., Kuhl, P. K., Chen, C., & Dong, Q. (2009). Sustained and transient language control in the bilingual brain. *NeuroImage*, *47*, 414–422.

Wang, Y., Xue, G., Chen, C., Xue, F., & Dong, Q. (2007). Neural basis of asymmetric language switching in second-language learners: An ER-fMRI study. *NeuroImage*, *35*, 862–870.

Yeung, N., Botvinick, M. W., & Cohen, J. D. (2004). The neural basis of error detection: Conflict monitoring and the error-related negativity. *Psychological Review*, *111*, 931–959.

Zou, L., Ding, G., Abutalebi, J., Shu, H., & Peng, D. (2012). Structural plasticity of the left caudate in bimodal bilinguals. *Cortex*, *48*, 1197–1206.

7 The Bilingual Brain Revisited

What Is Right and What Is Left?

Jyotsna Vaid

Introduction

From early case reports of non-*parallel impairment* or recovery of language in bilinguals following brain injury to *brain mapping* studies of brain-intact individuals, claims about the relationship between bilingualism and the brain continue to generate interest and controversy. A dominant issue, particularly in early discussions of this topic, based on clinical accounts (see Fabbro, 2001; Ijalba, Obler, & Chengappa, 2004; Paradis, 2001, 2004) and on studies with non-clinical populations, is whether or when there are distinct neural correlates of multiple language experience (see Hull & Vaid, 2005; Vaid, 2002, 2008; Vaid & Genesee, 1980; Wattendorf & Festman, 2008, for reviews and further discussion).

Without attempting a comprehensive review of the vast and growing literature on this topic, in this chapter I will highlight key points from previous reviews and point out areas where additional research may be informative. I will begin by providing a rationale for the study of the bilingual brain. Next, I will outline sources of evidence on this topic and will evaluate their merits and limitations. I will then discuss points of convergence or divergence across studies. I will conclude by suggesting that our understanding of the bilingual brain will be advanced not just by ongoing improvements in the sensitivity of measures of brain structure and function, but also by considering alternative ways of conceptualizing the study of bilingualism and of language itself (e.g., Vaid & Meuter, 2017).

Why Study the Bilingual Brain?

The study of language and the brain has been guided by a prevailing assumption that the prototypical language user is monolingual. This assumption is unfounded given that, on a global level, there are at least as many and probably more bilingual and/or multilingual language users than there are single language users. Thus, one reason to study the bilingual brain is simply to understand how language is acquired, processed, and represented among users who constitute the majority of language users.

Apart from the intrinsic value of conducting basic research on bilingual or multilingual populations, investigation of neural correlates of bilingualism is also important for what it can tell us about neural responsivity to variations in language experience. Just as variations in early *sensory* experience (e.g., congenital deafness or blindness) are known to affect brain organization differentially (e.g., Neville & Bavelier, 2002; Newport, Bavelier, & Neville, 2001), it is likely that variations in early *language* experience may also alter brain organization. Given that multiple language users differ from one another in a wide variety of ways (e.g., in how they became bilingual/multilingual and in how they use their languages, and in the structural properties of their languages), these sources of variation may interact and lead to a diverse array of outcomes at the behavioral and neurobehavioral level. As such, the study of bilingualism provides a fertile testing ground for questions about neuroplasticity related to language structure and function.

Questions about language and the brain in multiple language users were of interest as far back as the late 1880s and were often raised by neurologists who reported cases of selective or non-selective patterns of loss and recovery of the language of their patients following unilateral brain injury. These case studies document a variety of patterns of impairment and recovery following *aphasia* in multilingual (or *polyglot*) patients, including *selective aphasia*, where only one language is impaired; *differential impairment*, where the languages show different types of impairment; or successive impairment, where only one language is initially impaired but then another language is impaired. However, since most of these case studies were published in neurological outlets, often in languages other than English, this early literature was largely inaccessible until it was reviewed and made available within linguistics and psychology, thanks largely to the seminal monograph by Albert and Obler (1978) and the edited collection of case reports by Paradis (1983).

Findings of differential language impairment in polyglot aphasia hinted at the importance of language acquisition history as a possible mediator of neural organization of language. In a direct examination of this variable, Lambert and Fillenbaum (1959) noted that aphasics who had acquired their two languages in similar contexts tended to show parallel deficits across their languages whereas those who had acquired their languages at different periods and in different settings tended to show differential language impairment. Such an outcome was consistent with verbal learning and memory studies of bilingualism indicating that bilinguals who had acquired their two languages simultaneously and, in similar contexts, tended to show greater integration of the two linguistic systems, whereas those who had acquired the two languages successively and in different contexts showed a greater functional separation in lexical organization and retrieval (e.g., Lambert & Rawlings, 1969). In addition, a number of behavioral studies pointed to a cognitive advantage in mental flexibility and *metalinguistic awareness* in bilinguals versus monolinguals (see Ben-Zeev, 1977; Peal & Lambert, 1962). This early work ushered in a large number of empirical studies in recent years that have sought to examine possible reasons that may underlie these group differences. In particular, enhanced *executive control* has been widely claimed as a reason for the so-called *bilingual advantage*. Nevertheless, a number of challenges to this claim have appeared in recent years (see Paap, this volume). As a result, there is a growing recognition that a theory-driven approach that seeks to differentiate bilinguals in terms of their actual language use patterns (e.g., frequency of code-switching, or of informal translation) may offer a more promising avenue for exploring the basis of cognitive or neurocognitive repercussions of bilingualism (de Bruin & Della Sala, 2016).

Behavioral research on bilingualism has foregrounded bilinguals' ability to keep their two languages functionally distinct (as when interacting with monolingual speakers), while being able to move seemingly effortlessly between their two languages (as when interacting with other bilingual speakers; Lambert, 1969). This ability of bilinguals to manage and move between their two languages has informed psycholinguistic inquiry, which has been directed at understanding the cognitive architecture of the bilingual mental lexicon (see Dijkstra, 2003). Behavioral and psycholinguistic approaches have been supplemented by neurobehavioral investigations of language functioning in brain-intact bilinguals. We turn now to the different research approaches that have been taken to study the bilingual brain.

Sources of Evidence

Aphasia

An important source of evidence about the bilingual brain comes from clinical case studies of aphasia, or language disturbances following unilateral brain injury. In several cases, non-parallel language impairment and/or recovery patterns were reported. However, as many of the early reports were selected cases, and since case studies are more likely to be published if they present an unusual and thereby interesting pattern, estimates of the incidence of parallel versus non-parallel impairment based on selected case reports may not be representative. There are far fewer group studies of bilingual aphasia (i.e., studies of unselected cases). One group study of 20 cases found that parallel language impairment and/or recovery represented 65% of the cases (Fabbro, 2001). There is clearly a need for more group studies of unselected cases.

When non-parallel recovery occurs, it is important to understand what factors might influence which language is more impaired and/or recovers better. At least four different principles have been proposed. One principle is that skills learned *early* in life are the most resistant to loss following brain damage, as they are likely to be highly practiced. Applied to the domain of language, this would lead to the prediction that a patient's first learned language (*mother tongue*) would be selectively spared and/or the first to recover following aphasia. This claim has been described in the literature as the *rule of Ribot* (Ribot, 1881). An alternative claim, described as Pitres' rule, proposes that what matters is not *when* a language was learned, but *how much* it was used before the brain injury (Pitres, 1895). According to Pitres' rule, the language that was used the most prior to the injury should be the most resistant to impairment following aphasia. A third claim, proposed by Minkowski (1963), holds that that the emotional significance of the language for the patient is relevant in determining whether that language would be spared, whether or not that language happens to be the first learned language (L1) or the most practiced language. Yet another factor that has been noted as potentially important is the language of the patient's environment (e.g., Goral, Rosas, Conner, Maul, & Obler, 2012). In addition to these factors, it has also been suggested that there may be a different pattern of language impairment or recovery depending on whether a language had been acquired in a spoken mode or a primarily written mode (e.g., in school), and the damage was in the auditory or visual regions of the brain, respectively (Luria, 1960). Finally, research on bilingual aphasia is examining the role of structural differences between the bilinguals' languages (e.g., Vaid & Pandit, 1991).

What may one discern from the polyglot aphasia literature? One value of this literature is that it documents the variety and complexity of deficits that may arise in each of a patient's languages following brain injury. However, the sheer diversity of findings makes it difficult to form generalizations. Conclusions are also difficult to arrive at given that information about a person's linguistic competence prior to the injury is not likely to be objective or complete, since it is usually gathered after the injury, through family members. Without having a reliable account of the patient's language use and proficiency prior to the aphasia, it is difficult to fully account for their language profile after the injury. A further limitation in interpreting aphasia evidence is that patients are rarely systematically assessed in all their languages. If they are formally assessed, the language assessment typically does not cover all aspects of language competence (e.g., semantic, syntactic, pragmatic). To date, the most comprehensive aphasia test that has been standardized for multiple language users is the *bilingual aphasia test* battery, developed by Paradis (2011) and adapted for over 60 language pairs. Briefly, this test provides a detailed assessment of relevant distinctions at the level of grammar, morphology, phonology, and discourse for each language pair (see Miller Amberber & Cohen, 2012, for further discussion).

In terms of how to interpret patterns of selective language impairment or recovery in polyglot aphasia, one can distinguish between two views. One is what may be termed *the representational account*. In this view, observed patterns of impairment reflect damage to brain regions thought to subserve language, whether in the left cerebral hemisphere, or the right hemisphere. Of relevance here is a claim that there may be a higher incidence of crossed aphasia in bilinguals than in monolinguals, *crossed aphasia* being defined as aphasia following damage to the right hemisphere; however, the evidence on this issue is by no means clear cut (see Karanth & Rangamani, 1988; Vaid, 2002, for further discussion).

A different interpretation of *selective loss* or recovery in aphasia is *the functional account*. In this account, brain regions subserving each language may be intact, but what is disrupted are control mechanisms that govern access to a particular language (Green, 1998). In its present form, the evidence is compatible with either view, although the functional view provides a more parsimonious account.

Electro-Cortical Stimulation Mapping

Another source of evidence on brain organization of language in bilinguals comes from studies of bilingual epileptics undergoing a procedure known as *electro-cortical stimulation mapping*. This procedure is undertaken prior to surgery to remove areas of the brain to reduce the frequency of epileptic seizures in these patients. Determining which brain regions are language-relevant provides useful practical information as the surgeon can try to avoid removing tissue close to those regions.

In this procedure, electrodes are placed directly on the exposed *cortex* at different locations or sites. The effect of electrical stimulation is to render the person temporarily aphasic. That is, under electrical stimulation patients show speech arrests, hesitations, semantic errors, or have word-finding difficulties. By determining which cortical sites lead to these difficulties in language production, it is possible to map out in individual patients the language-relevant (*eloquent*) areas of the brain. The use of bilinguals introduces additional complexity since the location of cortical sites and the nature of the response to the tasks used (typically, object naming or reading aloud) must be assessed for each of the bilingual's languages.

The first cortical stimulation studies to test bilinguals in both their languages were conducted by Ojemann and Whitaker (1978) on two patients, and by Rapport, Tan, and Whitaker (1983) on a small number of patients. These studies documented what the authors termed *partially distinct* and *partially overlapping* cortical representations of the bilinguals' languages. That is, electrical stimulation of certain cortical regions selectively disrupted naming in only one of the languages, whereas stimulation of other regions disrupted naming in both languages. However, the particular regions in which selective disruption of naming were found differed across individuals. It was also noted that language-relevant cortical regions were more widely dispersed in the less proficient language as compared to the more proficient one (Rapport et al., 1983).

Additional work conducted since the early studies corroborate and extend these findings. For example, Roux and Tremoulet (2002) studied 12 right-handed French-speaking bilingual patients of differing language backgrounds on counting, word naming, and reading in each language. Seven of these (including three of the four patients in the sample who had acquired a second language before the age of seven years), showed language-specific cortical sites. Five patients showed an overlapping set of sites across languages. Of the four patients in the sample who were *early bilinguals*, defined in the study as having acquired a second language (L2) before the age of seven years, three showed naming or word-finding difficulty in only one language in response to stimulation of certain cortical sites. Of the six non-proficient bilingual patients tested, only one showed a wider dispersal of cortical sites disrupting naming in the less proficient language. In five of the two patients, an overlapping set of sites across languages was found, whereas in the remaining seven patients, areas were found that were language-specific, in frontal and in temporal-parietal areas of the brain.

A study by Roux et al. (2004) compared intra-operative mapping of cortical areas involved in picture naming and reading sentences aloud in a group of 19 bilingual or multilingual and 35 monolingual (French) patients. The bilinguals were subdivided into four groups on the basis of age and proficiency of L2. The results showed no significant difference between bilingual and monolingual groups in reading or naming site locations, nor was there a statistical difference between first and second language cortical sites. Eight of the 19 bilinguals showed at least one language-specific reading site.

Lucas, McKhann, and Ojemann (2004) reported data from 22 bilingual patients and 117 monolingual control patients on a cortical stimulation study of object naming to address whether multiple languages are functionally separated in the bilingual brain and whether language organization in bilinguals resembles that in monolinguals. Evidence was obtained for distinct cortical modules for different languages in 21 of the 22 bilinguals; that is, sites were found in which stimulation reliably produced naming deficits in only one of the languages. Furthermore, in 43% of the bilinguals, stimulation at one site selectively produced errors in L1, whereas stimulation at another site produced errors only in L2. Additionally, it was found that the overall extent of language-sensitive cortical sites did not differ across the two languages nor did it differ as a function of language proficiency. However, the sites associated with L1 versus L2 naming disruption did appear to differ in anatomical distribution, with posterior temporal and parietal regions being more associated with L2-specific sites whereas anterior regions tended to show shared sites. An analysis of L1 sites in the bilinguals versus monolinguals suggested that primary language representation in the two groups was virtually the same. However, an analysis of L2 sites in bilinguals compared with monolingual sites showed differences in seven of the 28 zones, particularly around classic receptive language areas, with an under-representation of sites in bilinguals than in monolinguals.

In summary, the cortical stimulation data illustrate considerable variability in anatomical distribution of language-relevant cortical sites on object naming, counting, and reading tasks performed in L1 versus L2 of late bilinguals, and between bilinguals on their L2 and monolinguals. The findings suggest that L1 and L2 representation may differ, which argues for electro-cortical mapping being undertaken in each language of bilingual patients to localize language-sensitive sites prior to surgery. However, no consistent support was found for an association between language proficiency and extent of cortical activation.

Although they are of clear practical value in guiding surgery decisions for individual patients, cortical stimulation studies have certain limitations as a tool for understanding brain organization of language. One limitation of these studies is that the cortical area examined using electro-cortical stimulation is restricted to the area of the craniotomy (i.e., surgical incision of the skull), thus regions that extend beyond the craniotomy are not accessible. Another limitation is that direct stimulation mainly maps the gyral surface, unlike other forms of brain mapping, such as *positron emission topography* (PET) or *functional magnetic resonance imaging* (fMRI), which allow examination of activation at the level of the sulci, or fissures. Finally, in view of the fact that cortical stimulation data are based on patients in whom a long history of seizures may have resulted in some neural reorganization, generalizations to the healthy brain must be made with caution (but Simos et al., 2001, did find a similar pattern of variability in language-receptive regions even in healthy bilinguals; see Schmidt & Roberts, 2009, for a review of Magnetoencephalography studies with L2 users).

More generally, observations based on studies of brain-impaired populations are of value in demonstrating clear effects associated with brain injury or cortical stimulation of the brain, but to fully understand language organization in the non-brain-injured individual, it is important to supplement lesion data and data from clinical populations with studies conducted with healthy or so-called brain-intact individuals. A promising approach in this regard is the use of transcranial direct current stimulation. This technique is increasingly being used with clinical populations as a therapeutic intervention, but is also being used with brain-intact populations (see Monti et al., 2013, for a review). To date there have been no investigations with bilinguals using this measure. We turn now to a consideration of other sources of evidence based on healthy bilinguals.

Behavioral Laterality Measures

The most extensive body of research on language and the brain in brain-intact bilinguals involves behavioral laterality studies of functional *hemispheric asymmetries* or *brain lateralization*. Laterality studies exploit the *contralateral* sensory organization of the brain. In visual half field studies, linguistic input is presented unilaterally in the left or the *right visual field*. Dichotic listening studies present linguistic input to the left or right ear. Performance asymmetries in the pattern of response are used to infer involvement of the left or right hemisphere in the processing of the input. In studies with monolinguals, a *right ear advantage* (REA; under conditions of dichotic presentation) or a right visual field advantage (in studies of *divided visual field* presentation) are typically observed for verbal stimuli. That is, verbal judgments of various kinds are made faster when the stimuli are initially directed to the left hemisphere (LH). The question of interest in studies of brain lateralization in bilinguals is whether knowing more than one language alters the pattern of left hemisphere dominance that characterizes monolingual language processing. That is, does use of two or more languages alter the way in which the two hemispheres process language, such that there may be greater involvement of the right hemisphere (RH), or greater bilateral involvement in one or both languages?

Laterality studies with bilinguals were particularly prominent in the 1970s and 1980s (see Obler, Zatorre, Galloway, & Vaid, 1982, for methodological issues). In 1980, Vaid and Genesee proposed an integrative model of bilingual lateralization in which language acquisitional factors were hypothesized to influence the strategies deployed to process language and, thus, the relative involvement of the two hemispheres. They proposed that hemispheric involvement in bilinguals would resemble that of monolinguals to the extent that the two languages of bilinguals were acquired simultaneously and in similar contexts; however, RH involvement in bilinguals was expected to be more likely the later the L2 was acquired, the more informal the exposure to the L2, and the earlier the stage of L2 acquisition. In other words, language lateralization patterns were hypothesized to differ in early versus late bilinguals (where early bilinguals are generally defined as those who mastered their two languages before the age of 6 years and late bilinguals are defined as those who mastered their second language after the age of 12 years).

To test these hypotheses, Vaid and Hall (1991) undertook a meta-analysis of 59 published and unpublished laterality studies of bilinguals. A *meta-analysis* is a quantitative review of a body of literature, in which data from individual studies are combined and then analyzed to determine patterns of lateralization, or relative reliance on the left hemisphere in processing language. In Vaid and Hall (1991), no differences between bilinguals and monolinguals in lateralization were found in the L1 studies that had included monolingual groups. However, among bilinguals, the variable of age of L2 acquisition was significant: early bilinguals were found to be less left lateralized than late bilinguals (Vaid & Hall, 1991). Subsequently, another bilingual/monolingual meta-analytic investigation, this one based on 28 studies that compared bilinguals with monolinguals, found that bilinguals were less left lateralized than monolinguals; this was particularly true of early bilinguals (Hull & Vaid, 2006). An additional meta-analysis, based on 69 studies that compared bilinguals on their two languages or with other bilinguals, corroborated the finding of age of onset of bilingualism effects in lateralization. That is, early bilinguals showed evidence of bilateral hemispheric involvement in language processing, whereas late bilinguals showed greater left lateralization. No differences in lateralization were found between the L1 and L2 of bilinguals (Hull & Vaid, 2007).

The finding that early bilinguals make use of both hemispheres in processing language raises the question as to why simultaneous acquisition of two languages appears to alter the relative use of the two hemispheres, as compared to acquisition of a single language or acquisition of a second language later in life. Some previous cognitive studies of bilingual adults that have compared early versus late bilinguals on various linguistic and other tasks (e.g., Lambert, 1969; Vaid, 2002) have suggested that early bilinguals appear to be more inclined to process for meaning, whereas late bilinguals show a preference for processing the form of utterances. Other studies comparing early versus late learners of a second language have argued that early exposure to a language is critical in achieving grammatical competence (Newport et al., 2001; Wartenburger et al., 2003). However, questions remain as to the nature of the interpretation of the observed laterality differences between early bilinguals and monolinguals, and between early bilinguals and late bilinguals. Given that the majority of studies with adult bilinguals have used late bilinguals, there is clearly a need for more cognitive and neurocognitive research on early bilinguals (e.g., Rao & Vaid, 2017).

The meta-analysis findings are instructive in showing that the critical difference in brain lateralization of language may involve differences between groups rather than between languages. Moreover, despite the large number of bilingual laterality studies that have appeared, not all groups or tasks have been studied to the same extent. More studies of non-English-speaking bilingual participants are needed, as are studies that compare bilinguals whose two languages are structurally similar or structurally different (e.g., d'Anselmo, Reiterer, Zuccarini, Tommasi, & Brancucci, 2013). Further, given that the majority of laterality studies have used single words as stimuli, more studies are needed that examine language processing at the sentence level or beyond, and that separate out different components of language for study (e.g., phonetic, semantic, syntactic, and pragmatic aspects).

A study by Cieślicka and Heredia (2011) of Polish–English late bilinguals is particularly noteworthy. It is one of the few studies in the bilingual laterality literature that has examined hemispheric asymmetries in the processing of figurative language (idioms). In the study, literally plausible idioms in each language were presented centrally, embedded in sentence contexts that were either unconstraining (and could lead to a literal interpretation) or favored the figurative interpretation of the idiom. Target words related to the literal or the figurative interpretation were then presented laterally, either immediately after the idiom was presented, or at two different time delays. The results showed an effect of language status, with priming for figurative meaning of idioms occurring immediately upon idiom offset for L1 idioms, but only after 300 ms for L2 idioms; moreover, for L2 idioms, the literal meaning showed greater activation than the figurative meaning across all time intervals and in both hemispheres. More studies are needed of bilingual figurative language processing to get a fuller understanding of the contribution of bilingual-related and figurative-language-related variables that may jointly moderate hemispheric functioning.

Although there is much more that can and should be explored within the realm of behavioral laterality studies with bilinguals, it is the case that laterality research, by definition, only allows study of interhemispheric differences and does not speak to the issue of potential differences among bilinguals in patterns of neural activation *within* each hemisphere. To address this issue, we turn to neurobehavioral studies of language functioning that have relied on measures of brain imaging.

Neurobehavioral Measures

Techniques that permit examination of neural activity within each hemisphere (as well as between the two hemispheres) include: (1) electroencephalographic measures, such as *electroencephalography* (EEG), and *event-related brain potentials* (ERP), and *magnetocephalographic measures*, also known as magnetic source imaging; (2) hemodynamic imaging, such as PET, fMRI, and *near infrared spectrometry* (NIRS); and (3) *transcranial magnetic stimulation* (TMS).

In electroencephalographic research, brain wave components reflecting the summed activity of several neurons are elicited by specific sensory, motor, or cognitive events. Differences in the amplitude and latency of ERP components allow researchers to infer the degree and timing of electrical activity in the brain during a specific cognitive activity. For example, one commonly studied ERP component is known as the *N400*. It is found when there is some unexpected semantic event and is elicited by presenting sentences with unusual endings. ERP research allows fine-grained analysis of the temporal unfolding of events at the millisecond level on up. As such, ERP studies provide an ideal, real-time measure to study linguistic processing.

Electrophysiological measures are being increasingly used with bilingual populations (see Hull & Vaid, 2005, for a comparison of ERP and laterality studies). Recent electrophysiological research suggests the importance of early language experience in influencing how neural subsystems underlying language will develop and function.

Measures based on hemodynamic indices include measures of deoxygenation of the blood (e.g., fMRI) and changes in blood flow (e.g., PET). Unlike cortical stimulation or lesion-deficit studies which allow one to infer that a particular brain area is essential for performing a particular linguistic task, functional neuroimaging studies point to an association between an area and a particular function, without being able to characterize with certainty the particular regions that are necessary for performing that function.

Despite this limitation, functional neuroimaging techniques of bilingual language processing (particularly using fMRI) have rapidly proliferated over the past three decades (see Higby, Kim, & Obler, 2013; Vaid & Hull, 2002; Vaid, 2008, for further discussion). We will focus on findings from the *hemodynamic measures* in the remainder of this chapter, highlighting relevant methodological and interpretive issues.

Hemodynamic Neuroimaging Studies

Hemodynamic imaging studies are based on the following rationale: the performance of any task places demands on the brain; these demands are met through changes in neural activity in various areas; changes in neuronal activity in turn produce changes in local cerebral blood flow, which are measured directly by PET and indirectly with fMRI or NIRS. PET studies use radioactive tracers to image blood flow or metabolism. Areas that have a higher blood flow will have a larger amount of tracer and will thus emit a stronger signal. fMRI measures changes in the relative amounts of oxygenated versus deoxygenated hemoglobin present in neural regions that are metabolically active during a task. Since it does not require the use of radionuclides, a participant in an fMRI study can undergo many more trials than would be feasible in a PET study. Furthermore, fMRI offers better temporal and spatial resolution than PET. NIRS is a relatively new and promising hemodynamic imaging technique that measures regional changes in the concentration of oxygenated and deoxygenated blood (reflecting changes in oxygen supply and oxygen consumption) in small vessels of the brain cortex. It has a high temporal resolution and a high signal-to-noise ratio permitting observation of oxygenation changes at the single trial level. It is more compact, portable, and affordable than fMRI, and there is no scanner noise problem affecting attention as there is in fMRI studies.

The typical paradigm in hemodynamic studies involves participants performing a cognitive task for some period of time and contrasting neural activity during that task period with activity during a baseline task. It is assumed that brain activity will change between the two tasks and will reflect task demands. Brain areas that show increases in activation are identified by noting which specific brain regions change their signal intensity as the task state changes from the baseline condition to the target task.

An important issue in hemodynamic imaging studies is how to identify areas where a significant change of activity has occurred. To address this issue, different statistical analyses have been developed. One of these restricts the regions to be surveyed based on *a priori* considerations of which areas are thought to be more relevant to the function in question. This is the *region of interest* (ROI) approach. In the case of language research, using this approach would mean looking only at the so-called classical language areas. Another approach is to survey images without *a priori* assumptions about the locations of significant changes. However, use of this approach presents more difficult statistical problems given the large number of spatial locations that are not statistically independent from one another and in which there are small numbers of observations. To avoid the possibility of falsely deciding that a region shows an increase in activation, the use of strict statistical cutoffs is routine in this approach.

Language imaging research with monolinguals has found that most regions showing activation changes involve the so-called classical language areas, established by lesion evidence (i.e., areas surrounding the Sylvian fissure in the left hemisphere). In addition, language-related activation has been observed in other areas in the left hemisphere and in certain right hemisphere regions. In short, the set of regions activated in functional imaging studies of language is larger and more variable than those typically observed from lesion-deficit data.

What needs to be kept in mind, though, is that assignment of regions to functions based on activation data alone is not definitive since some regions may be activated because they are critical for task performance, while activation of other regions may reflect task-irrelevant, ancillary mental activity. An additional variable constraining interpretation is that the activation changes noted on specific tasks will vary depending on the choice of the baseline task. Thus, the assignment of regions to linguistic functions is usually tentative.

With the above as context, we can now consider the emerging literature on functional neuroimaging of language in multiple language users. The predominant question examined in these studies has been whether the regions activated for an L2 spatially overlap with those activated for the first language and whether the degree of overlap is influenced by factors such as proficiency or age of second language acquisition. A related question has been whether the amount of neural activation varies across languages, also as a function of language proficiency and/or age of onset of bilingualism.

There is no clear consensus on either of these questions. Some studies show evidence of overlapping activation across the two languages of bilinguals in late bilinguals (Illes et al., 1999), or in early and late bilinguals (Frenck-Mestre, Anton, Roth, Vaid, & Viallet, 2005), whereas others show evidence of distinct regions (Dehaene et al., 1997; Kim, Relkin, Lee, & Hirsch, 1997; Perani et al., 1996). There are more studies showing overlapping activation profiles than those showing distinct language activation. Consideration of proficiency or age of onset of bilingualism has not clarified the picture, as some studies claim a difference in L1 versus L2 activation in late but not in early bilinguals (Kim et al., 1997), and other studies report an identical pattern of activation for the two languages in early and late bilinguals alike (Frenck-Mestre et al., 2005). With respect to extent of activation, some evidence suggests that less proficiency is associated with the recruitment of more regions (Hasegawa, Carpenter, & Just, 2002), but more research is needed to corroborate this possibility.

Although it is assumed that the presence or absence of spatially overlapping regions of activation means that the languages are represented in common or separate regions, one need not make this inference. Rather than reflecting differential neural representation of the languages, differences in activation found across languages may reflect other factors such as the fact that performing a task in one's second language may be more cognitively demanding and, thus, may require more resources (see Hasegawa et al., 2002). Alternatively, it may reflect the usual variability observed across imaging runs even in a single language when subjects are tested in more than one session (Mahendra, Plante, Magliore, Milman, & Trouard, 2003).

Interpretive difficulties are compounded when studies employ tasks that do not require overt responses (i.e., where participants are instructed simply to think about the response, without saying it out loud). Indeed, several hemodynamic studies with bilinguals have employed covert word generation tasks. The reason that covert tasks are used is to minimize movement artifacts produced by articulation; however, there is evidence to suggest that different brain regions are activated in overt versus covert versions of a given task. Furthermore, when using covert generation in the absence of any behavioral validation, as was the case in the Kim et al. (1997) study, where participants were to think about what they had eaten the day before for lunch or dinner, in one language or another, it becomes impossible to know the extent to which participants were actually carrying out the task as instructed. Additionally, the use of spatial smoothing or averaging techniques, a standard practice in functional imaging studies, may have the unintended effect of removing individual differences in neural activation. Finally, there is always the possibility that the presence of overlapping activation across languages is due to the lack of sufficiently fine-grained spatial resolution. That is, what appears as a lack of difference across languages in the specific neural regions activated may turn out to be misleading, if the measures are not sensitive enough to reveal differences in activation that may actually be present, but may go undetected at the level of spatial resolution of the imaging techniques in use. This particular problem is likely to become less of an issue with the development of more sensitive imaging techniques with higher spatial resolution.

Toward Convergence

Although most bilingual neuroimaging research has focused on differences in spatial activation within the language-dominant hemisphere, it would be instructive to consider what these studies have found with respect to the issue of interhemispheric activation. Only a handful of functional imaging studies have actually reported activation patterns across hemispheres. An fMRI study by Illes et al. (1999) compared fluent English–Spanish with Spanish–English bilinguals who had acquired their second language at around 12 years of age and found spatially overlapping frontal lobe activation patterns on a same/different synonym judgment task. Further analysis indicated that left frontal activation was greater than right frontal activation for both languages of the late bilinguals and particularly so for the L2 relative to the L1 (the latter trend was not significant, though). Dehaene et al. (1997) reported an fMRI study with moderately fluent French–English bilinguals who had acquired their second language during late childhood and showed increased RH participation during L2 (relative to L1) processing on a story listening task. Significant activation differences were found between the two languages. Chee, Tan, and Thiel (1999) reported an fMRI study using a word stem completion task with fluent Chinese–English late bilinguals. Interestingly, comparisons of laterality effect sizes for frontal lobe activation patterns of early and late bilinguals in this study showed a non-significant trend for increased RH participation on both languages of early bilinguals relative to participants with late L2 acquisition.

As we have already seen, meta-analytic results based on behavioral laterality studies with bilinguals point to less left lateralization in early bilinguals than in late bilinguals or monolinguals. However, since imaging studies have almost exclusively included comparisons across languages, they leave open the question of possible group differences. Very few bilingual imaging studies have included monolingual comparison groups and fewer still have compared different bilingual subgroups, such as early versus late bilinguals (Frenck-Mestre et al., 2005; Mahendra et al., 2003; Wartenburger et al., 2003). To resolve differences in findings across imaging studies, there need to be replications of studies that systematically compare performance across groups on each language. The sample of participants used in imaging studies needs to be increased as well to permit direct statistical comparisons across subgroups varying in proficiency or L2 acquisition age.

A majority of existing imaging studies seeking to make claims about the effect of a particular variable (e.g., age or proficiency) have not been designed to permit an actual test of the claims. An ideal test would require a comparison across groups selected to vary on a particular dimension, such as age of onset of bilingualism, and only on that dimension. An exemplary brain imaging study in this regard is that of Berken, Chai, Gracco, and Klein (2016), who compared two groups of French/English bilinguals in Montreal, carefully screened to be highly proficient in both languages but differing mainly in their age of onset of bilingualism (simultaneous, or after the age of five years). The groups were found to differ. The study sought to determine whether early versus late experience of a second language would be associated with different patterns of resting state functional connectivity in the region of the inferior frontal gyrus in each hemisphere, given prior work showing greater right IFG cortical thickness for early bilinguals (Klein, Mok, Chen, & Watkins, 2014). Berken et al. (2016) found evidence for greater functional connectivity between the left and right IFG among early bilinguals as compared to late bilinguals, with the degree of connectivity correlating negatively with the age of second language acquisition in the sequential bilinguals. These patterns of findings converge with the laterality findings of early/late bilingual differences.

From the laterality findings and recent neuroimaging studies we see the importance of including relevant comparisons between early and late proficient versus non-proficient bilinguals, as also between bilinguals and monolinguals. Also, considering neural activation underlying different components of language, such as phonology, or orthography, and between the relative structural distance of a particular component, would be more promising ways to approach future work, rather than looking at the whole of language in a global sense. In this regard, a recent meta-analysis of bilingual neuroimaging studies is of particular interest. Liu and Cao (2016) examined the role of age of onset of bilingualism, and relative orthographic transparency of the bilinguals' two languages as potential determinants of differences between L1 and L2 neural activation patterns. They found that L2 processing recruited more neural regions than L1 processing for late bilinguals than was the case for early bilinguals; early bilinguals also showed evidence for greater co-activation of L1 and L2 orthographies; furthermore, the same L2 languages showed different patterns of activation depending on whether they were more or less orthographically transparent ("shallow") than L1. These findings attest to the dynamic influence of L2 structural properties in interaction with L1 structural properties, as well as corroborating an effect of age of onset of bilingualism.

Summary and Conclusion

Our understanding about the bilingual brain has been shaped not only by the possibilities and limitations of available techniques to study language and the brain but also by the ways in which language, neurofunctional organization of language, and bilingualism itself have been conceptualized (see Vaid, 2002; Vaid & Meuter, 2016). Advances in our understanding of the bilingual brain will require the joint use of multiple, converging measures, behavioral and neurobehavioral, and multiple comparison groups (e.g., bilingual vs. monolingual, early vs. late bilingual, late proficient vs. non-proficient bilinguals, and users of linguistically similar vs. dissimilar language pairs). In addition, it will require an ongoing engagement with conceptual developments in bilingualism, language, and neurocognitive functioning.

Looking ahead, more research is needed on neurocognitive correlates of linguistic practices along which bilinguals differ from other bilinguals. Two examples are informal translation (or *language brokering*) and code-switching. In many refugee or immigrant communities bilingual children end up having to translate for family members or others in their community. What might be some neurocognitive implications of prolonged early experience in translation? Similarly, many bilinguals engage in code-switching when speaking with other bilinguals. With few exceptions, there is very little psycholinguistic and neurocognitive research on this important component of bilinguals' linguistic repertoire (Moreno, Federmeier, & Kutas, 2002; Ng, Gonzales, & Wicha, 2014). A greater consideration of code-switching would also serve to lessen the emphasis on treating the languages of bilinguals as autonomous entities and direct more emphasis on the dynamic and interactive aspects of bilingual language use (Grosjean, 1989; Vaid & Meuter, 2016).

A second area of interest for further inquiry is to examine the relationship between functional and structural neural correlates of bilingualism (Li, Legault, & Litcofsky, 2014). If acquiring a second language indeed alters brain functioning, it would be plausible to expect differences between bilinguals and monolinguals at the level of brain structure as well. Several studies have recently noted structural differences associated with acquisition of another language (see Klein et al., 2014; Wei et al., 2015).

Among the earliest reports of structural differences is a study by Mechelli et al. (2004), who found significantly greater gray matter density in the left inferior parietal cortex in bilinguals as compared to monolinguals. Furthermore, in another sample, the density of gray matter in the left inferior parietal cortex was found to increase with second language proficiency and decrease with later age of acquisition. What is particularly noteworthy is that the difference in brain density was most pronounced in early bilinguals, who showed greater gray matter density in both the left and the right hemisphere, a result that converges nicely with the findings from the laterality literature showing greater bilateral hemispheric involvement in language processing in early bilinguals as compared to monolinguals. Whether the increase in gray matter density observed in bilinguals is due to changes in neuronal size, or dendritic or axonal arborization could not be determined by the method used. Since this early study, other studies have noted differences in cortical thickness (Klein et al., 2014), other structural differences associated with differences in age of onset of bilingualism, and differences in language proficiency. What is needed now are longitudinal studies that track structural correlates with particular aspects of bilingual language acquisition history and patterns of use.

What have we learned thus far from the study of the bilingual brain? One generalization is that early cognitive and clinical approaches to the study of bilinguals anticipated what was later confirmed in experimental studies involving behavioral and neurobehavioral measures with brain-intact bilinguals, namely, that bilingualism and, in particular, early onset of bilingualism, significantly alters neural functioning. Specifically, the evidence to date, taken together, suggests that the neural repercussions of early bilingualism involve a reduced dependence on the left hemisphere for language processing and a greater bilateral hemispheric involvement than that characterizing single language users or late second language learners. It also appears that the two languages of bilinguals are not necessarily represented in separate neural regions, although depending on certain tasks, they may appear to be functionally dissociated. Finally, it appears that neural repercussions of knowing more than one language extend beyond the level of brain functioning to affect various aspects of brain structure. Thus, knowing and using two or more languages presents a rich and varied form of experience that has distinct neurocognitive consequences. It remains for future research to spell out in more fine-grained detail the nature of these consequences for differences among bilinguals in the particular languages they know and in *how* they use their languages.

List of Key Words and Concepts

Aphasia, Bilingual advantage, Bilingual aphasia test, Brain lateralization, Brain mapping, Contralateral, Cortex, Differential impairment, Divided visual field, Early bilinguals, Electro-cortical stimulation mapping, Electroencephalography (EEG), Event-related brain potentials (ERPs), Functional magnetic resonance imaging (fMRI), Hemispheric asymmetries, Hemodynamic measures, Language brokering, Late bilinguals, Laterality, Magnetocephalographic measures, Meta-analysis, Metalinguistic awareness, N400, Near infrared spectrometry (NIRS), Parallel impairment, Positron emission topography (PET), Region of interest (ROI), Representational account, Right ear advantage (REA), Right hemisphere (RH), Right visual field, Selective aphasia, Rule of Ribot, Selective loss, Transcranial magnetic stimulation (TMS)

Internet Sites Related to the Bilingual Brain

Bilingual Aphasia Test: https://www.mcgill.ca/linguistics/research/bat
Bilingualism, Brain and Behavior: What's the Connection? York Circle Lecture by Ellen Bialystok (36 min.). https://www.youtube.com/watch?v=gOniN0PMyJg
Lost in Translation: https://www.youtube.com/watch?v=v3qphH5j304

Discussion Questions

(1) What is a meta-analysis, and why is it useful?
(2) How might the way we define bilingualism affect the way we study the bilingual brain?
(3) In what ways do bilinguals differ from each other, and how might these differences in turn affect the way the brain processes language in bilinguals?
(4) How do the ways in which brain structure and brain function are studied affect what we may conclude about the bilingual brain?
(5) What are some of the major research issues or debates that are currently being discussed in the literature on the bilingual brain?

Suggested Research Projects

(1) Go to a psychological database (e.g., *PsychINFO* or *EBSCO*), and obtain a laterality study cited in the meta-analysis by Hull and Vaid (2007). Find out how these researchers measured *language lateralization*. Can you describe the technique used in their experiment?
(2) Analyze on the basis of recent titles of journal articles on the bilingual brain and keywords used by the authors of these articles what aspects of the brain and of bilingualism researchers have focused on across two different time periods (e.g., 1985–1995 vs. 2005–2015).
(3) Prepare a mini-review of recent studies of language lateralization in *early* versus *late bilinguals*, separating them by approach (lesion-based, behavioral laterality, neuroimaging). What can you conclude about the relationship between age of onset of bilingualism and brain lateralization?

Suggested Readings

Garcia, A. (2015). Translating with an injured brain: Neurolinguistic aspects of translation as revealed by bilinguals with cerebral lesions. *Meta: Translators' Journal, 60*(1), 112–134.
Khachatryan, E., Vanhoof, G., Beyens, H., Goeleven, A., Thijs, V., & Van Hulle, M. (2016). Language processing in bilingual aphasia: A new insight into the problem. *WIREs Cognitive Science, 7,* 180–196.

Author Notes

I thank Fred Genesee, Loraine K. Obler, Michel Paradis, Renata Meuter, and the editors of this volume for fruitful discussion over the years. This chapter is dedicated to the memory and legacy of Frantisek Lichtenberk, Wallace E. Lambert, and Elizabeth Bates.

References

Albert, M., & Obler, L. K. (1978). *The bilingual brain*. New York: Academic Press.
Ben-Zeev, S. (1977). The influence of bilingualism on cognitive strategy and cognitive development. *Child Development, 48*, 1009–1018.
Berken, J., Chai, X., Gracco, V., & Klein, D. (2016). Effects of early and late bilingualism on resting state functional connectivity. *The Journal of Neuroscience, 36*(4), 1165–1172.
Chee, M., Tan, E., & Thiel, T. (1999). Mandarin and English single word processing studied with functional magnetic resonance imaging. *The Journal of Neuroscience, 19*, 3050–3056.
Cieślicka, A., & Heredia, R. (2011). Hemispheric asymmetries in processing L1 and L2 idioms: Effects of salience and context. *Brain and Language, 116*, 136–150.

D'Anselmo, A., Reiterer, S., Zuccarini, F., Tommasi, L., & Brancucci, A. (2013). Hemispheric asymmetries in bilinguals: Tongue similarity affects lateralization of second language. *Neuropsychologia, 51*, 1187–1194.

de Bruin, A., & Della Sala, S. (2016). The importance of language use when studying the neuroanatomical basis of bilingualism. *Language, Cognition, and Neuroscience, 31*(3), 335–339.

Dehaene, S., Dupoux, E., Mehler, J., Cohen, L., Paulesu, E., Perani, D., van de Moortel, P., Lehéricy, S., & Le Bihan, D. (1997). Anatomical variability in the cortical representation of first and second language. *NeuroReport, 8*, 3809–3815.

Dijkstra, T. (2003). Lexical storage and retrieval in bilinguals. In R. van Hout, A., Hulk, F. Kuiken, & R. Towell (Eds.), *The interface between syntax and the lexicon in second language acquisition* (pp. 129–150). Amsterdam: John Benjamins.

Fabbro, F. (2001). The bilingual brain: Bilingual aphasia. *Brain and Language, 79*, 201–210.

Frenck-Mestre, C., Anton, J. L., Roth, M., Vaid, J., & Viallet, F. (2005). Articulation in early and late bilinguals' two languages: Evidence from functional magnetic resonance imaging. *Neuroreport, 16*, 761–765.

Goral, M., Rosas, J., Conner, P., Maul, K. K., & Obler, L. K. (2012). Effects of language proficiency and language of the environment on aphasia therapy in a multilingual. *Journal of Neurolinguistics, 25*(6), 538–551.

Green, D. (1998). Mental control of the bilingual lexico-semantic system. *Bilingualism: Language and Cognition, 1*, 67–81.

Grosjean, F. (1989). Neurolinguists beware! The bilingual is not two monolinguals in one person. *Brain and Language, 36*, 3–15.

Hasegawa, M., Carpenter, P., & Just, M. (2002). An fMRI study of bilingual sentence comprehension and workload. *Neuroimage, 15*(3), 647–660.

Higby, E., Kim, J., & Obler, L. K. (2013). Multilingualism and the brain. *Annual Review of Applied Linguistics, 33*, 68–101.

Hull, R., & Vaid, J. (2005). Clearing the cobwebs from the study of the bilingual brain: Converging evidence from laterality and electrophysiological research. In J. Kroll & A. M. B. de Groot (Eds.), *Handbook of bilingualism: Psycholinguistic approaches* (pp. 480–496). Oxford: Oxford University Press.

Hull, R., & Vaid, J. (2006). Laterality and language experience. *Laterality, 11*(5), 436–464.

Hull, R., & Vaid, J. (2007). Bilingual language lateralization: A tale of two hemispheres. *Neuropsychologia, 45*(9), 1987–2008.

Ijalba, E., Obler, L. K., & Chengappa, S. (2004). Bilingual aphasia. In T. K. Bhatia & W. C. Ritchie (Eds.), *The handbook of bilingualism* (pp. 71–89). Malden, MA: Blackwell.

Illes, J., Francis, W., Desmond, J., Gabrieli, J., Glover, G., Poldrack, R., Lee, C., & Wagner, A. (1999). Convergent cortical representation of semantic processing in bilinguals. *Brain and Language, 70*(3), 347–363.

Karanth, P., & Rangamani, G. N. (1988). Crossed aphasia in multilinguals. *Brain and Language, 34*, 169–180.

Kim, K., Relkin, N., Lee, K., & Hirsch, J. (1997). Distinct cortical areas associated with native and second languages. *Nature, 388*, 171–174.

Klein, D., Mok, K., Chen, J. K., & Watkins. K. E. (2014). Age of language learning shapes brain structure: A cortical thickness study of bilingual and monolingual individuals. *Brain and Language, 131*, 20–24.

Lambert, W. E. (1969). Psychological studies of interdependencies of the bilingual's two languages. In J. Puhvel (Ed.), *Substance and structure of language* (pp. 99–126). Los Angeles: University of California Press.

Lambert, W. E., & Fillenbaum, S. (1959). A pilot study of aphasia among bilinguals. *Canadian Journal of Psychology, 13*, 28–34.

Lambert, W. E., & Rawlings, C. (1969). Bilingual processing of mixed language associative networks. *Journal of Verbal Learning and Verbal Behavior, 6*, 604–609.

Li, P., Legault, J., & Litcofsky, K. (2014). Neuroplasticity as a function of second language learning: Anatomical changes in the human brain. *Cortex, 58*, 301–324.

Liu, H., & Cao, F. (2016). L1 and L2 processing in the bilingual brain: A meta-analysis of neuroimaging studies. *Brain & Language, 159*, 60–73.

Lucas, T. H., McKhann, G. M, & Ojemann, G. A. (2004). Functional separation of languages in the bilingual brain: A comparison of electrical stimulation language mapping in 25 bilingual patients and 117 monolingual control patients. *Journal of Neurosurgery, 101*, 449–457.

Luria, A. (1960). Differences between the disturbances of speech and writing in Russian and in French. *International Journal of Slavic Linguistics and Poetics, 3*, 13–22.

Mahendra, N., Plante, E., Magloire, J., Milman, L., Trouard, T. P. (2003). fMRI variability and the localization of languages in the bilingual brain. *NeuroReport, 14*(9), 1225–1228.

Mechelli, A., Crinion, J., Noppeney, U., O'Doherty, J., Ashburner, J., Frackowiak, R., & Price, C. (2004). Neurolinguistics: Structural plasticity in the bilingual brain. *Nature, 431*, 757–757.

Miller Amberber, A., & Cohen, H. (2012). Assessment and treatment of bilingual aphasia and dementia using the Bilingual Aphasia Test. *Journal of Neurolinguistics, 25*(6), 515–519.

Minkowski, M. (1963). On aphasia in polyglots. In L. Halpern (Ed.), *Problems of dynamic neurology* (pp. 116–119). Jerusalem: Hebrew University.

Monti, A., Ferrucci, R., Fumagalli, M., Mameli, F., Cogiamanian, F., Ardolino, G., & Priori, A. (2013). Transcranial direct current stimulation (tDCS) and language. *Journal of Neurology, Neurosurgery, and Psychiatry, 84*, 832–842.

Moreno, E., Federmeier, K., & Kutas, M. (2002). Switching languages, switching palabras (words): An electrophysiological study of code switching. *Brain and Language, 80*, 188–207.

Neville, H., & Bavelier, D. (2002). Human brain plasticity: Evidence from sensory deprivation and altered language experience. In M. Hofman, G. Boer, A. Holtmaat, E. Van Someren, J. Verhaagen, & D. Swaab (Eds.), *Progress in brain research* (pp. 177–188). Elsevier Science.

Newport, E., Bavelier, D., & Neville, H. (2001). Critical thinking about critical periods: Perspectives on a critical period for language acquisition. In E. Dupoux (Ed.), *Language, brain, and cognitive development: Essays in honor of Jacques Mehler* (pp. 481–502). Cambridge: MIT Press.

Ng, S., Gonzales, C., & Wicha, N. (2014). The fox and the cabra: An ERP analysis of reading code switched nouns and verbs in bilingual short stories. *Brain Research, 1157*, 127–140.

Obler, L., Zatorre, R., Galloway, L., & Vaid, J. (1982). Cerebral lateralization in bilinguals: Methodological issues. *Brain and Language, 15*, 40–54.

Ojemann, G., & Whitaker, H. A. (1978). The bilingual brain. *Archives of Neurology, 35*, 409–412.

Paradis, M. (1983). *Readings on aphasia in bilinguals and polyglots*. Montreal: Didier.

Paradis, M. (2001). Bilingual and polyglot aphasia. In R. Berndt (Ed.), *Handbook of neuropsychology* (Vol. 3, pp. 69–91). Amsterdam: Elsevier.

Paradis, M. (2004). *An integrated neurolinguistic theory of bilingualism*. John Benjamins.

Paradis, M. (2011). Principles underlying the Bilingual Aphasia Test (BAT) and its uses. *Clinical Linguistics and Phonetics, 25*, 427–443.

Peal, E., & Lambert, W. E. (1962). The relations of bilingualism to intelligence. *Psychological Monographs, 76*(27), 1–23.

Perani, D., Dehaene, S., Grassi, F., Cohen, S., Cappa, S., Dupoux, Fazio, F., & Mehler, J. (1996). Brain processing of native and foreign languages. *NeuroReport, 7*, 2439–2444.

Pitres, A. (1895). Etudes sur l'aphasie chez les polyglottes. *Revue de Medecine, 15*, 873–899.

Rao, C., & Vaid, J. (2017). Morphology, orthography, and the two hemispheres: A divided visual field study with Hindi/Urdu biliterates. *Neuropsychologia, 98*, 46–55.

Rapport, R. L., Tan, C. T., & Whitaker, H. A. (1983). Language function and dysfunction among Chinese- and English-speaking polyglots: Cortical stimulation, Wada testing, and clinical studies. *Brain and Language, 18*, 342–366.

Ribot (1881). *Diseases of memory: An essay in the positive psychology.* London: Paul.

Roux, F. E., Lubrano, V., Lauwers-Cances, V., Tremoulet, M., Mascott, C., & Demonet, J. F. (2004). Intra-operative mapping of cortical areas involved in reading in mono- and bilingual patients. *Brain, 127*, 1796–1810.

Roux, F. E., & Tremoulet, M. (2002). Organization of language areas in bilingual patients: A cortical stimulation study. *Journal of Neurosurgery, 97*(4), 857–864.

Schmidt, G. W., & Roberts, T. (2009). Second language research using magnetocephalography: A review. *Second Language Research*, *25*, 135–166.

Simos, P., Castillo, E., Fletcher, J., Francis, D., Maestud, F., Breier J., Maggio, W., & Papanicolaou, A. (2001). Mapping of receptive language cortex in bilingual volunteers by using magnetic source imaging. *Journal of Neurosurgery*, *95*, 76–81.

Vaid, J. (2002). Bilingualism. In V. S. Ramachandran (Ed.), *Encyclopedia of the human brain* (Vol. 1, pp. 417–432). San Diego: Elsevier.

Vaid, J. (2008). Neural substrates of language processing in bilinguals: Imagi(ni)ng the possibilities. In Srinivasan, N., Gupta, A. K., & Pandey, J. (Eds.), *Advances in cognitive science* (pp. 122–136). New Delhi: Sage Press.

Vaid, J., & Genesee, F. (1980). Neuropsychological approaches to bilingualism: A critical review. *Canadian Journal of Psychology*, *34*, 417–445.

Vaid, J., & Hall, D. G. (1991). Neuropsychological perspectives on bilingualism: Right, left, and center. In A. Reynolds (Ed.), *Bilingualism, multiculturalism and second language learning: The McGill Conference in Honour of Wallace E. Lambert* (pp. 81–112). Hillsdale, NJ: Lawrence Erlbaum Associates.

Vaid, J., & Hull, R. (2002). Re-envisioning the bilingual brain using functional neuroimaging: Methodological and interpretive issues. In F. Fabbro (Ed.), *Advances in the neurolinguistics of bilingualism* (pp. 315–355). Udine Forum: Udine University Press.

Vaid, J., & Meuter, R. (2016). Not through a glass darkly: Refocusing the psycholinguistic study of bilingualism through a 'bivocal' lens. In V. Cook & L. Wei (Eds.), *The Cambridge handbook of linguistic multicompetence* (pp. 77–96). Cambridge, UK: Cambridge University Press.

Vaid, J., & Meuter, R. (2017). Languages without borders: Reframing the study of the bilingual mental lexicon. In G. Libben, M. Goral, & M. Libben (Eds.), *Bilingualism: A framework for understanding the mental lexicon* (pp. 7–26). Amsterdam: John Benjamins.

Vaid, J., & Pandit, R. (1991). Sentence interpretation in normal and aphasic Hindi speakers. *Brain and Language*, 41, 250–274.

Wartenburger, I., Heekeren, H. R., Abutalebi, J., Cappa, S. F., Villringer A., & Perani, D. (2003). Early setting of grammatical processing in the bilingual brain. *Neuron*, *37*(1), 159–170.

Wattendorf, E., & Festman, J. (2008). Images of the multilingual brain: The effect of age of second language acquisition. *Annual Review of Applied Linguistics*, *28*, 3–24.

Wei, M., Joshi, A., Zhang, M., Mei, L., Manis, F., He, Q., Beattie, R. L., Xue, G., Shattuck, D. W., Leahy, R. M., Xue, F., Houston, S. M., Chen, C., Dong, Q., & Lu, Z.-L. (2015). How age of acquisition influences brain architecture in bilinguals. *Journal of Neurolinguistics*, *36*, 35–55.

Section III

Creativity and Developmental Principles

8 Bilingualism and Creativity

Anatoliy V. Kharkhurin

Introduction

During the past few decades, research in the area of bilingual cognitive and linguistic development has made tremendous progress and provided evidence supporting the notion that speaking more than one language extends, rather than diminishes, an individual's cognitive capacities (see Chapter 10). There is a strong argument in the literature that bilingual development may result in establishing specific architectures of the mind that are likely to promote later *cognitive advantages*. On the other side, according to the *creative cognition approach*, creativity is considered a product of *normative cognitive functioning*. The conceptual framework of creative cognition rests on two major assumptions. First, it characterizes creative products as novel (i.e., original or unexpected) and appropriate (i.e., useful or meeting task constraints; see Mayer, 1999, for an overview). Second, *ideas and tangible products that are novel and useful are assumed to emerge from the application of ordinary, fundamental cognitive processes to existing knowledge structures* (Ward, 2007, p. 28). One's creative performance can be understood in terms of the use of specific processes, and the richness and flexibility of stored cognitive structures to which these processes are applied (Ward, Smith, & Vaid, 1997). *Creative capacity*, therefore, is assumed as an essential property of *normative human cognition* (Ward, Smith, & Finke, 1999), and increase in general cognitive functioning may facilitate an individual's creative abilities. Thus, if bilingualism results in more elaborate cognitive structures and/or functioning, it may also facilitate creative functioning (Kharkhurin, 2012a).

In psychometric tradition, creative thinking is perceived as an ability to initiate multiple cycles of convergent and *divergent thinking* (Guilford, 1967), which create an active, attention-demanding process that allows generation of new, alternative solutions (Mumford, Mobley, Uhlman, Reiter-Palmon, & Doares, 1991). The fundamental difference between convergent and divergent thinking is that the former is a conscious, attention-demanding process, while the latter occurs in the unconscious mind, where attention is defocused (e.g., Kasof, 1997; Mendelsohn, 1976) and thought is associative (e.g., Koestler, 1964; Mednick & Mednick, 1967; Ward et al., 1997). *Convergent thinking* seeks one correct answer to the question or solution to a problem, which must have a single answer or solution (Runco, Dow, & Smith, 2006). Divergent thinking, on the other hand, involves a broad search for information and the generation of numerous novel alternative answers or solutions to a problem (Guilford, 1967). The solutions generated during divergent thinking are subsequently evaluated during convergent thinking, which narrows all possible alternatives down to a single solution.

Over the last half-century, numerous studies have provided evidence for the ability of divergent thinking tests to predict certain aspects of creative problem-solving performance and real-world creative achievement. Although as Runco (1991, p. ix) argued, *Divergent thinking is not synonymous with creative thinking*, many researchers believe that divergent thinking is a defining component of the creative process (Lubart, 2000). Guilford (1967) associated the properties of divergent thinking with four main characteristics: fluency (the ability to rapidly produce a large number of ideas or solutions to a problem); *flexibility* (the capacity to consider a variety of approaches to a problem simultaneously); *elaboration* (the ability to think through the details of an idea and carry it out); and originality (the tendency to produce ideas different from those of most other people). Factor analysis of these characteristics performed with several distinct sociocultural samples (Kharkhurin, 2008, 2009, 2011) revealed that they can be grouped together as two types of creative capacities: fluency, flexibility, and elaboration traits seem to represent the ability to generate and to elaborate on various, often unrelated, ideas; while the originality trait is likely to represent the ability to extract novel and unique ideas. The first type is referred to as *generative capacity*: It addresses the ability to activate a multitude of unrelated concepts and work through the concepts already activated. The second type is referred to as *innovative* capacity: it accounts for the ability to produce original and useful ideas.

Unfortunately, the relationship between bilingualism and creativity has not received adequate consideration in the scientific community. The reasons for this oversight can be inferred from the discussions in this volume. First, according to Simonton (2008), both theoretical constructs are fuzzily defined and researchers still struggle with a precise description of these phenomena. Second, the impact of bilingualism on creativity is mediated by the effects of *bicultural experience*. On one side, the term *culture* has numerous overlapping and misleading meanings, which hampers adequate quantitative analysis of its relation to one's cognitive functioning. On the other side, the influence of sociocultural context on an individual's creative abilities has received in itself substantial attention in the scientific community (e.g., Kaufman & Sternberg, 2006; Lubart, 1999; Niu & Sternberg, 2001). Third, the research into creativity has virtually no overlap with that of bilingualism. Each of these fields is largely developed and has received a substantial amount of empirical investigation. However, the studies focusing on the intersection of these two areas are few in number.

In her seminal review paper, Ricciardelli (1992b) reported 24 studies that took place between 1965 and 1992. In the following decade, this scarce research has been complimented by six dissertation works (Fleith, 1999; Garcia, 1996; Konaka, 1997; Martorell, 1992; Stephens, 1997; Stone, 1993), six peer-reviewed journal articles (Burck, 2004; Fleith, Renzulli, & Westberg, 2002; Garcia, 2003; Karapetsas & Andreou, 1999; Paduch, 2005; Palaniappan, 1994) and one book (Calderón & Minaya-Rowe, 2003), which addressed the theme in the context of bilingual education and its potential impact on students' creativity. Two more studies (Aguirre, 2003; Granada, 2003) focus on bilingual and gifted population. The concern of these works, however, appears with how to educate students who have been identified as bilingual and gifted. Altogether, bilingual research in creativity delivered approximately 40 studies over 40 years of work. Only recently, this theme was resuscitated and received systematic empirical investigation in the author's longitudinal project studying cognitive processes underlying bilingual creativity (Kharkhurin, 2005, 2007, 2008, 2009, 2010a, 2010b, 2011; Kharkhurin & Altarriba, 2015; Kharkhurin & Wei, 2014). After that, six additional studies addressing the relationship between bilingualism and creative and insightful problem-solving appeared in various publications (Adi-Japha, Berberich-Artzi, & Libnawi, 2010; Cushen & Wiley, 2011; Hommel, Colzato, Fischer, & Christoffels, 2011; Kostandyan & Ledovaya, 2013; Lee & Kim, 2011; Leikin, 2013).

This chapter provides an overview of empirical research on the relationship between bilingualism and creativity. The focus of most of these studies is primarily on the creative performance of bilingual and monolingual children and adults. Only recently, it has been shifted to creative performance of different types of bilinguals. After reviewing the empirical findings, we discuss their methodological issues and provide their theoretical interpretation.

Empirical Findings

Psychometric research provides evidence favoring bilinguals' creative abilities. Most of the studies have been conducted with children and only recently were they complemented by research with college students. In most of these studies, creativity was assessed by divergent thinking tests, and the comparison was made between bilingual and monolingual groups.

Psychometric Tools

The identification of creativity with divergent thinking spawned an array of divergent thinking tests such as *Alternative Uses* (Christensen, Guilford, Merrifield, & Wilson, 1960), *Consequences* (Christensen, Merrifield, & Guilford, 1953), *Instances Test* (Wallach & Kogan, 1965), *Plot Titles* (Berger & Guilford, 1969), *Remote Associates Test* (Mednick & Mednick, 1967), *Uses of Objects Test* (Getzels & Jackson, 1962), and *Torrance Tests of Creative Thinking* (TTCT; Torrance, 1966). The latter were developed to measure divergent thinking abilities in children. The TTCT were the most widely used (Davis, 1991) and most-referenced (Lissitz & Willhoft, 1985) tests of creativity that have been translated into more than 35 languages (Millar, 2002) and utilized in the educational field and the corporate world (Kim, 2006). These tests consist of relatively simple verbal and figural tasks that tap into divergent thinking abilities, as well as in other problem-solving skills. Since giving both the verbal and figural forms of the TTCT often requires considerable testing time (45 minutes for the verbal and 30 minutes for the figural), Torrance and his colleagues developed several abridged versions. The most recent adult version, the *Abbreviated Torrance Test for Adults* (ATTA; Goff & Torrance, 2002) contains three 3-minute verbal and figural tasks that are scored for fluency, flexibility, elaboration, and originality.

Research with Children

The majority of studies investigating the relationship between bilingualism and creativity in children reported bilingual advantages on various verbal and non-verbal divergent thinking tests (Garcia, 1996; Konaka, 1997; Stone, 1993; see also Ricciardelli, 1992b, for an overview of the earlier studies). Bilingual children outperformed their monolingual counterparts on divergent thinking traits such as fluency (e.g., Carringer, 1974; Jacobs & Pierce, 1966; Ricciardelli, 1992a), flexibility (e.g., Carringer, 1974; Konaka, 1997), elaboration (e.g., Srivastava & Khatoon, 1980; Torrance, Gowan, Wu, & Aliotti, 1970), and originality (c.g., Cummins & Gulutsan, 1974; Konaka, 1997; Leikin, 2013; Okoh, 1980). In a recent study, Adi-Japha et al. (2010) compared four- and five-year-old English–Hebrew and Arabic–Hebrew bilingual children and their monolingual peers on *Karmiloff-Smith's (1990) Task* of drawing a non-existent object, which is considered to be a measure of *cognitive flexibility*. They found that bilinguals exhibited a significantly higher rate of *interrepresentational flexibility* in their drawings (e.g., *a giraffe flower*, *a chair-house*, found in 28 of 54 drawings).

Only a few studies reported a different pattern of findings (e.g., Garcia, 1996; Gowan & Torrance, 1965). Whitney (1974) found no differences in the verbal TTCT scores obtained by 12- and 14-year-old German–English bilinguals and English monolinguals. Similarly, Stephens (1997) did not reveal any TTCT performance differences between Spanish–English bilinguals and their monolingual counterparts, although the former indicated greater social problem-solving abilities (assessed by the *Interpersonal Problem-Solving Scale*). In the same fashion, Fleith et al. (2002) demonstrated that placement in Portuguese monolingual or English bilingual classrooms was not related to Brazilian third to fifth grade students' TTCT performance. Finally, Torrance et al. (1970) compared Chinese– and Malayan–English bilingual and Chinese and Malayan monolingual children on figural TTCT. They found monolingual superiority on the fluency in different grades and flexibility in grades three and four.

The potentially *negative effect* of bilingualism on creativity could be explained by Cummins's (1976) *threshold hypothesis*. It states that bilinguals need to achieve a minimum (age-appropriate) proficiency threshold in both of their languages before bilingualism can promote cognitive advantages. This hypothesis was supported by studies with children (e.g., Diaz, 1985) showing that participants who did not reach a certain proficiency level in each of their languages performed poorer on a variety of cognitive tasks compared with monolinguals. For example, Ricciardelli (1992a) tested this theory with Italian–English bilingual and English monolingual children and found that only those bilinguals who scored high on both English and Italian versions of the *Peabody Picture Vocabulary Test* (Dunn, 1965), showed superior divergent thinking and metalinguistic abilities. Those bilinguals who had low proficiency in either one or both languages were statistically indistinguishable from the monolinguals. Therefore, negative effects of bilingualism on creativity reported in studies mentioned above could be explained simply by bilinguals' poor linguistic fluency in one or both of their languages. Unfortunately, this assumption cannot be confirmed due to the fact that many of these studies did not report what language assessment tools have been employed.

Research With Adults

The studies of the relationship between bilingualism and creativity in adults are thin on the ground. In her review paper of the early studies in the field, Ricciardelli (1992b) reported only one study conducted with adults. Lemmon and Goggin (1989) compared performance of undergraduate Spanish–English bilingual and English monolingual college students on cognitive ability tasks that required concept formation, *mental reorganization*, abstract and divergent thinking, and *mental flexibility*. The monolingual participants tended to score higher than their bilingual counterparts on most of the measures of cognitive skill. However, subsequent comparisons of the monolingual group with high and low proficiency bilingual subgroups (divided on the basis of their picture naming score in Spanish) indicated that this effect could be attributed to participants with limited skills in Spanish. In a later study, Karapetsas and Andreou (1999) found that fluent bilingual Greek–English adults outperformed their Greek monolingual counterparts on fluency in divergent thinking assessed by the Uses of Objects Test (Getzels & Jackson, 1962). In a recent study (Cushen & Wiley, 2011), the performance of monolingual and bilingual undergraduate colleague students was compared on *insight* and *non-insight problems*. An example of insight problem-solving task in this study presents a triangle formed out of ten coins arranged in such a way that it points towards the top of the page. The task is to move three coins to get the triangle to point to the bottom of the page while the coins still form a perfect triangle. This task probes an individual's ability to approach a problem in a non-traditional manner. An example of non-insight problem-solving task in this study encourages participants to find an exact number for a variable by selecting a smallest set of mathematical equations out of a larger set. Bilingual individuals who acquired two languages by the age of six demonstrated better rate of insight problem-solving than non-insight problem-solving, whereas their monolingual counterparts showed the opposite effect. Note however that bilinguals did not reveal better insight problem-solving abilities than monolinguals. These results could be due to inaccurate selection of bilingual sample, which included participants speaking English and a large variety of other languages, which proficiency was not controlled for. Hommel et al. (2011) demonstrated a high-proficient bilingual advantage for convergent thinking and a low-proficient bilingual advantage for fluency in divergent thinking. Ironically, this study used Mednick and Mednick's (1967) Remote Associates Test as a test of convergent thinking, whereas it is generally presented as a creativity test, which taps in ability to establish analogies. This study had other methodological inconsistencies, which are discussed in the following section.

In a series of studies initiated by the author in different geographic, linguistic, and cultural locations, bilingual college students revealed advantages on various creativity and cognitive tests compared with their monolingual counterparts. Russian–English bilingual immigrants in the US obtained greater ATTA fluency, flexibility, and elaboration scores than English monolinguals (Kharkhurin, 2008). An additional analysis of the same samples revealed bilingual advantage in *non-verbal creativity* and a monolingual advantage in *verbal creativity* (Kharkhurin, 2010a). The United Arab Emirates (UAE) resident Farsi–English bilinguals from the same educational group revealed advantages in innovative capacity compared with Farsi monolinguals (Kharkhurin, 2009). They also demonstrated greater ability to think beyond standard category properties (measured by a variation of the *Invented Alien Creature Test*; cf. Ward, 1994) and better *fluid intelligence* (assessed by Cattell's, 1973, *Culture Fair Intelligence Test*).

The reviewed studies demonstrate that both bilingual children and adults systematically outperform their monolingual counterparts on divergent thinking tests. A logical continuation of this research calls for systematic investigation of specific cognitive mechanisms facilitating creative performance, which may be encouraged by bilingual practice. The answer to this question, however, cannot be obtained from a comparison of bilinguals and monolinguals, for people in these two groups seem to have two distinct cognitive structures. This assumption receives growing support in linguistic multicompetence literature (see Cook & Wei, 2016, for discussion). Speaking multiple languages adds not only to an individual's linguistic repertoire, multilingual practice influences one's cognitive functions, conceptual representations, and even *personality traits*. Under this assumption, bilinguals and monolinguals appear to possess distinctively different minds, and therefore, their comparison would not shed any light on creative advantages of the former. Thus, a body of empirical data accumulated in bilingual creativity research would not illuminate the problem in question. Rather, we need to systematically investigate bilingual speakers with different histories of language acquisition and use to identify what factors can facilitate cognitive processes underlying creativity.

Bilingual Developmental Factors

Language Proficiency

Language proficiency appears to be the first factor that might have an impact on creative performance. Indirect evidence for the role of language proficiency in an individual's creative abilities comes from the studies comparing bilinguals with monolinguals. Mentioned above, Cummins's (1976) Threshold hypothesis predicted that bilinguals need to achieve high levels of proficiency in both of their languages before bilingualism can promote cognitive advantages. This was demonstrated in the studies with bilingual children and college students. They revealed greater divergent thinking performance of participants with high proficiency in both languages as compared to their linguistically unbalanced counterparts. For example, Ricciardelli's (1992a) study with Italian–English bilingual and English monolingual children revealed that only bilinguals with high proficiency in both languages showed greater fluency and imagination compared with their monolingual counterparts. Similarly, Lemmon and Goggin's (1989) study with Spanish–English bilingual college students found that the tendency of monolinguals to outperform their bilingual counterparts on fluency and flexibility was ascribed to those participants classified as a low proficiency group. In the same fashion, Konaka (1997) reported that the degree of bilingual balance (see the next section for details) significantly predicted performance on fluency, flexibility, and originality.

Few recent studies conducted with different types of bilinguals in various geographic locations and cultural contexts confirmed the effect of language proficiency on one's creative capacities. Bilinguals with high proficiency in both English and Russian performed better on elaboration than their less proficient counterparts (Kharkhurin, 2008). Similarly, Farsi–English bilinguals highly proficient in both languages outperformed their unbalanced and moderately proficient counterparts on fluency (Kharkhurin, 2009). Lee and Kim (2011) found that more balanced Korean–English bilinguals (whose level of bilingualism was assessed by the *Word Association Test*; Lambert, 1956) obtained higher creativity scores than their less balanced counterparts. These findings were complemented by the ones of another study conducted with bilinguals with different proficiency levels in English (Kharkhurin, 2011). This study revealed that more linguistically proficient bilinguals tended to score higher on originality and revealed more unstructured imagination (as measured by the Invented Alien Creature test; cf. Ward, 1994).

Age of Language Acquisition

The second factor refers to the age at which individuals acquired their languages. Traditionally, the distinction is made between *simultaneous* and *sequential bilinguals* (McLaughlin, 1984). The simultaneous bilinguals learn both of their languages from the onset of language acquisition. The sequential bilinguals learn their second language (L2) after age of five, when the basic components of first language (L1) are already in place. The sequential bilinguals are further divided into early and late ones, reflecting the age at which L2 acquisition occurred (Genesee, 1978). A group of simultaneous Armenian–Russian bilinguals scored higher on flexibility and originality than their sequential counterparts who started to learn one of the two languages two to four years later (Kostandyan & Ledovaya, 2013). There is also evidence that Russian–English bilinguals who acquired L2 at a younger age scored higher on fluency and flexibility (Kharkhurin, 2008). Similarly, bilinguals who acquired their L2 (English) by the age of six tended to solve insight problems more readily than their counterparts who acquired L2 after this age (Cushen & Wiley, 2011).

Sociocultural Context

The third factor reflects the context of language acquisition and use. The studies of bilingual creativity generally disregarded the fact that most participants in the target samples experience and participate in more than one culture. These individuals are primarily immigrants, migrant workers, members of the minority groups, or foreign students exposed to different educational systems. They acquire each of their languages in the respective cultural environments where different cultural cues are available (Pavlenko, 2000). Therefore, in addition to acquiring several languages, they could also adopt a range of multicultural values and beliefs. Acculturation studies support this view by demonstrating that language acquisition is often accompanied by adoption of the cultural values of the country in which this language is acquired (e.g., Birman, Trickett, & Vinokurov, 2002; Gordon, 1964). On the other hand, creativity research demonstrated that the specific economic, political, social, and cultural aspects of the environment can have a considerable influence both on levels of creative potential and on how creativity is evaluated (e.g., Lubart, 1999). Sociocultural values and norms determine and shape the concept of creativity, which in turn may influence the manner in which creative potential is apprehended and incarnated. Thus, if bilinguals acquire their languages in different countries, they are most likely to have been exposed to different sociocultural environments. This multicultural experience may encourage variations in the development of creative potential. Therefore, bilingual individuals' experience with multiple sociocultural settings may increase their creative potential.

This argument finds support in *cross-cultural research* demonstrating that the effect of bilingualism on creative performance is often confounded with the one of biculturalism (see Kharkhurin, 2012a, for a discussion). For example, Kharkhurin (2008) found that the length of residence in the new cultural environment related to Russian–English bilingual college students' fluency, flexibility, and elaboration above and beyond the effect of bilingualism. Similar findings were obtained by Maddux and Galinsky (2009), who found that the amount of time MBA students from 40 different nations had lived abroad significantly predicted creative solutions of the *Duncker's (1945) Candle-Mounting Problem* when the effect of bilingualism was controlled.

Another line of research proposes that, in addition to direct contribution to this performance, the specific settings of the sociocultural environment to which an individual was exposed may modulate the impact of bilingualism on creativity (e.g., Kharkhurin, 2010b; Leung, Maddux, Galinsky, & Chiu, 2008). This idea stems from the cross-cultural research in creativity demonstrating that variations in the manners of socialization, degrees of self-perception and self-expression, and education and social conduct may modulate the differences in creative performance of the representatives of different cultures (e.g., Kharkhurin & Samadpour Motalleebi, 2008; Niu & Sternberg, 2001; Zha, Walczyk, Griffith-Ross, Tobacyk, & Walczyk, 2006). If individuals' creative potential may be influenced by their experience with different cultures, the variations in bilinguals' cultural settings may have an impact on different aspects of their creative thinking. For example, Kharkhurin (2010b) compared Farsi–English bilingual and Farsi monolingual college students residing in the Middle East with their Russian–English bilingual and English monolingual counterparts residing in the US. The study demonstrated that the interaction between bilingualism and the sociocultural environment had a significant influence on creative performance. Moreover, this study speculated that the *cultural distance* between the environments to which bilingual groups were exposed in the respective countries could also play a role in an individual's creative behavior.

Code-Switching

The fourth factor addresses defining feature of bilingualism, namely, *code-switching*—the alternation and mixing of different languages in the same episode of speech production.

Code-switching has been argued to be a creative act (e.g., Wei & Wu, 2009). For example, linguists working in the linguistic ethnography tradition replaced code-switching with other terms such as *translanguaging* to capture its creative and dynamic nature (see a review in Garcia & Wei, 2014). They investigated the use of translanguaging in diverse contexts, from literature and drama, to pop songs, the new media, and public signs (e.g., Androutsopoulos, 2013; Chik, 2010; Jonsson, 2005; Sebba, Jonsson, & Mahootian, 2012). These studies took code-switching not simply as a juxtaposition of different grammatical structural elements, but as an expressive and creative performance. Bhatia and Ritchie (2008) revealed various facets of creativity through code-switching as it manifests itself in the day-to-day verbal behavior of a bilingual. They argued that code-switching is essentially an *optimizing* strategy rendering a wide variety of new meanings which the separate linguistic systems are incapable of rendering by themselves. The only empirical evidence for the relationship between code-switching and creativity demonstrated that those individuals who code-switch frequently and regularly obtained higher scores on originality than those who do not code-switch in their everyday practice (Kharkhurin & Wei, 2014).

Methodological Considerations

Interpreting the findings of bilinguals' creative advantages, one is tempted to draw a conclusion, which assumes their *eminent creativity*. That is, the mere fact of speaking multiple languages guarantees one's exceptional creative capacities. However, this assumption would be quite premature considering the lack of systematic examination of bilingualism—creativity relation outside a laboratory setting. Due to the fact that the psychometric research deals with mundane rather than eminent creativity, the real-life creative accomplishments of bilingual individuals have not been tested. Yet no *historiometric* study to date has directly investigated the relationship between bilingualism and eminent creativity. Moreover, the real state of affairs in bilingual countries discourages from making too optimistic assumptions. In spite of the fact that most nationals of these countries speak more than one language, we do not find an overall higher level of creativity in these countries compared to predominantly monolingual countries. In this regard, a survey *Europeans and their languages* (2012) reported frequency of use of first language different from the mother tongue for 27 EU member states. This data was compared with these countries' creative class (Florida, 2002), which presents the portion of a population that is involved in creative work. The creative class consists *of workers in fields spanning science and technology, business and management, healthcare and education, and arts, culture, and entertainment* (Florida, Mellander, & Stolarick, 2011, p. 29). Surprisingly, the correlation between the frequency of L2 use and the creative class barely exceeded zero.

In other words, real-life observations do not support empirical findings demonstrating greater creative performance of bilinguals. Several possible explanations can be advanced to account for the contradiction between empirical findings showing bilingual advantages on the creativity tests and the real-life observations showing no remarkable differences in creative performance between bilingual and monolingual populations. These explanations serve as a framework for methodological considerations of bilingualism—creativity research.

Conceptual Definitions

Theoretical constructs of bilingualism and creativity are fuzzily defined, and researchers still struggle with a precise description of these phenomena. Current research lacks common framework of creativity. Although creativity is traditionally defined in terms of novelty and utility (Mayer, 1999), Kharkhurin (2014), for example, challenged this definition as being biased by a *Western perception of creativity*. He proposed an alternative four-criterion construct of creativity, which, in addition to novelty and utility, considers two other characteristics typical for *Eastern perception of creativity*: aesthetics and authenticity. In the same fashion, Boden (2004), Simonton (2012), and Sternberg and Lubart (1995) argued for three criteria, and Runco (forthcoming) argued for just one. As a consequence, the tests employed in creativity research provide mixed assessments with no strong correlation among each other (e.g., Hocevar & Bachelor, 1989; Simonton, 2000). For example, the creative cognition approach (Ward et al., 1997) mentioned in the beginning of the chapter linked creative behavior to various cognitive processes and functions (such as divergent thinking; Guilford, 1967). Personality psychologists, likewise, suggested that some personality traits are linked to creative behavior (e.g., Baas, Roskes, Sligte, Nijstad, & De Dreu, 2013; Chávez-Eakle, Eakle, & Cruz-Fuentes, 2012; Fürst, Ghisletta, & Lubart, 2014; Helson, 1996). Others claimed that individuals' motivation, attitudes and intentions, or their past experiences are related to creative behavior (e.g., Collins & Amabile, 1999; Davis, 1999; Gardner, 1993; Rogers, 1961). Still others consider social, cultural, and political determinants of creative behavior (see Runco, 2014, for an overview). Each of these approaches uses its own strategy of *creativity assessment*. Hocevar (1981, p. 450) listed ten different types of creativity measurement: *tests of divergent thinking, attitude and interest inventories, personality inventories, biographical inventories, teacher nominations, peer nominations, supervisor ratings, judgments of products, eminence and self-reported creative activities and achievements.* All of them were employed to identify creative talent. Therefore, as Hocevar (1981, p. 457) noted, *since each method is purported to be measuring creativity, it is reasonable to predict that they be correlated, thus satisfying a minimum condition of convergent validity.* However, a relatively weak correlation among these tests provided no convincing evidence of convergent validity. Mayer (1999, p. 450) identified at least five points on which researchers may differ in their approach to creativity: *whether creativity refers to a product, process, or person; whether creativity is personal or social; whether creativity is common or rare; whether creativity is domain-general or domain-specific; and whether creativity is quantitative or qualitative.* These considerations prompted Kaufmann (2003, p. 235) to make a rather bitter conclusion that *the field of creativity research was declared somewhat of a scientific disaster area.* In his view, the major problem of this research is *the considerable fragmentation that characterizes the field of creativity, both on the level of theory, measurement and empirical research, as well as the difficulty in pointing to core ideas and research findings* (Kaufmann, 2003, p. 235).

Although the concept of bilingualism is well elaborated in scientific investigation, researchers still debate about the definition of this phenomenon. Bilinguals rarely have equal fluency in their languages. They usually acquire and use these languages for different purposes, in different domains in life, and with different people (Grosjean, 1998). There was a long-lasting discussion in the literature about limiting bilingual study to so-called *true bilinguals*—those equally skilled in both languages (cf. Peal & Lambert, 1962). However, there are indications that such individuals are extremely rare. For example, by this strict definition, out of 238 participants in Kharkhurin's (2005) dissertational study who indicated that they spoke both English and Russian, only seven could be considered as *perfectly balanced* or true bilinguals. What about the rest of the sample? They were not perfectly balanced, for their command of both languages was not identical. At the same time, they were representative of the majority of bilingual population for individuals speaking several languages rarely display equal command of these languages. Thus, while it might be conceivable to limit one's experimental sample to perfectly balanced bilinguals, this would greatly sacrifice the generalization to the bilingual population at large. Therefore, it is prudent to consider bilingualism in a broader sense including individuals who are fluent in all their languages, but also individuals who actively use, or attempt to use more than one language, even if they have not achieved fluency in all of them (Kroll & de Groot, 1997).

Thus, research grounded in two ambiguous constructs, appears to be intricate to conduct. The picture becomes ever more complicated if one realizes that creativity is a complex that can be prompted by a large variety of factors such as education, expertise, motivation, attitudes, personality traits, personal experience, and socioeconomic, sociocultural, and political conditions (Runco, 2014). Bilingualism may play here an insignificant role, and its effect can be overridden by those factors. In other words, specific aspects of individuals' development may have impact on their creative performance above and beyond the effect of bilingualism.

Psychometric Assessment

Creativity Assessment

The majority of the studies in the field used tests of divergent thinking, most frequently— one or more of the TTCT subtests or their variations (Cramond, 1994). The choice of this paradigm was supported by a large body of research, which provides evidence for the ability of these tests to predict certain aspects of creative problem-solving (see Plucker & Renzulli, 1999, for an overview). However, there is a meaningful argument questioning the validity of divergent thinking tests as a creativity measure, because there is remarkably little evidence showing a strong correlation between highly creative people and high scores on these tests. Moreover, as mentioned earlier, the divergent thinking tests show little convergent and divergent validity (Hocevar & Bachelor, 1989). Thus, it is entirely possible that the mundane cognitive processing assessed by the divergent thinking tests cannot predict eminent creative performance. Due to limited convergent validity of the tests, bilinguals' greater divergent thinking performance in psychometric studies should not automatically imply their overall greater creative accomplishments in real life.

At the same time, a multitude of other assessment techniques have been completely excluded from the bilingualism—creativity investigation. These methods include, but are not limited to, the *Invented Alien Creature Task* (Ward, 1994), the *Consensual Assessment Technique* (Amabile, 1982), the *Lifetime Creativity Scales* (Richards, Kinney, Benet, & Merzel, 1988), the *Creative Personality Scale* (Gough, 1979), and the *Barron-Welsh Art Scale* (Barron & Welsh, 1952). Instead of assessing divergent thinking, these tests tap into imagination, *openness* to experience, creative personality, *self-concept*, hobbies and interests, and other traits that seem to be more likely to express genuine creativity. It is feasible that these tests are more pertinent to uncovering bilingual creative advantages than those adopted in the psychometric research.

Language Assessment

An obvious limitation of the language proficiency tests generally employed in psychometric research is that they do not assess all four major language skills: speaking, writing, listening, and reading (cf. Padilla & Ruiz, 1973). Rather, they assess specific aspects of linguistic aptitude such as language perception, language production, and vocabulary knowledge (e.g., Bialystok, Craik, Klein, & Viswanathan, 2004; Kharkhurin, 2012b; Lemmon & Goggin, 1989).

Although these tests may have a limited scope of application, they provide at least some assessment of language skills, which helps to identify participants' linguistic background. However, many studies, especially early studies in the field did not use any of them and provided no assessment of participants' language proficiency at all. For example, Chorney (1978) found that Ukrainian–English six- to nine-year-old bilinguals outperformed their English monolingual counterparts on the figural TTCT measures of fluency, flexibility, and originality. However, the interpretation of these results in favor of bilingualism would be premature since participants' language proficiency was not assessed. Similarly, Torrance et al. (1970) did not specify what criteria they used to include Chinese–English and Malayan–English speaking children in the bilingual group. No scores of children's proficiency in two languages were obtained to ensure a bilingual–monolingual dichotomy (Hakuta, 1984). In the same fashion, Landry (1974) selected bilinguals from an urban elementary school with a *foreign language in the elementary school* program and monolinguals from another urban elementary school without this program. Findings of bilingual superiority on the verbal and figural TTCT should be taken with caution for no assessment of participants' language proficiency was administered.

Lack of proper assessment of language skills continues into the contemporary research. For example, English–Dutch bilinguals in the above-mentioned Hommel et al.'s (2011) study were claimed to be balanced bilinguals despite the fact that they were tested only in English, and their proficiency in Dutch had not been assessed. Kostandyan and Ledovaya (2013) compared divergent thinking performance of simultaneous and successive Armenian–Russian bilinguals, although no control over their proficiency in both languages was provided.

Study Participants

One of the major methodological glitches contaminating not only bilingual creativity research, but also bilingualism research at large, arises from a procedure that assigns participants to bilingual and monolingual groups. As Hakuta and Diaz (1985, p. 329) pointed out, *in the real world, there is no such thing as random assignment to a bilingual and monolingual group*, and it is almost impossible to control all variables that may have an impact on this distinction.

As mentioned above, most of the early studies of bilingual creativity did not control for participants' comparative language proficiency when selecting them for one or another group. For example, Price-Williams and Ramirez (1977) based participants' selection solely on their ethnic background. Children attending Catholic parochial schools in Houston, Texas, were included in the bilingual group if they were Mexican or African–American on the assumption that they speak languages other than English. In the same fashion, Carringer (1974) assigned to the bilingual group only those participants who scored high on the Word Association Test (used as a measure of language proficiency) in both languages, whereas all others were included in the monolingual group. The results of this study favored bilingual divergent thinking. However, they are likely to be misleading, because the participants in the monolingual group were not adequately controlled for their linguistic abilities (MacNab, 1979). Due to the selection strategy employed, the monolingual group consisted of participants speaking only one language (whose linguistic skills were not tested) and those who spoke more than one language, but with low proficiency in one of these languages. Therefore, it is entirely possible that divergent thinking performance differences between bilinguals and monolinguals were in fact the differences in individuals with high and low language proficiency. Moreover, a bias in favor of bilingual creative achievement could arise from disproportional linguistic skills of participants in different groups. If a bilingual group included individuals with high proficiency in both languages, and a monolingual group consisted of participants whose language skills were not controlled, the variation in the groups' creative performance could result from their linguistic rather than cognitive abilities.

Recent studies provided more careful assessment of participants' languages and considered the specific language skills of the individuals assigned to bilingual and monolingual groups. Despite this improvement, the problem of participants' selection cannot be resolved. On one hand, selection of monolingual participants presents an apparent challenge, as there are virtually no individuals in certain geographic areas who were never exposed to other languages. For example, studies conducted in the New York City area (e.g., Kharkhurin, 2008; Konaka, 1997) assumed that monolingual participants spoke no other language but English. However, due to a highly mixed linguistic environment, these individuals were likely to experience languages other than English. The mere fact of the tacit presence of the foreign languages in their linguistic surrounding poses a challenge to integrity of the monolingual group. In the above-mentioned Hommel et al.'s (2011) study, a monolingual group included German University students who actually attained relatively high proficiency in English, which was indicated by their performance on the English proficiency test.

On the other hand, some participants included in the bilingual group can speak more than two languages. For example, the majority of Russian–English bilingual participants in Kharkhurin's (2008) study were immigrants from different republics of the former Soviet Union who, in addition to Russian, were exposed to their ethnic languages (e.g., Ukrainian, Belarusian, Moldavian). Moreover, some of them reported that they took classes in foreign languages other than English. Although none of them indicated linguistic fluency, the mere fact of experience with these languages may defy homogeneity of the bilingual group. A similar problem was identified in the bilingual sample collected by Kharkhurin (2009) in the UAE. In addition to Farsi and English controlled in that study, participants selected for the bilingual group revealed knowledge of other languages acquired either in a classroom setting (e.g., French, Spanish) or from a natural multilingual environment of the country (e.g., Arabic, Urdu). Thus, these studies omit an important detail that most participants selected for a bilingual group are in fact multilingual. This nuance decreases the reliability of the findings due to methodological inconsistency: if the studies deal with multilingual samples, all participants' languages should be assessed and conclusions should be made about the multilingual (not bilingual) population.

Another important issue comes from a large dispersion of participants' linguistic and geographic backgrounds. The tested languages included Arabic, Chinese, Czech, English, Farsi, French, German, Greek, Italian, Kannada, Malayan, Polish, Russian, Spanish, Tamil, Ukrainian, Urdu, Welsh, and Yoruba. The participants were sampled in Asia, Africa, Europe, the Middle East, and North America. A large variety of language-location combinations could present a particular intricacy to convergent validity of these studies. Specifically, the contribution of bilingual development to creative potential may differ across linguistic and cultural groups. Kharkhurin (2010b) found that Russian–English bilinguals in the North American sample showed greater generative capacity, whereas Farsi–English bilinguals in the Middle Eastern sample revealed greater innovative capacity compared with their respective monolingual counterparts. These findings were explained by different creative strategies employed by individuals speaking different languages and residing in different *sociocultural contexts*. Most of the studies in the field, however, ignored these factors and therefore supplied incoherent results. Moreover, due to variations in these factors, the comparison of these results seems to be unreliable.

Despite the fact that bilingual participants were tested in a large variety of languages, in most studies they spoke their native language and English. Virtually no research was conducted with individuals speaking other language combinations. However, it is plausible to assume that the variation in lexical and conceptual characteristics of bilinguals' languages may determine their performance on linguistic, cognitive, and creativity tests. For example, Chou (2008) found that English language learners in the US perceived linguistic distance between languages as one of important factors in language acquisition. Moreover, this factor could significantly predict students' language proficiency. The variations in combination of languages may influence the organization of bilingual memory. Paradis (2004, p. 199) noted: *The greater the typological and/or cultural distance between the two languages, the greater the difference in the organization of mental representations corresponding to a word or utterance and its translation equivalent.* Thus, bilingual creativity research may need to take into consideration the typological and/or cultural distances between bilinguals' languages, and compare creative performance of the individuals speaking typologically similar languages (e.g., German and Dutch) and those speaking typologically distant languages (e.g., Russian and Chinese).

It is noteworthy that the reviewed studies made no specific distinction between participants with different histories of language acquisition and cultural experience. However, it is important to differentiate bilinguals who acquired their L2 in a decontextualized environment (e.g., in a classroom setting) from those who acquired this language in an environment where they used this language in everyday life and mapped it within culture-specific events (Pavlenko, 2000). Moreover, the latter ones also do not present a homogeneous group. These individuals could be immigrants, migrant workers, members of the minority groups, or foreign students. Their socioeconomic status can stipulate not only the degree of linguistic involvement and acculturation, but also their conceptual systems (e.g., de Groot, 2000; Paradis, 2000; Pavlenko, 2005). For example, literature suggests that the experience of the immigrants varies depending on their isolation or participation in a new culture as well as in a bilingual community (e.g., Birman et al., 2002; Birman & Trickett, 2001; Szapocznik, Scopetta, Kurtines, & Aranalde, 1978).

Finally, it is striking that the majority of the studies in the field were conducted with children and young teenagers (see Ricciardelli, 1992b). The focus was on the effect of bilingual development on cognitive growth. These studies showed an apparent gain of bilingual children over their monolingual counterparts. However, they did not answer the question as to whether the benefits of bilingualism detected in childhood persist into adulthood when linguistic and conceptual systems are well established. This issue was addressed in more recent studies that compared creative performance of bilingual and monolingual adults. However, the focus in these studies was on college students, and none of them looked into creative behavior of older adults.

Research Designs

Most research investigating a relationship between bilingualism and creativity uses a *cross-sectional design*, which can be subsequently divided in *between-* and *within-group designs*. The former compares bilinguals with monolinguals, whereas the latter focuses on bilinguals with different histories of language acquisition and use. The early studies in the field employed a between-group design, which posed particular methodological problems.

As discussed earlier, the criteria used to assign participants to bilingual and monolingual groups were often poorly specified and inconsistent from study to study. Moreover, individuals included in a bilingual group could have different levels of linguistic proficiency in each of their languages. The inconsistency in assigning participants to respective groups could cause biases in evaluation of groups' creative performance.

In addition, there is growing concern in bilingualism and multilingualism research whether it is worthwhile to compare bilinguals and monolinguals. This tradition goes back to a so-called *monolingual perspective*, in which L2 users were considered from the perspective of L1 users. L2 is added to L1 competence, and this extra competence was assessed against the only language of monolingual native speaker. This approach was criticized within the linguistic *multicompetence framework* (see Cook & Wei, 2016). These researchers claim that speaking multiple languages adds not only to an individual's linguistic repertoire, multilingual practice influences one's cognitive functions, conceptual representations, and even personality traits (Cook, 2016). Under this assumption, bilinguals and monolinguals appear to possess distinctively different minds, and therefore, their comparison would not shed any light on creative advantages of the former. Therefore, a direct comparison between bilingual and monolingual speakers does not sustain understanding of bilinguals' creative capacities (Kharkhurin, 2016).

These issues were addressed in a within-group design, which employed a continuous assessment of bilingualism. Instead of comparing bilingual and monolingual groups, these studies considered various factors in bilingual development (level of expertise in each language, age of acquisition of each language, and sociocultural context in which each language was acquired). This approach seems to tap into more subtle differences between different types of bilinguals and provides a more sophisticated analysis of potential bilingual creative advantages. For example, Konaka (1997) determined bilingual type based on the score computed from bilinguals' self-rating and the Word Association Test (Lambert, 1956), which was subsequently transformed into a five-point scale ranging from balanced bilingual to unbalanced bilingual. Konaka found that the degree of bilingual balance significantly predicted divergent thinking abilities of Japanese–English sixth-, and seventh-grade students living in the New York area. The within-group design allowed Lemmon and Goggin (1989) to determine that the negative effect of bilingualism on creative performance could be attributed to participants with limited skills in Spanish. Similarly, based on the scores on the English and Russian picture naming test, Kharkhurin (2008) divided bilingual participants in high (high scores in both languages), unbalanced (high score in one language and low in the other), and low (low scores in both languages) proficiency groups. Only a high proficiency group was found to outperform a monolingual group on the ATTA measure of elaboration. In the same study, the age of L2 acquisition was found to relate to the ATTA measures of fluency and flexibility, and length of exposure to new cultural environments—to fluency, flexibility, and elaboration.

Thus, the within-group cross-sectional design that employs group comparison of different types of bilinguals and monolinguals seems to provide a more plausible solution to studying the effect of bilingualism on human creativity. However, it is important to keep in mind that causal inferences in this design have low *internal validity* (Campbell & Stanley, 1963). The findings of bilingual creative advantages could be attributed to other factors not related to bilingualism *per se*. These include education, expertise, motivation, attitudes, personality traits, personal experience, and socioeconomic, sociocultural, and political factors. The potential impact of these factors can be eliminated or at least reduced in a within-subject *longitudinal design*. In this paradigm, creative performance could be regularly assessed as a person proceeds through bilingual education. For example, a group of students can be administered a battery of creativity measures every semester as they advance through the full series of language courses. This design would help to determine whether a person's creative abilities improve with increase in his or her linguistic skills while controlling for other potentially confounding factors. Unfortunately, longitudinal studies are extremely rare in the area of bilingual cognitive development (Hakuta & Diaz, 1985).

Confounding Variables

Earlier in the chapter, it was mentioned that creativity can be prompted by a large variety of factors such as education, expertise, motivation, attitudes, personality traits, personal experience, and socioeconomic, sociocultural, and political conditions. One or more of these factors may influence bilingual individuals' performance on creativity tests. The relationship between bilingualism and creativity becomes the spurious consequence of these *confounding variables*.

In most of the studies in the field, bilingual groups included migrants who, in addition to speaking two languages, were also likely to experience and participate in two cultures. This cultural element has been virtually ignored in the investigation of the possible cognitive impact of bilingualism. While this theme has been brought up in some theoretical considerations (e.g., Cummins & Gulutsan, 1974; Francis, 2000; Okoh, 1980), it has not received enough attention in the empirical research. However, it is likely that in addition to the virtue of speaking two languages, bilinguals who experience and participate in two cultures may benefit from the meta- and paralinguistic advantages of biculturalism, leading to an increase in their creative abilities. Lubart (1999) identified four ways that cultural influence might affect creativity: (1) people from different cultures may have different concepts of creativity; (2) people from different cultures may use different psychological processes when they engage in creative endeavors; (3) language may influence the development of creativity; and (4) environment can either promote or reduce people's creativity. These directions suggest that sociocultural values and norms determine and shape the concept of creativity, which in turn may influence the manner in which creative potential is apprehended and incarnated. If bilinguals acquire their languages in different countries, they are most likely to have been exposed to different cultural systems. This experience encourages a variation in the development of creative potential. Indeed, the empirical findings referenced in the previous section present a case for the impact of cross-cultural experience on an individual's creative potential.

Other two confounding variables—political situation and motivation—can be extracted from the above-mentioned study demonstrating a significant difference in the innovative capacity between Farsi–English bilinguals resided in the UAE and Farsi monolinguals resided in Iran (Kharkhurin, 2009). An alternative explanation of those findings referred to political situations in these respective countries. According to Kharkhurin and Samadpour Motalleebi (2008), the prescribed ritualistic patterns of behavior reinforced by a low tolerance for deviant groups in Iran could encourage Iranian monolingual participants to provide rather traditional responses. Instead of looking for original solutions to the problems as required by the ATTA procedure, they tended to provide the most common traditional ones. On the other hand, by the mere fact of leaving Iran and residing in a more individualistic environment of the UAE, bilingual participants could benefit from more freedom of expression compared to their monolingual compatriots residing in Iran. The experience with the more liberal social environment of the UAE could facilitate their innovative capacity and encourage them to find less traditional solutions to the ATTA problems.

Further, a detailed analysis of the history of Farsi–English bilinguals revealed that only those who presumably emigrated to the UAE for educational purposes showed significantly greater innovative capacity compared with their monolingual counterparts (Kharkhurin, 2010b). This finding suggested that they could be intrinsically motivated to move to a new country in search for alternative education. Current theories considering the role of motivation in creativity (see Collins & Amabile, 1999, for an overview) emphasize the necessity of *intrinsic motivation* in the creative process. Intrinsic motivation refers to motivation that is based on taking pleasure in an activity rather than on acquiring an external reward. It is driven by an individual's interest in the task itself rather than by external pressure. It is contrasted with *extrinsic motivation* that refers to the performance of an activity in order to attain an outcome that is externally rewarded by money, grades, coercion, etc. Intrinsic motivation exists within the individual, whereas extrinsic motivation comes from outside of the individual. Sternberg and Lubart (1991) included motivation as one of six required resources in their investment theory of creativity. The interactive models of the development of an individual's creative potential within the society emphasize intrinsic motivation as a personal characteristic contributing to creative abilities (e.g., Csíkszentmihályi, 1990; Gardner, 1993). The empirical studies also provide extensive support to the assertion that motivation is beneficial for creativity (e.g., Collins & Amabile, 1999; Heinzen, Mills, & Cameron, 1993). The confounding effects of bilingualism and motivation and sociocultural and political factors should be carefully examined in the future research investigating bilinguals' creative capacities.

Theoretical Interpretations

The previous edition of this chapter refrained from making any theoretical interpretations of the relationship between bilingualism and creativity. The primary reasons for this wary attitude were the lack of systematic empirical research and the vast methodological drawbacks identified in the existing studies. During less than ten years after the appearance of the first edition, we have accumulated sufficient empirical data to build a first theoretical construct that directly relates these two human endeavors. The newly built bilingual creativity platform can serve as a starting point for scientific investigation in the field.

So, why might bilinguals have advantages in creative performance? A growing number of empirical studies show that bilingualism extends one's cognitive capacities. In line with the previously presented creative cognition approach, creativity can be explained by enhanced normative cognition. There is evidence that bilingualism results in more elaborate cognitive structures and/or functioning. Therefore, the facilitatory effect of speaking more than one language on individuals' cognition may also manifest in their enhanced creative performance.

This section sketches cognitive mechanisms and personality traits, which on one hand can directly benefit from bilingual practice, and on the other hand, can stimulate creative performance. To complete the picture, one would expect to see how these mechanisms and traits can be mapped onto bilingual developmental factors discussed above (see Kharkhurin, 2016, for further information).

Cognitive Mechanisms of Bilingual Creativity

Recall that in psychometric literature, creative thinking is perceived as an ability to initiate multiple cycles of divergent and convergent thinking (Guilford, 1967). There is evidence that bilingual practice facilitates both divergent and convergent thinking. The former may benefit from specific architecture of bilingual memory, and the latter may benefit from bilinguals' highly developed *selective attention*.

Language Mediated Concept Activation

Divergent thinking refers to the ability to activate and process simultaneously a large number of unrelated ideas and access the concepts from distant categories (Guilford, 1967). The functioning of divergent thinking can be explained by an automatic *spreading activation mechanism* that simultaneously triggers a large number of mental representations. These representations are stored in conceptual memory. The latter is assumed as a pattern of spreading activation (McClelland & Rumelhart, 1985) over a large set of mutually linked units of meaning (or conceptual features) organized in conceptual networks (Lamb, 1999). The spreading activation mechanism transfers activation between conceptual features providing facilitation for related concepts and inhibition for unrelated ones. This property of the conceptual system was illustrated in priming studies (e.g., Meyer & Schvaneveldt, 1971) that show that semantically related words tend to influence each other. The associations between distant mental representations can be established due to the distributed nature of the conceptual system (see Kharkhurin, 2012a, for details). In light of this discussion, divergent thinking takes place when a large number of often unrelated conceptual representations are accessed simultaneously. Spreading activation among distributed conceptual representations may build the links between distant concepts. A large number of simultaneously activated ideas may establish a rich plane of thought from which original and novel ideas might be extracted.

The specific architecture of bilingual memory is argued to facilitate the greater spreading activation between conceptual representations and thereby stimulate divergent thinking (see Kharkhurin, 2012a, for a detailed discussion). This may be accomplished through *language mediated concept activation* (LMCA; Kharkhurin, 2007, 2008, 2017). The idea of this mechanism is based on the assumption that translation equivalents automatically activate each other through shared conceptual representations (e.g., concept mediated translation in Kroll & de Groot, 1997; see also Chapter 3). Although translation equivalents share most of the conceptual features, these representations are not identical (e.g., Paradis, 1997). Variations in the conceptual representations of translation equivalents may result in the simultaneous activation of additional concepts, which eventually may produce a large pattern of activation over unrelated concepts from different categories. The activation of these concepts is assumed to take place through the lemmas representing the translation equivalents in two languages and/or through the word forms (e.g., phonetic, orthographic) shared by these languages.

Thus, the elaborate LMCA may allow bilinguals to process a large number of unrelated concepts from different categories simultaneously; that is, it may stimulate their divergent thinking. The indirect evidence for the LMCA is provided by the cross-language studies using semantic (see Kroll & Tokowicz, 2005, for a review) and translation (see Altarriba & Basnight-Brown, 2007, for a review) priming paradigms. These studies revealed that automatic spreading activation takes place not only between translation equivalents in different languages, but between semantically related words in different languages as well. Recently, Kharkhurin (2017) tested this hypothesis with Russian–English bilinguals and Russian monolinguals using a translingual priming test. The latter presented participants with pairs of Russian words, which were unrelated in Russian, but related through their translation equivalents in English (e.g., филиал [branch] is unrelated to дерево [tree], but *branch* is related to *tree*). Bilingual participants showed stronger priming effects and revealed greater flexibility in thinking compared with their monolingual counterparts. These results demonstrated that bilinguals' divergent thinking can benefit from an elaborate LMCA.

Selective Attention

The purpose of convergent thinking is to find the single best (or correct) answer to a clearly defined problem (Cropley, 2006). This cognitive function appears inevitable when a large pool of ambiguous divergent thoughts needs to be narrowed down to a single creative solution. These possible candidates should be explored, criticized, and evaluated to select the best fit to the problem. Kharkhurin (2011) argued that individuals' efficient selective attention may support creative problem-solving at the stage where a conscious attention-demanding process assists in narrowing a multitude of possible alternatives down to a single original solution. At the same time, extensive research demonstrated that *attentional control* is enhanced by bilingual practice (review in Bialystok, 2005; meta-analysis in Adesope, Lavin, Thompson, & Ungerleider, 2010). Bilinguals' selective attention is facilitated by their extensive practice with two active language systems, during which they have to solve the conflicts in lexical retrieval, which are unraveled by efficient executive control (Bialystok, Craik, & Ryan, 2006; Bialystok & Feng, 2009). Kharkhurin identified two control mechanisms of selective attention that may contribute to the improvement of bilinguals' creative abilities. The facilitation of relevant information was likely to boost the ability to activate a multitude of unrelated concepts and work through the concepts already activated. The inhibition of irrelevant information seemed to enhance the capacity to produce original and useful ideas.

Personality Traits of Bilingual Creativity

In addition to influence on cognitive mechanisms underlying creative thinking, bilingual practice seems to have an impact on personality traits associated with creative behavior.

Cognitive Flexibility

Lambert (1977) suggested that bilingualism often entails repeated switching from one language to another and constant dealing with several code systems (phonological, grammatical, and lexical). Due to this experience, bilinguals may learn to encode and access knowledge in diverse ways. People speaking several languages learn that the same concept can have multiple referents in these languages. For example, an object can have a referent *table* in English, *der Tisch* in German, or *стол* in Russian. Individuals speaking these languages learn that this object can be referred to with all three words. They grasp an idea that there is no one-to-one match between an object and its referent, which in turn may encourage their cognitive flexibility and abstract thinking.

Cognitive flexibility is considered an important *creativity trait* (Guilford, 1968). This trait allows an individual to find different perspectives, to switch between perspectives, and to think outside the box. Flexibility in thinking may be highly suitable in situations requiring nontrivial manipulation of existing cognitive structures, especially when logical approaches fail to produce satisfactory results (Torrance & Safter, 1999). Recall that flexibility is included in Guilford's (1967) characteristics of divergent thinking. Bilingual individuals were found to outperform their monolingual counterparts on this trait (e.g., Carringer, 1974; Kharkhurin, 2008; Konaka, 1997). In addition, Kharkhurin (2009) reported the effect of bilingualism on *structured imagination* (cf. Ward, 1994). The latter limits individuals' thinking outside the box; that is, people have difficulties violating the conceptual boundaries of a standard category when creating a new exemplar of that category. The ability to violate these boundaries can be ascribed to cognitive flexibility as well. Farsi–English bilinguals were found to more readily violate the conceptual boundaries than their monolingual counterparts. Moreover, current research showed that both bilingual children and adults excel in non-linguistic tasks requiring cognitive flexibility (e.g., Adi-Japha et al., 2010; Carlson & Meltzoff, 2008; Costa, Hernandez, & Sebastián-Gallés, 2008). These studies focus on bilinguals' executive control functions and therefore hint to a possibility that cognitive flexibility builds on inhibitory control mechanisms, such as the aforementioned selective attention.

Tolerance of Ambiguity

Okoh (1980, p. 164) argued that bilingual cross-cultural experience opens *two windows or corridors through which to view the world*. Bilinguals can see the same phenomenon in two different ways and have two perspectives on the same situation. Because different cultural commonalities may provide different perspectives on the same phenomena (Ricciardelli, 1992b), bilinguals *may have a greater tolerance for ambiguity because they are comfortable with situations in which one basic idea may have different nuances* (Lubart, 1999, p. 344).

Tolerance of ambiguity appears to be another personality trait related to an individual's creative behavior (e.g., Zenasni, Besançon, & Lubart, 2008). Budner (1962, p. 29) defined this trait as the *tendency to perceive ambiguous situations as desirable*. In a search for a creative answer, people may face a situation in which they have to consider several contradictory ideas simultaneously. People perceive these situations as ambiguous and tend to avoid them by leaping to the first available solution. However, those of them who tolerate ambiguity may be able to keep a pool of possible solutions open long enough to work effectively on a larger set of ideas, which eventually may result in generating a creative idea. Speaking multiple languages was found to relate to the tolerance of ambiguity (Dewaele & Wei, 2013). In this study, individuals speaking more than two languages revealed greater tolerance of ambiguity in comparison with those speaking two or only one language. Second language acquisition researchers also identified this trait as an important contributor to successful L2 learning (e.g., Oxford & Ehrman, 1992; Rubin, 1975).

Open-Mindedness

Recent research provided evidence that advanced knowledge and frequent use of more languages was linked to *open-mindedness* (Dewaele & Stavans, 2012; Dewaele & van Oudenhoven, 2009). The operational definition of this trait refers to openness to different sociocultural constructs: *open and unprejudiced attitude towards outgroup members and towards different cultural norms and values* (Dewaele & van Oudenhoven, p. 449). By analogy, one can think about openness to new ideas and experiences, which has been always regarded as an important creativity trait (e.g., Feist, 1998; Silvia, Nusbaum, Berg, Martin, & O'Connor, 2009). People with high scores on openness to experience are artistic, inventive, and curious; they appreciate novel ideas and new experiences, consider a variety of perspectives and thoughts, and employ unconventional problem-solving strategies (McCrae & Costa Jr., 1997). There is no empirical evidence of a link between bilingual practice and openness to experience. Researchers who might become interested in this theme should look at bilinguals' multicultural experience, which was discussed earlier.

Motivation

Motivation has been shown to play a crucial role in both successful language learning (e.g., Engjn, 2009; Masgoret & Gardner, 2003; Wang, 2008) and prolific creative behavior (e.g., Amabile, 1996; Hennessey, 2010). Current theories considering the role of motivation in creativity (see Collins & Amabile, 1999, for an overview) emphasize that creativity generally prospers under conditions that support intrinsic motivation (stimulated by personal interest and inner potential) and suffocates under conditions accentuating the extrinsic motivation (such as rewards and incentives). Therefore, one may expect that individuals with a strong intrinsic motivation may succeed in both language learning and creative performance. For example, Kharkhurin (2010b) claimed that intrinsic motivation could mediate the effect of bilingualism on creativity. He based this argument on a speculative interpretation of his findings that only those bilingual participants who were intrinsically motivated to change their country of residence could have shown greater originality in thinking.

Summary and Conclusion

In this chapter, I presented a revived field of research investigating the relationship between bilingualism and creativity. Reviewed empirical findings revealed a clear tendency of bilingual individuals to obtain greater scores on the creativity tests compared with their monolingual counterparts. However, the interpretation of these findings should be wary considering a number of methodological drawbacks related to definitions of the concepts, psychometric assessments, selection of the participants, research design, and presence of confounding variables.

I made an attempt to provide a preliminary interpretation and build a theoretical platform of the relationship between these two human endeavors. The specific structure of bilingual memory may facilitate language mediated concept activation, which in turn may ensure a simultaneous activation of distant concepts thereby encouraging divergent thinking. At the same time, bilingual practice may encourage inhibition and facilitation mechanisms of selective attention. These mechanisms seem to play an important role in divergent and convergent thinking, and thereby foster an individual's creative performance. In addition, there is evidence that creative personality traits such as cognitive flexibility, tolerance of ambiguity, openness to new experience, and motivation can be developed as a result of bilingual practice. The proposed cognitive mechanisms and personality traits appear to benefit from various developmental factors, such as proficiency in languages and individual uses, age of acquisition of these languages, circumstances and extent to which an individual switches between these languages, and the sociocultural environment in which these languages are acquired and used.

It is evident that empirical data suggesting the links between bilingualism and creativity is highly scattered and often speculative. Overall, bilingual creativity lacks systematic research, especially one focusing on variation in bilinguals' creative capacities. Therefore, a systematic investigation of the proposed and possibly other factors in bilingual creativity is required.

At this point only one conclusion can be certain: using multiple languages has important ramifications for the human mind as a whole. It develops multiple competences, which facilitate cognitive abilities. In our case, it is likely to improve an individual's creative capacities. As mentioned earlier, creativity is a complex construct, which can be prompted by a large variety of factors such as education, expertise, motivation, attitudes, personality traits, personal experience, and socioeconomic, sociocultural, and political conditions. Although, the effect of bilingualism *per se* may be overridden by those factors, it may play a substantial role in their development. Therefore, the findings reviewed in this chapter should stimulate new ideas and serve as a benchmark for a vast research in bilingual creativity.

An interesting development of this research appears in a context of a widely discussed topic in both bilingualism and creativity that comes from pedagogical considerations. The reviewed data presented a case for a relationship between linguistic and creative competences. Both of them can be nurtured through education. It is evident that the creativity fostering programs operate separately from those offering bilingual instruction, and researchers and teachers have mutually exclusive training. They are educated in either creativity or language-related disciplines. As mentioned in the Introduction, the academic community generally disregards the potential relationship between bilingualism and creativity. Similarly, the benefits of merging programs fostering creative potential and bilingual abilities seem to escape the attention of the educators. However, the efficacy of a program combining both efforts can be directly inferred from the research reviewed in this chapter. Various aspects of individuals' bilingual practice were demonstrated to facilitate certain cognitive mechanisms underlying their creative capacities. Therefore, by combining bilingual and creative educational strategies, a far greater synergy could be generated—a bilingual creative education program would capitalize on the assets of both forms of education to establish an effective and comprehensive curriculum. The need for this type of program turns out to be immense, considering the outcomes of scientific investigation, initiatives advanced by governmental policies, and public opinion (see review in Kharkhurin, 2012a).

I proposed a *bilingual creative education program*, which constitutes a unified teaching model introducing both language learning and creativity-fostering instructions to the school curriculum. The rationale is not to establish a special program focusing on children with exceptional abilities, but to suggest modifications to existing curricula and/or the classroom environment to promote bilingualism and creativity in early schooling. The purpose of the program is to introduce students to a bilingual school curriculum and to foster the defining aspects of creativity. To accomplish this goal, the program would utilize a holistic approach that combines cognitive, personal, and environmental factors. This approach would consider not only educational aspects directly pertinent to the school curriculum, but also those reflecting a child's personality and extracurricular settings. Note that the presentation of the program in the current chapter intends to stimulate the creative thinking in education professionals rather than to provide an explicit step-by-step description of the program. I direct the interested reader to Kharkhurin (2012a), which presents a detailed description as well as theoretical and empirical considerations underlying the program.

List of Key Words and Concepts

Abbreviated Torrance Test for Adults (ATTA), Age of language acquisition, Alternative uses, Attentional control, Balanced bilinguals, Barron-Welsh Art Scale, Between-group design, Bicultural experience, Bilingual creative education program, Code-switching, Cognitive advantages, Cognitive flexibility, Confounding variables, Consensual Assessment Technique, Consequences, Convergent thinking, Creative capacity, Creative cognition approach, Creativity assessment, Creative Personality Scale, Creativity trait, Cross-cultural research, Cross-sectional design, Cultural distance, Culture Fair Intelligence Test, Decontextualized environment, Divergent thinking, Domain-general, Domain-specific, Duncker's Candle-mounting problem, Eastern perception of creativity, Elaboration, Eminent creativity, Executive control, Extrinsic motivation, Flexibility, Fluid intelligence, Generative capacity, Historiometric, Insight problem, Instances Test, Internal validity, Interpersonal Problem-Solving Scale, Interrepresentational flexibility, Intrinsic motivation, Invented Alien Creature Test, Karmiloff-Smith Task, Language mediated concept activation, Language proficiency, Lifetime Creativity Scales, Longitudinal design, Mental flexibility, Mental reorganization, Monolingual perspective, Multicompetence framework, Negative effect, Non-insight problem, Normative cognitive functioning, Normative human cognition, Open-mindedness, Openness, Peabody Picture Vocabulary Test, Personality traits, Remote Associates Test, Selective attention, Self-concept, Sequential bilinguals, Simultaneous bilinguals, Sociocultural context, Spreading activation mechanism, Structured imagination, Threshold hypothesis, Torrance Tests of Creative Thinking, Translanguaging, Translingual Priming Test, True bilinguals, Uses of Objects Test, Verbal creativity, Western perception of creativity, Within-group design, Word Association Test

Internet Sites Related to Bilingualism and Creativity

Diagnostic Language Test: http://www.lancaster.ac.uk/researchenterprise/dialang/about
European Council of High Ability: http://www.echa.info/
Multilingual Creative Cognition Center: https://www.facebook.com/multilingualcreativity/
Society for the Psychology of Aesthetics, Creativity, and the Arts: http://www.div10.org/
The European Association for Creativity & Innovation: http://www.eaci.net/
The International Centre for Innovation in Education: http://icieworld.net/

Discussion Questions

(1) Why has the empirical investigation of bilingual creativity not received sufficient interest in the scientific community?
(2) Does speaking multiple languages change the way we approach creative problems?
(3) What factors in individuals' multilingual development and practice may have an impact on their creative behavior?
(4) What cognitive mechanisms and personality traits underlying creativity can benefit from multilingual practice?
(5) Why is there a discrepancy between psychometric laboratory research in bilingual creativity and real-life observations of the creative behavior of people in multilingual countries?
(6) What does corrupt the psychometric research in bilingual creativity?
(7) What are the most essential methodological considerations pertinent to the empirical study of the relationship between bilingualism and creativity?
(8) What are the practical implications of the findings demonstrating bilinguals' advantages on a variety of creativity tests?

Suggested Research Projects

(1) Identify bilingual and monolingual students from your class or your university. Using the DIALANG (https://dialangweb.lancaster.ac.uk/) or the iPNT language proficiency tests (http://harhur.com/ipnt/), assess the linguistic skills of your participants. Please use a median split to identify bilinguals with high proficiency in both languages, with high proficiency in one of their languages, and with low proficiency in both

languages. Compare performance of different bilingual and monolingual groups on available creativity test (e.g., Instances Test; Wallach & Kogan, 1965). The hypothesis is that bilinguals with high proficiency in both languages demonstrate better creative performance than monolingual and other bilingual groups.

(2) Identify students speaking multiple languages and assess their code-switching practice (e.g., Code-switching attitudes and behaviors questionnaire; Kharkhurin & Wei, 2014). Correlate their code-switching with their performance on available creativity tests.

(3) Administer bilingual students surveys assessing their intrinsic and extrinsic motivation (e.g., The Work Preference Inventory: Assessing intrinsic and extrinsic motivational orientations; Amabile, Hill, Hennessey, & Tighe, 1994), their language learning motivation (e.g., Language Learning Orientations Scale—Intrinsic Motivation, Extrinsic Motivation, and Amotivation Subscales; Noels, Pelletier, Clément, & Vallerand, 2000), and their creative behavior (e.g., Creative Behavior Inventory; Hocevar, 1980). See if there is a relationship between overall and language learning intrinsic versus extrinsic motivation and creative behavior.

Suggested Readings

Cook, V., & Wei, L. (Eds.). (2016). *Cambridge handbook of linguistic multicompetence.* Cambridge, UK: Cambridge University Press.

Kaufman, J. C., & Sternberg, R. J. (Eds.). (2010). *The Cambridge handbook of creativity.* New York: Cambridge University Press.

Kharkhurin, A. V. (2012). *Multilingualism and creativity.* Bristol, UK: Multilingual Matters.

Kroll, J. F., & de Groot, A. M. B. (2005). *Handbook of bilingualism: Psycholinguistic approaches.* New York: Oxford University Press.

Runco, M. A. (2014). *Creativity: Theories and themes: Research, development, and practice* (2nd ed.). Boston, MA: Elsevier.

References

Adesope, O. O., Lavin, T., Thompson, T., & Ungerleider, C. (2010). A systematic review and meta-analysis of the cognitive correlates of bilingualism. *Review of Educational Research, 80,* 207–245.

Adi-Japha, E., Berberich-Artzi, J., & Libnawi, A. (2010). Cognitive flexibility in drawings of bilingual children. *Child Development, 81,* 1356–1366.

Aguirre, N. (2003). ESL students in gifted education. In J. A. Castellano (Ed.), *Special populations in gifted education: Working with diverse gifted learners* (pp. 17–28). Boston, MA: Allyn & Bacon.

Altarriba, J., & Basnight-Brown, D. M. (2007). Methodological considerations in performing semantic and translation priming experiments across languages. *Behavior Research Methods, Instruments, & Computers, 39,* 1–18.

Amabile, T. M. (1982). Social psychology of creativity: A consensual assessment technique. *Journal of Personality and Social Psychology, 43,* 997–1013.

Amabile, T. M. (1996). *Creativity in context: Update to "the social psychology of creativity."* Boulder, CO: Westview Press.

Amabile, T. M., Hill, K. G., Hennessey, B. A., & Tighe, E. M. (1994). The work preference inventory: Assessing intrinsic and extrinsic motivational orientations. *Journal of Personality and Social Psychology, 66,* 950–967.

Androutsopoulos, J. (2013). Networked multilingualism: Some language practices on Facebook and their implications. *International Journal of Bilingualism, 19*(2), 185–205. doi:10.1177/1367006913489198.

Baas, M., Roskes, M., Sligte, D., Nijstad, B. A., & De Dreu, C. K. W. (2013). Personality and creativity: The dual pathway to creativity model and a research agenda. *Social and Personality Psychology Compass*, *7*, 732–748.

Barron, F., & Welsh, G. S. (1952). Artistic perception as a possible factor in personality style: Its measurement by a figure preference test. *Journal of Psychology*, *33*, 199–203.

Berger, R. M., & Guilford, J. P. (1969). *Pilot titles*. Beverly Hills, CA: Sheridan Psychological Services.

Bhatia, T. K., & Ritchie, W. C. (2008). The Bilingual mind and linguistic creativity. *Journal of Creative Communications*, *3*, 5–21.

Bialystok, E. (2005). Consequences of bilingualism for cognitive development. In J. F. Kroll & A. M. B. de Groot (Eds.), *Handbook of bilingualism: Psycholinguistic approaches* (pp. 417–432). New York: Oxford University Press.

Bialystok, E., Craik, F. I. M., Klein, R., & Viswanathan, M. (2004). Bilingualism, aging, and cognitive control: Evidence from the Simon task. *Psychology and Aging*, *19*, 290–303.

Bialystok, E., Craik, F. I. M., & Ryan, J. (2006). Executive control in a modified antisaccade task: Effects of aging and bilingualism. *Journal of Experimental Psychology: Learning, Memory, and Cognition*, *32*, 1341–1354.

Bialystok, E., & Feng, X. (2009). Language proficiency and executive control in proactive interference: Evidence from monolingual and bilingual children and adults. *Brain and Language*, *109*, 93–100.

Birman, D., & Trickett, E. J. (2001). Cultural transitions in first-generation immigrants: Acculturation of Soviet Jewish refugee adolescents and parents. *Journal of Cross-Cultural Psychology*, *32*, 456–477.

Birman, D., Trickett, E. J., & Vinokurov, A. (2002). Acculturation and adaptation of Soviet Jewish refugee adolescents: Predictors of adjustment across life domains. *American Journal of Community Psychology*, *30*, 585–607.

Boden, M. A. (2004). *The creative mind: Myths and mechanisms*. London, UK: Routledge.

Budner, S. (1962). Intolerance of ambiguity as a personality variable. *Journal of Personality*, *30*, 29–50.

Burck, C. (2004). Living in several languages: Implications for therapy. *Journal of Family Therapy*, *26*, 314–339.

Calderón, M. E., & Minaya-Rowe, L. (2003). *Designing and implementing two-way bilingual programs: A step-by-step guide for administrators, teachers, and parents*. Thousand Oaks, CA: Corwin Press.

Campbell, D. T., & Stanley, J. C. (1963). *Experimental and quasi-experimental designs for research*. Boston, MA: Houghton, Mifflin.

Carlson, S. M., & Meltzoff, A. N. (2008). Bilingual experience and executive functioning in young children. *Developmental Science*, *11*, 282–298.

Carringer, D. C. (1974). Creative thinking abilities of Mexican youth: The relationship of bilingualism. *Journal of Cross-Cultural Psychology*, *5*, 492–504.

Cattell, R. B. (1973). *Manual for the Cattell culture fair intelligence test*. Champaign, IL: Institute for Personality and Ability Testing.

Chávez-Eakle, R. A., Eakle, A. J., & Cruz-Fuentes, C. (2012). The multiple relations between creativity and personality. *Creativity Research Journal*, *24*, 76–82.

Chik, A. (2010). Creative multilingualism in Hong Kong popular music. *World Englishes*, *29*, 508–522.

Chorney, M. (1978). *The relationship of bilingualism and creativity*. (Unpublished honors thesis). University of Adulate.

Chou, C.-T. E. (2008). *Factors affecting language proficiency of English language learners at language institutes in the United States*, *68*, ProQuest Information & Learning, US. Available from EBSCOhost psyh database.

Christensen, P. R., Guilford, J. P., Merrifield, P. R., & Wilson, R. C. (1960). *Alternative uses*. Beverly Hills, CA: Sheridan Psychological Services.

Christensen, P. R., Merrifield, P. R., & Guilford, J. P. (1953). *Consequences*. Beverly Hills, CA: Sheridan Psychological Services.

Collins, M. A., & Amabile, T. M. (1999). Motivation and creativity. In R. J. Sternberg (Ed.), *Handbook of creativity* (pp. 297–312). New York: Cambridge University Press.

Cook, V. (2016). Premises of multi-competence. In V. Cook & L. Wei (Eds.), *Cambridge handbook of linguistic multi-competence* (pp. 1–25). Cambridge, UK: Cambridge University Press.

Cook, V., & Wei, L. (Eds.). (2016). *Cambridge handbook of linguistic multi-competence*. Cambridge, UK: Cambridge University Press.

Costa, A., Hernandez, M., & Sebastián-Gallés, N. (2008). Bilingualism aids conflict resolution: Evidence from the ANT task. *Cognition, 106*, 59–86.

Cramond, B. (1994). The Torrance Tests of Creative Thinking: From design through establishment of predictive validity. In R. F. Subotnik & K. D. Arnold (Eds.), *Beyond Terman: Contemporary longitudinal studies of giftedness and talent* (pp. 229–254). Westport, CT: Ablex.

Cropley, A. (2006). In praise of convergent thinking. *Creativity Research Journal, 18*, 391–404.

Csíkszentmihályi, M. (1990). The domain of creativity. In M. A. Runco & R. S. Albert (Eds.), *Theories of creativity* (pp. 190–212). Thousand Oaks, CA: Sage.

Cummins, J. (1976). The influence of bilingualism on cognitive growth: A synthesis of research findings and explanatory hypothesis. *Working Papers on Bilingualism, 9*, 1–43.

Cummins, J., & Gulutsan, M. (1974). Some effects of bilingualism on cognitive functioning. In S. T. Carey (Ed.), *Bilingualism, biculturalism and education*. In *Proceedings from the Conference at College Universitaire Saint-Jean* (pp. 129–136). Edmonton: University of Alberta.

Cushen, P. J., & Wiley, J. (2011). Aha! Voila! Eureka! Bilingualism and insightful problem solving. *Learning and Individual Differences, 21*, 458–462.

Davis, G. A. (1991). Identifying creative students and measuring creativity. In N. Colangelo & G. A. Davis (Eds.), *Handbook of gifted education* (pp. 269–281). Boston, MA: Allyn and Bacon.

Davis, G. A. (1999). Barriers to creativity and creative attitudes. In M. A. Runco & S. R. Pritzker (Eds.), *Encyclopedia of creativity* (Vol. 1, pp. 165–174). San Diego, CA: Academic Press.

de Groot, A. M. B. (2000). On the source and nature of semantic and conceptual knowledge. *Bilingualism: Language and Cognition, 3*, 7–9.

Dewaele, J.-M., & Stavans, A. (2012). The effect of immigration, acculturation and multicompetence on personality profiles of Israeli multilinguals. *International Journal of Bilingualism, 8*(3), 203–221.

Dewaele, J.-M., & van Oudenhoven, J. P. (2009). The effect of multilingualism/multiculturalism on personality: No gain without pain for third culture kids? *International Journal of Multilingualism, 6*, 443–459.

Dewaele, J.-M., & Wei, L. (2013). Is multilingualism linked to a higher tolerance of ambiguity? *Bilingualism: Language and Cognition, 16*, 231–240.

Diaz, R. M. (1985). Bilingual cognitive development: Addressing three gaps in current research. *Child Development, 56*, 1376–1388.

Duncker, K. (1945). The structure and dynamics of problem-solving processes. *Psychological Monographs, 58*, 1–112.

Dunn, L. M. (1965). *Peabody picture vocabulary test*. Circle Pines, MN: American Guidance Service.

Engjn, A. O. (2009). Second language learning success and motivation. *Social Behavior and Personality, 37*, 1035–1042.

Europeans and their languages. (2012). *Special Eurobarometer, 386*. http://ec.europa.eu/commfront office/publicopinion/archives/ebs/ebs_243_en.pdf

Feist, G. J. (1998). A meta-analysis of personality in scientific and artistic creativity. *Personality and Social Psychology Review, 2*, 290–309.

Fleith, D. D. S. (1999). *Effects of a creativity training program on creative abilities and self-concept in monolingual and bilingual elementary classroom* (Doctoral dissertation). University of Connecticut. AAI9926248. Retrieved from http://digitalcommons.uconn.edu/dissertations/AAI9926248/

Fleith, D. D. S., Renzulli, J. S., & Westberg, K. L. (2002). Effects of a creativity training program on divergent thinking abilities and self-concept in monolingual and bilingual classrooms. *Creativity Research Journal, 14*, 373–386.

Florida, R. L. (2002). *The rise of the creative class: And how it's transforming work, leisure, community and everyday life*. New York: Basic Books.

Florida, R. L., Mellander, C., & Stolarick, K. (2011). *Creativity and prosperity: The global creativity index*. Toronto, Canada: Martin Prosperity Institute.

Francis, W. S. (2000). Clarifying the cognitive experimental approach to bilingual research. *Bilingualism: Language and Cognition, 3*, 13–15.

Fürst, G., Ghisletta, P., & Lubart, T. (2014). Toward an integrative model of creativity and personality: Theoretical suggestions and preliminary empirical testing. *The Journal of Creative Behavior, 50*(2), 87–108.

Garcia, J. H. (1996). *The influences of oral language proficiency and acculturation on the creative thinking of second grade children* (Doctoral dissertation), *57*, ProQuest Information & Learning, US.

Garcia, J. H. (2003). Nurturing creativity in Chicano populations: Integrating history, culture, family, and self. *Inquiry: Critical Thinking Across the Disciplines, 22*, 19–24.

Garcia, O., & Wei, L. (2014). *Translanguaging: Language, bilingualism and education*. London: Palgrave.

Gardner, H. (1993). *Creating minds: An anatomy of creativity seen through the lives of Freud, Einstein, Picasso, Stravinsky, Eliot, Graham, and Gandhi*. New York: Basic Books.

Genesee, F. (1978). Language processing in bilinguals. *Brain and Language, 5*, 1–12.

Getzels, J. W., & Jackson, P. W. (1962). *Creativity and intelligence: Explorations with gifted students*. New York: Wiley.

Goff, K., & Torrance, E. P. (2002). *Abbreviated Torrance test for adults*. Bensenville, IL: Scholastic Testing Service.

Gordon, M. M. (1964). *Assimilation in American life: The role of race, religion, and national origins*. New York: Oxford University Press.

Gough, H. G. (1979). A creative personality scale for the adjective check list. *Journal of Personality and Social Psychology, 37*, 1398–1405.

Gowan, J. C., & Torrance, E. P. (1965). An intercultural study of non-verbal ideational fluency. *The Gifted Child Quarterly, 9*(1), 13–15.

Granada, J. (2003). Casting a wider net: Linking bilingual and gifted education. In J. A. Castellano (Ed.), *Special populations in gifted education: Working with diverse gifted learners* (pp. 1–16). Boston, MA: Allyn & Bacon.

Grosjean, F. (1998). Studying bilinguals: Methodological and conceptual issues. *Bilingualism: Language and Cognition, 1*, 131–149.

Guilford, J. P. (1967). *The nature of human intelligence*. New York: McGraw-Hill.

Guilford, J. P. (1968). *Intelligence, creativity, and their educational implications*. San Diego, CA: R. R. Knapp.

Hakuta, K. (1984). *The causal relationship between the development of bilingualism, cognitive flexibility, and social-cognitive skills in Hispanic elementary school children [Final report]*. New Haven, CT: Yale University.

Hakuta, K., & Diaz, R. M. (1985). The relationship between degree of bilingualism and cognitive ability: A critical discussion and some new longitudinal data. In K. E. Nelson (Ed.), *Children's language* (Vol. 5, pp. 319–344). Hillsdale, NJ: Erlbaum.

Heinzen, T. E., Mills, C., & Cameron, P. (1993). Scientific innovation potential. *Creativity Research Journal, 6*, 261–269.

Helson, R. (1996). In search of the creative personality. *Creativity Research Journal, 9*, 295–306.

Hennessey, B. A. (2010). The creativity-motivation connection. In J. C. Kaufman & R. J. Sternberg (Eds.), *The Cambridge handbook of creativity* (pp. 342–365). New York: Cambridge University Press.

Hocevar, D. (1980). Intelligence, divergent thinking, and creativity. *Intelligence, 4*, 25–40.

Hocevar, D. (1981). Measurement of creativity: Review and critique. *Journal of Personality Assessment, 45*, 450–464.

Hocevar, D., & Bachelor, P. (1989). A taxonomy and critique of measurements used in the study of creativity. In J. A. Glover, R. R. Ronning, & C. R. Reynolds (Eds.), *Handbook of creativity* (pp. 53–75). New York: Plenum Press.

Hommel, B., Colzato, L. S., Fischer, R., & Christoffels, I. (2011). Bilingualism and creativity: Benefits in convergent thinking come with losses in divergent thinking. *Frontiers in Psychology*, *2*, 1–5. doi:10.3389/fpsyg.2011.00273.

Jacobs, J. F., & Pierce, M. L. (1966). Bilingualism and creativity. *Elementary English*, *40*, 499–503.

Jonsson, C. (2005). *Code-switching in Chicano theater*. Umeå, Sweden: Umeå University Press.

Karapetsas, A., & Andreou, G. (1999). Cognitive development of fluent and nonfluent bilingual speakers assessed with tachistoscopic techniques. *Psychological Reports*, *84*, 697–700.

Karmiloff-Smith, A. (1990). Constraints on representational change: Evidence from children's drawing. *Cognition*, *34*, 57–83.

Kasof, J. (1997). Creativity and breadth of attention. *Creativity Research Journal*, *10*, 303–315.

Kaufman, J. C., & Sternberg, R. J. (2006). *The international handbook of creativity*. New York: Cambridge University Press.

Kaufmann, G. (2003). What to measure? A new look at the concept of creativity. *Scandinavian Journal of Educational Research*, *47*, 235–251.

Kharkhurin, A. V. (2005). *On the possible relationships between bilingualism, biculturalism and creativity: A cognitive perspective* (Unpublished doctoral dissertation). City University of New York.

Kharkhurin, A. V. (2007). The role of cross-linguistic and cross-cultural experiences in bilinguals' divergent thinking. In I. Kecskes & L. Albertazzi (Eds.), *Cognitive aspects of bilingualism* (pp. 175–210). Dordrecht, the Netherlands: Springer.

Kharkhurin, A. V. (2008). The effect of linguistic proficiency, age of second language acquisition, and length of exposure to a new cultural environment on bilinguals' divergent thinking. *Bilingualism: Language and Cognition*, *11*, 225–243.

Kharkhurin, A. V. (2009). The role of bilingualism in creative performance on divergent thinking and Invented Alien Creatures tests. *Journal of Creative Behavior*, *43*, 59–71.

Kharkhurin, A. V. (2010a). Bilingual verbal and nonverbal creative behavior. *International Journal of Bilingualism*, *14*, 1–16.

Kharkhurin, A. V. (2010b). Sociocultural differences in the relationship between bilingualism and creative potential. *Journal of Cross-Cultural Psychology*, *41*, 776–783.

Kharkhurin, A. V. (2011). The role of selective attention in bilingual creativity. *Creativity Research Journal*, *23*, 239–254.

Kharkhurin, A. V. (2012a). *Multilingualism and creativity*. Bristol, UK: Multilingual Matters.

Kharkhurin, A. V. (2012b). A preliminary version of an internet-based picture naming test. *Open Journal of Modern Linguistics*, *2*, 34–41.

Kharkhurin, A. V. (2014). Creativity.4in1: Four-criterion construct of creativity. *Creativity Research Journal*, *26*, 338–352.

Kharkhurin, A. V. (2016). Multi-competence as a creative act: Ramifications of the multi-competence paradigm for creativity research and creativity fostering education. In V. Cook & W. Li (Eds.), *The Cambridge handbook of linguistic multi-competence* (pp. 420–444). Cambridge, UK: Cambridge University Press. doi:10.1017/CBO9781107425965.020.

Kharkhurin, A. V. (2017). Language mediated concept activation in bilingual memory facilitates cognitive flexibility. *Frontiers in Psychology*, *8*, 1–16. doi:10.3389/fpsyg.2017.01067.

Kharkhurin, A. V., & Altarriba, J. (2015). The effect of mood induction and language of testing on bilingual creativity. *Bilingualism: Language and Cognition*, *19*(5), 1079–1094. doi:10.1017/S1366728915000528.

Kharkhurin, A. V., & Samadpour Motalleebi, S. N. (2008). The impact of culture on the creative potential of American, Russian, and Iranian college students. *Creativity Research Journal*, *20*, 404–411.

Kharkhurin, A. V., & Wei, L. (2014). The role of code-switching in bilingual creativity. *International Journal of Bilingual Education and Bilingualism*, *18*(2), 1–17. doi:10.1080/13670050.2014.884211.

Kim, K. H. (2006). Can we trust creativity tests?: A review of the Torrance tests of creative thinking (TTCT). *Creativity Research Journal*, *18*, 3–14.

Koestler, A. (1964). *The act of creation*. Lewiston, NY: Macmillan.

Konaka, K. (1997). *The relationship between degree of bilingualism and gender to divergent thinking ability among native Japanese-speaking children in the New York area* (Doctoral dissertation). New York University. Retrieved from Univ Microfilms International database.

Kostandyan, M. E., & Ledovaya, Y. A. (2013). How the age of language acquisition relates to creativity. *Procedia - Social and Behavioral Sciences, 86*, 140–145.

Kroll, J. F., & de Groot, A. M. B. (1997). Lexical and conceptual memory in the bilingual: Mapping form to meaning in two languages. In A. M. B. de Groot & J. F. Kroll (Eds.), *Tutorials in bilingualism: Psycholinguistic perspectives* (pp. 169–199). Hillsdale, NJ: Erlbaum.

Kroll, J. F., & Tokowicz, N. (2005). Models of bilingual representation and processing: Looking back and to the future. In J. F. Kroll & A. M. B. de Groot (Eds.), *Handbook of bilingualism: Psycholinguistic approaches* (pp. 531–533). New York: Oxford University Press.

Lamb, S. (1999). *Pathways of the brain*. Amsterdam: John Benjamins.

Lambert, W. E. (1956). Developmental aspects of second-language acquisition: Associational fluency, stimulus provocativeness, and word-order influence. *The Journal of Social Psychology, 43*, 83–89.

Lambert, W. E. (1977). The effect of bilingualism on the individual: Cognitive and social consequences. In P. A. Hornby (Ed.), *Bilingualism: Psychological, social and educational implications* (pp. 15–27). New York: Academic Press.

Landry, R. G. (1974). A comparison of second language learners and monolinguals on divergent thinking tasks at the elementary school level. *Modern Language Journal, 58*, 10–15.

Lee, H., & Kim, K. H. (2011). Can speaking more languages enhance your creativity? Relationship between bilingualism and creative potential among Korean American students with multicultural link. *Personality and Individual Differences, 50*, 1186–1190.

Leikin, M. (2013). The effect of bilingualism on creativity: Developmental and educational perspectives. *International Journal of Bilingualism, 17*, 431–447.

Lemmon, C. R., & Goggin, J. P. (1989). The measurement of bilingualism and its relationship to cognitive ability. *Applied Psycholinguistics, 10*, 133–155.

Leung, A. K.-Y., Maddux, W. W., Galinsky, A. D., & Chiu, C.-Y. (2008). Multicultural experience enhances creativity: The when and how. *American Psychologist, 63*, 169–181.

Lissitz, R. W., & Willhoft, J. L. (1985). A methodological study of the Torrance tests of creativity. *Journal of Educational Measurement, 22*, 1–11.

Lubart, T. I. (1999). Creativity across cultures. In R. J. Sternberg (Ed.), *Handbook of creativity* (pp. 339–350). New York: Cambridge University Press.

Lubart, T. I. (2000). Models of the creative process: past, present and future. *Creativity Research Journal, 13*, 295–308.

McClelland, J. L., & Rumelhart, D. E. (1985). Distributed memory and the representation of general and specific information. *Journal of Experimental Psychology: General, 114*, 159–188.

McCrae, R. R., & Costa, P. T., Jr. (1997). Conceptions and correlates of openness to experience. In R. Hogan, J. Johnson, & S. Briggs (Eds.), *Handbook of personality psychology* (pp. 825–847). San Diego: Academic Press.

McLaughlin, B. (1984). *Second-language acquisition in childhood: Preschool children* (Vol. 1, 2nd ed.). Hillsdale, NJ: Erlbaum.

MacNab, G. L. (1979). Cognition and bilingualism: A reanalysis of studies. *Linguistics, 17*, 231–255.

Maddux, W. W., & Galinsky, A. D. (2009). Cultural borders and mental barriers: The relationship between living abroad and creativity. *Journal of Personality and Social Psychology, 96*, 1047–1061.

Martorell, M. F. (1992). *Language proficiency, creativity, and locus-of-control among Hispanic bilingual gifted children* (Doctoral dissertation). Retrieved from ProQuest Information & Learning, US.

Masgoret, A. M., & Gardner, R. C. (2003). Attitudes, motivation, and second language learning: A meta-analysis of studies conducted by gardner and associates. *Language Learning, 53*, 167–210.

Mayer, R. E. (1999). Fifty years of creativity research. In R. J. Sternberg (Ed.), *Handbook of creativity* (pp. 449–460). New York: Cambridge University Press.

Mednick, S. A., & Mednick, M. T. (1967). *Examiner's manual: Remote associates test*. Boston: Houghton Mifflin.

Mendelsohn, G. A. (1976). Associative and attentional processes in creative performance. *Journal of Personality*, *44*, 341–369.

Meyer, D. E., & Schvaneveldt, R. W. (1971). Facilitation in recognizing pairs of words: Evidence of a dependence between retrieval operations. *Journal of Experimental Psychology*, *90*, 227–234.

Millar, G. W. (2002). *The Torrance kids at midlife*. Westport, CT: Ablex Publishing.

Mumford, M. D., Mobley, M. I., Uhlman, C. E., Reiter-Palmon, R., & Doares, L. M. (1991). Process analytic models of creative capacities. *Creativity Research Journal*, *4*, 91–122.

Niu, W., & Sternberg, R. J. (2001). Cultural influences on artistic creativity and its evaluation. *International Journal of Psychology*, *36*, 225–241.

Noels, K. A., Pelletier, L. G., Clément, R., & Vallerand, R. J. (2000). Why are you learning a second language? Motivational orientations and self-determination theory. *Language Learning*, *50*, 57–85.

Okoh, N. (1980). Bilingualism and divergent thinking among Nigerian and Welsh school children. *Journal of Social Psychology*, *110*, 163–170.

Oxford, R. L., & Ehrman, M. (1992). Second language research on individual differences. *Annual Review of Applied Linguistics*, *13*, 188–205.

Padilla, A. M., & Ruiz, R. A. (1973). *Latino mental health: A review of literature*. Washington, DC: U.S. Government Printing Office, Dh.

Paduch, I. (2005). Musik als Erfahrungs- und Gestaltungsraum. Bericht über ein Musikprojekt 'Der Seelenvogel' mit Kindergartenkindern. [Music as a space for experiences and creative activity. Report on a music project with kindergarten children]. *Musiktherapeutische Umschau*, *26*, 156–195.

Palaniappan, A. K. (1994). Preliminary study of the bilingual version of creative motivation inventory. *Perceptual and Motor Skills*, *79*, 393–394.

Paradis, M. (1997). The cognitive neuropsychology of bilingualism. In A. M. B. de Groot & J. F. Kroll (Eds.), *Tutorials in bilingualism: Psycholinguistic perspectives* (pp. 331–354). Hillsdale, NJ: Erlbaum.

Paradis, M. (2000). Cerebral representation of bilingual concepts. *Bilingualism: Language and Cognition*, *3*, 22–24.

Paradis, M. (2004). *A neurolinguistic theory of bilingualism* (Vol. 18). Amsterdam: John Benjamins.

Pavlenko, A. (2000). New approaches to concepts in bilingual memory. *Bilingualism: Language and Cognition*, *3*, 1–4.

Pavlenko, A. (2005). Bilingualism and thought. In J. F. Kroll & A. M. B. de Groot (Eds.), *Handbook of bilingualism: Psycholinguistic approaches* (pp. 433–453). New York: Oxford University Press.

Peal, E., & Lambert, W. E. (1962). The relation of bilingualism to intelligence. *Psychological Monographs*, *76*, 1–23.

Plucker, J. A., & Renzulli, J. S. (1999). Psychometric approaches to the study of human creativity. In R. J. Sternberg (Ed.), *Handbook of creativity* (pp. 35–61). New York: Cambridge University Press.

Price-Williams, D. R., & Ramirez, M. (1977). Divergent thinking, cultural differences, and bilingualism. *Journal of Social Psychology*, *103*, 3–11.

Ricciardelli, L. A. (1992a). Bilingualism and cognitive development in relation to threshold theory. *Journal of Psycholinguistic Research*, *21*, 301–316.

Ricciardelli, L. A. (1992b). Creativity and bilingualism. *Journal of Creative Behavior*, *26*, 242–254.

Richards, R., Kinney, D. K., Benet, M., & Merzel, A. P. (1988). Assessing everyday creativity: Characteristics of the lifetime creativity scales and validation with three large samples. *Journal of Personality and Social Psychology*, *54*, 476–485.

Rogers, C. R. (1961). *On becoming a person*. Oxford, UK: Houghton Mifflin.

Rubin, J. (1975). What the "good language learner" can teach us. *TESOL Quarterly*, *9*, 41–51. doi:10.2307/3586011.

Runco, M. A. (1991). *Divergent thinking*. Westport, CT: Ablex.

Runco, M. A. (2014). *Creativity: Theories and themes: Research, development, and practice* (2nd ed.). Boston, MA: Elsevier Academic Press.

Runco, M. A. (forthcoming). *The new science of creativity*. London, UK: Taylor & Francis.

Runco, M. A., Dow, G., & Smith, W. R. (2006). Information, experience, and divergent thinking: An empirical test. *Creativity Research Journal, 18*, 269–277.

Sebba, M., Jonsson, C., & Mahootian, S. (2012). *Language mixing and code-switching in writing : approaches to mixed-language written discourse*. New York: Routledge.

Silvia, P. J., Nusbaum, E. C., Berg, C., Martin, C., & O'Connor, A. (2009). Openness to experience, plasticity, and creativity: Exploring lower-order, high-order, and interactive effects. *Journal of Research in Personality, 43*, 1087–1090.

Simonton, D. K. (2000). Creativity: Cognitive, personal, developmental, and social aspects. *American Psychologist, 55*, 151–158.

Simonton, D. K. (2008). Bilingualism and creativity. In J. Altarriba & R. R. Heredia (Eds.), *An introduction to bilingualism: Principles and processes* (pp. 147–166). Mahwah, NJ: Erlbaum.

Simonton, D. K. (2012). Taking the U.S. Patent Office criteria seriously: A quantitative three-criterion creativity definition and its implications. *Creativity Research Journal, 24*, 97–106.

Srivastava, A. L., & Khatoon, R. (1980). Effect of difference between mother tongue and another tongue as medium of instruction on achievement, mental ability and creativity of the Vll standard children. In E. Annamalai (Ed.), *Bilingualism and achievement in schools* (pp. 31–41). Mysore, India: Central Institute of Indian Languages.

Stephens, M. A. (1997). *Bilingualism, creativity, and social problem-solving, 58*, ProQuest Information & Learning, US.

Sternberg, R. J., & Lubart, T. I. (1991). An investment theory of creativity and its development. *Human Development, 34*, 1–31.

Sternberg, R. J., & Lubart, T. I. (1995). *Defying the crowd: Cultivating creativity in a culture of conformity*. New York: Free Press.

Stone, S. (1993). *Divergent thinking: Nontraditional or creative talents of monolingual, bilingual, and special education students in an elementary school, 53*, ProQuest Information & Learning, US.

Szapocznik, J., Scopetta, M. A., Kurtines, W., & Aranalde, M. D. (1978). Theory and measurement of acculturation. *Revista Interamericana de Psicología, 12*, 113–130.

Torrance, E. P. (1966). *Torrance test of creative thinking*. Princeton, NJ: Personnel Press.

Torrance, E. P., Gowan, J. C., Wu, J.-J., & Aliotti, N. C. (1970). Creative functioning of monolingual and bilingual children in Singapore. *Journal of Educational Psychology, 61*, 72–75.

Torrance, E. P., & Safter, H. T. (1999). *Making the creative leap beyond*. Buffalo, NY: Creative Education Foundation Press.

Wallach, M. A., & Kogan, N. (1965). *Modes of thinking in young children: A study of the creativity-intelligence distinction*. New York: Holt, Rinehart & Winston.

Wang, F. (2008). Motivation and English achievement: An exploratory and confirmatory factor analysis of a new measure for Chinese students of English learning. *North American Journal of Psychology, 10*, 633–646.

Ward, T. B. (1994). Structured imagination: The role of category structure in exemplar generation. *Cognitive Psychology, 27*, 1–40.

Ward, T. B. (2007). Creative cognition as a window on creativity. *Methods, 42*, 28–37.

Ward, T. B., Smith, S. M., & Finke, R. A. (1999). Creative cognition. In R. J. Sternberg (Ed.), *Handbook of creativity* (pp. 189–212). New York: Cambridge University Press.

Ward, T. B., Smith, S. M., & Vaid, J. (1997). *Creative thought: An investigation of conceptual structures and processes*. Washington, DC: American Psychological Association.

Wei, L., & Wu, C.-J. (2009). Polite Chinese children revisited: Creativity and the use of codeswitching in the Chinese complementary school classroom. *International Journal of Bilingual Education and Bilingualism, 12*, 193–211.

Whitney, C. (1974). *The relationship of bilingualism and biculturalism to divergent thinking.* Unpublished honor's thesis. University of Adulate.

Zenasni, F., Besançon, M., & Lubart, T. I. (2008). Creativity and tolerance of ambiguity: An empirical study. *Journal of Creative Behavior, 42*, 61–73.

Zha, P., Walczyk, J. J., Griffith-Ross, D. A., Tobacyk, J. J., & Walczyk, D. F. (2006). The impact of culture and individualism-collectivism on the creative potential and achievement of American and Chinese adults. *Creativity Research Journal, 18*, 355–366.

9 Bilingualism and Executive Functioning

Kenneth R. Paap

Introduction

Students facing elective choices, parents of younger children, educators, psycholinguists, cognitive scientists, and bilinguals themselves have taken a keen interest in the consequences of bilingualism for language skills, cognitive abilities, and general quality of life. All things considered, let me make clear that I believe that the advantages of bilingualism across a host of personal, economic, social, and cultural dimensions overwhelmingly outweigh any disadvantages. This chapter examines a much narrower question: does bilingualism enhance executive functioning as reflected in performance advantages in non-verbal tasks? Furthermore, this analysis does not consider tests on preschool children as these generally use different tasks and tend to rely on accuracy rather than latency as the primary *dependent variable* or measurement of interest.

Executive Functions

Executive functions (EF) consist of a set of general-purpose control processes that are central to the *self-regulation* of thoughts and behaviors and that are instrumental to accomplishing goals. Across theoretical frameworks these functions include planning, organizing, sequencing, problem-solving, decision-making, updating working memory, switching between task sets, *monitoring* for task-relevant information, inhibiting distraction, and suppressing dominant, but undesirable responses. Clearly, these are important abilities. The construct of EF is often viewed as a set of interrelated component processes all involving the *prefrontal cortex* with each component recruiting additional areas of cortical function.

Research on EF has often focused on the three components identified by Miyake and Friedman (2012) using latent variable analyses: *updating, switching*, and *inhibitory control*. In statistics, latent (i.e., hidden) variables are not directly observed, but are rather inferred through a mathematical model from other variables that are observed. For example, the latent variable of inhibitory control might be inferred from performance measures in three different tasks that all involve competition and therefore require some type of *conflict resolution*. Likewise, a general switching ability might be inferred from performance on three different tasks that frequently require participants to switch from one task (e.g., judgments about color) to another (e.g., judgments about shape). The third latent variable, updating, can be thought of as an estimate of general *working memory capacity* (WMC) and was inferred from three different memory tasks. Each of the three observed measures significantly loaded on the expected latent variable. Loosely speaking, observed measures are said to *load* on the same hidden variable if they are more correlated with one another than with the observed measures linked to other *latent variables*. For example, performance on the three switching tasks were correlated with one another more so than with performance on the tasks assumed to require updating or inhibitory control. This step establishes that updating, switching, and inhibitory control can be considered as separate abilities. However, at the higher level of the analysis, the three latent variables are also correlated with one another. This is consistent with the assumption that the latent variables are components of a common EF ability.

Miyake and Friedman (2012) now favor a variation on the simple hierarchical model described above. To review, a parsimonious view is that a general EF ability can be modeled as consisting of three latent variables (the updating, switching, and inhibitory components) that are each recruited to enable performance in a variety of different tasks. Miyake and Friedman compared the fit of this model to a more complex second-order ("nested") model where the nine observed measures are allowed to load on common EF, and the three latent variables compete in accounting for the remaining variance. The best solution for the second-order model resulted in all nine measures loading on the common EF and with only two of the *nested components* (updating and switching) still making unique contributions. Putting this together, the model supports a theory of a general EF ability with separate updating and switching components and an inhibition component that is not separable, but moderately linked to general EF ability. This analysis led Miyake and Friedman to conclude that EF has both *unity* (a common EF) and *diversity* (additional specific abilities associated with switching and updating).

There are other frameworks, also based on latent variable analyses, that are somewhat different, and it may be good practice to not feel wedded to a specific model as our understanding of EF is evolving. Using similar latent variable methods, Engelhardt, Briley, Mann, Harden, and Tucker-Drob (2015) used data from 505 third- through eighth-graders and 12 different tasks to test five different models, but the second-order unity-diversity model favored by Miyake and Friedman was not among those evaluated. The best-fitting model includes the inhibitory control and switching components, but also separates working memory from updating.

Executive Functions in Language Production and Comprehension

Switching

An aspect of language control unique to multilingualism is the need to switch from one language to another. For example, bilinguals switch languages to accommodate the language proficiencies of their conversational partners. Most theories assume that language switching involves the selection of a new *language-task schema*. When I enter an ongoing conversation, my Spanish-speaking friends know my knowledge of Spanish is limited and switch to English, presumably by activating their *Speak English* schema. An important question for this chapter is the degree to which switching languages involves the same executive functions (and same neural circuits) that are used for general task switching. To put this more concretely, does switching back and forth between mixing drinks and making salsa involve the same control mechanism as switching back and forth between English and Spanish? If it does, then bilinguals, especially those who switch languages frequently, should have an advantage in general task switching compared to otherwise similar monolinguals who do not receive this extra practice.

However, there is substantial behavioral evidence that language switching is not subsidiary to general task switching and that the functional overlap between the two types of switching is minimal. For example, Calabria, Branzi, Marne, Hernández, and Costa (2015) reported that language switching performance did not correlate with performance on non-linguistic switching tasks and that there were age-related changes in non-linguistic *switching costs*, but not in language switching costs. On the other hand, Festman and colleagues (Festman & Münte, 2012; Festman, Rodriguez, & Münte, 2010) reported an interesting association between language *switching errors* and performance on common measures of inhibitory control (e.g., the flanker effect) or switching (e.g., *Wisconsin Card Sorting Task*). In these studies participants are cued to switch languages in alternating runs (viz., RRGGRRGG … where R is picture naming in Russian and G is naming in German) and are partitioned into good and poor switchers on the basis of the number of "errors of interference," that is, responses that are semantically correct, but in the wrong language. Furthermore, De Baene, Duyck, Brass, and Carreiras (2015) reported that highly similar brain circuits are involved in language control and domain-general cognitive control. Still, the dissociations noted first motivate one to keep an open mind and not automatically presume that frequent switching between languages hones the domain-general switching component of EF. As De Baene et al. caution, demonstrating overlap in the distributed *frontoparietal network* does not necessarily imply a bilingual advantage. (See the sections on the alignment and *valence-ambiguity problem* for a discussion of the difficulties associated with interpreting *neuroscience* data.)

Inhibitory Control

A similar argument has been advanced that bilinguals accrue more practice in inhibitory control. The foundation for this argument rests upon many compelling demonstrations that even when bilinguals speak a single language, there is activation of both languages (see Kroll & Gollan, 2014 for a review). To take just one example, Costa, Caramazza, and Sebastián-Gallés (2000) showed that bilinguals are faster to name pictures when the translations are word cognates in their two languages than to name matched non-cognate controls. Thus, even when there was clear intent to name pictures in Spanish, Spanish–Catalan bilinguals were faster to name *gato* (the Catalan translation is the cognate *gat*) than *mesa* (the Catalan translation is the non-cognate *taula*). From studies like this, it is generally agreed that during speaking, listening, and reading, the translations of individual words become active and compete for selection. Yet unwanted intrusions from the unintended language are quite rare, and two approaches have been offered to account for why this is despite the fact that words in the other languages are always co-activated.

One possible explanation, originally offered by Costa et al. (2000), is that the words in the unintended language do not really compete because each word is tagged as a member of a specific language and these tags can be used to filter out all the words belonging to the unintended language and to consider only those in the intended language. Costa and Santesteban (2004) further suggested that the ability to effectively ignore activated words in the unintended language had to be acquired and, consequently, would be present in highly proficient and balanced bilinguals, but not in first language (L1) dominant bilinguals.

The second and most influential approach to managing the competition from activated words in the unintended language is to assume that the competition is managed through inhibitory control. Green's (1998) *inhibitory control model* (ICM) assumes that this is accomplished at multiple levels. Formulating the intention to switch and activating a new intended language schema (e.g., "Speak English") involves the inhibition of the old schema (e.g., "Speak Spanish"). When the switch is instantiated, there is a reactive and global inhibition of any activated words in the unintended lexicon (e.g., Spanish) that is proportional to their individual levels of activation. Finally, the selection of a specific lexical item (e.g., *cat*) locally inhibits its translation (e.g., *gato*) and any other active competitors. If inhibitory control is ubiquitous in bilingual language control and involves the same control processes used to resolve conflict in general, then bilingualism should also enhance the inhibitory control aspect of EF.

Monitoring

In very general terms, monitoring refers to surveying the current environment for information that may advance or impede progress toward the current goal. When the monitor detects goal-relevant information, it can trigger appropriate control that takes advantages of affordances that will advance the goal and counter those that impede progress. In the bilingualism literature the construct of monitoring is chameleon-like with respect to the target of the monitor. One important aspect is to monitor performance so that, for example, when errors are detected they can be corrected. A more subtle form of this is the *conflict monitor* that detects and registers the current amount of response competition and up regulates the goal-relevant pathways so as to decrease the probability that overt errors will occur in the future (Botvinick, Braver, Barch, Carter, & Cohen, 2001). An example is the Stroop color-word *interference task* where participants must name the actual color of a printed word that spells out a competing name (e.g., the word *blue* in red ink). The detection of substantial conflict between the correct response, *red*, and the competing response, *blue*, can lead to the strengthening of the name-the-color pathway.

Another target of monitoring is for information that signals the need to switch tasks: recognizing that Ken has joined the conversation and retrieving from memory the fact that he does not speak Spanish can lead to a cooperative switch to speaking English. In laboratory tasks that investigate task switching, a common paradigm randomly presents cues that signal whether the participant should continue performing the same task or switch to a different one. Thus, the participant must monitor for the onset of the cue and interpret its meaning. When a switch is required, the task schema (or language schema in the language switching scenario) must be reconfigured and held in working memory. It is this aspect of monitoring that led Miyake, Friedman, Emerson, Witzki, and Howerter (2000) to suggest that monitoring is part of the updating component of EF.

For these various aspects of monitoring, we ask the same question as we did about switching and inhibition: does the monitoring employed in bilingual language control involve the same general-purpose control process, and, if yes, does it seem likely that bilinguals exercise their monitoring ability significantly more than monolinguals? Stipulating, for now, a yes answer to the first part of the question, conflict monitoring seems to be an ideal candidate for enhancement in bilinguals because every lexical selection in either production or comprehension generates competition from its translation equivalent that presumably involves monitoring. Somewhat surprising, it is the monitoring of who enters or leaves the conversation as a potential signal to switch languages that is more often used as an example for why bilinguals should be better at monitoring (e.g., Costa, Hernández, Costa-Faidella, & Sebastián-Gallés, 2009).

EF in Monolingual Language Control

As discussed above, in order for bilingualism to enhance EF, it must be the case that the amount of EF recruited by bilinguals during language comprehension and production is significantly greater than that employed by monolinguals. Several aspects of bilingual language control have no counterparts for monolinguals: the need to monitor the communication environment for changes that trigger a language switch, the actual act of switching languages, and the need to inhibit the translation equivalents. However, speaking any language appears to require substantial amounts of monitoring, switching, and inhibitory control. To provide just a few examples (taken from Paap & Greenberg, 2013), conversational participants must monitor the environment for signals regarding turn-taking, misunderstandings, possible use of sarcasm, changes of topic, or changes in register. These lead to switches from speaker to listener, switches from one knowledge domain to another, and so forth. Although monolinguals do not need to suppress translation equivalents during production, they incessantly make word choices among semantically and syntactically activated candidates that include synonyms, hypernyms, and hyponyms. In addition monolinguals must use context to suppress the irrelevant meaning of homographs during comprehension. In summary, fluent bilinguals have additional needs for monitoring, switching, and inhibitory control, but these unique requirements may not be substantial enough to generate group differences in cognitive control.

Genetics

High Heritability of EF

Heritability is the proportion of variance of a *phenotype* explained by genetic influences in a population of individuals. Phenotype refers to a characteristic that has been measured and in this case might be performance on a task assumed to require EF or to a latent variable at the component level (e.g., switching) or to common EF. Heritability is often estimated from studies of *monozygotic* (MZ, identical) and *dizygotic* (DZ, fraternal) twins. The underlying logic is based on the fact that MZ twins share all of their genes whereas DZ twins share only about half their genes. If one further assumes that genes have additive effects and that both types of twins have the same shared environment, then several key inferences can be drawn from the correlations obtained within each type of twin. For example, the additive assumption suggests that a DZ correlation should be about half the size of the MZ correlation. If the DZ correlation is more than half the MZ correlation, then shared environment is implicated. To take another constraint, if genetic and shared-environment effects accounted for all the variance, then the MZ correlation should be 1.0. Thus, to the extent that the MZ correlation is less than 1.0 provides an index of the amount of unshared environmental influence. When these constraints are formally expressed in a structural-equation model, estimates can be derived for the variance explained by heritability, shared environment, and unshared environment.

Turning to the case at hand, we are considering the possibility that bilingualism enhances common EF or perhaps specific components of EF. The remainder of this section explores the plausibility of this hypothesis given that common EF appears to be entirely heritable. A provocative place to start is Friedman, Miyake, Young, DeFries, Corley, and Hewitt's (2008) large-scale twin study showing that the latent variables for both common EF (99%) and componential EFs (greater than 65%) are almost entirely genetic in origin. This places EFs among the most heritable psychological traits. Only the latent variable for *switching* shows a small (13%) significant contribution from the nonshared environment. Surprisingly the main theme is that both the unity and diversity of EF has genetic origins. Unity, of course, because shared EF is 99% heritable. But the separability of the updating and *shifting* components are not due to influences from the environment, but mostly from additional genetic influences that are independent from those accounting for common EF.

One caveat to any simple interpretation of these results is that possible *gene by environment* (G-E) interactions are subsumed into the "heritability" component (unless they are explicitly included in the model). G-E interactions occur when different genotypes respond differently to the same environment. Consider an infant born into a family of balanced bilinguals and two possible G-E interactions. It could be that rich exposure to two languages benefits only those with high genetic EF. Or, it could be the reverse. If either is true, then bilingualism can enhance EF, but only certain genotypes will reap the benefit. A related concept (see Plomin, DeFries, & Loehlin, 1977) is G-E correlation: different phenotypes are selectively exposed to different environments. Children with high (or low) EF are likely to be treated differently by others and to personally seek compatible environments. G-E correlations are important to consider in studies of *sequential bilingualism* when a second language is acquired after mastery of a native language. When measures of EF and L2 proficiency positively correlate, is it because managing two languages enhances EF, or is it because having high EF makes L2 learning easy and fun?

Friedman et al. (2008) warn that extremely high heritability does not imply that a trait is fixed and immutable because the methodology is based on explaining individual variation about a population mean attributable to genetic effects at a particular point in time. Consider a limiting case where there are no bilinguals in a test population. Obviously bilingualism has no chance of enhancing the EF score of any participant and cannot contribute to a shared environmental effect. At the opposite extreme, if everyone in the population is a balanced bilingual (and assuming, for the moment, that bilingualism does really enhance EF), then all individual scores and the population mean will be incremented from their baselines. In this hypothetical scenario, bilingualism could have a substantial influence on EF, but because it does not account for any of the individual variation about the population mean, this nurturing influence will be masked. Thus, the effects of bilingualism (or any other dichotomous environmental factor) are most likely to be detected if it is present in roughly half the population. The population of families near Boulder, Colorado, sampled by Friedman et al. in 1984 was about 90% Caucasian (N. Friedman, personal communication, July 3, 2012) suggesting that the incidence of bilingualism was quite low, and, consequently, any true effect of bilingualism on EF may not have influenced the estimates of either shared or unshared environment.

The recent study by Engelhardt et al. (2015) provides a second look at the heritability question and does so in a younger population (8- to 15-year-old twins and triplets) where heritability estimates of cognitive abilities are often much lower (Haworth et al., 2009). With only 65% of the sample identifying as non-Hispanic White, and with 31% reported having received a form of mean-tested public assistance, this sample drawn from central Texas was more diverse racially and socioeconomically than the sample from Colorado. Despite these differences in population, the results are strikingly similar at the highest level. The common EF factor was 100% heritable, indicating that correlations among the four components in their model (viz., inhibitory control, switching, working memory, and updating) are entirely attributable to shared genetics. One point of difference is that Engelhardt et al.'s study with children showed that both *working memory* and updating were also influenced by nonshared environment.

To summarize, all other things equal, EF is the least likely cognitive ability to be moderated by bilingualism. Because the influences of shared or nonshared experience are most likely to affect task-specific processes, an environmental effect stemming from managing two languages is not likely to occur in composite measures of EF where task differences tend to cancel out.

Genetic Influence on Switching

There is evidence that a genetic factor (viz., the *A1 allele* of the DRD2/ANKK1 taq1A polymorphism) plays a role in the availability of dopamine in neural structures involved in *non-verbal control tasks*. A study by Stelzel, Basten, Montag, Reuter, and Fiebach (2010) had participants perform a switching task (between odd/even and greater/less than 5) during a functional magnetic resonance imaging (fMRI) scan. Behaviorally, there was a medium to large effect of genotype on switching costs, with carriers showing smaller costs than non-carriers. With respect to the neural results, non-carriers showed increased switching related activity in regions of interests. As Hernandez, Greene, Vaughn, Francis, and Grigorenko (2015) state, the main question of interest for those interested in bilingualism is whether carrier status augments or interacts with language experience.

In a preliminary report, Hernandez et al. (2015) show that the distribution of this allele is markedly different in a sample of Spanish–English bilinguals who are Hispanic ($N = 84$), compared to English monolinguals ($N = 58$) who are Caucasian: about two-thirds of the Hispanics are carriers while only one-third of the Caucasians are carriers. The behavioral results are not yet known, but a number of interesting implications are possible. For example, the presence of the allele may account for the variability in EF to the exclusion of whether individuals were monolingual or bilingual. As Hernandez et al. (2015, p. 116) put it: *these preliminary results suggest the possibility that differences in cognitive control between monolinguals and bilinguals may be due to the underlying distribution of the A1 variant in the gene within our population.* The routine genotyping of our participants may be in our future. Looking at the past, failures to match groups on race and ethnicity may have been riskier compromises than we had hoped.

It may also turn out to be the case that there are informative G-E interactions. Individuals with the A1 allele who are naturally better switchers may not benefit from bilingualism because they are already at or near asymptotic switching performance. In this scenario, it is the non-carriers who would benefit from the extensive practice of managing two languages.

Brain Plasticity

The hypothesis that bilingualism enhances EF is one instance of the broader claim that practicing specific tasks can boost general cognitive abilities. Wagenmakers (2015, p. 334) expresses the issue as a hope many of us harbor: *to what extent are our cognitive processes malleable? Are we to accept the hand that nature has dealt us—a short attention span, a fallible memory, a limited perceptual system—or is there hope that, with the right training and dogged persistence, we can grease the cogwheels of our cognitive machinery, improving performance beyond its apparent boundaries?* Can training on specific memory tasks increase general WMC? Some researchers are optimistic (Jaeggi, Buschkuehl, Jonides, & Shah, 2011), but others are pessimistic (Shipstead, Redick, & Engle, 2012). Does playing violent video games at least lead to improvements in visual perception? Perhaps it does (Bejjanki et al., 2014), but probably not (van Ravenzwaaij, Boekel, Forstmann, Ratcliff, & Wagenmakers, 2014). The problem with empirically testing these hypotheses is the same as testing for bilingual advantages: positive results can arise from confounds or misinterpretations as discussed later in the chapter.

The Bilingual Advantage Hypothesis

The origins of the *bilingual advantage hypothesis* spring from Peal and Lambert's (1962) "myth-busting" indictment of the belief that learning more than one language has substantial adverse cognitive consequences. Peal and Lambert (1962, p. 20) concluded that the experiences of their French–English bilinguals with two language systems and in two cultures resulted in greater *mental flexibility*. Hilchey, Saint-Aubin, and Klein's (2015) updated review credits Bialystok's (2001) book, *Bilingualism in development: Language, literacy and cognition* with the next major advance as it developed a theoretical framework for investigating the relationship between bilingualism and cognition. Some of the key ideas include: (1) bilingual advantages in children tend to occur in tasks that establish a misleading context and moderate conceptual demands, (2) bilingual children appear to be able to inhibit attention to misleading information even when it is more salient, (3) the source of the inhibition is the prefrontal cortex, and (4) both of a bilingual's languages remain active during language comprehension and production. Bialystok (2001, p. 216) melds these ideas into the hypothesis that the extensive practice in inhibiting the non-relevant language *carries over to processing in highly disparate domains*.

Klein (2015) credits the influential article by Bialystok, Craik, Klein, and Viswanathan (2004) for having triggered widespread interest in the phenomena. Klein notes that this paper was the first to study if these advantages carried over to adulthood and that it is the second most frequently cited article in a search using "bilingualism" as the subject. The three experiments reported by Bialystok et al. used the *Simon task*. On each trial a target is presented to the left or right of fixation and participants must press either a left or right button based on the identity of the target and the rule that maps target identity to the response choices (e.g., if the target is a circle press the right-hand button). The impetus for the *Simon effect* is the natural tendency for the most proximal effector to respond to a stimulus (Hilchey, Ivanoff, Taylor, & Klein, 2011). The conflict occurs if the response hand required by the task rule is incongruent with the physical location of the target stimulus. The standard marker of inhibitory control in the Simon task is the difference in mean response time between *incongruent trials* that require conflict resolution compared to the congruent trials that do not. This difference is often referred to as the Simon (interference) effect. In all three experiments there was a significant bilingual advantage; that is, for each age level, bilinguals had significantly smaller Simon interference effects compared to monolinguals

With the benefit of hindsight, there were several aspects of Bialystok et al. (2004) that should have received greater attention. The three studies used language-group sizes ranging from 10 to 32 with a mean of 15.4. As discussed in detail later, these small *sample sizes* are risky. Bilinguals living in India or Hong Kong were compared to monolinguals living in Canada and, consequently, there were cultural as well as language differences. The bilingual advantages were primarily driven by extremely large Simon effects for the monolingual groups (e.g., 535 ms for the younger monolinguals and 1,713 ms for the older monolinguals). Klein (2015) notes that these Simon effects are "strikingly anomalous" given that the Simon effect for elderly participants ranges from 21 to 48 ms (Proctor, Vu, & Pick, 2005). These extreme outcomes may have been caused by the confluence of small samples sizes, inadequate matching, and an unusually small number of trials per condition (as few as 14 in Study 1).

Bilingual Advantage Effects

Inhibitory Control

The introductions to many articles investigating the bilingual advantage give the impression that bilingual advantages occur frequently and consistently. The more recent and systematic reviews and meta-analyses do not support this generalization. Hilchey and Klein (2011) published the first systematic review of bilingual advantages focusing on non-verbal interference tasks and the inhibitory control and monitoring components of EF. In addition to the Simon task, another frequently used non-verbal interference task is the *flanker task* and its hybrid cousin the *attentional network task* (ANT). In both versions, the task is to press the response button corresponding to the direction of a center arrow. The center arrow is flanked on both sides by pairs of arrows that either point in the same direction as the center arrow (congruent trials) or in the opposite direction (incongruent trials). The *flanker interference effect* is defined as the difference between mean RT on congruent and incongruent trials, and it is commonly assumed that smaller flanker effects reflect better inhibitory control. After collating the results of 31 published studies using these non-verbal interference tasks like the Simon and flanker task. Hilchey and Klein (2011, p. 629) concluded that, on balance, there is little evidence for a bilingual advantage in inhibitory control in either children or young adults. More emphatically they asserted that the collective evidence *is simply inconsistent with the proposal that bilingualism has a general positive effect on inhibitory control processes.*

Monitoring

Although there were no systematic differences with respect to interference effects, many studies showed a bilingual advantage on both incongruent and congruent trials. The advantage on congruent trials cannot be the result of superior inhibitory control because there is no conflict to resolve. Furthermore, if the bilingual advantage were no greater on the incongruent trials than on the congruent trials, parsimony would dictate that there is only one cause of the advantages in tasks and that it is not superior inhibitory control. In contrast to the analysis of inhibitory control, aspects of monitoring must take place on both types of trials and, thus, could account for the advantages in *global RT* (i.e., faster RTs across both congruent and incongruent trials). This line of argument led many researchers to shift away from inhibitory control and toward monitoring as the executive function that is enhanced by managing two languages, although the "monitoring" construct is alternatively referred to as mental flexibility, *coordination,* or the *bilingual executive processing advantage* (BEPA). Whatever one calls the mechanism responsible for bilingual advantages on both congruent and incongruent trials, Hilchey and Klein (2011, p. 645) reported that, *in young adults, the global RT advantage is detected ubiquitously on spatial Stroop and flanker interference tasks, though seemingly not in the Simon task.*

Before continuing the historical narrative, it is worthwhile to point out that global RT as a measure of the monitoring construct raises the task impurity problem (Burgess, 1997): overall performance in a task reflects not only the process of interest (e.g., conflict monitoring), but all other stages of processing, from perceptual encoding through response selection and execution. Thus, an individual (or small group) displaying a very fast global RT may not have superior EF, but rather may have speedier motor skills. One approach to filtering out these differences in basic processing is to take the difference in RTs between two tasks that differ only in terms of the process of interest. This, of course, is the logic behind using the differences between congruent and incongruent trials to try to isolate the inhibitory control process. Extending this to the monitoring function, the difference between mean RT on the congruent trials in a block that mixes both congruent and incongruent trials and the mean RT from a pure block of neutral (control) trials is sometimes used as a measure of monitoring. Because individual differences tend to cancel out in the subtraction, this measure is usually credited with being a more pure measure of the monitoring construct.

Using both of these measures of monitoring in a series of three experiments using larger-than-usual sample sizes and both the Simon and flanker tasks, Paap and Greenberg (2013) reported no significant differences between bilinguals and monolinguals (nor did they report any differences in inhibitory control). The publication of this large batch of null results may have been a harbinger (if not a catalyst) for things to come because, when Hilchey et al. (2015) updated their review, they stated that the influx of new data strongly opposed their earlier conclusion that bilingualism causes advantages in monitoring.

Paap, Johnson, and Sawi (2014, 2015) also surveyed the tests for bilingual advantages in non-linguistic tasks, but focused on the distribution of statistically significant bilingual advantages and on studies reported subsequent to Hilchey and Klein's (2011) review. Using, the database from Paap et al. (2015), only 20% of the 64 tests for bilingual advantages in inhibitory control yielded bilingual advantages. Even more diagnostic is the distribution of these statistical outcomes across sample size. On the left panel in Figure 9.1 is the frequency of non-significant tests across various samples sizes. Note that these null results occurred with small, medium, and all of the larger sample sizes. In contrast, as shown on the right panel, significant bilingual advantages in inhibitory control tend to occur with small and moderate samples sizes.

As shown in Figure 9.2, the same pattern obtains in recent studies of the monitoring component of EF. Only 13% of the 46 tests for bilingual advantages in monitoring (obtained in non-verbal interference tasks) yielded bilingual advantages. Furthermore, as shown for inhibitory control, the significant advantages in monitoring tend to occur with small sample sizes.

This is not the expected pattern if bilingualism truly does enhance EF. If the null is false, then as the sample size becomes arbitrarily large—the *t* value grows without bound, and the *p* value converges to zero. This is a good property because it implies that the null will always be rejected in the large-sample limit, if there is a real difference to detect. As Rouder, Speckman, Sun, Morey, and Iverson (2009, p. 226) put it: *researchers, therefore,*

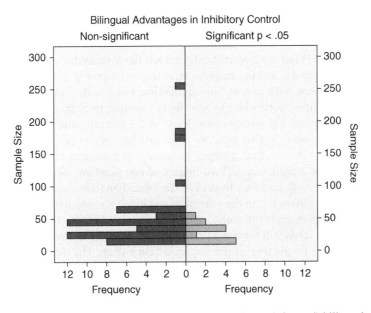

Figure 9.1   Histograms showing the frequency of non-significant (left panel) bilingual advantages in inhibitory control as sample size increases and the frequency of significant advantages (*p* < .05) on the right panel.

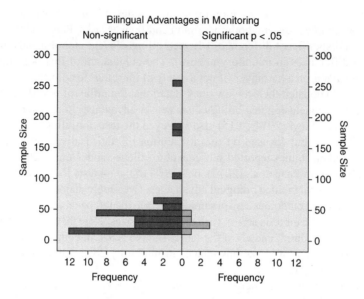

Figure 9.2   Histograms showing the frequency of non-significant (left panel) bilingual advantages in monitoring as sample size increases and the frequency of significant advantages ($p < .05$) on the right panel.

can rest assured that increasing sample size will, on average, result in a gain of evidence against the null when the null is, indeed, false. Thus, all other things being equal, one would expect significant effects to cluster at the higher end of sample sizes. A simple explanation for the pattern observed in Figures 9.1 and 9.2 is the combined assumption that the null is true and that there is a bias on the part of researchers and reviewers to prefer positive results to null results. *Publication bias* is addressed later in the chapter.

Switching

Hilchey and Klein (2011) did not systematically review the tests for bilingual advantages derived from switching tasks, and the analyses reported by Paap et al. (2014, 2015) combined the results obtained with non-verbal interference tasks with those obtained with switching tasks. Thus, it is worthwhile to separately examine tests for bilingual advantages using switching costs and *mixing costs*. Most of the relevant studies used a *color-shape switching task* similar to that used by Prior and MacWhinney (2010) and Paap and Greenberg (2013). On each trial, a target stimulus is presented: a blue circle, a blue triangle, a red circle, or a red triangle. Two fingers of one hand are used to make color decisions (e.g., blue or red), and two fingers of the other hand are used to make shape decisions (e.g., circle or triangle). In the critical mixed block a random precue, presented 250 ms before the target, signals if the upcoming decision should be on the basis of color or shape. Thus, half the trials will require a task switch (from color to shape or vice versa) and half will be repeated trials that do not require a task switch. The difference in mean RT between the switch and repeated trials in the mixed block is taken as a measure of general tasking switching ability and is referred to as switching costs. Participants also complete pure blocks of trials where a single task is performed on every trial. The difference in mean RT between the repeat trials in the mixed block and the mean RT on the single-task blocks reflect mixing costs, that is, the cost of being prepared to switch and having to encode the precue even though the repeated trial does not require a switch to the other task.

As indicated in Table 9.1, the seminal study by Prior and MacWhinney (2010) yielded a significant bilingual advantage in switching costs, but not mixing costs. A tour of the subsequent studies listed in Table 9.1 shows that the bilingual advantage in switching costs is very difficult to replicate. Prior and Gollan (2011) conducted a direct replication. The color-shape switching task was the same in all respects, but the young adults were recruited from a different university and included three groups: Spanish–English, Mandarin–English, and English monolinguals. The bilingual advantage failed to replicate for the Mandarin–English Bilinguals and did not replicate when the original analysis of variance (ANOVA) was run on the Spanish–English bilinguals. However, if the dependent measure was changed from absolute RT to a measure of relative speed and if *parent's educational level* (PED) was included as a covariate, then the difference between the Spanish–English and monolingual groups was significant. Furthermore, in a later replication, Prior and Gollan (2013) did not find any significant bilingual advantages, even for the Spanish–English group, when they used the same color-shape switching task but replaced keyboard responses with spoken responses.

Table 9.1 Results of Tests for Bilingual Advantages in Switching Tasks

Publication	Switching Costs	Mixing Costs
Prior & MacWhinney (2010)	B+	ns
Prior & Gollan (2011)		
Spanish–English bilinguals	B+	ns
Chinese–English bilinguals	ns	ns
Tare & Linck (2011)	ns	ns
Prior & Gollan (2013)		
Spanish–English bilinguals	ns	ns
Hebrew–English bilinguals	ns	ns
Chinese–English bilinguals	ns	ns
Paap & Greenberg (2013)		
Study 1	ns	ns
Study 2	ns	ns
Study 3	ns	ns
Hernández, Martin, Barceló, & Costa (2013)		
Experiment 1	ns	
Experiment 2	ns	
Experiment 3	ns	
Paap & Sawi (2014)	ns	ns
Mor, Yitzhaki-Amsalem, & Prior (2014)	ns	ns
Moradzadeh, Blumenthal, & Wiseheart (2014)	ns	ns
Wiseheart, Viswanathan, & Bialystok (2014)	ns	B+
von Bastian, Sousa, & Gade (2015)		
Color-shape task	ns	
Animacy-size task	ns	
Parity-magnitude task	ns	
Paap, Myuz, Anders, Bockelman, Mikulinsky, & Sawi (in press)		
Color-shape task	ns	ns
Letter-number task	ns	ns
Animacy-size task	ns	ns

Note. B+ = significant bilingual advantage at $p < .05$.

Although Prior and Gollan (2011) concluded that bilingual advantages may be restricted to bilinguals who switch languages frequently, it may be the case that the original advantage in switching costs reported by Prior and MacWhinney is simply an outcome that does not replicate.

Paap and Greenberg (Study 1, 2013) reported a direct replication of the Prior and MacWhinney study using undergraduate students and bilinguals who spoke a variety of languages in addition to English. Furthermore Paap and Greenberg (Study 2–3) and Paap and Sawi (2014) conducted three additional exact replications. The four studies averaged 65 participants per language group and there was no hint of a bilingual advantage in switching costs in any of them. Concurrently, Hernández, Martin, Barceló, and Costa (2013) were conducting a series of switching experiments comparing Catalan–Spanish bilinguals to Spanish monolinguals. Study 3 was a direct replication of Prior and MacWhinney's original color-shape switching task, but there were no language-group differences in switching costs. Although the first two studies used different switching tasks, they can be considered conceptual replications and that enabled Hernández et al. to combine the standardized switching costs from all three studies into a powerful test-based on responses from 292 participants. Even in this composite analysis the language-group differences were not significant. Mor, Yitzhaki-Amsalem, and Prior (2014) also reported null results for switching costs in a direct replication that compared 20 Russian–Hebrew bilinguals to 20 Hebrew monolinguals. Moradzadeh, Blumenthal, and Wiseheart (2014) in an interesting study examining both musical training and bilingualism found that musical training yielded both smaller mixing costs and switching costs in a *digit-number switching experiment* (and also on an updating measure), but there were no language differences on any of the measures.

In a final effort to unveil bilingual advantages in switching costs, we recently reported on a study using 218 college-student participants (55% bilingual) who each completed three standard switching tasks: color-shape, letter-number, and living-size (Paap et al., 2017). We replicated Friedman et al.'s (2008) report of significant correlations between the switching costs derived from each task, thus verifying that the three tasks show *convergent validity* as measures of switching ability. However, there were no differences between the groups of bilinguals and monolinguals in any of the three tasks for either mixing costs or switching costs. The cumulative evidence overwhelmingly favors the conclusion that there are no differences between bilinguals and monolinguals in switching ability. This should not be surprising given the earlier discussion that language switching and general task switching behaviorally dissociate and may have modest overlap, at best, with respect to the neural networks controlling the two types of switching.

Publication Bias

Biases in decision-making on the part of researchers, reviewers, and editors lead to a published database that is not representative of all studies. Rosenthal (1979) coined the phrase *file drawer problem* to describe the strong tendency of researchers to set aside experiments with null results rather than submit them for publication. Researchers may arrive at this decision for several related reasons: assuming that no one is interested in interventions that do not work, assuming that editors and reviewers will not publish null results, or believing that something must have been wrong with their study and deciding to do a better study rather than "mislead" the field with negative findings about an effect they are quite convinced exists. Rosenthal posited a worst-case scenario: that our journals are filled with the 5% of the studies that are *type 1 errors* (i.e., incorrectly rejecting the null hypothesis), and our file drawers are filled with the 95% that are correct failures to reject the null hypothesis. Even a mild case of the file drawer problem can severely skew the apparent size and consistency of a phenomenon.

Rubin (2011) remarks that in the late 1990s he conducted the first randomized experiment to evaluate the effectiveness of *eye movement desensitization and reprocessing* (EMDR), a treatment for trauma based on desensitization, with children and found no differences in outcome between the experimental and control groups. Although he did submit and publish the null results (Rubin et al., 2001), it is interesting that two colleagues known for their "leadership" in EMDR urged him to delay submitting his report because they were concerned that, if the null results were published first, then everyone would conclude that EMDR was ineffective with children. They apparently reasoned that the null results would be "misleading" and not at all a violation of research ethics, dictating that one should not stifle the dissemination of findings that challenge conventional wisdom.

When researchers resist the temptation to place their null results in a file drawer, they do so with the understanding that publishing null results, particularly ones that counter earlier published findings, will be an uphill fight. Reviewers and editors are well trained to respond favorably to results that are significant, novel, counterintuitive, and newsworthy, but not if the novelty takes the form of a failure to replicate an "established" finding. In these cases, editors may remind themselves that null results could be *type 2 errors* (i.e., incorrectly accepting the null hypothesis) or the product of poor methodology.

Although most psychologists seem willing to accept as fact that the peer-review system is biased against null results, there are experimental demonstrations of bias. Mahoney (1977) recruited journal reviewers to referee manuscripts reporting positive, negative, null, or mixed results. The methods and procedures were always identical, but the manuscripts reporting positive outcomes were judged to be methodologically superior and were more likely to be accepted with only minor or moderate revisions.

The field of bilingualism is not immune to these biases. De Bruin, Treccani, and Della Sala (2015a) provided evidence that the combined effects of researchers deciding what to submit and editors deciding which articles to publish were leading to a bias favoring studies with bilingual advantages over those reporting null and negative results. The primary evidence stemmed from examining the fate of 104 conference abstracts presented at 52 different national and international conferences. Fifty-two were eventually published in a scientific journal. Studies with results fully supporting the hypothesis that there are bilingual advantages in EF were most likely to be published (68%), followed by studies with mixed results, and those clearly challenging the hypothesis were published the least (29%).

De Bruin et al. (2015a) also report the results of a *meta-analysis* on the set of 41 published articles that included a total of 176 comparisons between bilinguals and monolinguals. The average weighted difference was $d = +.3$ and, following Cohen's (1992) guidelines, this is a *small effect size* (i.e., a small average difference between bilinguals and monolinguals in EF). However, any biases against null or negative effects will have inflated the true effect size and it is clearly smaller by an unknown amount. To assess this likely possibility, de Bruin et al. created the funnel plot shown in Figure 9.3.

Funnel plots are scatterplots of the inverse of the standard error as a function of effect size. Thus, the plotted point for each study indicates its positive effect size by displacement to the right and its precision as its displacement upward. In an unbiased meta-analysis, the points should be symmetrically distributed about the mean effect size, $d = +.3$ in this example. Furthermore, studies that have larger sample sizes and smaller standard errors should cluster near the mean effect size, whereas those with smaller sample sizes and larger standard errors will disperse across a wider range of effect sizes. Assuming a fixed "true" effect size, extreme values occur because of sampling error and are, of course, more

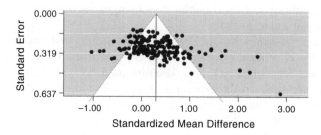

Figure 9.3   A funnel plot of a meta-analysis (adapted from de Bruin et al., 2015a). Each point represents the standard error and the standardized mean difference between bilinguals and monolingual for a single study. The white triangle represents the region where 95% of the data points would lie in the absence of a publication bias. The vertical line represents the average standardized mean difference of 0.30.

likely to occur when precision is low. The white triangle in Figure 9.3 represents the area about the mean effect size where 95% of the points should lie in the absence of publication bias. There are several extreme scores with low precision, but note that they are all positive effects. This apparent asymmetry suggests that the more extreme negative scores are missing, as one would expect if both file drawer effects and publication biases were operating. The asymmetry is expected for this meta-analysis because we already know that there were many abstracts with null or negative findings that were never published.

Because observed asymmetry in a funnel plot can be caused by chance, de Bruin et al. (2015a) used Egger et al.'s (1997) test to show that the asymmetry was significant ($z = 4.80, p < .0001$). Asymmetries can also occur if the true effect size is not constant and systematically varies across sample size. Thus, the funnel plot shown in Figure 9.3 may not reflect biases again null or negative results if it was plausible to argue that the studies with small sizes consistently recruited "better" bilinguals or used more sensitive tests of EF. Because there is no reason to suspect a systematic relationship between sample size and effect size and because there is every reason to suspect a publication bias, the latter stands as the most plausible explanation for the obtained asymmetry.

De Bruin et al. (2015a) note that the amount of bias favoring bilingual advantages in the total set of 104 abstracts is only the *tip of the iceberg*, as it is reasonable to assume that researchers with null and negative results most likely decided not to submit them for presentation at a major conference. If those relegated to the file drawer before submission to a conference could be added to the unpublished conference abstracts, they could easily cancel out the small effect size found in the meta-analysis of those conference abstracts that were eventually published. The interpretation of the de Bruin et al. (2015a) analysis has been challenged by Bialystok, Kroll, Green, MacWhinney, and Craik (2015), but see de Bruin, Treccani, and Della Sala (2015b) for an effective reply to the issues they raised. It is fair and accurate to state that only a small minority of tests for bilingual advantages in EF yield statistically significant group differences.

Bilingual Types

Although bilingual advantages are less general than first thought, might the small proportion of positive results point the way to the specific types of bilingual experiences that will benefit specific aspects of cognitive control? Paap et al. (2014, 2015) have provided a long answer to this question and concluded that, if bilingual advantages do exist, we have yet to discover the sufficient conditions for producing them. The leading nominees for special aspects of coordinating multiple languages are: proficiency and balance, *age of acquisition*, years of bilingual experience, frequency-of-switching, language similarity, and multilingualism.

Ideal Bilinguals

A common conception of an *ideal bilingual* is one who has acquired both languages early, has attained high levels of fluency in both, and who resides in a bilingual community where most people speak the same two languages and switching languages is commonplace. It is noteworthy that three large-scale studies using ideal bilinguals have been published and all yield null results on multiple measures of EF. Duñabeitia et al. (2014) compared Spanish monolinguals ($N = 252$) to Basque–Spanish bilinguals ($N = 252$) at six successive grades with respect to both a verbal Stroop task and a number-size congruency task. Bilinguals and monolinguals performed equivalently in these two tasks across all the indices of inhibitory control and across all grade levels. Antón et al. (2014) tested 180 Spanish–Basque bilinguals and 180 Spanish monolinguals in a child-friendly version of the ANT and found no significant differences in the magnitude of the flanker effect, in global performance, in alerting, or in orienting. These null results held for both speed and accuracy. The groups were exquisitely matched on three measures of *social economic status* (SES), two measures of intelligence, and on both reading and math scores. The balance between Spanish and Basque is assured because both are co-official languages and teachers are required to switch from one to the other language as they switch academic subject to achieve 50% of instruction in each language. As all the children are native to Spain, there are no differences in immigrant status and cultural experiences should be very similar. In a lifespan study testing seven age groups (from 3 to 60+), Gathercole et al. (2014) found no systematic language-group differences on three tasks assumed to reflect executive functioning: dimensional card sorting as a measure of switching ($N = 650$), the Simon task a measure of inhibition ($N = 557$), and a grammaticality judgment task that required semantic anomalies to be ignored ($N = 354$). Bilinguals were all highly proficient in both English and Welsh, but for purposes of analyses were classified as either coming from homes in which Welsh was dominant, English was dominant, or both were spoken. The English-speaking monolinguals resided just across the Welsh border into England.

As described above, ideal bilinguals have a combination of special experiences. There is always the possibility that one or more of these is detrimental and cancels out the enhanced EF caused by the others. To investigate that possibility we examine studies that focus on just one dimension at a time.

Highly Proficient and Balanced Bilinguals

It may be the proficiency of L2 relative to L1 that determines if bilingualism enhances EF. However, a rational argument can be constructed for predicting either that having high levels of proficiency and balance helps or that it hurts. The "helping" possibility assumes that the experience of coordinating two languages will enhance general EF only when the links to both translation equivalents are strong and/or there is a long history of managing both languages. This rationale predicts that highly proficient and balanced bilinguals should have better EF than bilinguals who have a clearly dominant language. Although these assumptions enjoy high plausibility, the argument becomes complicated if the task of managing two languages is viewed as one that varies along a dimension of automatic to *controlled processing*. Although the links between form and meaning may be stronger for highly fluent and balanced bilinguals, the mechanism for resolving the competition between translation equivalents may become automatic and more reliant on language-specific mechanisms within the bilingual lexicon (Costa, Santesteban, & Ivanova, 2006). If this is true, then the controlled processing regulated by EF may be exercised far more often by bilinguals with a clearly dominant language, especially when the non-dominant language is used often. Both possibilities were tested by Paap et al. (2014) by partitioning a composite database of 384 participants into groups based on the ratio of their L2 to L1 proficiencies. The groups included highly proficient and balanced bilinguals; bilinguals proficient in two languages, but with a dominant L1; and monolinguals with no or trivial exposure to an L2. Neither type of bilingual experience produced advantages in inhibitory control or monitoring, in mixing costs, or switching costs. Considering both the tests of ideal bilinguals and the analysis of Paap et al.'s composite database, there is no evidence supporting the hypothesis that a specific L2/L1 ratio is critical for producing bilingual advantages in EF.

Multilingualism

If coordinating two languages enhances EF, then managing three, four, and more should be even more fortifying. Intriguingly, Grogan et al. (2012) reported that multilinguals had higher gray matter density compared to bilinguals and the difference appeared to be related to age of acquisition of the second language (L2). Likewise, Bak, Nissan, Allerhand, and Deary (2014) compared a measure of *general fluid intelligence* (gF) at age 73 to a baseline measure taken when the cohort were 11 years old and reported that the subset of 85 multilinguals had higher gF scores compared to the 162 bilinguals or monolinguals. Although this finding bodes well for multilingualism, it is important to understand that gF and EF are highly correlated, but usually interpreted as separate constructs (Salthouse, 2005; Salthouse, Pink, & Tucker-Drob, 2008).

Examining the behavioral tests using standard measures of EF curbs one's enthusiasm. Poarch and van Hell (2012) reported advantages of trilinguals over monolinguals in flanker interference and of trilinguals over L2 learners in Simon interference, but in neither case were the trilinguals better than the bilinguals. Even more sobering, Humphrey and Valian (2012) reported no significant differences between trilinguals, bilinguals, and monolinguals in either the Simon or the flanker tasks testing for advantages in both inhibitory control and monitoring. Finally, but forcefully, Paap et al. (2014), using their composite database, report no significant differences favoring trilinguals on 13 measures of EF derived from four different tasks.

Frequency-of-Switching

Verreyt, Woumans, Vandelanotte, Szmalec, and Duyck (2015) compared balanced Dutch–French bilinguals who rarely switched to balanced bilinguals who switched frequently. The frequent switchers showed smaller flanker and Simon interference effects, but no differences in global RT. The small sample sizes ($N = 20$ and $N = 17$) warrant further investigation. Also, Verreyt et al. did not include a group of monolingual participants. If frequent switching between languages hones EF, then the high-switch bilinguals should show advantages compared to monolinguals as well as to the low-switch groups. In an analysis of a composite database Paap et al. (2017) selected 40 highly proficient bilinguals who switched frequently, 56 highly proficient bilinguals who switch infrequently, and 66 monolinguals with little or no exposure to an L2. These three language groups were compared in separate analyses of switching costs, mixing costs, Simon effects, and flanker effects. Results showed no advantages for high-switch bilinguals over low-switch bilinguals or for any bilingual group over the monolingual group. Thus, the data support the conclusion that high rates of language switching are not sufficient to consistently produce bilingual advantages in EF.

Script Similarity

Coderre and van Heuven (2014) hypothesized that similar-script bilinguals will have better EF because the greater overlap creates more cross-linguistic competition and presumably increases the daily demands on inhibitory control. They tested this hypothesis by comparing Arabic–English (low similarity), Polish–English (moderate similarity), and German–English bilinguals (high similarity) on measures of EF derived from a Stroop and a Simon task. In a commentary on the Coderre and van Heuven article, Paap, Darrow, Dalibar, and Johnson (2015) concluded that the evidence was inconsistent at best. More important, in an analysis of a composite database with much larger samples sizes, *script similarity* did not moderate the relationship between bilingualism and various measures of EF and no bilingual group showed an advantage compare to the monolingual group.

Age of Acquisition

A popular idea is that there is a *critical period* for acquiring an L2, after which the task requires more effort with limitations on the levels of achievement (DeKeyser, 2000). Consistent with this critical period notion, it has become increasingly clear that bilinguals have greater density of gray matter in the left inferior parietal cortex compared to monolinguals and that the difference is more pronounced in early compared to late bilinguals (Mechelli et al., 2004). Even if the effects of bilingualism on EF are not sensitive to age of acquisition *per se*, early bilinguals have more years of experience in managing two languages compared to late bilinguals. In a highly cited article, Luk, De Sa, and Bialystok (2011) reported the following pattern of differences across three language groups: an advantage in inhibitory control for early bilinguals over both late bilinguals and monolinguals with no language-group differences in monitoring. Among studies including all three of these groups, this specific pattern of results has never been replicated (Humphrey & Valian, 2012; Kalia, Wilbourn, & Ghio, 2014; Kapa & Colombo, 2013; Paap et al., 2014; Pelham & Abrams, 2014; Tao, Marzecova, Taft, Asanowicz, & Wodniecka, 2011). Not one of these subsequent studies resulted in a unique advantage of early bilinguals over both late bilinguals and monolinguals in inhibitory control. Given that the Luk et al. (2011) article is frequently cited as having demonstrated that an early age of acquisition is crucial to the development of bilingual advantages, the persistence of the belief provides a powerful demonstration of how an initial positive finding is rarely questioned, even when the core advantages (viz., early over late and early over monolingual) cannot be replicated.

Multiple Aspects of Bilingualism and EF

Von Bastian, Souza, and Gade (2015) have conducted a very large and complex study exploring how specific bilingual experience might influence specific components of EF. The study is unusual in its scope. Three aspects of bilingualism were used as continuous predictors of EF: age of acquisition, usage, and proficiency. A parallel analysis used *k-means clustering* (R Core Team, 2014) to create three groups that differed along a composite indicator formed from the three dimensions of bilingualism. The bilingualism measures were used to predict nine different components of EF and each of the nine components was measured with multiple tasks. Furthermore objective measures of SES and special activities (video-gaming, musical training, etc.) were matched across the three clusters. All of these measures were obtained from each of the 118 participants (students at Swiss universities)— a process requiring up to 4.5 hours per participant. The results are completely consistent: no aspect of bilingualism or interaction of aspects significantly predicts measures of inhibitory control, monitoring, switching, or a composite reflecting a generalized cognitive advantage. This further confirms the conclusions that age of acquisition, L2/L1 proficiency, proportion of language use, or combinations of these specific experiences are not related to EF. In fact, the von Bastian et al. study shows no relationship at all on any component of EF. Furthermore, near significant findings trend in the direction of advantages for the least bilingual group. In summary, there does not appear to be any cumulative progress in identifying aspects of bilingualism that are necessary or sufficient for potentiating bilingual advantages in EF. A lack of cumulative progress is what one expects if bilingualism does not enhance EF.

Inconsistent Bilingual Advantage Findings

Lack of Power

In *null hypothesis statistical testing* (NHST), power is the probability of rejecting the null hypothesis when, in fact, it is false. Statistics texts offer a guideline that desirable power should be at least .8 or 80%. Desirable levels of power are difficult to achieve when the effect size is likely to be small and recall that the mean effect size for bilingual advantages in the de Bruin et al. (2015a) meta-analysis was small, $d = .3$. Using the G*Power application (Faul, Erdfelder, Lang, & Buchner, 2007) it is easy to explore the number of participants needed to achieve a desired power given an effect size, significance level, a *one-* versus *two-tailed test*, and the ratio of N2/N1. For a simple independent samples *t-test* (e.g., comparing bilinguals to monolinguals on a single measure of EF), if one assumes an effect size of $d = .3$, groups with equal *N*, the standard alpha of .05, and a *two-tailed test* (a prudent choice given that significant monolingual advantages have been reported), then one would need 176 participants in each group to achieve the desired power! Are you interested in a compromise? If the effect of bilingualism on EF was generously estimated to be of medium size (Cohen's $d = .5$), and if we are willing to accept a power of only .67, then one still needs 48 participants in each of two language groups. This compromise means we will miss a true medium-size effect one-third of the time. And, if the effect size is truly smaller (e.g., $d = .3$), not medium, the design with only 48 participants in each group will have an anemic power of .31 and we will fail to correctly reject the null hypothesis two-thirds of the time. Looking back at Figure 9.1 the mean number of participants per language group for those studies reporting a statistically significant bilingual advantage in inhibitory control is only 28 ($SD = 11$). For those not showing a bilingual advantage the mean number per group is 47 ($SD = 44$). Clearly, we are doing grossly underpowered experiments, and consequently, it is not surprising that most experiments reporting bilingual advantages cannot be replicated. Furthermore, and acutely underappreciated, when underpowered designs are combined with questionable research practices, the probability of type 2 errors (*false positives*) also increases.

Small Sample Sizes and False Positives

Bakker, van Dijk, and Wicherts (2012) speculate that publication biases favoring positive results motivate researchers to conduct multiple studies with small sample sizes rather than a single study with a large sample size. If a researcher adopts this strategy, employs directional tests at *alpha* = .05 for each test, and stops and reports the first study that "works" (i.e., that yields a $p < .05$ in the predicted direction), then the combined probability of a type 1 error increases with the researcher's willingness to conduct two (.097), three (.142), four (.185), or five (.226) small experiments.

Only reporting those experiments that work should be considered a *questionable research practice* (QRP) because it can dramatically mislead fields of inquiry. Although one might conjecture that the incidence of putting this strategy into practice is low, John, Loewenstein, and Prelee (2012) surveyed over 2,000 research psychologists, and 48% admitted to having submitted papers that only reported the studies that "worked." Other prevalent practices from the John et al. survey include: (1) failing to report all of a study's dependent measures, 65% admission rate; (2) deciding to collect more data when the results are not significant, 57%; (3) rerunning analyses with outliers removed, 41%; (4) failing to report all of a study's conditions, 28%; and (5) "rounding off" a *p value* greater than $p = .050$ to a value $\leq .05$, 22%. In their simulation work Bakker et al. operationalized the first three QRPs from the list above and applied them sequentially to any simulated study that initially produced a non-significant result. Instantiating these QRPs caused the rate of false positives to jump to nearly .40.

In summary, the Bakker et al. (2012) simulations show that a strategy of conducting small-sample experiments, applying QRPs to the non-significant results, and reporting only those experiments that "work" leads to substantial rates of false positives when the true effect size is zero. Although it is not possible to pinpoint the rate of false-positive bilingual advantages it seems fair to conjecture that it is nontrivially greater than .05. Small sample sizes are especially risky when random assignments cannot be used because the comparison of interest is between two naturally occurring populations, an issue we turn to next.

Analysis of Covariance and Confounding Variables

Because random assignment is not possible in quasi-experimental studies comparing monolinguals to bilinguals, there is a likely possibility that bilingualism will covary with other factors that affect EF. This problem was raised early on by Morton and Harper (2007) and Carlson and Meltzoff (2008) and more recently by Hilchey and Klein (2011), Kousaie and Phillips (2012), Paap and Greenberg (2013), and Paap and Liu (2014). If a variable is confounded, one strategy is to analyze a subset of the participants by matching the two groups. For example, in Paap and Greenberg's study, there were no significant group differences in the Simon effect, but the mean parental education (PE) level for Paap and Greenberg's bilinguals was significantly lower than that for the monolinguals. In a supplementary analysis, they precisely matched 90 monolinguals to 90 bilinguals on PE scores and the results were the same, indicating that PE was not cancelling out a bilingual advantage. Matching was a very effective method in this study because the sample size was very large. Unfortunately, when matching is used on more typical sample sizes, the resulting group sizes can be very small and the risk of false negatives or positives can increase to undesirable levels. Another potential risk to using matching is that the selection itself may create a new confound. For example, eliminating the monolinguals from the most educated families could have produced a monolingual group with lower non-verbal intelligence. (It did not in the case of Paap and Greenberg's data.) It bears repeating that the standard paradigm for experimental control of extraneous variables consisting of the manipulation of an independent variable through random assignment to an experimental group (bilingualism) and control group (monolingualism) can only be used to study very small doses (weeks or months) of bilingualism.

The limitations of matching and random assignment noted above have led many researchers to rely on the analysis of covariance (ANCOVA) in order to take into account the effect of an extraneous factor (covariate) on the dependent measure. The appropriate use of ANCOVA can reduce the within-group error variance and thereby increase the likelihood of obtaining a significant group effect (Field, 2013). However, as Miller and Chapman (2001) point out it is a misapplication of ANCOVA to "statistically control" for factors that are confounded across the groups because this constitutes a violation of the independence assumption. Miller and Chapman argue that when the independence assumption is violated, the regression adjustment may either obscure part of the grouping effect (e.g., language effect) or produce spurious effects; thus the ANCOVA results are uninterpretable when there are systematic differences in the covariate across groups. Similarly, Field (2013) warns that when treatment groups differ on the covariate, putting the covariate into the analysis will not "control for" or "balance out" those differences.

As is true in almost every area of psychological science, the misapplication of ANCOVA is common and this holds true for the literature on the bilingual advantage. For example, Tao et al. (2011) compared early and late bilinguals to monolinguals and found bilingual advantages in both inhibition and monitoring, but only when measures of non-verbal intelligence (Raven's scores) and SES were used as covariates. The early bilinguals had significantly higher Raven's scores (Mean = 9.1) compared to the monolinguals (Mean = 6.9), with the late bilinguals falling in between (Mean = 8.2). The problem was not using covariates; it was using covariates that were confounded across groups. Having violated the independence assumption Miller and Chapman would caution that their results are uninterpretable.

Immigrant Status

Immigrant status is often associated with higher intelligence and more generally with a "healthy migrant effect" (Bak, 2015; Fuller-Thomson & Kuh, 2014; Kirk, Fiala, Scott-Brown, & Kempe, 2014). If the healthy immigrant effect generalizes to EF, then we would expect the group with a disproportionate number of immigrants to have better EF ability. Many reports of bilingual advantages have confounded immigrant status with bilingualism, especially in research testing older adults. In a study of older adults (Bialystok, Craik, & Luk 2008), 20 of the 24 bilinguals were immigrants. In a direct replication, Kirk et al. (2014) found no language-group differences in either the magnitude of the Simon interference scores or in global RT in five groups of older adults (Mean age = 70.8 years). In the research using older adults, language-group differences often occur when immigrant status is not matched (Bialystok et al., 2008; Gold, Kim, Johnson, Kryscio, & Smith, 2013; Salvatierra & Rosselli, 2011; Schroeder & Marian, 2012) and do not occur when it is (Billig & Scholl, 2011; Kirk et al., 2014; Kousaie & Phillips, 2012).

The importance of controlling for immigrant status is underscored by investigations of the role of bilingualism on the onset of mild cognitive decline or dementia. The first studies used *retrospective reports* of patients at memory clinics and showed that bilingualism delayed the onset of symptoms or diagnosis by several years. Some of these studies confounded bilingualism with immigrant status (Bialystok, Craik, & Freedman, 2007), while another found bilingual benefits within immigrant samples, but not between native samples (Chertkow et al., 2010). Immigrant status is important because it is associated with higher intelligence that, in turn, is associated with delays in dementia onset (Fuller-Thomson, 2015). Furthermore, the four studies that have used a *prospective cohort design* following individuals without dementia at baseline have all found no significant effects of bilingualism, and the trend in three of those favors the monolinguals (Crane et al., 2009; Lawton, Gasquoine, & Weimer, 2015; Sanders, Hall, Katz, & Lipton, 2012). Fuller-Thomson (2015) suggests that the *longitudinal design* is less open to biases in sampling, measurement, and publication. If the prospective studies are weighted more heavily than those using retrospective reports, there is little evidence that bilingualism protects against cognitive decline.

Culture

When immigrant status is confounded it is also likely that there are differences in culture across the language groups. Even when studies match the groups with respect to measured SES immigrant status, there may be cultural differences. Morton and Carlson (in press) present evidence for cultural differences in the development of EF and show how these differences can confound tests of bilingual advantages. A study by Carlson and Choi (2009) provides a dramatic demonstration of the entanglement between culture and bilingualism. Using six different measures of EF they found significant bilingual advantages comparing a group of Korean–English bilinguals living in the US to a "matched" sample of American monolinguals. However, the performance of the Korean–American bilinguals was indistinguishable from a third group of matched Korean monolinguals. This clearly questions an interpretation that the obtained group differences were due to bilingualism and strongly supports the view that cultural differences play an influential role in the development of EF.

Socioeconomic Status

In reviewing the research with children, Hilchey and Klein (2011) concluded that there was no evidence for bilingual advantages in inhibitory control obtained with the Simon task: across six different comparisons, there were no significance differences in the magnitude of the interference effect, but five of the six did show significant differences in global RT. The exception was the study by Morton and Harper (2007) that, in terms of task, methods, and design, was a direct replication of Bialystok et al. (2004). The main difference between the studies was that Morton and Harper used measures of PED and family income to ensure that the bilinguals and monolinguals were matched on SES. They were also matched in terms of ethnicity and immigrant status.

Convergent Validity in Inhibitory Control

In earlier sections, we discussed a variety of alternative explanations for why significant bilingual advantages in performance sometimes occur. This section raises a different concern, namely, that many of the standard measures of inhibition and monitoring obtained with non-verbal interference tasks lack convergent validity; that is, they do not correlate with one another. In contrast, mixing costs appear to have adequate levels of convergent validity (Paap et al., 2017; Paap & Sawi, 2014). If measures lack convergent validity, then individual or group differences are more likely to reflect a combination of chance factors and task-specific factors than differences in a domain-general component of EF.

Based on studies conducted in our laboratory and a very large number of others, Paap and Sawi (2014) concluded that there is little or no convergence between measures of inhibitory control. This may seem surprising given that Miyake and Friedman's latent variable analyses showed significant correlations between the task variables assumed to require inhibition. One piece of the puzzle is that Miyake and Friedman never included the Simon interference effect as one of their measures. But even different variants of the Stroop task do not correlate with one another (Shilling, Chetwynd, & Rabbitt, 2002), nor do different versions of the flanker task correlate with one another (Salthouse, 2010). These non-verbal interference tasks are sensitive to the conflict present on incongruent trials, but they do not appear to measure individual differences in domain-general inhibitory control.

In their seminal study of inhibition, Friedman and Miyake (2004) considered three categories of interference tasks, but the best model did not empirically separate response inhibition (viz., stop signal, antisaccade, Stroop) from interference control (e.g., resistance to distraction as in the flanker task). Unsworth et al. (2012, 2014), also treat both types of inhibition as a single latent variable. Thus, the outcome of these latent variable analyses does not mesh with studies assuming that bilinguals are better at interference control, but not response inhibition (e.g., Blumenfeld & Marian, 2014).

Convergent Validity in Monitoring

The convergent validity across these measures of monitoring has been examined in the three studies conducted by Paap and Greenberg (2013) and a fourth study reported in Paap and Sawi (2014). It is the case that global RT in the flanker task is highly correlated with global RT in the Simon task ($r = +0.60$), but as cautioned above, a host of nonexecutive processes may be contributing to the association. This possibility is reinforced by observing that the mixing costs (mean RT on congruent trials from a mixed block minus mean RT in a conflict-free baseline condition) for the Simon and flanker tasks yield correlations near zero. Because mixing costs in the color-shape switching task are also assumed to reflect the monitoring component of EF, this measure can also be correlated with the mixing costs obtained in the Simon and flanker tasks: the correlation between mixing in the switching task and mixing in the flanker or Simon task in our studies is usually near zero and in one case was slightly negative. These results reinforce the need for additional work in operationally defining constructs like monitoring, coordination, or mental flexibility and establishing their validity as measures of EF.

Significant bilingual advantages obtained with only a single measure of the EF component are likely to be caused by task-specific factors and unlikely to replicate with a conceptually similar measure derived from a different task. Only studies using two or more measures that converge with each other offer compelling evidence that differences in performance reflect differences in a specific component of EF.

Interaction Effects

Paap et al. (2015) and Hilchey et al. (2015) discuss several examples where significant congruency by language-group interactions were interpreted as evidence for a bilingual advantage in inhibitory control when the interpretation was not warranted. For example, the interaction shown in Figure 9.4 (equivalent to the bottom-right "quartet" of interactions from Wagenmakers, 2015) is clearly due to a monolingual advantage on the congruent trials and no difference on the incongruent trials. The interactions originate solely from

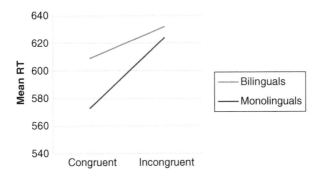

Figure 9.4   A pattern of congruency × language-group interaction sometimes interpreted as a bilingual advantage in inhibitory control (adapted from Wagenmakers, 2015, p. 335, Figure 1).

an unexplained performance difference for the congruent condition. This pattern cannot possibly support the hypothesis that bilinguals have superior inhibitory control.

Variations in Task Selection

Another factor that likely contributes to inconsistent results is that too many studies introduce new tasks or variations of old tasks without apparent motivation. It is a generally accepted lore that small changes in the displays and/or proportion of test stimuli can substantially alter performance on choice RT tasks, especially when the intent is to test for individual or group differences in specific stages of processing. Rather than admonish those who have practiced unmotivated variation (although Paap and Greenberg's choice of "Z" and "/" as targets in their Simon task would be a good example), it is more productive to illustrate the point with a counter example of excellence.

In a study designed to test for bilingual advantages in inhibitory control and conflict monitoring, Mendes (2015) meticulously justifies the choice of tasks and the specific versions of those tasks. Two tasks, the Simon and ANT, are chosen and potentially bilingual advantages can be demonstrated in two different tasks providing strong evidence that the advantages are not task-specific. Although both tasks provide measures of inhibitory control and conflict monitoring, they also offer an interesting contrast between interference control (ANT) and competition with a prepotent response (Simon). The specific instantiation of the Simon task was based on Bialystok et al.'s (2004) study 2, not simply for its historical significance, but because it is frequently argued that bilingual advantages in young adults are more likely to occur when task difficulty is high (e.g., Kroll & Bialystok, 2013). This version of the Simon task includes two additional conditions where two colors, rather than just one, are assigned to each response and consequently the demands on WMC and overall task difficulty are increased. One of the virtues of the ANT task is that it enables measures of two additional networks (alerting and orienting), as well as the flanker interference effect. More important for present purposes, the version of the ANT selected (viz., 50% congruent and 50% incongruent trials) is one that Costa et al. (2009) has shown to maximize the need for conflict monitoring and that is sufficient to produce bilingual advantages in inhibitory control, at least in the initial block of trials. The careful consideration of measures and tasks is mirrored with respect to several of the issues discussed earlier. Immigrant status is controlled for in a novel way, all of the 38 English monolinguals and the 77 English–other bilinguals are immigrants to New Zealand with at least five years of residency and a mean of about 11 years. The language groups are matched on measures of SES, educational level, fluid intelligence, English proficiency, playing video games, music performance, physical exercise, and *meditation*. The results of this careful design are, if nothing else, completely consistent. In both the Simon and ANT task there were no significant group differences in measure of inhibitory control (congruency), monitoring (global RT), or the magnitude of sequential-dependency effects. There were no differences in updating, a component measured only in the Simon task by comparing the four versus two color conditions. There were no differences in orienting effects or alerting effects that were measured only in the ANT task. Treating age of onset of active bilingualism, language balance, and language switching frequency as continuous variables, separate regression analyses on only the bilingual data showed no influence of these aspects of bilingualism on any of the measures of EF when controlling for age, fluid intelligence, and gender. In summary, the Mendes study is another example of a well-designed study using multiple measures of EF and larger-than-usual samples that yields no evidence that bilingual experience enhances EF.

Neuroscience and the Bilingual Advantage

Many researchers believe that the inconsistent evidence for the bilingual advantage in behavioral data has been strengthened by the studies that have jointly explored both behavioral and neuroscience measures. Although we agree that this could be so in theory, we have argued that this has yet to happen (Paap, 2014; Paap et al., 2014, 2015; Paap, Sawi, Dalibar, Darrow, & Johnson, 2014, 2015), principally because of two problems that we have dubbed the *alignment problem* and the valence-ambiguity problem. The interested reader is encouraged to consult one of our earlier treatments for more examples and an extended discussion, but the gist of these problems is presented next.

The Alignment Problem

In general, cortical areas shown to be involved in managing two languages overlap with those shown to be involved with inhibitory control and switching (Bialystok, Craik, & Luk, 2012). Furthermore, it is clear from the neuroimaging results that the neural processing of bilinguals and monolinguals differs during the performance of EF tasks. This is consistent with the view that coordinating two languages leads to a reorganization of neural networks in cortical areas involved in EF. However, reorganization to accommodate bilingualism does not logically need to result in more efficient performance. Alternatively, it could lead to comparable performance or even to a compromise that results in inferior performance. Thus, it is imperative that the observed neural differences be aligned with the behavioral differences so that bilingual advantages in actual performance can be confirmed. We propose that the existence of a behavioral phenomenon can only be adjudicated at the behavioral level, an argument first advanced by Hilchey and Klein (2011) and recently also seconded by Duñabeitia and Carreiras (2015).

A simple example of the alignment problem occurs in a study by Luk, Anderson, Craik, Grady, and Bialystok (2010), who claim to have shown neural correlates of a bilingual advantage in inhibitory control when participants were performing a flanker task. However, this conclusion runs counter to the actual behavioral results. With respect to the RT data, there was neither a main effect of group nor a significant Group x Trial Type interaction. Thus, there was no behavioral evidence for either a monitoring or inhibitory control advantage. With respect to neural differences, Luk et al. reported that the regions associated with faster responding were the same on both congruent and incongruent trials for monolinguals, but with different regions for bilinguals. This additional and different pathway employed by bilinguals on incongruent flanker trials led Luk et al. to conclude that bilinguals have superior inhibitory control. This is an interesting speculation, but one that should be advanced with great caution because: (1) the flanker effects for the two groups in this study were nearly identical, and (2) as reviewed earlier, the evidence, in general, for bilingual advantages in inhibitory control in young adults is very weak, at best.

The Valence-Ambiguity Problem

The interpretation of neural differences is very risky in the absence of behavioral data that show the same pattern of significant differences. When alignment problems occur, the ambiguity of many neural differences is exposed. *Valence ambiguity* (Paap, Sawi, Dalibar et al., 2014) occurs when increasing neural scores are interpreted as having a positive effect on performance by some researchers and as having a negative effect by others. In considering behavioral measures like speed or accuracy in choice RT tasks, it seems to be inherently the case that individuals or groups who are faster and/or more accurate enjoy a performance advantage over those who are slower and/or less accurate. Speed-accuracy tradeoffs can complicate the interpretation, but the point remains that within each measure, faster is better and more accurate is better. Differences in neural measures have no such *face validity* and they must be interpreted in the context of their behavioral consequences.

Fernandez, Acosta, Douglass, Doshi, and Tartar (2014) compared English monolinguals to Spanish–English bilinguals on both auditory and visual *go/nogo tasks* while recording *event-related potentials* (ERPs). An ERP is the measured brain response that is the direct result of a specific sensory, cognitive, or motor event. The N2 (or N200) negative peak occurs approximately 150–400 ms after stimulus onset and has been associated with the detection of response conflict in both children and adults. As predicted, bilinguals showed larger *N2 amplitudes* during the auditory nogo trials, which require inhibitory control, but no differences during the go trials. In contrast, there were no group differences in N2 amplitude during the visual nogo trials. A disadvantage of the go/nogo task is that one cannot check to see if the behavioral differences align with the N2 differences because there are no behavioral responses on a nogo trial unless the participant false alarms, and, in this study, false alarms were too rare to analyze. Fernandez et al. concluded that bilinguals have *enhanced inhibitory control*.

In a commentary on this study, Paap, Sawi, Dalibar et al. (2015) ask if larger N2 amplitudes are really indicative of better inhibitory control. Some of the most compelling evidence comes from developmental studies showing that N2 amplitude in the go/nogo task declines over the span of seven to sixteen years (Lamm, Zelazo, & Lewis, 2006). Similarly, Espinet, Anderson, and Zelazo (2012) found that three- to four-and-a-half-year-old children who can pass the dimensional change card sort (DCCS) task have significantly smaller N2 amplitudes during the post-switch phase of the task compared to those who perseverate and fail the test. The last result is compelling because the neural results align with the behavioral performance results (viz., success on the DCCS aligns with small N2 amplitude). These studies strongly suggest that a smaller N2 amplitude reflects superior performance.

Summary and Conclusions

The hypothesis that managing two languages enhances common or specific components of EF was examined. The hypothesis is predicated on the assumption that coordinating two languages is subsidiary to cognitive control, in general, and that bilingual control is sufficiently frequent and challenging to significantly enhance EF above the level of matched monolinguals. Although this underlying logic is attractive and the assumptions plausible, there is evidence suggesting dissociations between bilingual language control and general cognitive control. Furthermore, EF is highly heritable and individuals may achieve their genetically determined upper limits through a combination of daily tasks, special interests, and the language control required to understand and produce a single language.

Systematic reviews of the published literature show that about 80% of the tests for bilingual advantages yield null results, that those resulting in significant advantages tend to have small sample sizes, and that the mean effect size is quite small. Furthermore, the published research is biased in favor of positive results (i.e., bilingual advantages) and against null and negative results to the extent that the unbiased effects may be very close to zero. Compounding the problem of publication bias, small sample sizes in combination with questionable research practices can substantially increase the rate of false positives. Some positive findings are likely to have been caused by failures to match on demographic factors (e.g., SES, culture, immigrant status); others may have yielded significant differences only with an inappropriate use of the ANCOVA to "control" for these factors. Although direct replications are under-utilized, when they are, the results of seminal studies cannot be replicated. Furthermore, most studies testing for bilingual advantages use measures and tasks that do not have demonstrated convergent validity, and any significant differences in performance may reflect task-specific mechanisms and not domain-free EF abilities. Brain imaging studies have made only a modest contribution to evaluating the bilingual-advantage hypothesis, mainly because the neural differences frequently do not align with the behavioral differences and also because the neural measures are often ambiguous with respect to whether greater magnitudes should cause increases or decreases in performance. Based on this array of evidence, it seems reasonable to suggest that bilingual advantages in EF simply may not exist.

The possibility that bilingualism enhances EF, but that the effect is small, was also considered. The "real but small" scenario fits the fact that significant group differences occur infrequently and are small in average magnitude, but it does not fit the fact that the studies with the largest sample sizes yield null results. A more likely scenario is that bilingual advantages accrue only in very specific circumstances that pair the right set of bilingual experiences with the resonating set of EF measures. However, based on studies that have investigated age of acquisition, L2/L1 ratio, multilingualism, language similarity, and other aspects of bilingualism, it appears that the results are inconsistent. The most comprehensive efforts to match specific aspects of bilingualism with specific measures of EF have yielded consistent, but null results. Thus, those hypothesizing that bilingual advantages occur in only specific circumstances seem obligated to admit that, at this point in time, the sufficient circumstances for producing bilingual advantages are undetermined.

Recommendation for Future Studies

We have drawn a roadmap for persuading skeptics that bilingual advantages exist (Paap & Greenberg, 2013; Paap, Johnson, & Sawi, 2015). Studies should start with a theory of how two or more languages are coordinated and specify which (if any) of the control mechanisms employ domain-general executive functions. This should lead to the identification of the particular type (or combination of types) of bilingual experience that is most important to enhancing that component of EF. That critical experience should play the lead role in predicting which bilingual groups should have better EF and, in turn, be better than monolinguals. The groups should be matched on SES, immigrant status, culture, and so forth, using operationally defined measures. Tasks and measures should be selected that have demonstrated convergent validity, and, even then, it is best to have two measures, derived from two different tasks, included in the study so that one can rule out the concern that any obtained bilingual advantage in performance is task-specific. The number of participants in each group should be determined in advance and based on a reasonable level of desired power. In estimating power, a small effect size should be assumed given the meta-analysis reported by de Bruin et al. (2015a) and the effect sizes reported in Hilchey and Klein (2011) and Hilchey et al. (2015).

List of Key Words and Concepts

A1 allele, Age of acquisition, Alignment problem, Animacy-size task, Attentional network task (ANT), Balanced bilingual, Bilingual advantage hypothesis, Bilingual executive processing advantage (BEPA), Color-shape switching task, Conflict monitor, Conflict resolution, Congruent trials, Controlled processing, Convergent validity, Coordination, Critical period, Dependent variable, Digit-number switching experiment, Dimensional change card sort task (DCCS), Dizygotic (DZ), Event-related potentials (ERPs), Executive functions (EF), Eye movement desensitization and reprocessing (EMDR), Face validity, False positives, File drawer problem, Flanker interference effect, Flanker task, Fraternal twins, Frontoparietal network, Funnel plots, Gene by environment (G-E), General fluid intelligence (gF), Global RT, Go/nogo task, Grammaticality judgment tasks, Heritability, Ideal bilingual, Inhibitory control, Interference task, K-means clustering, Language-task schema, Latent variables, Letter-number task, Longitudinal design, Matched samples, Meditation, Mental flexibility, Meta-analysis, Mixing costs, Monitoring, Monozygotic (MZ), N2 amplitude, Nested components, Neuroscience, Non-verbal control tasks, Null hypothesis statistical testing (NHST), Parent's educational level (PED), Parity-magnitude task, Phenotype, Prefrontal cortex, Prospective cohort design, Publication bias, Questionable research practice (QRP), Retrospective report, Sample sizes, Script similarity, Self-regulation, Sequential bilingualism, Shifting, Simon effect, Simon task, Social economic status (SES), Stroop effect, Switching costs, Switching errors, Task selection, Unity-diversity, Updating, Valence-ambiguity problem, Wisconsin card sorting task, Working memory capacity (WMC)

Internet Sites Related to the Psycholinguistics of Bilingualism

Are Bilinguals Really Smarter? http://scienceline.org/2014/07/are-bilinguals-really-smarter/
Bilingualism and Language Learning: http://www.bilingualism-matters.ppls.ed.ac.uk/
Cognitive Advantages in Bilingualism: https://en.wikipedia.org/wiki/Cognitive_advantages_of_bilingualism
François Grosjean: http://francoisgrosjean.ch
Myths about Bilingualism: http://www.francoisgrosjean.ch/myths_en.html

Discussion Questions

(1) What are executive functions (EF)? Why do Miyake and Friedman conclude that EF has both "unity" and "diversity"?
(2) What is the underlying theory for why speaking two languages should lead to improvements in EF? What assumptions of that theory are likely to be wrong, if it turns out that bilingual advantages do not exist?

(3) Bilinguals may sometimes outperform monolinguals on tests of EF for reasons other than their experience in managing two languages. List these factors and indicate how their influence might be controlled, eliminated, or at least minimized.

(4) What specific aspects of bilingualism have been studied? What type of bilingual do you think is most likely to have superior EF ability? Why?

(5) Has neuroscience data contributed to our understanding of the relationship between bilingualism and EF? How does the "alignment problem" and the "valence ambiguity" problem complicate the interpretation of neuroscience data?

Suggested Research Projects

(1) Critique a recent study testing for bilingual advantages in EF. Assuming that any bilingual advantage will have a small effect size, does the design have adequate power? What extraneous variables were measured? Were any of them confounded across the language groups? Were there potential confounding variables that were not measured? How was bilingualism operationally defined? Were any specific bilingual experiences investigated, for example, age of acquisition, L2/L1 ratio, number of languages spoken, frequency-of-language switching, interactional context? Was the selection of the dependent measure(s) justified with respect to validity and/or reliability? Did the results completely, partially, or not-at-all support the research hypothesis?

(2) Alternatively, compare how several studies treat the problem of extraneous variables such as SES, parent's education, participant's education, immigrant status, cultural differences, and non-verbal intelligence. Were the variables measured, were they matched, and was the use of ANCOVA appropriate?

(3) Download a version of the flanker task (e.g., millisecond.com) and run yourself through several sessions keeping track of the mean RT on congruent and incongruent trials. Does your flanker interference effect continue to decrease across sessions? Assuming you are a young adult, what implications, if any, does this have for the hypothesis that young adults have reached their peak ability in inhibitory control?

(4) In tests of verbal fluency participants are asked to name as many instances of a target category as they can in 60 seconds. In "semantic" verbal fluency tasks the targets are categories like animals or musical instruments. In "letter" verbal fluency tasks the targets are words beginning with a specific letter like "F" or "P". Letter-fluency is thought to require more EF than does semantic-fluency. Describe an experimental design that could test this assumption. What do you predict if bilinguals were compared to monolinguals on your test?

Suggested Readings

Baum, S., & Titone, D. (2014). Keynote paper: Moving toward a neuroplasticity view of bilingualism, executive control and aging. *Applied Psycholinguistics, 5*, 857–894.

Hartsuiker, R. J. (2015). Why it is pointless to ask under which circumstances the bilingual advantage occurs. *Cortex, 73*, 336–337.

Morton, J. B. (2014). Sunny review casts a foreboding shadow over status quo bilingual advantage research. *Applied Psycholinguistics, 5*, 929–931.

Paap, K. R. (2015). Do many hones dull the bilingual whetstone? *Bilingualism: Language and Cognition, 18*(1), 41–42.

Valian, V. (2015). Bilingualism and cognition. *Bilingualism: Language and Cognition, 18*(1), 3–24.

References

Antón, E., Duñabeitia, J. A., Estévez, A., Hernández, J. A., Castillo, A., Fuentes, L. J., Davidson, D. J., & Carreiras, M. (2014). Is there a bilingual advantage in the ANT task? Evidence from children. *Frontiers in Psychology: Language Sciences, 5*, 1–12.

Bak, T. H. (2015). Beyond a simple "yes" and "no." *Cortex, 73*, 332–333.

Bak, T. H., Nissan, J. J., Allerhand, M. M., & Deary, I. J. (2014). Does bilingualism influence cognitive aging? *Annals of Neurology, 75*(6), 959–963.

Bakker, M., van Dijk, A., & Wicherts, J. M. (2012). The rules of the game called psychological science. *Perspectives in Psychological Science, 7*, 534–554.

Bejjanki, V. R., Zhang, R., Li, R., Pouget, A., Green, C. S., Lu, Z.-L., & Bavelier, D. (2014). Action video game play facilitates the development of better perceptual templates. In *Proceedings of the National Academy of Sciences of the United States of America, 111*, 16961–16966.

Bialystok, E. (2001). *Bilingualism in development: Language, literacy and cognition.* Cambridge, UK: Cambridge University Press.

Bialystok, E., Craik, F. I. M., & Freedman, M. (2007). Bilingualism as a protection against the onset of dementia. *Neuropsychologia, 45*(2), 459–464.

Bialystok, E., Craik, F. I., Klein, R., & Viswanathan, M. (2004). Bilingualism, aging, and cognitive control: Evidence from the Simon task. *Psychology of Aging, 19*(2), 290–303.

Bialystok, E., Craik, F. I. M., & Luk, G. (2008). Cognitive control and lexical access in younger and older bilinguals. *Journal of Experimental Psychology: Learning, Memory, and Cognition, 34*(4), 859–873.

Bialystok, E., Craik, F. I. M., & Luk, G. (2012). Bilingualism: Consequences for mind and brain. *Trends in Cognitive Science, 16*(4), 240–250.

Bialystok, E., Kroll, J. F., Green, D. W., MacWhinney, B., & Craik, F. I. M. (2015). Publication bias and the validity of evidence: What's the connection? *Psychological Science, 26*(6), 944–946.

Billig, J. D., & Scholl, A. P. (2011). The impact of bilingualism and aging on inhibitory control and working memory. *Organon, 51*, 39–52.

Blumenfeld, H. K., & Marian, V. (2014). Cognitive control in bilinguals: Advantages in stimulus-stimulus inhibition. *Bilingualism: Language and Cognition, 17*(3), 610–629.

Botvinick, M. M., Braver, T. S., Barch, D. M., Carter, C. S., & Cohen, J. D. (2001). Conflict monitoring and cognitive control. *Psychological Review, 108*, 624–652.

Burgess, P. W. (1997). Theory and methodology in executive function research. In P. Rabbit (Ed.), *Methodology of frontal and executive function* (pp. 81–116). Hove, UK: Psychology Press.

Calabria, M., Branzi, F. M., Marne, P., Hernández, M., & Costa, A. (2015). Age-related effects over bilingual language control and executive control. *Bilingualism: Language and Cognition, 18*(1), 65–78.

Carlson, S. M., & Choi, H. P. (2009, April). *Bilingual and bicultural: Executive function in Korean and American children.* Paper presented at the 2009 Biennial Meeting of the Society for Research in Child Development, Denver, Colorado.

Carlson, S. M., & Meltzoff, A. N. (2008). Bilingual experience and executive functioning in young children. *Developmental Science, 11*(2), 282–298.

Chertkow, H., Whitehead, V., Phillips, N., Wolfson, C., Atherton, J., & Bergman, H. (2010). Multilingualism (but not always bilingualism) delays the onset of Alzheimer disease: Evidence from a bilingual community. *Alzheimer Disease and Associated Disorders, 24*(2), 118–125.

Coderre, E. L., & van Heuven, W. J. B. (2014). The effect of script similarity on executive control in bilinguals. *Frontiers in Psychology, 5*, 1–16.

Cohen, J. (1992). "A power primer." *Psychological Bulletin, 112*(1), 155–159.

Costa, A., Caramazza, A., & Sebastián-Gallés, N. (2000). The cognate facilitation effect: Implications for models of lexical access. *Journal of Experimental Psychology: Learning, Memory, and Cognition, 26*(5), 1283–1296.

Costa, A., Hernández, M., Costa-Faidella, J., & Sebastián-Gallés, N. (2009). On the bilingual advantage in conflict processing: Now you see it, now you don't. *Cognition, 113*, 135–149.

Costa, A., & Santesteban, M. (2004). Lexical access in bilingual speech production: Evidence from language switching in highly-proficient bilinguals and L2 learners. *Journal of Memory and Language, 50*, 491–511.

Costa, A., Santesteban, M., & Ivanova, I. (2006). How do highly proficient bilinguals control their lexicalization process? Inhibitory and language-specific selection mechanisms are both functional. *Journal of Experimental Psychology: Learning, Memory, and Cognition, 32*(5), 1057–1074.

Crane, P. K., Gibbons, L. E., Arani, K., Nguyen, V., Rhoads, K., McCurry, S. M., Launer, L., Masaki, K., & White, L. (2009). Midlife use of written Japanese and protection from late life dementia. *Epidemiology, 20*(5), 766–774.

De Baene, W., Duyck, W., Brass, M., & Carreiras, M. (2015). Brain circuit for cognitive control is shared by task and language switching. *Journal of Cognitive Neuroscience, 27*(9), 1752–1765.

de Bruin, A., Treccani, B., & Della Sala, S. (2015a). Cognitive advantage in bilingualism: An example of publication bias. *Psychological Science, 26*(1), 99–107.

de Bruin, A., Trecanni, B., & Della Sala, S. (2015b). The connection is in the data: We should consider them all. *Psychological Science, 26*(6), 947–949.

DeKeyser, R. M. (2000). The robustness of critical period effects in second language acquisition. *Studies in Second Language Acquisition, 22*(4), 499–533.

Duñabeitia, J. A., & Carreiras, M. (2015). The bilingual advantage: Acta et fabula? *Cortex, 73*, 371–372.

Duñabeitia, J. A., Hernández, J. A., Antón, E., Macizo, P., Estévez, A., Fuentes, L. J., & Carreiras, M. (2014). The inhibitory advantage in bilingual children revisited. *Experimental Psychology, 61*(3), 234–251.

Egger, M., Smith, D., Schneider, M., & Minder, C. (1997). Bias in meta-analysis detected by a simple graphical test. *BMJ, 15*, 629–634.

Engelhardt, L. E., Briley, D. A., Mann, F. D., Harden, K. P., & Tucker-Drob, E. M. (2015). Genes unite executive functions in childhood. *Psychological Science*, 1–13.

Espinet, S. D., Anderson, J. E., & Zelazo, P. D. (2012). N2 amplitude as a neural marker of executive function in young children: An ERP study of children who switch versus perseverate on the dimensional change card sort. *Developmental Cognitive Neuroscience, 1*, S49–58.

Faul, F., Erdfelder, E., Lang, A. G., & Buchner, A. (2007). G*Power 3: A flexible statistical power analysis program for the social, behavioral, and biomedical sciences. *Behavioral Research Methods, 39*(2), 175–191.

Fernandez, M., Acosta, J., Douglass, K., Doshi, N., & Tartar, J. L. (2014). Speaking two languages enhances an auditory but not a visual neural marker of cognitive inhibition. *AIMS Neuroscience, 1*(2), 145–157.

Festman, J., & Münte, T. F. (2012). Cognitive control in Russian-German bilinguals. *Frontiers in Psychology, 3*(115), 1–7. https://doi.org/10.3389/fpsyg.2012.00115

Festman, J., Rodriguez-Fornells, A., & Münte, T. F. (2010). Individual differences in control of language interference in late bilinguals are mainly related to general executive abilities. *Behavioral and Brain Function, 6*(5), 1–10. https://behavioralandbrainfunctions.biomedcentral.com/articles/10.1186/1744-9081-6-5

Field, A. (2013). *Discovering statistics using IBM SPSS statistics* (4th ed.). London: Sage.

Friedman, N. P., & Miyake, A. (2004). The relations among inhibition and interference control functions: A latent-variable analysis. *Journal of Experimental Psychology: General, 133*(1), 101–135.

Friedman, N. P., Miyake, A., Young, S. E., DeFries, J. C., Corley, R. P., & Hewitt, J. K. (2008). Individual differences in executive functions are almost entirely genetic in origin. *Journal of Experimental Psychology: General, 137*, 201–225.

Fuller-Thomson, E. (2015). Emerging evidence contradicts the hypothesis that bilingualism delays dementia onset. *Cortex, 66*, 170–172.

Fuller-Thomson, E., & Kuh, D. (2014). The healthy migrant effect may confound the link between bilingualism and delayed onset of Alzheimer's disease. *Cortex, 52*, 128–130.

Gathercole, V. C. M., Thomas, E. M., Kennedy, I., Prys, C., Young, N., Vinas-Guasch, R., Roberts, E. J., Hughes, E. K., & Jones, L. (2014). Does language dominance affect cognitive performance in bilinguals? Lifespan evidence from preschoolers through older adults on card sorting, Simon, and metalinguistic tasks. *Frontiers in Psychology, 5*(11), 1–14. https://doi.org/10.3389/fpsyg.2014.00011

Gold, B. T., Kim, C., Johnson, N. F., Kryscio, R. J., & Smith, C. D. (2013). Lifelong bilingualism maintains neural efficiency for cognitive control in aging. *The Journal of Neuroscience*, *33*(2), 387–396.

Green, D. W. (1998). Mental control of the bilingual lexico-semantic system. *Bilingualism: Language and Cognition*, *1*, 67–81.

Grogan, A., Jones, O. P., Ali, N., Crinion, J., Orabona, S., Mechias, M. L., Ramsden, S., Green, D. W., & Price, C. J. (2012). Structural correlates for lexical efficiency and number of languages in non-native speakers of English. *Neuropsychologia*, *50*, 1347–1352.

Haworth, C. M. A., Wright, M. J., Luciano, M., Martin, N. G., De Geus, E. J. C., Van Beijsterveldt, C. E. M., & Plomin, R. (2009). The heritability of general cognitive ability increases linearly from childhood to young adulthood. *Molecular Psychiatry*, *1*, 1112–1120.

Hernandez, A. E., Greene, M. R., Vaughn, K. A., Francis, D. J., & Grigorenko, E. L. (2015). Beyond the bilingual advantage: The potential role of genes and environment on the development of cognitive control. *Journal of Neurolinguistics*, *35*, 109–119.

Hernández M., Martin, C. D., Barceló, F., & Costa, A. (2013). Where is the bilingual advantage in task-switching? *Journal of Memory and Language*, *69*, 257–276.

Hilchey, M. D., Ivanoff, J., Taylor, T. L., & Klein, R. M. (2011). Visualizing the temporal dynamics of spatial information processing responsible for the Simon effect and its amplification by inhibition of return. *Acta Psychologica*, *136*(2), 235–244.

Hilchey, M. D., & Klein, R. M. (2011). Are there bilingual advantages on nonlinguistic interference tasks? Implications for plasticity of executive control processes. *Psychonomic Bulletin & Review*, *18*, 625–658.

Hilchey, M. D., Saint-Aubin, J., & Klein, R. M. (2015). Does bilingual exercise enhance cognitive fitness in non-linguistic executive processing tasks. In J. W. Schwieter (Ed.), *Handbook of bilingual processing* (pp. 572–586). New York: Cambridge University Press.

Humphrey, A. D., & Valian, V. V. (2012, November). *Multilingualism and cognitive control: Simon and flanker task performance in monolingual and multilingual young adults*. Paper presented at the 53rd Annual Meeting of the Psychonomic Society, Minneapolis, MN.

Jaeggi, S. M., Buschkuehl, M., Jonides, J., & Shah, P. (2011). Short-and long-term benefits of cognitive training. In *Proceedings of the National Academy of Sciences of the United States of America*, *108*, 10081–10086.

John, L. K., Loewenstein, G., & Prelec, D. (2012). Measuring the prevalence of questionable research practices with incentives for truth-telling. *Psychological Science*, *23*(5), 524–532.

Kalia, V., Wilbourn, M. P., & Ghio, K. (2014). Better early or late? Examining the influence of age of exposure and language proficiency on executive function in early and late bilinguals. *Journal of Cognitive Psychology*, *26*(7), 699–713.

Kapa, L. L., & Colombo, J. (2013). Attentional control in early and later bilingual children. *Cognitive Development*, *28*, 233–246.

Kirk, N. W., Fiala, L., Scott-Brown, K., & Kempe, V. (2014). No evidence for reduced Simon cost in elderly bilinguals and bidialectals. *Journal of Cognitive Psychology*, *26*(6), 640–648.

Klein, R. (2015). Is there a benefit of bilingualism for executive functioning? *Bilingualism: Language and Cognition*, *18*(1), 29–31.

Kousaie, S., & Phillips, N. A. (2012). Ageing and bilingualism: Absence of a "bilingual advantage" in Stroop interference in a nonimmigrant sample. *The Quarterly Journal of Experimental Psychology*, *65*(2), 356–369.

Kroll, J. F., & Bialystok, E. (2013). Understanding the consequences of bilingualism for language processing and cognition. *Journal of Cognitive Psychology*, *25*(5), 497–514.

Kroll, J. F., & Gollan, T. H. (2014). Speech planning in two languages: What bilinguals tell us about language production. In V. Ferreira, M. Goldrick, & M. Miozzo (Eds.), *The Oxford handbook of language production* (pp. 165–181). Oxford, UK: Oxford University Press.

Lamm, C., Zelazo, P. D., & Lewis, M. D. (2006). Neural correlates of cognitive control in childhood and adolescence: disentangling the contributions of age and executive function. *Neuropsychologia*, *44*, 2139–2148.

Lawton, D. M., Gasquoine, P. G., & Weimer, A. A. (2015). Age of dementia diagnosis in community dwelling bilingual and monolingual Hispanic Americans. *Cortex, 66*, 141–145.

Luk, G., Anderson, J. A. E., Craik, F. I. M., Grady, C., & Bialystok, E. (2010). Distinct neural correlates for two types of inhibition in bilinguals: response inhibition versus interference suppression. *Brain and Cognition, 74*, 347–357.

Luk, G., De Sa, E., & Bialystok, E. (2011). Is there a relation between onset age of bilingualism and enhancement of cognitive control? *Bilingualism: Language and Cognition, 14*, 588–595.

Mahoney, M. J. (1977). Publication prejudices: An experimental study of confirmation bias in the peer review system. *Cognitive Therapy and Research, 1*, 161–175.

Mechelli, A., Crinion, J. T., Noppeney, U., O'Doherty, J., Ashburner, J., Frackowiak, R. S., & Price, C. J. (2004). Structural plasticity in the bilingual brain: Proficiency in a second language and age at acquisition affect grey-matter density. *Nature, 431*, 757–757. doi: 10.1038/431757a.

Mendes, C. G. (2015). *The impact of bilingualism on conflict control* (Unpublished doctoral dissertation). University of Otago, Dunedin, New Zealand.

Miller, G. A., & Chapman, J. P. (2001). Misunderstanding analysis of covariance. *Journal of Abnormal Psychology, 110*(1), 40–48.

Miyake, A., & Friedman, N. P. (2012). The nature and organization of individual differences in executive functions: Four general conclusions. *Current Directions in Psychology, 21*(1), 8–14.

Miyake, A., Friedman, N. P., Emerson, M. J., Witzki, A. H., & Howerter, A. (2000). The unity and diversity of executive functions and their contributions to complex "frontal lobe" tasks: A latent variable analysis. *Cognitive Psychology, 41*, 49–100.

Mor, B., Yitzhaki-Amsalem, S., & Prior, A. (2014). The joint effect of bilingualism and ADHD on executive functions. *Journal of Attention Disorders, 19*(6), 527–541.

Moradzadeh, L., Blumenthal, G., & Wiseheart, M. (2014). Musical training, bilingualism, and executive function: A closer look at task switching and dual-task performance. *Cognitive Science, 39*, 1–29.

Morton, J. B., & Carlson, S. M. (in press). In M. Hoskyn, G. Iarocci, & A. Young (Eds.), *The bilingual advantage: Evidence and alternative views*. Oxford: Oxford University Press.

Morton, J. B., & Harper, S. N. (2007). What did Simon say? Revisiting the bilingual advantage. *Developmental Science, 10*, 719–726.

Paap, K. R. (2014). The role of componential analysis, categorical hypothesizing, replicability and confirmation bias in testing for bilingual advantages in executive functioning. *Journal of Cognitive Psychology, 26*(3), 242–255.

Paap, K. R., Darrow, J., Dalibar, C., & Johnson, H. A. (2015). Effects of script similarity on bilingual advantages in executive control are likely to be negligible or null. *Frontiers in Psychology, 5*, 1–16.

Paap, K. R., & Greenberg, Z. I. (2013). There is no coherent evidence for a bilingual advantage in executive processing. *Cognitive Psychology, 66*, 232–258.

Paap, K. R., Johnson, H. A., & Sawi, O. (2014). Are bilingual advantages dependent upon specific tasks or specific bilingual experiences? *Journal of Cognitive Psychology, 26*(6), 615–639.

Paap, K. R., Johnson, H. A., & Sawi, O. (2015). Bilingual advantages in executive functioning either do not exist or are restricted to very specific and undetermined circumstances. *Cortex, 69*, 265–278.

Paap, K. R., & Liu, Y. (2014). Conflict resolution in sentence processing is the same for bilinguals and monolinguals: The role of confirmation bias in testing for bilingual advantages. *Journal of Neurolinguistics, 27*(1), 50–74.

Paap, K., Myuz, H. A., Anders, R. T., Bockelman, M. F., Mikulinsky, R., & Sawi, O. M. (2017). No compelling evidence for a bilingual advantage in switching or that frequent language switching reduces switch cost. *Journal of Cognitive Psychology, 29*(2), 89–112.

Paap, K. R., & Sawi, O. (2014). Bilingual advantages in executive functioning: Problems in convergent validity, divergent validity, and the identification of the theoretical constructs. *Frontiers in Psychology, 5*(962), 1–15.

Paap, K. R., Sawi, O., Dalibar, C., Darrow, J., & Johnson, H. A. (2014). The brain mechanisms underlying the cognitive benefits of bilingualism may be very difficult to discover. *AIMS Neuroscience, 1*(3), 245–256.

Paap, K. R., Sawi, O., Dalibar, C., Darrow, J., & Johnson, H. A. (2015). Beyond panglossian optimism: Larger N2 amplitudes probably signal a bilingual disadvantage in conflict monitoring. *AIMS Neuroscience, 2*(1), 12–17.

Peal, E., & Lambert, W. E. (1962). The relation of bilingualism to intelligence. *Psychological Monographs: General and Applied, 76*, 1–23.

Pelham, S. D., & Abrams, L. (2014). Cognitive advantages and disadvantages in early and late bilinguals. *Journal of Experimental Psychology: Learning, Memory, and Cognition, 40*(2), 313–325.

Plomin, R., DeFries, J. C., & Loehlin, J. C. (1977). Genotype–environment interaction and correlation in the analysis of human behavior. *Psychological Bulletin, 84*(2), 309–322.

Poarch, G. J., & van Hell, J. G. (2012). Executive functions and inhibitory control in multilingual children: Evidence from second-language learners, bilinguals, and trilinguals. *Journal of Experimental Child Psychology, 113*, 535–551.

Prior, A., & Gollan, T. (2011). Good language-switchers are good task-switchers: Evidence from Spanish–English and Mandarin–English bilinguals. *Journal of International Neuropsychological Society, 17*, 1–10.

Prior, A., & Gollan, T. H. (2013). The elusive link between language control and executive control: A case of limited transfer. *Journal of Cognitive Psychology, 25*(5), 622–645.

Prior, A., & MacWhinney, B. (2010). A bilingual advantage in task switching. *Bilingualism: Language and Cognition, 13*, 253–262.

Proctor, R. W., Vu, K. P. L., & Pick, D. F. (2005). Aging and response selection in spatial choice tasks. *Human Factors: The Journal of the Human Factors and Ergonomics Society, 47*(2), 250–270.

R Core Team. (2014). *A language and environment for statistical computing.* Vienna, Austria: R Foundation for Statistical Computing. Retrieved from http://www.R-project.org/

Rosenthal, R. (1979). The file drawer problem and tolerance for null results. *Psychological Bulletin, 86*, 638–641.

Rouder, J. N., Speckman, P. L., Sun, D., Morey, R. D., & Iverson, G. (2009). Bayesian t tests for accepting and rejecting the null hypothesis. *Psychonomic Bulletin & Review, 16*, 225–237.

Rubin, A. (2011). *Practitioner's guide to using research for evidence-based practice.* Hoboken, NJ: John Wiley & Sons.

Rubin, A., Bischofshausen, S., Conroy-Moore, K., Dennis, B., Hastie, M., Melnick, L., Reeves, D., & Smith, T. (2001). The effectiveness of EMDR in a child guidance center. *Research on Social Work Practice, 11*, 435–457.

Salthouse, T. A. (2005). Relations between cognitive abilities and measures of executive functioning. *Neuropsychology, 19*, 532–545.

Salthouse, T. A. (2010). Is flanker-based inhibition related to age? Identifying specific influences of individual differences on neurocognitive variables. *Brain and Cognition, 73*, 51–61.

Salthouse, T. A., Pink, J. E., & Tucker-Drob, E. M. (2008). Contextual analysis of fluid intelligence *Intelligence, 36*, 464–486.

Salvatierra, J. L., & Rosselli, M. (2011). The effect of bilingualism and age in inhibitory control. *International Journal of Bilingualism, 15*, 26–37.

Sanders, A. E., Hall, C. B., Katz, M. J., & Lipton, R. B. (2012). Non-native language use and risk of incident dementia in the elderly. *Journal of Alzheimer's Disease, 29*(1), 99–108.

Schroeder, S. R., & Marian, V. (2012). A bilingual advantage for episodic memory in older adults. *Journal of Cognitive Psychology, 24*(5), 591–601.

Shilling, V. M., Chetwynd, A., & Rabbitt, P. M. A. (2002). Individual inconsistency across measures of inhibition: an investigation of the construct validity of inhibition in older adults. *Neuropsychologia, 40*, 605–619.

Shipstead, Z., Redick, T. S., & Engle, R. W. (2012). Is working memory training effective? *Psychological Bulletin, 138*, 628–654.

Stelzel, C., Basten, U., Montag, C., Reuter, M., & Fiebach, C. J. (2010). Frontostriatal involvement in task switching depends on genetic differences in D2 receptor density. *The Journal of Neuroscience, 30*(42), 14205–14212.

Tao, L., Marzecova, A., Taft, M., Asanowicz, D., & Wodniecka, Z. (2011). The efficiency of attentional networks in early and late bilinguals: The role of age of acquisition. *Frontiers in Psychology, 2*, 1–19.

Tare, M., & Linck, J. (2011, November). *Exploring bilingual cognitive advantages when controlling for background variables.* Poster presented at the 52nd Annual Meeting of the Psychonomic Society, Seattle, WA.

Unsworth, N., Fukuda, K., Awh, E., & Vogel, E. K. (2014). Working memory and fluid intelligence: Capacity, attention control, and secondary memory retrieval. *Cognitive Psychology, 71*, 1–26.

Unsworth, N., McMillan, B. D., Brewer, G. A., & Spillers, G. J. (2012). Everyday attention failures: An individual differences investigation. *Journal of Experimental Psychology: Learning, Memory, and Cognition, 38*(6), 1765–1772.

van Ravenzwaaij, D., Boekel, W., Forstmann, B., Ratcliff, R., & Wagenmakers, E.-J. (2014). Action video games do not improve the speed of information processing in simple perceptual tasks. *Journal of Experimental Psychology: General, 143*, 1794–1805.

Verreyt, N., Woumans, E., Vandelanotte, D., Szmalec, A., & Duyck, W. (2015). The influence of language switching experience on the bilingual executive control advantage. *Bilingualism: Language and Cognition, 19*(1), 181–190.

von Bastian, C. C., Sousa, A. S., & Gade, M. (2015). No evidence for bilingual cognitive advantages: A test of four hypotheses. *Journal of Experimental Psychology: General, 145*(2), 246–258.

Wagenmakers, E.-J. (2015). A quartet of interactions. *Cortex, 73*, 334–335.

Wiseheart, M., Viswanathan, M., & Bialystok, E. (2014). Flexibility in task switching by monolinguals and bilinguals. *Bilingualism: Language and Cognition. 19*(1), 141–146. doi:https://doi.org/10.1017/S1366728914000273.

10 Bilingual Linguistic and Cognitive Development

Elena Nicoladis and Lisa Smithson

Introduction

Child: *Mon ventre est presque full de water!*
        "My belly is almost" full "of" water!

The first author's daughter, a French–English bilingual, said the above sentence when she was five years old. To someone familiar only with monolingual conversations, this sentence might sound as if she were arbitrarily using words from her two languages, making a kind of language salad. When parents of bilingual children hear *mixed-language* sentences, they sometimes worry that learning two languages confuses their children. Does bilingualism confuse children?

One of the earliest studies of a bilingual child's language development showed that bilingualism did not confuse the child. Ronjat (1913) kept a diary of the words and sentences used by his son, Louis, who was being raised speaking both French and German. Ronjat himself spoke only French to Louis, while Louis' mother spoke only German. By the time Louis was 16 months old, he chose the appropriate language for his parents, saying *Brot* (*bread* in German) to his mother and *pain* (*bread* in French) to his father. At the age of 28 months, Louis addressed the French cook in German, but he quickly learned to use the correct language. Louis learned German faster than he did French, and until he was about 43 months of age, he occasionally borrowed a German word when he was trying to speak French. Almost all of his language mixes could be attributed to a gap in Louis' French vocabulary. Ronjat attributed Louis' lack of confusion to the fact that both he and his wife always addressed Louis in their native tongue and did not themselves mix languages. He concluded that bilingualism did not have to lead to confusion.

This conclusion was questioned by the results of another *diary study* of a German–English bilingual child who grew up in the US. Leopold (1949) spoke only German to his daughter, Hildegard, and his wife spoke only English. Hildegard produced mixed-language utterances. Leopold concluded that Hildegard passed through a stage of assuming that German and English were a single linguistic system. According to her father, Hildegard did not differentiate her two languages until she was about three years of age.

On the basis of these two diary studies, it is impossible to draw any general conclusions about whether bilingualism confuses children. These diary studies only address the language outcomes for two children and additionally, there is a methodological difficulty with diary studies. In both cases, the diarist could only observe his child's behavior when he was present. The presence of one parent could affect the behavior of the child (Genesee, 1989). For example, in Hildegard Leopold's case, it is possible that she spoke as much German as possible when her father was present and never spoke it when he was absent. A diary study cannot tell us about behavior when the diarist is absent.

More recent research has corrected for this possibility by videotaping children in *spontaneous conversation* with a variety of people who speak different languages (Genesee, Nicoladis, & Paradis, 1995). For example, in a study of a Portuguese–English bilingual child growing up in the US, the researchers videotaped the child playing in his home in two different contexts: (1) with the Portuguese-speaking father, videotaped by a native Portuguese speaker and (2) with the English-speaking mother, videotaped by a native English speaker (Nicoladis & Secco, 2000). Results of studies like these show that bilingual children can reliably choose the language preferred by their interlocutor from at least two years of age (e.g., Nicoladis & Genesee, 1996). This same pattern can even be observed among young trilingual children (Quay, 2012).

In fact, by the age of two years, bilingual children even show sensitivity to a stranger's language choice. Genesee, Boivin, and Nicoladis (1996) observed four French–English bilingual two-year-olds growing up in Canada. All four children were learning French from one parent and English from another, although all the parents had some knowledge of the other language. The researchers first videotaped each child interacting with each parent in *spontaneous play* situations in the families' homes. Then, on the basis of parental reports and each child's videotaped production, the researchers identified each child's weaker language (for two children, it was French and for the other two it was English). The researchers then asked a stranger who spoke only the child's weaker language to play with the child while being videotaped. Three of the four children spoke significantly more of the stranger's language with the stranger than with the relevant parent. These results suggest that the bilingual children were sensitive to the stranger's language use and produced as much of that language as they could.

Young bilingual children might also be sensitive to how their parents respond to their language mixing. Lanza (1992) observed a Norwegian–English bilingual girl, Siri, growing up in Norway with her Norwegian-speaking father and English-speaking mother. The father seemed to be more accepting of the child's language mixing: when Siri mixed languages, the father allowed the conversation to continue. For example, when Siri used the English word *hug* with him, he responded mostly in Norwegian, including the English word *hug*. In contrast, Siri's mother responded to mixed languages as if she did not understand the Norwegian words. Lanza argued that Siri was more likely to mix languages with her father because she learned that he accepted either language.

The language choice in parent–child interactions is not determined solely by the parents (see Quay, 2012, for discussion). Prevoo, Mesman, Van IJzendoorn, and Pieper (2011) found that Turkish-speaking mothers in the Netherlands started to use more Dutch with their children when they started attending daycare. These results suggest that as the children started using more Dutch at home, the parents also started to use more Dutch. There is growing evidence that the language choice of siblings and other family members, as well as the language of the community, can also make a difference in parent–child language choices (Schwartz, 2010).

Taken together, these studies suggest that bilingualism does not confuse children. The language mixing that Leopold thought was evidence for confusion is actually a clever use of linguistic resources on the part of bilingual children. Bilingual children can clearly differentiate their languages from at least two years of age on and can negotiate the appropriate language of a conversation. While bilingual children can differentiate their languages, they do not use their languages exactly like two monolinguals (Byers-Heinlein, 2014). Why does bilingualism affect language and cognitive development? Clearly, the answer is at least somewhat implicit in the question: bilingual children know two languages and monolinguals know one. What is it about the knowledge of two languages that makes development different? In this chapter, we will discuss four ways in which researchers have documented differences between bilinguals and monolinguals: delay in language development, acceleration in language development, cross-linguistic influence, and cognitive differences. At the outset, we would like to note that the differences between bilinguals and monolinguals are often small (see De Houwer, 2005). Nevertheless, the detectable differences can shed some light onto how language and cognitive development unfold in all children.

Before turning to a review of the observed differences, it is important to note how we are characterizing bilingualism. We will concentrate on bilingual development in the first five years of life. Most of the studies have concerned *simultaneous bilinguals* (that is, children acquiring two languages from birth). Because it is possible that there will be differences in development if two languages are acquired sequentially (Gross, Buac, & Kaushanskaya, 2014), we will note if a study concerns *sequential bilingual* development. We will also concentrate on children who have been exposed to two languages on a regular basis. This characterization of bilingualism allows for the possibility of passive knowledge of one language. Because we are using such a liberal characterization of bilingualism, it is important to note, where possible, how variations in children's proficiency or degree of knowledge of the two languages affect our conclusions about where and why there are differences in development due to bilingualism (see Paradis, 2011, for discussion of the impact of individual differences on early *sequential bilingualism*).

Delay in Language Development

Does bilingualism delay language development? To answer this question reliably, it is important to compare a group of typically developing bilingual children with a group of typically developing monolingual children. However, it is very difficult to find an appropriate group of bilinguals because bilinguals form a heterogeneous group. The heterogeneity comes from a variety of sources. Bilingual children are often more proficient in one language than another, with their proficiency varying considerably between individuals and over time. For example, Leopold (1949) reported that his daughter's German was weaker than her English until they went on a trip to Germany for several weeks. Variations in bilingual development might also be manifested in terms of the language pairs known (e.g., Chinese and English vs. Vietnamese and French). The attitudes toward bilingualism that parents and people in the general public have could also influence how well children end up speaking their two languages.

The heterogeneity of bilinguals is a challenge to devising norms for bilingual development. Nevertheless, researchers have been interested in what domains of language bilingualism might slow down. Before turning to the research results, we would like to caution the reader that few bilingual children have been studied in each of the domains we will mention, with the exception of vocabulary.

In some domains of language development, bilingual children seem to show no delays. One of the earliest developmental markers of language behavior is the onset of *canonical babbling*, or babbling composed of consonant-vowel-consonant-vowel forms, like *dada*. Some researchers have argued that canonical babbling allows children to practice word-like forms before actually saying words (Vihman, 1996). One study recorded the babbling produced by infants who heard both Spanish and English on a regular basis (Oller, Eilers, Urbano, & Cobo-Lewis, 1997). This study showed that the age at which the bilingual infants started to use canonical babbling was the same age as has been reported for monolingual infant. Other researchers have replicated this finding (Maneva & Genesee, 2002).

There is evidence of delays in language acquisition in other domains. We will mention two here: vocabulary size and production of past tense verbs. Bilingualism may affect vocabulary size most significantly among very young children. In one study, Pearson, Fernández, and Oller (1993) asked the parents of 25 Spanish–English bilingual children between 8 and 30 months of age to fill out vocabulary checklists of words that their children used spontaneously. They found that the average bilingual vocabulary score was about half that of a monolingual in each language. However the total vocabulary size of bilingual children was approximately equivalent to the vocabulary scores reported by parents of monolingual children. In a follow-up study, the researchers compared the ratio of vocabulary between the two languages of an individual child with the time the parents reported that the child spent interacting in each language (Pearson, Fernández, Lewedag, & Oller, 1997). They found that the more time the children spent interacting in a language, the greater their vocabulary in that language. Similar results have been reported in a more recent study (Place & Hoff, 2011). These results suggest that there may be some limits on children's vocabulary size in the first few years of life and that the frequency of exposure to a language will be related to which words a child learns. It is possible that the limits on vocabulary size are limited to the first few years of life.

Research tends to show a *receptive* vocabulary disadvantage for bilingual preschoolers in comparison to monolingual preschoolers (aged 3–5 years; Allman, 2005; Bialystok, Luk, Peets, & Yang, 2010; Doyle, Champagne, & Segalowitz, 1978). However, much of this research has been conducted among bilingual speakers who are speaking a minority language at home (e.g., Allman, 2005; Bialystok et al., 2010). Bilingual performance on tests of receptive vocabulary tends to be quite different when assessed in a sociocultural context that supports both bilingual languages. In a study by Thordardottir (2011), the receptive vocabulary of 4;6 to 5;0 year-old French–English bilinguals was compared with age-matched monolinguals. Importantly, these children were living in a context supporting both bilingual languages (Montreal, Canada). The results indicated that bilinguals who were equally exposed to both languages did not differ in terms of receptive vocabulary in comparison to monolinguals. Thordardottir attributed this outcome to the supportive language learning environment in Montreal, Canada. Similarly, in a study by Smithson, Paradis, and Nicoladis (2014), French–English bilingual preschoolers performed significantly above the standard mean on both French and English receptive vocabulary assessments and performed comparably to age-matched monolinguals on both French and English receptive vocabulary assessments. Older bilingual children and bilingual adults residing in a sociocultural context that supports both bilingual languages showed similar results (Smithson et al., 2014).

Research conducted by Thordardottir (2011) and Smithson et al. (2014) suggests that if bilinguals reside in a sociocultural context that supports both of their languages, they can score comparably to monolinguals on tests of receptive vocabulary. It is possible, then, that the delay in vocabulary acquisition in bilinguals in a language is a short-lived phenomenon, restricted to the first few years of language acquisition. We will return to this point below, when we address cognitive differences between bilinguals and monolinguals.

Another example of delay in language acquisition to be discussed here is in the acquisition of past tense verbs. One study reported such a delay in French–English bilingual children between the age of four and six years (Nicoladis, Palmer, & Marentette, 2007). The researchers showed a cartoon to a group of bilingual children, a group of English monolingual children, and a group of French monolingual children. They asked the children to tell back the story to someone who had not seen the cartoon. The bilingual children told the story twice, once to a French speaker and once to an English speaker. The researchers found that the bilingual children used fewer correct past tense forms to tell a story than monolinguals in both languages. The differences were particularly noticeable with irregular past tense forms; the bilingual children made more errors by adding *–ed* to irregular verbs, like *goed* or *runned*. Because irregular past tense verbs are irregular, there is no way to learn them except by hearing them repeatedly (e.g., Bybee, 1995). Monolinguals also make the same kinds of errors, but they do so earlier in development. Thus, the researchers concluded that the bilingualism delayed the children's acquisition of past tense verbs. Indeed, this same pattern of delay was observed among French–English bilingual preschoolers when particular verbs were elicited in the past tense (Nicoladis & Paradis, 2012). This delay could be due to the fact that they hear less of each language than monolinguals and practice using verbs less often as well. In support of this argument, young school-aged French–English and Chinese–English bilingual children still used slightly fewer irregular past tense forms relative to reported results with English monolinguals (Nicoladis, Song, & Marentette, 2012).

In summary, we have mentioned here two domains in which delay in language acquisition has been observed in bilingual children: vocabulary size and past tense verb forms (particularly irregulars). In these domains, the frequency of exposure to and use of a particular language is thought to play a crucial role in acquisition.

While delays might be attributed to frequency, it does not necessarily follow that no delay means that frequency is not an important variable in the acquisition of that particular aspect of language. The domains in which no delay has been reported are domains in which exposure to *any* language may be crucial. For example, as long as a child is hearing language on a regular basis, he/she will produce his/her first word around 13 months of age (Petitto et al., 2001). There is no reason to suspect that bilingual children will be delayed in all domains of language development.

Acceleration in Language Development

Acceleration in language development among bilinguals has been mentioned in the literature less often than delays. However, at this point, this cannot necessarily be taken to mean that bilingualism delays development more often than it accelerates it. As mentioned in the last section, it is difficult to compare a few bilingual children's development with norms for monolinguals.

Bilinguals have been shown to have difficulty in linguistic tasks requiring the rapid retrieval of specific words, but this difficulty is not apparent in more general linguistic and conceptual processing (Bialystok, Craik, & Luk, 2008). One possibility for this difficulty is that bilinguals process lexical terms more deeply than monolinguals. In a study by Proctor, Uccelli, Dalton, and Snow (2009, p. 319), grade 5 bilinguals (with fluency in a variety of languages in addition to English), and English monolinguals were asked to learn new words and, given a picture, asked to come up with ways of making this picture *come alive* by providing a caption that illustrated their understanding of the words. The bilingual children tended to outperform monolinguals on this task (though this effect was not significant), even though their vocabulary scores in English were significantly lower than monolinguals. The semantic depth scores predicted the children's reading proficiency (though bilingual/monolingual status did not). So, in this study, the results could be due to bilinguals being slightly better at reading proficiency. In another study with children in which reading proficiency did not seem to be a factor, Marinova-Todd (2012) reported that bilinguals accurately guessed the meanings of novel words with less information than same-aged monolinguals.

Accelerated language development among bilinguals has also been demonstrated in a study in which children were asked to name some machines that were performing an action on an object (Nicoladis, 2003). For example, one machine was catching butterflies. In English, the children were encouraged to produce compound words like *butterfly catcher* (object-verb-*er*) and in French, *chasse-papillons* (literal translation: *chase-butterflies*). Compounds of the form verb-object are grammatical in French (e.g., *casse-noisettes —break-hazelnuts*—refers to a nutcracker), although there are few examples of them in the language. The preschool French–English bilingual children produced more compound words in French than monolingual children, once the vocabulary scores were statistically controlled for. How could the bilingual children's knowledge of English help them produce more *verb-object compounds* in French? To understand these results, it is important to know that monolingual English-speaking children produce ungrammatical verb-object compounds around the age of four years of age when an object-verb-*er* compound would be expected (Clark, Hecht, & Mulford, 1986). For example, they might say *a wash-bottle* to refer to someone who washes bottles, while adults are more likely to say *a bottle washer*. Nicoladis argued that the French–English bilingual children produced more verb-object compounds in French than monolinguals because they had access to verb-object compounds in English as well (for whatever reason monolingual English-speaking children use them).

Bilingual children may use whatever knowledge they have, even if it comes from the inappropriate language for the context. Gawlitzek-Maiwald and Tracy (1996) explored this issue using data from a German–English bilingual girl whose German was more proficient than her English. They recorded the child in spontaneous conversation with a variety of speakers. They showed that soon after the child started using auxiliary verbs in German, she also started using these German auxiliary verbs in her otherwise mostly English utterances. For example, she said *ich hab gemade you much better* (*I have ge-made you much better*), where the morpheme *ge-* in German can mark a verb as being in the past tense. By using auxiliary verbs in German, this girl could clearly refer to events in the past in English, at a point in time when she could not do so in English alone. The researchers argued that the child's use of two languages allowed her to create utterances of a greater complexity than her English knowledge alone would allow her to do. They refer to this phenomenon as *bilingual bootstrapping*.

If the interpretation of these studies is correct, then knowledge of the underlying structure in one language (even if it is ungrammatical, as with the verb-object compounds) can bootstrap bilingual children into producing a similar structure in their other language. This production can happen earlier than one might expect, given the children's proficiency. If the two languages share a structure, then bilingual children might be more advanced in development than monolingual children at a similar stage of linguistic development. What happens when two languages differ in structure?

Cross-Linguistic Influence

Bilingual children sometimes use constructions in one language that seem to be based on a structure from the other language. For example, a Spanish–English bilingual child might talk about *the shoe of my father*, rather than the more usual *my father's shoe*, based on the Spanish construction *el zapato de mi papá* (literal translation: *the shoe of my father*). We use the terms *cross-linguistic influence* (CLI) to refer to the structural influence of one language on another. The resulting construction in the above example is grammatical in English, although the result of CLI could be an ungrammatical construction. For example, one Italian–German bilingual child growing up in Italy said *Von Lisa klein klein* (*from Lisa little little*; Volterra & Taeschner, 1978). Most adjectives in Italian typically appear after nouns while adjectives in German typically appear before nouns. The child may have been using the Italian word order in German. Another example comes from a Cantonese–English bilingual child who said, *Where's the Santa Claus give me the gun?*, meaning to refer to the gun that Santa Claus had given him (Yip & Matthews, 2000). The researchers argue that the child was using a word order allowed in Cantonese.

CLI has not just been observed in word order. For example, Holm and Dodd (1999) described the pronunciation of particular consonants in Cantonese by two children who started learning English after their second year. Both children were living in Australia and were the children of immigrants from Hong Kong. The researchers made regular recordings of the children's pronunciation of words in conversation for about six months. The children initially pronounced their Chinese words with Chinese sounds. After a few months of exposure to English, however, they started to use some English-sounding consonants in their pronunciation of Cantonese words.

Researchers have been exploring several explanations of CLI. We will briefly mention two here: (1) *idiosyncratic input*, and (2) speech production. Note that these explanations are not necessarily mutually exclusive. It is possible that *influence* is a complex phenomenon with many sources.

Idiosyncratic input could account for some cases of CLI. Quay and Montanari (2016) pointed out that bilingual children often hear their languages from bilingual adults who, themselves, may show CLI. In one study, researchers focused on the spontaneous productions of a Spanish–English bilingual child who was growing up in Great Britain (Paradis & Navarro, 2003). In Spanish, it is possible to produce a grammatical sentence without specifically mentioning the subject of the sentence. For example, it is possible to say *Yo como la manzana* (literal transltation: *I eat the apple*) and *Como la manzana* (literal translation: *eat the apple*). The researchers were interested if the bilingual child would produce more subjects of sentences in her Spanish sentences because they are required to make grammatical sentences in English. They found that the child did, in fact, produce more subjects in Spanish than two monolingual Spanish-speaking children of the same age. Before concluding that the child's idiosyncratic Spanish was due to knowledge of English, the researchers calculated how often the parents produced subjects of sentences. They discovered that both parents of the bilingual child also produced more subjects than did the mothers of monolingual children. The researchers could not rule out the possibility that the child was learning an idiosyncratic version of Spanish.

Another possible explanation of CLI is that it appears in the normal process of putting words to ideas in the act of producing speech (Nicoladis, 2006). Nicoladis came to this explanation on the basis of data from French–English bilingual children. She showed preschool children pictures of objects and encouraged them to label the objects with adjective-noun constructions (like *a sad dog* or *a striped dinosaur*). The bilingual children did two sessions, one in English with a native English speaker and one in French (on a different day) with a native French speaker. In English, adjectives almost always appear before nouns, and in French, most adjectives appear after nouns (e.g., *carte blanche*; literal translation: *card white*), although some adjectives appear before nouns (like *grand–big*; and *nouveau–new*). Before discussing the results that pointed to evidence for CLI, it is important to note that most of what the bilingual children said was grammatical for the target language. The bilingual children reversed more adjectives in English (e.g., *a dog sad*) than monolingual children. The bilingual children also reversed more adjectives in French than monolingual children (e.g., *un rayé éléphant–a striped elephant*; this adjective would typically appear after the noun). Finally, the bilingual children reversed more adjectives in French than in English.

Nicoladis (2006) argued that the CLI observed in the above study and in other studies of bilingual children comes from how speakers put words to the concepts they wish to convey. Previous studies of monolinguals have shown that speech errors are likely to occur when speakers have to choose between two linguistic structures that convey the same message (Ferreira & Dell, 2000). For example, a person who uses both the words *sofa* and *Chesterfield* might occasionally say *chofa*. Nicoladis (2006) argued that CLI can be seen as a kind of speech error or lexical blending. Any time bilinguals have to choose between linguistic structures (either within a language or between languages), they are more likely to make errors. According to this interpretation, the reason bilingual children make more errors in French than in English with adjective placement is because there are two options of where to place adjectives in French. This explanation is supported by research showing that CLI often represents only a small proportion of children's productions (e.g., Nicoladis & Gavrila, 2015).

In sum, while much of what bilingual children say is grammatical in the target language, it is clear that they produce some constructions that are influenced by knowledge of their other language. Several factors might contribute to children's likelihood to display cross-linguistic influence, including idiosyncratic input (for other possible factors, see Müller & Hulk, 2001). It is also possible that CLI is due, at least in part, to children's having to choose between a variety of different ways of conveying a message. If this is true, then, the CLI observed in bilingual children may not be all that different from the kinds of speech errors observed in monolingual children.

Cognitive Differences

Several researchers have argued that bilingual children's cognitive development would benefit from knowing two languages and having a contrast in two linguistic systems. The contrast would facilitate bilingual children's insight into the separability of words from their referents. Starting in the 1960s and 1970s, researchers have documented cognitive differences between bilinguals and monolinguals, with a *bilingual advantage* in *cognitive flexibility* (e.g., Ben-Zeev, 1977), intelligence (Peal & Lambert, 1962), and *creativity* (Bialystok & Shapero, 2005). These researchers argued that experience with choosing languages permitted bilinguals to create more flexible connections between words and referents. More recently, researchers have narrowed in on a few ways in which bilinguals think differently from monolinguals. In this section, we will discuss four: *communicative competence*, *theory of mind*, strategy use, and control of attention.

Communicative competence refers to the ability to communicate effectively, taking into account the interlocutor's knowledge and conversational needs. Bilingual children have extensive experience of choosing languages for the pragmatic context, such as a particular person or a topic. As a result of their experience choosing different languages, they might become sensitive to other people's communicative needs. For example, consider the results of one study with two-year-old French–English bilingual children growing up in Montreal (Comeau, Genesee, & Lapaquette, 2003). In this study, the researchers visited the children three times and, on each visit, calibrated the rate of language mixing that they used in speaking to the children. On the first visit, the rate of mixing was low, on the second visit it was higher, and on the third visit it was low again. The children's rate of language mixing mirrored that of the researchers. This result suggests that bilingual children can modify their rate of mixing to correspond to that of their interlocutor. Another example of communicative competence comes from a study of two Estonian–English bilingual siblings who were raised in the US (Vihman, 1998). They were recorded in free play situations over the course of about four years, starting when the older sister was almost six and the younger brother was about two-and-a-half years old. Vihman noticed that the children used English (the language of school and outside the home) for dramatic play and Estonian (the language of the home and the children's stronger language) to negotiate the rules of play. Thus, the children seemed to associate each language with a function.

The results of the previous studies suggest that bilingual children can make online adjustments of their language choice, depending on what language is spoken to them. Are they simply reacting to the language spoken to them at that moment? Or do they know something about how much linguistic knowledge they share with their interlocutor? One way to assess the source of bilingual children's sensitivity to an interlocutor's linguistic knowledge is to see how they behave with languages they do not speak. The results of one study suggest that bilinguals might be more sensitive than monolinguals to an interlocutor's knowledge when the interlocutor speaks a language that the children do not. Nicoladis, Kwong See, and Rhemtulla (2005) compared English monolinguals and French–English bilinguals on whether or not they understood that they did not understand what a Chinese speaker meant. The study was based on research showing that children tend to assume that novel words refer to objects for which they do not know a name (e.g., Markman, Wasow, & Hansen, 2003). Nicoladis and her colleagues asked two- and three-year-old children to indicate whether a novel word that was used by a speaker who only spoke in Chinese referred to an object for which they already knew a name (like an apple) or an unfamiliar object (like a Zimmer frame). If children understood that Chinese words could refer to objects for which they already had a name in English, they should pick randomly between familiar and unfamiliar objects. In fact, this is what the bilingual children did. In contrast, the monolingual children were less likely to pick familiar objects, suggesting that they treated Chinese words much like novel English words. Other studies with bilingual children have shown the opposite pattern of results, with bilinguals accepting more words within a language to refer to the same object than monolinguals (e.g., Byers-Heinlein & Werker, 2013). The results of the study with younger children suggest that bilingual children may be sensitive to their interlocutor's linguistic knowledge. It is not yet clear why different studies are showing different results.

To see the extent to which bilingualism leads to sensitivity to other people's knowledge, researchers have tested the hypothesis that bilingual children have an advantage over monolinguals in the development of theory of mind. Theory of mind refers to the ability to think about others' thoughts, especially the ability to know that others can have different thoughts from oneself (Bartsch & Wellman, 1995). Because bilingual children have the experience of changing languages according to the interlocutor, they might develop an early understanding that other people's thoughts can differ from their own. One task used to assess children's theory of mind is a *false belief task* (Perner, Leekam, & Wimmer, 1987). For example, children might be shown a Smarties box and asked what is inside. They usually say that there are Smarties inside. The researcher then opens up the box to reveal something else, like pencils. The children are then asked to predict what another person who was not present for the opening of the Smarties box will say is in the box. Three-year-old children often say *pencils* while four-year-old children are more likely to say *Smarties* (Perner et al., 1987). Researchers have interpreted these findings to mean that three-year-old children assume that everyone shares the same knowledge as they themselves have, while four-year-olds are capable of considering the possibility that someone could have different beliefs and that these beliefs could be false. Goetz (2003) showed that Mandarin–English bilingual children were more likely to pass a false belief task than English monolingual children. It should be noted that other studies have shown no bilingual advantage in theory-of-mind tasks (e.g., Jean-Louis, 1999) or an advantage only after vocabulary had been controlled (e.g., Bialystok & Senman, 2004). In a study by Nguyen and Astington (2014), English–French bilingual, English monolingual, and French monolingual preschoolers completed a false belief task. The monolingual and bilingual groups did not differ significantly with respect to parental income and education. Bilinguals performed significantly better than monolinguals on the false belief task, but only after statistically controlling for both age and *language proficiency*. Interestingly, the bilingual advantage in the false belief task continues into adulthood (Rubio-Fernández & Glucksberg, 2012). In summary, the bulk of the results point to the possibility that bilingualism leads to increased sensitivity to the knowledge of other people.

Another area of cognitive development that bilingualism might affect is the use of implicit strategies in communicating. Previous research with bilingual adults has shown that bilinguals learn words after fewer exposures than monolinguals (Gollan & Silverberg, 2001). Recall the point that was raised earlier in this chapter that preschool bilingual children sometimes have lower vocabularies than monolinguals in any one language (e.g., Pearson et al., 1993). What strategies might account for such rapid word learning?

One possible answer to this question is a stronger reliance upon spatial strategies among bilinguals in comparison to monolinguals. According to the *bilingual dual coding model* (Paivio & Desrochers, 1980), bilinguals have one set of verbal representations for each language that they speak (identified as V1 and V2 for language one and two, respectively) and an imagery system (I). V1, V2, and I are interconnected in such a way that translation equivalents can converge on shared imagistic representations (Paivio, Clark, & Lambert, 1988). According to McLeay (2003, p. 426), *conceptual sharing between languages in the form of non-verbal image generators may be of assistance to bilinguals in performing spatial tasks as well as other problems where mental imagery is helpful*. It may be the case that the bilingual reliance upon shared imagistic representations is associated with stronger imagery abilities.

Some evidence supports this possibility. For example, in a study by Bialystok (2011), eight-year-old monolinguals and bilinguals participated in auditory and *visual classification* tasks. These tasks involved classifying visual and auditory stimuli as either musical instruments or animals. When tasks were presented in the visual or auditory format, participants in both language groups performed comparably. When a dual-task paradigm was used (i.e., when both visual and auditory stimuli were used simultaneously), bilinguals were more accurate than monolinguals, particularly on the visual task (Bialystok, 2011). These results suggest that the use of difficult tasks may more clearly elucidate differences among monolinguals and bilinguals with respect to performance on visuospatial tasks.

The emergence of a spatial advantage for bilinguals may occur early in development. In a study by Gorrell, Bregman, McAllister, and Lipscomb (1982), spatial abilities were examined among monolingual and bilingual first-grade children (approximately six years of age) using the WISC-R Block Design test. This test requires children to duplicate a visual pattern and is thought to serve as a measure of *perceptual ability*. Bilinguals were found to outperform monolinguals on this task.

Another possible manifestation of bilinguals' reliance of visuospatial processing is the use of *co-speech gestures*. Co-speech gestures are gestures produced while speaking; they often convey similar meaning to the speech (Goldin-Meadow, 2000). The use of gestures may help speakers package information, particularly about spatial information and particularly in difficult tasks (e.g., Alibali, Kita, & Young, 2000). Bilinguals tend to use more gestures than monolinguals (Nicoladis, Pika, & Marentette, 2009; Nicoladis, Pika, Yin, & Marentette, 2007; c.f. Smithson, Nicoladis, & Marentette, 2011). In a study of four- to six-year-old bilinguals, French–English bilingual children watched a Pink Panther cartoon and told back the story (Nicoladis, Pika, & Marentette, 2005). Story-telling relies heavily on visuospatial abilities for speakers to remember the events from the story. The bilinguals used more manual gestures while speaking than either English or French monolingual children (who used gestures at about the same rate). These results are compatible with the idea that bilinguals gesture to help package spatial information for telling stories.

One possible outcome of bilingual children's experience with choosing the appropriate language for a particular person or context is enhanced *selective attention* to the relevant variables, particularly for formal linguistic tasks (Bialystok, 2001) and other related cognitive functions (Blom, Küntay, Messer, Verhagen, & Leseman, 2014). For example, Bialystok (2001) reviewed a number of studies showing that bilingual children can perform better on *grammaticality judgments* of sentences that are also semantically anomalous (e.g., *Colourless green ideas sleep furiously*). In order to judge a semantically anomalous sentence as grammatical or ungrammatical, it is necessary to attend selectively to the syntax and ignore the meaning. These results have been replicated by other researchers (see Barac, Bialystok, Castro, & Sanchez, 2014, for a review). It is not clear that the bilingual advantage extends to all aspects of formal linguistic knowledge at all ages (e.g., Bialystok, Majumder, & Martin, 2003). Nevertheless, the experience of choosing the appropriate language(s) for the context may give bilinguals some cognitive benefits over monolinguals.

In summary, bilingual children may have some differences from monolinguals in cognitive development in terms of communicative competence, theory of mind, strategy use, and selective attention (see Paap, this volume). In this section, we have described these four components of cognition as if they were separate. It is clearly plausible that all four are manifestations of a single underlying cognitive process. Alternatively, it is quite likely that all four are minimally interrelated (Tare & Gelman, 2010). For example, it could be the experience of choosing languages for a context that allows the bilingual advantages in taking other people's perspective (thus, enhanced theory of mind). This enhanced theory of mind might allow children's control of attention to relevant formal linguistic properties. It would be interesting to know how these aspects of cognitive development are related in both bilinguals and monolinguals.

Conclusion

The purpose of this chapter was to ask: why does bilingualism affect language and cognitive development? As we noted at the beginning of the chapter, it is not surprising to find that the answer is at least partially definitional: bilingual children know two languages and monolinguals know one. What is it about the knowledge of two languages that makes development different? We reviewed four areas in which differences between bilinguals and monolinguals have been documented: delay in language development, acceleration in language development, CLI, and cognitive differences. There are small but detectable differences between bilinguals and monolinguals in these areas. These differences can shed some light onto how language and cognitive development unfold in all children. We have reviewed each of the major differences in turn, in hopes of highlighting what the differences might tell us about language and cognitive development in general.

There is some evidence of bilinguals acquiring some aspects of language more slowly than monolinguals. Recall, however, that bilinguals do not seem to be delayed in all aspects of language. The delays observed thus far are often with aspects of language that are thought to be highly dependent on frequency. Bilingual children may hear and use less of either language than monolingual children. For example, bilingual children's delay in learning irregular past tense forms (Nicoladis et al., 2007) should come as no surprise. There is no other way to learn a truly irregular past tense except by memorization (e.g., Bybee, 1995). Bilinguals' less frequent experience with either language should cause delays in the aspects of language in which frequency is crucial for acquisition. Some language theorists have argued that much of language is learned on the basis of children's own usage (e.g., Tomasello, 2000). Bilingual acquisition allows an interesting testing ground for such theories.

Language acquisition is not based on frequency of usage alone. At some point in development, children must make generalizations about the patterns of linguistic combinations that can exist in their languages. In this chapter, we argued that when bilinguals have two similar underlying structures in their two languages, they could be accelerated in their usage of that structure relative to what we might expect from their level of proficiency (see Nicoladis, 2003). If bilinguals have two different underlying structures available, then there may be some CLI, at least when they produce speech. If this interpretation is correct, then bilingual children's generalizations about possible structures in their two languages are not completely distinct by language (see discussion in Paradis & Genesee, 1996). If true, then children's generalizations about underlying structures may go beyond what they have heard or used themselves. To some extent at least, children's underlying linguistic knowledge might not be linked to knowledge of a specific language.

Lastly, bilingual children have shown slight advantages over monolingual children in terms of communicative competence, theory of mind, and selective attention. Researchers have argued that these advantages are due to bilingual children's experience with choosing appropriate language(s) for the context (e.g., Bialystok, 2001; Nicoladis, Pika, & Marentette, 2005). If this interpretation is correct, then children's early experience with language choice could lead them to early insight into the minds of others and attention to relevant cues, at least in linguistic and social domains. To test this interpretation, it would be particularly crucial to document changes in theory of mind and selective attention longitudinally as children acquire a second language in the preschool years.

In closing, it is clear that bilingualism impacts both language and cognitive development in small and systematic ways. Bilingualism does not lead to confusion in development, as once feared by researchers and parents alike. In fact, bilinguals can differentiate their languages early in development. The differences between bilingualism and monolingualism allow us insights into how development unfolds. For example, we can uncover where experience using a language makes a difference in how that language develops (e.g., Tomasello, 2000). As further research with bilinguals is carried out, we will gain further insights into how development takes place in all children.

List of Key Words and Concepts

Accelerated language, Babbling, Bilingual advantage, Bilingual bootstrapping, Bilingual dual coding model, Canonical babbling, Co-speech gestures, Cognitive flexibility, Communicative competence, Creativity, Cross-linguistic influence (CLI), Diary study, False belief task, Grammaticality judgments, Idiosyncratic input, Language proficiency, Mixed-language, Perceptual ability, Receptive vocabulary, Selective attention, Sequential bilingual, Simultaneous bilinguals, Spontaneous conversation, Spontaneous play, Theory of mind, Verb-object compounds, Visual classification

Internet Sites Related to the Psycholinguistics of Bilingualism

Baby Center: http://www.babycenter.com/0_raising-a-bilingual-child-the-top-five-myths_10340869.bc

Children Communication: http://www.hanen.org/Helpful-Info/Articles/Bilingualism-in-Young-Children--Separating-Fact-fr.aspx

Multilingual Parenting: http://multilingualparenting.com/2014/02/26/12-things-parents-raising-bilingual-children-need-to-know/

Discussion Questions

(1) What advice would you give to a parent who wanted to raise a bilingual child?
(2) What differences would you expect for simultaneous and sequential bilingual children and why?
(3) How might the country in which a bilingual child grew up impact his/her development? Why would this impact be seen?
(4) Would you expect any differences in development for children who are bilingual because they have been adopted versus children who are bilingual growing up with their birth families? Why or why not?
(5) If one of the languages that a bilingual child was learning was a signed language, would you expect any different outcomes relative to children learning two spoken languages? What about two signed languages?

Suggested Research Projects

(1) Ask an adult who grew up speaking two languages if he/she thinks differently, feels differently, or acts differently when processing the two languages.
(2) Ask a bilingual adult to generate an example of code-mixed utterances. Are the utterances ungrammatical in only one language, both languages, or no languages? What do your results suggest for when code-mixing is likely to occur?

Suggested Readings

Bialystok, E. (2001). *Bilingualism in development: Language, literacy, and cognition.* Cambridge: Cambridge University Press.

De Houwer, A. (2009). *An introduction to bilingual development* (Vol. 4). Bristol, UK: Multilingual Matters.

Yip, V., & Matthews, S. (2007). *The bilingual child.* Cambridge: Cambridge University Press.

References

Alibali, M. W., Kita, S., & Young, A. J. (2000). Gesture and the process of speech production: We think, therefore we gesture. *Language and Cognitive Processes, 15,* 569–613.

Allman, B. (2005). Vocabulary size and accuracy of monolingual and bilingual preschool children. In J. Cohen, K. T. McAlister, K. Rolstad, & J. MacSwan (Eds.), *ISB4: Proceedings of the 4th International Symposium on Bilingualism* (pp. 58–77). Somerville, MA: Cascadilla Press.

Barac, R., Bialystok, E., Castro, D. C., & Sanchez, M. (2014). The cognitive development of young dual language learners: A critical review. *Early Childhood Research Quarterly, 29*(4), 699–714.

Bartsch, K., & Wellman, H. M. (1995). *Children talk about the mind.* New York: Oxford University Press.

Ben-Zeev, S. (1977). Mechanisms by which childhood bilingualism affects understanding of language and cognitive structures. In P. A. Hornby (Ed.), *Bilingualism: Psychological, social, and educational implications* (pp. 29–55). New York: Academic Press.

Bialystok, E. (2001). *Bilingualism in development: Language, literacy, and cognition*. New York: Cambridge University Press.

Bialystok, E. (2011). Coordination of executive functions in monolingual and bilingual children. *Journal of Experimental Child Psychology, 110*, 461–468.

Bialystok, E., Craik, F., & Luk, G. (2008). Cognitive control and lexical access in younger and older bilinguals. *Journal of Experimental Psychology: Learning, Memory, and Cognition, 34*, 859–873.

Bialystok, E., Luk, G., Peets, K. F., & Yang, S. (2010). Receptive vocabulary differences in monolingual and bilingual children. *Bilingualism: Language and Cognition, 13*, 525–531.

Bialystok, E., Majumder, S., & Martin, M. M. (2003). Developing phonological awareness: Is there a bilingual advantage? *Applied Psycholinguistics, 24*, 27–44.

Bialystok, E., & Senman, L. (2004). Executive processes in appearance–reality tasks: The role of inhibition of attention and symbolic representation. *Child Development, 75*, 562–579.

Bialystok, E., & Shapero, D. (2005). Ambiguous benefits: The effect of bilingualism on reversing ambiguous figures. *Developmental Science, 8*, 595–604.

Blom, E., Küntay, A. C., Messer, M., Verhagen, J., & Leseman, P. (2014). The benefits of being bilingual: Working memory in bilingual Turkish–Dutch children. *Journal of Experimental Child Psychology, 128*, 105–119.

Bybee, J. (1995). Regular morphology and the lexicon. *Language and Cognitive Processes, 10*, 425–455.

Byers-Heinlein, K. (2014). Languages as categories: Reframing the "one language or two" question in early bilingual development. *Language Learning, 64*, 184–201.

Byers-Heinlein, K., & Werker, J. F. (2013). Lexicon structure and the disambiguation of novel words: Evidence from bilingual infants. *Cognition, 128*, 407–416.

Clark, E. V., Hecht, B. F., & Mulford, R. C. (1986). Coining complex compounds in English: Affixes and word order in acquisition. *Linguistics, 24*, 7–29.

Comeau, L., Genesee, F., & Lapaquette, L. (2003) The modeling hypothesis and child bilingual code-mixing. *International Journal of Bilingualism, 7*, 113–126.

De Houwer, A. (2005). Early bilingual acquisition: Focus on morphosyntax and the separate development hypothesis. In J. Kroll & A. M. B. de Groot (Eds.), *The handbook of bilingualism* (pp. 30–48). Oxford: Oxford University Press.

Doyle, A.-B., Champagne, M., & Segalowitz, N. (1978). Some issues in the assessment of linguistic consequences of early bilingualism. In M. Paradis (Ed.), *Aspects of bilingualism* (pp. 13–20). Columbia, SC: Hornbeam Press.

Ferreira, V. S., & Dell, G. S. (2000). Effect of ambiguity and lexical availability on syntactic and lexical production. *Cognitive Psychology, 40*, 296–340.

Gawlitzek-Maiwald, I., & Tracy, R. (1996). Bilingual bootstrapping. *Linguistics, 34*, 901–926.

Genesee, F. (1989). Early bilingual development: One language or two? *Journal of Child Language, 16*, 161–179.

Genesee, F., Boivin, I., & Nicoladis, E. (1996). Bilingual children talking with monolingual adults: A study of bilingual communicative competence. *Applied Psycholinguistics, 17*, 427–442.

Genesee, F., Nicoladis, E., & Paradis, J. (1995). Language differentiation in early bilingual development. *Journal of Child Language, 22*, 611–631.

Goetz, P. J. (2003). The effects of bilingualism on theory of mind development. *Bilingualism: Language and Cognition, 6*, 1–15.

Goldin-Meadow, S. (2000). Beyond words: The importance of gestures to researchers and learners. *Child Development, 71*, 231–239.

Gollan, T. H., & Silverberg, N. B. (2001). Tip-of-the-tongue states in Hebrew-English bilinguals. *Bilingualism: Language and Cognition, 4*, 63–83.

Gorrell, J. J., Bregman, N. J., McAllister, H. A., & Lipscomb, T. J. (1982). *The Journal of Genetic Psychology, 140*, 3–10.

Gross, M., Buac, M., & Kaushanskaya, M. (2014). Conceptual scoring of receptive and expressive vocabulary measures in simultaneous and sequential bilingual children. *American Journal of Speech-Language Pathology*, *23*, 574–586. doi:10.1044/2014_AJSLP-13–0026.

Holm, A., & Dodd, B. (1999). A longitudinal study of the phonological development of two Cantonese-English bilingual children. *Applied Psycholinguistics*, *20*, 349–376.

Jean-Louis, B. (1999). *Does childhood bilingualism facilitate the development of theory of mind?* (Unpublished doctoral dissertation). Yale University.

Lanza, E. (1992). Can bilingual two-year-olds code-switch? *Journal of Child Language*, *19*, 633–658.

Leopold, W. (1949). *Speech development of a bilingual child* (Vol. 4). Evanston, IL: Northwestern University Press.

McLeay, H. (2003). The relationship between bilingualism and the performance of spatial tasks. *Bilingual Education and Bilingualism*, *6*(6), 423–438.

Maneva, B., & Genesee, F. (2002). Bilingual babbling: Evidence for language differentiation in dual language acquisition. In B. Skarabela, S. Fish, & A. H.-J. Do (Eds.), *Boston University Conference on Language Development 26 Proceedings* (pp. 383–392). Somerville, MA: Cascadilla Press.

Marinova-Todd, S. H. (2012). "Corplum is a core from a plum": The advantage of bilingual children in the analysis of word meaning. *Bilingualism: Language and Cognition*, *15*, 117–127.

Markman, E. M., Wasow, J. L., & Hansen, M. B. (2003). Use of the mutual exclusivity assumption by young word learners. *Cognitive Psychology*, *47*, 241–275.

Müller, N., & Hulk, A. (2001). Crosslinguistic influence in bilingual language acquisition: Italian and French as recipient languages. *Bilingualism: Language and Cognition*, *4*, 1–21.

Nguyen, T.-K., & Astington, J. W. (2014). Reassessing the bilingual advantage in theory of mind and its cognitive underpinnings. *Bilingualism: Language and Cognition*, *17*(2), 396–409.

Nicoladis, E. (2003). Cross-linguistic transfer in deverbal compounds of preschool bilingual children. *Bilingualism: Language and Cognition*, *6*, 17–31.

Nicoladis, E. (2006). Cross-linguistic transfer in adjective-noun strings by preschool bilingual children. *Bilingualism: Language and Cognition*, *9*, 15–32.

Nicoladis, E., & Gavrila, A. (2015). Cross-linguistic influence in Welsh-English bilingual children's adjectival constructions. *Journal of Child Language*, *42*, 903–916.

Nicoladis, E., & Genesee, F. (1996). A longitudinal study of pragmatic differentiation in young bilingual children. *Language Learning*, *46*, 439–464.

Nicoladis, E., Kwong See, S., & Rhemtulla, M. (2005). *Are mutual exclusivity violations guided by children's assumptions about people's word knowledge?* Paper presented at the Jean Piaget Society, Vancouver, B. C., Canada.

Nicoladis, E., Palmer, A., & Marentette, P. (2007). The role of type and token frequency in using past tense morphemes correctly. *Developmental Science*, *10*(2), 237–254.

Nicoladis, E., & Paradis, J. (2012). Acquiring regular and irregular past tense morphemes in English and French: Evidence from bilingual children. *Language Learning*, *62*(1), 170–197.

Nicoladis, E., Pika, S., & Marentette, P. (2005). *Gesturing bilingually: French–English bilingual children's gestures.* Paper presented at the International Congress for the Study of Child Language, Berlin, Germany.

Nicoladis, E., Pika, S., & Marentette, P. (2009). Do French–English bilingual children gesture more than monolingual children? *Journal of Psycholinguistic Research*, *38*(6), 573–585.

Nicoladis, E., Pika, S., Yin, H., & Marentette, P. (2007). Gesture use in story recall by Chinese-English bilinguals. *Applied Psycholinguistics*, *28*, 721–735.

Nicoladis, E., & Secco, G. (2000). The role of a child's productive vocabulary in the language choice of a bilingual family. *First Language*, *58*, 3–28.

Nicoladis, E., Song, J., & Marentette, P. (2012). Do young bilinguals acquire past tense morphology like monolinguals, only later? Evidence from French–English and Chinese–English bilinguals. *Applied Psycholinguistics*, *33*, 457–479.

Oller, D. K., Eilers, R. E., Urbano, R., & Cobo-Lewis, A. B. (1997). Development of precursors to speech in infants exposed to two languages. *Journal of Child Language*, *24*, 407–425.

Paivio, A., Clark, J. M., & Lambert, W. E. (1988). Bilingual dual-coding theory and semantic repetition on recall. *Journal of Experimental Psychology: Learning, Memory, and Cognition, 14*(1), 163–172.

Paivio, A., & Desrochers, A. (1980). A dual-coding approach to bilingual memory. *Canadian Journal of Psychology, 34*(4), 388–399.

Paradis, J. (2011). Individual differences in child English second language acquisition: Comparing child-internal and child-external factors. *Linguistic Approaches to Bilingualism, 1*(3), 213–237.

Paradis, J., & Genesee, F. (1996). Syntactic acquisition in bilingual children: Autonomous or interdependent? *Studies in Second Language Acquisition, 18,* 1–25.

Paradis, J., & Navarro, S. (2003). Subject realization and crosslinguistic interference in the bilingual acquisition of Spanish and English: What is the role of the input? *Journal of Child Language, 30,* 371–393.

Peal, E., & Lambert, W. E. (1962). The relation of bilingualism to intelligence. *Psychological Monographs, 76,* 1–23.

Pearson, B. Z., Fernández, S. C., Lewedag, & Oller, D. K. (1997). The relation of input factors to lexical learning by bilingual infants (ages 10 to 30 months). *Applied Psycholinguistics, 18,* 41–58.

Pearson, B. Z., Fernández, S. C., & Oller, D. K. (1993). Lexical development in bilingual infants and toddlers: Comparison to monolingual norms. *Language Learning, 43,* 93–120.

Perner, J., Leekam, S. R., & Wimmer, H. (1987). Three-year-olds' difficulty with false belief: The case for a conceptual deficit. *British Journal of Developmental Psychology, 5,* 125–137.

Petitto, L. A., Katerelos, M., Levy, B. G., Gauna, K., Tétreault, K., & Ferraro, V. (2001). Bilingual signed and spoken language acquisition from birth: Implications for the mechanisms underlying early bilingual language acquisition. *Journal of Child Language, 28,* 453–496.

Place, S., & Hoff, E. (2011). Properties of dual language exposure that influence 2-year-olds' bilingual proficiency. *Child Development, 82*(6), 1834–1849.

Prevoo, M. J. L., Mesman, J., Van IJzendoorn, M. H., & Pieper, S. (2011). Bilingual toddlers reap the language they sow: Ethnic minority toddlers' childcare attendance increases maternal host language use. *Journal of Multilingual and Multicultural Development, 32,* 561–576.

Proctor, C. P., Uccelli, P., Dalton, B., & Snow, C. E. (2009). Understanding depth of vocabulary online with bilingual and monolingual children. *Reading and Writing Quarterly, 25,* 311–333.

Quay, S. (2012). Discourse practices of trilingual mothers: Effects on minority home language development in Japan. *International Journal of Bilingual Education and Bilingualism, 15*(4), 435–453.

Quay, S., & Montanari, S. (2016). Early bilingualism: From differentiation to the impact of family language practices. In E. Nicoladis & S. Montanari (Eds.), *Bilingualism across the lifespan* (pp. 23–42). Washington, DC: de Gruyter and American Psychological Association.

Ronjat, J. (1913). *Le développement du langage chez un enfant bilingue.* Paris: Champion.

Rubio-Fernández, P., & Glucksberg, S. (2012). Reasoning about other people's beliefs: Bilinguals have an advantage. *Journal of Experimental Psychology: Learning, Memory, and Cognition, 38*(1), 211–217.

Schwartz, M. (2010). Family language policy: Core issues of an emerging field. *Applied Linguistics Review, 1*(1), 171–192.

Smithson, L., Nicoladis, E., & Marentette, P. (2011). Bilingual children's gesture use. *Gesture, 11,* 330–347.

Smithson, L., Paradis, J., & Nicoladis, E. (2014). Bilingualism and receptive vocabulary achievement: Could sociocultural context make a difference? *Bilingualism: Language and Cognition, 17,* 810–821.

Tare, M., & Gelman, S. A. (2010). Can you say it another way? Cognitive factors in bilingual children's pragmatic language skills. *Journal of Cognition and Development, 11,* 137–158.

Thordardottir, E. (2011). The relationship between bilingual exposure and vocabulary development. *The International Journal of Bilingualism, 15,* 426–445.

Tomasello, M. (2000). First steps toward a usage-based theory of language acquisition. *Cognitive Linguistics, 11,* 61–82.

Vihman, M. M. (1996). *Phonological development*. Cambridge, MA: Blackwell.

Vihman, M. M. (1998). A developmental perspective on codeswitching: Conversations between a pair of bilingual siblings. *International Journal of Bilingualism, 2*, 45–84.

Volterra, V., & Taeschner, T. (1978). The acquisition and development of language by bilingual children. *Journal of Child Language, 5*, 311–326.

Yip, V., & Matthews, S. (2000). Syntactic transfer in a Cantonese-English bilingual child. *Bilingualism: Language and Cognition, 3*, 193–208.

Section IV

Social and Sociocultural Processes

11 Social Psychology of Bilingualism

Luis A. Vega

Introduction

There are over 6000 languages in the whole world. We lose one every two weeks. Hundreds will be lost within the next generation. By the end of this century, half of the world's languages will have vanished.

Grubin (2015)

Globalization has increased how we relate to each other, increasing the homogenization of communication. Of the many languages that humans speak, 50 percent are in demise (Grubin, 2015). Others have called this a *language apocalypse*, stating that *many tongues are already all but dead* (Meinzer, 2015, p. 1). This is especially true of oral languages, exemplified by Charlie Mangulda from Australia, who is the last person who speaks *Amurdak*, a language that is thousands of years old. *Amurdak* is a language with no writing system, kept alive through oral tradition—poetry in the case of Charlie Mangulda (Grubin, 2015).

A similar fate has befallen many Native American languages, with many of their languages disappearing due to neglect from American society on groups of people who have been called the *invisible minority* (Leavitt, Covarrubias, Perez, & Fryberg, 2015). If the homogenization of communication is responsible for languages disappearing, its effects need to be understood. This is especially true because the language(s) we speak are at the core of who we are, how we see ourselves, what we feel, and the actions we take as we relate to others. What implications do these changes mean for the future of bilingualism?

Language is a social tool of influence that needs to be understood at the level of the person and context. Social psychologist Kurt Lewin (1951), the father of experimental psychology, explained it best when he stated that *behavior* is a *function* of the *person* and the *situation*, denoted as $B = P*S$. In this notation, bilingualism use, the *behavior (B)*, is influenced by a *person's (P) social identity* and perceptions of positive or negative attitudes found in the community or particular situation (S). Thus, if the situation is such that a person's language is at risk of extinction due to a low number of speakers ($-P$) and dominant society's assimilation pressures ($+S$), then we can predict a low survival probability for that language ($-B$), such as the case with Charlie Mangulda above. In this instance, applying Lewin's notation describes how bilingualism is used and viewed in relation to how the variables are weighted.

However, often the weight of variables is more complicated, for Charlie Mangulda may be a proud man who refuses to learn English, at great personal and monetary costs to him ($-P$). Also, his ethnic pride may result in efforts to maintain his native tongue ($+P$), especially now that means of recording and transcribing his language are available ($+P$).

But if society does not value his language (–*S*), he may decide it is not worth the effort (–*P*). The different permutations of Lewin's notion of how behavior, person, and situation relate to each other captures the definition of *social psychology*, which is how people perceive, think about, feel about, and act towards the implied, imagined, or actual presence of others (Allport, 1954a). How humans negotiate language, and bilingualism in particular, from a social psychology perspective then is the focus of this chapter.

In the first edition of this book, my social psychology of bilingualism chapter offered explanations of how bilingualism is negotiated at multiple levels of social perception, including attitudes, cultural groups, group status, social norms, and expectations (Vega, 2008). For this chapter, I use a more integrative approach, based primarily on the use of *social identity theory* (SIT; Tajfel & Turner, 1979) and *social categorization theory* (SCT; Turner, 1978). Briefly, social identity refers to *social psychological processes of intergroup phenomena* such as identification with an *in-group* but not an *out-group* (Us-versus-Them), whereas social categorization theory refers to *social cognitive processes of self-categorization* and how behavior is explained within and between groups, such as stereotyping and conformity (Postmes & Branscombe, 2010, pp. 8–9). This integration allows for more coherent explanations of how bilingualism is perceived, practiced, and predicted to change given prevailing and forthcoming social contexts.

The Influence of Perceptions and Contexts

As a tool of *social influence*, language use in the form of bilingualism is assumed to be socially valued, as two languages provide more tools for communication to the bilingual, even more to the multilingual and the polyglot. And yet perceptions do matter in how bilingualism is perceived, both from objective and subjective perspectives. This can be seen reflected in the Bible's story of the *Tower of Babel* (Genesis 11: 1–9 KJV). According to the story, God created many languages to limit people's God-like ambitions, which they had manifested in trying to build a tower that would reach heaven. It was thought the Babylonians were not following the ways of religion, what might be considered a subjective interpretation.

On the other hand, a plausible objective interpretation of this story lies in the name Babel. *Babel* is the Hebrew name for Babylon, translated as *gate of god*. It is known that the Hebrews had no liking for the Babylonians, and that the Hebrews may actually have meant the name *balal*, translated as *confound* or *confused* (The Tower of Babel, 2015). Of these two explanations, the latter can be considered more objective in the sense that this Bible story may reflect the desire for the Hebrews to see themselves (in-group or own-tribe) as different from the Babylonians (out-group or other-tribe), and what better way to do it than by differentiating their languages? This perception of who is in the in-group or out-group, or intergroup differences, will be shown to be crucial in the acceptance and thriving of bilingualism.

Bilingualism and Objective Considerations

Practical or objective considerations can influence bilingualism. For example, Papua New Guinea is composed of 600 islands, and as of 2013, the count of individual languages was 851, with 12 described as extinct and 839 living but in a state of flux (Papua New Guinea, 2016). The high number of languages can be inferred to be the result of the islands' geography comprising this country. More so true given the *isolation* brought about by dense rain forests, the world's largest swamps, and the geographic spread of its smaller islands over a large body of water.

Similarly, the many languages of European countries might be due to some degree of isolation, for in early times, people did not travel, had no outside communication, and had limited literacy, ensuring language silos (Explain Like I Am Five, 2015). Where bilingualism, or multilingualism flourished, as with the Dutch people who were merchants, such outcome can be explained on the opposite continuum of isolation, still an objective factor. Geographical, transportation limitations, and isolation, illustrated by un-contacted Amazonian tribes even to this day (http://www.uncontactedtribes.org/brazilfootage), can pose limitations to bilingualism. Thus, context must be acknowledged as an objective consideration in how bilingualism flourishes, either through isolation or out of necessity.

To the degree that bilingualism can confer advantage, objective considerations can also be involved. Consider the widespread use of the English language throughout the world. According to Martinez (2014), compared to many other languages, English is a practical language that is linguistically a neutral language, not needing gender distinctions as in the Romance languages, nor class or general distinctions referring to status (boss, elder, stranger) or familiarity (friend, subordinate, child) as in some Asian languages. These practicalities have aided English to become a predominant second language (L2) in the world (Martinez, 2014). Additionally, the homogenization of communication has also made English the native language of popular culture, including music, movies, sports, and even science. Furthermore, English *is the official language in more countries than any other language* (para. 11), even though in terms of speakers of English (508 million), it is not the most spoken language in the world; Mandarin is (1 billion +) (Jamie, 2008). These objective considerations further explain the popularity and use of English as a second language.

There are objective and biologically related considerations to bilingualism as well. For example, greater emotionality is present in the first language (L1) than in the L2 (Dewaele, 2010). This may be the case because of parallel language and emotional brain regulation systems. Later language development may be more cortically represented, less connected to subcortical areas, or L1 may even be encoded at the neural level (Proverbio, Adorni, & Zani, 2009). Thus, biological factors on language, be L1 or L2, are undeniable, as are their differential effects in language(s) acquisition, processing, and expression. But the social aspects are more likely to have a malleable effect, subjectively bound, and perhaps just as important on how bilingualism is influenced, perceived, and manifested given objective considerations.

Bilingualism and Subjective Considerations

That objective, concrete considerations play a role in bilingualism is undeniable, but perhaps more important influences may be found at the subjective level. Specifically, perceptions of security, control, and expectations are conflated with our social identity and survival-instincts to the degree that they become survival-traits (Darwin, 1859). Our early ancestors foraging for food in the savanna needed to determine friend from foe. Allegiance to one's tribe ensures survival—even manifested at the primordial level, such as when children intuitively know to be afraid of strangers. A strong in-group identification with our tribe, clan, or social group accords benefits, and out-group trust with other-tribe, competitor, or enemy can carry costs. In this sense, the nature of our intergroup contacts, dealings between and among groups, determine the degree of our interactions with others, from our willingness to engage and embrace them (valuing bilingualism), to our willingness to disparage and discriminate against them (devaluing bilingualism).

Tajfel (1970) created an experimental paradigm to examine the role of intergroup relations via *Us-versus-Them* (in-group/out-group) dynamics, which can help us understand bilingualism perceptions. In what he called the *minimal group paradigm*, he asked a group of strangers to estimate the number of dots in a piece of paper. Then, he would tell them that some people were over- and others under-estimators. Irrespective of the estimate participants provided, Tajfel would tell half of them they were over-estimators (Group 1) and the other half that they were under-estimators (Group 2), with assignment done randomly and based on chance along. In fact, any marker can be used to separate groups, hence the term minimal group, which can be arbitrary. The importance of this is that it controls for history effects, as the participants in each group come to the experiment with clean slate, without past prejudices, grievances, or animosities. In fact, the two groups do not even have to see each other to get at the nature of groups' perceptions, as it is next described.

Once participants are told they are in a group, they are asked to complete a series of competition games with differing *pay-off matrixes*; that is, they can award points (rewards) to their group (G1) and the other group (G2) in forced choices (A, B, C), such as the one depicted below:

		Choice	
Group	*A*	*B*	*C*
G1	5	10	25
G2	1	11	27

Columns are arranged in terms of points awarded between the groups. For example, Choice A would denote G1 being awarded 5 points, and G2 one point. The following is a simplification and summary of what participants are asked to do. Put yourself in this experiment as G1; if forced to pick one choice of three, which one would you choose, A, B, or C? Most people pick *Choice A*, they give their in-group 5 points, and the out-group (G2) 1 point. In doing so, they sacrifice compromise (Choice B), where they could *double* their profit and about break even with the out-group (10 to 11). Even better, they could *quintuple* (5 times) their profit, a form of cooperation securing the biggest profit for both groups, but G2 (out-group) would benefit more (25 to 27). These findings are most shocking because it pits the norm of fairness versus groupness, with the latter winning. Can you see crucial points of human nature displayed in these results?

Tajfel (1970) showed the preferred choice was A, reflecting *maximum group differentiation* and the one that increased *maximum in-group profit*, a form of *in-group favoritism* that is not the most rational decision. Specifically, for G1 the maximum group differentiation occurred in the in-group/out-group competition under Choice A (5 − 1 = 4 points), which also had maximum in-group profit (4 points for Choice A, versus −1 in Choice B, and −2 in Choice C), and this in-group favoritism cost them 20 points had they chosen to maximize actual profit, as denoted in Choice C, a loss of 20 points (25 − 5). Thus, the most *rational decision* would have been Choice C, maximizing join profit, or fairness, and a choice picked not as often. Most importantly, these choices reveal that out-group discrimination was reflected in Choice A, the one most often chosen. This is consistent with the tribal mentality reflected in evolutionary theory that suggests that we prefer our own group, for they give us a sense of belonging and provide protection, such as our family. We must keep in mind that in this experiment, participants had no history, previous animosity, or any emotional conflicts to air, just a cognitive sense of in-group versus out-group (Us–Them). Bring those factors into the intergroup dynamics of in-group/out-group, and we can see why it has been so difficult to solve ongoing conflicts (e.g., Palestine–Israel conflict) throughout the world.

Bilingualism and Language Status

Because language is such a strong marker of group identity (Us-versus-Them), Tajfel's (1970) principles of social identity have significant relevance to bilingualism and intergroup relations. Discrimination among groups, such as racism, has changed from blatant to subtler ways. For example, a person may not be denied service at a restaurant for speaking poor English but they may be denied a job. Race, ethnicity, and mother-language other than English can serve as markers of in- or out-groupness (Jones, Dovidio, & Vietze, 2013). Language is more likely to be used as a marker of in-group/out-group identification with real-life consequences. For example, research on aversive racism, where non-racist people nonetheless may discriminate, shows that such discrimination is not due to out-group derogation, but rather in-group favoritism (Gaertner & Dovidio, 1986). Thus, a person for whom English is a second language or who speaks English with an accent may be denied a job, not because English is their second language or is seen as part of an out-group, but because the person offering the job may have a preference for those whose English is their primary language, or an in-group person. Consequently, language use is intimately related to social identity and social categorization, often with consequential outcomes, as the above example illustrates.

Bilingualism often takes place in an intergroup setting with groups of different statuses. The in-group favoritism found by Tajfel (1970) is most likely to be manifested by the group of higher status, with the lower status group as the out-group, often a minority. Language is a marker that can produce the maximum differentiation (Choice A in the matrix above), where one language will be favored and one will be ostracized. Particular examples of how this might be manifested can be seen in the push for *English Only* movement in the US, with the marginalization of Spanish (Crawford, 1992, 2015; Hurtado & Rodriguez, 1989), and in Canada, where Aboriginal languages have been subject to *linguicide* (Wright & Taylor, 2010) and where bilingual education has been a tool to ensure the survival of some languages (Taylor, Caouette, Usborne, & Wright, 2008). In some cases, such as the case in the United Kingdom, where English came to be seen as the language of the future and Welsh as a *sign of regional backwardness* (Lewis, 2012, p. 5), laws have been enacted (*Welsh Language Act* of 1993) to protect it, but with continued group differentiation and discrimination (Lewis, 2012). Again, social identity playing a large role in how bilingualism and language attitudes play out.

Bilingualism and the Influence of Stereotypes

Tajfel (1981) showed that intergroup differentiation takes place through social *stereotypes*, often products of language markers. The need for distinctiveness is best summarized as, *the social group is seen to function as a provider of positive social identity for its members through comparing itself and distinguishing itself, from other comparison groups, along salient dimensions which have a clear value differential* (Commings & Lockwood, 1979, pp. 281–282). In this regard, social categorization theory posits that language provides a tool to validate one's group identity and to validate discrimination against the out-group, which is parlayed through mechanisms of self-cognition that substantiate, create, and legitimize stereotypes that mark group differences (Postmes & Branscombe, 2010; Tajfel, 1981).

Most notably, a language value differential through stereotypes of a group was investigated in a recent study by Ortiz and Behm-Morawitz (2015). These researchers showed how stereotypes of Latinos permeate group-based attitudes and beliefs in both English- and Spanish-language television. They use the *cultivation theory*, which states that portrayals of self- and group-image in the media validates, reinforces, and more generally speaking, legitimizes how Latinos see themselves represented in television, be it in a positive or negative light. Results of a survey ($N = 209$) with Latino respondents showed that in the English media, Latinos see prejudice against their group, but not discrimination (likely because of political correctness); but importantly, they see legitimization and implicit acceptance of negative Latino stereotypes (i.e., criminals, lazy, speaking poor English). No significant findings were found for Spanish media, even though it stereotypes in favor of the young and light-skinned. Given such outcomes, how do low-status groups fight these stereotypes?

According to Allport (1954b) and Tajfel and Turner (1979), low-status groups have several strategies at their disposal. These can include militancy, denial of group membership, self-hate, neuroticism, strategies generally known as *compensatory behaviors* on the part of victims (Allport, 1954b, p. 160b). Tajfel and Turner (1979) formalized these into *social strategies* available to low-status groups: *Social-mobility*, moving into the high-status group; *-Creativity*, reframing negative into positive stereotypes; *-Competition*, challenging the high-status group; and *-Change*, changing the social-order through protests or even revolution.

In the case of Latinos in the US, *social-competition* has been used by fighting for bilingual education, but it has been a losing strategy in the face of the English Only movement (Crawford, 2015). If anything, bilingualism has come in the losing end also on social-mobility, a winning strategy for English monolingualism, as shown by Spanish-to-English shift across generations (Hurtado & Vega, 2004), as well as English media consumption (Villarreal, 2015). Where social-competition has been tried, some chaos has followed, as can be seen in the Welsh Language Act described above. In all, research shows that as long as a group sees the system open or accessible for mobility, a low-status group will opt for this strategy to pass into the high-status group (Wright, Taylor, & Moghaddam, 1990) and a diminishing role for bilingualism.

Differential Social Value of Languages

The mere presence of group status affords a language greater or lesser value. Common sense dictates that a lesser valued language would fall out of favor, perhaps even disappear (Grubin, 2015; Lambert, 1977). That is not always the case, however, countervailing predictions. As a marker of identity, often as immutable as phenotype, language server as social validation for the in-group, and this in itself ensures survivability through what Lambert (1977) has termed *additive bilingualism* or the bilingual advantage effect (see de Bot & Houtzager; Paap, this volume). This is consistent with Allport (1954b) and Tajfel and Turner (1979), who state that a low-status group can opt to strengthen in-group ties and *social creativity* (i.e., *black is beautiful*).

A low-status group can also engage in what is known as *cultural frame switching* (Benet-Martinez, Leu, Lee, & Morris, 2002) as a compensation strategy and cognitive process. That is, *[low status groups can] have access to multiple cultural meaning systems and switch between different culturally appropriate behaviors depending on the context* (Benet-Martinez et al., 2002, p. 493). This strategy works because it has been shown that individuals can hold orthogonal information-processing streams for dual languages and *in-group* identities, depending on activation triggers. Thus, this cultural frame switching can explain why an African–American may opt to speak *Ebonics (blending the words "ebony 'black' and phonics 'sounds,'") an English dialect spoken among African Americans and literally translated as "black speech," created in 1973 by African American scholars in repudiation of stigmatizing terms such as "Nonstandard Negro English"* (Rickford, 2016, p. 1). This might explain why Mexican–American speakers might maintain Spanglish while being fluent in English and Spanish. It may also explain why Yiddish, *Jewish German*, at one time classified as a dirty language that servant girls and manual workers spoke, continues to survive and strive to this day (Hacillo, 2014).

The word value of a language carries two meanings, both related to the social identity of an in-group. It can refer to the *status value* of the language *vis-à-vis* the status of the group (minority/majority). This can be seen when a high-status group's language is conferred the status of *official language*. In contrast, it also carries *affective value*, or emotional weight. For example, French was the premiere international *lingua franca* of diplomacy until English displaced it after World War II. However, because of the emotional value attached to the language, France has a long-instituted blockade of the English language, from the 1635 language protecting laws by the *Académie Française*, to fixed quotas for French songs played on radio, to the 1994 *Toubon Law*, decreeing all public advertising to be in the French language (Samuel, 2015). Although an end to this English language blockade has been called for by France's Culture Minister, there is no denying the French emotional attachment to their language. This again is explained by the role that social identity plays on bilingualism attitudes, be positive or negative.

Social Valuation and Validation in Bilingualism

Attitudes are central constructs in social psychology and are defined as evaluations, negative or positive, of an object, person, idea, or activity (Allport, 1935). From an instrumental perspective, people should have a positive attitude about bilingualism, adding to the repertoire of human potential, increasing communication, and expanding access to the human mind, economic benefit, and emotional expansion. And yet, our review of social identity demonstrates that a negative attitude about bilingualism can prevail, no matter how irrational, to the degree that in-group/out-group attitudes intermingle as part of social categorization (Turner & Reynolds, 2010). Left in default, it would appear that negative attitudes about bilingualism would be more predominant.

From a social identity perspective, a high-status group will confer their language more value. Such value could be codified into law, such as the English Only laws enacted in various American states, or language statuses enacted in various countries (i.e., 1994 Toubon Law in France). Social value of a language can also manifest in terms of discrimination, such as Spanish-speaking students in Texas being disciplined in school for speaking Spanish, or speakers of a low-status language being ostracized (aboriginal languages in Canada, Welsh in England, and Native American languages in Mexico). From this perspective, the role of the situation in Lewin's notion of how behavior, person, and context are related would appear to doom bilingualism. By context, or the situation, favoring one language, by law or discrimination, it would seem that most people would be steered to speak the most valued language.

However, context can work in both directions; it can work against bilingualism, but it can also encourage and protect it. The merchant benefits the Dutch derived from bi-, or tri-lingual abilities, accrued from the context in which they live. Laws can also serve to create a *protected* context for bilingualism, such as laws of bilingual education in Canada and the US, as well as more than one official language in some countries—eleven official languages in the case of South Africa. But there is no denying that context can exert negative influence on attitudes about bilingualism, emerging from tribal (in-group/out-group) and cognitive processes (Turner & Reynolds, 2010). Yet, in social psychology changing norms (Allport, 1954b; Asch, 1956; Sherif, 1935, 1936) can bring about attitude change, from negative to positive (Festinger, 1957).

Attitudes can be shifted from negative to positive, changing how the languages of bilingualism are valued, and this can come about by focusing on the context and accordingly changing it. This valuation (change in value) can then be said to be validated when speakers of a group accept it. Validation means acceptance, but such acceptance may or may not be tacit (Festinger, 1957; Gaertner, Mann, Murrell, & Dovidio, 1986).

Specifically, an explicit acceptance of bilingualism can be tacitly manifested, where speakers go along with language laws and norms, such as the case in how English monolingual speakers might view translated documents in presidential elections in the US for Spanish speakers. In reality, some English monolinguals can hold negative attitudes that they may not manifest in public. Spanish speakers, in turn, may manifest in-group validation and in-group loyalty by using Spanish material rather than English, though at the price of perceived discrimination from the out-group. So, while bilingualism may be legitimized by the law, inequities may still simmer underground, with high/low status for each language remaining, or through aversive forms of discrimination. Having a changed context may not lead to changed minds, in how bilingualism is perceived and valued. Again, this would still be fueled by social identity, inasmuch as laws and norms attempt to check-and-balance the value afforded to speakers of different languages.

Bilingualism and Permeable Boundaries of Social Identity

If social identity is so *minimal*, evolutionarily based through tribal behaviors, and important to the social validation of self and group, are not negative attitudes about intergroup behavior such as use of bilingualism inevitable and of permanence? According to Jones, Dovidio, and Vietze (2013), as our world becomes more diverse, tribal boundaries become more permeable. Perhaps it is the homogenization of communication integrating our world, or secularization of in-group/out-group differences, but evidence shows that it is possible to reduce the Us-versus-Them mentality.

The empirical evidence suggests several pathways: increasing cooperation has been one approach to get groups to converge on a goal (Sherif, 1958). So too, increasing co-dependency on a task for individuals of different group backgrounds, through what is called the *jigsaw technique* (Aronson, 1978). To the degree that a common objective, or goal, for people of different groups can be maintained, positive attitudes among members of the different groups will be sustained.

More recent studies show that social identity can be reduced through two additional processes. The first one is *de-categorization*, where people distance themselves from the group (Hewstone & Brown, 1986), and reducing what Tajfel (1970) called the *groupness norm*. Gaertner, Mann, Murrell, and Dovidio (1989) also show another effective method to reduce intergroup conflict, through what they call *re-categorization*, or bringing the out-group closer to the in-group, and what Aronson (1978) called *mutual interdependence* by creating a new, merged group. It should be noted that the above processes involved not only changes to context, but also changes in people's perceptions, completing Lewin's notion that behavior is a function of both, person and situation. Thus, efforts to reduced group boundaries are possible, even if more work than (*the minimal effort in*) creating them is required.

Importantly, reducing group boundaries does not ensure sustained bilingualism. Ironically, it can contribute to reduced bilingualism. Spanish television in the US has enjoyed more than 50 years of sustained growth until now, when a generation of bilingual *millennials* have started to gravitate away from *novelas* (Spanish soap operas) and brassy variety shows (Univision's 53-year-old *Sábado Gigante*, which kept losing advertising sponsors). The Spanish television network, Univision, has called this generation *billennials*, and they are moving in droves to English only media. This Spanish-to-English language shift, demonstrated by Hurtado and Vega (2004), is further corroborated by recent surveys (Taylor, Lopez, Martinez, & Velasco, 2012), which show that English is the dominant language of third-generation Latinos (at least one parent born in the US). This shift has prompted Spanish television to introduce bilingual programming through sister stations (Telemundo for NBC and UniMax for Univision), to mixed results and with irreversible trends towards English only media for billennials (Villarreal, 2015).

Bilingualism and Binary (Social and Biological) Benefits

The universal pull of English is not only true for Latinos in the US, but so too in Wales and even France, where an end to the boycott of English language words has been called. From this perspective, it appears that contextual imperatives drive the need for bilingualism and attitudes people possess. To the degree that personal choice matters, we could say a juggling process of context and person-perspective takes place.

Choice and ability can dictate how bilinguals will navigate their social world, learning or not an L2. But even for bilinguals, they must be *mental jugglers* (Fields, 2012), keeping both languages active at all the time, which research implies brings benefit to the bilingual person (see de Bot & Houtzager; Paap, this volume). These benefits may include better executive control, and the ability to activate or suppress what is important/unimportant, given their use of language (L1 or L2) at any given time (Fields, 2012).

More indirect health benefits have also been shown, with bilingualism called a *cognitive reserve* for Alzheimer's disease, being diagnosed 4.3 years later and with reported symptoms appearing 5.1 years later than in monolinguals (Craik, Bialystok, & Freedman, 2010). Bilingualism even has benefits in the Us-versus-Them tribal dichotomy, where loyalty to the in-group is maintained (Allport, 1954b), while interaction with the out-group is increased (Pettigrew & Tropp, 2005).

Conclusion

Social identity plays in important role on perceptions of bilingualism, and likely, in its manifestation. Intergroup differences are not only manifested across languages, but even within a language, as gleaned by the society wide disdain shown to speakers who do not speak Standard English, or whatever that country's official language might be. To the degree that group boundaries fall, through the homogenization of communication, bilingualism may have a limited life expand. To the degree that situations demand bilingualism or polyglotism, due to financial gain or other practical matters, we can expect its continuous existence. To the degree that tribal (in-group) loyalty demands it, bilingualism or adherence to a mother tongue will continue. In either case, Lewin's notion that *Behavior* is influenced by the *Person* and *Situation* ($B = P*S$) will continue to play a large role in how individuals come to perceive and adapt to bilingualism.

List of Key Words and Concepts

Additive bilingualism, Affective value, Cognitive reserve, Compensatory behaviors, Cultivation theory, Cultural frame switching, De-categorization, Groupness norm, In-group, In-group favoritism, Invisible minority, Jigsaw technique, Maximum group differentiation, Maximum in-group profit, Minimal group paradigm, Mutual interdependence, Out-group, Pay-off matrixes, Re-categorization, Social categorization theory, Social competition, Social creativity, Social identity theory, Social influence, Social strategies, Status value, Stereotype, Toubon Law, Tower of Babel, Us-versus-Them, Welsh Language Act

Internet Sites Related to Social Psychology and Bilingualism

Journal of Language and Social Psychology: http://jls.sagepub.com/
Language and Culture: http://languageasculturespring11.blogspot.com/2011/03/social-influences-of-language-assets.html
Social Psychology Network: http://www.socialpsychology.org/

Discussion Questions

(1) Discuss the role of social perception on the *valuation* and *validation* of bilingualism in a society.
(2) Explain how a society can use a group's status to discourage or encourage bilingualism?
(3) Why might a low-status person embrace bilingualism compared to a high-status person?
(4) What are the conditions that can encourage a person to assimilate to the dominant language?
(5) How do stereotypes influence the value of bilingualism?
(6) Explain how social context can encourage or discourage bilingualism?
(7) Analyze scenarios where bilingualism may precede the loss of one language?
(8) What is the role of *Us-versus-Them* ideology in bilingual attitudes?
(9) Can we apply biological knowledge to understand the effects of bilingualism?
(10) What does social psychology have to say about the polyglot person?

Suggested Research Projects

(1) Choose three related articles on bilingualism and social psychology from the *Journal of Language and Social Psychology, Journal of Social Issues*, or from any other psychological journal related to language and social psychology. Write an analysis for each article, focusing on the (a) validity of the premises and conclusions of the study, (b) methodological strengths and weaknesses of how the study was conducted, and (c) alternative explanations of the findings and whether or not they can be ruled out. These exercises will help you understand the empirical nature of research on bilingualism and social psychology.

(2) Please read any major newspaper in your city to find any articles that involved the social psychology of bilingualism. This article should be about an extemporaneous topic, such as bilingualism and legislation, culture and language, media issues, or a topic that you can relate to issues discussed in this chapter. Critically analyze the topic with principles of this chapter, noting how the issue involves social influence, attitudes, emotions, actions, or any other relevant role that perceptions might play on a critical outcome. Is bilingualism being encouraged, discouraged? Is social identity involved? Should the context be changed?

(3) Sports competitions are prime examples of intergroup relation dynamics and a good place to see in-group/out-group differences manifested through language. Apply principles from this chapter to the 2016 Copa America tournament, where Mexican fans were chastised by the American media for homophobic chants of "Eeeh, puto," a hurtful slur. Read the following source for background: Krauze, L. (2016, June 21). Mexican soccer fans need to stop this homophobic chant: Why Univision is broadcasting a statement denouncing the "Eeeh, puto!" cheer. *The Washingtonpost*. Retrieved on June 21, 2016, from https://www.washingtonpost.com/posteverything/wp/2016/06/21/mexican-soccer-fans-need-to-stop-this-homophobic-chant/

Suggested Readings

Chen, S. X. (2015), Toward a social psychology of bilingualism and biculturalism. *Asian Journal of Social Psychology*, *18*, 1–11.

Harwood, J., & Vincze, L. (2015). Ethnolinguistic identification, vitality, and gratifications for television use in a bilingual media environment. *Journal of Social Issues*, *71*, 73–89.

Holtgraves, T. (2010) Social psychology and language: Words, utterances, and conversation. In S. Fiske, D. Gilbert, & G. Lindzey (Eds.), *Handbook of social psychology* (Vol. 2, 5th ed.) (pp. 1386–1422). Hoboken, NJ: John Wiley & Sons.

Hurtado, A. (2016). The social psychology of Spanish/English bilingualism in the United States. In M. J. Gelfand, C. Chiu, & Y. Hong (Eds.), *Handbook of advances in culture and psychology* (Vol. 6, pp. 157–208). New York: Oxford University Press

Montaruli, E., Bourhis, R. Y., Azurmendi, M. J. (2011). Identity, language, and ethnic relations in the bilingual autonomous communities of Spain. *Journal of Sociolinguistics*, *15*, 94–121.

Walters, J. (2014). *Bilingualism: The sociopragmatic–psycholinguistic interface*. New York: Psychology Press.

References

Allport, G. (1935). Attitudes. In C. M. Murchison (Ed.), *Handbook of social psychology* (pp. 798–844). Worcester, MA: Clark University Press.

Allport, G. W. (1954a). The historical background of modern social psychology. In G. Lindzey & E. Aronson (Eds.), *The handbook of social psychology* (Vol. 1, pp. 1–80). Reading, MA: Addison-Wesley.

Allport, G. W. (1954b). *The nature of prejudice* (1st ed.). Menlo Park, CA: Addison-Wesley.

Aronson, E. (1978). *The jigsaw classroom*. Beverly Hills, CA: Sage.

Asch, S. (1956). Studies of independence and conformity: A minority of one against a unanimous majority. *Psychological Monographs*, *70*, 1–70.

Benet-Martinez, V., Leu, J., Lee, F., & Morris, M. (2002). Negotiating biculturalism: Culture frame switching in bicultural and oppositional versus compatible cultural identities. *Journal of Cross-Cultural Psychology*, *33*, 492–516.

Commings, B., & Lockwood, J. (1979). The effects of stress differences, favoured treatment and equity on intergroup comparisons. *European Journal of Social Psychology*, *9*, 281–289.

Craik, F. I., Bialystok, E., & Freedman, M. (2010). Delaying the onset of Alzheimer disease: Bilingualism as a form of cognitive reserve. *Neurology, 75*, 1726–1729.

Crawford, J. (1992). *Hold your tongue: Bilingualism and the politics of English only.* Reading, MA: Addison-Wesley.

Crawford, J. (2015). *James Crawford's language policy web site & emporium.* Retrieved on September 30, 2015, from http://www.languagepolicy.net/

Darwin, C. R. (1859). *On the origin of species by means of natural selection, or the preservation of favoured races in the struggle for life.* London: John Murray.

Dewaele, J. M. (2010). *Emotions in multiple languages.* London: Palgrave Macmillan. doi:10.1057/9780230289505.

Explain Like I Am Five (2015). *ELI5: How did so many different languages develop, particularly in countries that border on to each another?* Retrieved on September 31, 2015, from https://www.reddit.com/r/explainlikeimfive/comments/39vc5t/eli5how_did_so_many_different_languages_develop/

Festinger, L. (1957). *A Theory of cognitive dissonance.* Stanford, CA: Stanford University Press.

Fields, H. (2012). Speaking your mind: Bilingual language, culture, and emotion. *Observer: Association of Psychological Sciences, 25*(5), 15–19.

Gaertner, S. L., & Dovidio, J. F. (1986). The aversive form of racism. In J. F. Dovidio & S. L. Gaertner (Eds.), *Prejudice, discrimination, and racism* (pp. 61–89). Orlando, FL: Academic Press.

Gaertner, S. L., Mann, J., Murrell, A., & Dovidio, J. F. (1989). Reducing intergroup bias: The benefits of recategorization. *Journal of Personality and Social Psychology, 57*(2), 239–249.

Grubin, D. (2015, January 19). *Language matters, with Bob Holman.* Public Broadcasting System. Retrieved on September 31, 2015, from http://www.languagemattersfilm.com/

Hacillo, A. (2014). *Can a language without a home survive? New internationalist blog.* Retrieved on September 31, 2015, from http://newint.org/blog/2014/04/17/yiddish-language-survival/

Hewstone, M., & Brown, R. J. (1986). Contact is not enough: An intergroup perspective on the contact hypothesis. In M. Hewstone & R. J. Brown (Eds.), *Contact and conflict in intergroup encounters* (pp. 1–44). Oxford: Blackwell.

Hurtado, A., & Rodriguez, R. (1989). Language as a social problem: The repression of Spanish in south Texas. *Journal of Multilingual and Multicultural Development, 10*, 401–419.

Hurtado, A., & Vega, L. A. (2004). Shift happens: Spanish and English transmission between parents and their children. *Journal of Social Issues, 60*, 137–155.

Jamie, F. (2008). Top 10 most spoken languages in the world. *Listverse* (26 June 2008). Retrieved on September 31, 2015, from http://listverse.com/2008/06/26/top-10-most-spoken-languages-in-the-world/

Jones, J. M., Dovidio, J. F., & Vietze, D. L. (2013). *The psychology of diversity: Beyond prejudice and racism.* West Sussex, UK: Wiley-Blackwell.

Lambert, W. E. (1977). The effects of bilingualism on the individual: Cognitive and sociocultural consequences. In P. A. Hornby (Ed.), *Bilingualism: Psychological, social and educational implications* (pp. 15–27). New York: Academic Press.

Leavitt, P. A., Covarrubias, R., Perez, Y. A., & Fryberg, S. A. (2015). "Frozen in time": The impact of Native American media representations on identity and self-understanding. *Journal of Social Issues, 71*, 39–53.

Lewin, K. (1951). *Field theory in social science.* (Edited by D. Cartwright.) New York: Harper.

Lewis, R. (2012, November 25). Save Wales from the Welsh: Children told they can't go to the loo if they ask in English. Architects shunned if their plans aren't in Welsh. ROGER LEWIS on Welsh Language Society 'nutters'. *Dailymail.com.* Retrieved on September 31, 2015, from http://www.dailymail.co.uk/news/article-2238472/Save-Wales-Welsh-Children-told-loo-ask-English-Architects-shunned-plans-arent-Welsh-ROGER-LEWIS-nutty-Welsh-Language-Society.html

Martinez, A. (2014, November 15). English will grow as the most popular language. *The Bakersfield Californian.* p. B7.

Meinzer, K. (Producer). (2015, January 26). The language apocalypse is coming, and many tongues are already but dead. *The Takeaway* [Public Radio broadcast]. New York: Public Radio

International, WGBH and WNYC. Retrieved on January 26, 2015, from http://www.pri.org/stories/2015-01-26/language-apocalypse-coming-and-many-tongues-are-already-all-dead

Ortiz, M., & Behm-Morawitz, E. (2015). Latinos' perceptions of intergroup relations in the United States: The cultivation of group-based attitudes and beliefs from English- and Spanish-language television. *Journal of Social Issues, 71*, 90–105.

Papua New Guinea (2016). *Ethnologue: Languages of the world.* Retrieved on July 8, 2016, from http://www.ethnologue.com/country/PG

Pettigrew, T. F., & Tropp, L. R. (2005). Allport's intergroup contact hypothesis: Its history and influence. In J. F. Dovidio, P. Glick, & L. Rudman (Eds.), *On the nature of prejudice: Fifty years after Allport* (pp. 262–277). Malden, MA: Blackwell.

Postmes, T., & Branscombe, N. R. (2010). Sources of social identity. In T. Postmes & N. R. Branscombe (Eds.), *Key readings in social psychology: Rediscovering social identity* (pp. 1–12). New York: Psychology Press.

Proverbio, A. M., Adorni, R., & Zani, A. (2009). Inferring native language from early bio-electrical activity. *Biological Psychology, 80*, 52–63.

Rickford, J. R. (2016). *What is Ebonics (African American Vernacular English)?* Washington, DC: Linguistic Society of America. Retrieved on July 8, 2016, from http://www.linguisticsociety.org/content/what-ebonics-african-american-english

Samuel, H. (2015). France must drop 'ineffective' blockade against English language. *The Telegraph.* Retrieved on September 31, 2015, from http://www.telegraph.co.uk/news/worldnews/europe/france/11467624/France-must-drop-ineffective-blockade-against-English-language.html

Sherif, M. (1935). A study of some social factors in perception: Chapter 2. *Archives of Psychology, 27*(187), 17–22.

Sherif, M. (1936). *The psychology of social norms.* New York: Harper & Row.

Sherif, M. (1958). Superordinate goals in the reduction of intergroup conflicts. *American Journal of Sociology, 63*, 349–356.

Tajfel, H. (1970). Experiments in intergroup discrimination. *Scientific American, 223*, 96–102.

Tajfel, H. (1981). Social stereotypes and social groups. In J. C. Turner & H. Giles (Eds.), *Intergroup behavior* (pp. 144–167). Oxford, UK: Blackwell.

Tajfel, H., & Turner, J. C. (1979). An integrative theory of intergroup conflict. In W. G. Austin & S. Worchel (Eds.), *The social psychology of intergroup relations* (pp. 33–47). Monterey, CA: Brooks-Cole.

Taylor, D. M., Caouette, J., Usborne, E., & Wright, S. C. (2008). Aboriginal languages in Québec: Fighting linguicide with bilingual education. *Diversité Urbaine: Plurilinguisme et identités au Canada*, Automne, 69–89.

Taylor, P., Lopez, M. H., Martinez, J., & Velasco, G. (2012). *When Labels don't fit: Hispanic and their views of identity.* Pew Research Center: Hispanic Trends. Retrieved from http://www.pewhispanic.org/2012/04/04/iv-language-use-among-latinos/

The Tower of Babel (2015). *Christian Bible Reference Site.* Retrieved on September 31, 2015, from http://www.christianbiblereference.org/story_TowerOfBabel.htm

Turner, J. C. (1978). Differentiation between social groups: Studies in the social psychology of intergroup relations (pp. 235–250). In T. H. Tajfel (Ed.), *Social categorization and social discrimination in the minimal group paradigm.* London: Academic Press.

Turner, J. C., & Reynolds, K. J. (2010). The story of social identity. In T. Postmes & N. R. Branscombe (Eds.), *Key readings in social psychology: Rediscovering social identity* (pp. 13–32). New York: Psychology Press.

Vega, L. A. (2008) Social psychological approaches to bilingualism. In J. Altarriba & R. R. Heredia (Eds.), *An introduction to bilingualism: Principles and practices* (pp. 185–198). Mahwah, NJ: Lawrence Erlbaum.

Villarreal, Y. (2015, July 18). The billennial generation: How bilingual millennials are changing Spanish-language TV. *Los Angeles Times.* Retrieved on September 31, 2015, from http://www.latimes.com/entertainment/envelope/cotown/la-et-ct-latino-millennials-univision-20150719-story.html

Wright, S. C., & Taylor, D. M. (2010). Justice in Aboriginal language policy and practices: Fighting institutional discrimination and linguicide. In D. R. Bobocel, A. C. Kay, M. P. Zanna, & J. M. Olson (Eds.), *The psychology of justice and legitimacy* (pp. 273–298). New York: Psychology Press.

Wright, S. C., Taylor, D. M., & Moghaddam, F. M. (1990). Responding to membership in a disadvantaged group: From acceptance to collective protest. *Journal of Personality and Social Psychology, 58*, 994–1003.

12 The Social and Cultural Contexts of Bilingualism

*Flavia C. Peréa, Viviana Padilla-Martínez,
and Cynthia García Coll*

*There can be no divided allegiance here... We have room for but one language here, and
that is the English language, and we intend to see that the crucible turns our people out as
Americans.*

(Twenty-sixth US President Theodore Roosevelt, to the
American Defense Society, January 3, 1919)

*So if you want to really hurt me, talk badly about my language. Ethnic identity is twin skin
to linguistic identity–I am my language... Until I am free to write bilingually and to switch
codes without having always to translate, while I still have to speak English or Spanish when
I would rather speak Spanglish, and as long as I have to accommodate the English speakers
rather than having them accommodate me, my tongue will be illegitimate.*

(Anzaldúa, 1987, p. 59)

*Our new immigrants must be part of our One America... We have a responsibility to make
them welcome here; and they have a responsibility to enter the mainstream of American life.
That means learning English.*

(Forty-second US President William Clinton, State of the
Union Speech, January 19, 1999)

*Now, I agree that immigrants should learn English. I agree with that. But understand this.
Instead of worrying about whether immigrants can learn English—they'll learn English—
you need to make sure your child can speak Spanish. You should be thinking about, how can
your child become bilingual? We should have every child speaking more than one language.*
(Forty-fourth US President Barack Obama, Presidential Campaign Event,
Powder Springs, GA, July 8, 2008)

Introduction

Language diversity is not a relatively new phenomenon, and concerns about language
diversity can be found in some of the world's oldest stories and mythologies. The Bible
story of Babel, related in *Genesis*, is one example (*Genesis* 11:4–9). According to the bib-
lical story, people once spoke only one common language until they angered God and he
punished them. As the story goes, after the Flood, Noah's descendants decided to build a
mighty tower that would reach up to Heaven. God, however, was offended by their efforts,
and chose to punish the people for their arrogance by making them all speak different
languages. Because they were unable to speak to each other, they couldn't cooperate and
build the tower. Known as the *Curse of Babel*, the story characterizes linguistic diversity
as a punishment and multilingualism as a liability that makes it hard, if not impossible, for
people to cooperate and work together. In the story, language is portrayed as a limiting and

debilitating obstacle, suggesting that multilingualism, or, rather, the absence of a single, common language, serves to divide and hinder people's abilities to cooperate and advance.

Historically, various languages have been present within the current political borders of the US. Hundreds of languages were spoken in North America before European contact with the Native Peoples who had populated the continent for centuries. Immigrants and incorporated peoples from all parts of the world have also retained aspects of their language as they have become residents and citizens of this country. Contrary to the popular perception of the US as a homogeneous, English monolingual and monocultural state, language diversity has been and remains an important feature of US society. But, in spite of the fact that the US has been multilingual from its inception, there is no question that English is by far the dominant language and *lingua franca* in the US as it is throughout the world. English is, for all practical intents and purposes, the *de facto* official language; is without doubt the dominant language of politics, business, and education; and is spoken (with varying degrees of fluency and in many different dialects) by the vast majority of people in the US. However, an official language or national language policy does not exist. Rather, there are various policies that do not reflect a consistent theory of language use and choice, or ideology about language rights, which often reflect different values and competing ideas about language.

This chapter operates under the assumptions that there is an inextricable link between the prevalent definitions of race/ethnicity, culture, and language (between what is popularly deemed a *foreign language* and the imposition of an ascribed non-American *foreign origin* in the US). As much as *e pluribus unum* (one out of many) is undoubtedly a great strength, it is also a point of tension and, as US history shows, has often been a source of strife. The conflict over language policy has deep social and cultural foundations, and the debate about language use and choice reflects tension between bilingualism and individual, group, and national identity. As Hakuta (1986, p. 9) writes, *Bilingualism, in addition to being a linguistic concept, refers to a constellation of tensions having to do with a multitude of psychological, societal and political realities.* There is a clear social and cultural context that underlies *language laws* and policies, which are inseparable from historical factors, immigration laws, and prevailing social attitudes that are intimately coupled with issues of difference, race/ethnicity, and culture. Ideas about language use and choice also have everything to do with prevailing notions of *American identity*.

This chapter will discuss the social and cultural contexts of bilingualism in the US at the dawn of the 21st century. In order to capture the various angles that define the social and cultural contexts of bilingualism, the chapter is divided into three parts: Historical, Demographic, and Language Laws and Policies. First, the chapter will discuss the historical record and national language policy; US *expansion, Americanization* and diversification; and immigration and language diversity at the turn of the twentieth century. Second, it will discuss changing demographics and growth among the language minority population today, present a case study on Latin American immigration, and discuss questions surrounding the *integration* of Latinos. Lastly, it will discuss federal protections offered to language minorities, the English only movement, English only laws and policies, and take a close examination of the education of language minority students.

This chapter will discuss the historical records regarding language policy since the inception of this country. It will illustrate how language policies have been and continue to be used as one tool to incorporate new Americans and which often reflect anti-immigrant attitudes and competing values about identity and language rights. In the past, increased immigration triggered fear, and evolving diversity caused concern about the incorporation of immigrants, stemming from notions of what it means for new Americans to enter US society. More often than not, population changes were met with anti-immigrant attitudes and policies that restricted the options and rights of immigrants and minority groups. As part of efforts to incorporate new peoples, often forcibly, *assimilationist* strategies were employed, meaning tactics intended to force minority groups to adopt the culture, language customs, and way of life of the majority while giving up those of their home/native countries and cultures of origin. As shall be discussed, language was historically recognized as the powerful tool that it is, and it was often used to further the goals of full cultural and linguistic *assimilation* of immigrant and minority groups into the dominant Anglo-American culture. Such was the case with Native Americans and immigrants in the early 20th century, and such is the case with Latinos today. As we shall see, language was used and continues to be used as a proxy for race/ethnicity and as a tool to exclude immigrant and minority groups, notably during periods of profound demographic change. New immigrants need appropriate policies that will help to integrate them into the US mainstream. The new post-1965 immigration and the growth among the Latino population, in particular, has raised a host of social policy issues and placed new demands on government and its ability to integrate the new Americans who are re-shaping America. This chapter will show how the absence of an official language or national language policy has resulted in various actions taken at various levels of government and civil society, measures that reflect different values and ideas about identity and language rights. This chapter will explore questions of language and bilingualism and their relationship to those goals today and in the past.

Historical Context and National Language Policy

Unlike the Spanish who imposed strict language policies on their colonies in the Americas, the English implemented no such policies on the (White, Anglo-Saxon, Protestant) citizenry as they colonized the US. Although English has effectively been the dominant language since the founding of the 13 colonies, most people would be surprised to learn that English is not the official language in the US. One important question is, why didn't the nation's founders name an official language?

Because language is intimately tied to culture and heritage, it is possible that the early colonists saw native language maintenance and language choice as part of their right to preserve their heritage (Crawford, 1999). However, as shall be presented, there has always been an intimate link between language and power, and throughout US history, language has reflected the relationship between majority and minority groups, as language dominance has been the privilege of the group that holds power. For example, African slaves were forbidden from using their native languages and were punished by their White slave owners if they did. However, they were also forbidden from learning to read and write in English and risked doing so under fear of brutal punishment. Teaching slaves to read and write was considered a crime for both Whites and Blacks. White slave owners clearly recognized that language, education, and emancipation were intimately tied. Denying African slaves their languages and the ability to become literate helped to strengthen white domination and ensure the enslavement of African peoples.

Clearly, the potential for conflict over language existed in the US from its inception. Hechinger (1978) and Ovando (2003) argued that the founders envisioned *a country with a unified history, with unified traditions, and with a common language* (Hechinger, 1978, p. 130). Given the nation's history, it is hard to believe otherwise. As John Jay poignantly wrote in Federalist Paper Number 2: *With equal pleasure I have as often taken notice that Providence has been pleased to give this one connected country to one united people—a people descended from the same ancestors, speaking the same language, professing the same religion, attached to the same principles of government, very similar in their manners and customs.* It would seem that the founders assumed America would be a culturally homogeneous White, Anglo-Saxon, Protestant nation and that they had no reason to make English the official language because all those considered *true Americans* already spoke it (Schildkraut, 2004, p. 11).

In keeping with the views of John Jay, some of the founders felt the designation of a common official language was necessary for the success of the country. John Adams proposed establishing an *English Language Academy* to set standards for English. However, it was debated and subsequently rejected by the Continental Congress because it was believed to be an inappropriate role for government and deemed incompatible with the American freedom of spirit (Heath, 1976). At the time, the Continental Congress published many important official documents in English, French, and German (Perea, 1998b). As Marshall (1986, p. 11) writes, *The founding fathers of our country did not choose to have an official language precisely because they felt language to be a matter of individual choice.* The first bill concerning language the US Congress ever voted on was in 1795. The proposed bill, which was rejected, would have allowed the government to print its laws in both English and German. A second bill to follow later that year mandated that all federal statutes be published in English only. The bill was approved by the Congress and signed by George Washington (Schildkraut, 2004, p. 12).

The historical record indicates that, at the nation's founding, some of the founders felt an official language would compromise the ability to form and sustain a union, whereas others felt an official language was necessary to do so. In spite of, or perhaps because of, this conflict, the nation's founders did not adopt *an official language nor a government-sanctioned body to regulate speech* (Crawford, 1999, p. 22). Arguably, at the time, it is possible that the government somewhat supported multilingualism and the use of languages other than English, as the founders generally promoted a nationalism based on agreement over democratic principles and not language and culture (Crawford, 2000). For example, after the Revolutionary War, the *Articles of the Confederation* were published in English, French, and German (Perea, 1998b). This would support the hypothesis that the founders sought to transcend linguistic differences and build a nation based on principles, and without language as a prerequisite. However, some believe that there was a policy of *official English* from the beginning. Hernandez-Chavez (1995) argues that because the *Declaration of Independence*, the Constitution, and all key US documents are written in English, it is tantamount to an official English policy. He concludes that, therefore, English was clearly meant to be the official language of the new nation, the language of citizenship and of all legislative, judicial, and administrative matters (Hernandez-Chavez, 1995, p. 141). From the perspective that English as the official Language was implied or understood, Hernandez-Chavez may be right. However, although it may, at best, have been implied, official English was not explicitly defined, and therefore, arguably, any implication holds no water.

The question of official English is open to interpretation. That there is no mention of an official language in the US Constitution, in light of the fact that the issue was discussed among the nation's founders, can be interpreted to mean either an implicit tolerance of multilingualism or the absence of such. Did the founding fathers *intend* for there to be an official language? Did they understand official English as implicit, as something obvious that went without saying, or did the founding fathers—who were quite thorough in the design and wording of the documents that are the foundation of the US as a nation—deliberately not include any mention of an official language out of tolerance for multilingualism? Did they intend for language to be a right, a freedom like speech and religion, a personal liberty and matter of individual choice? Did they mean for it to be a state's right? Whatever the reason, in the US, language is not centrally regulated and this was done so on purpose. Indeed, as we have seen, the historical record indicates that the question of official language was discussed by the nation's founders and the institution of an official language was an issue that was not accidentally overlooked.

The historical record explaining the absence of a national language policy has been detailed. In the next section, this chapter will discuss the growth and diversification of the US and present the country's history of enactment of restrictive language policies on conquered peoples. It will discuss how language measures have been enacted in the past and the motives that drove such actions in the absence of an official language.

Expansion, Americanization, and Diversification

The social and cultural contexts of bilingualism are directly related to prevailing social and cultural attitudes towards diversity. Concerns about language diversity would not be an issue today if diversity itself were not. Therefore, understanding the US historical context—how the US came to be the diverse place it is and knowing the mechanisms by which different population groups came to be incorporated into the US—is critical for understanding the social and cultural contexts of bilingualism today (see Table 12.1 for a timeline of important historical events).

The US's expansion westward during the 19th century was driven in large part by the doctrine of *Manifest Destiny*. Manifest Destiny was the 19th-century belief that America was created to be expanded and that the US had a divine mission to expand across the continent of North America towards the Pacific Ocean. The idea, which means obvious or undeniable fate, was never a specific policy. Rather, it was an ideology that combined elements of American nationalism, *expansionism*, and *exceptionalism* (the belief that the nation is exceptional and does not conform to any pattern or norm). The doctrine professed the cultural and racial superiority of White Europeans and often characterized White people as *God's chosen* who were destined and required by divine providence to overcome and *Americanize* uncivilized, non-European peoples, meaning to make them *American* in culture.

During the 1840s, Manifest Destiny was used to justify and advance the US desire to appropriate North America and displace non-European peoples. Westward *expansion* entailed the acquisition of land and the exclusion and oppression of non-European peoples, prompting conflict with Native Americans and the sovereign nation of Mexico. As the US pushed westward, the *Indian Wars* resulted. Native Peoples were displaced as their land was taken by settlers and by military force through forcible *Indian Removal*. *Mexicanos*, *Tejanos*, and *Californios* in what today is the US Southwest were squeezed by settlers and eventually incorporated into the US when their land was annexed by the US after Mexico lost the Mexican–American War.

Language assimilation as part of cultural assimilation was a strategy employed in the conquest of the Americas and the US annexation of land. Arguably, one of the most effective ways to exterminate a people is to destroy their culture by robbing them of their language. In the 1880s, the US government established the notorious Indian boarding schools as part of its explicit federal policy to assimilate Native Peoples into the dominant Anglo-American culture. This essentially called for the extermination of Native American cultures through the forced integration and Anglicization of Native Peoples (Spolsky, 2004, p. 94). The intention of the Indian boarding schools was to replace traditional

Table 12.1 Important Historical Events

1795	US Congress rejects first language bill. Bill would have allowed the government to print all laws in English and German.
	US Congress approves a second language bill that is signed by George Washington. Bill requires all federal statutes to be published in English only.
1846	*Mexican–American War*. Ends with the signing of the Treaty of Guadalupe 1848 Hidalgo.
1879	Carlisle Indian School, first of the *Indian Boarding Schools*, founded in Pennsylvania.
1898	*Spanish–American War*. Puerto Rico becomes a US territory.
1901	*Foraker Act*. Formally establishes the territorial relationship between the US and Puerto Rico.
1902	US declares both English and Spanish as the official languages of Puerto Rico, and imposes English as the language of instruction in Puerto Rican schools.
1909	*Olmstead Act*. Gives the US President a direct role in Puerto Rican affairs.
1916	English language requirement for Puerto Rican schools relaxed to allow for use of Spanish in classroom instruction in lower elementary grades.
1917	*Jones Act* grants Puerto Ricans US citizenship. Puerto Rico officially becomes an unincorporated US territory.
1930	English language requirement for Puerto Rican schools ends.
1952	Puerto Rico becomes a commonwealth.
1991	Spanish becomes the official language in Puerto Rico, and the official language of instruction in Puerto Rican schools.

Native American life-ways, like culture, language, and religion, with life-ways sanctioned by the US government. One of the first, and most notorious, schools established was the Carlisle Indian School in Pennsylvania, founded in 1879 by Captain Richard Henry Pratt, an assimilationist who professed the superiority of White people and the inferiority of Native Peoples. From the 1880s through the 1920s, federal *Indian education* policy called for the forcible removal of Native American children from their families and people and enrollment at a US government-run boarding school. The policy-makers argued that by eliminating exposure to Indian peoples and culture, and by immersion in American *cultural norms* through an American education, the Indians could become *civilized* just like any other (White) American. However, it is doubtful that the oppression of Native Americans was solely an issue of culture. It seems obvious that the oppression of Native Peoples was, and continues to be, as much about race/ethnicity as it was about culture. For example, it is unlikely that the *civilizing* of Native Peoples would ever result in their being perceived or categorized as Americans, a designation that is arguably reserved for Whites only. The fact that Native Americans like other hyphenated Americans are not just *American* makes the point.

Clearly, mastery of English was considered a primary requirement for assimilation into American culture and society. Perhaps the *Commissioner of Indian Affairs*, T. J. Morgan, captures the sentiment of the times and the guiding beliefs underlying the establishment of the boarding schools best when he described English as *the language of the greatest, most powerful and enterprising nationalities beneath the sun* (Marr, n.d.). Clearly, the establishment of the Indian boarding schools was based in part, if not entirely, on the belief that Native American cultures and life-ways, such as their languages, were inferior to those of Whites. In keeping with this attitude, bilingualism, or the maintenance of native languages, was explicitly prohibited at the boarding schools, and children caught *speaking Indian* were harshly punished. Similarly, this is also what a lot of Mexican-Americans/Chicanos reported as they attended public schools in California and throughout the Southwest.

The belief in Manifest Destiny that encouraged the conquest and Americanization of Native Peoples also prompted the Mexican–American War (1846–1848). In 1845, President James Polk announced to the US Congress that the country should strictly enforce the *Monroe Doctrine*[1] and aggressively expand into the West. Mexicans, in what became the US Southwest, were involuntarily incorporated into the US after the Mexican–American War. The two-year war ended with the (controversial and disputed) signing of the *Treaty of Guadalupe Hidalgo*, which necessitated that Mexico sell almost half its land to the US (this includes what today is Texas, New Mexico, Arizona, California, Nevada, Utah, most of Colorado, and some small parts of Kansas, Oklahoma, and Wyoming; Schmidt, 2000, p. 102). Mexicans living in the newly acquired land had, in theory, the *choice* to stay in the US or return to Mexico. Those who *chose* to stay in the US were granted US citizenship. However, in spite of the fact that Mexicans living in the US Southwest were granted citizenship, they were not allowed to vote. Voting rights were denied legally and through restrictive property laws, language and literacy requirements, as well as through widespread intimidation and violence (Ricento, 1995).

As a former Spanish colony, and with a huge indigenous population, the newly American *Mexicanos* were not English speaking. They spoke Spanish and the US chose to incorporate those Spanish-speaking people into the US. Similar to Native Americans, when *Mexicanos* became part of the US, English was imposed as the language of instruction in schools. Children were not allowed to speak Spanish in school. Like Native Americans, language was a primary tool used to try to Americanize Mexicans. Spanish-speaking Mexican children were schooled to behave and act civilized like White Americans, which entailed learning English. As Texas Governor (1915–1927) James Ferguson so eloquently put it (with reference to Spanish being taught in Texas public schools): *If English was good enough for Jesus Christ, it ought to be good enough for the children of Texas* (circa 1924).[2] In spite of US efforts to Americanize Mexican peoples, the impact of Mexican culture on the US, as evident in the Southwest today, was and is profound. As a result of the annexation of this vast Mexican, Spanish-speaking area, the US Southwest was infused with and, to some degree, culturally determined by, its non-White Anglo-Saxon, Protestant, non-English-speaking cultures. To this day, the US Southwest has the highest concentration of Spanish speakers, the highest concentration of non-English speakers, and the highest concentration of Latinos in the US (Mexican-origin people are the largest Latino national group in the US, and comprise two-thirds of the Latino population). In part due to this, the US is one of the largest Spanish-speaking countries in the world.

Similar to much of Mexico, the island of Puerto Rico became a US territory after military conflict, when it was ceded to the US after its victory in the Spanish–American War of 1898. The War ended with the signing of a peace treaty between the US and Spain, under which the US gained control of Puerto Rico. The Foraker Act of 1901 formally established the territorial relationship between Puerto Rico and the US, and many of its provisions still hold to this day. In 1909, the Olmstead Act gave the US President a direct role in Puerto Rican affairs. It wasn't until the Jones Act of 1917 that Puerto Ricans were granted US citizenship and Puerto Rico officially became an unincorporated US territory. In 1952, Puerto Rico became a commonwealth with its own legislature and constitution, granting the island its own internal self-government.

When the US gained control of Puerto Rico, the country was a Spanish-speaking country, as it is today. In 1902, the US declared both English and Spanish the island's official languages and imposed English as the language of instruction in the schools reflecting a consistent policy of incorporation through public school instruction in English. Upon arrival, the US determined that Spanish-language Puerto Rican schools were in need of English language reform, and declared English *the official language of school reform throughout the island* (Crawford, 2000, p. 17). As was the case with Native Americans and Mexicans in the Southwest, language was used as a tool by the government to Americanize Puerto Ricans.

President Theodore Roosevelt firmly believed that immigrants and newly incorporated Americans had to become English speakers and adopt Anglo-American cultural ways to become American. Roosevelt understood that the schools were a powerful tool through which the US colonial mission in Puerto Rico could be carried out and, consequently, was a staunch advocate of English instruction in the schools. In 1937, after 38 years under US control, President Roosevelt appointed a new education commission for the island with the purpose of intensifying English instruction in the schools (Crawford, 2000). Roosevelt found it *regrettable* that *hundreds of thousands of Puerto Ricans have little and often virtually no knowledge of the English language ... Only through the acquisition of this language will Puerto Rican Americans secure a better understanding of American ideals and principles* (Crawford, 2000, p. 18). This statement clearly illustrates the prevailing sentiment at the time that becoming American meant learning English because it was within language, at least in part, that fundamental American principles were located, a model that was different from that of many of the founders who believed American citizenship and identity was a function of shared beliefs in democratic principles and not a common language and culture.

Although the language requirements in Puerto Rican schools were relaxed somewhat in 1916 to allow for use of the native language in classroom instruction in the lower elementary grades, the US imposed English as the language of instruction in the schools until 1930. It wasn't until almost 100 years after the US gained control of the Spanish-speaking island that Spanish once again became the island's official language in 1991. At that time, Spanish became the official language of instruction in the schools.

So what does it mean to be an American, and what did that mean for new peoples to become American? As we have seen, language is a powerful tool and marker of identity, and there is an intimate relationship between power, notions of cultural superiority, and language. As the examples of Native Americans, Mexicans, and Puerto Ricans illustrate, language was used as a tool to incorporate new Americans and Americanize them as the country was forming and expanding. American identity was widely believed to be a function of culture, of which a common language was a fundamental component. Furthermore, becoming American meant acting civilized, meaning like White Americans, which entailed learning English. Hence, English language skills were understood as a requirement for entrance and participation in US society because becoming American necessitated adopting American culture and values which could, perhaps only, be found in language. This meant not just proficiency in English, but rather English monolingualism as a result of cultural coercion and forced sociocultural and linguistic assimilation resulting in loss of the native language. Language assimilation was *piggy-backed* to cultural assimilation, and language policies at various levels of government were enacted to further that belief. The language policies that were adopted functioned effectively as a form of *social engineering*, as the policies were designed to effect conformity, and produce sociocultural homogeneity and linguistic uniformity through assimilation and Anglo-American enculturation, although not necessarily integration (the proposition that integration can result from segregation and exclusion is arguably nonsensical). The prevailing belief was that only through English could American ideals and values be understood. This was a sharp departure from the ideas of some of the founders who believed that American identity was rooted in shared principles and values, and not a common language and culture; and as the 20th century unfolded, these widely held beliefs only became more prominent.

How the US enacted restrictive language policies on conquered peoples has been detailed. In addition to the involuntary incorporation of conquered people, immigration has played an equally important, if not greater role, in making the US into the diverse country it is. In the next section, European immigration at the turn of the 20th century will be presented. As shall be discussed, how Native Peoples, Mexicans, and Puerto Ricans were treated foreshadowed a widespread anti-immigrant backlash and the enactment of various anti-immigration and restrictive language policies.

Immigration and Language Diversity

Since the founding of this country to the present day, views towards diversity, language, and bilingualism among the US population, as reflected in various official and unofficial government policies, have fluctuated and varied. They have moved from being tolerant and accepting to resentful and intolerant. This dynamic has largely been dependent on who—racially/ethnically, culturally, nationally—the speakers of a language were and has been tied to immigration trends. Language has also been closely tied to (actual and perceived) citizenship and immigrant status, which is highly correlated with prevailing notions of American identity. It is a dynamic that historically has been about power and notions of cultural superiority.

In the beginning, bilingualism among Americans and European immigrants was mostly appreciated, and non-English languages were protected and socially and politically encouraged until the late 19th century (Fitzgerald, 1993, p. 37). However, this changed with the increase in immigration in the late 1800s. Germans were one of the first immigrant groups to be the targets of anti-immigrant sentiments in colonial Pennsylvania (Crawford, 2000). At the time, German immigration was high and they were settling in large numbers in Pennsylvania. As the German population grew and adopted a noticeable presence, concerns about English language displacement began to emerge as they began to be perceived as a threat to the sociocultural and political integrity of the country. As none other than Benjamin Franklin remarked: *Unless the stream of their importation could be turned from this to other Colonies ... they will soon so out number us, that all the advantages we have will not in My Opinion be able to preserve our language, and even our Government will become precarious* (*The papers of Benjamin Franklin*, as cited in Crawford, 2000, p. 11). And as he went on to conclude in *Observations Concerning the Increase of Mankind*, Franklin:

> *[W]hy should the Palatine Boors be suffered to swarm into our Settlements, and by herding together, establish their Language and Manners, to the Exclusion of ours? Why should Pennsylvania, founded by the English, become a colony of **Aliens**, who will shortly be so numerous as to Germanize us instead of our Anglifying them, and will never adopt our Language or Customs, any more than they can acquire our Complexion.*

> (as cited in Crawford, 2000, p. 11, emphasis in original)

The hostile and exclusionary tones of these remarks are poignantly obvious. They also foreshadow the *nativist attitudes* (meaning to favor the interests of established inhabitants over those of immigrants) that would come to mark the US in the late 1800s and well into the 20th century. It clearly illustrates the fear that accompanied the increase among one national and linguistic group in particular and exemplifies notions of White, Anglo-Saxon, Protestant cultural superiority. These sentiments have historically greeted whoever has been considered a non-White, Anglo-Saxon, Protestant group, especially as they begin to establish a presence in the US and as a measure by which to exclude their access to resources and power.

The diversity of the US and its ongoing struggle with language issues is evident in past state level language policies. Like education, language policy has primarily been a function of state and local governments and the development and implementation of language policies within their purview. During the 1800s, many states were officially bilingual in the sense that they had a *Statutory or constitutional recognition of languages other than English* (Perea, 1998b, p. 589): Pennsylvania in English and German, California and New Mexico in Spanish and English, and Louisiana in French and English (Perea, 1998b). During that time, there were also movements in Ohio to recognize German as the official language (Spolsky, 2004, p. 94).

When the Louisiana Territory was purchased in 1803, Native Americans and non-English-speaking Europeans, mostly French, became part of the US along with the land. It was a huge territory where English was not the dominant language. As a result, shortly after the purchase all federal laws applicable to the Louisiana Territory were printed in English and French. Interestingly, according to Schildkraut (2004), Louisiana was the first state to declare an English language requirement in 1812 (Schildkraut, 2004, p. 14).[3] However, it was not an English only law, and French continued to be used in state government. Louisiana's 1845 Constitution guaranteed a bilingual legislature (Crawford, 2000, p. 13). However, the republican constitutions imposed by Union troops after the Civil War in 1864 and 1868 terminated French language rights as punishment for their support of the Confederacy (Crawford, 2000). But this was reversed about a decade later at the end of Reconstruction, when the Constitution of 1879 restored the legal status of French, although to a lesser degree than before, which remained in effect until 1921 (Crawford, 2000). With the exception of Louisiana, however, there was little state level action on the issue of language until 1920, when Nebraska amended its constitution and made English the official language (Schildkraut, 2004, p. 14).

The early examples of state level efforts to *deal with* the issue of language diversity foreshadowed the problems that were looming on the horizon as immigration began to increase in the late 1800s. The 19th and early 20th century saw high numbers of immigrants, primarily from Europe, arrive in the US during the great wave of European immigration between 1880 and 1920. However, during this peak in immigration, immigrants shifted from northern European to primarily southern and eastern European origin. Unlike Native Americans, Mexicans, Puerto Ricans, and African origin peoples, in the beginning, European immigrants were shown more tolerance with regard to native language use. The difference in treatment was tied to sociocultural perceptions of who belongs, who can be *American*, and who is defined as *Other* by mainstream US society, as determined by different points of origin as manifest in non-northern European racial/ethnic phenotological features and cultural characteristics. It is this designation as Other which resulted in different racial/ethnic, cultural, and national groups receiving different treatment with regard to native language use. The case of bilingual education helps to illustrate this point.

Until the late 1800s, bilingual education among European immigrants was fairly common, as was school instruction solely in the native language. For example, Germans set up schools where instruction was both in German, as well as bilingual in both English and German (Crawford, 1999; Fitzgerald, 1993; Hakuta, 1986). In 1839, Ohio became the first of many states to allow bilingual German–English instruction. A few years later in 1847

Louisiana passed a law allowing bilingual instruction in public schools (Crawford, 2000). The practice was followed by other immigrant groups—Italians and Greeks, among others—who also incorporated instruction in their native languages in their schools, with and without state authorization (Crawford, 2000).

Although bilingual instruction was prevalent, once non-English speakers began to grow in numbers and have a noticeable presence, language became an issue of concern. When non-northern European immigration peaked, efforts to restrict native language use and institute English only laws emerged across the country. Not coincidentally, support for native language instruction in the schools plummeted with the increase in the number of immigrants. Beginning in the 1880s, some states passed laws preventing instruction in any language other than English, particularly German. With increased immigration and the emergence of anti-German sentiments during and after World War I, paranoia and *xenophobia* (fear of foreigners and what is perceived as foreign) swept the nation along with a strong sense of patriotism. Coupled with a national desire to do away with any allegiance to a foreign state, there was a new emphasis placed on learning English and doing away with foreign languages. Theodore Roosevelt (US President 1901–1909) believed that English was an integral part of what it meant to be an American, and if immigrants spoke a foreign language that that they would be divided in loyalty. He proposed setting up schools for immigrants and sending them back to their native country if, in five years, they had not learned English (Spolsky, 2004). Thirty states passed laws mandating that persons who could not speak English had to attend evening school (Spolsky, 2004, p. 95). By 1923, 34 states had banned native language instruction and made English the only language of instruction in the public schools and in some cases private schools as well. However, in 1923, the Supreme Court ruled in *Meyer vs. Nebraska* that state laws banning native language instruction in school violated the due process clause and found such laws unconstitutional. It was the first case regarding language rights ever heard by the Supreme Court. However, the damage had been done, and the xenophobia of the 1920s was already firmly entrenched. Perhaps Theodore Roosevelt captured the prevailing attitude of the times best when he declared: *There can be no divided allegiance here … We have room for but one language here, and that is the English language, and we intend to see that the crucible turns our people out as Americans* (Theodore Roosevelt, in a letter to the president of the American Defense Society, Jan. 3, 1919).

The paranoia and xenophobia that consumed the US during the early part of the 20th century emerged during a period of high immigration from countries that until that point had not traditionally been the sources of new immigrants to the states. They were not Anglo-Saxon or Protestant and, at the time, those from southern and eastern Europe were not even considered white. These *new immigrants* did not come from northern Europe and did not have northern European cultural traditions. They were different, and fear of differences as a threat to the dominant culture and way of life is what drove the country to implement anti-immigrant policies and the restrictive language policies that came along with them. In fact, it was through language policies that anti-immigrant policies were put into effect and efforts to exclude immigrants and disenfranchise *non-American* ethnic/ racial and cultural groups were implemented.

The presence of racial/ethnic, cultural, and linguistic minorities, and the increase of languages other than English, came to be regarded as a danger to the wellbeing of the nation. Consequently, English language requirements for naturalization were enacted with The *Nationality Act* of 1906, which required immigrants to speak English in order to be naturalized as citizens. It was the first piece of federal legislation imposing any kind of language requirement on residents or prospective citizens. It remains in effect today.

The policy was intended to *Improve the 'quality' of naturalized citizens* (Perea, 1998a, p. 568). As the Commissioner of Naturalization in 1905 poignantly articulated the widespread view: *The proposition is incontrovertible that no man is a desirable citizen of the United States who does not know the English language* (as cited in Perea, 1998a, p. 568). The purpose of the language requirement was to exclude the number of people whose cultures and ethnicities differed from the White American mainstream cultural majority and demonstrates how language was used as a proxy for race/ethnicity and culture with the purpose of excluding immigrants based on national origin. It is a policy of tremendous symbolic importance. The policy demonstrates a culturally specific federal policy that equates the English language with being American, as it is through the naturalization process and applicable laws that the criteria for admission to American society are established (Perea, 1998a).

During the early 20th century, the prevailing belief was not only that bilingualism was of no social value, but that non-English languages were socially damaging, encouraged separatism, were indicative of allegiance to a foreign state, and even came to be associated with low intelligence and a lack of patriotism (Fitzgerald, 1993; Hakuta, 1986; Spolsky, 2004). Historically, *hereditarian* views of bilingualism and bilinguals (an advance of the theory that individual differences among people can be primarily explained by genetics) were rooted in a deficit-model of the genetic and cultural inferiority of bilingual people and non-English speakers. Bilingualism was thought to be the cause of low intelligence as it was thought to result from low intelligence—*a catch 22*. Notably, this prevailing idea was popular among scientists, elected officials, and the public during a period of high immigration from non-Western European countries (Hakuta, 1986).

These widely held beliefs were driven by the fear of the times. Between 1910 and 1950, more than 1,000 people were incarcerated for *subversive speech*, and thousands of cases were brought to trial citing use of a non-English language as a *clear and present danger* (Fitzgerald, 1993, p. 39; Trueba, 1989). The US had entered a heightened period of isolationism and xenophobia, and immigrants and those not of northern European ancestry were going to bear the brunt. It was one example of one of many periods in US history when culture, race/ethnicity, and language were collectively used to disenfranchise and exclude large numbers of people from the American mainstream or prevent them from entering the US at all. It demonstrates how language was a convenient symbol under which racial, ethnic, and cultural discrimination could be carried out.

With anti-immigrant attitudes peaking, *immigrant quotas* were adopted in the 1920s. Because mass immigration resumed after World War I, the US government adopted the national origins quota system. The immigration acts of 1921 and 1924 limited immigration by assigning each nationality a quota. The goal of the policy was not just to increase the number of immigrants, but to give priority to Northern European immigrants who were believed to be more *suitable* and easier to assimilate (Spolsky, 2004, p. 102). The quotas had the desired effect of stemming the flow of immigrants and the number of non-English-speaking people to the US. In 1952, the *Immigration and Nationality Act* (INA) brought under one comprehensive statute all the multiple laws which had governed immigration and naturalization until that point. Although it perpetuated the already existing immigration statutes and did not abolish the quota system, it did, among other important modifications, eliminate race as a bar to immigration and naturalization. The changes can be called progressive because they lifted racial barriers to immigration and eliminated blatant race-based criteria for admission to the US. However, such progress was limited as the changes left, intentionally or not, cultural/ethnic barriers in place by not lifting the national origin quotas. Such policies appear as racially neutral; however, culture and ethnicity have historically functioned as proxies for race. Thus, in practice, leaving the quotas in place had the effect of a race-based policy without being racist on its face.

But monumental sociopolitical changes were on the horizon. The *Civil Rights Movement* brought racial and social justice issues to the fore during the 1960s. During the struggle for social change, the INA was amended in 1965, and the national origins quota system repealed. The changes to the INA marked a shift within the federal government and the attitudes of the nation as a whole. The changes illustrate the power of political will when driven by profound and widespread sociocultural change and public demands to correct historic and deeply entrenched injustices and protect minority rights. This change was the most extensive revision of immigration policy since the 1920s. Most importantly, it replaced the quota system with a system based primarily on family reunification and the intent of attracting immigrants with needed skills to the US. It is a system that exists to this day and which, in part, opened the door for the massive demographic changes taking place in the US today—changes which, decades later, would bring language issues to the forefront of public discourse and result in efforts to implement the same kinds of restrictive language policies witnessed in the past.

In the proceeding sections, immigration since 1965 will be discussed. In particular, the demographic changes taking place in the US at the turn of the 21st century, notably the growth among the language minority population will be presented. Because immigration from Latin America has exerted profound influence on US population change, a case study of the Latino population in the US will be presented. The large and steadily growing Latino population presents numerous important policy issues, among them questions about language and bilingualism. The pros and cons of Spanish–English bilingualism and English or Spanish monolingualism will be presented. Increased immigration, specifically growth among the Latino population, has triggered anti-Latino immigrant fears similar to those that accompanied European immigration in the past. These issues will be discussed in the proceeding sections as well.

The Post-1965 Immigration

The dramatic demographic changes unfolding in the US today are a defining issue of the present day as population changes impact every US social, political, and economic institution. There has been an explosion in the immigrant population since the 1960s, but especially since the 1980s.

Population Change in the US Today

In 2010, the *American Community Survey* (ACS) of the US Census identified 39,955,854 immigrants living in the US. During the 2000s, the immigration population gained 22.5 million people (legal, illegal, and by birth; Camarota, 2012). The number of immigrants currently living in the US is unprecedented. According to the *Migration Policy Institute* (MPI) statistics, immigrants accounted for 13% of the total population—the highest percentage since 1920. During the early 20th century, the number of immigrants living in the US was only less than half of what it is today (13.5 million in 1910; Camarota, 2002). The 1990s in particular were marked by a dramatic rise in immigration after a growth of 40% in the foreign-born population during the 1980s alone. Over 13 million people entered the US during the decade—more than a million people per year (Capps, Fix, & Passel, 2002). During the 1990s the foreign-born population increased by more than 50%, from 7.9% in 1990 to 11.1% in 2000, to 28% in 2010 (Camarota, 2012, p. 13). From the 40 million immigrants, 9 million came to US in 2000 or later. This is a ratio of 1.3 to 1.4 million per year during the 2000s. For 2050, estimations are that one in five Americans (19%) will be foreign born and 53% of the total population will be identified as Hispanic, Black, or Asian (Passel & Cohn, 2008). The total growth will be of 129%.

The recent population changes in the US have been driven by the increase in immigration from Latin America and, to a lesser degree, from Asia, as well as high birth rates among Latinos. In fact, immigration from Latin America has stalled and has been outpaced by growth of US-born Latinos (Krogstad & Lopez, 2014). In 2013 the Hispanic population was 54 million and the Asian population was 19.4 million. This represents a growth of 2.1% and 2.9%, respectively, in comparison with 2012 (Krogstad & Lopez, 2014). Remarkably, in 1980 Latinos and Asians together accounted for only 8% of the US population (Kolankiewicz, 2000). Demographic projections predict that over the course of the next 50 years, the racial/ethnic, cultural, and linguistic diversity of the country will continue to expand significantly. The current majority white population is growing more slowly than that of the other major racial and ethnic groups and by mid-century is expected to cease to be the majority and continue to shrink after 2100. It is projected that the US will be a majority-minority nation for the first time in 2043 (US Census, 2012). The minority population in the US is projected to increase from 37% in 2012 to 57% in 2060. But the non-Hispanic white population will remain the biggest group when counted separately (US Census, 2012).

Immigration is a critical factor in US population change, as overall population growth across the US in the 1990s was largely driven by an increase in the foreign-born population and a relative decrease in the growth of the native population. Interestingly in 2010, the immigrant population in the South experienced the most rapid growth. Immigrants today are settling in large numbers in states that historically have not attracted large numbers of immigrants. In addition to traditional gateway states, like California, Texas, New York, and Florida, which have historically attracted immigrants, immigrants are settling in areas of the country that do not have a history of receiving large numbers of immigrants.

Immigration has increased the most in non-traditional immigrant states and has grown there by a higher percentage than in states like New York and Florida. For example, during the 2000s Alabama saw an increase of 92.1% in the foreign-born population, South Carolina 84.4%, and Tennessee 81.8% (Camarota, 2012), whereas New York's foreign-born population increased by 11.1% and Florida by 37%. Nevertheless, more than half of the foreign-born population lived in California, New York, Texas, and Florida in 2010 (Camarota, 2012).

These new and dynamic immigration patterns raise critical questions about how to best integrate new immigrants and puts a new spin on key policy issues, such as language policy, as states that were more or less predominantly White non-Latino, or culturally, racially/ethnically static, if not homogeneous, for decades are becoming more diverse. As of 2010, there were four majority-minority states: California, New Mexico, Texas, and Hawaii (which has never had a white majority). The District of Columbia is also a majority-minority area. In fact, seven of the 15 most populated cities in the US were majority-minority in 2012, including Los Angeles, San Diego, and New York (Czekalinski & Nhan, 2012). In addition, currently 14 states have a child population 5 years or younger that is majority-minority. For example, in Hawaii only 15.2% of children between 0–5 years are white, followed by New Mexico and California with 24.9% and 25.1%, respectively (Frey, 2013). This is the context upon which attitudes and policies about bilingualism are projected and presently enacted. The implications are that issues that were once the concern of a certain few states are now of national concern. Such is the case with language policy as increased immigration has resulted in tremendous growth among language minorities.

Growth Among Language Minorities

Greater language diversity has accompanied increased immigration, which has caused growth among language minority groups and the presence of languages other than English in the US. Whereas the US population age five and above grew 37.6% between 1980 and 2010, the number who spoke a language other than English grew 158.2% (Ryan, 2013).

According to the 2011 ACS, 60.6 million people aged five or older (21% of the general population) speaks a language other than English at home. This figure increased from 13.8% in 1990 and 11% in 1980. There are approximately 381 languages spoken in the US, according to the US Census Bureau.

The US is also home to a sizable bilingual population, which has been increasing along with immigration. The US Census Bureau reports that, of the number of people who reported speaking a language other than English on the 2010 census, 79% spoke English well or very well and 21% spoke English *less than well*. Of the approximately 61 million people who spoke a language other than English in 2011, 42% spoke English less than very well. However, the proportion of people who speak English less than very well has steadily grown from 4.8% in 1980, to 6.1% in 1990, to 8.1% in 2000, to 8.7% in 2011.

The US is clearly not a monolingual country, and one could reasonably expect the number of bilinguals and multilinguals will continue to grow far into the future. Language diversity in the US is so great that the 2010 Census questionnaire used six languages, English, Spanish, Korean, Mandarin Chinese, Vietnamese, and Tagalog, in addition to 59 language assistance guides (which provide in-language translations of the English questionnaire and explain how to complete the census questionnaire in English).

The new immigration to the US is different from previous waves of immigration because it is part of a global trend and is not solely a US phenomenon. *Globalization* has led to the large-scale migration of people on a global scale, which is driving US population change as well as demographic changes around the world, notably in Europe. People are migrating primarily for economic reasons and are moving from rural areas and developing countries to cities and developed countries on a scale like never before. Because the US is in such close proximity to so many Latin American countries, and because of the political and economic relationship between the US and Latin America, the new immigration is primarily from within the hemisphere. Latin American immigration has had, is having, and will continue to have a tremendous sociocultural impact on the US, and Latinos are shaping the future of the nation.

Latin American Immigration

Immigration from Latin America and the consequent growth of the Latino population has had a profound impact on the US population. In 2000, Latinos became the largest minority group in the US, and in 2012 comprised 16.9% of the total population, up from 12.5% in 2000. According to the Pew Research Center, the Latino population has increased by sixfold since 1970. The population of 53 million people in 2010 is projected to increase to 129 million by 2060, which would make it 31% of the US population—making the US effectively 33% Latino. Latinos are and will remain the largest ethnic, linguistic, and minority group in the US well into the future.

There has been a nativity shift, however, and since 2000, the primary source of growth of the Latino population has changed from immigration to native births (Krogstad & López, 2014). Since 2000, US births accounted for 60% of Latino population growth (Krogstad & López, 2014). This underscores the important fact that not all Latinos are immigrants—the majority are not. In 2012, 35.5% of all Latinos were born abroad, down from 40% earlier in the 2000s (Krogstad & López, 2014).

Latinos have lived within the borders of the US since before its inception. To refer to all Latinos as immigrants is simply inaccurate. In particular, many Mexican-origin peoples in the Southwest and California are not immigrants; they are US citizens by birth and the descendants of people who lived within the borders of the US since before the nation existed. Furthermore, migrant laborers today, the majority of whom are Mexican, are following migratory lines that have existed for generations and which transcend political borders.

Puerto Ricans are not immigrants either. Puerto Rico is a US territory and Puerto Ricans are US citizens. Immigrants are people who leave one country to settle permanently in another, whereas migrants are people who move from one place to another to find work or better living conditions, or who move back and forth between regions or countries for economic reasons, such as Latin American migrant laborers who work in agriculture. Although there are varying perspectives in the scholarly literature, it is the position of the authors that, because Puerto Ricans who leave the island of Puerto Rico to live in the continental US are moving within the US and its territories, they are migrants, not immigrants.

Nevertheless, the increase among recent Latino immigrants has created new pressures, since more than three-quarters speak Spanish (but not all Latinos speak Spanish; see sections below). The US has a huge Spanish-speaking population, and Spanish is the most spoken language in the US after English. It is expected that, in 2020, the US will have between 39 and 43 million people that speak Spanish (Ortman & Shin, 2011).

The influence of the Spanish language in the Americas and its impact on the US cannot be underestimated. President Thomas Jefferson, who spoke five languages, offered some advice in the 18th century that is highly relevant today: *Spanish. Bestow great attention on this and endeavor to acquire an accurate knowledge of it. Our future connections with Spain and Spanish America will render that language a valuable acquisition. The ancient history of a great part of America, too, is written in that language* (Thomas Jefferson, in a letter to Peter Carr, Paris, Aug. 10, 1787). More than 200 years later, Spanish is the most widely spoken language in the US after English, and the US is the second largest Spanish-speaking country in the world; Mexico is the largest.

As the US Latino population has grown, the debate surrounding bilingualism has become more intense. For a country with high levels of immigration, it is questionable if assimilationist language policies are appropriate and effective for integrating such a large percentage of the population that primarily speaks one language—namely, Spanish. High immigration and the fluid, transnational dynamics it has created have cast doubt on the efficacy of political borders and have arguably made their relevance questionable. People are blending, moving back and forth, in many ways, resulting in an arbitrary and ambiguous borderland—neither here nor there, but both, or as it is nicely put in Spanish, *ni (de) aquí, ni (de) allá.* Such is the case in the US Southwest.

Romaine (2004) argues that the diversity and linguistic realities of the US reflect changing political boundaries. As a result of various historical factors, many bilinguals have become concentrated in regions where use of a language other than the dominant language is the norm (Romaine, 2004). In the US, the annexation of land necessitated the enclosure of various cultural, ethnic/racial, and linguistic groups within the country's borders.

The resulting dynamic of, for example, a high concentration of Spanish speakers within a large swathe of geographic area, illustrates the societal and sometimes legal imposition of the dominant language on those groups, and the efficacy, if not the legitimacy, of the forced incorporation of peoples through assimilationist tactics. In an area where a political border was drawn through a national and linguistic group, it logically follows that such a border area will be linguistically diverse (Romaine, 2004, p. 390). Such is the case with Mexican-origin peoples in the Southwest, Puerto Ricans on the island of Puerto Rico, and to a lesser degree, Native Americans.

Nevertheless, whatever the causes are, the fact remains that the US has a large and steadily growing Spanish-speaking Latino population. How to best integrate the population into the US mainstream and promote their social, economic, and political participation—not segregation or exclusion—is a fundamental concern for policy-makers, elected officials, researchers, the business community, and the general population.

Bilingualism and the Social and Cultural Integration of Latinos

The noticeable growth among Latin American immigrants has raised concerns about their ability to acculturate, enter the US mainstream, and become American. This understandably has raised questions about the ability of these new immigrants to learn English, which is without question the dominant language of the country and is essentially required to *make it* in the US—but this should not be taken to mean that learning English should come at the expense of losing the native language, and that English monolingualism is what is required to make it.

Linguists have documented the steady linguistic assimilation of immigrants. Most agree that by the third generation, the native language is lost, as the second and then third generations experience a *language shift* and become English monolinguals (Hakuta, 1986; Rodriguez, 2001). However, whether this pattern holds for current immigrants is a subject of debate. Unlike previous waves of immigration, there is a huge Latino migrant population today that moves back and forth between the US, and primarily, Mexico. For this migratory group, there are clear incentives to learn English, but there are also clear incentives to maintain the native language. Therefore, for this sub-population, this migratory dynamic could possibly result in subsequent generations not experiencing a language shift to English dominance or monolingualism as rapidly.

There are difficulties in measuring the rate at which today's Latino immigrants acquire English language skills and the rate at which subsequent generations become fluent English speakers or English monolinguals. Measurement may be complicated by there being a fairly steady stream of Spanish-speaking immigrants entering the US that replenishes new immigrant and Latino ethnic communities. New immigrants could possibly mask the number of persons attaining English proficiency in a particular community or in the Latino population in general, making it appear as if there are fewer individuals learning English than there actually are. However, the steady and high presence of Spanish speakers in Latino communities presents an incentive to maintain the native language, which could possibly negatively impact the need to learn English if it is not necessary for life and survival. This raises issues of residential segregation and other complex social inequities beyond the scope of this chapter. The important point is that racial/ethnic, immigrant, linguistic, and other minority communities come together as a result of numerous interrelated historical, economic, political, and sociocultural factors. The problems that accompany segregated minority communities are not a function of the concentration of racial minority groups or ethnic enclaves. It is not Blackness any more than it is the Spanish language, but housing discrimination, racism, oppression, socioeconomic marginalization, and a system of *de facto* segregation that is at the root of our most pervasive social problems and which are deeply entrenched in a vicious cycle of social reproduction (García Coll et al., 1996).

Nevertheless, research suggests that Spanish-speaking immigrants today are learning English as quickly as earlier European immigrants (Rodriguez, 2001). Current research is confirming what linguists have argued for decades: the first generation is monolingual, the second bilingual, and the third, if they haven't become English monolinguals, prefer to speak English. Some scholars have even suggested that the speed of Anglo-American assimilation and shift to English language dominance among immigrants is increasing and quickly approaching a two-generation pattern, particularly among Spanish speakers (Crawford, 2000; Rodriguez, 2001). This finding would indicate that while the number of people who speak a language other than English is increasing, linguistic assimilation is on the rise, as well.

The incentives to learn English are many, and the evidence suggests that they work. It is doubtful that making English the official language would increase the incentive to learn English (Schildkraut, 2004). In their study of second-generation immigrant children in Florida and California, Portes and Rumbaut (2001) found evidence of the same pattern of linguistic assimilation and language shift that the evidence from linguistics suggests. Portes and Rumbaut found that the children of immigrants learn English quickly; they come to prefer it to their native language and soon lose fluency in their native language. They found that preference for English was stronger among children born in the US than among those who immigrated to the US with their parents. They also found that the generational language shift, one component of the process of *acculturation* (the form of cultural transmission experienced by individuals and groups that results from contact with, and influence from, institutions and people that are of a different culture than their own, which leads them to incorporate certain culturally specific and appropriate behaviors into their repertoires; Berry, Poortinga, Segall, & Dasen, 2002, p. 21), can lead to tension and conflict within families. It would seem important to assure that those people who become English-speaking monolinguals do not develop negative attitudes towards bilinguals or Spanish speakers.

Globalization and the advent of the internet have also brought about the global dominance of English. Coupled with the dominance of English in the US, the world's only current superpower, English has become the world's common international language. English is the language of the internet, our global economy, business, technology, and politics. There are overwhelming social and economic incentives, if not a fundamental need, for Spanish-speaking Latino immigrants to learn English to make it in the US, as well as the world—no one person knows the value of English more than someone who does not speak it. Spanish-speaking Latino immigrants face the challenge of learning English in order to make it, a reality that is intensified by the demands of our globalized economy in our technology-driven information age.

Just as there is a need to learn English, there are clear reasons to learn a second language and become bilingual. In an era of globalization and increased immigration, the value of multilingualism goes without saying. The ability to effectively communicate cannot be overstated, and the more languages a person speaks, the more people a person is able to communicate with. The job market advantages of being able to communicate in more than one language are obvious. For these reasons, it would seem in the best interest of the nation to build on the strengths and abilities of its new immigrants and for the government to adopt policies that promote bilingualism as an asset.

Although bilingualism is an asset, there is a stigma associated with being bilingual in the US, which is widely perceived as a transitional period leading up to full (cultural and linguistic) assimilation into English monolingualism (Hakuta, 1986, p. 7). In addition, bilingualism and limited English language skills are frequently associated with low socio-economic status, poor levels of educational attainment, and undocumented immigrant status (Hakuta, 1986, p. 7). For these reasons, bilinguals are widely perceived as possessing both a linguistic and cultural handicap, instead of a skill. The impact of these attitudes is exacerbated for Spanish speakers, who also grapple with the social stigma associated with the Spanish language in and of itself, as well as pervasive racism. There are cultural, social, and political values attached to certain languages, such as English, and not to others, notably Spanish. Although there is little to no evidence of support or enthusiasm for languages other than English in the US, there is a clear negative association, a stigma, with Spanish and those who speak it.

There is no evidence to suggest that bilingualism or language accommodations slow the acquisition of English language skills or promote cultural and ethnic fragmentation, only anecdotes that have no scientific value. Nevertheless, as we shall see, advocates of restrictive language policies claim that bilingualism and the use of a language other than English encourages cultural and ethnic separatism and discourages assimilation into the US mainstream. These are claims that have been made throughout US history and have gained new strength in recent years, as evidenced by the highly charged and polarized 2016 Presidential election, where, for example, Spanish speakers or speakers of languages other than English, were widely portrayed as a threat to national security. Current fears about a linguistic and cultural takeover by Spanish-speaking Latinos are coupled with a *nativist* and racist stance that echoes the xenophobic attitudes and beliefs of cultural superiority heard in the past.

Latinos, Language, and Fear

As the impact of the new immigration on US society became clear, anti-immigrant sentiments and negative attitudes toward certain ethnic and national groups re-emerged with newfound strength in the 1980s, with a particular focus on Latinos and Latin Americans. The English only/language restriction movement was an outgrowth of the anti-immigration movement at the end of the 20th century, appealing to similar attitudes and with similar followers. It is worth noting that the anti-immigration movement has the support of eugenicists and white supremacist organizations

Although language had been an issue in the past, it was not until the 1980s that the notion English was endangered and therefore in need of legal protection, surfaced (Crawford, 2000). The English only movement emerged from a fear that English is threatened because its dominance is being challenged by the growth of other languages, particularly Spanish, as embodied by the increased presence of other, non-White, non-American, Spanish-speaking Latinos. The movement seeks to defend what is wrongly perceived as a nation-wide cultural shift to other foreign languages and to Spanish, in particular. The notion of a linguistic threat and looming linguistic displacement is the product of a perceived cultural threat that has the potential to displace the dominant culture unless *something is done*. Proponents of restrictive language laws believe that the Spanish language (and high immigration from Latin America) threatens the sociocultural and political integrity of the US.

Bilingualism and concerns about language are issues that are closely tied to the Latino population. While the debate over bilingualism and language policy does not pertain only to Latinos, the sheer size of the population in the US makes it very much a Latino issue. The impact of what is frequently labeled as a Latino population explosion, can be seen everywhere. Arguably, the definition of American is changing, as aspects of Latino and Latin American cultures are being incorporated into what is popularly thought of as *American culture*, just as aspects of Italian, German, French, and Irish culture were incorporated in the past. The fact that Latin American and Latino cultures are having such a profound impact is unsettling to many Americans. Unfortunately, this change has resulted in the widespread misconception that Latinos are *taking over*, a view that has largely been driven and inflated by fear of a Latino cultural and linguistic invasion or *Hispanophobia*. This tension has resulted in a conflict between groups; what has sometimes been called a *culture war*. Perhaps Harvard University Professor Samuel Huntington, in his essay *The Hispanic Challenge* (2004, p. 1), sums it up best:

> *The persistent inflow of Hispanic immigrants threatens to divide the United States into two peoples, two cultures and two languages. Unlike past immigrant groups, Mexicans and other Latinos have not assimilated into mainstream US culture, forming instead their own political and linguistic enclaves ... and rejecting the Anglo-Protestant values that built the American dream. The United States ignores this challenge at its peril.*

That concerns about language policy and bilingualism are popularly associated with Latinos and the Spanish language goes without saying. Furthermore, there is a clear negative association with Spanish in the US, as the language is popularly associated with poverty, crime, and illegal status. These are *stereotypes* that exist parallel to stereotypes about Latinos and are evidenced by the way the language issue is framed as an English/American/US citizen versus Spanish/Latino (undocumented) immigrant issue, and polarized as an *Us-versus-Them* problem (see Vega, this volume). Additionally, there is a prevalent misconception in the US that English is *competing* with Spanish. There is no language in the US today that is as widely spoken as English or which has the potential to replace English as the dominant language in the future, and there is no evidence to support those assertions. Although Spanish is the most widely spoken language in the US after English, contrary to some beliefs, the Spanish language does not have the potential to overtake English as the dominant language. This widespread fear of the *Latinization* of America, or the Mexicanization of California or the Southwest (see for example, Victor Davis Hanson, 2003), and the perceived cultural threat from the Spanish language reflects the xenophobic and nativist attitudes that have fueled and continue to fuel the English only movement. John Tanton, co-founder of US English (see section *English only movement and English only laws* in this chapter*)*, perhaps captured this attitude best:

> *In this society, will the present majority peaceably hand over its political power to a group that is simply more fertile? Can 'homo contraceptives' compete with 'horno progenitivo' if our borders aren't controlled? ... Perhaps this is the first instance in which those with their pants up are going to be caught by those with their pants down. As whites see their power and control over their lives declining, will they simply go quietly into the night? Or will there be an explosion? ... We're building in a deadly disunity.*

This was from an official, although private, memo Tanton wrote to other members of US English in 1988. Its racist and vulgar tones are obvious and help to draw the connection between the anti-immigration and restrictive language movements. Not surprisingly, when the internal memo was acquired by the media and made public, Tanton promptly stepped down in 1988.

The attitudinal shift towards immigrants, Latinos, and language minorities that emerged in the late 20th century reflects a stark change from the socially progressive attitudes of the 1960s and the early 1970s that sought to empower minorities. Current attitudes towards Latino immigrants and the Spanish language mirror the same concerns about *divided allegiance* expressed by Theodore Roosevelt and echo the nativist and racist thoughts of Benjamin Franklin. It is for these reasons that the progress made during the Civil Rights Era is especially important in an age when, as we shall see, the rights of language minorities are being threatened and slowly chipped away. Thus, in order to contextualize current efforts to curb language minority rights and understand the impact of restrictive language laws and policies today, it is important to know the rights and protections the federal government offers (and once offered) linguistic minorities. In the following sections, measures taken during the Civil Rights Era to protect the rights of linguistic minorities will be presented, and current language policies and measures to socioculturally integrate language minorities into the US mainstream, will be discussed.

Federal Recognition and Protection of Language Minority Rights

During the 1960s and into the 1970s, monumental social and political achievements were reached to protect the rights of oppressed groups. It was during this period that the US government recognized the civil rights of language minorities and took critical steps to protect those rights (see Table 12.2). Two of the most notable, and controversial, were in the field of education, and another was in the area of voting rights.

The Bilingual Education Act

The *Bilingual Education Act* (BEA) expired in 2002. Although it is no longer in effect, it is an important milestone in federal language legislation. In its absence, it helps to illustrate the impact of recent actions impacting language minorities today.

In 1968, Congress passed the BEA, or *Title VII* of the *Elementary and Secondary Education Act* (ESEA), and the issue has been controversial ever since. Title VII is a legacy of the Great Society initiatives of President Lyndon Johnson, which sought to provide equal economic and educational opportunities for oppressed groups—civil rights issues that were brought to the forefront of US popular discourse during the Civil Rights Movement of the 1960s and which gave rise to the Great Society. From its inception, bilingual education has been about rights: *From the outset, then, bilingual education was justified as a means of promoting greater educational success, which, in turn, would lead to greater social mobility and therefore greater social equality for language minority children and their communities* (Schmidt, 2000, p. 131). Title VII provided educational support to poor children who were considered *educationally disadvantaged because of their inability to speak English* (Crawford, 1992, p. 32). Title VII was designed to overcome language barriers and give language minority students equal educational opportunities.

The BEA provided financial incentives for school districts to implement bilingual education. Because it only funded bilingual education, the BEA identified native language instruction as the preferred approach for educating language minority students. The BEA highlighted the importance of native language instruction as a means of giving voice and access to a largely ignored population of students. The BEA emphasized students'

Table 12.2 Federal Protection of Language Minorities since the 1960s and 1970s

1968	The Bilingual Education Act becomes law
1974	*Lau vs. Nichols* decided by the US Supreme Court
1975	The 1965 Voting Rights Act amended with Section 203 (a temporary provision that must be reauthorized by Congress; last reauthorization was in 2006 for 25 years)
2002	Bilingual Education Act Expired

educational and civil rights to learn content knowledge in their native language and was not focused solely on learning English, thus advocating the use of bilingual education. However, the BEA did not specify a program/instructional approach, mandate bilingual education, or specify a method for the education of language minority students, which has allowed for various interpretations of what constitutes *bilingual education* and contributed to much of the current confusion surrounding bilingual education today.

Lau vs. Nichols

The US Supreme Court has been central in advancing the rights of language minority students outlined in Title VII. In *Lau vs. Nichols* in 1974, parents of non-English-speaking Chinese children sued the San Francisco schools. They argued that their children could not access general education instruction because of the language barrier and were not receiving any special instruction and therefore were denied equal opportunities to learn. It was the second case the Court had heard regarding language rights. In this case, the Supreme Court ruled that school districts were required to provide non-English-speaking students with equal educational opportunities, and that the San Francisco school district had failed to do so. It held that the 1964 *Civil Rights Act* meant that the failure of the school district to provide non-English speakers with instruction in a language they can understand discriminated on the basis of race and national origin, as language minority students were not receiving equal benefits as the English-speaking students and were, consequently, denied a meaningful opportunity to participate in school. The *Lau* decision set major legal precedent on language rights as inextricably linked to civil rights by mandating that the government provide adequate language accommodations. As stated in the majority ruling:

> *There is no equality of treatment merely by providing students with the same facilities, textbooks, teachers, and curriculum; for students who do not understand English are effectively foreclosed from any meaningful education. Basic English skills are at the very core of what these public schools teach, imposition of a requirement that, before a child can effectively participate in the educational program, he must already have acquired those basic skills is to make a mockery of public education. We know that those who do not understand English are certain to find their classroom experiences wholly incomprehensible and in no way meaningful.*
>
> (*Lau vs. Nichols*, 1974)

The Court ruled that schools must provide language minority students with some sort of *affirmative steps to rectify the language deficiency in order to open its instructional program to these students*. The ruling made explicit that children have a right to learn in a language they can understand and obligated school districts to provide meaningful education to students in that language. However, like the BEA, the ruling did not mandate bilingual education, require or state a preference for one educational method or instructional technique over another, and did not specify how the assistance was to be implemented, leaving this important decision to the states and individual school districts, hence the various programs and practices found under bilingual education today. This is reflected in the continued debate about whether bilingual education is intended to provide transitional support or produce individuals who are bilingual, a debate which is as old as the BEA. The *Equal Educational Opportunity Act* (EEOA) of 1974 codified the standards of *Lau*, by requiring states and school districts *to take appropriate action to overcome language barriers that impede equal participation by its students in its instructional programs.*

Bilingual Elections and the Voting Rights Act

The *Equal Protection Clause* of the Fourteenth Amendment to the US Constitution passed in 1868 was supposed to guarantee equal protection to all US citizens under the law. The Fifteenth Amendment passed in 1870 was supposed to guarantee the voting rights of all US citizens and end voting discrimination at any level of government on the basis of race, color, or previous servitude. Nevertheless, it took almost 100 years until the Civil Rights Movement in the 1960s for the US government to enforce the Fourteenth and Fifteenth Amendments and to recognize that all US citizens have equal rights and are entitled, by virtue of citizenship, to equal access to all government and public institutions, as well as the right to full and free participation in public and political life without discrimination.

In response to a clash in *Selma*, Alabama, in March 1965 known as *Bloody Sunday*, where peaceful Black civil rights marchers led by the Rev. Dr. Martin Luther King Jr. encountered white police officers with clubs, President Lyndon Johnson created the *Voting Rights Act* (VRA) of 1965. The VRA is a benchmark of the Civil Rights Movement and was primarily enacted to bring an end to the widespread discrimination against Blacks, particularly in the South. It is widely considered to be one of the most effective pieces of legislation ever enacted. The permanent provisions of the VRA banned racial discrimination in voting nationwide, guaranteed all US citizens equal rights in voting, and eliminated various direct and indirect techniques used to disenfranchise voters, such as English literacy tests and poll taxes.

In 1975, the VRA was amended with the addition of *Section 203*, which extended voting protections to Native American, Alaskan Native, Asian American, and Latino language minority groups—groups whom the political process has historically excluded. Section 203 was enacted in response to the considerable evidence that language minorities were systematically barred from participating in the political process through language barriers and discrimination on the basis of national origin. Section 203 is a temporary provision of the VRA, which must be renewed by Congress to remain in effect. It requires under certain conditions[4] that certain state and local jurisdictions provide ballots and voting information in languages other than English to voters who are not literate or fluent in English. Under the mandate, election officials must provide ballots, voting information, and assistance in all voting-related activities and materials, and poll workers must also be able to provide oral instructions and assistance in registration and voting at polling places. In July 2002 the US Census Bureau determined that there were 31 states covered in whole or in part by Section 203.

As President Johnson expressed at the time, the Civil Rights Movement was an effort to *overcome the crippling legacy of bigotry and injustice* that every American must overcome so that all citizens may enjoy *the full blessings of American life* (From President Lyndon B. Johnson's historic "We Shall Overcome" speech to the US Congress about the voting Rights Act. Delivered on March 15, 1965, a week after "Bloody Sunday," the day deadly racial violence erupted in Selma, Alabama when peaceful and unarmed African–Americans prepared to march to Montgomery, Alabama, to protest voting rights discrimination, and were attacked by white state troopers and police officers). The absence of discrimination as a basic human, civil, and Constitutional right, and the concept of free and equal access to participation in public and political life are fundamental tenets of American life. However, the pursuit of these, which arguably continue to be in many ways, ideals, is an ongoing challenge. Language requirements have historically been used to prevent US citizens who speak languages other than English from voting, and since its enactment the VRA has been subject to various legal challenges. The VRA together with *Title VI* of the 1964 Civil Rights Act, which prevents exclusion from participation in, and discrimination under, federally assisted programs (such as education) on the basis of race, color, and national Origin, are two critical pieces of legislation that have been the foundation for numerous laws and policies forbidding language discrimination and discrimination on the basis of national origin.

Before bilingual elections, many language minorities, particularly Spanish speakers, did not register to vote because they were unable to understand election materials and could not communicate with poll workers. Bilingual elections have encouraged Spanish-speaking citizens to register and vote and participate in democratic process. The notion that bilingual elections promote cultural division is misplaced criticism. Bilingual elections encourage the political participation of peoples who have historically been prevented from participating in the democratic process because of their inability to understand the English language. They do not promote separatism, but promote participation and the social and political integration of historically excluded and disenfranchised groups. Furthermore, contrary to widely held beliefs, language assistance in voting is not excessively costly when well-implemented, bilingual elections account for only a small fraction of the cost of the total election. It is arguably a compelling state interest for the provision of language assistance in the political process to remain in effect, as the social and political costs of eliminating those protections are steep. They would hinder progress and effectively take the country backwards. In a country where voter participation rates loom around 45%, such steps would be devastating and are incongruent with democratic ideals and the promotion of civic participation.

In light of these important federal provisions, language minorities do not have rights and protections equal to those of racial or ethnic minority groups—no piece of Civil Rights legislation explicitly bars discrimination on the basis of language (it is national origin that is used as a proxy for language). Existing protections are, simply put, not as numerous and not as strong. Furthermore, there has been a profound social and political attitudinal shift since the progressive 1960s and early 1970s which has resulted in less concern over minority rights in general and the adoption of what are arguably socially and politically regressive measures that have stymied efforts to effect positive social change. Consequently, as shall be presented, in the absence of solid federal protections and guarantees, numerous efforts have been made at the state and local levels to curb the rights of language minorities and impose restrictive language policies. With some important exceptions, they reflect prevailing values that are drastically different from those that led to the BEA and VRA, and which also reflect competing values about language rights and the most appropriate ways to integrate linguistic minorities. As we shall see, these efforts have been most successful through the efforts of the English only movement and the adoption of English only laws at the state level. In the preceding sections, recent language laws and policies at the federal, state, and local levels will be discussed.

The English Only Movement and English Only Laws

The first official language measure ever considered at the federal level was brought to the Congressional floor in 1923 by Washington J. McCormick, a Republican Congressman from Montana. The bill proposed to displace English by making American the official language of the US. The measure died in committee, but was later adopted at the state level by Illinois. It wasn't until the 1980s that the question of an official language was again raised.

Congress considered declaring English the official language for the first time in 1981, when California Senator Samuel Ichiye Hayakawa, an immigrant himself, introduced a *Constitutional English Language Amendment*. The amendment was dismissed. Not long afterwards, he left Congress and, together with John Tanton, the founder of *Federation for American Immigration Reform* (FAIR), founded US English in 1983. Chilean immigrant Mauro Mujica succeeded Hayakawa as the leader of the organization. The organization is a *citizen action group* dedicated to preserving the unifying role of the English language in the US (US English). As their mission statement says: *US English believes that the passage of English as the official language will help to expand opportunities for immigrants to learn and speak English, the single greatest empowering tool that immigrants must have to succeed.* English Only is the largest and arguably the most influential organization of its kind, although there are other similar organizations, such as English First founded in 1986, and *English for the Children* founded in 1997, which is solely dedicated to ending bilingual education.

In 1996, the US House approved a Bill to make English the official language. However, the Bill failed because it lacked Senate support. Similar bills have appeared in every Congress since then (Schildkraut, 2004). Although most died in committee, in 1996 the *Emerson English Language Empowerment Act* passed in the US House of Representatives. It failed in the Senate, but has been reintroduced since then (Ricento, 1998). If the Act had been approved, it would have made English the official language of the US government, required that naturalization ceremonies take place exclusively in English, and repealed the bilingual voting requirements of the VRA. In addition, it stated that *no person shall be denied services, assistance, or facilities, directly or indirectly provided by the Federal Government solely because the person communicates in English* (Schildkraut, 2004, p. 13). Two similar bills were sent to Congressional committee in 2003.

Although proponents of English only have lacked success at the federal level, they have had tremendous success at getting English only laws and amendments adopted in various states. As of this writing, 31 states have enacted some types of English only or official English laws and policies. In addition, at least 15 states have considered English language laws and constitutional amendments, and only seven, at most, have not publicly considered taking such action (Schildkraut, 2004). Some states, such as Massachusetts in 1975, have English only policies in place as a result of a court ruling instead of legislative action. Such action has not gone unchallenged, however. For example, Arizona passed an *English only amendment* in 1988; however, it was declared unconstitutional in 1999 on the grounds that it violated the First Amendment Right to free speech. Recently in May 2005, the Governor of Arizona vetoed an English only bill that would have required the state to conduct all official business in English only. The Governor vetoed the bill because she disagreed with the notion that a restriction on other languages would be the best way to encourage immigrants to learn English.

In 1988, Alaska voters approved a law requiring government workers to only speak English when conducting public business. However, the law was challenged in state court and was never enforced. The court ruled that the law violated the Constitutional right to free speech and that it served no compelling public interest. Alaska subsequently passed a constitutional amendment in 1998; however, it was overturned by the Alaska Supreme Court in 2002.

In spite of the success for English only at the state level, there are two officially bilingual states. Hawaii is officially bilingual in English and Hawaiian, as prescribed by the Constitution of Hawaii adopted in 1978. The Constitution requires Hawaiian to be used in all official state business such as public acts, documents, and laws. In New Mexico, the state Constitution has provisions which protect Spanish, and the state officially recognizes both English and Spanish in the state. Official bilingualism in New Mexico dates back to 1848 and the Treaty of Guadalupe Hidalgo, which included provisions to protect the language and culture of Mexicans who chose to stay after their land was annexed by the US.

It is important to note that any state level action taken is unrelated to the process of a Constitutional amendment to make English the official language. Nevertheless, in addition to English only laws, various other types of language policies have been adopted at all levels of government as well as within civil society. These measures have been taken, in part, to address some of the many social policy issues posed by increasing language diversity and illustrate the competing values that frame language conflict. These initiatives have had a tremendous impact and will have profound long-term consequences for language minorities. They also raise fundamental questions about the appropriateness and legality of restrictive language policies.

Language Laws and Policies at the Federal Level

The new immigration and the growth among linguistic minorities have raised a host of social, political, and economic issues, which have come to the forefront over the last two decades. In particular, demographic changes are raising important policy questions about the provision of public and social services for immigrants, who are overwhelmingly Latin American. They also pose questions about language rights, exactly what kinds of protections language minority groups have, how and if they are different from those extended to racial/ethnic minorities, and why. There are challenges inherent in designing effective policies to help immigrants adapt and become involved members of their communities and society in general, challenges that are inherent to the design of any public policy. Language diversity is one issue that poses challenges in education, healthcare, the workplace, social services, and in every aspect of US society. The government and our most fundamental institutions have responded to increased linguistic diversity in various ways. In some instances, measures taken have clearly served to integrate and protect the rights of US citizens and residents who happen to speak a language other than English. In others, they have served to exclude immigrants and language minorities from full participation in US society. How to best integrate and meet the needs of a large and growing number of people who speak a language other than English has resulted in different responses at all levels of government reflecting competing values about language and bilingualism. Two fairly recent actions in particular merit discussion: the case of *Hernández vs. New York*, and *Executive Order 13166*.

Hernández vs. New York

In 1991, the US Supreme Court heard the case *Hernández vs. New York*. The case was the third and last time to date that the court has heard a case regarding language rights. In the criminal case, the victims and the defendant were all Latino. The prosecutor excluded potential jurors solely based on their ability to speak Spanish because he believed that such jurors would not accept a translator's version of the evidence presented. The defense argued that because language skills are closely tied to ethnicity, it is not race neutral to exclude jurors based on their Spanish-language abilities alone and doing so constitutes discrimination on the basis of race and national origin. Nevertheless, the prosecutor only challenged potential jurors with Spanish surnames, and the result was a case tried without any Latino jurors—so much for the right to be tried by a jury of one's peers, and it would appear to be as equally unjust as a Black person being tried by an all-white jury.

In criminal cases, jurors cannot be challenged on the basis of race, and the Supreme Court heard the case because potential Latino jurors were excluded from the jury on the basis of language. In *Hernández vs. New York*, the Court ruled that potential jurors may be eliminated based solely on their ability to speak a language other than English. Although jury duty is a fundamental component of active citizenship, the courts have consistently treated bilingualism and multilingualism as sufficient grounds to exclude persons from participating in this important and indispensable American sociopolitical and democratic institution, and basic aspect of US citizenship (Rodriguez, 2001). In 1968, the US Congress adopted a law requiring that persons sitting on a federal jury must be able to speak English and *read, write, and understand the English language with a degree of proficiency sufficient to fill out satisfactorily the juror qualification form* (Del Valle, 2003, p. 187). However, the critical ruling in *Hernández* means that a US citizen may be excluded from a jury solely because of her/his ability to communicate in a language other than English, irrespective of their ability to communicate in English.

The case reflects issues at the intersection of race/ethnicity and language which have been pushed to the forefront by the new immigration. It also illustrates the tension surrounding the differentiation and integration of Latinos into US mainstream culture, where the black–white racial paradigm prevails, but within which it is impossible to squeeze a minoritized group not defined by race or color, but overwhelmingly by language and culture that has effectively served to "racialize" Latinos as a distinct (ethnic) group. The court, however, neglected to address the race issue, but instead essentially marginalized prospective jurors based on language (Del Valle, 2003)—an arguably immutable characteristic that has historically served as a proxy for race and a tool with which to exclude immigrants and ethnic and cultural minorities.

Executive Order 13166

On August 11, 2000, then-President William Clinton signed into law Executive Order 13166 entitled *Improving access to services for persons with limited English proficiency*. The order requires any organization, agency, or institution receiving federal funds to provide services in a language other than English if necessary. For example, private physicians, clinics, and hospitals that accept Medicare and Medicaid must provide translators for patients who are *limited English proficient* (LEP) at their own expense. The goals of the order are to improve access to federally operated and assisted programs and services by persons with limited English skills, and ensure that such programs and services do not violate Title VI of the Civil Rights Act. In a way, and to a certain extent, the order promotes federal support of multilingualism. Some, namely US English, argue that it has made the federal government, to a certain extent, multilingual.

The order signed by President Clinton demonstrated support for the needs of language minorities at the federal level and established some level of responsibility the government has in ensuring limited English speakers have access to fundamental social and public services. Nevertheless, it is not a comprehensive language policy or tantamount to a federal policy of multilingualism. Rather, it is one piece of a complex web of language policies that are in effect at various institutional and governmental levels. These policies often compete with each other to further the professed goal of sociocultural and political integration of linguistic minorities.

Language Laws and Policies at the State and Local Levels

The sizable language minority population in the US poses significant public policy challenges to state and local governments. Conflicts over language have become increasingly common as the racial/ethnic and cultural composition of the country has evolved. As the country has struggled with immigration and population change, these two issues have presented serious challenges at all levels of government, but have largely been left up to the states to address. Some feel that this is an example of the federal government wanting to stick responsibility for tackling these issues to the states, while others feel it is a state's rights issue. Others argue that this is an example of the influence of corporations and big business on the federal government, who arguably profit from immigration policy as it currently is because it provides a steady stream of cheap labor that allows them to keep costs down and maintain high profit margins. Some simply argue that this is what happens in a period with strong political and social opposition to big government and a greater emphasis on state's rights and power. Whether or not all or any of these things are true is a matter of perspective and opinion.

The language policy debate has largely shifted from the federal government to states and localities. Efforts toward an English Language Amendment or the institution of official English have somewhat subsided in recent years. This can be attributed to the challenges to adopting such a measure at the federal level, whereas efforts towards such measures at the state and local levels are more likely to succeed—and, as we shall see, have been quite successful. Moreover, given the number of language minority persons who are predominantly Spanish-speaking Latino and constitute a large and growing percentage of US voters, such a move at the national level would be politically difficult. For these and perhaps other reasons, proponents of English only have focused their efforts on states and localities, where numerous laws and policies have been adopted in recent years. Official English laws and policies mandate that all official government business, including regulations and legislation, public record keeping and documentation, hearings and public meetings, be conducted solely in English. As of this writing, 31 states have some form of official English law in effect. Some of the more recent states to adopt these measures include Oklahoma (2010), Kansas (2007), Idaho (2007), Arizona (2006), Iowa (2002), and Missouri (2008).

English Plus has emerged in stark contrast to the English only movement. English Plus is a policy alternative that encourages bilingualism, emphasizes inclusion and the integration of language minority groups, and, in strict departure from the monolingualism advocated for by proponents of English only, advocates for policies that would provide opportunities for all members of our society to learn a second or multiple languages. English Plus policy encourages investments in language education for *all* US citizens, while strengthening programs that teach English. Notably, Representative Jose Serrano of New York introduced a nonbinding English Plus resolution in 2001 in the 107th Congress. Similar measures passed on the State level in New Mexico (1989), Oregon (1989), Rhode Island (1992), and Washington (1989).

Although language minorities have certain rights and protections guaranteed by the federal government, in the absence of a single language policy and the presence of contradictory theories of language rights at the federal level, competing values and theories of language rights are playing out at the state and local levels. States such as Alabama have attempted to implement English only driver's tests and laws, and localities such as Atlanta, Georgia, have instituted ordinances requiring signs to be written primarily in English (Schildkraut, 2004). Sometimes such efforts indicate legitimate attempts to deal with a challenging and emerging social issue for which resources are limited, and others are examples of blatantly discriminatory policies that have directly targeted a specific ethnic or linguistic group. Together, these diverse policies illustrate the tension and ambivalence in the design and objective of language policy resulting from the absence of a single coherent ideology of language use and choice. Laws and policies for the education of language minority students can be used to illustrate this point.

The Education of Language Minority Students

The education of language minority students is the most prominent and contentious issue raised by the new immigration. As the foreign-born population has grown, language minority students have become increasingly visible, and their education has evolved into a highly controversial public issue. Children of immigrant families comprised 24% of all US children as of 2010, a group that accounts almost entirely for the growth in the child population between 1990 and 2008. According to the National Center for Education Statistics (NCES), in 2014, for the first time in US history, the majority of students in public school were non-white, the majority of whom were Latino, followed by African–Americans (McFarland et al., 2017). Schools educate 11 million children of immigrants, and approximately 10% of public school children speak English poorly or not at all (Dillon, 2003). Of the bilingual students who enter US schools, 67% are born in the US and 85% speak Spanish.

The LEP student population has more than doubled between 1989–1990 and 2003–2004 (Padolsky, 2005b), and the US Census Bureau predicts that by the 2030s, students whose home language is not English will comprise 40% of the school-age population. In 2010 LEP individuals accounted for 9% of the US population five years and older (Chhandasi, Batalova, & McHugh, 2011), approximately 25.2 million people. Of these, 68% are dispersed in the following six states: California, Texas, New York, Florida, Illinois, and New Jersey.

The National Clearinghouse for English Language Acquisition and Language Instruction Educational Programs (NCELA) estimates that there were fewer than 5 million students in some type of bilingual education program in the US in grades kindergarten through 12 during the 2003–2004 school year (Padolsky, 2005a). Estimates indicate LEP students represent a small share of the total US student population at 10.3% in 2010. Also, of the 21.8% of children and youth ages 5 to 14 that speak a language other than English at home, 76.2% spoke English very well, and 23.8% had difficulty speaking English (Ryan, 2013).

The debate over bilingual education intensified in the 1990s when immigration that was and still is largely Latin American, increased. Bilingual education has become the heart of the language debate, and the controversy over bilingual education in many ways can be used to gauge prevailing attitudes towards immigrants and non-English speakers. Most states designate English language learners (ELL) students as LEP for only a short period of time. The implications are that students lose their LEP status before becoming fully English proficient. This is particularly concerning given demographers estimate that 40% of the school-aged population will be comprised of English language learners by the 2030s

Notably, it is in education that the English only movement has had significant achievements by successfully championing the end of bilingual education in three states. Many important policy changes impacting language minority students have taken place since the late 1990s (see Table 12.3). Not long after President Clinton signed Executive Order 13166 into law, the BEA was eliminated as part of then-President George W. Bush's sweeping federal education policy, *No Child Left Behind* (NCLB). Under NCLB, the BEA was replaced by the *English Language Acquisition Act* (ELAA). The change was a complete reversal of 34 years of education policy for language minority students. Whereas the BEA sought to develop English language skills and, to the extent possible, develop native language skills, under NCLB, the emphasis is on the acquisition of English language skills only. Illustrating how bilingual education has been dismantled at the federal level, the policy switch affirms Hakuta's (1986) position that in the US, bilingualism is widely understood as a transitional period leading to English monolingualism.

The change at the federal level illustrates the federal government's renege on its commitment to language minority students as spelled out in the BEA in 1968, as well as waning social and political support of language assistance for linguistic minorities. Furthermore, although the *Lau* decision is supposed to guarantee the Constitutional rights of language minority students to learn in their native language, more drastic steps have been taken at the state level. The English for the Children Campaign spearheaded by Ron Unz has successfully used the citizen's initiative process in California, Massachusetts, and Arizona to eliminate bilingual education in those three states and replace it with mandated one-year English immersion. Popularly known as *Unz initiatives*, the anti-bilingual education voter referenda passed in California, Arizona, and Massachusetts (see Table 12.3). Ironically, Massachusetts was the first state in the country to pass bilingual education legislation in 1971. A similar referendum failed in Colorado in 2002.

The Unz initiatives have effectively enacted an ideology of monolingualism by dictating language use in public schools (Stritikus, 2002). This reflects current attitudes towards language diversity that perceive bilingualism as irrelevant and of questionable social value. The controversy over bilingual education also highlights the perceived threat of a cultural and linguistic takeover posed by bilingualism and which drives the language policy conflict. As Espinoza-Herold (2003, p. 8) poignantly states:

> *Bilingual education in the United States has been successfully utilized by conservative and racist political groups as an anti-immigrant weapon and as a way to instill fear among the White population of a growing Mexican cultural and linguistic invasion.*

Importantly, language minority students in California, Massachusetts, and Arizona have become the only student population in the US to be enrolled in public education programs subject to the regulation of instructional content and methodology. It would seem that the *Lau vs. Nichols* decision means that mandated English immersion for all language minority students is a violation of their Constitutional rights. However, the voter initiative process has been used to sidestep the legislative process and institute lawfully and constitutionally questionable policies that are arguably discriminatory, as they primarily target Spanish-speaking Latinos, as well as being potentially pedagogically unsound. In 1998, a class action lawsuit was filed to block *Proposition 227* from going into effect in

Table 12.3 Policy Changes Impacting Language Minority Students since the Late 1990s

1998	Proposition 227 eliminates bilingual education in California.
2000	Proposition 203 eliminates bilingual education in Arizona.
2002	The 1968 Bilingual Education Act expires and is replaced by the English Language Acquisition Act under the larger federal education policy No Child Left Behind.
2002	Question 2 eliminates bilingual education in Massachusetts. A similar voter referendum fails in Colorado.

California. The case, *Valeria G. vs. Wilson,* was based on the claim that the policy violated the educational and civil rights of LEP students under the law. However, the US District Court for the Northern District of California upheld the Constitutionality of Proposition 227. The ruling was appealed.

Scientific evidence seems to overwhelmingly indicate the importance of native language instruction for the acquisition of English language skills and overall academic achievement of language minority students. In the largest, and perhaps most important, study on language minority education to date, Thomas and Collier (1997, 2001) conducted a longitudinal study of thousands of LEP students between 1985 and 2001. The study sought to determine the amount of time LEP students needed native language instruction before they could perform on grade level in English, and what were the variables that effected long-term academic achievement. Researchers found that students in bilingual programs scored at or above their native English-speaking peers, and that students schooled bilingually had higher levels of academic achievement than students schooled monolingually. The research also found that LEPs in English immersion had the highest number of school drop-outs. They concluded that skill and the amount of instruction in the native language were the best predictors of English language achievement, and that native language instruction was the most effective program type for educating language minority students. Their research demonstrated that it takes a minimum of four years for LEPs to reach grade-level performance in English, and a minimum of five years to attain English language skills and academic achievement levels equal to their native English-speaking peers. They recommended that students with no English skills should not be placed in one- to three-year English immersion programs. These findings were echoed by August and Hakuta (1997) in their report to the *National Research Council*, where they reported that bilingual education produced better results than English immersion on key outcome variables. They reported no significant evidence that native language instruction impedes the development of English language skills or the overall academic achievement of LEP students, and that effective programs for LEP students include some use of the native language (August & Hakuta, 1997). Furthermore, Hakuta, Goto, and Witt (2000) found it takes three to five years to develop oral English proficiency, and four to seven years to develop academic proficiency.

Research on bilingualism has yielded evidence indicating the various cognitive advantages of bilingualism (see de Bot & Houtzager; Kharkhurin; Paap, this volume). Additionally, although the literature is mixed, research has not conclusively demonstrated the superiority of native language instruction for all LEP students in all contexts, and the evidence weighs heavily in favor of native language instruction. Numerous studies have found bilingual education to be more effective. However, evidence suggests there are various program types that would be successful in educating LEP students. In the not-too-distant past, the National Clearinghouse for English Language Acquisition (NCELA), which works to support the mission of the Office of English Language Acquisition (OELA) within the US Department of Education, emphasized the importance of multilingualism for language minority students to achieve academically in the second language. Although this statement has long since been removed from the NCELA website, this succinct statement illustrates how multilingualism was previously by federal policy:

> *The more the native language is academically supported, in combination with balanced second language development, the higher language minority students are able to achieve academically in the second language each succeeding year, in comparison with those instructed only in the second language.*
>
> (NCELA, 2005, no longer available)

No longer solely a question of appropriate educational practice, the anti-bilingual education referenda have made the education of language minority students into an important legal, political, and civil rights issue. In particular, questions about who in particular is affected, if not targeted, by the policy shift is paramount to understanding its impact and determining its legitimacy and legality. Evidently, the policy shift impacts a large and growing segment of the US school-age population that is predominantly Spanish-speaking Latino. This raises important questions about a policy that—intentionally or not—primarily affects one ethnic and linguistic minority group in particular. In light of the facts, such a policy cannot constitute an ethnically neutral policy. Whether or not one-year English immersion and the elimination of native language programs for LEP students is legally viable is one question; whether or not it is appropriate and Constitutional to have a *de facto* policy based on ethnicity, language, and minority status is another. This raises a plethora of civil rights issues and questions about whether such policies violate the equal protection clause and discriminate on the basis of race/ethnicity and national origin. These are not insignificant consequences that can be dismissed as unintended. The controversy over language education policy mirrors nationwide concerns over how to socially integrate and meet the needs of immigrants and people with limited English language skills, an issue which in large part is driven by questions about how to integrate and meet the unique needs of Spanish-speaking Latinos into the existing and evolving US sociocultural context, which is rapidly changing due to the growth among Spanish-speaking Latinos.

The Social and Cultural Contexts of Language Conflict

Language conflict is about values, and the language policies that result are about values as well. Some fundamental American ideals are central to the debate over language in the US; freedom, individualism, economic opportunity, participatory democracy, and tolerance are ideals championed by both opponents and proponents of English only policies and restrictive language laws. What these ideals and the people who call on them have in common is that they both seek to protect what they believe is American (Schildkraut, 2004, p. 4). Individual feelings about national identity drive people's opinions on language and immigration issues and consequently their political and policy views. These ideas and opinions sometimes lead people to think that making English the official/national language is in the best interest of the nation, while others feel it would impinge on some of our basic rights and freedoms and run against what America stands for (Schildkraut, 2004, p. 5).

It would seem that unity based on conformity is in conflict with some of the most fundamental American principles. For many Americans, the notion of an official/national religion, such as one might find in a dictatorship or in a country governed by religious law, would be unfathomable, and with good reason. In the US, separation of church and state is a cornerstone of our constitutional democracy. Religion is not centralized nor within the purview of the government, and freedom of religion is a right enshrined in the US Constitution. Although Judeo-Christian faiths have had a tremendous impact on our nation and institutions, there is no institutionalized religious practice in the US—rather, we have the exact opposite. Freedom of religion and separation of church and state do not compromise national unity or forsake a national identity. To suggest that bilingualism or the absence of a national language has that effect contradicts the most fundamental American values of freedom and individualism. As Rodriguez (2001, p. 142) states, *the response should be to accommodate linguistic difference, much in the way that the law struggles to accommodate religious minorities and to enable the free exercise of religion.*

Language, like race/ethnicity or culture, is an immutable aspect of identity and is not a matter of personal choice. As Rodriguez (2001) argues, choice of language, like choice of culture, is a fictional construct. That certain population groups have been treated differently *because of their language* is discriminatory on the basis of race/ethnicity and national origin and a violation of the equal rights and protections guaranteed to all US citizens by the Constitution. Whether or not and under what circumstances English only laws and restrictive language policies violate the equal protection clause and infringe upon the Constitutional and civil rights of language minority persons are critical questions upon which the controversy over language policy hinges today. Federal protection of language minorities has weakened and remaining provisions are in danger. The courts have generally ruled in favor of protecting the rights of language minorities; however, recent court rulings have had the ironic effect of curbing the civil rights protections of those who do speak English simply because they speak another language. It is doubtful that such an approach promotes sociocultural integration and fosters a sense of national unity.

The language policy conflict is also about identity politics. Both opponents and advocates of restrictive language laws would agree that language is a central aspect of individual and group identity and more than simply a communication tool. Some argue that language is a critical aspect of national identity and is necessary for national unity. Others argue that language is *a symbol of cultural allegiance* (Rodriguez, 2001, p. 133). But in a multicultural country like the US that is increasingly becoming more diverse, the concept of cultural allegiance is ambiguous. Should immigrants have to *give up* their native/home culture for an American culture? If so, culture is akin to religion, in which case should immigrants or any person within the political borders of the US have to give up their religion in order to participate in American life and become an American? If we are a nation of many cultures, which culture should people have allegiance to? If it is American culture, what exactly is American culture if America is multicultural? Is it White, Anglo-Saxon, Protestant culture that holds this country together and to which citizens should have allegiance to, or is it our Constitution and *Bill of Rights* that holds this diverse country together and our civil liberties and social and political freedoms which citizens should have allegiance to and that defines us as American?

Proponents of English only laws argue that a common language is necessary for national unity and a prerequisite for US citizenship. They argue that being American means learning English, and that English language skills are a central aspect of American life and identity. The conflict over language reflects, in part, a cultural conflict between what is believed to be American culture and what is perceived as foreign. Language is related to different social and cultural networks, and those networks are coupled to value systems. In part, the social and political values attached to certain languages result from competing values about individual, group, and national culture, identity, and what it means to be an American. The issue is exactly which of those values are necessary for participation in American life and integration into US society. Are they values that transcend language, such as a belief in participatory democracy, or are they values that proscribe specific behaviors, such as organized prayer, and impinge on our civil liberties, such as prohibiting *religious dress* in public?

There is no reason to suggest that the presence of multiple languages results in social unrest, a lack of social cohesion, or conflict between groups. The conflict over language in the US is not about language itself, but rather is, in part, about the deeper social and personal issues of racism and the profound social inequalities that exist between groups of people who happen to speak different languages. It is a conflict rooted in cultural differences, questions about socioeconomic status, and our pervasive and deeply entrenched socioeconomic inequalities which are related to, but do not necessarily result from, tensions between individual, group, and national identity. It may also be a conflict rooted in a fear of competition, in the sense that bilinguals could be better prepared for jobs than monolinguals.

Monolingualism is not the norm, not in the US or in any other country. It is doubtful that it is possible or in the best interest of the nation to try to absorb linguistic minority groups into a monolingual, *Monocultural Americana* because such a country is a fictional construct. Most importantly, the legitimacy and legality of restrictive language policies is, at best, debatable. Furthermore, it is questionable if assimilationist policies are appropriate in a country for which immigration has been, and remains, integral to shaping its demographic make-up. Demographic realities in the foreseeable future suggest that an appropriate policy response would be to design policies that have immigrant integration as their primary goal. Only through such efforts will the country incorporate concerned and involved citizens. As Rodriguez (2001, p. 135) states: *the principle of free and equal access to participation in public life animates the language debate and should be at the heart of any effort to protect and empower linguistic minorities*. It is questionable if restrictive language policies are an effective means to achieve the goal of integration, and it is probable that they may have the opposite effect.

Summary and Conclusion

Bilingualism has powerful sociocultural and political significance. From one perspective, it could be argued that the US was meant to be a country founded by and for Whites, meaning the descendants of (northern) European immigrants, possessing a White, Anglo-Saxon, Protestant, English-speaking culture. Although the US is not, demographically, a culturally and linguistically monolithic place, and never has been, because the founders intended or expected it to be that way, cultural and linguistic minorities must not just adapt, but be subjugated to live under a culture of white domination. On the other hand, the US is and has always been a multicultural country comprised of people from all over the world, and to believe and promote otherwise is to inhibit sociocultural and political progress. It is to shun the very values that this country purports to stand for.

The US has no official language, although the nation's founders discussed the issue when the country was in its infancy. Nevertheless, throughout US history, language has shaped the way in which people conceptualize their understanding of conflicts between different cultural and immigrant groups. As US history shows, language has often served as a proxy for the exclusion of immigrants, and cultural and ethnic minority groups when such groups are perceived as a threat. The US has a history of systematically denying and restricting minority people, their culture, and their language in an effort to ensure and strengthen their subordinate, minority status under a system of domination and oppression. Unfortunately, such realities are as much a part of our current reality as they are a part of our past. Language has been used and continues to be used today as a tool to Americanize immigrants and minority groups and further the full cultural and linguistic assimilation— as opposed to acculturation—of new Americans. The fear of difference and immigrants that drove such language-based anti-immigrant measures in the past are the same ones that inform restrictive language policies primarily targeted toward Spanish-speaking Latinos today. As we have seen, such laws and policies promote segregation and exclusion, serve to maintain the social stratification system present of the US, and do not foster sociocultural integration. There are few, if any, reasons to believe that the effect of such measures could have a different impact today.

Current concerns about language and bilingualism are directly related to concerns about evolving diversity largely driven by Latin American immigration. As Samuel Huntington states: *the single most immediate and most serious challenge to America's traditional identity comes from the immense and continuing immigration from Latin America* (Huntington, 2004, p. 2). Huntington and other proponents of restrictive immigration and language laws believe that Latin American immigration poses a threat to the cultural and political integrity of the country and will lead to a *de facto* split within a Spanish-speaking and English-speaking US (Huntington, 2004). Because current restrictive language policies primarily impact one ethnic and linguistic minority group (Spanish-speaking Latinos), they are examples of *de facto* ethnically based, sociocultural policies. As such, they cannot be ethnic or culturally neutral policies any more than share cropping policies in the US South after the Civil War can be construed as racially neutral.

The story of Babel portrays bilingualism as an obstacle and impediment to human progress. However, the assertion that bilingualism is a sociocultural and political liability is completely dumbfounding. Language skills are a tremendous resource and asset. However, the US does not have a single language policy. Instead, various types of language laws and policies exist at various levels of government, some of which have resulted from Court rulings and not through any legislative process, and others which have been implemented through voter referenda. These policies do not reflect a consistent theory of language use and choice or ideology of language rights, but rather they illustrate the many beliefs and contradictory ideas about language and bilingualism. Even though language minority groups are undergoing linguistic assimilation similar to, if not faster than, previous immigrant groups, the fact that immigration is high, steady, and shows no indication of slowing suggests that, for at least far into the future, there will always be a substantial population of non-English speakers. Furthermore, even as subsequent generations become English monolingual speakers, the fluidity of borders and the constant stream of immigrants ensure the presence of diverse cultures and, consequently, a linguistically diverse populace. Are restrictive language policies the best way to integrate the New Americans into US society? Is there any evidence that suggests restrictive language policies have achieved this goal in the past and will advance it in the future, or does simply the pursuit of such restrictive policies result in a sociocultural and political conflict that could otherwise be avoided, resulting in discord instead of unity?

Most previous immigrants suffered some degree of social, political, and cultural exclusion. Nevertheless, they were eventually integrated into US society. However, the new immigration is drastically different from previous waves. Immigrants overwhelmingly come from within the hemisphere, many go back and forth, and huge numbers are undocumented. They are not European, and they are not white in culture, race, or ethnicity. Economic structures have changed. The ability to work up the socioeconomic ladder, from the poor or working class to the middle class, has become almost non-existent with the disappearance of manufacturing, increased automation, and the high degree of specialization required in so many jobs. Against the backdrop of globalization, income inequality and the gap between the rich and poor has grown exponentially over the past 40 years. The mechanisms which allowed previous immigrants to climb the ladder—entry-level, blue collar, factory work requiring limited skills and education—has basically been eliminated by technological and industrial advances connected to macroeconomic and geopolitical changes. The old model of immigrant integration does not apply to the new immigration. There are aspects of the new immigration and characteristics of new immigrants that set it apart from previous immigrants. Importantly, the new immigration, overwhelmingly

Latino, has a social stigma attached to it unlike any other previous immigrant groups. How can that stigma be transcended for the benefit of the nation? How can society and the government respond? That the US is undergoing massive population changes is a reality to which appropriate responses must be developed and implemented at all levels of government and within civil society. Measures that are taken should protect the rights of language minorities just as racial and ethnic minorities should be protected from discrimination. Immigration is not a temporary phenomenon that will go away. Language diversity has been omnipresent within the borders of the US, and linguistic diversity will be an integral aspect of the nation in the future. The new immigrants are here to stay, and they are bringing their languages and cultures with them. They are the New Americans. As Huntington (2004, p. 12) writes, *There is no Americano dream. There is only the American dream created by an Anglo-Protestant society. Mexican Americans will share in that dream and in that society only if they dream in English.* Is this the kind of constructive attitude that will promote the integration of new immigrants into our democracy and ensure a prosperous future for the nation, or is it destructive? History offers some insights, but only time will tell.

List of Key Words and Concepts

Acculturation, American Community Survey (ACS), American identity, Americanization, Articles of the Confederation, Assimilationist, Bilingual Education Act (BEA), Bill of Rights, Bloody Sunday, Civil Rights Act, Civil Rights Movement, Commissioner of Indian Affairs, Constitutional English Language Amendment, Culture war, Curse of Babel, Declaration of Independence, Elementary and Secondary Education Act (ESEA), Emerson English Language Empowerment Act, English for the Children, English Language Academy, English Language Acquisition Act (ELAA), English only amendment, English only movement, English Plus, Equal Educational Opportunity Act (EEOA), Equal Protection Clause, Exceptionalism, Executive Order 13166, Expansionism, Federation for American Immigration Reform (FAIR), Foraker Act, Foreign language, Globalization, Hereditarian, *Hernández vs. New York*, Hispanophobia, Immigrant quotas, Immigration and Nationality Act (INA), Indian boarding schools, Indian education, Integration, Jones Act, Language assimilation, Language diversity, Language laws, Language shift, Latinization, *Lau vs. Nichols*, Limited English proficient (LEP), Manifest Destiny, Mexican–American War, *Meyer vs. Nebraska*, Migration Policy Institute (MPI), Monocultural Americana, Monroe Doctrine, National Research Council, Nationality Act, Nativist attitudes, No Child Left Behind (NCLB), Official English, Olmstead Act, Proposition 227, Section 203, Selma, Social engineering, Spanish–American War, Stereotypes, Title VI/VII, Treaty of Guadalupe Hidalgo, Unz initiatives, Us-versus-Them, *Valeria G. vs. Wilson*, Voting Rights Act (VRA), Xenophobia

Internet Sites Related to the Social and Cultural Contexts of Bilingualism

Bilingual Research Journal, the Journal of the National Association of Bilingual Education: http://www.tandfonline.com/loi/ubrj20/
Center for Applied Linguistics: http://www.cal.org/
English for the Children: http://www.onenation.org/
James Crawford's Language Policy Web Site and Emporium: http://www.languagepolicy.net/

Leadership Conference on Civil and Human Rights: http://www.civilrights.org
National Association for Bilingual Education: http://nabe.org/publications
Office of English Language Acquisition, US Department of Education: https://ed.gov/about/offices/list/oela/index.html
The National Education Policy Center: http://nepc.colorado.edu/
US Census Bureau: http://www.census.gov/
US English: https://www.usenglish.org/

Discussion Questions

(1) What kinds of policies would be most appropriate to help integrate language minorities?
(2) What kinds of policies would be most appropriate in helping limited English proficient persons attain English language proficiency?
(3) Do current policies promote the integration of immigrants and language minorities or do they serve to exclude? How and why?
(4) Does the government have a responsibility in the area of language policy, and if so, at what level? Is federal involvement tantamount to *big government*? Should language policy be a state, local, and/or private issue?
(5) What is the sociocultural and political benefit of bilingualism?
(6) What is the sociocultural and political benefit of monolingualism?
(7) Are anti-bilingual education/English immersion voter referenda, which limit instruction in a language other than English, Constitutional, legitimate, and appropriate or do they constitute discrimination on the basis of national origin, as held under *Lau vs. Nichols*?
(8) Is a common language necessary for national unity, and in a multicultural country, what does the English language have to do with being *American*?
(9) Does immigration to the US entail cultural and linguistic sacrifices, and if so, what and how?
(10) Can a balance between the home/native culture and language and the dominant culture and language in the US be found?

Suggested Research Projects

(1) *How are bilinguals or Spanish speakers depicted? Is Spanish or bilingualism depicted as an asset, liability, or both? What messages are communicated to young children, explicitly or implicitly about Spanish, bilingualism, and speakers of languages other than English? What values are ascribed to bilingualism?* Engaging with texts or other media for children, students can explore the portrayal of bilingualism or the use of Spanish in children's literature, television programming, music, and/or other media. Understanding how Spanish and bilingualism is represented in materials and entertainment directed to children can increase understanding of the values assigned to language diversity. It can also shed light on how the representation of bilinguals and Spanish speakers may influence children's understanding of bilingualism and languages other than English, as well as the values ascribed to linguistic diversity that may be internalized by children, influencing the development of their attitudes and personal beliefs.
(2) *Are there relationships among community demographics (racial/ethnic composition, percent poverty, or foreign born, etc.), and school-district-wide language education*

programs? Are there differences between the language education programs prevalent in largely immigrant or Latino communities (e.g., immersion or transitional bilingual programs) and those in more affluent or majority white communities (e.g., dual language)? Examining language education programs within school districts, and exploring possible differences in language instruction in demographically distinct neighborhoods, can increase understanding of how attitudes towards language education programs and policies about bilingualism are enacted in different contexts. This can also provide insights into attitudinal and programmatic variations linked to second language instruction for native English speakers compared to English language instruction for speakers of languages other than English.

(3) *How are language policy issues framed and by whom? What are the dominant voices in the language policy debate? Are all perspectives included in faming the issue? What groups are excluded from the policy debate? How do different political and ideological groups and segments of society frame and approach questions about language policy, and how are these evident in current events?* Examining newspapers and/or other sources of news can increase understanding of the perspectives shaping current debates about language, immigrant integration, and appropriate policy responses at different levels of government or within different sectors of community life. News sources with different sociopolitical perspectives, for example, Republican or Democratic; left-wing or right-wing; conservative, liberal, progressive, or libertarian, can help to illustrate how language policy debates play out in the media and how popular perspectives are shaped.

Suggested Readings

Crawford, J. (2000). *At war with diversity: US language policy in an age of anxiety.* Clevedon, UK: Multilingual Matters, Ltd.

Del Valle, S. (2003). *Language rights and the law in the United States: Finding our voices.* Clevedon, UK: Multilingual Matters.

Hakuta, K. (1986). *Mirror of language: The debate on bilingualism.* New York: Basic Books.

Hanson, V. D. (2003). *Mexifornia: A state of becoming.* San Francisco: Encounter Books.

Huntington, S. P. (2004). The Hispanic challenge. *Foreign Policy*, March/April 2004. Retrieved March 14, 2004, from http://www.foreignpolicy.com

Pullum, G. K. (1991). *The great Eskimo vocabulary hoax and other irreverent essays on the study of language.* Chicago, IL: University of Chicago Press.

Rodriguez, C. M. (2001). Accommodating linguistic differences: Towards a comprehensive theory of language rights in the US. *Harvard Civil Rights-Civil Liberties Law Review*, 36, 133–223.

Schildkraut, D. J. (2004). *Press one for English: Language policy, public opinion, and American identity.* Princeton, NJ: Princeton University Press.

Schmidt, R. (2000). *Language policy and identity politics in the United States.* Philadelphia, PA: Temple University Press.

Notes

1   The Monroe Doctrine, issued by President James Monroe in 1823, declared that the Americas should be closed to colonization by European countries in the future, and that sovereign states in the Americans should be free from European interference. It also proclaimed that the US would remain neutral in wars between European countries and their colonies, but would consider any European interference with sovereign states in the Americas as a hostile act toward the US. The Doctrine was intended to declare the US' opposition to colonialism. However, during the Falklands War in 1982, between Argentina and the UK, the US did not intervene. Whether the US

under Ronald Reagan either ignored the conflict over the Falklands or chose to ignore the Monroe Doctrine and not to intervene in South America, is a subject of debate. Nevertheless, in strict departure from its professed moral objections, the US did assume, and continues to have to this day, colonial rule over the island nation of Puerto Rico.

2   This quote has been attributed to various people in addition to James Ferguson. Its exact origin is unknown.

3   There is some disagreement on this point, which Schildkraut (2004) acknowledges. Spolsky (2004) states that, after the Louisiana Purchase, the new governor required that English be used for all public matters; however, the 1845 constitution provided for bilingualism at the legislature. This was later reversed by the 1879 constitution.

4   A state or locale is required to provide such language assistance under two conditions: (1) if one of the protected language minority groups is more than 5% of the voting-age citizen population in a jurisdiction and have limited English proficiency, or (2) where more than 10,000 voting-age citizens in a jurisdiction belong to a single language minority group and are limited English proficient, and the illiteracy rate of that group exceeds the national illiteracy rate.

References

Anzaldúa, G. (1987). *Borderlands la frontera: The new Mestiza*. San Francisco: Aunt Lute Books.

August, D., & K. Hakuta. (1997). *Improving schooling for language minority children: A research agenda*. Washington, DC: National Academy Press.

Berry, J. W., Poortinga, Y. H., Segall, M. H., & Dasen, P. R. (2002). *Cross cultural psychology: Research and applications* (2nd ed.). Cambridge, UK: Cambridge University Press.

Camarota, S. (2012). *Immigrants in the United States: A profile of America's foreign-born population*. Center for Immigrant Studies. Retrieved from http://cis.org/2012-profile-of-americas-foreign-born-population

Camarota, S. A. (2002). *Immigrants in the United States-2002: A snapshot of America's foreign-born population*. Washington, DC: Center for Immigration Studies. Retrieved from http://www.cis.org/articles/2002/back1302.html

Capps, R., Fix, M., & Passel, J. (2002, November 26). The dispersal of immigrants in the 1990s. *Immigrant Families and Workers: Facts and Perspectives* [Video Series, Brief No. 2]. Washington, DC: Urban Institute. Retrieved from http://www.urban.org/url.cfm?ID=410589

Chhandasi, P. Batalova, J., & McHugh, M. (2011). *Limited English proficient individuals in United States: Number, share, growth, and linguistic diversity*. Migration Policy Institute. National Center in Immigrant Integration Policy.

Crawford, J. (1992). *Hold your tongue: Bilingualism and the politics of "English only"*. Reading, MA: Addison-Wesley.

Crawford, J. (1999). *Bilingual education: History, politics, theory and practice*. Los Angeles: Bilingual Educational Services.

Crawford, J. (2000). *At war with diversity: US language policy in an age of anxiety*. Clevedon, UK: Multilingual Matters.

Czekalinski, S., & Nhan, D. (2012). 7 of 15 most populous US cities are majority-minority. *National Journal*. Retrieved from http://www.nationaljournal.com/thenextamerica/demographics/7-of-15-most-populous-u-s-cities-are-majority-minority-20120702

Del Valle, S. (2003). *Language rights and the law in the United States: Finding our voices*. Clevedon, UK: Multilingual Matters.

Dillon, S. (2003, November 5). School districts struggle with English fluency mandate. *The New York Times*. Retrieved from: http://www.nytimes.com/2003/11/05/nyregion/school-districts-struggle-with-english-fluency-mandate.html

Espinoza-Herold, M. (2003). *Issues in Latino education: Race, school culture, and the politics of academic success*. Boston: Allyn and Bacon.

Fitzgerald, J. (1993). Views on bilingualism in the United States: A selective historical review. *Bilingual Research Journal, 17*(1&2), 35–56.

Frey, W. (2013). Shift to a majority-minority population in the US happening faster than expected. *Brookings*. Retrieved from http://www.brookings.edu/blogs/up-front/posts/2013/06/19-us-majority-minority-population-census-frey

García Coll, C., Lamberty, G., Jenkins, R., McAdoo, H., Crnic, K., Wasik B., & Garcia, H. (1996). An integrative model for the study of developmental competencies in minority children. *Child Development, 67*, 1891–1914.

Hakuta, K. (1986). *Mirror of language: The debate on bilingualism.* New York: Basic Books.

Hakuta, K., Goto, Y., & Witt, D. (2000). *How long does it take English language learners to attain proficiency?* [Policy Report 2000–1]. Retrieved from The University of California Linguistic Minority Research Institute, Stanford University website: http://www.stanford.edu/%7ehakuta/Docs/HowLong.pdf

Hanson, V. D. (2003). *Mexifornia: A state of becoming.* San Francisco: Encounter Books.

Heath, S. B. (1976). A national language academy? Debate in the new nation. *International Journal of the Sociology of Language, 11*, 9–43.

Hechinger, F. M. (1978). Political issues in education: Reflections and directions. In W. I. Israel (Ed.), *Political issues in education* (pp. 127–135). Washington, DC: Council of Chief State School Officers.

Hernandez-Chavez, E. (1995). Language policy in the United States: A history of cultural genocide. In T. Skutnabb-Kangas & R. Phillipson (Eds.), *Linguistic human rights: Overcoming linguistic discrimination* (pp. 141–158). New York: Mouton de Gruyter.

Huntington, S. P. (2004, March/April). The Hispanic challenge. *Foreign Policy*. Retrieved March 14, 2004, from http://www.foreignpolicy.com

Kolankiewicz, L. (2000) *Immigration, population, and the new census bureau projections.* Washington, DC: Center for Immigration Studies. Retrieved from http://www.cis.org/articles/2000/back600.html

Krogstad J. M., & López, M. H. (2014, April 29). *Nativity shift: US births drive population growth as immigration stalls.* Retrieved from Pew Research website: http://www.pewhispanic.org/2014/04/29/hispanic-nativity-shift/

Lau v. Nichols, 483 F.2d 791 (9th Cir. 1973) rev'd 414 U.S. 563 (1974).

McFarland, J., Hussar, B., de Brey, C., Snyder, T., Wang, X., Wilkinson-Flicker, S., Gebrekristos, S., Zhang, J., Rathbun, A., Barmer, A., Bullock Mann, F., & Hinz, S. (2017). *The Condition of Education 2017* (Report NCES 2017-144). Washington, DC: National Center for Education Statistics.

Marr, C. J. (n.d.). *Assimilation through education: Indian boarding schools in the Pacific Northwest.* University of Washington Libraries: Digital Collections. Retrieved July 26, 2005, from http://content.lib.washington.edu/aipnw/marr.html

Marshall, D. F. (1986). The question of an official language: Language rights and the English Language Amendment. *International Journal of the Sociology of Language, 6*, 7–75.

National Clearinghouse for English language acquisition and language instruction educational programs (NCELA). (2005). *NCELA FAQ No. 4: How does native language development influence academic achievement in a second language?* Washington, DC: National Clearinghouse for English language acquisition and language instruction educational programs. Retrieved from http://www.ncela.gwu.edu/expert/faq/04academic.htm

Ortman, J., & Shin, H. (2011). Language projections: 2010–2020. *Population Division U.S. Census Bureau.* Social, Economic, and Housing Statistics Division U.S. Census Bureau. Retrieved from http://www.census.gov/hhes/socdemo/language/data/acs/Ortman_Shin_ASA2011_paper.pdf

Ovando, C. J. (2003). Bilingual education in the United States: Historical development and current issues. *Bilingual Research Journal, 27*, 1–24.

Padolsky, D. (2005a). *NCELA FAQ No. 1: How many school-aged English language learners are there in the US?* Washington, DC: National Clearinghouse for English language acquisition and language instruction educational programs. Retrieved from http://www.ncela.gwu.edu/expert/faq/01leps.htm

Padolsky, D. (2005b). *NCELA FAQ No. 8: How has the English language learners (ELL) population changed in recent years?* Washington, DC: National Clearinghouse for English language

acquisition and language instruction educational programs. Retrieved from http://www.ncela.
gwu.edu/expert/faq/08leps.htm

Passel, J. S., & Cohn, D. (2008) *U.S. Population Projections: 2005–2050.* Washington, DC: Pew
Hispanic Center. Retrieved from: http://www.pewhispanic.org/files/reports/85.pdf

Perea, J. (1998a). American languages, cultural pluralism, and official English. In R. Delgado & J.
Stefancic (Eds.), *The Latino/a condition: A critical reader* (pp. 566–573). New York: New York
University Press.

Perea, J. (1998b). Death by English. In R. Delgado & J. Stefancic (Eds.), *The Latino/a condition:
A critical reader* (pp. 583–595). New York: New York University Press.

Portes, A., & Rumbaut, R. G. (2001). *Legacies: The story of the immigrant second generation.*
Berkeley: University of California Press.

Ricento, T. (1995). *A brief history of language restrictionism in the United States.* Retrieved July 21,
2005, from http://faculty.coehd.utsa.edu/tricento/OfficialEnglish.htm

Ricento, T. (1998). Partitioning by language: Whose rights are threatened? In T. Ricento & B.
Burnaby (Eds.), *Language and politics in the United States and Canada* (pp. 317–330). London:
Lawrence Erlbaum Associates.

Rodriguez, C. M. (2001). Accommodating linguistic differences: Towards a comprehensive theory
of language rights in the US. *Harvard Civil Rights-Civil Liberties Law Review, 36,* 133–223.

Romaine, S. (2004). The bilingual and multilingual community. In T. K. Bhatia & W. C. Ritchie
(Eds.), *The handbook of bilingualism* (pp. 385–405). Malden, MA: Blackwell.

Ryan, C. (2013). Language use in the United States: 2011. *American Community Survey Reports.*
Retrieved from http://www.census.gov/prod/2013pubs/acs-22.pdf

Schildkraut, D. J. (2004). *Press one for English: Language policy, public opinion, and American
identity.* Princeton, NJ: Princeton University Press.

Schmidt, R. (2000). *Language policy and identity politics in the United States.* Philadelphia: Temple
University Press.

Spolsky, B. (2004). *Language policy.* Cambridge, UK: Cambridge University Press.

Stritikus, T. (2002). *Immigrant children and the politics of English-only: Views from the classroom.*
New York: LFB Scholarly Publishing.

Thomas, W. P., & Collier, V. (1997). *School effectiveness for language minority students.*
Washington, DC: National Clearinghouse for Bilingual Education. Retrieved from www.ncela.
gwu.edu/ncbepubs/resource/effectiveness/Thomas-collier97.pdf

Thomas, W. P., & Collier, V. (2001). *A national study of school effectiveness for language minority
students' long-term academic achievement.* Center for Research on Education, Diversity and
Excellence. Retrieved from http://www.crede.ucsc.edu/research/llaa/1.1_final.html

Trueba, H. T. (1989). *Raising silent voices: Educating the linguistic minorities for the 21st Century.*
New York: Newbury House. Retrieved from http://usenglish.org/inc

United States Census Bureau. (2012). *U.S. census bureau projections show a slower growing, older,
more diverse nation a half century from now.* News Release, December 12.

13 The Sociolinguistics of Bilingualism

Barbara E. Bullock and Almeida
Jacqueline Toribio

Introduction

It is often noted that there is more *linguistic variation* between speakers within bilingual (or *plurilingual*) communities than within monolingual ones (Meyerhoff & Nagy, 2008) as well as more inter-individual variation between bilingual participants in controlled studies compared to monolinguals (De Houwer, 2011). So, not only are bilinguals observed to differ significantly from monolinguals on a range of linguistic tasks, but they are also seen to differ from one another. This frequent finding has led scholars across a range of disciplines to situate this variation in the *proficiency* disparities that distinguish bilingual individuals and to focus their efforts on disentangling the maturational, cognitive, and experiential factors that underlie them (Birdsong, 2014). Our purpose here is to demonstrate that bilinguals can vary in their linguistic performance in ways that are not bound by their proficiency.

The focus of this chapter is on linguistic variation, by which we mean the ways in which individuals or groups construct and use diverse forms for expressing the same meanings. For bilingual populations, variation can emerge as a consequence of possessing two (or more) languages. This is generally construed as a sign of language interference, although, as we will argue, this is not necessarily the case. It can also ensue, as it does for everyone, from how we use language for social interaction and how such uses are judged. In this chapter, then, we discuss variation from the perspective of *sociolinguistics* to demonstrate that some of the differences observed within groups of bilingual speakers or between bilinguals and monolinguals are socially motivated and not correlated directly with factors unique to bilinguals.

We launch the chapter with an overview of how variation has been conceptualized and accounted for in the scholarly literature on bilingualism. We briefly discuss how bilingual and contact communities have been studied traditionally, drawing parallels between the notions of *restricted speakers* and *language shift* in the sociolinguistic and language contact literature and proficiency and *language dominance* in psychology. Our objective is to show that these fields, though disparate in their goals, have been similarly engaged in accounting for the variation observed, particularly within bilingual communities, as a function of proficiency and dominance. From here, we turn to the factors that contribute to language variation that are less often explored in the empirical literature on bilingualism and discuss current work that has begun to consider the effects of *socio-indexical* and interactional factors on bilingual performance, particularly at the phonetic level. Socio-indexicality refers to the ways in which speakers project aspects of their identity through the forms their utterances take. We conclude this chapter with a discussion of the implications of these studies for future research in bilingualism.

The Conception of Variation in Bilingual Studies

Variation in language can result as a consequence of inherent physiological and matura-tional differences between members of a community. For instance, men tend to have lower fundamental frequency than women as a function of their vocal tract size. Inter-individual differences brought about by physical and developmental causes are not normally within the purview of bilingual studies. Instead, researchers tend to focus on variation that sig-nals something about the speakers' bilingualism. This type of variation can affect any level of the grammar: word selection (Kroll & Stewart, 1994), expression of subject pro-nouns (Otheguy, Zentella, & Livert, 2007), word order (Gavarro, 2003), phonetic cat-egories (Caramazza, Yeni-Komshian, Zurif, & Carbone, 1973), phonological distributions (Purnell, Salmons, & Tepeli, 2004), *semantic categorization* (Ameel, Storms, Malt, & Sloman, 2005), *discourse markers* (Sankoff, Thibault, Nagy, Blondeau, Fonollosa, & Gagnon, 1997), for example.

There are two broad strands of quantitative empirical research in bilingualism. In the first case, bilinguals are studied relative to monolinguals in order to gauge whether they acquire, store, process, and produce a language, usually their weaker one, in the same way that monolingual speakers do. In the second case, bilinguals are studied with an eye toward understanding phenomena that are arguably exclusive to bilingualism: *code-switching* (i.e., the mixing of languages) and cross-linguistic interaction (also called transfer, inter-ference, or convergence). We say *arguably* since bidialectal speakers have shown such effects (Hazen, 2001) as have those who attempt to *cross* ethnic or other identity-based boundaries (Rampton, 2005). What often unites these strands of research is that variation is conceived of primarily as deviation from an optimal variety, wherein some productions are assumed to be more correct (i.e., monolingual-like) than others by the analyst. Under this view, variants are not all considered equally valid communicative options.

When bilinguals are compared to monolinguals, as is most often the case, it is the pro-duction or perception of the latter group that is taken as the norm under the assumption that bilinguals strive to match the monolingual variety. In the phonetic literature, bilin-guals have been frequently observed to produce and perceive sound categories that do not overlap exactly with those of natives, even when they have acquired both languages from infancy (Pallier, Bosch, & Sebastián-Gallés, 1997). This has been interpreted to mean that, regardless of age of acquisition, a bilingual can be observed to deviate from a monolingual in a measurable way (Mack, 2003). And in cases when bilinguals are compared to one another, those with more signs of *linguistic transfer* or those who use a less diverse set of structures are often assumed to be not as fluent as those with less overt signs of contact and more structural complexity in their speech.

This etic conception of linguistic variants as falling along a continuum of correctness or complexity has historically pervaded the study of bilingualism at both micro and macro levels. Within psycholinguistics, factors such as linguistic proficiency and language domi-nance are evoked to account for the variation attested between bilingual and monolingual speakers, on the one hand, and between individual bilinguals on the other. Moving from the focus on individuals to the study of communities, scholars of language contact tend to correlate types and degrees of language contact phenomena with different contact set-tings in a manner that casts proficiency and dominance as community-level characteristics (Muysken, 2005). *Contact linguists* hypothesize that certain types of linguistic borrow-ing are practiced by fully proficient (i.e., native) speakers, whereas linguistic interference beyond the lexical level is theorized to occur with increased frequency at all levels of the grammar only in communities of restricted speakers who are undergoing language shift

(Thomason & Kaufman, 1988). Across various subfields of linguistic inquiry, there has been a tendency to view some of the variation produced by bilinguals as suboptimal when measured against a monolingual standard variety that is often more imagined than real.

Consider the examples in 1–3, below, of attested utterances from bilinguals in the US who hail from long-standing bilingual communities. In (1), we see a case of borrowing (or code-switching) where a speaker from the border town of El Paso, Texas, inserts chunks of English language into an otherwise Spanish clause. An apparent case of convergence is illustrated in (2) in the speech of a French–English bilingual from a language-isolated community in Pennsylvania. Note that while all the lexemes that he uses are French, the word order is English. And in (3), a Cajun French–English bilingual uses a preposition followed by a bare noun, rather than the form of the preposition that encodes the definite article. In each case, the corresponding reference form options are given in italics.

(1) Y era lo que les dije a mis hijas, *high school* (*Translation: la preparatoria*) son los *four years* (*Translation: cuatro años*) más bonitos de tu vida (Speaker AF006), Spanish in Texas Corpus Project (Bullock & Toribio, 2012).
     And what I said to my daughter was, high school are the best four years of your life.
(2) Et pi' je travaillais à une **grosse éléctrique ligne** (*Translation: ligne éléctrique*; Speaker NB, Frenchville Pennsylvania, US, Bullock fieldnotes 2007).
     And then I worked on a big electric line.
(3) Et là ils m'ont envoyé **à** Colorado (*Translation: au Colorado*; Dubois & Noetzel, 2005, p. 138).
     And then they sent me to Colorado.

These structures diverge in a salient way from the structures that might be found in contemporary reference grammars of the Romance languages depicted. Yet in the absence of additional information about the speakers and the linguistic norms of their communities, we cannot know whether the use of certain forms over others is indeed dictated by the speakers' proficiency and/or language dominance, or whether the forms are instead circulated widely among other speakers in their social networks. In order for researchers to accurately categorize the types of behavior that they elicit from bilingual individuals, they need to investigate the range of factors that are known to condition variation in monolingual communities, where proficiency and dominance are not a concern. Some of these factors are overviewed in the following sections.

Factors that Contribute to Language Variation

Sociolinguists study how a language varies as a function of *social factors*. For instance, in his seminal study, Labov (1963) observed that the vocalic portion of the diphthongs in words like *tight* and *house* in men's speech in Martha's Vineyard were centralizing to a schwa-like vowel. A multivariate analysis of 69 individuals, categorized according to age, region, occupation, and ethnicity showed that these changes were correlated to speaker identity, with those who expressed the most regional pride and the strongest resistance to non-islanders presenting the most change. The implication is that linguistic variation reflects socially constructed categories.

Sociolinguistic studies are typically localized to examine variation within a given *speech community* whose members are assumed to share the same language variety and patterns of use. Bilinguals have idiosyncratic patterns of use; they use different languages according to environment and conversation partners, and they can have asymmetric patterns of literacy and education. Thus, in practice, the concept of the speech community is uneasily applied in bilingual environments and, for this reason, there are few large-scale, quantitative studies of variation *within* bilingual communities to parallel those that exist for the study of variation in monolingual ones (for exceptions, see Mougeon, Nadasdi, & Rehner, 2005; Poplack, 1980). More often than not, then, bilinguals are grouped together in a study (or in an experiment) as a macro-level variable juxtaposed to monolinguals. Alternatively, when not compared to monolinguals, they are grouped according to their language dominance or proficiency, either self-assessed or as measured by the researcher, even though it is widely recognized that there are many social confounds underlying these components of group difference (Flege, Mackay, & Piske, 2002; Treffers-Daller, 2011).

A more useful concept to investigate variation between bilingual individuals is found in the notion of a *community of practice*, which is defined by its members and by the practices they engage in (Eckert & McConnell-Ginet, 2007). The community of practice model allows us to consider the possibility that some of the variation commonly observed in bilingual studies might reflect *style* rather than *variety* (Quist, 2008). Individuals align with multiple communities of practice, and they fashion and project their identities and allegiances through selecting and recombining linguistic variables. That this often leads to variations perceived by naïve listeners as non-native has become evident in the flurry of studies focused on speakers of youth languages and ethnolects in urban centers worldwide: in Canada (Hoffman & Walker, 2010), Denmark (Quist, 2008), France (Jamin, Trimaille, & Gasquet-Cyrus, 2006), the US (Mendoza-Denton, 1997), Belgium (Blommaert, 2014), England (Kerswill, 2013), Sweden (Magnusson & Stroud, 2012), Senegal (Swigart, 1989), Germany (Keim, 2002), and China (Lefort, 2012). Importantly, because these are native speakers who are dominant in the national language that surrounds them, sociolinguists interpret the choices these individuals make as a product of and a conscious response to globalization and immigration rather than as a reflection of their linguistic proficiency or language dominance.

Research on bilingualism, in general, has been slow to explore the range of social variables that are known to contribute to language variation, such as sex, age, ethnicity, and social class, although each is known to contribute to variation in significant ways. A community of practice orientation to bilingual research, similar to that taken for urban youth languages and ethnolects, encourages us to consider, as well, the social affiliations of bilingual speakers and the identities they forge for themselves in each of their languages. One such example, a study of *ethnolectal* phonetic variation among second-generation Punjabi–English bilingual speakers in London, revealed that their self-identification as *Asian* or *British–Asian* was a significant predictor of how they produced rhotic sounds in English (Hirson & Sohail, 2007). The authors of the study interpret the different labels to indicate a participant's sense of integration or alienation in British society. Those who chose the label British–Asian produced mostly non-rhotic variants, typical of the accent of the area, while all the self-identified Asian participants produced rhotic accents, some with the retroflex taps used in Punjabi. The stance of the speakers *vis-à-vis* their Britishness proves to be an important social factor contributing to variation between them.

There is accumulating empirical evidence that we cannot rule out the possibility that some of the variation attributed to language interference or to proficiency among bilingual study participants is intentional and performative (Heselwood & McChrystal, 2000; Sharma & Sankaran, 2011). Bilingual speakers have been shown to deliberately adopt or shed stereotypically native-like features in order to pass as native-speakers (Piller, 2002) or voice the speech of others (Flege & Hammond, 1982; Zuengler, 1988). This means that bilinguals can also adopt and project various identity-based styles in their languages, which sometimes make them appear *non-native*. It is often observed that bilinguals, when in conversation with one another, have recourse to code-switching for stylistic purposes (Bell, 1984; Gumperz, 1970; Zentella, 1997). The deployment of code-switching might well constitute style shifting on some occasions, but it is not the only means by which bilinguals project their various social affiliations or stances. Nevertheless, the focus on code-switching as the first resort for style shifting has eclipsed research into the possibility that bilinguals can make stylistic moves by alternating within their languages rather than by alternating between them. As a consequence, the signs of convergence in bilingualism are too freely interpreted as emanating from interference, rather than from planning.

There is a movement in linguistics to supplant the construct of *language* as a conventionalized, objectively defined and static system with a more dynamic, subjective, and inclusionary model. The current call to reconceptualize language follows from a recognition of the diversity and unboundedness of linguistic forms found in multilingual societies worldwide (Makoni & Pennycook, 2007) and as a reaction to the linguistic changes accompanying the societal changes that have resulted from increased immigration toward western Europe (Blommaert & Rampton, 2011). This dismantling of hermetically defined languages parallels the rejection of the concept of the *native-speaker* who possesses a target grammar that adult second language learners aspire to attain (Cook, 1999).

The pressing insistence on debunking *ideologies* of standard languages and native speakers bears on the important factor of *input* in bilingualism and the fact that most speakers worldwide do not have access to the normative model of language for which the putative native-speaker represents the standard bearer. In point of fact, with its emphasis on the vernacular, sociolinguistics serves to inform us over and over again that monolingual speakers also ignore prescriptive norms and fashion their own speech patterns according to conventions that have local currency. Monolinguals show more vernacular variants in their talk than formal ones in most circumstances. Likewise, we should expect bilingual speakers to show very different patterns of use according to the type of input they are exposed to and according to how they wish to be viewed, with some demonstrating more frequent colloquial variants and others favoring formal or normative ones in one or the other language. Work on Anglophones acquiring French in Montreal reveal such a bifurcated pattern among bilinguals; those who acquired French in immersion school use significantly less frequent subject doubling, a strong feature of the spoken vernacular, than naturalist French acquirers (Nagy, Blondeau, & Auger, 2003). The authors of that study raise the possibility that this pattern may be revelatory of identity rather than proficiency:

> *It remains an open question whether these findings indicate partial mastery of the L1 grammar (i.e., a sort of* interlanguage status*) or whether L2 speakers in this social situation do not wish to acquire L1 patterns that would identify them as Francophone, at the risk of losing their Anglophone identity.*
>
> (Nagy et al., 2003, p. 99)

To isolate the role of socio-indexical and input factors in bilingualism from those that are viewed as uniquely bilingual variables (proficiency and dominance), analysts need two primary sources of data. First, we need large corpora of the vernacular speech varieties that monolinguals and bilinguals alike produce and are exposed to in order to examine their frequency and distribution patterns. This would allow us to situate individuals' performance in their proper ecological context rather than relative to an abstract, and possibly, absent normative input. Efforts are underway to gather these types of corpora, but spoken corpora are time consuming and costly to develop and curate (Barnett et al., 2000; Bullock & Toribio, 2012; Léglise & Alby, 2013; Travis & Cacoullos, 2013).

Absent this data, we are still able to observe variation on a smaller scale by exposing bilinguals to different conditions, as we do with monolinguals. Comparing how the same individuals perform in differing contexts nullifies the effects of proficiency and focuses instead on how they respond to other factors. In the next section, we review contemporary empirical work that has begun to address the effects of socio-indexical and interactional factors *within* bilingual populations. It should be noted that few works attend to bilinguals' performances in each of their component languages, perhaps in part because it is difficult to find linguistic variables that are similar enough to be compared across languages. Our focus is particularly on studies of phonetic variation because pronunciation is regarded as the most salient marker of regional and social differences and speakers have been shown to be particularly attuned to how small acoustic differences index socially constructed categories such as race (Walton & Orlikoff, 1994), *gender* (Strand, 1999), and nativeness (Cheong, 2007). A focus on phonetics also permits an exploration of variables that are continuous, rather than discrete, so that researchers can probe degrees of socially conditioned linguistic variation.

Gender

Socio-indexical linguistic variables are those that serve to point toward recognizable socially relevant categories. A seminal study on bilingual language use investigated language shift patterns among Hungarian speakers in the linguistic enclave of Oberwart, Austria (Gal, 1978, 1979). Gal's results indicated that young women were at the forefront of shift to the majority language, German, while older speakers with more network ties to the peasant community were the most likely to maintain Hungarian, as were young men. She argued that the factor of sex is correlated with the identity a speaker wished to project; women expressed a desire to distance themselves from their association with the bilingual, peasant community by claiming a new social status via assimilation to the majority language, German.

While women have repeatedly been shown to be the first to adopt and diffuse linguistic innovations, this is not necessarily the case. In a study of the prosodic correlates of focus marking among bilingual K'ichee'–Spanish speakers in Guatemala—Baird (2014) compared speakers from two different communities, one closer to an urban center (Cantel) where Spanish is prevalent, and one more remote (Nahualá). This study is one of the few to test bilinguals in each of their component languages. The findings indicated an interaction between sex and location; women in the more rural community were more likely to show K'ichee' features in their Spanish than men from the same community, but there were no *between-gender* differences in their K'ichee'. There were also no significant between-gender differences in either Spanish or K'ichee' for the speakers from Cantel. A plausible explanation for these finding is that women in Nahualá have less access to Spanish speakers than do men, who have more mobility (Baird, 2014).

Contributing to the growing body of research on Catalan–Spanish bilingualism, Simonet (2010) investigated whether the dark laterals of Catalan and the light laterals of Spanish were converging due to contact and bilingualism. Two findings of note with respect to the variable of gender were revealed. First, when the participants were speaking Spanish, listeners had more difficulty in classifying females as native or non-native than males, irrespective of whether the speaker was Catalan- or Spanish-dominant. Spanish-dominant men were judged to be more native-like in Spanish than Spanish-dominant females, and Catalan-dominant men were judged to be more non-native-like in Spanish than were Catalan-dominant females. This could suggest that the men assume more marked native

(Spanish-dominant) or non-native (Catalan-dominant) pronunciations in Spanish, perhaps to index their backgrounds or their stance toward the language, than do the women. A second finding notes that only younger Spanish-dominant females were observed to produce a single, merged lateral category for their two languages, characterized by high values of the second formant (F2), indicating a tendency toward clearer (more Spanish-like) laterals. Simonet sees this as a potential way for young Spanish-dominant females to *distance themselves from what they perceive as Catalan-accented Spanish* (Simonet, 2010, p. 676) and concludes that some signs of transfer found in *quasi-balanced* bilingual communities may be due to indexicality rather than to an inability to acquire native-like categories.

Poplack's (1980) seminal multivariate analysis of the code-switching patterns of a Puerto Rican *barrio* community in New York City also revealed an effect of gender on code-switching. While Poplack's main hypothesis of the study held that more syntactically integrated forms of code-switching would correlate with a higher degree of bilingual fluency (a hypothesis that was supported by the findings), she also found that women produced far more instances of the *fluent* intra-sentential form of code-switching than did men. These studies illustrate that issues that appear to ensue from language dominance and proficiency might be dependent on access to linguistic input or to the projection of gendered identities. Speakers are not granted, nor do they always seek, equal access to certain types of linguistic input. Instead, their speech forms are aligned according to the affiliations that they maintain or to which they aspire. Gender differences, particularly in minority language contexts where access to the majority language may be compromised for some speakers, may play a much larger role in contributing to bilingual variation than they have been afforded to date.

Race and Ethnicity

Just as they have been shown to give rise to ethnolectal variants in English and other languages (Boberg, 2004; Hoffman & Walker, 2010; Jamin, Trimaille, & Gasquet-Cyrus, 2006; Quist, 2008; Rampton, 2005), the social categories of race and ethnicity can also influence a bilingual's language choices. Toribio (2003) conducted an ethnographic exploration of the impact of perceived racial discrimination on the language choices of two families of Dominican speakers in New York. She observes that those from the family whose members perceive themselves to have been subject to racial discrimination use their languages, both Spanish and Spanish-accented English, as a means of foregrounding their identity as Dominican, rather than African–American, while *(f)or white Dominicans, the minority language may be in competition with acculturation into the dominant social structure* (Toribio, 2003, p. 9). Thus, it might be easier for those whose ethnic status is not visible to lose the linguistic features that index them as members of a minority community. This is a point made, as well, in a study of ethnolects of Toronto English (Hoffman & Walker, 2010). In that context, the between-group differences in linguistic behavior found between three generations of Chinese and Italian immigrants and a British–Irish reference group were taken to reflect ethnic identities that the authors acknowledge might be more visible for some groups than for others.

There is also empirical evidence that linguistic performance of an individual can be affected by his/her orientation toward the local political importance of language as a marker of ethnic identity (Bourhis & Giles, 1976; Gatbonton, Trofimovich, & Segalowitz, 2011). Gatbonton et al. (2011) examined Quebec Francophones' pronunciation of the English interdental phoneme /ð/ (as in *things, rather, lathe*) as a correlate of four measures of ethnic group affiliation to find that the stronger they identified as Francophones, the more accented their English was found to be. This lends support to the notion that *non-native* accents can serve as markers of ethnic identities, and in certain cases, of a speaker's bilingualism.

Affect and Emotion

Cultural differences have an impact on bilingual performance in ways that exceed the expression of ethnic identity. Different cultures vary in their expectations with regard to social conventions, and bilinguals' linguistic choices can be guided by these cultural norms. For example, Korean has an elaborate system of honorific markings, and Chinese–Korean bilinguals in Yanji, an autonomous Korean prefecture in China, have been shown to prefer to switch to Korean when speaking to a superior but to Chinese when talking among equals (Ma, 2005). By contrast, American-raised bilingual students of Korean heritage in the US profess to prefer to speak English to their Korean elders in order to avoid making a mistake in attempting to use honorific forms.

Different cultural expectations can also impact the way affect is encoded in language (Besnier, 1990). Bilinguals often remark that they experience affect and emotions differently in their two languages (Besemeres, 2004; Pavlenko, 2002; Wierzbicka, 2005). Based on her ethnographic work with Portuguese–French bilinguals in France, Koven (2004) argues that bilinguals have access to different *repertoires of personas* through which they can perform different affective associations. In her case study, her participant feels and is perceived as more forceful and aggressive in French than in Portuguese, and she finds herself unable to talk back to her mother in Portuguese like she does in French. Koven notes that her participant might not feel free to do so because she may not have a "back-talking" persona in Portuguese.

If bilinguals can be seen to enact different personas across their languages, then some of the variation observed in their performances in the laboratory or in the field may result from the types of tasks that they are asked to complete. Standard methodology for sociolinguistic interviews attempts to elicit the most casual style of speech possible from interviewees, often by asking them to recount vivid memories, such as near-death experiences, which would engage them emotionally so that they monitor their speech less. But reacting with high affect to certain themes might be easier for a bilingual participant to do in one language than the other, not necessarily because the speaker lacks the linguistic ability to do so but because he or she may not feel as comfortable doing so.

Second language learners have been shown to opt for more formal linguistic features, arguably reflecting the type of styles they have been exposed to in the classroom, even when these are immersive (Mougeon, Nadasdi, & Rehner, 2010). But regardless of their proficiency, all types of bilinguals may consciously avoid adopting particular styles in one of their languages if their use of those styles might be perceived as awkward or inauthentic. Many bilinguals may find it *safer* to simply adopt neutral or formal variants than to attempt to use variants that index identities or stances that they feel they cannot lay claim to in one of their languages even if they very familiar to them. So, though they might correlate with measures of proficiency and/or dominance, restrictions in style might as easily correlate with identity-based variation.

Audience and Accommodation

An important factor in examining styles in linguistics is audience (Bell, 1984). In *Bell's model of audience design*, speakers can be perceived to adapt their speech to various interlocutors, both real (audience) and imagined (referee). In audience design, speakers can be observed to shift styles to converge to or away from their conversation partners as a psychosocial form of communication accommodation (Giles, 1984; Sachdev & Giles, 2006). While convergence signals alignment, divergence generally has been taken to signal disagreement with the speaker's stance or affiliations (Babel, 2012; Bourhis & Giles, 1976; Kim, Horton, & Bradlow, 2011). In a manifestation of accommodation in bilinguals, Chinese–Thai bilingual children used Thai-accented variants with Thai interlocutors significantly more than with Chinese listeners (Beebe, 1981). In recent work on adults, it was found that speakers who shared the same dialect and the same language converged more than speakers in dyads who shared the same language but not the same dialect or those who differed in their native languages altogether (Kim et al., 2011). Other researchers have found signs of both divergence and convergence on a variety of prosodic parameters among speakers of different native languages when performing a task together in their common language (Rao, 2013).

Murphy (2014) investigated *phonetic accommodation* among native and non-native speakers of French in a design that paired English-speaking French learners of various proficiencies with native and non-native French-speaking interviewers. Surprisingly, the native-speaking French interviewer was observed to converge her vowels significantly toward those of the non-natives. It was also the more proficient learners who converged most toward their interviewers, in particular toward the French interviewer. Proficiency and age of acquisition did not contribute to the learners' convergence for specific vowels; instead, the only factor contributing to convergence was the interviewers' native language. The author speculates that the strong effect of the interviewers' background on the learners may have occurred because the learners *wished to emulate the native speaker more* (Murphy, 2014, p. 446). The implication of this study is that speakers do not accommodate automatically in conversation; they only do so with speakers for whom they feel a strong affiliation.

In seminal sociophonetic work on bilingual children's accommodation, Khattab (Khattab, 2002a, 2002b, 2006, 2009, 2013) demonstrates how several bilingual Arabic–English children in the UK accommodate using accented, non-accented, and code-switched variants. Importantly, her work suggests that bilinguals acquire and store multiple phonetic variants for the same forms. She shows that the children's choice among variants is conditioned by the social-communicative situation and that they can be observed to move between different styles accordingly. That the children might possess *accented* and *unaccented* variants of the words they use is a claim consistent with a growing body of literature in sociophonetics, and in linguistics more broadly, pointing to the notion that socio-indexical information is acquired and stored as an essential part of a linguistic representation (Foulkes, 2010).

A different type of audience is conveyed in *referee design* (Bell, 1984), in which a speaker initiates a performance that corresponds with his or her stereotype of a persona, as if it were being performed to an audience. Bilinguals, who have a versatile and flexible linguistic repertoire (Blommaert & Backus, 2012), have been shown to deliberately deploy non-native features to project stereotyped personas. Magnusson and Stroud (2012) investigate a group of young multilinguals in Sweden who identify themselves to be Assyrian–Syrians. The youths are observed to take on deliberate stereotyped performances of immigrants in an act of *passing as a non-native speaker* (Pennycook, 2012, p. 97).

The degree to which patterns of accommodation have a long-term effect on local language forms is still unknown (Hoffman & Walker, 2010; Sankoff, 2002; Sharma &

Sankaran, 2011). In their study of Punjabi bilinguals in the UK, Sharma and Sankaran (2011) find that older second-generation speakers employ strongly Punjabi-inflected English phonetic variables that correlate with Punjabi language use. However, within the group of younger second-generation speakers, these same variables come to index gender, indicating that the enregisterment (Agha, 2005) of this variable has evolved from its origin as an index of Punjabiness, in general.

Phonetic markers reflect regional and social accents, and accents can easily take on meanings that are emblematic of distinct identities. There is also evidence that convergence can impact areas of grammar that may be less easily evaluated for social meaning, like syntax. For instance, different dialects of Spanish vary according to the linguistic constraints that condition the presence or absence of a subject pronoun with a tensed verb. A landmark, corpus-driven study of US- and foreign-born Spanish speakers in New York City (NYC) documented, among other effects, a significant increase in overt pronoun use among NYC-born speakers relative to immigrants (Otheguy & Zentella, 2012). These changes appear to result from dialect leveling (toward the Caribbean dialects with higher frequency of expressed subject pronouns) and from contact with English. From these results, it would appear that convergence via accommodation in some immigrant contexts can have long-term linguistic consequences, leading to structural differences in the language as spoken in the immigrant context from its form as spoken in the homeland.

Language Mode

In a series of publications, Grosjean has elaborated the concept of *language mode*, which envisions bilinguals moving along a continuum of bilinguals' states between monolingual endpoints depending on psychological, linguistic, and contextual factors (Grosjean, 1998, 2001; Grosjean & Miller, 1994; Grosjean & Soares, 1986). The ability of bilinguals to adjust the ratio of one language to another in various modes (e.g., English, Swedish, and English–Swedish modes) had been observed earlier in descriptions of natural speech produced with different interlocutors in bilingual contexts (Hasselmo, 1970). The bilingual language mode has proven to be a particularly apt metaphor for conceptualizing code-switching as the dual activation of languages, although it is intended to apply broadly to all types of bilingual phenomena, including convergence and *language drift* (Sancier & Fowler, 1997). In language drift, individuals can be observed to modulate their performance in each of their languages so that they vary in tandem according to one or other monolingual endpoint. Sancier and Fowler (1997) document the case of a bilingual who produced more Portuguese-like short-lag voiceless stops in her Portuguese and her English during and immediately after a stay in Brazil, but manifested more English-like longer-lag stops in both her languages after her return to the US.

Language mode theorizes the impact of contextual factors on the degree of mixing a bilingual undertakes, and it has been operationalized by comparing the phonetic outputs of speakers when they perform in only one language versus when they use them both in the same speech event while switching. Such studies have yielded mixed results, with some researchers exposing a significant effect of code-switching in real time in one or both languages and others finding little to no effect (Balukas & Koops, 2015; Bullock, Toribio, González, & Dalola, 2006; Grosjean & Miller, 1994; Grosjean & Soares, 1986; Khattab, 2003). In a study of the Catalan mid-vowels that indirectly tests the effect of code-switching (bilingual mode), Simonet (2014) manipulated the language of the stimuli

(Catalan-only versus mixed Catalan–Spanish) in a reading task to find that the same speakers produced significant differences between the vowels depending only on language context. Significantly, the studies that manipulate language mode are among the very few studies in the experimental literature that attend to a bilinguals' performance without reference to an external monolingual control group.

A different application of language mode is one that primes a speaker to expect either more monolingual or more bilingual context by varying the cue for language in a naming task (Goldrick, Runnqvist, & Costa, 2014; Olson, 2013, 2016). Olson (2013) demonstrates that bilinguals are more sensitive to unexpected switches than to expected ones. Olson created three different language modes: English mode, where 95% of the stimuli were to be named in English to 5% Spanish; Spanish mode, with a ratio of 95% Spanish to 5% English; and bilingual mode, with a balanced ratio of stimuli, 50% Spanish to 50% English. The results showed that bilinguals produced a significant difference in stop consonant production between the balanced conditioned and the more monolingual modes for the non-switched tokens (those that are to be named in the same language as the previous token). In the bilingual mode, English stops were produced with more Spanish-like values, and Spanish stops were produced with more English-like ones. This implies that speakers' expectations about the language or languages to be used in an interaction affect their behavior.

Investigations of language mode highlight the dynamic nature of bilingual performance and the potential that convergence can be transient, reflecting *bilingual style* rather than interference. Language mode can be induced by a host of social factors, including conversation partner, switching habits, ideologies and attitudes, content of the message, function of the speech act, and physical environment in which the utterance takes place. Overall, language mode reflects a speaker's perception of the style warranted or expected of a given interaction. If social and linguistic information are learned, stored, and processed together, then questions of accuracy cannot be fully disaggregated from questions of styles/modes. Studies of code-switching operationalized as language mode demonstrate that language is dynamic and shifts according to the socio-pragmatic and indexical context of the utterance, and appears to be partially dependent on the speaker's prior experiences, expectations, and audiences (e.g., Hay, Jannedy, & Mendoza-Denton, 1999; Niedzielski, 2010).

Ideologies

Throughout this chapter, we have focused on the social and contextual sources that help give rise to the variation produced by bilinguals. But it is as important that we give due consideration to how variation itself is evaluated. Standard linguistic ideologies have a pervasive effect on how *sociolinguistic variation* is represented (Bauman & Briggs, 2003; Schieffelin, Woolard, & Kroskrity, 1998), and we inhabit a world where the prestige accorded to localized language practices is always trumped by the perception that *purer* forms and practices are used elsewhere. So, while linguists might argue, as we have done here, that variation can arise intentionally from the performance of identity-based styles that can be highly valued in a bilingual's network, these styles may nonetheless be evaluated harshly both locally and externally. Such attitudes can become internalized, engendering linguistic insecurity and language shift in some and emboldening others to perform over-the-top bilingual personas (Magnusson & Stroud, 2012). In addition, it can hardly be denied that the public discourse on the *non-nativeness* of some immigrants and their children in the US and in Europe is infused with an undercurrent of racial and ethnic stereotyping. The effect of such attitudes remains to be fully investigated as a factor in bilingualism.

Conclusion

Grosjean (1998) argues that the conflicting findings from research on bilingualism emanate, in part, from insufficient attention to the factors that differentiate bilingual participants and their language modes. We have proposed here that, in addition, some of the variation that is found in observations of bilinguals in the lab or in the field may result from under-studied social factors that crosscut bilingual groupings; however, they may be defined on the basis of proficiency or dominance. Variables like sex, age, identity, ethnicity, language mode, and language ideologies contribute to produce linguistic variations among bilingual speakers that mirror the characteristics that are assumed to index *non-nativeness*. This implies that, going forward, researchers might wish to focus on understanding the ways in which bilinguals themselves evaluate and value variations within their communities of practice, as local and individual practices may deviate substantially from normative ones in ways that cannot be circumscribed by proficiency or dominance.

List of Key Words and Concepts

Bell's model of audience design, Between-gender, Bidialectal, Bilingual style, Code-switching, Contact linguists, Discourse markers, Ethnolectal, Gender, Ideologies, Inter-language status, Language dominance, Language drift, Language mode, Language shift, Linguistic transfer, Linguistic variation, Phonetic accommodation, Plurilingual, Proficiency, Quasi-balanced, Referee design, Repertoires of personas, Semantic categorization, Social factors, Socio-indexical, Sociolinguistics

Internet Sites Related to the Sociolinguistics of Bilingualism

Heritage Language Variation and Change in Toronto: http://projects.chass.utoronto.ca/ngn/ HLVC/0_0_home.php
The World in Words: http://www.pri.org/collections/world-words

Discussion Questions

(1) One factor not mentioned here is *religion*. How might religion affect bilingual speech performance?
(2) In her book *Growing up Bilingual*, Zentella noted that male Spanish–English bilingual adolescents use more African–American inflected variants in English than do female adolescents. What *socio-indexical* considerations might account for this difference?
(3) What differences might you predict would be observed in a study of bilingual immigrant speakers in an area where they are welcomed versus an area where immigrants are scapegoated?

Suggested Research Projects

(1) Conduct a meta-study on published studies of the cognitive benefits of bilingualism. Do any of the studies consider gender, race, or ethnicity as independent variables?

References

Agha, A. (2005). Voice, footing, enregisterment. *Journal of Linguistic Anthropology, 15*(1), 38–59.

Ameel, E., Storms, G., Malt, B. C., & Sloman, S. A. (2005). How bilinguals solve the naming problem. *Journal of Memory and Language, 53*(1), 60–80.

Babel, M. (2012). Evidence for phonetic and social selectivity in spontaneous phonetic imitation. *Journal of Phonetics, 40*(1), 177–189.

Baird, B. O. (2014, January 1). *An acoustic analysis of contrastive focus marking in Spanish–K'ichee' (Mayan) bilingual intonation* (Doctoral dissertation). University of Texas.

Balukas, C., & Koops, C. (2015). Spanish–English bilingual voice onset time in spontaneous code-switching. *International Journal of Bilingualism, 19*(4), 423–433.

Barnett, R., Codó, E., Eppler, E., Forcadell, M., Gardner-Chloros, P., van Hout, R., & Sebba, M. (2000). The LIDES coding manual: A document for preparing and analyzing language interaction data. *International Journal of Bilingualism, 4*(2), 131–271.

Bauman, R., & Briggs, C. L. (2003). *Voices of modernity: Language ideologies and the politics of inequality.* Cambridge, UK: Cambridge University Press.

Beebe, L. M. (1981). Social and situational factors affecting the communicative strategy of dialect code-switching. *International Journal of the Sociology of Language, 32*, 139–149.

Bell, A. (1984). Language style as audience design. *Language in Society, 13*(2), 145–204.

Besemeres, M. (2004). Different languages, different emotions? Perspectives from autobiographical literature. *Journal of Multilingual and Multicultural Development, 25*(2–3), 140–158.

Besnier, N. (1990). Language and affect. *Annual Review of Anthropology, 19*, 419–451.

Birdsong, D. (2014). Dominance and age in bilingualism. *Applied Linguistics, 35*, 374–302.

Blommaert, J. (2014). Infrastructures of superdiversity: Conviviality and language in an Antwerp neighborhood. *European Journal of Cultural Studies, 17*(4), 431–451.

Blommaert, J. M. E., & Backus, A. (2012). Super diverse repertoires and the individual. *Tilburg Papers in Cultural Studies, 24.* Tilburg University, the Netherlands.

Blommaert, J., & Rampton, B. (2011). Language and superdiversity. *Diversities, 13*(2), 3–21.

Boberg, C. (2004). Ethnic patterns in the phonetics of Montreal English. *Journal of Sociolinguistics, 8*(4), 538–568.

Bourhis, R. Y., & Giles, H. (1976). The language of cooperation in Wales: A field study. *Language Sciences, 42*, 13–16.

Bullock, B. E., & Toribio, A. J. (2012). *The Spanish in Texas corpus project COERLL.* Austin: The University of Texas at Austin. Retrieved from http://www.spanishintexas.org

Bullock, B. E., Toribio, A. J., González, V., & Dalola, A. (2006). Language dominance and performance outcomes in bilingual pronunciation. In M. G. O'Brien, C. Shea, & J. Archibald (Eds.), *Proceedings of the 8th Generative Approaches to Second Language Acquisition Conference (GASLA 2006): The Banff Conference* (pp. 9–16), Somerville, MA: Cascadilla Press.

Caramazza, A., Yeni-Komshian, G., Zurif, E., & Carbone, E. (1973). The acquisition of a new phonological contrast: The case of stop consonants in French–English bilinguals. *The Journal of the Acoustical Society of America, 54*(2), 421–428.

Cheong, S. H. (2007). *The role of listener affiliated socio-cultural factors in perceiving native accented versus foreign accented speech* (Unpublished doctoral dissertation). The Ohio State University.

Cook, V. (1999). Going beyond the native speaker in language teaching. *TESOL Quarterly, 33*(2), 185–209.

De Houwer, A. (2011). Language input environments and language development in bilingual acquisition. *Applied Linguistics Review, 2*, 221–240.

Dubois, S., & Noetzel, S. (2005). Intergenerational pattern of interference and internally-motivated changes in Cajun French. *Bilingualism: Language and Cognition, 8*(2), 131–143.

Eckert, P., & McConnell-Ginet, S. (2007). Putting communities of practice in their place. *Gender and Language, 1*(1), 27–37.

Flege, J. E., & Hammond, R. M. (1982). Mimicry of non-distinctive phonetic differences between language varieties. *Studies in Second Language Acquisition, 5*(1), 1–17.

Flege, J. E., Mackay, I. R. A., & Piske, T. (2002). Assessing bilingual dominance. *Applied Psycholinguistics, 23*(4), 567–598.

Foulkes, P. (2010). Exploring social-indexical knowledge: A long past but a short history. *Laboratory Phonology, 1*(1), 5–39.

Gal, S. (1978). Peasant men can't get wives: Language change and sex roles in a bilingual community. *Language in Society, 7*(1), 1–16.

Gal, S. (1979). *Language shift: Social determinants of linguistic change in bilingual Austria.* New York: Academic Press.

Gatbonton, E., Trofimovich, P., & Segalowitz, N. (2011). Ethnic group affiliation and patterns of development of a phonological variable. *Modern Language Journal, 95*(2), 188–204.

Gavarro, A. (2003). Economy and word order patterns in bilingual English–Dutch acquisition. *Bilingualism: Language and Cognition, 6*(1), 69–79.

Giles, H. (1984). The dynamics of speech accommodation. *International Journal of the Sociology of Language, 46*, 1–155.

Goldrick, M., Runnqvist, E., & Costa, A. (2014). Language switching makes pronunciation less nativelike. *Psychological Science, 25*(4), 1031–1036.

Grosjean, F. (1998). Studying bilinguals: Methodological and conceptual issues. *Bilingualism: Language and Cognition, 1*(2), 131–149.

Grosjean, F. (2001). The bilingual's language modes. In J. L. Nicol (Ed.), *One mind, two languages: Bilingual language processing* (pp. 1–22). Oxford: Blackwell.

Grosjean, F., & Miller, J. L. (1994). Going in and out of languages: An example of bilingual flexibility. *Psychological Science, 5*(4), 201–206.

Grosjean, F., & Soares, C. (1986). Processing mixed language: Some preliminary findings. In J. Vaid (Ed.), *Language processing in bilinguals: Psycholinguistic and neuropsychological perspectives* (pp. 145–179). Hillsdale, NJ: Erlbaum Associates.

Gumperz, J. (1970). Verbal strategies and multilingual communication. In J. E. Alatis (Ed.), *Report of the Twenty-First Annual Round-Table Meeting on Linguistics and Language Studies* (pp. 129–147). Washington, DC: Georgetown University Press.

Hasselmo, N. (1970). *Code-switching and modes of speaking.* Berlin: de Gruyter.

Hay, J., Jannedy, S., & Mendoza-Denton, N. (1999). Oprah and/ay: Lexical frequency, referee design and style. In *Proceedings of the 14th International Congress of Phonetic Sciences* (pp. 1389–1392). Berkeley, CA: University of California.

Hazen, K. (2001). An introductory investigation into bidialectalism. *University of Pennsylvania Working Papers in Linguistics, 7*(3), 85–99.

Heselwood, B., & McChrystal, L. (2000). Gender, accent features and voicing in Panjabi-English bilingual children. *Leeds Working Papers in Linguistics and Phonetics, 8*, 45–70.

Hirson, A., & Sohail, N. (2007). Variability of rhotics in Punjabi–English bilinguals. In *Proceedings of the 16th International Congress of Phonetic Sciences*, 1501–1504.

Hoffman, M. F., & Walker, J. A. (2010). Ethnolects and the city: Ethnic orientation and linguistic variation in Toronto English. *Language Variation and Change, 22*(1), 37–67.

Jamin, M., Trimaille, C., & Gasquet-Cyrus, M. (2006). Convergence within divergence: The case of ethnically diverse neighborhoods in France. *Journal of French Language Studies, 16*(3), 335–356.

Keim, I. (2002). Social style of communication and bilingual speech practices: Case study of three migrant youth groups of Turkish origin in Mannheim/Germany. *Turkic Languages, 6*(2), 284–299.

Kerswill, P. (2013). Identity, ethnicity and place: The construction of youth language in London. In P. Auer, M. Hilpert, A. Stukenbrock, & B. Szmrecsanyi (Eds.), *Space in language and linguistics: Geographical, interactional, and cognitive perspectives* (pp. 128–146). Berlin: de Gruyter.

Khattab, G. (2002a). /l/ Production in English–Arabic bilingual speakers. *International Journal of Bilingualism, 6*(3), 335–353.

Khattab, G. (2002b). /r/ Production in English and Arabic bilingual and monolingual speakers. *Leeds Working Papers in Linguistics and Phonetics, 9*, 91–129.

Khattab, G. (2003). Age, input, and language mode factors in the acquisition of VOT by English–Arabic bilingual children. In *Proceedings of the 15th International Congress of Phonetic Sciences*, Barcelona, Spain (pp. 1–4).

Khattab, G. (2006). Phonological acquisition by Arabic-English bilingual children. In Z. Hua & B. Dodd (Eds.), *Phonological development and disorders in children: A multilingual perspective* (pp. 383–412). Clevedon: Multilingual Matters.

Khattab, G. (2009). Phonetic accommodation in children's code-switching. In B. E. Bullock & A. J. Toribio (Eds.), *The Cambridge handbook of linguistic code-switching* (pp. 142–160). Cambridge: Cambridge, UK: Cambridge University Press.

Khattab, G. (2013). Phonetic convergence and divergence strategies in English–Arabic bilingual children. *Linguistics, 51*(2), 439–472.

Kim, M., Horton, W. S., & Bradlow, A. R. (2011). Phonetic convergence in spontaneous conversations as a function of interlocutor language distance. *Laboratory Phonology, 2*(1), 125–156.

Koven, M. (2004). Getting 'emotional' in two languages: Bilinguals' verbal performance of affect in narratives of personal experience. *Text-Interdisciplinary Journal for the Study of Discourse, 24*, 471–515.

Kroll, J. F., & Stewart, E. (1994). Category interference in translation and picture naming: Evidence for asymmetric connection between bilingual memory representations. *Journal of Memory and Language, 33*(2), 149–174.

Labov, W. (1963). The social motivation for sound change. *Word, 19*, 273–309.

Lefort, J. (2012). Can recent linguistic developments in Dongxiang be categorized as a youth language? *Langage & Société, 141*, 71–98.

Léglise, I., & Alby, S. (2013). Les corpus plurilingues, entre linguistique de corpus et linguistique de contact. *Faits de Langues, 41*, 95–122.

Ma, C. (2005). *Language practice and identity of Korean–Chinese bilinguals in Yanji* (Unpublished doctoral dissertation). Michigan State University.

Mack, M. (2003). The phonetic systems of bilinguals. In M. T. Banich & M. Mack (Eds.), *Mind, brain, and language: Multidisciplinary perspectives* (pp. 309–349). Mahwah, NJ: Erlbaum.

Magnusson, J. E., & Stroud, C. (2012). High proficiency in markets of performance: A sociocultural approach to nativelikeness. *Studies in Second Language Acquisition, 34*(2), 321–345.

Makoni, S., & Pennycook, A. (Eds.). (2007). *Disinventing and reconstituting languages*. Clevedon, UK: Multilingual Matters.

Mendoza-Denton, N. C. (1997). *Chicana/Mexicana identity and linguistic aariation: An ethnographic and sociolinguistic study of gang affiliation in an urban high school* (Unpublished doctoral dissertation). Stanford University, California.

Meyerhoff, M., & Nagy, N. (2008). *Social lives in language sociolinguistics and multilingual speech communities: Celebrating the work of Gillian Sankoff* (Vol. 24). New York: John Benjamins.

Mougeon, R., Nadasdi, T., & Rehner, K. (2005). Contact-induced linguistic innovations on the continuum of language use: The case of French in Ontario. *Bilingualism: Language and Cognition, 8*(2), 99–115.

Mougeon, R., Nadasdi, T., & Rehner, K. (2010). *The sociolinguistic competence of immersion students*. Bristol, UK: Multilingual Matters.

Murphy, M. (2014). Sociophonetic convergence in native and non-native speakers of French. *Concordia Working Papers in Applied Linguistics, 5*, 435–450.

Muysken, P. (2005). Modeling language contact (otra vez) Bilingual optimisation strategies. In G. Banti, A. Marra, & E. Vineis (Eds.), *Atti del 4° congresso di studi dell'Associazone Italiana di Linguistica Applicata* (pp. 11–36). Perugia: Guerra Edizioni.

Nagy, N., Blondeau, H., & Auger, J. (2003). Second language acquisition and "real" French: An investigation of subject doubling in the French of Montreal anglophones. *Language Variation and Change, 15*(1), 73–103.

Niedzielski, N. (2010). Linguistic security, ideology, and vowel perception. In D. R. Preston & N. Niedzielski (Eds.), *A reader in sociophonetics* (pp. 253–264). Berlin/New York: De Gruyter Mouton.

Olson, D. J. (2013). Bilingual language switching and selection at the phonetic level: Asymmetrical transfer in VOT production. *Journal of Phonetics, 41*(6), 407–420.

Olson, D. J. (2016). The impact of code-switching, language context, and language dominance on suprasegmental phonetics: Evidence for the role of predictability. *International Journal of Bilingualism, 20*(4), 453–472. doi:1367006914566204.

Otheguy, R., & Zentella, Z. C. (2012). *Spanish in New York: Language contact, dialectal leveling, and structural continuity*. New York: Oxford University Press.

Otheguy, R., Zentella, A. C., & Livert, D. (2007). Language and dialect contact in Spanish in New York: Toward the formation of a speech community. *Language, 83*(4), 770–802.

Pallier, C., Bosch, L., & Sebastián-Gallés, N. (1997). A limit on behavioral plasticity in speech perception. *Cognition, 64*(3), B9–B17.

Pavlenko, A. (2002). Bilingualism and emotions. *Multilingua, 21*(1), 45–78.

Pennycook, A. (2012). *Language and mobility: Unexpected places*. Bristol, UK: Multilingual Matters.

Piller, I. (2002). Passing for a native speaker: Identity and success in second language learning. *Journal of Sociolinguistics, 6*(2), 179–208.

Poplack, S. (1980). Sometimes I'll start a sentence in Spanish y TERMINO EN ESPANOL: Toward a typology of code-switching. *Linguistics, 18*(7–8), 581–618.

Purnell, T., Salmons, J., & Tepeli, D. (2004). German substrate effects in Wisconsin English: Evidence for final fortition. *American Speech, 80*(2), 135–164.

Quist, P. (2008). Sociolinguistic approaches to multiethnolect: Language variety and stylistic practice. *International Journal of Bilingualism, 12*(1–2), 43–61.

Rampton, B. (2005). *Crossing: language and ethnicity among adolescents* (2nd ed.). Manchester: St. Jerome.

Rao, G. N. (2013). *Measuring phonetic convergence: segmental and suprasegmental speech adaptations during native and non-native talker interactions* (Unpublished doctoral dissertation). The University of Texas at Austin.

Sachdev, I., & Giles, H. (2006). Bilingual accommodation. In T. K. Bhatia & W. C. Ritchie (Eds.), *The handbook of bilingualism* (pp. 353–378). Oxford: Blackwell.

Sancier, M. L., & Fowler, C. A. (1997). Gestural drift in a bilingual speaker of Brazilian Portuguese and English. *Journal of Phonetics, 25*(4), 421–436.

Sankoff, G. (2002). Linguistic outcomes of language contact. In J. K. Chambers, P. Trudgill, & N. Schilling-Estes (Eds.), *The handbook of language variation and change* (pp. 638–668). Malden, MA: Blackwell.

Sankoff, G., Thibault, P., Nagy, N., Blondeau, H., Fonollosa, M.-O., & Gagnon, L. (1997). Variation in the use of discourse markers in a language contact situation. *Language Variation and Change, 9*(2), 191–217.

Schieffelin, B. B., Woolard, K. A., & Kroskrity, P. V. (Eds.). (1998). *Language ideologies: practice and theory*. New York: Oxford University Press.

Sharma, D., & Sankaran, L. (2011). Cognitive and social forces in dialect shift: Gradual change in London Asian speech. *Language Variation and Change, 23*(3), 399–428.

Simonet, M. (2010). Dark and clear laterals in Catalan and Spanish: Interaction of phonetic categories in early bilinguals. *Journal of Phonetics, 38*(4), 663–678.

Simonet, M. (2014). Phonetic consequences of dynamic cross-linguistic interference in proficient bilinguals. *Journal of Phonetics, 43*, 26–37.

Strand, E. A. (1999). Uncovering the role of gender stereotypes in speech perception. *Journal of Language and Social Psychology, 18*(1), 86–100.

Swigart, L. (1989). Practice and perception: A look at code-switching and mixing in Dakar. *Réalités Africaine et Langue Française, 23*, 25–39.

Thomason, S. G., & Kaufman, T. (1988). *Language contact, creolization, and genetic linguistics*. Berkeley, CA: University of California Press.

Toribio, A. J. (2003). The social significance of Spanish language loyalty among Black and White Dominicans in New York. *Bilingual Review/La Revista Bilingüe*, 3–11.

Travis, C. E., & Cacoullos, R. T. (2013). Making voices count: Corpus compilation in bilingual communities. *Australian Journal of Linguistics, 33*(2), 170–194.

Treffers-Daller, J. (2011). Operationalizing and measuring language dominance. *International Journal of Bilingualism*, *15*(2), 147–163.

Walton, J. H., & Orlikoff, R. F. (1994). Speaker race identification from acoustic cues in the vocal signal. *Journal of Speech Language and Hearing Research*, *37*(4), 738–745.

Wierzbicka, A. (2005). Universal human concepts as a tool for exploring bilingual lives. *International Journal of Bilingualism*, *9*(1), 7–26.

Zentella, A. C. (1997). *Growing up bilingual: Puerto Rican children in New York*. Malden, MA; Oxford: Blackwell.

Zuengler, J. (1988). Identity markers and L2 pronunciation. *Studies in Second Language Acquisition*, *10*(1), 33–49.

14 Code-Switching

Dalia Magaña

Introduction

Code-switching (CS), switching languages at the word, phrase, clause, or sentence level (Valdés, 1988), is part of the bilingual reality of numerous communities and occurs both in formal and informal situations. Institutionalized contexts where CS may have an important communicative role, such as medical interactions, have received little attention. As part of my doctoral dissertation (Magaña, 2013) I studied doctor–patient interactions in Spanish and noticed that patients would switch into English for contextual reasons (e.g., naming a medical term). The doctor would also switch into English following the code-switch. The doctor's linguistic choice was meaningful since its effect had important implications in the medical environment in which it occurred. While doctors and patients have social disparities in terms of power, the doctor in my study aimed to mitigate these. One of the discursive strategies that the doctor uses to achieve this is by CS when bilingual patients code-switch, which serves to create a more interpersonal relationship with patients while also gaining their trust. Through his switches, the doctor demonstrates that he understands the bilingual/bicultural situation of patients, even though he was not raised in the US. He also displays affective involvement since CS is intimate, reserved for in-group use and is stigmatized outside of its speakers.

CS occurs naturally across language pairs and in distinct political and geographic contexts where languages are in contact (e.g., Hindi–English in India or Spanish–English in the US). CS differs from *borrowing* (using a borrowed term from another language, such as *el sangüich*), even though each phenomenon results from languages being in contact. In the following examples, sentence (1a) is considered a code-switch because the word *pillow* is not adapted into Spanish phonology (i.e., the sound system of a language), therefore there is a switch into English. However, sentence (1b) is considered Spanish monolingual discourse because the word *disability* is phonologically integrated into Spanish.

(1a)   *Me voy con mi pillow [pʰɪ.ɬou] en la mano* (Translation: *I leave with my pillow in my hand*).
(1b)   *¿Por qué esta en disability* [de.sa.bi.li.te]? (Translation: *Why are you on disability?*)
(1c)   *El dime* [dai.me] … (Translation: *The dime …*)

In addition to *phonological integration*, borrowing can also feature morphological integration (i.e., assigning gender to English nouns as in sentence (1c) above (Magaña, 2013)).

In monolingual speech, when a speaker switches into a different speech style (i.e., register), this can also be seen as a similar phenomenon as CS. For instance, monolinguals may switch their speech style according to the interlocutor they address and the context in which the interaction takes place. The contextual setting, the interlocutor's age, gender, race, socioeconomic status, and knowledge of the other speaker are all factors that influence language choices. A monolingual may also switch registers for a certain social effect, such as to emphasize something, or to make a side comment or a joke.

Compared to monolinguals, we could think of bilinguals as having more language choices at their disposal when they switch languages. They have a larger speech repertoire, and, therefore, CS can be seen as a linguistic resource. Valdés (1988), a linguist who has contributed significantly to knowledge about Spanish–English bilinguals in the US, uses the following guitar metaphor to explain the bilingual language repertoire:

> *By alternating between their languages, bilinguals are able to use their total speech repertoire, which includes many levels and styles and modes of speaking in two languages. It is helpful to imagine that when bilinguals code-switch, they are in fact using a twelve string-guitar, rather than limiting themselves to two six-string instruments.*

Many Spanish–English bilinguals are proud of their ability to code-switch. Bilinguals demonstrate this implicitly by engaging in CS and explicitly by claiming they speak *Spanglish*. As an example, some bilinguals will add to their Facebook profile that Spanglish is one of their languages.

However, CS remains widely misunderstood by the general population. Negative views of CS are captured constantly in online commentaries found in social networks, news sources, blogs, and dictionaries. Some view code-switchers as less competent individuals who do not speak either language well, or see CS as a mixture or *hodge-podge* of languages that negatively affects the languages. The Royal Spanish Academy's definition of Spanglish originally included the term "deforming" to explain the effects of CS.

> *Modalidad del habla de algunos grupos hispanos de los Estados Unidos, en la que se mezclan, deformándolos, elementos léxicos y gramaticales del español y del inglés.*

> (*Modality of speaking of some groups of Hispanics in the United States, in which they mix lexical and grammatical elements of Spanish and English, deforming them.*)

However, that definition is not linguistically informed since three decades of literature has shown that CS reflects linguistic dexterity, follows certain grammatical rules, and is used stylistically and strategically. (Various sociolinguists requested removal of the term *deformándolos* and the Royal Spanish Academy approved the request.)

The literature on CS across the disciplines is very extensive. Rather than a comprehensive overview, this chapter focuses on key concepts in that literature regarding grammar, functions, and current CS issues in psycholinguistics (such as costs). The chapter ends with a discussion about the advantages of an interdisciplinary approach to CS.

CS and Bilingual Competence

The literature on CS and *bilingual competence* has offered important insights about the grammatical dexterity of code-switchers. Briefly, bilingual competence refers to the knowledge speakers have in each of their languages that enables them to complete various communicative tasks. In her study, on 20 Puerto Rican bilinguals with ranging language levels of Spanish and English, linguist Poplack (1982) observed that bilinguals engaged in different types of CS depending on their *language proficiency*. For instance, non-fluent bilinguals and non-group members preferred more *tag-like* CS and switching single nouns, (i.e., *emblematic switching*). These types of switches require minimal proficiency in the L2 (second language), as in sentence 2 below:

(2) <u>*Yeah*</u>, *y a la hora que sea* (Translation: *Yeah, and at any time*).

In contrast, the more fluent bilinguals and in-group members tended to produce more intra-sentential CS or switching within the sentence (i.e., *intimate code-switching*), for example:

(3) *Sí, yo tomaba para esconder, agarrar esos sentimientos y <u>put them away and forget</u> <u>for</u> un ratito* (Translation: *Yes, I'd drink to hide, get those feelings, and put them away and forget for a bit*).

Sentence (3) provides an example of intra-sentential CS. In this case, the main language of the interaction is Spanish (or the *matrix language*; Myers-Scotton, 1995) with switches into English (the embedded language which is inserted into the overall Spanish discourse). Poplack (1982) suggested that intra-sentential CS was linked to solidarity or intimacy. Furthermore, these types of switches indicate the degree of bilingual competence since bilinguals transition between L1 (first language) and L2 elements, without false starts, hesitations, or lengthy pauses (Poplack, 1982). Poplack also probed into two grammatical CS constraints: one dealing with morphology (word structure), the *free morpheme constraint*, and the other with syntax (sentence structure), the *equivalence constraint* (Poplack, 1981). According to the free morpheme constraint, CS could not happen within a word as in "*EAT-iendo*" (*the structure is ungrammatical) or within phrases such as *cross my fingers and hope to die*, which behaves similar to a bound morpheme (switching at the morpheme level) since speakers do not tend to switch within these phrases. The equivalence constraint explains why CS occurs where the L1 and the L2 elements are juxtaposed and how the switch does not violate the grammatical rules of either language. These constraints accounted for all the CS patterns in the data. To illustrate the equivalence constraint examples, (4a) and (4b) offer two versions of the same sentence. The ellipses indicate permissible points where CS can take place.

(4a) *El ... doctor ... me dijo ... que ... me tomara ... estas ... pastillas.*
(4b) *The ... doctor ... told me ... that ... I should take ... these ... pills.*

Any other combination that does not violate these permissible points is acceptable, for example (4c) and (4d):

(4c) *El doctor me dijo que I should take estas pills.*
(4d) *El ... doctor ... me dijo ... que ... I should take ... estas ... pills.*
(4e) **The doctor ... me told ... que ... I tomara ... estas ... pills.*

However, when the grammatical structures are not parallel between the languages, as in *me dijo*/"told me," or *me tomara*/"I should take" we would not find a switch. Therefore, it is very unlikely that a bilingual speaker will produce a sentence such as (4e) since it violates the equivalence constraint in two structures and makes part of the sentence ungrammatical: **me told* and **I tomara*.

Toribio (2000) further probed into these CS constraints. The study presented Spanish–English bilinguals with stories containing grammatical and ungrammatical CS. She found that for the stories that did not follow CS constraints (ungrammatical CS), the participants found the text to be less accessible and confusing compared to the text that contained permissible and grammatical CS. Toribio's study provides evidence that bilinguals develop a strong competency in the grammatical patterns of CS.

Socio-Pragmatic Functions of CS

A common (non-linguistic) view about CS is that bilinguals use both languages due to *language gaps* (i.e., not having sufficient language proficiency in one or the other languages). Heredia and Altarriba (2001, p. 165) provide key arguments for why CS is not necessarily due to language gaps, among them that CS might be *due to failure to retrieve the correct word*, and CS is necessary when a word does not have an equivalent match in the other language. Zentella's (1997) groundbreaking ethnographic study on Puerto Rican bilinguals provides evidence for debunking the language gap misconception as the sole purpose for CS. Zentella observed that even though a bilingual code-switched into English for a certain word, in another instance, that bilingual had produced the word in Spanish. This demonstrates the speaker knew the word, but perhaps at the time of the code-switch had failed to retrieve it or wanted to switch for a social or *pragmatic effect*.

Sociolinguistics research has informed us extensively about the social and pragmatic purposes for CS. Different studies have proposed different typologies, but there are noteworthy similarities among them. The classifications that Gumperz (1982) proposed have been particularly influential. Gumperz found that CS functioned for quotation, addressee specification, interjection, repetition, message qualification (where the speaker separates statements from commentary), and personification versus objectivities (where the speaker contrasts her personal viewpoints with objective ones). The list however, is not exhaustive. Subsequent research on Spanish–English CS in the US (Jacobson, 1982; Valdés, 1982; Zentella, 1997) revealed similar functions.

One of Zentella's (1997) CS categorizations is *apposition switch*, which occurs when the speaker switches languages in order to add information or details about the topic of interaction. For instance, in sentence (5), a male patient begins explaining a difficult point in his life in Spanish and then switches momentarily into English to add more information about how he felt. The patient admits to his doctor there was a time where he felt he made bad choices (*Iba por muy mal camino*). He then switches into English, an apposition switch, to add additional details about how he felt (saying *I'd forget about myself*) and switches back into Spanish, the main language of the interaction.

(5) *Sí iba por muy mal camino. I'd forget about myself. Y entonces no* (Translation: *Yes, I was going down a very wrong way. I'd forget about myself. And well no*).

CS for topic shifts occurs when a switch indicates a topic change (Zentella, 1997). However, the topic shift does not necessarily trigger a switch to the associated language. In sentence (6), a patient offers the doctor information about her medical history in Spanish and when she switches topic she switches into English.

(6) *Estuve en terapia por dos años, pero ahora estoy mejor. The other day* … (Translation: *I was in therapy for two years, but now I feel better. The other day* …)

CS for topic shifts prevents disruption in the flow of the conversation since using the other language eases the transition (Zentella, 1997), such as in sentence (6). Monolinguals may mark topic switches through *paralinguistic markers*, for instance through intonation, pitch, volume, and gestures. Zentella (1997) explains that, *[w]hereas monolinguals adjust by switching phonological, grammatical, and discourse features within one linguistic code, bilinguals alternate between the languages in their repertoire as well* (p. 80).

CS also occurs when a bilingual speaker directly or indirectly quotes someone, *not necessarily in the language used by the person quoted* (Zentella, 1997, p. 94). As we see in sentence (7) below, the patient strategically uses CS to separate the quote from her own discourse.

(7) *Le dije [al doctor] "do it." Y me dijo, "I like the way you think"* (Translation: *I told the doctor "do it." And he said to me, "I like the way you think"*).

Bilinguals may switch languages for emphasis in order to draw special attention to something they have uttered. In some cases speakers may repeat a word in the other language in order to draw emphasis as a patient does in sentences (8a-b):

(8a) Doctor: *¿[Tienes] pesadillas?* (Translation: *Any nightmares?*)
(8b) Patient: *Before–antes sí* (Translation: *Before–before yes I did*).

This type of switch provides further evidence that CS is not due to language gaps since the speaker immediately translates the term. As has been shown, CS occurs for complex reasons.

Contextual CS is a category that overlaps with numerous other CS typologies (or categorizations) and has also been referred to as *domain* or *topic shifts* (Jacobson, 1982). This type of switch is triggered by a situation or topic being linked to the other language (Valdés, 1982). In Jacobson's (1982) study, the home/family and church domains trigger a switch into Spanish, yet employment, school, and business trigger a switch into English.

In a doctor–patient interaction, bilingual patients tended to switch into English for medical terms and numbers since they may have been associating these terms with an English-language context, as in sentence (9).

(9) *Cuando vine para la casa me estaba checando mi sangre y si subía arriba de one hundred and fifty me tenía que dar un injection* (Translation: *When I got back I was checking my blood sugar y if it went over onehundred and fifty I had to give myself an injection*).

Contextual shifts into Spanish also appear when no English equivalent exists, as in *quinceañera* or *friolento* (i.e., someone with a tendency to be cold).

Psycholinguistic research reveals CS triggers have several similarities with contextual switches. According to de Bot, Broersma, and Ludmila (2009, p. 88), CS triggers include, *[a] sound from the other language, the thought of an event specific to a particular language setting, the occurrence of a word, sound, gesture or construction from the other language.* Within their theoretical framework, de Bot et al. (2009, p. 89) argue that, *[s]electing an element from the other language may lead to the activation of elements from that language at other levels … lexical concepts, words, syntactic procedures, discourse, gestures, syllables and sounds.* For instance, a cognate between languages can act as a trigger for CS. In addition, the more the languages' features overlap, the more triggering can be expected. The authors point out an important difference regarding CS triggers among bilinguals: *in the habitual switcher, the two languages are both highly activated, which leads to a critical state in which it is difficult to predict what happens. For the occasional switcher, more simple mechanisms such as lack of knowledge or low availability may suffice to describe patterns of CS* (de Bot et al., 2009, p. 100). De Bot et al. (2009) do not try to account for all the possible CS triggers, nor do they claim that their model can predict CS, but they offer the field insights about the language production of multilinguals.

CS classification is a methodologically complex process given that a single stance of CS may have a number of functions (Nilep, 2006). For these reasons, ethnographic knowledge of the population that enables researchers to take into account the way speakers index their social and cultural backgrounds alleviates the problem of *reducing analysis to a simple 'category check'* (Androutsopoulos, 2013, p. 683).

CS and Social Identity

Sociolinguistic research in diverse geographical and political contexts has offered insights as to the social and identity factors that may influence CS among bilinguals.

According to Gumperz's (1982) influential study, CS may serve as a contextualization cue that offers some indication of how the exchange should be interpreted. Gumperz's work, based on the language pairs Spanish–English, Slovenian–German, and Hindi–English, proposed the concepts of *we-code* or *they-code*. We-code refers to the minority language used for in-group and informal activities. They-code refers to the majority language within a bilingual society; bilingual speakers use it in *the more formal, stiffer and less personal out-group relations* (Gumperz, 1982, p. 66). For Spanish–English bilinguals in the US, Valdés argues that a *switch into Spanish, for example, by a Mexican American bilingual who is speaking English to another bilingual of the same background, may signal greater solidarity or a reference to values associated with the ethnic language* (Valdés, 2000, p. 114). However, Gumperz warns that the content of an interaction will not always coincide with the associated language code. More recent research across distinct language pairs and social contexts complicates the concepts of we-code and they-code (Androutsopoulos, 2006; Auer, 1995, 2005; Sebba & Wootton, 1998). Sebba and Wootton (1998) propose that for bilingual speakers, either language can represent we- or they-code depending on the social identity they want to index. We also have to take into account that these identities may fluctuate and shift through the speaker's life. Poplack (1982) contends that CS may occur in a specific interaction, meaning that it can be the we-code and the expected register among some bilinguals. Hinrichs (2006) further explores these ideas through analysis of emails among Jamaicans. While Jamaicans prefer using English in email, during face-to-face interactions, they code-switched using both English and Jamaican Creole. He explains that this pattern reflects a lack of standard written form for Jamaican Creole. Interestingly, his data included switches into Jamaican Creole for self-identification that serve to distinguish the we- and they-code in narratives, as well as serving stylization purposes, and double-voicing.

Myers-Scotton (1993) offers an in-depth look at the identity roles of speakers when they code-switch. She proposes that, *speakers have a sense of markedness regarding available linguistics codes for any interaction, but choose their codes based on a persona and/ or relation with others which they wish to have in place* (Myers-Scotton, 1993, p. 75). In other words, code choices are explained in terms of speaker motivations.

Within the *markedness model, code-choices are understood as indexing rights-and-obligations sets (RO sets) between participants in a given interaction type. The unmarked RO set is derived from whatever situational features are salient for the community for that interaction type* (Myers-Scotton, 1993, p. 84). Myers-Scotton further explains that marked (unexpected) and unmarked (expected) choices are not universal, but what is universal is that speakers perceive linguistic choices as marked/unmarked relative to RO sets.

Whereas the *unmarked switch* is more common because it is the *expected* choice within a given situational context, the marked choice is more unusual and unexpected. One of the parameters that Myers-Scotton proposes for identifying unmarked switching is that speakers must be bilingual peers, meaning that there is not a socioeconomic differential between speakers. An additional parameter for unmarked CS is that *the interaction has to be of a type in which speakers wish to symbolize the dual memberships that CS calls up. Typically such interactions will be informal and involve only in-group members* (Myers-Scotton, 1993, p. 119).

Through her data from speakers in Kenya and Zimbabwe, Myers-Scotton illustrates how unmarked switches are realized. In one example, Myers-Scotton notes that two young men switch from Shona or Swahili to English even though they are able to speak one or the other language. The author explains that these young men are not satisfied with using either language since, *they see the rewards in indexing both identities for themselves* (Myers-Scotton, 1993, p. 122). Myers-Scotton (1993, p. 122) concludes that, *[CS] itself becomes their unmarked choice for making salient simultaneously two or more positively evaluated choices*. Similarly, Myers-Scotton (1993) perceives some of the literature on Spanish–English CS in the US as unmarked switches where speakers index dual identities.

On the other hand, for CS as the marked choice, Myers-Scotton (1993, pp. 131–132) proposes that, *the speaker simply dis-identifies with the expected RO set*. The general motivation for marked choice is *to negotiate a change in the expected social distance holding between participants, either increasing or decreasing it*. The author offers examples of how speakers code-switch into English to increase the distance between interlocutors since English is the language of power and authority in the African communities she studied.

CS Research in Psycholinguistics

The research on CS within psycholinguistics is an emerging area of study compared to CS studies within sociolinguistics. However, psycholinguistic research thus far has helped us to gain a better understanding of CS phenomena, including the role of language competency and cognitive abilities among bilinguals.

Grosjean is an important scholar in psycholinguistics who has contributed to many areas of bilingualism. Among them, his idea of *language mode* has been highly influential. The idea behind language mode is that bilinguals are able to activate, at different levels, their L1 or L2 depending on the situation in which they are engaged. Further, the language mode should be seen on a continuum according to language activation. In his 1997 study, Grosjean tested the language mode of 15 French–English bilinguals living in Boston. In the task, participants heard a story in French with switches into English and then retold the story to three imaginary interlocutors. The interlocutors were bilinguals whose language backgrounds ranged from:

(i)   A French student who had recently arrived to the US. This speaker read and wrote in English, but had speaking difficulties.
(ii) A French person who had been in the US for seven years, who spoke French at home and at work, but was bilingual.
(iii) A French person who had also been in the US for seven years, but spoke French and English at home and in the work place.

The results revealed numerous interesting findings, one of them that the participants' amount and extent of CS depended on the language background of the imaginary interlocutors.

For instance, the participants hesitated less in CS with fully bilingual interlocutors. The study offers insights about how the context of an interaction (the interlocutors and their backgrounds) strongly influences the language choices that speakers make.

CS processing costs is an important area of study in psycholinguistic approaches to CS. With respect to CS, these cognitive costs deal with time, meaning slower responses, in relation to time, compared to monolingual speech when bilinguals switch languages (Finkbeiner, Almeida, Janssen, & Caramazza, 2006; Meuter & Allport, 1999). Bilinguals tend to react slower to a language task where they have to switch trials than for non-switch trials (Grainger & Beauvillain, 1987; Kolers, 1966; Meuter & Allport, 1999). However, within the debate on CS costs, research has provided us with a more complex view of the factors that influence CS. Studies have reported that these costs range depending on variables such as language fluency, whether the switch occurs out of choice or is prompted, and the complexity in switch type.

CS processing costs may vary depending on whether bilinguals switch into their L1 or L2. Meuter and Allport (1999) studied 16 bilingual adults that spoke English and another European language. The participants' task included naming numbers in either their first or second language. The results revealed that participants had a slower response time when switching into their L1 (stronger language) from the L2 (weaker language) than the other way around. The study explained that due to the relative strength of the participants' two languages it is more difficult to suppress the more dominant language of the speaker, in other words, it requires more effort than suppressing the L2.

Unlike many CS studies, which prompt participants to switch languages, Gollan and Ferreira (2009) designed their experiment so that participants were given the choice of switching into whichever language they preferred when they preferred. For instance, the task did not direct the participant to switch or name things in one language or the other. This setting reflected more closely what occurs during natural interactions. When participants are given these choices, switching cost is minimized or absent. Further, when given these choices, the task is facilitated even for unbalanced bilinguals, meaning the bilingual is much stronger in one language than the other (Gollan & Ferreira, 2009).

Language proficiency is also an important variable when it comes to CS costs. In their study on highly proficient Spanish–Catalan bilinguals, Costa and Santesteban (2004) revealed that there were no *switching costs*. CS costs could also depend on the type of CS that bilinguals use for instance, whether the switch occurs within the sentence level or outside the sentence level.

Gullifer, Kroll, and Dussias (2013) conducted a series of experiments using proficient Spanish–English bilinguals. One of the experiments probed into lexical access when switching languages inter-sententially, meaning when language switching occurs after a complete sentence (and not within a sentence). The authors found that cognates were named faster than non-cognates in both languages. They also found that *there is no cost to inter-sentential switching when participants are required to name words embedded in sentences, and that inter-sentential switching does not influence the magnitude of language co-activation* (Gullifer et al., 2013, p. 7).

Fewer studies have examined how late bilinguals (meaning speakers who acquire another language after childhood, after age 13) process CS. However, Guzzardo Tamargo and Dussias (2013) reveal not only how late bilinguals process different types of CS, but also how they behave similarly or differently to early bilinguals (meaning speakers who acquire another language during childhood, before age 13). Specifically, they explored the following questions: Do late bilinguals recognize tendencies in natural CS? Do they attain native-like CS? The study consisted of 18 participants that were Spanish native speakers.

They had learned English after 13 years of age. Participants were given 32 code-switched sentences on a computer screen to which they had to answer yes-no comprehension questions (see sentences 10a-d). The sentences varied in CS at the following grammatical structures:

Auxiliary in a progressive structure:

(10a) *El director confirmó que los actores **are rehearsing** their lines for the movie* (Translation: The director confirmed that the actors …).

Participle in a progressive structure:

(10b) *El director confirmó que los actores están **rehearsing** their lines for the movie.*

Auxiliary in a perfective structure:

(10c) *El director confirmó que los actores **have rehearsed** their lines for the movie.*

Participle in a perfective structure:

(10d) *El director confirmó que los actores han **rehearsed** their lines for the movie.*

In order to contrast this group of *late bilinguals* to *early bilinguals*, the authors used data from their other study on early bilinguals, in which they used the same materials. The results demonstrated that, in sentences (10a) and (10b), early and late bilinguals processed code-switched sentences similarly. Both groups read sentences with the perfect structures and the past participle more slowly when the switch occurred at the participle than when it occurred at the auxiliary. These findings are critical because they also inform us about CS phenomena, since the overall study and the participants' responses mirrored natural CS production. The more common types of CS (e.g., at the progressive auxiliary) were processed faster than less common types of CS (i.e., the past participle; Guzzardo Tamargo et al., 2013).

Phonological environment is another factor that affects CS recognition (Grosjean, 1988; Li, 1996). A phonotactic structure that has received attention from researchers is initial consonant–vowel clusters (CV) compared to initial consonant clusters (CC). Grosjean (1988) studied this phonotactic structure in French–English bilinguals. While English has more initial consonant clusters than French, in French CV is more common than in English. Grosjean's (1988) study revealed that when the phonotactic environment of a word is associated with one language, the switch is recognized sooner. It is noteworthy to specify that both English and French permit CC and CV clusters, while other languages, such as Chinese (and its dialects), only permit CV clusters. In order to understand any potential differences in CS recognition among languages such as Chinese and English, Li (1996) studied Chinese–English bilinguals. The experiment demonstrated that word recognition depends on phonological, structure, and contextual factors.

The aforementioned studies provide us with insights about CS costs. As we can see, this is not a simple binary concept but rather a much more complex one. For that reason, we should perceive CS costs on a continuum with different factors or variables influencing the cost and the extent of the cost.

Psycholinguistic studies on CS have also revealed advantages that bilinguals have over monolinguals. For instance, research has shown that bilinguals are superior when switching non-linguistic tasks (Prior & Gollan, 2011; Prior & MacWhinney, 2010). Prior and Gollan (2011) studied three groups of speakers: a monolingual English-speaking group, a group of Spanish–English bilinguals, and a group of Mandarin–English bilinguals. The study provided evidence that participants who reported CS in their daily lives (Spanish–English bilinguals) showed more advantages in non-linguistic *switching tasks* than the group that reported not switching as much (Mandarin–English bilinguals). This study offers convincing support that language switching is a cognitively demanding skill and one that positively affects other cognitive areas.

An Interdisciplinary View of CS and CS Across Domains

Psycholinguistic studies on CS provide us with concrete quantitative results, which help shape knowledge about the bilingual mind. These studies control for many factors and are carefully planned. However, aspects of a psycholinguistic approach could be enriched if there were more cross-disciplinary integration of, for example, sociolinguistic and discourse analysis approaches and qualitative-oriented methodology. Addressing CS issues using an interdisciplinary framework offers us a more complete picture of the language situation and CS functions or triggers.

Psycholinguistic studies on CS could be improved if they considered more of the social factors that may influence how speakers communicate, for instance, by incorporating the ideas behind *register theory*. According to Halliday (1994), of all the variables that may influence a language choice, the register variables are the most important. These include the *tenor*, or the relationship between the interlocutors, the *mode*, meaning the role of the language in an interaction, and the field, referring to the topic of the conversation. For instance, in inspecting the register variables, some problematic observations stand out from a social point of view (Guzzardo Tamargo & Dussias, 2013). With respect to mode, it is significant to note that the language in the experiment is written; it is displayed on a computer screen. However, CS tends to occur in more informal spaces, be it face-to-face or written informal interactions (such as the language in social networks or texting). The topic and language that participants engaged in, dealing with a director, is formal, grammatical, and carefully crafted, whereas CS is spontaneous, non-rehearsed, and deals with everyday topics. The variable that seems the most problematic is tenor, given that natural CS interactions involve two or more speakers in dialogue who most likely know each other. In that study, though, there is no interaction since participants are to read the text.

CS can be an intimate way to communicate solidarity with someone, but that factor is not taken into consideration in some of the psycholinguistic studies. Even more, these studies could be improved by including more in-depth information about language use. For example, they should take into account information about the mixed levels of acquisition and English–Spanish use, the sociolinguistic situation of these speakers, and specifically whether they code-switch and their CS attitudes—all of which could be important factors that further inform us about the results. Because CS conveys a lot about the speaker's social identity, ideologies, and culture, CS for bilinguals can be a sociopolitically charged use of languages. As has been discussed, there are strong attitudes about CS from both sides: negative attitudes come from those who misunderstand the phenomena and critique its speakers and positive attitudes come from bilinguals who defend this use of Spanglish. However, these elements are absent in psycholinguistic studies that perceive CS as a neutral option for using languages.

It is also important to make efforts to educate the general population and those in different sectors about bilingualism and CS research since negative views about CS could be damaging. In his study of court interpreters, Angermeyer (2010) finds that interpreters explicitly tell claimants to speak the non-English language when they switch into English even for a word. He finds that because interpreters viewed CS as stigmatized *it may be taken as a sign of an inability to find the appropriate translation equivalent in English* (Angermeyer, 2010, p. 475). However, by legitimizing this typically stigmatized language use, speakers are encouraged to express themselves using the linguistic resources available in their language repertoires across distinct public and private spheres.

In educational spheres some teachers, administrators, and parents are concerned that CS will confuse bilinguals, or they view bilinguals as not speaking either language well. However, if children are given opportunities to code-switch, their identities are not only empowered, they have more linguistic resources available to them, allowing them to express themselves better. Zentella (1997, p. 120) argues the language situation of Puerto Rican children in New York: *[b]ecause they had a foot in both worlds, they never spoke in one for very long without acknowledging and incorporating the other, especially in informal speech.*

In healthcare CS also plays an important role in communication. Mondada (2007) analyzes the interaction between doctors, a medical team and a group of medical professionals via teleconference. In this case, English is the *lingua franca* with strategic switches into French (they are all native French speakers) to make side comments. Mondada (2007, p. 314) explains that CS is used systemically, *[e]ven though English as a lingua franca is presented and dealt with as the official language of the event being broadcasted, French is another resource contributing to the intelligibility of the organization of talk and action in a context of multi-activity.* Additionally, patients may be willing to share more in one language than in the other and should be encouraged to code-switch, since *a bilingual approach that incorporates the use of both Spanish and English can potentially lead to more effective therapeutic outcomes for Hispanics* (Altarriba & Santiago-Rivera, 1994, p. 392).

It is enriching to uncover the different uses of CS across diverse contextual settings where we encompass informal to formal language, oral to written, and everything in between (e.g., Internet language). In our digital age, we have numerous opportunities for online interactions via different modes (email, social networks, texting, chat). Because this form of communication has become part of our daily lives, it is crucial to have more insights about these codes of speaking. Research on online CS has recently received the attention of linguistics (Androutsopoulos, 2006; Magaña, 2016; Montes-Alcalá, 2005, 2007; Negrón Goldbarg, 2009), but it is still in incipient stages. In his online ethnographic study on German-based diasporic websites, Androutsopoulos (2006) inspected the relationship between language use and ethnic identity. The websites were predominantly German-language with switches into English and various minority languages (Arabic, Greek, Hindi, Persian, Punjabi). The author found that *home languages undergo transformations, the most visible aspect of which is their Romanized transliteration* (Androutsopoulos, 2006, p. 541).

On Spanish–English CS, Negrón Goldbarg (2009) examined email messages from bilingual graduate students and found that subjects used Spanish for group identification and that among native Spanish speakers using English only breaks with the interpersonal conventions. In one of her studies on CS in personal notes, Montes-Alcalá (2005) found that bilinguals code-switched for both stylistic and communicative effects, and in another, she reported that bilingual bloggers code-switched for reasons pertaining to *bicultural expression* (Montes-Alcalá, 2007). Interestingly, in these communicative domains, bilinguals use some of the CS socio-pragmatic functions that we find in the literature on face-to-face interactions, for instance, speakers switched languages for: greetings, contextualization of topic shifts, emphasis/repetition, quotations, questions, and interpersonal alignment.

When we look at several disciplines, we see that they may have similar or complementary findings, even though they have different perspectives and methods. It is crucial that we continue to make efforts to inform the general population about the research across disciplines on CS particularly for several reasons. This approach would provide a holistic picture of this linguistic phenomenon. Furthermore, arguments are more powerful when we encounter similar findings across disciplines and modes of communication, such as the patterns about the benefits of bilingualism and of CS.

Summary and Conclusions

CS has been studied widely across various disciplines and with distinct methodologies. This chapter has provided an overview of CS within sociolinguistics and psycholinguistics. The sociolinguistics literature informs us that CS is not only a natural language practice with specific socio-pragmatic functions (e.g., repetition, quotation, topic shift etc.), but also conveys information about bilinguals' identity and their political and solidarity stances. The CS literature on bilingual competency informs us that bilinguals follow intuitive grammatical rules when they switch languages. The more proficient bilinguals are those who are able to produce intra-sentential switches, which require grammatical knowledge of both languages. Research in psycholinguistics has shown that switching languages requires more processing time or cost when compared to speaking in one language. However, within that debate there are numerous factors that can influence this cost, including whether speakers are given the choice to switch, the type of switch they are to engage in, and their language proficiency (e.g., it is easier for bilinguals to inhibit their L2s than their L1; Meuter, 2005).

This chapter also pointed to a need for more cross-disciplinary dialogue and mixed methodology in CS research. The chapter has also proposed considerations that could be taken into account when conducting experiments to better help us interpret the results, such as collecting ethnographic information about language use. This is important because a speaker may be more dominant in certain registers than others and these can also fluctuate throughout time and the speakers' life experiences. As Heredia and Altarriba (2001, p. 167) point out: *bilingual lexical representation is not a static but a dynamic representation system in which the first language can fall in strength, while the second language becomes the dominant.* Research studies should not only rely on self-reported data about language use and attitudes to obtain an accurate representation of the participants' language background. Rather, we need to supplement self-reported data with indirect methods (e.g., match-guise technique for obtaining language attitudes) as well as longitudinal and ethnographic data on language use.

The sociolinguistics literature provides numerous models for collecting ethnographic data on language use, but has heavily focused on informal interactions that occur face-to-face. There is a need to complement research on CS in informal interactions with language use across other sectors and modalities of interaction. We need more research studies on Internet language, both formal and informal communication that occurs in formal institutions (e.g., medical interactions and courts), where CS has an important role. This wider representation of language use would offer a more accurate picture of CS phenomenon and bilingual speakers in contextualized and authentic interactions.

List of Key Words and Concepts

Apposition switch, Bicultural expression, Bilingual competence, Borrowing, Code-switching (CS), Contextual CS, Contextual shifts, Dominant language, Early bilinguals, Embedded language, Emblematic switching, Equivalence Constraint, Free morpheme constraint, Inter-sentential switching, Intimate code-switching, Intra-sentential CS, Language gap, Mode, Language proficiency, Late bilinguals, Markedness Model, Matrix language, Paralinguistic markers, Phonological integration, Pragmatic effect, Register theory, Relative Strength Hypothesis, Rights-and-obligations sets (RO sets), Switching costs, Switching tasks, Tag-like, Tenor, They-code, Topic shift, Unbalanced bilinguals, Unmarked switch, We-code

Internet Sites Related to Code-Switching

Academia Mexicana De La Lengua: http://www.academia.org.mx/
Espanglish Community Facebook Page: https://www.facebook.com/espanglishpr
Evaluating Convergence Via Code-Switching: http://nmcode-switching.la.psu.edu/
La Página Del Idioma Español: http://www.elcastellano.org/
LIPPS (Language Interaction in Plurilingual and Plurilectal Speakers) and LIDES (Language Interaction Data Exchange System) Project: http://www.ling.lancs.ac.uk/staff/mark/lipps/lipps.htm

Discussion Questions

(1) Name five examples of borrowings from English into any other language.
(2) What types of CS attitudes have you experienced or encountered from others?
(3) What are some of the places where you have witnessed CS? What was its effect?
(4) Briefly explain the *free morpheme constraint* and provide your own example that violates the constraint.
(5) Explain the Equivalence Constraint and provide two examples of your own: one that follows and one that violates the constraint.
(6) Name five socio-pragmatic reasons for CS.
(7) Explain what CS *costs* are and two elements that may affect the extent of a cost in CS.
(8) What conclusions can we make from Grosjean (1997) study?
(9) What do the findings in the study by Guzzardo Tamargo and Dussias (2013) inform us about language use?
(10) Discuss the advantages and disadvantages of an interdisciplinary approach to research.

Suggested Research Projects

(1) *Interdisciplinary Literature Search:* Search for recent articles on CS reported in different disciplines (Sociology, Psychology, Linguistics). Compare and contrast the methodologies and findings of these studies, and then offer a critique of ways in which they could each be improved using an interdisciplinary approach.
(2) *Conduct a Study:* Design a psycholinguistic study to explore an aspect of your choice (e.g., costs, competence) about CS. Propose a research question and explain: the criteria for your participants, the methodology, hypothesis, and potentials challenges.
(3) *CS Functions:* Collect CS data based on authentic interactions found either online (bilingual blogs, social networks, etc.) or face-to-face (interactions with a cash register, interactions between friends, etc.). Describe the socio-pragmatic functions that account for the CS samples you collected.
(4) *CS Competence:* Replicate an experiment similar to Toribio's (2000). Provide bilingual participants with sample texts of CS that are grammatical and ungrammatical. The materials could be distributed online and participants could also be recruited

online. Include both participants that tend to code-switch and those that do not to reveal whether use accounts for discrepancies.

(5) *Language Contact Attitudes:* Collect attitudes about CS or language *borrowing* between any two languages of your choice online. You can look at Facebook, online news commentaries, dictionary discussion forums. Dictionary discussion forums are usually filled with strong language attitudes, for example, the one in Wordreference. com. Use Wordreference.com and search for several borrowed terms of your choice and identify any patterns you notice.

Suggested Readings

Altarriba, J., & Heredia, R. R. (Eds.). (2008). *An introduction to bilingualism: Principles and processes.* Mahwah, NJ: Erlbaum.

Auer, P. (1998). *Code-switching in conversation: Language, interaction, and identity.* London: Routledge.

Bullock, B. E., & Toribio, J. A. (2012). *The Cambridge handbook of linguistic code-switching.* Cambridge: Cambridge University Press.

Gardner-Chloros, P. (2009). *Code-switching.* Cambridge: Cambridge University Press.

Isurin, L., Winford, D., & de Bot, K. (2009). *Multidisciplinary approaches to code switching.* Amsterdam/Philadelphia: John Benjamins.

Kharkhurin, A. V., & Wei, L. (2015). The role of code-switching in bilingual creativity. *International Journal of Bilingual Education and Bilingualism, 18*(2), 153–169.

MacSwan, J. (2016). Code-switching in adulthood. In E. Nicoladis & S. Montanari (Eds.), *Bilingualism across the lifespan: Factors moderating language proficiency. Language and the human lifespan series* (pp. 183–200). Washington, DC: American Psychological Association.

Martinez, G. A. (2006). *Mexican Americans and language: Del dicho al hecho.* Tucson: The University of Arizona Press.

Milroy, L., & Muysken, P. (Eds.). (1995). *One speaker, two languages: Cross-disciplinary perspectives on code-switching.* Cambridge: Cambridge University Press.

Schwieter, J. W. (2015). *The Cambridge handbook of bilingual processing.* Cambridge: Cambridge University Press.

References

Altarriba, J., & Santiago-Rivera, A. L. (1994). Current perspectives on using linguistic and cultural factors in counseling the Hispanic client. *Professional Psychology: Research and Practice, 25*(4), 388–397.

Androutsopoulos, J. (2006). Multilingualism, diaspora, and the Internet: Codes and identities on German-based diaspora websites. *Journal of Sociolinguistics, 10*(4), 524–551.

Androutsopoulos, J. (2013). Code-switching in computer-mediated communication. In S. C. Herring, D. Stein, & T. Virtanen (Eds.), *Pragmatics of computer-mediated communication* (pp. 667–694). Berlin/Boston: de Gruyter Mouton.

Angermeyer, P. S. (2010). Interpreter-mediated interaction as bilingual speech: Bridging macro- and micro-sociolinguistics in codeswitching research. *International Journal of Bilingualism, 1*(4), 466–489.

Auer, P. (1995). The pragmatics of code-switching: A sequential approach. In L. Milroy & P. Muysken (Eds.), *One speaker, two languages: Cross-disciplinary perspectives on code-switching* (pp. 115–135). Cambridge: Cambridge University Press.

Auer, P. (2005). A post-script: Code-switching and social identity. *Journal of Pragmatics, 37*(3), 403–407.

Costa, A., & Santesteban, M. (2004). Lexical access in bilingual speech production: Evidence from language switching in highly proficient bilinguals and L2 learners. *Journal of Memory and Language, 50,* 491–511.

de Bot, K., Broersma, M., & Ludmila, I. (2009). Sources of triggering in code switching. In L. Isurin, D. Winford, & K. de Bot (Eds.), *Multidisciplinary approaches to code switching* (pp. 85–102). Amsterdam/Philadelphia: John Benjamins.

Finkbeiner, M., Almeida, J., Janssen, N., & Caramazza, A. (2006). Lexical selection in bilingual speech production does not involve language suppression. *Journal of Experimental Psychology: Learning, Memory and Cognition, 32*, 1075–1089.

Gollan, T. H., & Ferreira, V. S. (2009). Should I stay or should I switch? A cost-benefit analysis of voluntary language switching in young and aging bilinguals. *Journal of Experimental Psychology: Learning, Memory and Cognition, 35*(3), 640–665.

Grainger, J., & Beauvillain, C. (1987). Language blocking and lexical access in bilinguals. *Quarterly Journal of Experimental Psychology, 39A*, 295–319.

Grosjean, F. (1988). Exploring the recognition of guest words in bilingual speech. *Language and cognitive processes, 3*, 233–274.

Grosjean, F. (1997). Processing mixed languages: Issues, findings and models. In A. M. B. de Groot & J. Kroll (Eds.), *Tutorials in bilingualism: Psycholinguistic perspectives* (pp. 225–254). Mahwah, NJ: LEA.

Gullifer, J., Kroll, J. F., & Dussias, P. E. (2013). When language switching has no apparent cost: Lexical access in sentence context. *Frontiers in Psychology, 4*, 1–13.

Gumperz, J. (1982). *Discourse strategies.* Cambridge: Cambridge University Press.

Guzzardo Tamargo, R., & Dussias, P. E. (2013). Processing of Spanish–English code switches by late bilinguals. In S. Baiz, N. Goldman, & R. Hawkes (Eds.), *Proceedings of the 37th Boston University Conference on Language Development* (pp. 134–146). Somerville, MA: Cascadilla Press.

Halliday, M. A. K. (1994). *An introduction to functional grammar* (2nd ed.). London: Edward Arnold.

Heredia, R. R., & Altarriba, J. (2001). Bilingual language mixing: Why do bilinguals code-switch? *Current Directions in Psychological Science, 10*, 164–168.

Hinrichs, L. (2006). *Codeswitching on the web.* Amsterdam/Philadelphia: John Benjamins.

Jacobson, R. (1982). The social implications of intra-sentential code-switching. In J. Amastae & L. Elías-Olivares (Eds.), *Spanish in the United States: Sociolinguistic aspects* (pp. 182–208). Cambridge: Cambridge University Press.

Kolers, P. A. (1966). Interlingual facilitation in short-term memory. *Journal of Verbal Learning and Verbal Behavior, 5*, 314–319.

Li, P. (1996). Spoken word recognition of code-switched words by Chinese–English bilinguals. *Journal of Memory and Language, 35*, 757–774.

Magaña, D. (2013). *Language, Latinos and healthcare: Discourse analysis of the Spanish psychiatric interview* (Unpublished doctoral dissertation). University of California, Davis.

Magaña, D. (2016). Code-switching in social-network messages: A case-study of a bilingual Chicana. *International Journal of the Linguistic Association of the Southwest, 32*(1), 43–65.

Meuter, R. (2005). Language selection in bilinguals: Mechanisms and processes. In J. F. Kroll & A. M. B. de Groot (Eds.), *Handbook of bilingualism: Psycholinguistic approaches* (pp. 349–370). New York: Oxford University Press.

Meuter, R. F. I., & Allport, A. (1999). Bilingual language switching in naming: Asymmetrical costs of language selection. *Journal of Memory and Language, 40*, 25–40.

Mondada, L. (2007). Bilingualism and the analysis of talk at work: Code-switching as a resource for the organization of action and interaction. In M. Heller (Ed.), *Bilingualism. A social approach* (pp. 297–318). Basingstoke: Macmillan.

Montes-Alcalá, C. (2005). Mándame un e-mail: Cambio de códigos español-inglés online. In L. A. Ortiz López & M. Lacorte (Eds.), *Contacto y contextos lingüísticos: El español en los Estados Unidos y en contacto con otras lenguas* (pp. 173–185). Iberoamericana/Vervuert.

Montes-Alcalá, C. (2007). Blogging in two languages: Code-switching in bilingual blogs. In J. Holmquist, A. Lorenzino, & L. Sayahi (Eds.), *Selected proceedings of the third workshop on Spanish sociolinguistics* (pp. 162–170). Somerville, MA: Cascadilla Proceedings Project.

Myers-Scotton, C. (1993). *Duelling languages: Grammatical structure in codeswitching*. Oxford: Clarendon Press.

Myers-Scotton, C. (1995). A lexically based model of code-switching. In L. Milroy & P. Muysken (Eds.), *One speaker, two languages: Cross-disciplinary perspectives on code-switching* (pp. 233–266). Cambridge: Cambridge University Press.

Negrón Goldbarg, R. (2009). Spanish/English code-switching in e-mail communication. *Language @Internet*, *6*(1), 29–52.

Nilep, C. (2006). Code switching in sociocultural linguistics. *Colorado Research in Linguistics*, *19*, 1–22.

Poplack, S. (1981). Syntactic structure and the social function of code switching. In R. P. Durán (Ed.), *Latino language and communicative behaviour* (pp. 169–184). Norwood, NJ: Ablex.

Poplack, S. (1982). Sometimes I'll start a sentence in Spanish Y TERMINO EN ESPANOL: Toward a typology of code-switching. In J. Amastae & L. Elías-Olivares (Eds.), *Spanish in the United States: Sociolinguistics aspects* (pp. 230–263). Cambridge: Cambridge University Press. Reprinted in L. Wei (Ed.), *The bilingualism reader* (pp. 221–256). New York: Routledge.

Prior, A., & Gollan, T. H. (2011). Good language switchers are good task-switchers: Evidence from Spanish–English and Mandarin–English bilinguals. *Journal of the International Neuropsychological Society*, *17*, 682–691.

Prior, A., & MacWhinney, B. (2010). A bilingual advantage in task switching. *Bilingualism: Language and Cognition*, *13*, 253–262.

Real Academia Española (2014). *Diccionario de la lengua española* (23rd ed.). Madrid: Espasa Calpe. Retrieved October 24, 2014, from http://lema.rae.es/drae/?val=spanglish

Sebba, M., & Wootton, T. (1998). We, they and identity. In P. Auer (Ed.), *Code-switching in conversation: Language interactions and identity* (pp. 151–172). Amsterdam/Philadelphia: John Benjamins.

Toribio, A. J. (2000). Spanglish?! Bite your tongue! Spanish-English code-switching among Latinos. In R. Flores (Ed.), *Reflexiones 1999* (pp. 115–147). Austin, TX: Center for Mexican American Studies.

Valdés, G. (1982). Social interaction and code-switching patterns: A case study of Spanish–English alternation. In J. Amastae & L. Elías-Olivares (Eds.), *Spanish in the United States: sociolinguistics aspects* (pp. 209–229). Cambridge: Cambridge University Press.

Valdés, G. (1988). The language situation of Mexican Americans. In S. L. McKay & S. C. Wong (Eds.), *Language diversity* (pp. 111–139). San Francisco: Newbury House Publishers.

Valdés, G. (2000). Bilingualism and language use among Mexican Americans. In S. L. McKay & S. C. Wong (Eds.), *New immigrants in the United States* (pp. 99–136). Cambridge: Cambridge University Press.

Zentella, A. C. (1997). *Growing up bilingual: Puerto Rican children in New York*. Cambridge, MA: Blackwell.

Linguistics, Second Language Acquisition, and Communication Disorders

15 Linguistic Contributions to Bilingualism

Vivian Cook

These are some facts about people who speak a second language:

(1) People's pronunciation of sounds like /t/ and /d/ in their first language (L1) is affected by the other languages that they know. You can tell whether a Frenchman speaks English by their accent in French.

(2) Second language (L2) learners rapidly learn the appropriate pronunciations for their own gender. For instance, while women L2 learners of English tend to pronounce the -*ing* ending of the continuous form *going* as /ɪŋ/, men tend to use /ɪn/.

(3) Ten days after brain injury from a road accident, a bilingual Moroccan could speak French but not Arabic; the next day Arabic but not French; the next day she went back to fluent French and poor Arabic; three months later she could speak both.

(4) Five-year-old Bengali children in the East End of London learn the regular spoken past tense endings /t/ *learnt* and /d/ *played* before the ending /ɪd/ *waited*. People acquire the elements of an L2 in a fixed common order.

(5) In London restaurants, Spanish is a *lingua franca* among many non-Spanish-speaking workers just as Italian is in Toronto.

(6) Children who know two languages perform better in noisy classrooms than children who know only one.

This chapter tries to show how linguistics may help or hinder us from explaining some of these apparent facts. It reviews some of the ways that linguistics has been used in *second language acquisition* (SLA) and bilingual research, ranging from overall linguistic theories to research techniques, and evaluates the relationship between linguistics and SLA research.

Introduction

The people who study the acquisition and use of languages other than the mother tongue come from a variety of backgrounds. Some are linguists concerned with testing out the latest linguistic theory. Some are psycholinguists concerned with the processing and use of second languages. Others are teachers trying to establish the best foundation for language teaching. Some call themselves applied linguists, some SLA researchers, some bilingual researchers. All of these have their own traditions for thinking about language and feel uncomfortable with the world view of the others: some linguists dislike what they perceive as the psychologists' view of words as coins with two faces, one inscribed in each language; some psychologists cannot fathom why linguists are so interested in the minutiae of *syntax* or grammar, such as past tense endings; some teachers deplore the lack of practical applicability of both camps to the multifaceted classroom situation. In an ideal world, the discipline of linguistics would set out the nature of language in general and would describe individual languages in particular. Linguists would provide maps of the different aspects of language from *phonology* to *semantics*, which could then be appropriated by those who want to study the use and acquisition of more than one language. In that the domain of linguistics is language itself—the actual subject matter that the others are drawing on for their own purposes—it should have a role in any discipline concerned with language. Just as you go to a geologist to find properties of land, so you would go to a linguist to find properties of language.

We can start with a quotation from the eminent linguist Roman Jakobson (1953), who claimed that *bilingualism is for me the fundamental problem of linguistics.* On the one hand, this reassures the researcher of the importance of bilingualism; on the other hand, it is a warning that linguists see bilingualism as a problem, an exception to the rule of monolingualism rather than the normal condition of human beings. Indeed Chomsky (1986) argued that the pure idealized form of language knowledge should be the first object of study, rather than the muddy waters of bilingualism. He has always tended to see bilingualism as an unnecessary complication for his theories. By and large, linguists implicitly believe that the monolingual native speaker is the norm: *From Saussure to Chomsky 'homo monolinguis' is posited as the man who uses language—the man who speaks* (Illitch & Sanders, 1988, p. 52). L2 users are defined in relation to monolingual native speakers, not as a type of human being in their own right (Cook, 2016). The acceptance of this assumption has tended to separate SLA researchers from bilingualism researchers, who usually reject it, resulting in a major fissure in the field of SLA research. Whenever linguistics is drawn on for SLA research, it must be remembered that it is seldom neutral, but takes a position about the relative unimportance of SLA as opposed to first language acquisition and makes a number of other implicit assumptions, as we shall see.

Comparing Linguistics and SLA Research

As a quick way in, let us see whether linguists and SLA researchers share the same idea of language by comparing the weighting given to particular areas in linguistics and SLA research sources. The *Blackwell Handbook of Linguistics* (Aronoff & Rees-Miller, 2001) provides a useful source for linguistics. Its chapter headings deal with such technical linguistic areas as phonetics, phonology, morphology, the lexicon, semantics, syntax, pragmatics, discourse analysis, sociolinguistics, neurolinguistics, and indeed SLA. An adequate account of linguistics, as represented on, say, an undergraduate degree course in linguistics, could hardly omit any of these. And surely, neither could an adequate account of SLA. Somewhere all these areas play their part in the second language. Our introductory examples, for instance, require answers involving the areas of phonetics (how people pronounce /p/), sociolinguistics (how the /ɪn/ pronunciation of -*ing* goes with a particular social grouping), neurolinguistics (how brain damage affects language), and morphology (how the past tense -*ed* is pronounced in three different ways).

Representative sources for SLA research can be Rod Ellis' (1994) mammoth 824-page *Study of Second Language Acquisition* (henceforward *SoSLA)* and the second edition of Josiane Hamers and Michel Blanc's 468-page, "state-of-the-art" *Bilinguality and Bilingualism* (henceforward *BaB*) (Hamers & Blanc, 2000). The only area of linguistics that appears to be missing from the SLA contents list and the indexes of *SoSLA* and *BaB* is phonetics. SoSLA, and most SLA books, uses morphology to refer to *grammatical morphemes*—the *function words* like *to* and inflections like past tense -*ed*—not to the wider discipline concerned with the structure of words that is found in linguistics. The vocabulary store called the lexicon, crucial to linguistics is reflected in the SLA sources only in *lexical errors* and *lexical phrases*, not through how words are related to each other. The meanings of words, covered in semantics, in linguistics is barely touched on in SLA research; neuro-linguistics, too, is mentioned only in the context of age. In *BaB* the major linguistic area of syntax—the way sentences are structured grammatically—is not referred to except in the context of *syntactic processing*, though *grammar* occurs on a handful of pages.

Do the main descriptive categories used by the *Handbook of Linguistics* occur in the L2 sources? The *phoneme* (the minimal sound difference between pairs of words such as *bang* and *pang*, crucial to many phonological analyses in linguistics) is mentioned only in passing in *SoSLA* in connection with coding ability; the *allophone* (the non-significant difference between, for example, the two *l*s in *lip* and *pill*, an important feature of *foreign accent*) is not mentioned in either book as a phonological term, nor is the *vowel* apart from the context of infant acquisition. The *sentence*—the major unit in virtually all syntax in linguistics—is barely mentioned; *grammatical gender* (the difference in meaning between *she* and *he* in English)—a major element of syntax which differs very much between lan-guages is absent, as is *tense* (another vital area covering present *he goes* versus past *he went* versus tenseless *to go*). The major types of words for linguists are hardly mentioned: the *verb* is briefly touched on in *SoSLA*, but not in *BaB;* the *noun* occurs in *SoSLA* only in *noun phrase* and does not exist in *BaB*. The overall linguistic term, lexicon, for vocabulary occurs in both books, but the more detailed terms *lexical item* (a unit of vocabulary which may be a word *look* or a phrase *look up to*), *collocation* (how some words go together so that *strong* goes with *tea* but not *car*, while *powerful* goes with *car* but not with *tea*), or indeed the general idea that there are structural relationships between words such as synonyms and antonyms are not discussed. The all-pervasive linguistic term *feature*—*distinctive feature* (i.e., the features that distinguish /p/ from /b/ of voicing and aspiration), *semantic feature* (i.e., the meaning difference between *boy* and *girl*, *fox* and *vixen*)—is absent from both SLA books.

This brief survey highlights how little overlap there is between linguistics and the ortho-doxies of SLA and bilingual research. More recent books tend to be more specialized and not to aim at the scope or size of *SoSLA* and *BaB*. The large-scale Gass and Selinker (2008) shows little change; 12 pages out of 593 are devoted to phonology, 28 to the lexicon; *phoneme*, *allophone*, *sentence*, and *gender* do not appear in the index. Obviously, there are exceptions in the form of linguistically based studies of L2 syntax, such as Hawkins (2001), or of L2 phonology, such as Archibald (1993). The lack of interest in whole areas of linguistics in the SLA introductions, nevertheless, gives a fair picture of much SLA research. On the face of it, the SLA research mainstream is unrelated to the core concerns and categories of linguistics. Whatever the *L* in SLA research stands for, it is not language in the linguist's sense—for good or for ill. Perhaps you do not have to know the theory of the internal combustion engine to measure a sparking gap, but you do at least have to be able to recognize a sparking plug when you see one.

One point that emerges from this is the two levels at which linguistics can be involved in bilingualism and SLA research. The area that has received most debate is the general ideas about language and language learning. Researchers tend overtly to accept or deny particular overall models of linguistics: they are for or against Chomskyan linguistics or Complexity Theory.

But there is also the level at which linguistics provides the categories for analyzing language. A researcher may deny that they are using linguistics, yet they will casually use such terms as noun and verb, phoneme and morpheme, word and syllable, as if these were primitive terms that needed no justification, rather than categories within specific linguistic theories: it is assumed that these have nothing to do with linguistics, just facts of life. The danger is that researchers unwittingly fall back on the views of language instilled in them at school, drawn mostly from the tradition of Latin-based grammar in Europe. For example, nouns are seen in terms of school grammar, represented, say, by Priestley (1761), *a noun ... is the name of any thing*, or Cobbett (1819), *nouns are the names of persons and things,* or indeed Wikipedia (2014), *a noun ... is a word that functions as the name of some specific thing or set of things*. Linguists have often inveighed against such semantic definitions of parts of speech on the grounds of their woolliness (the noun *fire* is hardly an object, the verb *seem* hardly an action), and their overlap (*request* is both a noun and a verb, *up* can be a preposition *up the hill*, a noun *ups and downs*, and a verb *Up the grant!*). No two people would agree on whether many words were nouns or verbs by these subjective definitions; at best, there is a statistical tendency that a noun will refer to an object, a verb to an action (Lyons, 1968). Instead, linguists have preferred to define syntactic categories in terms of formal structural properties; Fries (1952) defines words that can be inflected for number and can be preceded by a determiner as Word Class 1 (i.e., nouns are defined structurally rather than notionally). Other linguists have treated noun and verb as primitive terms—*certain fixed categories (noun, verb, etc.) can be found in the syntactic representation of the sentences of any language* (Chomsky, 1965, p. 28); these are substantive universals—*items of a particular kind in any language must be drawn from a fixed class of items* (Chomsky, 1965, p. 28)—a built-in aspect of the human mind. Even Sapir (1921, p. 96) has a universal leaning: *There must be something to talk about and something must be said about this subject of discourse ... No language wholly fails to distinguish noun and verb, though in particular cases the nature of the distinction may be an elusive one*. Oddly enough, many of those who reject the Chomskyan idea of innate universals of language are quite happy to use nouns and verbs (and indeed words) as self-evident universal categories. But even Chomsky's definition refers to syntactic properties; it is an empirical question whether there are two groups of word-classes that can be isolated in all languages on the grounds of syntactic properties (Robins, 1952). When Evans and Levinson (2009, p. 439) say *each word class we add to the purported universal inventory would then need its own accompanying set of syntactic constraints*, they are putting the cart before the horse: a word class is precisely the label for a set of words that have the same syntactic constraints, not a concept in search of its syntactic characteristics. Anything that describes language involves a linguistic theory; it might as well be an explicit current theory as one whose categories are based on the grammars of the 18th century.

Views of Language and Views of Second Language Acquisition

What researchers think language *is* dictates their views about how people acquire it. If you conceive of language primarily as behavior—things people do in the visible world, such as greeting each other or signing contracts—they learn patterns of behavior by actually behaving. If you think of language chiefly as knowledge—invisible ideas in the mind, people planning their day or deciding what to have for supper—they learn abstract rules and items through mental processes. If you think of language as social interaction—how people relate to each other in society, whether as customers or boyfriends—they learn by interacting with their parents and caretakers. And these are only three of the many possible positions discussed in Cook (2010). It is like looking at a landscape from the viewpoints of a geologist, a landscape painter, and a farmer: the observer's purpose dictates what is seen.

Hence one problem with relating linguistics to other disciplines has been the sheer multiplicity of linguists' views and the amount of time and energy they spend ridiculing those who do not share them. Relating linguistics to L2 acquisition and use necessitates first of all defining what one means by linguistics (i.e., which school or theory is supported). A reviewer of *Linguistics and Second Language Acquisition* (Cook, 1993), for example, argued that linguistics meant linguistic theory and that there was only one tenable linguistic theory, namely the generative (Gregg, 1995). But linguistics is about many things, not just linguistic theory (imagine music being defined as music theory) in particular, description of languages; there are, in any event, many linguistic theories, not just one and *generative theory* is now the possession of a specialized minority of linguists with their own journals and conferences. Above all, science should attempt to explore all avenues rather than just one (Feyerabend, 1975). The multifaceted nature of language demands multiple approaches.

As language is involved in every aspect of human life, non-linguists also have strong opinions about it, sometimes echoing those of linguists, sometimes not, mostly reflecting the by-gone traditions of school grammar teaching. The mass media, for instance, display prescriptive attitudes to language almost every week, regarding spelling and grammar mistakes as signs of moral turpitude. The present chapter only touches on a few of the types and areas of linguistics that have been used in SLA research.

Since two or more languages are involved in SLA research, the same type of linguistics needs to be implemented for two language systems. Ideally this would mean using descriptive techniques that encompass all languages (e.g., the inventory of all the sounds that can occur in human languages or universal theories that apply to all languages with specified parameters of variation). More often, the SLA researcher has the task of reconciling two languages described with linguistic approaches that differ to a greater or lesser degree.

Competence and SLA

Since Chomsky (1965) first divided *linguistic competence* (the knowledge of language of the idealized native speaker) from *performance* (the actual concrete use of language), it has been axiomatic that all normal adult human beings have linguistic competence in their first language: competence is indeed defined as whatever it is that native speakers possess; *any* native speaker can then stand for *all* native speakers. All children, with rare exceptions, succeed in learning their first language over roughly the same period of time: they become native speakers. They do so in a language environment, the properties of which are familiar to everyone, and are usually surrounded by a small cast of parents and other caretakers. Research into L1 acquisition tries to see how the child reaches a destination that is relatively constant and in a primal human child-rearing situation.

L2 acquisition, however, has no settled final linguistic competence, common to all, or even most, learners. Few L2 learners acquire a native-like competence in the second language. Their final state ranges from near-beginners able to say a few L2 words in a classroom to writers of world-class literature, (e.g., Conrad or Nabokov). There is no standard L2 learner or L2 user in the sense that there is a standard native speaker. The environment of L2 learners varies immensely, say from schools to refugee camps, compared to the family child-rearing situation. The age of L2 learners varies from early childhood to old age, unlike the lock-step development of age and L1 acquisition. Rather than being typical of all human beings, L2 learners and users are a far from a random selection of people, chosen by education, migration, job needs, and many other factors. SLA research has to describe multiple routes to diverse destinations rather than the single route to the sole destination of L1 research.

A major influence on SLA research has been the concept of *interlanguage—the exist-ence of a separate linguistic system* (Selinker, 1972) in the L2 learner's mind from the L1 and the L2. This is clearly derived from the Chomskyan notion that linguistic competence is whatever it *is*, rather than reflecting what it is *not*, called the *independent grammars assumption* (Cook, 1993); children are not failures for not speaking like adults, but chil-dren in their own right with competences of their own. L1 researchers such as McNeill (1966) indeed tried to write grammars for particular points of development, say the gram-mar of the two-year-old as an independent system. Interlanguage took this concept over into SLA research, insisting that the first goal of SLA research was to describe the L2 learner, not to evaluate how they mangle native speaker language. This has remained an implicit part of SLA research that is seldom questioned. It is now partly subsumed by the multicompetence idea that interlanguage is only one factor in the L2 user's total language system, which encompasses both the first language and the interlanguage (Cook, 2016).

Overall Views of Learning

Linguistics has, in its time, spawned a multitude of theories of L1 acquisition, some com-ing directly from linguistic theories such as Chomsky's *universal grammar* (UG), which sees the knowledge of language as consisting partly of innate language principles, partly of limited variation and masses of lexical items that have to be learned. Others are spin-offs from psychological theories, such as the *adaptive control of thought model* (ACT*; Anderson, 1983), which see language acquisition as a process of automatizing large amounts of language information, called *declarative knowledge*, into a set of procedures, called *procedural knowledge*, developed by Ullmann (2001). So it is hard to speak of a unified linguistic approach to L1 acquisition that can be *transferred* to L2 acquisition. L2 approaches have borrowed all the way from say the UG model (White, 2003) to ACT* (Dechert, 1984) to chaos theory (Larsen-Freeman, 1997). Inasmuch as linguists agree about anything, it is probably nowadays no more than the assumption that language is a complex system of its own, hence lining themselves up against psychological theories, such as ACT*, that believe it makes use of the same learning and production processes as any other skilled activity. Linguists typically insist that a specific account of language acquisition is needed rather than an extrapolation to language from general theories of human learning such as *connectionism*, going back to Chomsky's scorn of a theory of language learning based on the behavior of rats (Chomsky, 1957). The response from psychologists is often on the lines of, *well, linguists would, wouldn't they*? If language is not distinct, linguists do not have a role of their own in the academic community. In other words, much psychology-based SLA research adopts what Chomsky (2013) calls the *no-language* position: language is simply an intersection of cognitive processes and has no existence in its own right.

The division between external *E-language* and internal *I-language* (Chomsky, 1986) provides a useful broad categorization of two distinct ways of approaching language, language learning, and research methodology. E-language is the actual occurrence of sentences in the world outside, whether as conversation, newspapers, or whatever; I-language is the knowledge of language stored inside a person's mind. Phrased in terms of L2 acquisition, the data for an E-language approach is naturally occurring samples of learners' language, whether tape-recordings, emails or whatever; these are analyzed to see the patterns, frequencies, and regularities in people's processing; what people do is established chiefly from example of what they have done. The data for an I-language approach might be *grammaticality judgments* (asking people to judge whether sentences are grammatical, or acceptable), reaction time measures (timing how long people take to respond to various L1 and L2 stimuli), eye tracking measures looking at how learners process text, and many others designed to test hypotheses about what learners know; knowledge of the language is established by indirect means, not necessarily from things they actually say. This I-language versus E-language distinction is all pervasive in SLA research, as we shall see.

SLA Theories Derived from Linguistics

Contrastive Analysis

Some SLA research shows its origins in linguistics fairly obviously, particularly when it is associated with older forms of linguistics. A classic E-language approach to L2 acquisition was *contrastive analysis* (CA), both in the European schools described in Sajavaara (1981) and the American school exemplified by Lado (1957). Linguistics provided descriptions of two languages; the differences between the two descriptions are taken to be the major contribution to the learners' difficulties with the second language, as in Stockwell, Bowen, and Martin's (1965) comparison of English and Spanish.

Linguistic description was then the main driving force. In syntax, this took the form of *phrase structure* grammar through which the relationship between the L1 and the L2 could be stated in two-dimensional syntactic trees or in the columns of substitution tables. In phonology, it was phoneme theory, particularly the tool of *minimal pairs* (e.g., *bit/bat*), which treated speech as a succession of discrete sounds in a chain. Most language teaching has used these approaches to syntax and phonology ever since, presumably because they are straightforward to apply.

American CA also relied on the *structuralist learning theory* of Bloomfield (1933) and his followers. To Lado (1964), for example, speakers control habits that produce speech automatically without thinking; these are acquired through exposure and practice; habits learned for one task or language are transferred to new tasks or languages or may interfere with them. The learning model is thus a form of *behaviorism* relying on frequency of occurrence and on imitation. As such, its modern developments do not come within the scope of this chapter. The term behaviorism has been a red rag to a bull to linguists ever since Chomsky's elegant demolition of behaviorist approaches to language in his celebrated review of B. F. Skinner's *Verbal Behavior* (Chomsky, 1959). Linguists do not consider that it matters how often you say something and deny that rules could be learned by imitation. Nevertheless such approaches have continued to be developed in psychology, as seen for example in *The New Psychology of Language* (Tomasello, 1998).

Since SLA research is about minds with two languages, the relationships between these languages, both in the learners' development and in their final state of knowledge, inevitably have to form a major part of its domain. The concept of transfer from one language in the learner's mind to the other is then necessary in one shape or another; for instance, Spanish learners may transfer the Spanish sentence structure to English to get subjectless sentences (e.g., *is raining*) and may transfer Spanish syllable structure to get *eschool* by adding an initial vowel. The danger with terms such as *transfer* and *interference* is, however, their negative associations with this largely discredited CA theory. Whatever the terminology or theory that is used, the relationships between the two languages that they denote stand at the center of SLA research. If the L2 and the L1 were entirely separate in the mind, there would indeed be no separate discipline of SLA research as L2 acquisition would be a special case of L1 acquisition.

Universal Grammar and SLA

Since the 1950s, Chomsky's I-language theories have been crucial to linguistics, whether people react for or against them. Chomsky emphasized how the individual mind created knowledge of language from the evidence available to it, conceptualized first as a *language acquisition device* (LAD) that produced knowledge of language in the child's mind, then as UG having invariable principles that govern the structures of all languages and variable parameters that are set differently for each language (Chomsky, 1986), currently rephrased as the *minimalist program* (MP; Chomsky, 1995), which has reduced language knowledge to an even sparser set of principles.

UG theory had the advantage for SLA research that it treated all languages as variations on a theme, called by Rizzi (2004) *comparative syntax*, rather than languages varying indefinitely from each other without constraint, as they often seemed to do in structuralist theories—*languages could differ from each other without limit and in unpredictable ways* (Joos, 1957, p. 96). It automatically provided an overall framework within which the L1 and the L2 could be compared. For example, the *null subject parameter* distinguishes languages like English where the pronoun subject of the sentence is compulsory from those like Spanish where it is not. So in English you have to say *he talks*, not *talks*; in Italian you typically say *parla*, without a subject rather than *il parla*. But it is not just English and Italian that this applies to: all languages have to choose whether to be like English or Italian, even if the majority adopt the Italian solution. This neat difference between languages has provided a useful tool for SLA research and has been a favorite topic from White (1986) to, say, Amaral and Roeper (2014).

UG theory also had the bonus of providing its own learning theory through its claims that much language knowledge is already built-in to the mind and that input activates it in circumscribed ways by setting parameters for the particular language and providing vocabulary. It is then an I-language theory that takes the individual mind as its model. But, unlike CA, it is primarily a theory of monolingual L1 acquisition, with SLA studies mostly riding on the back of the L1. The debates about UG in SLA research have centered on whether it can be extended to L2 acquisition—is there *access* to UG in L2 acquisition (Cook, 1985a; White, 2003)?—and whether its properties suit one version or another of contemporary syntactic description (Hawkins & Chan, 1997), rather than proposing distinct SLA research questions of its own.

Distinctive L2 Views

In addition to the broad CA and UG approaches above, which import a linguistic movement into SLA research, there have been more specifically L2 models that have drawn on linguistics to some extent.

Krashen's Input Hypothesis Model

Krashen's theory of SLA reached its full form in the *input hypothesis* of the 1980s (Krashen, 1985). Its main claims were the division between acquisition—the *natural* implicit process of acquiring a language—and learning—the formal explicit learning of language, available to older learners. Its linguistic antecedents were Chomskyan in its reliance on the inherent capacity of the human mind to acquire languages, but it concentrated on the conditions which fostered or hindered successful attainment rather than making suggestions how this worked. Indeed, it is anathema to Chomskyan theory to claim that specific conditions are necessary for language acquisition: virtually all children learn language despite the inefficiencies of their parents; the only thing that can harm them is lack of *any* language input at all.

The Krashen view of language partly comes out of 1960s L1 acquisition research, which in turn derived rather remotely from linguistics. For instance, SLA research took over the concept of grammatical morpheme from the first language work of Brown (1973). Brown selected an eclectic and arbitrary selection of so-called grammatical morphemes consisting of aspects of the inflectional morphology of the verb (progressive -*ing*), and the noun (possessive -*s*) mixed with articles (*the* and *a*) and others, and scored how well children produced them over the first years of life, establishing a common order for their acquisition.

A massive amount of SLA research was devoted to testing this out in SLA, starting with Dulay and Burt (1973), who found that there was indeed an order of difficulty for these grammatical morphemes for Spanish-speaking learners of English. The easiest was the plural'-*s* in *books*, followed by the continuous -*ing* in *going*; the most difficult, the third person -*s* in *likes* and the possessive -*s* in *John's*. Similar orders were found for L2 learners of English whether they came from Japan or from Italy and whether they were taught English or learned it informally. Hannan (2004) used it to show a similar sequence for Bengali-speaking children in East London, and Wei (2000) used it to compare Japanese and Chinese learners of English. It remains the only aspect of morphology to be covered to any extent in SLA research; a meta-analysis of selected studies can be found in Goldschneider and DeKeyser (2001).

One of the planks of the input hypothesis model was the *natural order hypothesis* (Krashen, 1985), based on this research: the rules of language are necessarily acquired in a particular order. This has remained a persistent and virtually unchallenged claim about SLA to this day for many theories and many areas of acquisition. The problem with Krashen's version is partly that it is based on a restricted set of syntax, mostly that no real reason is provided why the order is necessary. It cannot be, for example, that the natural order for English grammatical morphemes is an innate part of the mind as this would mean that *ing* and *s* and the rest are built-in to the brain, rendering other languages impossible to learn. It must be that these are covered by more general principles at an abstract level, which Krashen never discusses.

European Models

European SLA research often took a different turn under the influence of the long-standing European tradition of linguistics typified by de Saussure (1916) and Halliday and Mattheisen (2013), known as *functionalism*. In these theories the meaning and function of the sentence and its contribution to social exchange and communication are seen as more important than its sheer structure. It is how people use language in the real world that matters.

One example is the large-scale research program involving six first languages and five second languages known as the European Science Foundation (ESF) project. This regarded the interlanguage as based on a set of organizational principles—phrasal (how words are put in structures), semantic (how one referent in the sentence controls another), and pragmatic (how each sentence answers an implied question; Klein & Perdue, 1997). Large-scale research with adult migrant workers in Europe unearthed a basic grammar common to all L2 learners consisting of three simple rules, namely: a sentence may consist of a noun phrase (NP) followed by a verb, optionally followed by another NP (*girl take bread*); or of an NP followed by a copula and another NP or an adjective (*it's bread*); or of a verb followed by an NP (*pinching its*). And that is it, so far as the basic L2 grammar is concerned. This is true almost regardless of which first or second language is involved. L2 learners not only have an interlanguage grammar, they all have the same interlanguage grammar.

An alternative approach, first called the *multidimensional model* (Meisel, Clahsen, & Pienemann, 1981), also looked beyond statements of order to underlying explanations. It had at its core how the order of sentence elements such as subject, verb, and object is modified by syntactic movement that displaces the elements of the sentence to other places, familiar from the formation of passives, *Poland was invaded by Germany* (*Germany invaded Poland*), and questions, *which country did they invade?* (*they invaded which country*). First the L2 learners progressed from saying one word or phrase (e.g., *ticket*) to using the most typical word order for the language (e.g., Subject verb object: *you buy ticket*). Then they went on to modify this basic structure by moving elements around in the sentence to generate, *yesterday I buy ticket*, before acquiring the question movement, *which ticket do you want?* Finally they get the order in subordinate clauses (e.g., *he asked which ticket I wanted*). These stages of development were caused by the constraints of language processing, starting from the minimal single-word sentences people could handle and expanding to encompass more and more complex movement as their processing capacity allowed. This explanation based upon the capacity to move elements in the sentence evolved into the *processability model* (Pienemann & Kessler, 2011), though the syntax became more rigorous, based on the ideas of Joan Bresnan (2001) known as *lexical functional grammar*.

Using Different Areas of Linguistics

Sometimes SLA research has not just taken its cue from linguistic theories but has also taken over descriptive techniques used by linguists from different traditions. The danger is that such tools are seldom neutral but can commit SLA research to a particular view of language and language acquisition. The phonological descriptions used in CA were, for example, based essentially on a description of the phonemes and allophones used in the phonological theories of the 1950s rather than more modern ideas, such as *Optimal Phonology*. These continue to be tools in much SLA research, but SLA researchers have to be careful about the underlying structuralist assumptions about language learning that they might not wish to take on board. Furthermore, the tools of linguistics, being designed to handle the monolingual native speaker, may not properly cover L2 acquisition appropriately, as we elaborate below. Let us then see two mainstream uses of linguistic apparatus in the service of SLA research: phonology and sociolinguistics.

Phonetics and Phonology in SLA Research

A particular close link between phonetics and SLA research has been the measurement of *voice onset time* (VOT), an aspect of phonetic variation between languages that lends itself well to precise measurement and experimentation reviewed in Watson (1991), going from Williams (1977), to Kehoe, Lleo, and Rakow (2004). VOT refers to the timing of voicing in the production of *plosive consonants* such as /p~b/, /t~d/, and /k~g/. Plosive consonants are made by completely closing some part of the mouth with the tongue or the lips and so preventing air from coming out; then the air is released, giving *plosion*. Plosives may be either voiced, like the /g/ in *got*, or unvoiced, like the /k/ in *cot*. But whether we perceive them as voiced depends, not just on the vibration of the vocal cords, but also on when voicing starts. Using the moment of release of air from the obstruction as a reference mark, voicing can start *before* the release, *shortly after* the release or *some time after* the release; deciding whether a plosive is voiced depends on the length of the silent gap between the release and the start of voicing—the VOT. In the voiced English /g/ in *gut*, the voicing starts anytime between 88 milliseconds (ms) before the release and 21 ms after; in the voiceless /k/ in *cut*, the voicing starts about 80 ms after the release. The difference is then at least 60 ms.

While there are pairs of voiced and voiceless plosives in many languages, the VOT difference between the voiced and unvoiced forms varies from one language to another. For example the voiced Spanish /g/ has an early VOT of 88 ms before the release similar to English, but the voiceless Spanish /k/ has a VOT of 29 ms shortly after the release. While both languages have a pair of voiced and unvoiced consonants, there is quite a difference between them in the timings. The Spanish /k/ starts voicing much earlier than its English counterpart /k/, almost within the range for the English /g/, hence acquiring the pronunciation of a second language may involve not just learning the overall contrast between pairs of plosive consonants, but also altering the perception and production of VOT.

A long tradition of SLA experiments dealing with multiple language pairs has shown that L2 learners neither match the target language VOTs fully nor retain their first language VOTs completely. Indeed, more recently, Wrembel (2011) has shown that third language VOTs are affected by both L1 and L2. Thus L2 learners end up differing from monolingual speakers of both L2 *and* L1. This is supported by research ranging from Spanish/English (Zampini & Green, 2001), Hebrew/English (Obler, 1982), and German/Spanish (Kehoe et al., 2004). Some of the original phonetics research may give a false impression of monolinguals: Kato (2004) has pointed out that the supposedly monolingual VOTs often come from bilingual subjects tested in their L1 and hence may have already been influenced by the L2.

The VOT area then shows the close relationship that can arise between linguistic techniques and SLA research, more or less independently of the linguistic theory to which they were originally attached. Other tools used in phonetics are also starting to have an impact. For instance, event-related potentials (ERPs) show carryover of perception of vowel duration from Russian to Finnish L2 for Russian-similar vowels but not for dissimilar (Nenonen, Shestakova, Huotilainen, & Näätänan, 2005). Analysis of speech intonation in terms of fundamental frequencies showing how the pitch goes up and down have demonstrated the effects of L2 Greek on location of intonational peaks in L1 Dutch questions (Mennen, 2004) and of Turkish on intonation by Turkish/German bilingual children (Queen, 2001). Such techniques are used by experimental phoneticians such as Flege (1990) and Major (2001) to support a number of theories of L2 phonological development. VOT is a highly testable area of phonetics in SLA research; the problem is whether techniques such as VOT have much to say for other aspects of phonology, let alone L2 acquisition in general. Nevertheless they do show that SLA research has progressed beyond the concept of the phoneme. And they show how second language research can usefully borrow research techniques from linguistics without being overwhelmed by them.

Sociolinguistics in SLA Research

SLA research has also drawn on sociolinguistics, in particular on the kind called *variationism*. This concerns itself chiefly with the varying pronunciations of different social groups, such as Labov's famous study of the pronunciation of /r/ in New York department stores (Labov, 1966) and Trudgill's account of women using the more upwardly mobile /ɪn/ pronunciation of -*ing* versus men using the downwardly mobile /ɪn/ pronunciation (Trudgill,

1974), arguably a worldwide phenomenon in English-speaking countries. The sociolinguistic techniques for investigating different native groups can then be extended to L2 learners. Take, for example, the variable pronunciation of the -*ing* verbal ending. Not only is the /ɪn/ pronunciation used by men rather than women, but also by working-class speakers rather than middle-class, and in informal circumstances rather than formal, as shown by the spelling variant <*in'*> in advertising campaigns for whiskey <*a sippin' whiskey*> and for fast food <*i'm lovin' it*>. L2 learners soon learn the gender bias; male L2 students tested by Adamson and Regan (1991) say /ɪn/ four times as often as female students.

Rehner, Mougeon, and Nadasdi (2003) applied variationism to the acquisition of French pronouns by English-speaking students in Canada, showing that they preferred the more formal first person pronoun *nous* to the informal *on* compared with both native speakers and their own teachers. Cook (1985b) similarly found that L2 learners preferred more formal forms of thanking such as *thank you very much indeed* over informal forms such as *thanks*. So far, the variation that has been studied by SLA researchers has been matching variants established from native speaker norms; that is, there is little research dealing with variation between the situations and L2 users rather than native speakers, apart perhaps from the variable of contact with native speakers as in year-abroad studies (Collentine, 2009; but see Dewaele, 1994, 2004; Dewaele & Regan, 2002). The danger is seeing the L2 learner as being deficient compared to the native speaker; it may be that extra formality for instance is expected of non-native speakers and so is the correct thing for them to do while talking with native speakers.

SLA research has extended its sociolinguistics methodology in several directions. One is the social *network theories* used in Wei's (1994) study of the Chinese community in Newcastle, concerned with the varying contacts that members of a minority group may have with the majority community. Another is the notion of power—how one group controls another group through language. Partly, this may be a matter of the power relationships between different language groups in a multilingual society such as Singapore which has English, Chinese, Bahasa Indonesia, and Tamil, or Northern Ireland which has English and Ulster Scots; or in the US with the English only movement. At an overall level the issue has become one of native speaker power: do native speakers have the sole rights over a language (Cook, 1999; Rampton, 1996)? L2 users have rights as second language users in their own right, not just according to the extent to which they accommodate to native speakers.

Perhaps the main contact areas between linguistics and SLA research have been syntax and vocabulary. Syntax of various types underlies much of the above discussion, whether UG, the ESF project or the input hypothesis model. Syntax and vocabulary have not been expanded here at length mostly because they are well covered in books such as *SoSLA* and Nation (2013). But also much syntactic discussion in SLA research has now become a test of linguistic theories from L2 data rather than SLA research that uses linguistics and so not part of SLA research proper; much work with vocabulary is based on ideas from psychology or testing rather than linguistics.

The Methodology of SLA Research

The I-language versus E-language division runs through the methodology of SLA research. Some researchers are interested in naturally occurring samples of language, for example, tape-recordings of L2 learners' speech, their emails, their essays, or indeed any other source of spoken or written language produced by L2 learners—classic E-language data. From these different types of text, we can derive regularities, frequencies for what happens in L2 users' speech, as in the ESF analysis of corpora (Klein & Perdue, 1997). Other researchers employ I-language approaches such as reaction time experiments, grammaticality judgments and the like to find out what the L2 user knows rather than what they have done (Yuan, 1997). In practice, this distinction may be blurred: the fact that a learner has written something may be used to show both E-language frequency and I-language knowledge. Nevertheless the difference in orientation is there, E-language seeing its main responsibility as the faithful reporting of what has already occurred, I-language as accounting for what the user might potentially say.

The I- and E-language division is also sometimes at cross-purposes with the competence/performance distinction; do grammaticality judgments count as competence (i.e., underlying knowledge of the language) because they involve knowledge, or as performance (i.e., processes involved in using language) because they are established by a process task? Corpora data exist such as the L2 students' essays in the International Corpus of Learner English (http://www.uclouvain.be/en-cecl-icle.html)—what learners have actually said. Experimental studies of reaction times are equally obviously measures of performance—how learners do something. In between comes a gray area where performance data such as grammaticality judgments are used to say something about competence. Some people, mostly from the psychological domain, deny that the competence/performance distinction is necessary. Others pay it lipservice, for instance, by accepting grammaticality judgments as evidence for underlying knowledge without taking in the processes they use.

In a sense, the use of grammaticality judgments is an extrapolation from the linguists' idea of linguistic intuition, prevalent from Chomsky (1957) onwards. Linguists usually ask themselves whether a single sentence, such as *Is Sam is the cat that black?*, is grammatical and get a yes/no/don't know answer; their intuition depends on self-assessment of a sentence or two. SLA researchers ask many subjects to judge many examples of the same structure and establish a frequency of scores rather than an absolute answer. The linguistic intuition method of the linguists is then closer to a single sentence competence mode, the SLA researchers' grammaticality judgments test to an experiment-based approach: linguists rarely give the statistical significance of their intuitions, SLA researchers almost invariably do for their grammaticality judgments. The trap that SLA research sometimes falls into is comparing the intuitions of native speakers with the grammaticality judgments of L2 learners; however good their intuitions, native speakers are very far from perfect at grammaticality judgment tests even in areas where their grammatical structures seem well attested in their competence, say *John is easy/eager to please*. The only valid comparison is between like and like—L2 grammaticality judgments compared with L1 grammaticality judgments, or L2 intuitions compared with L1 intuitions. The latter is interestingly never done for the reason that researchers cannot readily admit that L2 users have valid intuitions, since native speakers are the gold standard from which L2 users depart.

Questioning Linguistic Ideas in Second Language Acquisition Research

The use of grammaticality judgments in SLA research can then be seen as a potentially misleading reinterpretation of a concept from linguistics. This section argues that this reflects a more general problem when SLA research takes over other core assumptions from linguistics. While such assumptions are not necessarily wrong in their original context, they may not be appropriate for SLA research, particularly when they are axiomatic rather than derived from theories or descriptions of language.

The Dominance of Speech

Throughout linguistics, it is assumed that speech is the primary form of language, writing a secondary derived form, whether it is Aristotle from the 4th Century BC asserting *writing is a symbol of vocal sounds* (as cited in Harris, 2000), or Lyons from the 20th century AD claiming that *writing is essentially a means of representing speech in another medium* (Lyons, 1968, p. 38), or the founding father of American linguistics Bloomfield insisting *writing is merely a way of recording language by means of visible marks* (Bloomfield, 1933, p. 21). Yet written language affects our lives in many ways that spoken language does not; its advantages of permanency, density of lexical content, and neutrality of social roles for reader and writer are precisely that it is *not* spoken language (Cook, 2004). Once we have learned to read, few of us read aloud, except for newsreaders or parents: we do not necessarily convert what we read into speech but use the different technique of silent reading. English people read entire novels by Dostoyevsky or J. R. Tolkien where they cannot pronounce the names of the characters. Far from being dependent on spoken language, written English differs in grammar and vocabulary as well as in the unique systems of punctuation and spelling; Haas (1970) indeed talked of the relationship between speech and writing in terms of translation between languages. For literate people, speech and writing are in parallel rather than writing being a slave system. The arguments for the *primacy of speech* have little to do with our everyday experience. Of course, written language does slip in to linguistics by the backdoor; every time Chomsky cites a sentence such as *John said he was looking for a cat, and Bill did too* (Chomsky, 1995, p. 126), he, like all linguists, is surreptitiously relying on our knowledge of left-to-right direction, word spaces, capital letters and punctuation—the sentence would be ungrammatical if *<Bill>* were all in lower case *<bill>*.

Since the 1880s, language teaching has adopted the same creed of speech being primary, writing secondary. This was seen explicitly in the *direct method*, which started in the later 20th century and was characterized by its emphasis on spoken language. It was most extreme in the audiolingualism of the mid-20th century, which emphasized the spoken language to the extent that it banned the written word from the first stages of second language learning (Lado, 1964). It survived implicitly in the recent communicative language teaching approach or indeed the contemporary *task-based learning method*: these emphasize the importance of spontaneous communication in the classroom but see such communication as essentially through speech rather than writing; the written language is used in teaching as an aid to the spoken language rather than as a major component in its own right: *The literature on tasks, both research-based or pedagogic, assumes that tasks are directed at oral skills, particularly speaking* (Ellis, 2003, p. 6).

SLA research has then adopted this spoken language bias almost without question, leading to the dominance of the spoken language over the written. CA was based on comparison between the L1 and L2 phonologies, as in Stockwell et al. (1965), not between writing systems; learner errors to be analyzed were spoken, not written; sequences of acquisition were based on speech data, not written (Dulay & Burt, 1973), and so on. SLA research has throughout used the notion of the *lexical sentence* from spoken language with its *complete* grammatical structure, rather than that of the *textual sentence* with its *incomplete* sentence fragments (Cook, 2004). But again the messages are mixed: Bigelow and Tarone (2004) point out that virtually all SLA research has concerned learners and users who are already literate and whose minds and lives have therefore been transformed in all sorts of ways by literacy itself. This is particularly dangerous when investigating whether success in L2 acquisition is related to the age of the learner; younger learners will either be non-literate or learning literacy; older learners will mostly be literate—those who are not will probably be untypical of the rest of the community because of isolation or learning disability. Hence it may be impossible to disentangle the two effects of age and literacy.

Why should speech be more important than writing in SLA research where literate L2 users are concerned? It is irrelevant for L2 acquisition that children acquire their first language before their first writing system or that speech comes historically before writing in the human race, the usual arguments for the primacy of speech. Literate adult L2 users have been through the transformation that written language makes in their lives, and they approach language quite differently from non-literate adults and children (Goody, 2000). Their view of language, for instance, depends upon the main type of writing system they are familiar with in their L1, whether meaning-based like Chinese or sound-based like Italian. Transferring from one major system to another can have serious long-term disadvantages, as for example, Chinese learners of English (Haynes & Carr, 1990).

Speech before writing is then a shibboleth adopted from linguists, now sometimes challenged even within linguistics itself (Aronoff, 1992; Derwing, 1992). At one extreme, many of the categories of spoken language used by linguists in the 20th century are claimed to be artifacts subconsciously projected from linguists' first-acquired writing systems. The phoneme, for example, looks suspiciously like the invention of people with an alphabetic writing system rather than the character-based kanji system of Japanese; the word was the invention of people who use word spaces to separate words in writing, not found, for example, in Chinese. If modern linguistics had started in China, it might not have found the need for either the phoneme or the word.

Most SLA research has then been conducted on the spoken language, devaluing the writing system, which is probably just as important to most L2 users in the world today, who contact each other through emails, text-message, Twitter, and Facebook rather than spoken conversation. The sole reference to written language in *SoSLA* is in the context of illocutionary acts; *BaB* mentions the writing system briefly on seven pages, chiefly in connection with aphasia and brain functioning. Overall the effects of the primacy of speech assumption have been that SLA research has overemphasized the importance of the spoken language and has neglected the specific properties of the writing system.

Research specifically on L2 writing systems is starting to be carried out, as seen in Cook and Bassetti (2005). Much of it mirrors the early days of SLA research, overwhelmingly concerned with the transfer of the L1 writing system to the L2 writing system in a CA mode (though mostly concerned with processing) and with assigning the errors of L2 learners to their L1 phonology and L1 writing system in an *Error Analysis* fashion. For instance, readers with meaning-based L1 writing systems are faster at word naming in Chinese as an L2 writing system than readers with sound-based L1 writing systems (Yang, 2000).

The Pre-Eminence of the Monolingual Native Speaker

We have already alluded to the largely unspoken assumption that the subject matter of linguistics is the monolingual native speaker. This can be traced back at least to Bloomfield (1933, p. 43): *The first language a human being learns to speak is his **native language**; he is a **native speaker** of this language* (emphasis in the original). The clearest statement of this linguist's point of view is perhaps Chomsky's *River Charles metaphor* in a famous interview with François Grosjean (for the benefit of readers without a knowledge of US geography, the Charles River flows through Boston by MIT):

Why do chemists study H_2O and not the stuff that you get out of the Charles River? You assume that anything as complicated as what is in the Charles River will only *be understandable, if at all, on the basis of discovery of the fundamental principles that determine the nature of all matter, and those you have to learn about by studying pure cases.*

This can be called the *purity argument* for using monolinguals in linguistics: bilingual minds are in some sense impure, contaminated by the pollutants of another language. The true *pure* state of linguistic competence is a mind with one language. This applies to groups as well as to individuals: the language of a mixed community:

would not be pure in the relevant sense, because it would not represent a single set of choices among the options permitted by UG but rather would include contradictory choices for certain of these options.

(Chomsky, 1986, p. 17)

While Chomsky's quotations relate primarily to the UG model, these do show the basic monolingual assumption in linguistics. SLA research implicitly takes over this assumption: language is what native speakers know and do. The native speaker is the touchstone against which all other speakers are tested—*an idealized monolingual native speaker, who is held to be the ultimate yardstick of linguistic success* (Ortega, 2009, p. 140). Anything that does not conform to native speaker language is wrong. Judged by this criterion, there are indeed very few successful L2 learners, some might say none; Towell and Hawkins (1994, p. 14) typically claim that *very few L2 learners appear to be fully successful in the way that native speakers are*: well yes, if the only successful person by definition is the native speaker. As Sridhar and Sridhar (1986, p. 413) point out, *paradoxical as it may seem, Second Language Acquisition researchers seem to have neglected the fact that the goal of SLA is bilingualism.*

Bilingualism researchers are more reluctant to subordinate their bilingual subjects to monolinguals than SLA researchers. Romaine (1994, p. 282) insists that *it is clear that a reasonable account of bilingualism cannot be based on a theory which assumes monolingual competence as its frame of reference.* The overall emphasis is an acceptance of the L2 user *as an L2 user* to be measured by the standards of L2 users. The L2 user is a genuine bilingual, not an imitation monolingual in the L2: bilingualism is not double monolingualism but a different state (Grosjean, 1989). The *ultimate attainment* of SLA is not, and could never be, monolingual competence (Cook, 2016).

One retort to Chomsky's *River Charles metaphor* is that H_2O is not pure but a molecule built up from two hydrogen and one oxygen atoms; if we decompose it to its pure state, we would no longer be studying water as such but the properties of hydrogen and oxygen. The natural *molecule* for human languages is the complex multicompetence state, not the pure monolingual one; monolinguals are missing an atom from the usual language molecule, so to speak. A Chomskyan argument called the *uniformity requirement* by Cook and Newson (2007) undermines the linguist's reliance on monolingual native speakers. This claims that a theory of language acquisition has to apply to all children in all circumstances; language acquisition does not depend on the precise nature of the input language available, provided there is some input available. Our theory of language acquisition has then to accommodate what *all* children can potentially do. We know that children exposed to two languages acquire both of them, even if differently from monolinguals; children exposed to one language become monolinguals. The difference is then input-specific, a matter of the environment, and not part of a general theory of acquisition accounting for the potential for all human beings regardless of situation. Monolinguals do not acquire a second language because they are deprived of the necessary input, just as children deprived of L1 input do not acquire a first language (Curtiss, 1977); monolingualism is a particular case of an input-starved situation. Any human being has the potential to acquire more than one language. Indeed, even in terms of sheer numbers, there are probably more people in the world who use more than one language than those who use one.

Conclusion

Linguistics has then been both a source of inspiration and a curse to SLA research. Linguists' ideas about language are a major driving source, yet they can insidiously undermine research if their assumptions are not re-examined for appropriateness to the issues of L2 acquisition and use. However, if linguistics is ignored, SLA research often falls back on common-sense folk-linguistic views of language or ideas derived from the school grammar tradition. Perhaps any linguistics is better than none.

The relationship between SLA researchers and linguists has sometimes shown a lack of mutual understanding; linguists feel SLA research is misusing ideas long past their sell-by date, SLA researchers regret they are not getting usable tools and concepts from linguists and increasingly criticize the emphasis in linguistics on the monolingual native speaker. Hopefully, this impasse will be resolved and SLA research will be better able to assert its independence from linguistics and to achieve its own goals of addressing the puzzle of one mind with two languages. While we have gone some way to answering most of our initial questions, the answers are far from complete.

List of Key Words and Concepts

Adaptive control of thought model (ACT*), Behaviorism, Collocation, Comparative syntax, Connectionism, Contrastive analysis (CA), Declarative knowledge, Direct method, Dominance of speech, E-language, Error analysis, European models, Foreign accent, Function words, Functionalism, Generative theory, Grammatical gender, Grammatical morphemes, Grammaticality judgments, I-language, Independent grammars assumption, Input hypothesis, Interference, Interlanguage, Krashen's input hypothesis model, Language acquisition device (LAD), Lexical errors, Lexical functional grammar, Lexical phrases, Lexical sentence, Lexicon, Linguistic competence, Minimal pairs, Minimalist program, Morphology, Multicompetence state, Multidimensional model, Natural order hypothesis, Network theories, Null subject parameter, Optimal phonology, Performance, Phonology, Phrase structure, Plosive consonants, Pragmatics, Primacy of speech, Procedural knowledge, Processability model, Purity argument, Second language acquisition (SLA), Semantics, Sociolinguistics, Structuralist learning theory, Syntactic processing, Syntax, Task-based learning method, Textual sentence, Transfer, Uniformity requirement, Universal grammar, Variationism, Voice onset time (VOT)

Internet Sites Related to Linguistics and Bilingualism

American Association for Applied Linguistics: http://www.aaal.org/
Center for Applied Linguistics: http://www.cal.org/
National Clearinghouse for English Language Acquisition and Language Instruction
Educational Programs: http://www.ncela.gwu.edu/
Second Language Acquisition: http://www.viviancook.uk/SLA/Index.htm
Stephen Krashen's Theory: http://www.sk.com.br/sk-krash.html

Discussion Questions

(1) Do you think there is a single discipline that studies the acquisition and use of second languages or that there are really several disciplines (SLA research, bilingualism, psychology) that happen to use L2 evidence but have little in common?
(2) Does or should linguistics have a monopoly on ideas about language itself?
(3) Can any one view of language, linguistics, or language learning ever be completely right?
(4) Do you agree that we should treat learners as people with independent language systems of their own, or as people with language systems that are deficient versions of the target, whether adults in L1 acquisition or native speakers in L2 acquisition?
(5) To what extent do you think that the languages you know are indeed similar to each other or different?
(6) How important do you feel is the actual language input that L2 learners receive?
(7) Is the use of hi-tech techniques of linguistic investigation such as VOT necessary to investigate L2 acquisition, or is there a place for such traditional techniques as *grammaticality judgments*?
(8) Do you believe that particular areas of language, such as syntax, should form the core of SLA research or do you feel all areas are equally important?
(9) Are the ideas of the primacy of speech and the pre-eminence of the native speaker valid for SLA research as well as for most mainstream linguistics?
(10) What areas of linguistics do you feel could be most usefully exploited in SLA research without sacrificing its own research agenda?

Suggested Research Projects

(1) Take a particular grammatical construction in two languages, such as articles or questions, that you know and look up parallel grammatical descriptions in current grammar books. Could you really compare them? Do the differences correspond to the kinds of *mistakes* that learners actually make in your experience?
(2) Suppose that you wanted to test a hypothesis about variation in L2 learning (e.g., whether left-handed learners are better). Choose an appropriate area of linguistics to use and design a linguistically sound research method that shows whether there was an actual correlation.
(3) Take a sample of recent articles from the SLA research literature from your library and see what use it makes of standard linguistic terms such as morpheme, phoneme, and word order. Does this demonstrate a closeness or a separation from linguistics?

References

Adamson, H., & Regan, V. (1991). The acquisition of community norms by Asian immigrants learning English as a second language: A preliminary study. *Studies in Second Language Acquisition, 13*(1), 1–22.
Amaral, L., & Roeper, T. (2014). Multiple grammars and second language representation. *Second Language Research, 30*(3), 3–36.
Anderson, J. R. (1983). *The architecture of cognition.* Cambridge, MA: Harvard University Press.
Archibald, J. (1993). *Language learnability and L2 phonology: The acquisition of metrical parameters.* Dordrecht: Kluwer.
Aronoff, M. (1992). Segmentalism in linguistics: The alphabetic basis of phonological theory. In P. Downing, S. D. Lima, & M. Noonan (Eds.), *The linguistics of literacy* (pp. 71–82). Amsterdam: John Benjamins.

Aronoff, M., & Rees-Miller, J. (2001). *The handbook of linguistics*. Oxford: Blackwell.

Bigelow, M., & Tarone, E. (2004). The role of literacy level in second language acquisition: Doesn't who we study determine what we know? *TESOL Quarterly*, *38*(4), 689–700.

Bloomfield, L. (1933). *Language.* New York: Holt.

Bresnan, J. (2001). *Lexical-functional syntax.* Oxford: Blackwell.

Brown, R. (1973). *A first language: The early stages*. London: Allen and Unwin.

Chomsky, N. (1957). *Syntactic structures.* The Hague: Mouton.

Chomsky, N. (1959). Review of B.F. Skinner verbal behavior. *Language*, *35*, 26–58.

Chomsky, N. (1965). *Aspects of the theory of syntax*. Cambridge, MA: MIT Press.

Chomsky, N. (1986). *Knowledge of language: Its nature, origin and use*. New York: Praeger.

Chomsky, N. (1995). *The minimalist program*. Cambridge, MA: MIT Press.

Chomsky, N. (2013). Problems of projection. *Lingua*, *130*, 33–49.

Cobbett, W. (1984). *A grammar of the English language*. Oxford: Oxford University Press. (Original work published 1819).

Collentine, J. (2009). Study abroad research: Findings, implications and future directions. In M. Long & C. Doughty (Eds.), *The handbook of language teaching* (pp. 218–233). New Jersey, NJ: Wiley-Blackwell.

Cook, V. J. (1985a). Chomsky's universal grammar and second language learning. *Applied Linguistics*, *6*, 1–18.

Cook, V. J. (1985b). Language functions, social factors, and second language teaching. *IRAL*, *13*(3), 177–196.

Cook, V. J. (1993). *Linguistics and second language acquisition*. London: Macmillan.

Cook, V. J. (1999). Going beyond the native speaker in language teaching. *TESOL Quarterly*, *33*(2), 185–209.

Cook, V. J. (2004). *The English writing system*. London: Edward Arnold.

Cook, V. J. (2010). Prolegomena to second language learning. In P. Seedhouse, S. Walsh, & C. Jenks (Eds.), *Conceptualising language learning* (pp. 6–22). London: Palgrave Macmillan.

Cook, V. J. (2016). Premises of multi-competence. In V. Cook & L. Wei (Eds.), *The Cambridge handbook of linguistic multi-competence* (pp. 1–25). Cambridge: Cambridge University Press.

Cook, V. J., & Bassetti, B. (Eds.). (2005). *Second language writing systems*. London: Edward Arnold.

Cook, V. J., & Newson, M. (2007). *Chomsky's universal grammar: An introduction* (3rd ed.). Oxford: Blackwell.

Curtiss, S. (1977). *Genie: A psycholinguistic study of a modern-day wild child*. New York: Academic Press.

De Saussure, F. (1916). *Course in general linguistics*. London: Peter Owen. (Original work published Bally, C., & Sechehaye, A. (Eds.). *Cours de linguistique générale* (1916)).

Dechert, H. (1984). Second language production: Six hypotheses. In H. Dechert, D. Möhle, & M. Raupach (Eds.), *Second language productions* (pp. 211–230). Tubingen: G. Narr.

Derwing, B. L. (1992). Orthographic aspects of linguistic competence. In P. Downing, S. D. Lima, & M. Noonan (Eds.), *The linguistics of literacy* (pp. 193–210). Amsterdam: Benjamins.

Dewaele, J. M. (1994). Variation synchronique de taux d'exactitude: Analyse de fréquence des erreurs morpholexicales dans trios styles d'interlangue française. *International Review of Applied Linguistics*, *32*, 275–300.

Dewaele, J. M. (2004). Retention or omission of the 'ne' in advanced French IL: The variable effect of extralinguistic factors. *Journal of Sociolinguistics*, *8*(3), 433–450.

Dewaele, J. M., & Regan, V. (2002). Maîtriser la norme sociolinguistique en interlangue française: Le cas de l'omission variable de 'ne'. *Journal of French Language Studies*, *12*, 123–148.

Dulay, H., & Burt, M. (1973). Should we teach children syntax? *Language Learning*, *3*, 245–57.

Ellis, R. (1994). *The study of second language acquisition*. Oxford: Oxford University Press.

Ellis, R. (2003). *Task-based language learning and teaching*. Oxford: Oxford University Press.

Evans, N., & Levinson, S. (2009). The myth of language universals: Language diversity and its importance for cognitive science. *Behavioral and Brain Sciences*, *32*, 429–448.

Feyerabend, P. (1975). *Against method*. London: Humanities Press.

Flege, J. E. (1990). English vowel production by Dutch talkers: More evidence for the "similar" vs. "new" distinction. In J. Leather & A. James (Eds.), *New Sounds 90: Proceedings of the Amsterdam symposium on the acquisition of second-language speech* (pp. 255–293). Amsterdam: University of Amsterdam.

Fries, C. C. (1952). *The structure of English*. New York: Harcourt Brace.

Gass, S., & Selinker, L. (2008). *Second language acquisition: An introductory course*. London: Routledge.

Goldschneider, J. M., & DeKeyser, R. M. (2001). Explaining the "natural order of L2 morpheme acquisition" in English: A meta-analysis of multiple determinants. *Language Learning, 51*(1), 1–50.

Goody, J. (2000). *The power of the written tradition*. Washington, DC: Smithsonian Institute.

Gregg, K. R. (1995). Review of Cook, V. Linguistics and second language acquisition. *Second Language Research, 11*(1), 90–94.

Grosjean, F. (1989). Neurolinguists, beware! The bilingual is not two monolinguals in one person. *Brain and Language, 36*, 3–15

Haas, W. (1970). *Phonographic translation*. Manchester: Manchester University Press.

Halliday, M. A. K., & Mattheisen, M. I. M. (2013). *Halliday's introduction to functional grammar*. (4th ed.), Abingdon: Routledge.

Hamers, J., & Blanc, M. (2000). *Bilinguality and bilingualism* (2nd ed.). Cambridge: Cambridge University Press.

Hannan, M. (2004). *A study of the development of the English verbal morphemes in the grammar of 4–9 year old Bengali-speaking children in the London Borough of Tower Hamlets* (Unpublished doctoral dissertation). Essex University, UK.

Harris, R. (2000). *Rethinking writing*. Indiana: Indiana University Press.

Hawkins, R. (2001). *Second language syntax*. Oxford: Blackwell.

Hawkins, R., & Chan, C. (1997). The partial availability of universal grammar in second language acquisition: The failed functional features hypothesis. *Second Language Research, 13*(3), 187–226.

Haynes, M., & Carr, T. H. (1990). Writing system background and second language reading: A component skills analysis of English reading by native-speaking readers of Chinese. In T. H. Carr & B. A. Levy (Eds.), *Reading and its development: Component skills approaches* (pp. 375–421). San Diego: Academic Press.

Illitch, I., & Sanders, B. (1988). *ABC: Alphabetisation of the popular mind*. Berkeley: North Point Press.

Jakobson, R. (1953). Results of the conference of anthropologists and linguists. *International Journal of American Linguistics, Memoir 8*, 19–22.

Joos, M. (1957). *Readings in linguistics*. Chicago, IL: The University of Chicago Press.

Kato, K. (2004). *Second language (L2) segmental speech learning: Perception and production of L2 English by Japanese native speakers* (Unpublished doctoral dissertation). University of Essex, UK.

Kehoe, M., Lleo, C., & Rakow, M. (2004). Voice onset time in German/Spanish bilinguals. *Bilingualism: Language and Cognition, 7*(1), 71–88.

Klein, W., & Perdue, C. (1997). The basic variety (or: Couldn't natural languages be much simpler?). *Second Language Research, 13*(4), 301–347.

Krashen, S. (1985). *The input hypothesis: Issues and implications*. New York: Longman.

Labov, W. (1966). *The social stratification of English in New York City*. Washington, DC: Centre for Applied Linguistics.

Lado, R. (1957). *Linguistics across cultures*. Ann Arbor: University of Michigan Press.

Lado, R. (1964). *Language teaching: A scientific approach*. Chicago, IL: McGraw-Hill.

Larsen-Freeman, D. (1997). Chaos/complexity science and second language acquisition. *Applied Linguistics, 18*, 141–165.

Lyons, J. (1968). *Introduction to theoretical linguistics*. Cambridge: Cambridge University Press.

McNeill, D. (1966). Developmental psycholinguistics. In F. Smith & G. A. Miller (Eds.), *The genesis of language: A psycholinguistic approach* (pp. 15–84). Cambridge: MIT Press.

Major, R. C. (2001). *Foreign accent: The ontogeny and phylogeny of second language phonology.* Mahwah, NJ: Lawrence Erlbaum Associates.

Meisel, J., Clahsen, H., & Pienemann, M. (1981). On determining developmental stages in natural second language acquisition. *Studies in Second Language Acquisition, 3*(2), 109–135.

Mennen, I. (2004). Bi-directional interference in the intonation of Dutch speakers of Greek. *Journal of Phonetics, 32*, 543–563.

Nation, I. S. P. (2013). *Learning vocabulary in another language* (2nd ed.). Cambridge: Cambridge University Press.

Nenonen, S., Shestakova, A., Huotilainen, M., & Näätänan, R. (2005). Speech-sound duration processing in a second language is specific to phonetic categories. *Brain and Language, 92*, 26–32.

Obler, L. (1982). The parsimonious bilingual. In L. Obler & L. Menn (Eds.), *Exceptional language and linguistics* (pp. 339–346). New York: Academic Press.

Ortega, L. (2009). *Understanding second language acquisition.* London: Hodder Education.

Pienemann, M., & Kessler, J. (2011). *Studying processability theory.* Amsterdam: John Benjamins.

Priestley, J. (1761). *The rudiments of English grammar.* London: R. Griffiths.

Queen, R. M. (2001). Bilingual intonation patterns: Evidence of language change from Turkish-German bilingual children. *Language in Society, 30*, 55–80.

Rampton, B. (1996). Displacing the native speaker: Expertise, inheritance and affiliation. In T. Hedge & N. Whitney (Eds.), *Power, pedagogy and practice* (pp. 17–22). Oxford: Oxford University Press.

Rehner, K., Mougeon, R., & Nadasdi, T. (2003). The learning of sociolinguistic variation by advanced FSL learners: The case of *Nous* versus *On* in Immersion French. *Studies in Second Language Acquisition, 25*, 127–156.

Rizzi, L. (2004). On the study of the language faculty: Results, developments, and perspectives. *The Linguistics Review, 21*, 323–344.

Robins, R. H. (1952). Noun and verb in universal grammar. *Language, 28*, 289–298.

Romaine, S. (1994). *Bilingualism.* Oxford: Blackwell.

Sajavaara, K. (1981). Contrastive linguistics past and present and a communicative approach. In J. Fisiak (Ed.), *Contrastive linguistics and the language teacher* (pp. 33–56). Oxford: Pergamon.

Sapir, E. (1921). *Language: An introduction to the study of speech.* Reprinted n.d. by New York: Harcourt Brace and Co.

Selinker, L. (1972). Interlanguage. *International Review of Applied Linguistics, X*(3), 209–231.

Sridhar, S. N., & Sridhar, K. K. (1986). The syntax and psycholinguistics of bilingual code mixing. *Canadian Journal of Psychology, 34*(4), 407–416.

Stockwell, R., Bowen, J., & Martin, J. (1965). *The grammatical structures of English and Spanish.* Chicago, IL. University of Chicago.

Tomasello, M. (Ed.). (1998). *The new psychology of language.* Mahwah, N.J: Lawrence Erlbaum.

Towell, R., & Hawkins, R. (1994). *Approaches to second language acquisition.* Clevedon, Bristol: Multilingual Matters.

Trudgill, P. (1974). *The social differentiation of English in Norwich.* Harmondsworth: Penguin.

Tsimpli, T., Sorace, A., Heycock, C., & Filiaci, F. (2004). First language attrition and syntactic subjects: A study of Greek and Italian near native speakers of English. *International Journal of Bilingualism, 3*, 257–278.

Ullmann, M. (2001). A neurocognitive perspective on language: The declarative/procedural model. *Nature Neuroscience, 2*, 717–726.

Watson, I. (1991). Phonological processing in two languages. In E. Bialystok (Ed.), *Language processes in bilingual children* (pp. 26–48). Cambridge: Cambridge University Press.

Wei, L. (1994). *Three generations, two languages, one family: Language choice and language shift in a Chinese community in Britain.* Clevedon: Multilingual Matters.

Wei, L. (2000). Unequal election of morphemes in adult second language acquisition. *Applied Linguistics, 21*, 106–140.

White, L. (1986). Implications of parametric variation for adult second language acquisition: An investigation of the pro-drop parameter. In V. J. Cook (Ed.), *Experimental approaches to second language acquisition* (pp. 55–72). Oxford: Pergamon.

White, L. (2003). *Second language acquisition and universal grammar*. Cambridge: Cambridge University Press.

Williams, L. (1977). The perception of consonant voicing by Spanish English bilinguals. *Perception and Psychophysics*, *21*(4), 289–297.

Wrembel, M. (2011). Crosslinguistic influences in third language acquisition of voice onset time. *ICPhS XVII*, 2157–2160.

Yang, J. (2000). Orthographic effect on word recognition by learners of Chinese as a foreign language. *Journal of the Chinese Language Teachers Association*, *35*(2), 1–18.

Yuan, B. P. (1997). Asymmetry of null subjects and null objects in Chinese speakers' L2 English. *Studies in Second Language Acquisition*, *19*, 467–497.

Zampini, M. L., & Green, K. P. (2001). The voicing contrast in English and Spanish: the relationship between perception and production. In J. Nicol (Ed.), *One mind, two languages* (pp. 23–48). Oxford: Blackwell.

16 Second Language Acquisition and Bilingualism

Susan Gass and Margo Glew

Introduction

The following anecdotes reveal how, even after many years of experience with another language, there are still areas that make *non-native speakers* (NNS) of a language different from *native speakers* (NS) of that language.

(1) One morning, Mrs. G, a native speaker of English now living in Israel, was doing her daily shopping at the local supermarket. As she was pushing her shopping cart, she unintentionally bumped into Mr. Y, a native Israeli. Her natural reaction was to say, *I'm sorry* (in Hebrew). Mr. Y turned to her and said, *Lady, you could at least apologize.* On another occasion the very same Mr. Y arrived late for a meeting conducted by Mr. W (a native speaker of English) in English. As he walked into the room he said, *The bus was late*, and sat down. Mr. W, obviously annoyed, muttered to himself, *These Iraelis, why don't they ever apologize!* (Olshtain & Cohen, 1989, p. 53).

(2) From Goldschmidt (1996, p. 255)
> NNS: *I have a favor to ask you.*
> NS: *Sure, what can I do for you?*
> NNS: *You need to write a recommendation for me.*

(3) A Chilean jockey, after winning the Kentucky Derby, was accused of carrying something in his hand other than his whip. Apparently, he had told a reporter that he wore a Q-Ray, which is a therapeutic bracelet used for arthritic conditions. What had been understood was a *cue-ring*, which apparently the reporter had never heard of (probably because it does not exist).

While these non-native speakers are able to speak a second language (L2) with grammatical accuracy, they have not learned to use language appropriately, or in the case of example 3, to pronounce language according to standard norms. Further, with regard to example 3, despite the fact that the reporter didn't know what a *cue-ring* was, he assumed it to be something illegal. Had the reporter minimally recognized that perception of non-native speech often occurs through the filter of our native language sound system, and that that perception is not always accurate, the problem might have been avoided. That, coupled with the fact that he had never heard of a *Q-ring*, might have suggested the need to seek greater clarification, and the 2–3-day scandal that resulted could have been avoided.

The study of *second language acquisition* (SLA) is concerned with what language learners know and don't know about a new language and how they come to know it. The field is broad and includes not only learner knowledge of the grammatical, lexical, and phonological features of a new language, but also includes ways in which that knowledge is put to use. As such, it also deals with communication difficulties such as the ones exemplified above.

Conceptual Definitions

The second/foreign language literature and the bilingualism literature often deal with the same or similar phenomena, but with different terminology. Because this chapter appears in a book devoted primarily to the field of bilingualism and because this chapter draws on literature from a different (albeit related) field, SLA, it is particularly important to attempt to sort out some of the terminological differences. In the first part of this chapter, we deal with some of the varying definitions common in the discourse of these two fields, providing the conventional use of the words and terms in the SLA literature. It is hoped that this section contributes to the unpacking, and hence understanding, of some of the terms used in both fields. We use the term SLA quite broadly in this chapter. It includes the study of the acquisition of any language learned after the first language. The construct of first language (L1) is difficult to define given that in many parts of the world, multiple languages are learned simultaneously and not sequentially. The term SLA is vague as to whether the language being learned is actually the second, third, or fourth language. SLA, in a strict sense, refers to language learning in the environment where the language being learned is spoken, whereas foreign language learning refers to learning in an environment where the native language, not the target language is spoken; however, the term SLA is used as a general cover term, frequently referring to languages learned in either a second or foreign language environment. Thus, the conventional use of the term *SLA* is quite broad, referring to any language learned after the first in either a second or foreign language environment. This is not to say that SLA researchers do not recognize important differences in the environment or in the chronological ordering of learning, as these factors are important considerations in SLA studies (see Gass, 2004, for a discussion of the relevance of the environment in learning and Cenoz & Gorter, 2015; Cenoz & Jessner, 2000, for discussions focused on the acquisition of languages beyond the second); however, a detailed treatise of these issues is beyond the scope of this chapter.

Native Speaker

The term native speaker seems, at first glance, quite an easy term to understand and, for some, it is a quite clear and uncontroversial term. A native speaker is a person who, having learned the language in question from birth, has fully acquired and has full competence in that language. For example, a monolingual speaker who learns only one language from birth, is probably uncontroversially a native speaker of his/her one (and only) language.

However, Davies (1991, 2003a, b) points out that even this seemingly clear concept is not without different interpretations and ambiguities. This is particularly the case when speakers acquire a given language from a very young age and the distinction between native and *near-native* speaker is ambiguous. Davies (2003a, p. 435) provides six ways in which the term native speaker can be characterized.

A native speaker:

(i)   Acquires the L1 in childhood.
(ii) Has intuitions about his/her idiolectal (individual) grammar.
(iii) Has intuitions about those features of the *Standard Language* grammar which are distinct from his/her idiolectal grammar.
(iv) Has a unique capacity to produce fluent spontaneous discourse. In both production and comprehension, the native speaker exhibits a wide range of communicative competence.
(v)   Has a unique capacity to write creatively.

(vi) Has a unique capacity to interpret and translate into the L1. Disagreements about the deployment of an individual's capacity are likely to stem from a dispute about the Standard Language.

Different definitions each draw, to varying degrees, on different combinations of some of the factors listed above. As previously mentioned, the concept is not without controversy. For example, issues of identity figure into who is considered to be a native speaker of what. That is, individuals may begin life as native speakers of one language and, at a certain point in life, find themselves in a different environment where use of the native language is severely limited. The question arises in a situation such as this as to what the *native language* is and even what a native speaker is. In instances such as these, it may be more important to consider an individual's *most comfortable* language. One must realize that whatever criteria we use, we are referring to an idealized abstraction because individuals vary as to their knowledge of their L1 depending on many factors, some of the most common being, social or regional, to name just two.

Near-Native Speaker

Closely related to the concept of native speaker is the near-native speaker. Most individuals know or have heard someone who speaks an L2 as well as a native speaker (perhaps with the exception of pronunciation). An example of this is the diplomat Henry Kissinger (born in Germany) who came to the US at about age 15. In many measures of his language ability, he would meet anyone's criterion of a native speaker of English. The use of the term near-native speaker comes primarily from the literature on ultimate attainment. The main question is the extent to which an adult learner can structure and organize his/her L2 in the way a native speaker does. In other words, can *nonprimary language acquisition ... be 'complete'?* (Sorace, 1993, p. 22). But, the definition of near-native speaker is operational and not absolute. For example, White and Genesee (1996, p. 242) described near-native speakers as *Virtually indistinguishable from native speakers* and identified a group of near-native speakers on the basis of evaluations by native speakers on the following categories: pronunciation, morphology, syntax, vocabulary choice, fluency, and *overall impression of nativeness*. Sorace (1993, p. 35) determined near-nativeness through individual interviews with the criterion used for the determination being *native-like performance from the point of view of fluency and accuracy* (although phonological accuracy was not taken into account). As Sorace acknowledges, this is clearly impressionistic, although she did ensure some degree of validity by making sure that the individuals could perform at a high level for a minimum of ten minutes.

In general, we have two different ways of thinking of the concepts of native and near-native—the practical and the technical. In practical terms, native speakers are those who, in everyday conversation, are indistinguishable from other native speakers, and near-native speakers are highly proficient speakers who are distinguishable from native speakers, but only in small ways. The technical definition refers to a native speaker as someone who is indistinguishable in a scientific sense (e.g., through comparative performance on tests designed specifically to measure the outer reaches of proficiency) from other native speakers—a near-native speaker is an individual who in casual conversation may be indistinguishable from native speakers but who may differ in subtle ways from native speakers, as the examples at the beginning of this chapter show. While these fine distinctions between native and near-native are, practically speaking, unimportant given that most near-native speakers are indistinguishable, or nearly so, from native speakers, the difference is nonetheless important in a linguistic sense.

Advanced Language Learner

Another term that appears in the literature with numerous uses is *advanced language learner*. This term is particularly vague and refers to a wide range of abilities. In fact, this term (and similar ones such as *beginner* and *intermediate* learner) is notoriously problematic in the L2 literature and in the psycholinguistics of bilingualism in that it is difficult to compare research results from one study to another because one researcher's intermediate-level learner may be another's advanced learner. In many cases, what is meant by advanced language learner is what others call near-native, the difference being the theoretical tradition within which they are operating. Bardovi-Harlig (2004, pp. 9–10) reviews the literature on the advanced language learner with particular relation to the acquisition of pragmatics in a second/foreign language, noting the following different ways in which researchers have identified advanced language learners:

(i)   Other-identification—researchers use others (e.g., friends, colleagues, teachers of potential participants) for purposes of classification;
(ii)   Other-identification in combination with tests of language proficiency;
(iii)   Evaluation by trained judges;
(iv)   Length of residence (controlling for age of arrival);
(v)   Length of residence (not-controlling for age of arrival);
(vi)   Years of study in language program;
(vii)   Use of language in occupational contexts;
(viii) Test scores in a language program;
(ix)   Comparison with native speakers;
(x)   Scores on standardized tests.

In reviewing 46 studies that focused on the advanced language learner (in the context of pragmatics), Bardovi-Harlig (2004) finds a wide range of definitions. Some of these are provided below:

(i)   Length of residence about 2 years;
(ii)   International faculty using English for communication;
(iii)   Mean *Test of English as a foreign language* (TOEFL) score of 593;
(iv)   TOEFL scores greater than 525;
(v)   Elite of the country, studying to be English teachers;
(vi)   Graduate students in a university in the US;
(vii)   Length of stay 5–7 years;
(viii) Length of residence about 2 years;
(ix)   University enrollment upper division literature and linguistics courses;
(x)   Greater than 6 semesters classroom instruction plus exposure to *target language* environment;
(xi)   Program placement test;
(xii)   Sufficiently proficient to successfully pass regular academic classes in a US university.

These are but a few of the examples of how advanced learner is defined. They range from vague to contradictory, or, minimally, are non-compatible (e.g., length of stay five to seven years vs. length of residence about two years). Thus, in any specific reading of the literature, one has to determine carefully the relevance of the definition to one's own research interests and concerns (see also Bartning, 1997; Kasper & Rose, 2002).

Yet another way of determining proficiency and thereby determining the degree to which non-native speakers approximate NS behavior is to use standard rubrics, such as those developed for English by TOEFL or those developed for other languages by the American Council on the Teaching of Foreign Languages (ACTFL), or tests developed using the framework of the Common European Framework of Reference.

Heritage Language Speaker

Heritage language speakers are, broadly speaking, those who have been exposed to a language of personal connection (Fishman, 2001). This generally refers to immigrant or indigenous languages or, in some contexts, to colonial languages. Valdés (2001, p. 38) notes that, *it is the historical and personal connection to the language that is salient and not the actual proficiency of individual speakers. Armenian, for example, would be considered a heritage language for American students of Armenian ancestry even if the students were English-speaking monolinguals.* As Montrul and Polinsky (2011, p. 59), citing Au, Knightly, Jun, and Oh, 2002, note, *[h]eritage speakers are notorious for the tremendous variance within their populations—from very high proficiency cases where some registers may be affected, to so-called overhearers.*

The term heritage language speaker has only recently become prevalent, having its origins in the education literature. Until 1996, according to Valdés (2001), heritage speakers of Spanish had been primarily equated with native speakers of Spanish. More recently, this group of speakers has been of interest to L2 researchers. However, the interests of these two research groups (educators and L2 researchers) are quite different with the former asking questions of language maintenance and even language revitalization and the latter asking questions relating to what early/home exposure means for language learning.

For second or foreign language research, the important issue is the exposure and use of the language in childhood. And here, as can be easily imagined, there are numerous problems, since exposure and use can vary from individual to individual. Unlike much of the literature on heritage language learners which considers the language of the ancestral family with or without exposure and use, Polinsky (2008, p. 149) defines heritage language as the language *which was first for an individual with respect to the order of acquisition but has not been completely acquired because of the switch to another dominant language. An individual may use the heritage language under certain conditions and understand it, but his/her primary language is a different one.*

The recognition of heritage language learners as a variable in L2 research is recent. Often, the concept of heritage language speaker is (often unknowingly) ignored, and these individuals are consequently included in the database of studies (as either *native speakers* or L2 learners). Sorace (1993, p. 35) is an exception in that she explicitly controlled for heritage language speakers in her study on the acquisition of Italian by eliminating them from her database, stating that *none had Italian origins.* In recent years, specific studies have been devoted to an understanding of what language knowledge heritage speakers have (e.g., Benmamoun, Montrul, & Polinsky, 2013a,b; Gass & Lewis, 2005; Montrul, 2004; Polinsky, 2008, 2015). A journal, *Heritage Language Journal* (see suggested internet sites), is devoted to the study of heritage languages. Begun in 2002, it *provide[s] a forum for scholars to disseminate research and knowledge about heritage and community languages.* Valdés (2005) presents a view in which heritage language learning/teaching are a part of L2 research and argues for greater flexibility in disciplinary boundaries.

A slight, but particularly interesting variation on the theme of heritage language learning is what Polinksy (2015, p. 163) refers to as *heritage-speakers-turned learners.* By this, she means those learners who *re-learn* their heritage language after the so-called L2 has become the dominant language. These learners are better at learning the phonetics/phonology of their heritage language, even when learning involves a variety of the heritage language (e.g., a prestige variety) that was not the variety exposed to at home. This suggests a strong influence from the L1. However, when it comes to morphosyntax, the greatest influence comes from the L2 (now the dominant language). This brief description suggests the complexity of separating each of these research areas into discrete categories. Rather, it is important to consider all aspects of the multi-language learning process.

Second Language Learner

In the L2 literature, second language learners are the object of study. As noted earlier, this term encompasses a wide range of abilities (beginner, intermediate, advanced) and a wide range of means of getting to a given point of linguistic knowledge (e.g., exposure, study). The details of these learners are specified in most research reports by providing information such as amount of time studying the language, amount of exposure to the language, and test scores. However, the main point is that these individuals are *learners* and the emphasis is on the *processes* involved in learning and the knowledge they have of the L2.

Second Language Speaker

The term second language speaker refers to a person who speaks a language other than the native language. The term second language speaker can refer to a person who speaks a second, third, or fourth language. The term *second* simply means any language other than the first and focuses on the chronological order of learning. This term, therefore, designates someone who learned an L2 after having learned the first, but does not necessarily entail that the person is still a learner. The example given above of Henry Kissinger is a case in point. While he is no longer learning English (at least not any more than an adult native speaker is still learning his/her native language), he is, nonetheless, a second language speaker of English. His language learning history might be the object of theoretical inquiry. The question is what the final stage of learning can look like in *non-primary language acquisition, that is, whether such a state is quantitatively and/or qualitatively different from the monolingual steady state* (Sorace, 2003, p. 130).

Bilingual

The concept of *bilingualism* is interpreted differently in the field of SLA and fields such as psychology and education. That is, L2 researchers reserve use of bilingual for those who are shown to be the equivalent of native speakers of two languages, as assessed through a given linguistic measure. Thus, from the perspective of L2 researchers, bilingual is a difficult term. In its strict meaning, it refers to someone whose language is in a steady state, who has learned and is highly proficient in two languages. That is, bilingual refers to an end point, someone is bilingual. Within an L2 research context, this interpretation of the term is generally not a focus of inquiry. Rather, L2 researchers, because of their interest in discovering the SLA process, focus on all stages of acquisition up to and including near-native speakers or advanced language learners.

The use of the term, as just described, does not generally appear to be the case in some of the psychological and educational literature on bilingualism. For example, Edwards (2004) starts off his article on the foundations of bilingualism by saying, *everyone is bilingual. That is, there is no one in the world (no adult, anyway) who does not know at least a few words in languages other than the maternal variety. If, as an English speaker, you can say 'c'est la vie' or 'gracias' or 'guten Tag' or 'tovarisch' – or even if you only understand them – you clearly have some command of a foreign tongue ... The question, of course, is one of degree.* He goes on to say, *It is easy to find definitions of bilingualism that reflect widely divergent responses to the question of 'degree'* (Edwards, 2004, pp. 7–8). Bhatia (2004, p. 5) states this in an interesting way when he refers to *the process of second language acquisition—of becoming a bilingual.* In other words, the end result of SLA is a bilingual speaker. Given that bilingualism is seen as the end result, and given that we know that native-like competence in a second language is rare, there is some difficulty in discussing bilingualism in this way. Thus, Bhatia and Edwards refer to two different phenomena. Edwards argues that one is bilingual at any point in the second language learning process, whereas Bhatia refers only to the end point and does not deal with whether or not that end point has to be native or not. In other words, the issue seems to be a matter of degree (whether or not one is bilingual even if not a native speaker of the L2), and of end point (whether or not one is bilingual if still in the process of acquisition). L2 researchers are more likely to reserve use of the term for the end state.

Valdés (2001, p. 40) also discusses the issue of degree when she says, *the term 'bilingual' implies not only the ability to use two languages to some degree in everyday life, but also the skilled superior use of both languages at the level of the educated native speakers.* She acknowledges that this is a narrow definition for it considers the bilingual as someone who can *Do everything perfectly in two languages and who can pass undetected among monolingual speakers of each of these two languages* (Valdés, 2001, p. 40). This she refers to as the *mythical bilingual.* She argues that there are, in fact, different types of bilinguals and that it is, therefore, more appropriate to think of bilingualism as a continuum with different amounts of knowledge of the L1 and L2 being represented. In this view, talking about bilinguals can refer to the process of learning as well as the end result, the product of learning.

Some researchers make a distinction between second language learners and bilinguals, as is clear from the title of an article by Kroll and Sunderman (2003): *Cognitive processes in second language learners and bilinguals.* In this article, the authors refer to *skilled adult bilinguals,* presumably the rough equivalent of advanced language learners.

Finally, Deuchar and Quay (2000, p. 1) define bilingual acquisition as *the acquisition of two languages in childhood,* although they point to the difficulties involved in this definition given the many situations that can be in place. They point to De Houwer (1995) who talks about *bilingual L1 acquisition,* referring to situations when there is regular exposure to two languages within the first month of birth and *bilingual SLA,* referring to situations where exposure begins later than one month after birth but before the age of two.

Throughout this and subsequent discussions, it is important to keep in mind that there is a difference between on the one hand, what knowledge of language entails and the age of onset of acquisition, and, on the other, the context and frequency of use. This chapter focuses on the former.

Multilingual

Often the term *bilingual* is used loosely to incorporate multilingualism, as is clear from the Introduction to a section of a book by Bhatia and Ritchie (2004). Bhatia states that *the investigation of bilingualism is a broad and complex field, including the study of the nature of the individual bilingual's knowledge and use of two* [or more] *languages* (emphasis ours; Bhatia and Ritchie, 2004, p. 5). Cenoz (2005) in her review of this book states, *The editors make a remark in the introduction about the use of the word bilingualism in the title of the book and say that they do not exclude additional languages and that the chapters in the book include the full range of multilingualism. However, the use of the term bilingualism is problematic because the Latin prefix bi means two* (p. 638). It seems that most scholars use *bilingualism* to incorporate *multilingualism* in a way similar to which the term SLA includes third, fourth, and fifth language acquisition.

Conclusion

When it comes to identifying different types of language learners, different levels of language proficiency, and different language learning experiences, there are many gray areas which present a problem for second language researchers. As can be seen from this brief discussion, the terminology used in various literatures is vague, at times contradictory, and often limited to a narrow domain. It is frequently the case that two groups of researchers refer to the same phenomenon by different names (e.g., advanced language learners in the second language literature versus bilinguals in the bilingual literature, or heritage language learners by those who are concerned with language maintenance versus second language learners by those concerned with learning). It is thus crucial to understand exactly how various terms are used as one meanders through research reports.

Creating a Language System

Perhaps the most fundamental concept in studying how people learn a second language is the notion of a linguistic system. Just as language is systematic and children create a linguistic system as they learn their L1, L2 learners also create a system which is largely unconscious. A learner's developing linguistic system is most commonly known as an *interlanguage*.

The Nature of the Developing System

There are a few features of interlanguages that we point out: (1) they are dynamic, (2) they are systematic, (3) they follow stages of development, (4) the system may include prefabricated (chunked) patterns, and (5) learners often appear to be regressing when, in fact, their interlanguage is continuing to develop.

Dynamic

Unlike someone's native language which, at least by adulthood, is relatively stable (possibly with the exception of vocabulary), interlanguages are in a state of flux as learners learn new forms and attempt to integrate them within their current system. As new information enters the system, the old system is restructured. In fact, research focuses on just this aspect of L2 learning; it is known by various names, including complexity theory, chaos theory, or dynamic systems theory (see de Bot, 2008; Ellis & Larsen-Freeman, 2006; Larsen-Freeman, 2011, 2012).

Systematic

Despite the fact that interlanguages often do not have the same degree of sophistication as a fully formed language, they are nonetheless systematic. Consider the sentences in

(4) below. These come from an Arabic speaker in the early stages of learning English. The intended meaning (gleaned from context) is provided in parentheses in e-g.

(4)   Data from Hanania (1974)
(4a) *He's sleeping.*
(4b) *She's sleeping.*
(4c) *It's raining.*
(4d) *He's eating.*
(4e) *Hani watch TV.* (Hani is watching.)
(4f) *Read the paper.* (He is reading the paper.)
(4g) *Drink the coffee.* (He is drinking the coffee.)

Although at first glance, this learner appears to use the verb *to be* inconsistently, where the third singular *is* is present at some times and not at others, a closer examination of the learner's use of *to be* suggests an underlying *system*. In sentences 4a-d, the learner uses a contraction followed by the progressive form of the verb when there is no direct object. On the other hand, when there is a direct object (as in sentences 4e-g), the simple form of the verb is used (with or without the subject) and the copula *is* is missing. An explanation of this distinction goes beyond the scope of this paper although we might speculate that it may have to do with processing limitations. The important point is that what at first glance may appear random, on closer examination reveals regularity. In other words, SLA is not an idiosyncratic phenomenon, but develops in a systematic and often regular way that cuts across individual differences.

Stages of Development

In many areas of acquisition, there are predictable stages of acquisition. Table 16.1, from Mackey (1995), adapted from Pienemann and Johnston (1987), shows the development of English question formation. What is interesting is that this *acquisition order* holds for learners of English regardless of the L1 of the learner, and is relatively impervious to instruction (although see Mackey, 1999, for evidence of learners being able to move through stages at different rates).

Prefabricated Patterns

Very often, in learning an L2, a learner may hear what sounds like one word, but which may actually be a *blend* of more than one word. These are called *prefabricated patterns* or *chunks*. As an example, Hakuta (1974) presents interesting data, given in (2) from Uguisu, a child Japanese speaker learning English. In Uguisu's first month in the US, she says the following:

(5)   Data from Hakuta (1974)
(5a) *Do you know?*
(5b) *How do you do it?*
(5c) *Do you have coffee?*
(5d) *Do you want this one?*

These appear to be well-formed English questions. However, upon considering her English a month later, we note the following (intended meaning in parentheses):

(5e)   *What do you doing, this boy?* (What is this boy doing?)
(5f)   *What do you do it, this, froggie?* (What is this froggie doing?)
(5g)   *What do you doing?* (What are you doing?)
(5h)   *What do you drinking, her?* (What is she drinking?)

How can we account for the fact that at one point, she can form complex English questions with *do*, but a month later, she can no longer do so? The most plausible explanation is that she does not analyze *do you* as a complex question form, but rather has heard it when someone is clearly asking her a question. She has consequently learned it as a chunk, that is, as a single word or unit. This learner only appears to have acquired English questions in month 1; once the questions become more complex with the introduction of *what* in her lexicon, we are able to see that *do you* was probably not made up of two words at all (in month 1 or month 2), but only serves to indicate a question. This is a prefabricated pattern, and it is

Table 16.1 Developmental Stages of English Question Formation (adapted from Mackey, 1995, and reprinted by permission of author)

Developmental Stage	Example
Stage 1: Single Units	
Single words.	What?
Single Units.	What is your name? [This is often an unanalyzed chunk of speech whereby a learner thinks of this as a single unit or single word, as if it were *whatisyourname*?]
Stage 2: Subject Verb Object (*SVO*)	
Basic word order with question intonations.	It's a monster? Your cat is black? You have a cat? I draw a house here?
Stage 3: *Fronting:* (*wh-* word/*do*)	
Direct questions with main verbs and some form of fronting.	Where the cats are? What the cat doing in your picture?
	Do you have an animal? Does in this picture there is a cat?
Stage 4: Pseudo inversion: yes/no questions, verb *to be*	
In yes/no questions an auxiliary or modal (e.g., *can/could*) is in sentence-initial position.	Have you got a dog? Have you drawn the cat?
In *wh-* questions the verb *to be* and the subject change positions.	Where is the cat in your picture?
Stage 5: *Do*/auxiliary second	
Q-word → auxiliary/modal → subject (main verb, etc.).	Why (Q-word) have (auxiliary) you (subject) left home?
Auxiliary verbs and modals are placed in second position after *wh-* question words and before subjects (applies only in main clauses/ direct questions).	What do you have? Where does your cat sit? What have you got in your picture?
Stage 6: *Can* inversion, negative question, tag question	
Can inversion: *wh-* question inversions are not present in embedded clauses.	Can you see what the time is? Can you tell me where the cat is?
Negative question: A negated form of *do*/auxiliary is placed before the subject.	Doesn't you cat look black? Haven't you seen a dog?
Tag question: An auxiliary verb and a pronoun are attached to the end of a main clause.	It's on the wall, isn't it?

only with time that this *chunk* will become *unpackaged* into its component parts of *do* and *you*. This would become obvious, for example, when researchers start to observe her using *does* appropriately. Chunking or formulaic language is seen as an important part of learning (see Siyanova & Schmitt, 2008, and Siyanova-Chanturia, Conklin, & Schmitt, 2011).

U-Shaped Learning

The example above appears, on the surface, to show that this learner has regressed. *U-shaped learning* refers to the phenomenon whereby learners seem to have *unlearned* what they apparently knew at an earlier time. When one investigates further, however, it becomes clear that what seemed to be correct was only correct by accident and not because any target-like system had been learned, as we saw with the *do you* example above. Thus, *chunked learning*, that is, the learning as a single undifferentiated unit of what a native speaker might consider two or even three words, becomes a way for a learner to use language before she or he is fully able to *unpack* the unit into appropriate component parts. This may have the consequence of appearing to be regression. One might even say, then, that regression is a part of learning.

The Starting Point

As learners set about the task of acquiring a language, it is important to consider what knowledge or information they bring to the task. What expectations or assumptions do learners have at the start of the acquisition process? With regard to children learning their L1, a predominant view is that children have an innate capacity to acquire human language (Chomsky, 1981). Chomsky and other *nativist* linguists argue that children are born with an innate capacity to learn their native language. Just as all children, barring any physical impairment, eventually learn to walk, all human children, barring any language impairment or other unusual circumstances, become proficient speakers of their native language. Additionally, all child language learners, regardless of the language they are acquiring, follow roughly similar timetables and acquisition stages. Thus, a child in Kenya learning Swahili will begin *babbling*, utter her first word, and begin making two-word sentences at roughly the same age as a child in China learning Chinese. Furthermore, linguists have suggested that the only logical explanation for how young children come to learn all the complex rules of their native language, given the limited language samples that they are exposed to, is that children have a biological capacity for language acquisition as well as innate assumptions and expectations about the language they are learning.

   This biologically endowed capacity to acquire one's native language includes the child's inherent expectations and assumptions about how human languages work. These expectations, or *linguistic principles*, provide limits or constraints on how human languages can be constructed, thereby ruling out certain linguistic impossibilities. This collection of linguistic principles, which are claimed to be universal, and the learner's inherent knowledge about how exactly these principles can be realized in human languages, form part of what is referred to as *universal grammar* (UG). UG helps make the task of developing a complex linguistic system much easier for the child. Another component of UG are *parameters* which can vary from language to language (e.g., some languages, such as English, have mandatory pronouns—*I speak English*—whereas other languages, such as Spanish, have optional discourse-based constraints on pronoun use—*hablo español*). A child must be exposed to the language in order to determine exactly how each parameter is realized in the given language.

Excluding children with specific impairments, UG enables children to fully acquire their native language. Adult L2 learners, however, exhibit much greater variability in their ability to fully acquire another language, and their achievement of native-like competence in a second language is, according to many researchers, quite rare, if not impossible, a point taken up in greater detail below. Thus, the question of what role, if any, UG plays in the SLA process is a topic of much interest and research (see White, 2003, for thorough coverage on this topic).

L2 researchers have taken positions on all sides of this issue. One position is that UG is available to second language learners in the same way that it is available to the child first language learner. That is, second language learners begin the acquisition task with the assumptions and expectations about the new language that are available, through UG, to children (Epstein, Flynn, & Martohardjono, 1996).

While it is not unreasonable to suggest that adult language learners are still able to access UG in order to help with the acquisition process, second language learner behavior indicates that the language acquisition process may be different for adult second language learners than it is for a child learning his or her native language due, in part, to the fact that the second language learner has already acquired an L1. Data from second language learners indicate that the rules and conventions of the first language play a potentially important role in various stages of the acquisition process in that rules and conventions from the first language are often used to the context of the *new language*, a point discussed in detail in a later section.

Rather than beginning the SLA task simply with UG, some researchers have suggested that second language learners begin the acquisition task by equating the new L2 grammar with the grammar of their L1 and then rely, according to an earlier view of language, on UG principles and parameters to guide the subsequent learning process. Proponents of variations of this position argue that the second language learner transfers most or all of the L1 grammar to the L2 context and assumes that the L2 grammar is the same as the L1 grammar until the learner notices properties of the L2 that are inconsistent with the L1, at which time the learner is able to rely on the constraints provided by UG in order to restructure the developing grammar so that it conforms to the L2. There is still much discussion and controversy surrounding this and questions of the starting point for learning.

A more recent view of the role of formal linguistics on second language learning comes from innovations within linguistic theory, namely the *minimalist program* (Chomsky, 1995). The basic unit consists of *formal features* (e.g., gender, case, number) and *conceptual meaning features* (e.g., definiteness). The way features are bundled on particular lexical items varies from language to language. For example, in some languages both number and gender are "bundled" together in one form. In Italian, the difference between *ragazzo, ragazza, ragazzi, ragazze* lies in whether the word means *boy, girl, boys, girls*. In English, the only overt marking is the plural "s". The task for a second language learner is to figure out how features are bundled in the L2. This has been referred to as the *feature reassembly hypothesis* (Lardiere, 2008, 2009) and entails a reconfiguration of the features that bundle together in the L1 to appropriate configurations of features in the L2.

In addition to models arguing that second language learners are able to make full use of the principles and parameters of UG, there are those who argue that adult second language learners must rely exclusively on general learning mechanisms to acquire the language and do not make use of the constraints provided by UG at all. For example, in the *processability approach* of Pienemann (1989, 1998), the underlying notion is that there is a predictable acquisition order. Rather than simply providing a statement of acquisition order, the processability approach attempts to provide an explanation for that order based on processing difficulties and limitations. In sum, there are numerous theoretical approaches to the study of SLA that emphasize the linguistic system that learners start with and the means available to them as they attempt to learn a second language.

The Role of L1

In addition to the potential role of UG in the SLA process, the learner's L1 also plays a potentially significant role. In the 1950s and 1960s, the L1 was seen to be of major importance to the SLA process. At that time, in the behaviorist tradition, language learning was viewed as a process of habit formation. According to this view of language learning, learners automatically relied on rules of the L1 and applied them to the L2 context. Language learning, then, involved eliminating the inappropriate L1 rules/forms while maintaining the appropriate L1 forms. Proficient speakers of the L2 with whom the learner interacted, such as a language teacher, facilitated acquisition by providing positive modeling and reinforcement of good language habits as well as negative reinforcement, such as error correction, for the learner. In this sense, the role of the L1 was viewed to be a potential source for both facilitation and interference. For features of the L2 similar to those of the L1, positive transfer of the L1 feature was predicted to occur and the learner would acquire that feature of the L2 without difficulty. In areas where the features of the L2 differed from those of the L1, the L1 rule was predicted to cause interference, and the learner would need to eliminate the bad habit of the L1 rule.

As views of the language learning process developed and changed, and more researchers focused attention on the role of the L1 in the SLA process, the straightforward *same = easy* and *different = hard* explanation for L1 influence was challenged. L1 influences were viewed to be much more complex and were found to affect the language acquisition process in a more complex way, operating in conjunction with other factors, such as perceptions of distance between the L1 and the L2 (Gass, 1996; Odlin, 2003).

Given that the L1 is only one of a number of factors that affect the course and pace of language acquisition, it is important to consider what specific features of a learner's L1 are most likely to be candidates for use in the L2 context. Researchers make the case that all areas of language—grammar, pronunciation, rules of language use, word formation, and even writing—have features that learners apply to the L2 context (see Gass, 1996; Gass & Selinker, 1992; Odlin, 1989, 2003, for an overview). Though language learners *transfer* components from all areas of language and apply them to the L2 context, learners are more likely to transfer some features of language than others.

Kellerman (1977, 1978, 1979) was one of the first to challenge the behaviorist view of language transfer and argued that transfer is not an automatic process. The individual learner's judgments about similarities and differences between the L2 and the L1 are key to determining which language features are transferable to the L2 and which are not. In some cases when learners perceive a similarity between the L2 and the L1, transfer is more likely than when they perceive a great difference.

In addition to perceived similarity, researchers have suggested that learners also judge the transferability of different language features based on such features as transparency. Thus, a phrase that the learner perceives to have a straightforward or transparent meaning is intuitively more "transferable" than a phrase that the learner perceives to be more idiosyncratic in meaning. For example, a phrase such as make a difference is more likely to be transferred to an L2 than kick the bucket, given the greater transparency of meaning of the first in comparison to the second.

One way in which transfer can have an effect on the acquisition process relates to the interaction of transfer and learner progress through second language developmental stages of acquisition. For example, Henkes (1974) conducted a longitudinal investigation of the acquisition of English of three children, native speakers of French, Spanish, and Arabic. One area of concern was the copula (the verb *to be*), which is present in French and Spanish, but not in Arabic. A common developmental pattern is the omission in English of the copula *is* in equational sentences. In (6) below are examples from the native languages of the three children in question.

(6)   Examples of equational sentences from French, Spanish, and Arabic
    French   *sa maison est vieille*
               his house is old
    Spanish *su casa es vieja*
               his house is old
    Arabic   *baytuhu qadimun*
               house his old

None of the three children used the copula in English consistently, so one could argue that this was a developmental issue rather than a transfer issue. However, Zobl (1982) pointed out that there was a definite, but more subtle, influence of the native language in the form of learning rates. The French and Spanish children regularly used the copula after the early stages of learning, whereas the Arabic child (possibly finding a counterpart in the native language) continued variable usage for a much longer period of time.

Current thinking about the role of the L1 in the second language process has evolved since the early behaviorist views of L1 transfer. L1 influence is viewed as a complex process affected by factors such as perceived similarity and distance between L2 and L1 features as well as the transparency of a given feature. Furthermore, the L1 can interact with the developmental stages of acquisition through which all second language learners progress, in that learners may remain longer in a particular developmental stage if that stage is similar to the L1 rule.

End Point

As discussed earlier, many researchers support the position that children have a biologically driven capacity for acquiring language. All human children, born into an environment where they are provided the opportunity to interact in the language, eventually become fully proficient in that language. It is only in rare and unusual circumstances, such as when a child has a severe brain impairment or injury or is somehow deprived of basic exposure to language, that complete acquisition of language fails to take place.

This picture changes dramatically as children mature and set out to learn a language as teenagers or adults. Adult language learners are much less likely to successfully acquire a language to the degree that they are indistinguishable from native speakers. In fact, some researchers have suggested that it is impossible to be completely successful at language learning when one begins this task later in life (for a review of research on the age and its potential effect on SLA, see Birdsong, 1999; Hyltenstam & Abrahamsson, 2003; Long, 2007; Moyer, 2004; Singleton & Lengyel, 1995; Singleton & Ryan, 2004).

Because language acquisition is essentially universally successful among normal first language learners and significantly less so among adults, researchers have suggested that there exists a critical or sensitive period in the maturation process during which humans are able to acquire language, and after which the *window of opportunity* closes so that adults are no longer able to be completely successful at acquiring language. This is often referred to as the *critical or sensitive period hypothesis* (see Lenneberg, 1967).

Cases of children who were deprived of language stimulation during childhood show that when first language acquisition begins later in life, after the *sensitive period* for language acquisition, language learners are unable to fully acquire language.

One dramatic case is the case of *Genie*. At the age of 2.5 years, Genie was confined to a room where she received essentially no verbal interaction until the day that she was rescued at the age of 13 years and 7 months of age. In addition to the psychological trauma that she suffered, Genie was also deprived of the opportunity to learn language until after the critical period for language learning. Because of this, Genie's language was severely impaired and remained so despite extensive attempts to teach her language. Akmajian, Demers, Farmer, and Harnish (1995, p. 478) presented the following sample of Genie's speech, recorded by Susan Curtiss, the linguist who worked with Genie to study her language development:

> *Genie could not memorize a well-formed WH-question. She would respond to "What do you say?" demands with ungrammatical, bizarre phrases that included WH question words, but she was unable to come up with a phrase she had been trained to say. For example, instead of saying the requested "Where are the graham crackers?" she would say "I where is graham cracker," or "I where is graham cracker on top shelf." In addition, under pressure to use WH-question words, she came out with sentences such as:*
> *Where is tomorrow Mrs. L.?*
> *Where is stop spitting?*
> *Where is May I have ten pennies?*
> *When is stop spitting?*
>
> (Curtiss, 1977, p. 31)

As this language sample shows, Genie's linguistic development was severely impaired due to the linguistic isolation she experienced during the sensitive period. Cases of other children such as *Chelsea* (Curtiss, 1988) and others who were deprived of the opportunity to acquire language during the sensitive period show similar language impairments. These children, like Genie, suffered significant and permanent language impairment because they were not given the opportunity to acquire language during the sensitive period.

While there is little doubt that children who do not acquire their first language during the sensitive period are significantly affected and, in fact, are unable to acquire more than the most rudimentary features of language, the picture for second language learners is more complex. Second language learners are different from first language learners such as Genie and Chelsea in that second language learners have fully acquired a native language during the developmental window of opportunity for language learning.

In studies comparing intuitions about what is acceptable or unacceptable in a language (for example, is the following an acceptable English sentence: *There's two people at the door?*), learners who began acquiring a second language early in life exhibit much more native-like intuitions than those who began the task later, with later learners exhibiting more variable degrees of attainment with many, if not most, falling significantly short of native-like performance on linguistic tests (see Birdsong, 1992; Coppieters, 1987; DeKeyser, 2000; Johnson & Newport, 1989; Moyer, 1999; Patkowski, 1980).

While there is little disagreement over the differential success of early language learners over late learners, there remains significant controversy over nearly every other aspect of the issue, such as the age at which learners lose their language learning advantage, whether it is impossible for late learners to reach native-like competency in the L2, whether the maturational effects are indeed best characterized as a critical or sensitive period, and whether the cause of differential success is due to maturational constraints or to other social, neurobiological, or psychological factors.

Hyltenstam and Abrahamsson (2003) make the case that *biological scheduling, exercise* of the language acquisition system, and social/psychological factors interact in complex ways in determining the ultimate success of second language learners, with universal success only in the earliest language learners. As age of onset of second language learning increases and the biological advantage of early learning declines, environmental factors play an increasingly larger role in the ultimate attainment of the language learner. Hyltenstam and Abrahamsson (2003, p. 575) suggest that,

> *the role of social/psychological factors becomes increasingly important with age. At least up to the age of onset of 6 or 7, all learners will automatically reach levels that allow them to pass as native speakers—provided that there is sufficient input and that the learning circumstances are not deficient. The relatively early phase of the maturation process thus allows for learning to result in seemingly native-like proficiency from mere L2 exposure. With increasing age of onset after this age, however, certain social/psychological factors must be increasingly advantageous in order to compensate for the successively negative effects of maturation.*

Thus, while early learners have the clear advantage over late language learners, there are many cases where L2 learners achieve extremely high proficiency in another language. As Hyltenstam and Abrahamsson (2003) suggest, other factors that do not necessarily play a major role in normal first language acquisition do have the potential to positively affect the SLA process.

Input, Interaction, Output

In the previous section we discussed issues related to the creation of an L2 system. We emphasized various linguistic factors that are crucial to the understanding of the types of linguistic systems that learners are able to create in learning a second language. In the following section we will deal with individual characteristics that are known to impact language learning. In this section we begin with a discussion of the ways in which learners obtain the linguistic information that serves as the basis for their linguistic generalizations.

Input

A common belief about second language learning, particularly learning that takes place in a classroom context, is that it proceeds best when teachers (via textbooks and materials) present new linguistic information, perhaps accompanied by explanation. This is followed by practice in which learners use the new linguistic information as a way of reinforcing what has been presented. In this section, we will see that learning involves a complex interplay of information, language use, and feedback. Learners are not passive recipients of new linguistic information but rather are individuals who actively try to sort out information about the language being learned. In other words, they are actively creating interlanguages with relevant information from the input.

Input is the linguistic data that learners are exposed to as they are learning another language. These data are available through reading or listening (or signing in the case of Sign Languages). Another term used for input is *positive evidence* which comes from a UG framework and, simply put, refers to the linguistic information which is used to create a grammar (in the case of second language learners, an interlanguage). One could say that input is the most important part of the process because languages are not learned in a vacuum and language learning cannot take place without input.

Given the importance of input, it is necessary to consider what the nature of input is. The following example in Table 16.2 illustrates its changing nature depending on the proficiency level of the learners. Kleifgen (1985) finds differences in the way a single teacher (in this case a teacher of a kindergarten class) addresses different students in a class.

As can be seen from Table 16.2, as the proficiency level of the learner decreases, so does the teacher's syntactic sophistication and the level of vocabulary (e.g., *great big pointed hat* versus *big, big, big hat*). Other characteristics of modified input (also known as *foreigner talk*) are: slower rate and clearer articulation, differences in vocabulary (e.g., higher frequency vocabulary items less slang and few idioms), simpler syntax (e.g., short and simple sentences, new information at end of sentence).

In understanding how second and foreign languages are learned, we need to consider what the functions are of modified speech. Although we do not have studies of motivation for this type of reduced speech, we can assume that at least one factor is comprehension: by hearing speech that has been simplified in the ways just described, the second language learner will be better able to understand. And, it is uncontroversial to state that without understanding, learning will not take place. Although understanding alone does not guarantee that learning will occur, it does set the scene to enable learning to take place. Crucial to the success of any conversation and to language learning in general is the ability to understand and to be understood.

Another area of input that needs to be considered is frequency of occurrence. Within certain frameworks of language learning (namely the innatist view discussed earlier), no mention is made of frequency. That is, it is not specified whether a one-time encounter with a particular language feature is sufficient to trigger a change in a learner's representation of language or whether multiple instances are required. Ellis (2002, 2012), taking a *usage-based approach* to acquisition, maintained that learning takes place on the basis of the frequency of exemplars in the input. That is, learners are sensitive to the frequency of exemplars as they abstract regularities from the input. As Ellis (2002) states, *frequency*

Table 16.2 Talk to a Kindergarten Class

To a NS group of kindergarten students:
These are babysitters taking care of babies. Draw a line from *Q* to *q*.
From *S* to s and then trace.
To a single NS:
Now, Johnny, you have to make a great big pointed hat.
To an intermediate level NS of Urdu:
Now her hat is big. Pointed.
To a low intermediate level NS of Arabic:
See hat? Hat is big. Big and tall.
To a beginning level NS of Japanese:
Big, big, big hat.
To a beginning level NS of Korean:
Baby sitter. Baby.

is a necessary component of theories of language acquisition and processing. In some guises it is a very rudimentary causal variable. Learners analyze the language input that they are exposed to; practice makes perfect. In other guises it is incredibly complex. The multiplicity of interacting elements in any system that nontrivially represents language makes the prediction of the patterns that will eventually emerge as difficult as forecasting the weather, the evolution of an ecological system or the outcome of any other complex system (Ellis, 2002, p. 178). Note, however, that Ellis claims that frequency is a necessary factor, but he does not say that it is a sufficient condition. In other words, frequency is not the sole explanation for acquisition, but interacts with other factors such as salience and complexity among others.

Interaction

As mentioned above, when one thinks of a typical language classroom, in many instances, a grammatical form is presented and then practice comes in the form of using that structure, often in a conversational setting. Research has shown that what happens during a conversation is more than just practice and can actually contribute to learning (Gass, 1997; Gass & Varonis, 1994; Mackey, 1999, 2012). This is known as the *Interaction Hypothesis* and we turn now to an explanation of how this happens. Long (1996, pp. 451–452) puts it as follows:

> *"Negotiation for meaning," and especially negotiation work that triggers "interactional" adjustments by the NS or more competent interlocutor, facilitates acquisition because it connects input, internal learner capacities, particularly selective attention, and output in productive ways.*

Negotiation for meaning refers to those instances in conversation when participants interrupt the flow of the conversation in order for both parties to understand what the conversation is about. In conversations between learners and native speakers or proficient speakers of the second language, negotiations are frequent. An example of a negotiation exchange in (7) below comes from Pica (1987, p. 6). In this case, the negotiation occurs following a pronunciation problem. The learner is made aware of the problem through the native speaker's indications of nonunderstanding (in c and e).

(7)   Negotiation exchange (NS = native speaker; NNS = non-native speaker)
(7a)   NNS: *And they have the chwach there.*
(7b)   NS: *The what?*
(7c)   NNS: *The chwach—I know someone that—*
(7d)   NS: *What does it mean?*
(7e)   NNS: *Like um like American people they always go there every Sunday.*
(7f)   NS: *Yes?*
(7g)   NNS: *You kn—every morning that there pr-that -the American people get dressed up to got to um chwach.*
(7h)   NS: *Oh to church—I see.*

It is negotiation that allows learners to understand the conversation and hence the input. And, importantly, as we noted earlier, comprehension is an essential element of learning. Beyond that, the negotiation itself provides a form whereby the learner focuses attention on problem areas, in this instance a pronunciation problem.

Not only are there numerous instances of negotiation, but conversations involving learners and proficient speakers are modified in other ways. Long (1980) was the first to point out that conversations involving non-native speakers exhibited forms that did not appear to any significant degree when only native speakers interacted. For example, confirmation checks (*Is this what you mean?*), comprehension checks (*Do you understand? Do you follow me?*), and clarification requests (*What? Huh?*) are peppered throughout conversations in which there is a non-proficient, non-native speaker participant. In addition, one finds different questions, which appear to be used to help the learner. Long (1983, p. 180) provides the example in (8) in which, in response to an indication of nonunderstanding (*huh?*), the native speaker narrows down the topic (California Los Angeles) to make it easier for the learner to respond appropriately.

(8) Narrowing down the topic
  NS: *Do you like California?*
  NNS: *Huh?*
  NS: *Do you like Los Angeles?*
  NNS: *Uhm...*
  NS: *Do you like California?*
  NNS: *Yeah, I like it.*

These conversational tactics provide the non-native speaker with as much information as possible as she attempts to ascribe meaning to the native speaker's stream of sounds. At times, a proficient speaker will ask an *or-choice* question, as in example (9) which comes from an *English as a second language* (ESL) classroom. This exchange took place during the first class after a long holiday break. The teacher had asked a student what he did over the break. He responded that he had just relaxed.

(9) Or-choice question
  NS: *Where did you relax?*
      Silence
  NS: *Did you relax out of town or in East Lansing?*
  NNS: *East Lansing.*

In these examples, the effect of native speaker and non-native speaker modifications (whether intentional or not) is to aid the non-native speaker in understanding. Thus, the learner is assisted (possibly as a show of solidarity—see work by Aston, 1986; Hawkins, 1985) by others in understanding and in producing language appropriate to the situation. However, one must remember that comprehension is not the same as acquisition; comprehension, in the usual sense of the word, refers to a single event, whereas acquisition refers to a permanent state, or a process.

In thinking more specifically about the function of interaction, Long (1996, p. 414) provides the following explanation:

> *It is proposed that environmental contributions to acquisition are mediated by selective attention and the learner's developing L2 processing capacity, and that these resources are brought together most usefully, although not exclusively, during "negotiation for meaning." Negative feedback obtained during negotiation work or elsewhere may be facilitative of L2 development, at least for vocabulary, morphology, and language-specific syntax, and essential for learning certain specifiable L1–L2 contrasts.*

Long refers to two important concepts: *negative feedback* and *attention*. Negative feedback refers to information provided to a learner that there is a problem with something that she or he has said. What negative feedback does not do, however, is provide information about the nature of the error or what has to be done to *fix* it. Thus, in (10), the learner of Italian understands that there is a problem with what she has said (she has used the incorrect ending on *tazzi*), but doesn't know what the correct form is.

(10)   From Mackey, Gass, and McDonough (2000) (INT = Interviewer)
   NNS: *C'è due tazzi* (Translation: *There is two cups [masculine plural ending, but should be feminine plural]*).
   INT: *Due tazz-come?* (Translation: *Two cup—what?*)
   NNS: *Tazzi, dove si puó mettere té, come se dice questo?* (Translation: *Cups [masculine plural], where one can put tea, how do you say this?*)

But, importantly, the learner's attention is drawn to the problem. This, it has been argued, sets the scene for later learning (Gass, 1997). As a first step to learning, a learner must be aware of a need to learn. Negotiation and feedback of the sort that take place in conversation are a means to focus a learner's attention on just those areas of language that do not *match* those of the language being learned.

We now turn to the mechanism that may be at the heart of the Interaction Hypothesis (as Long, 1996, noted)—selective attention. Negotiation and other types of correction focus learners' attention on parts of their language that diverge from the language they are learning. And, it has been claimed that attention is a crucial part of learning. For example, according to Schmidt (2001, p. 3) attention *is necessary in order to understand virtually every aspect of second language acquisition*. He also argues that *LA is largely driven by what learners pay attention to and notice in target language input* (Schmidt, 2001, p. 4).

What is generally agreed upon in the field of SLA is that attention is important in order to account for the ways that learners sort through the large amounts of sometimes incoherent and seemingly contradictory data that they are exposed to. It is uncontroversial to state that learners are exposed to more input (raw data) than they can cope with. Therefore, there must be some mechanism to help isolate parts of the input as learners create and test hypotheses. One way in which the input can be made more manageable is to focus attention on a limited and, hence, controlled amount of data at a given point in time. This returns us to the topic of negotiation, the question being: what happens during a negotiation event that allows learners to utilize the content of the negotiation to advance their own knowledge? Long's (1996) statement, given earlier, suggests an important role for attention, as does Gass' (1997, p. 132) argument that *attention, accomplished in part through negotiation is one of the crucial mechanisms in this process*.

It is through interaction that a learner's attention is focused on a specific part of the language, particularly on mismatches between target language (TL) forms and learner-language forms. This can happen through negotiation, as noted above or even through less direct means, such as recasts, as in the examples in (11) below from Philp (2003).

(11)   Recasts
   NNS: Why they want to sell to the house?
   NS: Why do they want to sell the house?
   NNS: Why do they want to sell the house?
   NNS: Does does he uh the hand uh on the hand ah what what.

NS: What is he carrying?
NNS: Yeah what he is carry?

In the first example, the learner corrects her error, whereas in the second she gets it only partly correct. But, in both cases, it is possible that if learning does not necessarily take place *on the spot* (which it probably does not), there is at least recognition of a problem and the scene is set for later learning.

Of course, a prerequisite to viewing the role of attention within an interactional context in the way that we have described is that learners are capable of noticing mismatches. Schmidt and Frota (1986) reported on the learning of Portuguese in which the learner documented the noticing and subsequent learning of new forms. In this study, the learner kept a language learning diary and therefore provided evidence of what he had noticed. The authors were able to relate instances of noticing with later use.

The importance of attention is widely recognized although there is controversy over whether attention relies on capacity limits. Are attentional resources limited or unlimited? One model, the interference model is essentially a non-capacity limited model. As Robinson (2003, pp. 644–645) states,

> *Increasing the number of stimuli and response alternatives or the similarity between them will sometimes lead to confusion, reducing performance efficiency. This can be caused by competition for the same types of codes during information flow, or by "cross-talk" between similar codes.*

In this view, there are no limits to attentional capacity; rather, interference is a matter of involuntary attention shift.

However, in other views, it is assumed that the human brain is equipped with a single, limited attentional processing system that allows for a certain amount of input to be attended to at one time (Anderson, 1983; Kahneman, 1973; Kihlstrom, 1987). Then, the fact that learners are constantly exposed to input, not all of which is of use, is explained in terms of *cognitive overload*. In this view, learners have a mechanism that allows them to filter out some language stimuli from the input, resulting in input that is ultimately more manageable and easily *digestible*, thus ready for further processing. What is isolated is clearly dependent on a learner's stage of development and readiness to learn (Gass, Svetics, & Lemelin, 2003; Mackey, 1999).

The role of memory in connection with attention is also important. Williams (1999) found a strong relationship between individual differences in memory capacity and learning outcomes in an experiment involving a semiartificial form of Italian. He also recognized the importance of the relationship between long-term memory and vocabulary learning.

Mackey, Philp, Egi, Fujii, and Tatsumi (2002) considered the relationship between working memory capacity and learner reports of noticing in an interactional context. They found a relationship between the composite scores on a working memory test and their reports of noticing. This may be one factor (although clearly not the only one) in determining noticing. Other factors may include proficiency level and other individual differences across learners.

Gass, Behney, and Uzum (2013) did not find the same effects for working memory. Rather, they found an effect for inhibitory control that is the ability of second language learners to inhibit irrelevant information. So this supports the first view—that working memory capacity is less relevant than the ability to shift attention.

Output

The final area we consider in this section is the role of *output*, or, more simply put, production or language use. A limitation of input is that one can often understand language by interpreting the meanings of individual words without regard to the order or grammatical structure of those words. For example, if one hears only the words *girl, jumped, on, table* it is likely that the meaning *The girl jumped on the table* is the one that will be assumed rather than the more unusual but grammatically correct *The table jumped on the girl*. Little knowledge, other than knowing the meanings of the words and knowing something about real-world events, is needed for correct understanding. However, when producing language, certain decisions have to be made as to the order of words and other necessary features of the syntax. Production, then, *may force the learner to move from semantic processing to syntactic processing* (Swain, 1985, p. 249). Swain (1995, p. 128) further claimed that *output may stimulate learners to move from the semantic, open-ended, nondeterministic, strategic processing prevalent in comprehension to the complete grammatical processing needed for accurate production. Output, thus, would seem to have a potentially significant role in the development of syntax and morphology.*

We present four possible ways that language learning takes place through production: (1) testing hypotheses about the structures and meanings of the TL; (2) receiving crucial feedback for the verification of these hypotheses; (3) developing automaticity in *interlanguage production*; and (4) forcing a shift from more meaning-based processing of the second language to a more syntactic mode.

Producing language can be a way of testing a hypothesis, either consciously or unconsciously. To relate this to our previous discussion on interaction, through negotiation and through feedback, learners can be made aware of an erroneous hypothesis. That is, the activity of using language helps create a degree of analyticity that allows learners to think about language. The example in (12) comes from a study by Mackey, Gass, and McDonough (2000), who used a stimulated recall format (see Gass & Mackey, 2000) to elicit learners' thoughts about interactions. In this example, the learner and interviewer (fluent speaker of Italian) are trying to identify differences in two similar pictures.

(12)   Language production as a way of thinking about language
      NNS: *poi un bicchiere* (Translation: *then a glass*)
      INT: *un che, come?* (Translation: *a what, what?*)
      NNS: *bicchiere* (Translation: *glass*)

Watching a video of the interaction immediately following the interaction and reflecting on it, the learner said:

> *I was drawing a blank. Then I thought of a vase but then I thought that since there was no flowers, maybe it was just a big glass. So, then I thought I'll say it and see. Then, when she said "come" (what?), I knew that it was completely wrong.*

The comment *I'll say it and see* suggests that she was using the conversation as a way to see if a hypothesis was correct or incorrect.

A second important function of producing language is feedback. Feedback itself provides information to the learner of a potential problem (or of a correct form). Feedback often results in negotiation of the problem by providing learners with information about incorrect forms, as can be seen in (13) below from Nobuyoshi and Ellis (1993, p. 204):

(13)   Feedback
      NNS: *He pass his house.*
      NS: *Sorry?*
      NNS: *He passed, he passed, ah, his sign.*

It is important to note that we are often left with the unknown factor of longer-term retention.

If we are to claim that feedback and negotiation are important to learning, we have to determine the extent to which learners are aware of the information that is being provided through feedback or the negotiation sequence. The issue is: What do learners perceive? In a study by Mackey, Gass, and McDonough (2000), data were collected from ten learners of English as an L2 and seven learners of Italian as a foreign language. The study explored learners' perceptions about feedback provided to them through interaction. In the interactions, learners received feedback focused on a range of morphosyntactic, lexical, and phonological forms. After completing the tasks, learners watched videotapes of their previous interactions and were asked to introspect about their thoughts at the time the original interactions were in progress. The results showed that learners were relatively accurate in their perceptions about lexical, semantic, and phonological feedback. However, morpho-syntactic feedback was generally not perceived as such. Consequently, it is not always clear that learners perceive feedback in the way it was intended (see also, Hawkins, 1985). A further complication comes from research by Gass and Lewis (2005) who found different perceptual emphases of true L2 learners and heritage language learners with the former perceiving feedback more often as grammatical feedback and the latter perceiving feedback more often as semantic feedback.

The third function we point out reflects the traditional view of output; that is, as a means for developing fluency and automaticity of processing. Certain processes are deliberate, requiring a significant amount of time and working memory capacity. Others are routine and automatic, involving less time and capacity. McLaughlin (1987, p. 134) claimed that automatization involves *a learned response that has been built up through the consistent mapping of the same input to the same pattern of activation over many trials.* Here we extend this notion to output, claiming that the consistent and successful mapping (practice) of grammar to output results in automatic processing (see also Loschky & Bley-Vroman, 1993).

The final area we look at is an understanding of the difference between meaning-based and grammatically based use of language. Swain's initial hypothesis stated that *output may force the learner to move from semantic processing to syntactic processing* (1985, p. 249). In other words, the learner moves from meaning-based processing to word order-based processing. As Gass with Behney and Plonsky (2013, p. 374) put it:

> Output provides learners the opportunity to produce language and gain feedback, which through focusing learners' attention on certain local aspects of their speech may lead them to notice either (a) a mismatch between their speech and that of an interlocutor (particularly if as part of the feedback a linguistic model is provided) or (b) a deficiency in their output. Noticing, then, leads to reassessment, which may be an on-the-spot reassessment or involve longer-term complex thinking about the

*issue. This latter process may be bolstered by the gathering of additional informa-
tion through a variety of sources (e.g., input, direct questioning, looking in grammar
books, and dictionaries). This, in essence, is the process of learning.*

Individual Factors

In previous sections we discussed how the age of the learner, the learner's first language,
and the linguistic environment can impact the acquisition process. In addition to these
factors, there are other factors that can vary from individual to individual that also play a
potential role in the rate of acquisition and ultimate success of a given language learner.
Considering the many ways in which individuals can vary, numerous *individual factors*
have the potential to impact, either positively or negatively, the process of learning an
L2. For example, researchers have explored the potential impact on language learning
of individual characteristics such as anxiety, introversion versus extroversion, empathy,
memory, inhibition, risk taking, self-esteem, motivation, aptitude, learning styles, and
learning strategies, which are behaviors or thought processes that the learner engages
in that potentially facilitate or inhibit learner success, but this is beyond the scope of
this paper (the interested reader is invited to refer to Dörnyei, 2005, for a discussion of
this topic).

Summary and Conclusion

This brief chapter has provided some of the major concepts needed to understand how
learning a second or foreign language takes place. We have shown that learners are actively
involved in forming grammars. There are many elements that are potentially involved,
namely the possible role of UG age of acquisition, the first language, the amount and quality of input and interaction as well as other individual factors, such as motivation, aptitude,
and attitude. We have argued that factors such as the specific language learners are exposed
to (input), the conversational interactions that learners are engaged in, and their own linguistic production (output) serve important functions as learners work to create second
language grammars. We have also pointed out that such factors as attitude, aptitude, and
motivation may affect learning.

Learning an L2 is a long, difficult, and arduous process and is rarely complete, in the
sense of knowing the second language as native speakers of that language do. This does
not mean that L2 speakers cannot be fully functional in the L2, only that there are generally
endpoint differences, for example differences in pronunciation as well as frequent differences in morphology, syntax, and pragmatics.

List of Key Words and Concepts

Acquisition order, Advanced language learner, Babbling, Chunked learning, Cognitive
overload, Conceptual meaning features, English as a second language (ESL), Feature
reassembly hypothesis, Foreign language, Fronting, Genie, Heritage language, Individual
factors, Input, Interaction hypothesis, Interference, Interlanguage production, Involuntary
attention shift, Linguistic principles, Minimalist program, Mythical bilingual, Native
speakers (NS), Nativist, Negative feedback, Negative reinforcement, Non-native speakers (NNS), Non-capacity limited model, Output, Parameters, Positive evidence, Positive
modeling, Positive transfer, Prefabricated patterns, Principles, Processability approach,
Reinforcement, Second language acquisition (SLA), Sensitive period hypothesis, Standard
Language, Target language (TL), Test of English as a foreign language (TOEFL), Transfer,

Transparency, U-shaped learning, Universal grammar (UG), Usage-based approach, Word formation

Internet Sites Related to Second Language Acquisition

Center for Advanced Research on Language Acquisition: http://www.carla.umn.edu/
European Second Language Association: http://www.eurosla.org/
Heritage Language Journal: http://www.heritagelanguages.org
Second Language Acquisition and Second Language Learning: http://www.sdkrashen.com/articles.php?cat=6
Second Language Acquisition Topics: http://www.viviancook.uk/SLA/index.htm

Discussion Questions

(1)   Find two empirical articles from a journal of second language acquisition research (e.g., *Studies in Second Language Acquisition, Language Learning, The Modern Language Journal*). What level learners do they use? How is this level defined?

(2)   Frequently teachers present language information to their students expecting them to learn it after much practice in class. Often, however, this is not the case; the same mistakes continue. Why do you think this is the case?

(3)   The term L2 learning refers to a wide range of learning environments, including, (a) learning in a classroom where the language being learned is spoken, (b) learning in the environment where the language being learned is spoken, but not in a classroom, and (c) learning in a classroom in an environment where the language being learned is not spoken—that is, the language is for all practical purposes only available in the classroom. What might the actual differences be in terms of learning in these three contexts?

(4)   A child learner of English (native speaker of Japanese) said the following:

(4a)   *Do you know?*
(4b)   *How do you do it?*
(4c)   *Do you have coffee?*
(4d)   *Do you want this one?*

(5)   Do you think that this child has learned how to ask questions in English? Now consider the following questions, said by the same child one month later.

(5a)   *What do you doing, this boy?* [= What is this boy doing?]
(5b)   *What do you do it, this, froggie?* [= What is this froggie doing?]
(5c)   *What do you doing?* [= What are you doing?]
(5d)   *What do you drinking, her?* [= What is she drinking?]

(6)   Do you still think that she knows how to form English questions? What generalization has she made about English questions? Does the second set of data cause you to rethink your conclusions about the first set of data? Why or why not?

(7)   Some languages have possessive phrases that follow nouns, as in the following French example:

(7a)   *Le chien de mon ami.*
(7b)   *The dog of my friend.*

(8)   In English, the situation is more complicated and two structures are possible, one in which the possessor follows the noun and one in which it precedes it.

(8a)   *The dog of my friend.*
(8b)   *My friend's dog.*

(9)   Whereas both of these English sentences are possible, the first one (a) sounds strange. On the other hand, of the following two groups of sentences in English:

(9a)   *The leg of the table.*
(9b)   *A leg of lamb.*
(9c)   *The table's leg.*
(9d)   *A lamb's leg.*

(10)   It is the second group (9c and 9d) that is less likely to be said. How would you explain this? What would you predict regarding a learner's interlanguage production? Considering both *transfer* and input, how would a French learner of English figure out the facts of English?

(11)   A French speaker learning English has to go from one form to two, whereas an English learner learning French would go from two forms to one. Which do you think would be more difficult, and why?

(12)   What do you think are characteristics of good language learners?

(13)   If you were designing a study on *advanced language learners*, how would you operationalize the concept? That is, how would you determine who should or should not be in your subject pool?

Suggested Research Projects

(1)   Make a drawing of a nonsense object or animal. Tell a young child that that is a "wug." Next, show the child a picture of two of these objects and say to the child: "Now there are two_____." Have the child fill in the blank. Do this a few times with different words. Try this with children of different ages starting with young children. At what age do they start using the regular English plural? What can you conclude about the children's ability to generalize forms?

(2)   Now try the same activity with children of different first languages who are learning English (or another language). Do the same patterns hold? Vary the ages of the children and determine at what age child learners of English begin to acquire regular English plurals. Do this with children learning a second language as well as those who are growing up bilingual.

(3)   Find an article that deals with the acquisition of a language that you are interested in. Make sure that there is enough detail to conduct a replication. Find appropriate participants and replicate the study. Do your results coincide with those of the original author(s)? If not, why do you think that that is the case?

Suggested Readings

Gass, S. (1997). *Input, interaction, and the second language learner*. Mahwah, NJ: Lawrence Erlbaum Associates.

Gass, S. with Behney, J., & Plonsky, L. (2013). *Second language acquisition: An introductory course* (4th ed.). New York: Routledge.

Lightbown, P., & Spada, N. (2013). *How languages are learned* (4th ed.). Oxford: Oxford University Press.

Lüdi, G., & Py, B. (2002). *Etre bilingue* (2nd ed.). Bern, Germany: Peter Lang.

Mackey, A. (2012). *Input, interaction and corrective feedback in L2 classrooms.* Oxford: Oxford University Press.

VanPatten, B. (2003). *From input to output: A teacher's guide to second language acquisition.* Boston: McGraw-Hill.

References

Akmajian, A., Demers, R. A., Farmer, A. K., & Harnish, R. M. (1995). *Linguistics: An introduction to language and communication*. Cambridge, MA: MIT Press.

Anderson, J. (1983). *The architecture of cognition*. Cambridge, MA: Harvard University Press.

Aston, G. (1986). Trouble-shooting in interaction with learners: The more the merrier? *Applied Linguistics*, *7*, 128–143.

Au, T., Knightly, L., Jun, S., & Oh, J. (2002). Overhearing a language during childhood. *Psychological Science*, *13*, 238–243.

Bardovi-Harlig, K. (2004). *Pragmatic competence of the advanced learner*. Focused Research Review for the High-Level Language Ability Research Hub, University of Maryland, February 29th, 2004.

Bartning, I. (1997). L'apprenant dit avancé et son acquisition d'une langue étrangère: Tour d'horizon et esquisse d'une caractérisation de la variété avancée. *Acquisition et Interaction en Langue Étrangère*, *9*, 9–50.

Benmamoun, E., Montrul, S., & Polinsky, M. (2013a). Heritage languages and their speakers: Opportunities and challenges for linguistics. *Theoretical Linguistics*, *30*, 129–181.

Benmamoun, E., Montrul S., & Polinsky, M. (2013b). Defining an "ideal" heritage speaker. *Theoretical Linguistics*, *39*, 259–294.

Bhatia, T. (2004). Introduction. In T. Bhatia & W. Ritchie (Eds.), *The handbook of bilingualism* (pp. 5–6). Oxford: Blackwell.

Bhatia, T., & Ritchie, W. (Eds.). (2004). *The handbook of bilingualism*. Oxford: Blackwell.

Birdsong, D. (1992). Ultimate attainment in second language acquisition. *Language*, *68*, 706–755.

Birdsong, D. (Ed.). (1999). *Second language acquisition and the critical period hypothesis*. Mahwah, NJ: Lawrence Erlbaum Associates.

Cenoz, J. (2005). Review of T. Bhatia & W. Ritchie (Eds.), The handbook of bilingualism. *Studies in Second Language Acquisition*, *27*, 638–639.

Cenoz, J., & Gorter, D. (Eds.). (2015). *Multilingual education: Between language learning and translanguaging*. Cambridge: Cambridge University Press.

Cenoz, J., & Jessner, U. (Eds.). (2000). *English in Europe: The acquisition of a third language*. Clevedon, UK: Multilingual Matters.

Chomsky, N. (1981). Principles and parameters in syntactic theory. In N. Hornstein & D. Lightfoot (Eds.), *Explanation in linguistics: The logical problem of language acquisition* (pp. 32–75). London: Longman.

Chomsky, N. (1995). *The minimalist program*. Cambridge, MA: MIT Press.

Coppieters, R. (1987). Competence differences between natives and near-native speakers. *Language*, *63*, 544–573.

Curtiss, S. (1977). *Genie: A psycholinguistic study of a modern-day "wild child."* New York: Academic Press.

Curtiss, S. (1988). Abnormal language acquisition and the modularity of language. In F. J. Newmeyer (Ed.), *Linguistics: The Cambridge survey* (Vol. 2, pp. 99–116). Cambridge: Cambridge University Press.

Davies, A. (1991). *The native speaker in applied linguistics*. Edinburgh: Edinburgh University Press.

Davies, A. (2003a). *The native speaker: Myth and reality*. Clevedon, UK: Multilingual Matters.

Davies, A. (2003b). The native speaker in applied linguistics. In A. Davies & C. Elder (Eds.), *Handbook of applied linguistics* (pp. 431–450). New York: Blackwell.

De Bot, K. (2008). Introduction: Second language development as a dynamic process. *The Modern Language Journal*, *92*, 166–178.

De Houwer, A. (1995). Bilingual language acquisition. In P. Fletcher and B. MacWhinney (Eds.), *The handbook of child language* (pp. 219–250). Oxford: Blackwell.

DeKeyser, R. M. (2000). The robustness of critical period effects in second language acquisition. *Studies in Second Language Acquisition*, *22*, 493–533.

Deuchar, M., & Quay, S. (2000). *Bilingual acquisition: Theoretical implications of a case study*. Oxford: Oxford University Press.

Dörnyei, Z. (2005). *Psychology of the language learner: Individual differences in second language acquisition*. Mahwah, NJ: Lawrence Erlbaum Associates.

Edwards, J. (2004). Foundations of bilingualism. In T. Bhatia & W. Ritchie (Eds.), *The handbook of bilingualism* (pp. 7–31). Oxford: Blackwell.

Ellis, N. (2002). Frequency effects in language processing. *Studies in Second Language Acquisition*, *24*, 143–188.

Ellis, N. (2012). Frequency-based accounts of second language acquisition. In S. Gass & A. Mackey (Eds.), *The Routledge handbook of second language acquisition* (pp. 193–210). New York: Routledge.

Ellis, N., & Larsen-Freeman D. (Eds). (2006). Language emergence: Implications for applied linguistics. [Special issue]. *Applied Linguistics*, *27*, 558–589.

Epstein, S., Flynn, S., & Martohardjono, G. (1996). Second language acquisition: Theoretical and experimental issues in contemporary research. *Brain and Behavioral Sciences*, *19*, 677–758.

Fishman, J. (2001). 300-plus years of heritage language education in the United States. In J. Peyton, D. Ranard, & S. McGinnis (Eds.), *Heritage languages in America preserving a national resource* (pp. 81–97). Washington, DC: Center for Applied Linguistics.

Gass, S. (1996). Second language acquisition and linguistic theory: The role of language transfer. In W. Ritchie & T. K. Bhatia (Eds.), *Handbook of second language acquisition* (pp. 317–345). San Diego, CA: Academic Press.

Gass, S. (1997). *Input, interaction, and the second language learner*. Mahwah, NJ: Lawrence Erlbaum Associates.

Gass, S. (2004). Language teaching: Environment, presentation & complexity. In W. Hu (Ed.), *ELT in China: Papers presented at the International Conference on ELT in China in 2004*. Beijing: Foreign Studies University.

Gass, S., Behney, J., & Plonsky, L. (2013). *Second language acquisition: An introductory course* (4th ed.). New York: Routledge.

Gass, S., Behney, J., & Uzum, B. (2013). Inhibitory control, working memory, and L2 interaction gains. In K. Droździał-Szelest & M. Pawlak (Eds.), *Psycholinguistic and sociolinguistic perspectives on second language learning and teaching: Studies in honor of Waldemar Marton* (pp. 91–114). New York: Springer.

Gass, S., & Lewis, K. (2005). *Perceptions of interactional feedback: Differences between heritage and non-heritage language learners*. Paper presented at EUROSLA, Dubrovnik, Croatia.

Gass, S., & Mackey, A. (2000). *Stimulated recall methodology in second language research*. Mahwah, NJ: Lawrence Erlbaum Associates.

Gass, S., & Selinker, L. (Eds.). (1992). *Language transfer in language learning*. Amsterdam: John Benjamins.

Gass, S., Svetics, I., & Lemelin, S. (2003). Differential effects of attention. *Language Learning*, *53*, 495–543.

Gass, S., & Varonis, E. (1994). Input, interaction and second language production. *Studies in Second Language Acquisition*, *16*, 283–302.

Goldschmidt, M. (1996). From the addressee's perspective: Imposition in favor–asking. In S. Gass & J. Neu (Eds.), *Speech acts across cultures* (pp. 241–256). Berlin: Mouton de Gruyter.

Hakuta, K. (1974). Prefabricated patterns and the emergence of structure in second language learning. *Language Learning*, *24*, 287–297.

Hanania, E. (1974). *Acquisition of English structures: A case study of an adult native speaker of Arabic in an English-speaking environment* (Unpublished doctoral dissertation). Indiana University, Bloomington.

Hawkins, B. (1985). Is an "appropriate response" always so appropriate? In S. Gass & C. Madden (Eds.), *Input in second language acquisition* (pp. 162–178). Rowley, MA: Newbury House.

Henkes, T. (1974). *Early stages in the non-native acquisition of English syntax. A study of three children from Zaire, Venezuela, and Saudi Arabia* (Unpublished doctoral dissertation). Indiana University, Bloomington.

Hyltenstam, K., & Abrahamsson, N. (2003). Maturational constraints in SLA. In C. Doughty & M. H. Long (Eds.), *The Handbook of second language acquisition* (pp. 539–588). Oxford: Blackwell.

Johnson, J. S., & Newport, E. (1989). Critical period effects in second language learning: The influence of maturational state on the acquisition of English as a second language. *Cognitive Psychology*, *21*, 60–99.

Kahneman, D. (1973). *Attention and effort.* Englewood Cliffs, NJ: Prentice Hall.

Kasper, G., & Rose, K. R. (2002). *Pragmatic development in a second language.* Oxford: Blackwell.

Kellerman, E. (1977). Towards a characterization of the strategy of transfer in second language learning. *Interlanguage Studies Bulletin*, *21*, 58–145.

Kellerman, E. (1978). The empirical evidence for the influence of L1 on interlanguage. In A. Davies, C. Criper, & A. P. R. Howatt (Eds.), *Interlanguage* (pp. 98–122). Edinburgh: Edinburgh University.

Kellerman, E. (1979). Transfer and non–transfer: Where we are now. *Studies in Second Language Acquisition*, *2*, 37–57.

Kihlstrom, J. (1987). The cognitive unconscious. *Science*, *237*, 1445–1452.

Kleifgen, J. (1985). Skilled variation in a kindergarten teacher's use of foreigner talk. In S. Gass & C. Madden (Eds.), *Input in second language acquisition* (pp. 59–85). Cambridge, MA: Newbury House.

Kroll, J., & G. Sunderman (2003). Cognitive processes in second language learners and bilinguals: The development of lexical and conceptual representations. In C. Doughty & M. H. Long (Eds.), *Handbook of second language acquisition* (pp. 104–129). Oxford: Blackwell.

Lardiere, D. (2008). Feature assembly in second language acquisition. In J. M. Liceras, H. Zobl, & H. Goodluck (Eds.), *The role of formal features in second language acquisition* (pp. 106–140). New York: Lawrence Erlbaum Associates.

Lardiere, D. (2009). Some thoughts on the contrastive analysis of features in second language acquisition. *Second Language Research*, *25*, 173–227.

Larsen-Freeman, D. (2011). A complexity approach to second language development/acquisition. In D. Atkinson (Ed.), *Alternative approaches to second language acquisition* (pp. 48–72). New York: Routledge.

Larsen-Freeman, D. (2012). Complexity theory. In S. Gass & A. Mackey (Eds.), *The Routledge handbook of second language acquisition* (pp. 73–87). New York: Routledge.

Lenneberg, E. (1967). *Biological foundations of language.* New York: Wiley.

Long, M. H. (1980). *Input, interaction and second language acquisition* (Unpublished doctoral dissertation). University of California, Los Angeles.

Long, M. H. (1983). Linguistic and conversational adjustments to non-native speakers. *Studies in Second Language Acquisition*, *5*, 177–193.

Long, M. H. (1996). The role of the linguistic environment in second language acquisition. In W. Ritchie & T. Bhatia (Eds.), *Handbook of second language acquisition* (pp. 413–468). San Diego, CA: Academic Press.

Long, M. H. (2007). *Problems in SLA.* Mahwah, NJ: Lawrence Erlbaum Associates.

Loschky, L., & Bley-Vroman, R. (1993). Grammar and task-based methodology. In G. Crookes & S. Gass (Eds.), *Tasks and language learning: Integrating theory and practice* (pp. 122–167). Clevedon, UK: Multilingual Matters.

Mackey, A. (1995). *Stepping up the pace—input, interaction and interlanguage development: An empirical study of questions in ESL* (Unpublished doctoral dissertation). University of Sydney, Australia.

Mackey, A. (1999). Input, interaction and second language development. *Studies in Second Language Acquisition*, *21*, 557–587.

Mackey, A. (2012). *Input, interaction and correct feedback in L2 classrooms.* Oxford: Oxford University Press.

Mackey, A., Gass, S., & McDonough, K. (2000). How do learners perceive implicit negative feedback? *Studies in Second Language Acquisition*, *22*, 471–497.

Mackey, A., Philp, J., Egi, T., Fujii, A., & Tatsumi, T. (2002). The outcomes of implicit feedback in conversational interaction: An exploration of the role of aptitude in phonological short-term memory. In P. Robinson (Ed.), *Individual differences and instructed language learning* (pp. 181–210). Amsterdam, the Netherlands: John Benjamins.

McLaughlin, B. (1987). *Theories of second language learning.* London: Edward Arnold.

Montrul, S. (2004). Subject and object expression in Spanish heritage speakers: A case of morpho-syntactic convergence. *Bilingualism: Language and Cognition, 7,* 125–142.

Montrul, S., & Polinsky, M. (2011). Why not heritage speakers? *Linguistic Approaches to Bilingualism, 1,* 58–62.

Moyer, A. (1999). Ultimate attainment in L2 phonology: The critical factors of age, motivation, and instruction. *Studies in Second Language Acquisition, 21,* 81–108.

Moyer, A. (2004). *Age, accent and experience in second language acquisition.* Clevedon, UK: Multilingual Matters.

Nobuyoshi, J., & Ellis, R. (1993). Focused communication tasks and second language acquisition. *English Language Teaching, 47,* 203–210.

Odlin, T. (1989). *Language transfer.* Cambridge: Cambridge University Press.

Odlin, T. (2003). Cross-linguistic influence. In C. Doughty & M. Long (Eds.), *The handbook of second language acquisition* (pp. 436–486). Malden, MA: Blackwell.

Olshtain, E., & Cohen, A. D. (1989). Speech act behavior across languages. In H. W. Dechert & M. Raupach (Eds.), *Transfer in production* (pp. 53–67). Norwood, NJ: Ablex.

Patkowski, M. S. (1980). The sensitive period for the acquisition of syntax in a second language. *Language Learning, 30,* 449–472.

Philp, J. (2003). Constraints on "noticing the gap": Nonnative speakers' noticing of recasts in NS-NNS interaction. *Studies in Second Language Acquisition, 25,* 99–126.

Pica, T. (1987). Second-language acquisition, social interaction, and the classroom. *Applied Linguistics, 8,* 3–21.

Pienemann, M. (1989). Is language teachable? Psycholinguistic experiments and hypotheses. *Applied Linguistics, 10,* 52–79.

Pienemann, M. (1998). *Language processing and second language development: Processability theory.* Amsterdam, the Netherlands: John Benjamins.

Pienemann, M., & Johnston, M. (1987). Factors influencing the development of language proficiency. In D. Nunan (Ed.), *Applying second language acquisition research* (pp. 45–141). Adelaide, Australia: National Curriculum Resource Centre, AMEP.

Polinsky, M. (2008). Heritage language narratives. In O. Kagan & D. Brinton (Eds.), *Heritage languages: A new field emerging* (pp. 149–164). New York: Routledge.

Polinsky, M. (2015). When L1 becomes an L3: Assessing grammatical knowledge in heritage speakers/learners. *Bilingualism: Language and Cognition, 18,* 163–178.

Robinson, P. (2003). Attention and memory during SLA. In C. Doughty & M. H. Long (Eds.), *Handbook of second language acquisition* (pp. 631–678). Oxford: Blackwell.

Schmidt, R. (2001). Attention. In P. Robinson (Ed.), *Cognition and second language instruction* (pp. 3–32). Cambridge: Cambridge University Press.

Schmidt, R., & Frota, S. (1986). Developing basic conversational ability in a second language: A case study of an adult learner of Portuguese. In R. Day (Ed.), *Talking to learn: Conversation in second language acquisition* (pp. 237–326). Rowley, MA: Newbury House.

Singleton, D., & Lengyel, Z. (Eds.). (1995). *The age factor in second language acquisition.* Clevedon, UK: Multilingual Matters.

Singleton, D., & Ryan, L. (2004). *Language acquisition: The age factor* (2nd ed.). Clevedon, UK: Multilingual Matters.

Siyanova, A., & Schmitt, N. (2008). L2 learner production and processing of collocation: A multi-study perspective. *The Canadian Modern Language Review, 64,* 429–458.

Siyanova-Chanturia, A., Conklin, K., & Schmitt, N. (2011). Adding more fuel to the fire: An eye-tracking study of idiom processing by native and non-native speakers. *Second Language Research, 27,* 1–22.

Sorace, A. (1993). Incomplete vs. divergent representations of unaccusativity in non-native grammars of Italian. *Second Language Research*, *9*, 21–47.

Sorace, A. (2003). Near-nativeness. In C. Doughty & M. H. Long (Eds.), *Handbook of second language acquisition* (pp. 130–151). Oxford: Blackwell.

Swain, M. (1985). Communicative competence: Some roles of comprehensible input and comprehensible output in its development. In S. Gass & C. Madden (Eds.), *Input in second language acquisition* (pp. 235–253). Rowley, MA: Newbury House.

Swain, M. (1995). Three functions of output in second language learning. In G. Cook & B. Seidlhofer (Eds.), *Principle and practice in applied linguistics* (pp. 125–144). Oxford: Oxford University Press.

Valdés, G. (2001). Heritage language students: Profiles and possibilities. In J. Peyton, D. Ranard, & S. McGinnis (Eds.), *Heritage languages in America preserving a national resource* (pp. 37–57). Washington, DC: Center for Applied Linguistics.

Valdés, G. (2005). Bilingualism, heritage language learners, and SLA research: Opportunities lost or seized? *The Modern Language Journal*, *89*, 410–426.

White, L. (2003). *Second language acquisition and universal grammar*. Cambridge: Cambridge University Press.

White, L., & Genesee, F. (1996). How native is near-native? The issue of ultimate attainment in adult second language acquisition. *Second Language Research*, *12*, 233–265.

Williams, J. (1999). Memory, attention, and inductive learning. *Studies in Second Language Acquisition*, *21*, 1–48.

Zobl, H. (1982). A direction for contrastive analysis: The comparative study of developmental sequences. *TESOL Quarterly*, *16*, 169–83.

17 Bilingualism and Communication Disorders

M. Adelaida Restrepo, Ashley Adams,
and Beatriz Barragan

Introduction

Communication disorders in general are deficits in communicating due to speech, language, motor, sensory, cognitive, or a combination of these difficulties. Communication deficits in children or adults can range from mild to devastating effects in the person's everyday functioning at home, school, or work environment. Language is the primary tool for communication in humans, and thus, when there are language deficits, the individual with a communication disorder experiences difficulty in social interactions.

Language disorders can be developmental in nature, with no known etiology, or they can have neurological, cognitive, or *sensory etiologies*. In addition, language disorders can be acquired through neurological events, such as strokes, head injury, seizure disorders, tumors, or other neurological diseases. This chapter will focus on developmental language disorders in bilingual children and on acquired language disorders in bilingual adults. We will cover some general issues in relation to communication disorders in bilingual children and adults, and then we will focus on those that impact language primarily. Language disorders in bilingual populations provide a window to help us in understanding the nature of these disorders and how languages are organized and processed in the brain.

Language Ability versus Language Proficiency in Bilinguals

Language ability refers to the child's developmental language aptitude and resources inherent to the child that make the native language(s) fluent, functional, and efficient (*simultaneous bilinguals* have two native languages; *sequential bilinguals* have one native language, or L1, and one second language, or L2). Children with *primary language impairment* (PLI) present with low language ability in their L1 because they have not developed one or more language milestones in reference to what is considered normal native acquisition for their specific age and sociolinguistic group. In contrast, children with typical language development present language like their reference group in terms of syntax, morphology, and possibly other aspects of language. Thus, when authors discuss language disorders or PLI, they are often referring to impairment of language ability.

Language proficiency, on the other hand, is the extent to which a language has developed, and it is often used in reference to an L2 (Smyk, Restrepo, Gorin, & Gray, 2013). While we assume that the child is proficient in his or her native language(s) and can have typical language development or PLI, the child may have a different level (e.g., intermediate or advanced) of proficiency in the L2. Therefore, when the child is learning an L2, the child is proficient in the L1(s) and goes through the different stages of L2 acquisition (Tabors, 2008). For example, a child learning English as an L2 may speak Spanish as the

L1, have normal language ability, but demonstrate intermediate levels of English proficiency as an L2 after one or two years of schooling in English.

Distinguishing language differences from language disorders can be difficult in bilingual populations. Some children may have low language proficiency resulting from limited contact with one or both of the languages. For example, children in the process of acquiring an L2 can exhibit errors that resemble the language of a child with language impairment. Further, when the child is in the process of becoming proficient in their L2 and has limited input in the L1 at home, the development of the L1 is affected. The child can present with protracted language development, incomplete language acquisition, or *language loss* (Castilla-Earls et al., 2015). Multiple factors, external (e.g., quality of input in the language environment, parental education, SES) and internal (e.g., *working memory*, language ability, and cognitive abilities) can influence children's language development. The most significant factor is the quality and quantity of input in the L1, especially when there is no schooling in that language or low stimulation in the home (Chondrogianni & Marinis, 2011; Restrepo et al., 2010). The child's L1 development may be protracted when its growth slows down compared to monolingual or sequential bilinguals who have good quality input in each language. Incomplete acquisition occurs when some aspect of the language does not fully develop, such as clitics (i.e., direct object pronouns may show gender agreement errors) in Spanish speakers (Morgan, Restrepo, & Auza, 2013). Language loss occurs when the child loses the ability to retrieve the language and the lexical or grammatical skills may become less accurate compared to a previous time (Anderson, 2012). Further, children and adults can shift proficiency and dominance from the L1 to an L2 when there is loss or limited use of the native language.

When language loss or incomplete acquisition impact grammar, it is difficult to differentiate low language ability from low language proficiency because some of the grammatical characteristics typical of bilingual children in the L1 and L2 can resemble difficulties seen in monolinguals with PLI (Paradis, Schneider, & Duncan, 2013). For example, Spanish monolingual children with PLI may demonstrate gender agreement difficulties; however, bilingual Spanish speakers with typical language development in English only education contexts can also demonstrate gender agreement errors in Spanish, their L1 (Morgan et al., 2013).

Studying language disorders in bilingual populations presents a variety of challenges, as well as insights, into the nature of these disorders. For example, some areas (such as past tense in English) are difficult for L2 learners and for children with language disorders, and thus, error patterns may look similar in both groups. In addition, these areas are also more vulnerable in language loss (such as gender agreement in Spanish), when there is not sufficient stimulation in the language. Bilingual effects can be positive when there is transfer across languages, and thus, some forms are learned faster, such as the use of verb inflections in young children who speak Spanish and are learning Italian as an L2. These effects can also be negative, or they can change the developmental trajectory, such as the influence of *word order* in Spanish speakers learning English as an L2 in noun + adjective constructions (Blom & Paradis, 2013; MacSwan & Rolstad, 2005). These bilingual language effects can complicate the assessment and diagnostic process in bilingual children for a variety of reasons and depending on the context.

Bilingualism in children can occur in *additive-* and *subtractive-language* environments. Additive-language environments are those in which both languages are valued, are vital in the community, and are used in the children's education. Subtractive-language environments are those in which the children's L1 is not valued in the community, and thus, it is not well accepted socially, nor used in the children's education. Subtractive-language environments often occur when the L1 is a minority language in the community. In subtractive environments, children may demonstrate slower language development of grammatical skills, such as syntax and morphology (Morgan et al., 2013; Restrepo et al., 2010) in the L1 than monolingual or bilingual peers in additive-language environments. Additive-language environments, such as in some contexts in Canada and Europe, value languages, and the negative effects of language contact are minimal, especially when there is literacy instruction in the two languages.

In additive contexts in which children receive bilingual education, when the two languages are valued in the community or when the family makes the effort to ensure that language and literacy continue to develop in the two languages, the children's language skills in the L1 show development more similar to monolingual children. Further, the ability to develop literacy skills in the L1 helps them solidify their grammatical skills and improve their vocabulary.

Vocabulary development is best captured when examined across languages because it is distributed knowledge and is learned only in the context of each language (e.g., Core, Hoff, Rumiche, & Señor, 2013; Pearson, Fernández, & Oller, 1993). Although it has been argued that vocabulary is delayed in each language for a bilingual child, if both languages are combined in an analysis, the child ultimately will demonstrate typical vocabulary development overall, as a combined score accounts for *all* of the child's experiences in both languages together. *Conceptual vocabulary* scoring is a method that researchers developed to examine vocabulary because counting labels in each language seems to overestimate development, and counting only one language underestimates development. Therefore, when conceptual scoring is used, the developmental norms for bilingual children match those of monolingual peers, resulting in a vocabulary score that indicates typical language development (Pearson et al., 1993). Although Core et al. (2013) argued that using the total vocabulary across languages is a better representation of the children's vocabulary development, it is clear that accounting for only one language does not accurately represent the child's overall vocabulary development. Total vocabulary scores give credit for the labels in all the languages the child produces. On the other hand, conceptual vocabulary scores give credit for the words in either language, but only counts them once if the labels are available in the two languages. For example, the child produces the following: jugo, leche, coke, lemonade, limonada, coffee, milk, horchata. The English score is 4 words, the Spanish score is 4 words, the total score is 8 words, and the conceptual score is 6 words (2 only in English, 2 only in Spanish, and 2 in both languages).

Brain Representation of Language Proficiency

Research on the brain representation of bilingual language has been of interest for several decades. Research findings in this area have significant implications for primary language disorders in children and adults, because they provide a better understanding of the nature of the disorders and the impact of a neurological event in bilingual adults. Research indicates that in proficient bilinguals, overlapping brain regions are activated when the individual performs language tasks in both languages. In less proficient bilinguals, it is typical to find significant neural activation differences between the L1 and L2. In one research study, Chinese students with limited knowledge of the English language were asked to judge whether two words were semantically related or not (*cat-dog* vs. *table-juice*; the first are semantically related). As expected, the students were faster and more accurate in their responses in Chinese than in English, even though the imaging data showed similar activation for both languages in the left inferior frontal gyrus, fusiform cortex, occipital cortex, and subcortical regions (Xue, Dong, Jin, Zhang, & Wang, 2004). These similarities in neural activation suggest that there are shared neural substrates for *semantic processing* even in low-proficient bilinguals. However, significantly more activation was observed for English in the anterior cingulate area, posterior cingulate area, and the left inferior parietal lobe. These differences could be attributed to an increase in the computational requirement of L2, as processing of a low proficiency language requires significantly more attention and working memory resources (Xue et al., 2004).

Proficiency is a neuromodulator that controls the recruitment of additional brain regions to process the language. Spanish–English bilinguals whose L1 was Spanish, but as young adults were more proficient in L2, required significantly more time to read words in the less proficient L1 (Spanish) than in their more proficient L2 (English). Increased neural activation for Spanish words was observed in articulatory motor processing regions such as the supplementary motor area, putamen, and insula moreso than for English words, suggesting that the less proficient language (even if it is the native language) requires the recruitment of additional brain regions during reading than the more proficient language (Meschyan & Hernandez, 2006).

Language Disorders in Bilingual Children

Language disorders in children in general can impact semantic, grammatical, or pragmatic skills. They can have neurological etiologies, such as seizure disorders; sensory etiologies, such as hearing impairment (not all children with hearing impairment present with language disorders, although they can impact oral language development); and *cognitive etiologies*, such as developmental disorders; and *Down's syndrome*. In addition, language disorders can impact different language modalities, such as *receptive* and *expressive language*, and reading and writing skills.

Children with developmental cognitive delays tend to have difficulties in all aspects of language: form, content, and use (grammar, semantics, and pragmatics). These difficulties are present to different degrees, and children can differ in strengths and weaknesses. Pragmatic skills, for example, can be a strength for some children, while they can be a primary deficit for other children. In children with Down's syndrome, grammatical skills are below those of children with similar mental ages, and vocabulary development can lag behind or be on par with their developmental age (Bird et al., 2005; Eadie, Fey, Douglas, & Parsons, 2002). On the other hand, children with *autism*, by definition, have social/pragmatic difficulties, and, depending on their cognitive skills, their language can vary from non-verbal to highly verbal. Many clinicians may experience concern from parents or teachers that bilingualism may be difficult or confusing for children with developmental cognitive delays; however, research does not support this conclusion. Bilingual children with cognitive delays can learn two languages as well as their monolingual peers learn one (Bird, 2009). Thus, recommending that the children focus on learning only one language is not warranted, and doing so can have a major and negative impact on the families' communication at home (Kohnert, Yim, Nett, Kan, & Duran, 2005).

Primary Language Impairment in Bilinguals

PLI is a disorder in which language skills fail to develop at the expected rate and age. Compared to typical peers, children with PLI frequently present with slower processing speed and mild attentional and cognitive differences that are not clinically significant

(Leonard, 1998). Thus, the clinical and primary deficit is language, and it can impact school performance. Bilingual children with PLI demonstrate deficits in the same areas as monolingual children in each of their languages. These deficits occur primarily in grammar in the early years and develop into more semantic deficits in later years; however, grammatical deficits can remain in written language, and often are still seen in oral language (Tomblin, Zhang, & Buckwalter, 1997; Tomblin, Zhang, Buckwalter, & O'Brien, 2003).

Grammatical deficits in children with PLI who speak English often include the verb system, such as in the use of past tense; copulas (*the girl * happy with the new puppy*); and the third-person singular (Rice & Wexler, 1996). In monolingual Spanish, on the other hand, grammatical deficits tend to impact the noun system and noun phrases (e.g., articles, pronouns, and prepositional phrase) more than the verb system (Morgan, Restrepo, & Auza, 2009, 2013). In other languages, grammatical skills are affected in the most vulnerable aspects of the language (e.g., Dromi, Leonard, Adam, & Zadunaisky-Ehrlich, 1999; Leonard, Sabbadini, Leonard, & Volterra, 1987), and they differ across each language. Bilingual children with PLI will therefore demonstrate deficits in the two languages, and each language may have different deficit patterns (Restrepo, 2003). When deficits are only observed in one language, clinicians do not regard the child as having PLI.

Bilingual children with PLI may demonstrate significant deficits as compared to monolingual peers when they live in subtractive-language contexts. For example, in two case studies, Restrepo (2003) found that bilingual children with PLI demonstrated significant language loss despite living in monolingual Spanish-speaking homes, but attending English only schools, where there was no L1 instruction and very few language peers. These children demonstrated significant changes in syntax, morphology, and vocabulary over a one-year period. One child reduced the mean length of utterance from 3.18 to 1.94 words per sentence, whereas the second child increased mean length of utterance from 2.57 to 4.92, but also increased the number of ungrammatical sentences. In addition, these two children demonstrated grammatical deficits not seen in monolingual children. One child, for example, substituted the clitic pronoun (*le*) for the articles (*el, la, los,* and *las*). This is not a type of error we see in monolingual Spanish-speaking children.

On the other hand, bilingual children with PLI attending additive-educational contexts have language skills comparable to those of monolingual children with PLI (Bruck, 1982; Paradis, 2005). Their grammatical skills do not differ from their same-age peers with similar disorders. Therefore, additive-language environments do not have negative effects on language development; however, subtractive-language environments can cause protracted growth, language loss, or no growth, and these effects can complicate the diagnostic process. Given these complexities, distinguishing between language difference and language disorder becomes more difficult for clinicians. Research on bilingual PLI indicates that obtaining bilingual norms in the specific tasks is helpful (Morgan et al., 2013), and examining the child across the two languages is essential in distinguishing language difference from language disorder and in obtaining a global view of a child's strengths and weaknesses.

As with grammatical skills, bilingualism can cause some differences in processing skills and executive function skills (e.g., Bialystok & Feng, 2005; Kroll & Bialystok, 2013). Certain aspects in executive function can actually be better when compared to monolinguals, although in some areas one can also see slightly slower processing rates (Kohnert, Windsor, & Yim, 2006). These slower rates, however, are not identifiable in everyday life, and the benefits of bilingualism outweigh the slight slowing in processing speed. Some authors argue that bilingual children need to switch back and forth between the languages; thus, to be successful in this task, prefrontal executive control is required to overcome prepotent automatic behavior (inhibition of the dominant language) and select the correct words in the appropriate language. This constant cognitive effort could give an executive function advantage to bilingual individuals, specifically in the inhibitory control component (Bialystock, Luk, & Kwan, 2005). Further, research has shown that the bilingual advantage in executive control could extend even to non-verbal domains. In one study, six-year-old bilingual children completed the *trail-making task* and *global-local task* more rapidly than monolingual same-age peers. Both tasks require perceptual processing of general and particular features of complex stimuli, selective attention to some features while ignoring others, and switching in conflicting situations. This result indicates that the bilingual executive function advantage could extend beyond the inhibitory control of language to a broader range of cognitive processes (Bialystok, Craik, & Freedman, 2010). On the other hand, despite the significant evidence of the bilingual advantage in executive control, not all research supports this view. An important group of researchers have argued that the bilingual advantage found in previous studies is the result of methodological issues, such as small sample sizes, the use of measures that do not demonstrate convergent validity, hidden demographic factors, and inadequately matched groups (Paap & Greenberg, 2013; Paap, Johnson, & Sawi, 2015; Paap & Sawi, 2014; see also Paap, this volume).

While the topic is still controversial, it seems plausible that bilingual children with PLI can benefit from the bilingual experience. *Metalinguistic skills* are those skills in which children are aware of the language structures and their use, such as *phonological awareness*, where the child is able to manipulate the sounds and syllables of the language. These skills are important to adequately produce and comprehend speech. Children with PLI demonstrate metalinguistic difficulties and executive function differences when compared to children with typical language development (Boudreau & Hedberg, 1999; Catts, 1991; Im-Bolter, Johnson, & Pascual-Leone, 2006). Bilingualism helps to improve metalinguistic skills, and executive function abilities (Bialystok et al., 2005; Bialystok & Feng, 2005); therefore, it is possible that bilingual children with PLI may have an advantage in developing metalinguistic and cognitive skills important for communication. However, research in this area is needed. If the hypothesis is supported, additive-language education may provide cognitive and metalinguistic benefits to children with PLI.

Neurobiological Evidence Associated with PLI

Neurobiological studies conducted with children with PLI evidence a *sound discrimination* problem due to a temporal lobe processing deficit. This deficit may cause discrimination difficulties when perceiving L2 phonemes (Pihko et al., 2007). *Functional magnetic resonance imaging* (fMRI) studies found this temporal deficit when comparing members of a family with PLI and a control group with normal language development. While hearing real words and pseudo words, members of the family with PLI showed smaller and weaker bilateral activations of the temporal lobes, concentrated in the upper posterior part of the superior temporal gyrus, and significantly less activation in the anterioventral areas of the superior temporal gyrus and medial temporal gyrus than the control group (Hugdahl et al., 2004). Activation of these temporal regions is associated with speech processing and phonological awareness, which could explain the *phoneme discrimination* difficulties observed in children with PLI.

Another characteristic of children with PLI is an impaired ability to discriminate between *rapid successive sounds*, which also suggests temporal processing deficits. The *event-related potentials* (ERPs) technique is an electrophysiological response related to a cognitive event, which is recorded through the scalp and has become a very useful technique to study brain responses to discrimination tasks. A *mismatch negativity* (MMN) is a component in the ERPs technique observed when a deviant stimuli (e.g., a grammatical error or a semantic inconsistency) is presented among a sequence of standard sounds; therefore, it has been associated with automatic change detection (Moreno, Rodriguez-Fornells, & Laine, 2008). When the MMN of a group of 8-week-old infants with a family history of PLI and considered at risk for the disorder were compared to a group of infants who had no family history and no risk for PLI, researchers observed a delayed processing of an auditory stimulus change. The differences found revealed that even at a very early age, children at risk of PLI are already affected in their temporal processing, which could affect the ability to categorize sounds (Friedrich, Weber, & Friederici, 2004).

ERPs technology is also revealing important information related to the bilingual neural processing of semantic and grammatical skills. In monolingual adults, different neural systems are involved in the processing of lexical/semantic information and grammatical information: semantic processing requires more activation in posterior temporal-parietal regions, and anterior temporal activation is necessary for grammatical processing. Apparently, both systems have different developmental time courses; young children show a similar ERP pattern of response to adults listening to semantically deviant sentences (i.e., sentences grammatically correct but semantically nonsensical: *The little girl drove her mother to school*). In contrast, the pattern of response to grammatical information changes with time, and it reaches a mature pattern only during the middle teen years (Neville & Mills, 1997). Therefore, in the bilingual population, grammatical processing is more sensitive to the age of L2 acquisition than is semantic processing. The differential cerebral organization for semantic and grammatical aspects of language in bilingual children is fostered by the amount of language experience. Even when children are exposed to an L2 very early in life, between one and three years of age, differences in neural organization for grammatical processing are observed. On the other hand, high proficiency minimizes the effects of cerebral organization on semantic processing, and similar neural activation patterns can be displayed for the L1 and L2 (Meschyan & Hernandez, 2006). For example, in Chinese–English bilinguals, very long delays (16 years) in exposure to the English language had little effect on the neural organization associated with *lexical*/semantic processing. In contrast, delays of only four years in exposure to the English language revealed important effects on neural organization related to grammatical processing. Interestingly, children with PLI showed similarly limited brain functional organization for grammatical processing as children with delayed exposure to language; that is, they present with less activation within anterior regions of the *left hemisphere* (Neville & Mills, 1997).

Examination of neural waveform patterns has revealed additional similarities between children with PLI and bilingual children with typical development when processing words in a low proficiency language. When typically developing children listen to a word, ERP waveforms are characterized by a positive bilateral component at 100 ms (*P100*) after the onset of the word. Thirteen-month-old infants with a large vocabulary displayed a larger P100 over the temporal and parietal left hemisphere in comparison to the *right hemisphere*. Infants at the same age with a small vocabulary and at risk of PLI displayed a symmetrical and smaller P100 response in the left and right hemispheres. This difference between the two groups of infants was maintained at 20 and 30 months of age, suggesting that a small and symmetrical P100 is associated with PLI (Neville & Mills, 1997). Similarly, bilingual children performing in the dominant and non-dominant languages show a similar P100 effect. Conboy and Mills (2006) conducted a study with 19- to 22-month-old infants exposed to English and Spanish prior to 6 months of age. Infants were assigned to a *high-total-conceptual vocabulary* size group or a *low-total-conceptual vocabulary* group based on their performance on the English and Spanish versions of the *MacArthur-Bates Communicative Development Inventories*—words and sentences. While hearing a list of words in both languages, infants in the high-total-conceptual vocabulary group displayed a larger P100 for the dominant language over the left hemisphere, while a symmetrical P100 for the non-dominant language was observed. The researchers argued that the left asymmetry for the P100 indicated the use of a more efficient processing system for the dominant language. In contrast, infants in the low-total-conceptual vocabulary group showed symmetrical P100 for both languages similar to monolingual infants at risk of PLI. It was concluded that language proficiency shapes the organization of language processing in the brain.

Assessment in Bilingual Children with PLI

As discussed above, language assessment in bilingual children with PLI can be difficult because of the variability in the quality and quantity of language input and the representation of the disorder, when they are exposed to an L2, the type of languages they speak, and the interaction between these languages. Differences in language proficiency could be mistakenly interpreted as PLI, and bilingual children with PLI could mistakenly be labeled as an L2 learner, or have delayed identification because clinicians may attribute the L2 difficulties to lack of proficiency in that language.

The availability of measures with standardized language norms for bilingual populations and in languages other than English is quite limited. Therefore, the language assessment process requires multiple sources of evidence to determine whether the bilingual child has PLI. In addition, many cultural factors impact how a child performs on a given task. For example, Peña and Iglesias (1992) found that bilingual, Spanish-speaking children performed poorly on measures that required children to name or label objects; however, when they received a *dynamic assessment* that focused on teaching these skills, the children with typically developing language (TD) performed well, and those with PLI continued to demonstrate difficulties on the task. These results indicated that finding converging evidence might require different types of assessment and alternative assessments, such as dynamic assessment, parent interviews, teacher interview, and *language sampling*. For example, Restrepo (1998) found that the use of language sampling procedures in combination with parent report were accurate methods for identifying primarily Spanish-speaking children with PLI who were learning English as an L2. Other studies have also found that language sampling procedures and parent interviews seem to improve accuracy in identification of PLI in bilingual populations (Bedore, Peña, Joyner, & Macken, 2011; Gutierrez-Clellen & Kreiter, 2003). Examples of language sample procedures include obtaining data from conversations or story retelling in which children's mean length of utterance, vocabulary, and grammatical skills are analyzed.

Clinicians may find that developing tasks that target vulnerable or difficult areas in a language may be useful in identifying whether a child has PLI when no other measures are available. However, comparing monolingual and bilingual performance may not be useful. For example, Morgan et al. (2013) found that in an *elicited grammatical task* (i.e., asking a child to complete a sentence with the correct article or pronoun), bilingual children in general scored significantly below same-age monolingual peers in morphological skills, and thus, using cutoff scores designed for monolingual children over-identified typical bilingual children as presenting with PLI. In addition, Barragan, Castilla-Earls, Martinez-Nieto, Restrepo, and Gray (2017) found that a standardized measure with bilingual norms still over-identified bilingual children as having PLI. However, these children had several other risk factors, including low socioeconomic status, low parent education, and English only education. So even when bilingual norms are available, these may not be appropriate for the population, given variability due to external factors.

For assessment purposes, we recommend that bilingual children be assessed in all the languages they speak; that clinicians consider the quality and quantity of input the children receive at home, school, and childcare; that they consider the relative proficiency in each language; and that they obtain converging evidence from multiple sources and informants. Different sources of information include dynamic assessment, language sampling, parent and teacher interviews, standardized assessment, classroom observation, curriculum-based products, and *portfolio assessments*. The parent interview examining in detail the history of contact with a language, speakers at home of each language, the language the child uses with the different speakers, and the language of instruction in educational contexts are critical pieces of information to make appropriate clinical decisions.

Establishing what typical performance in a group of bilinguals is may require understanding the population's culture and examining the characteristics of the language. The clinician must investigate the syntactic, morphological, and phonological characteristics of the different languages the child speaks. In addition, the clinician should possibly interview the family or community members to better understand not only the language, but also the cultural factors and socialization practices that impact language. Assessments of bilingual children should also examine their written language skills. Because many bilingual children start learning to read in a language that they do not speak or in which they are not very proficient, they often present with reading and writing levels well below their monolingual peers. However, difficulties are secondary to low language proficiency, especially when the children learn to read only in the least proficient language, and may not be indicative of language disorders. Bilingual children with PLI, however, can present with additional written language difficulties above and beyond those seen in typical language development bilingual children.

Language Intervention in Bilingual PLI

Research is limited on how to intervene in bilingual children with PLI. Regardless, intervention for bilingual children requires that the clinician understand what language components transfer across languages. In addition, the clinician may need to determine whether some methods shown to work in one language and in monolingual children are also efficacious in bilinguals.

The evidence, however, is clear that the bilingual child needs intervention in both languages. When a clinician treats the bilingual child in only one language, the benefits of intervention may be in that language only (e.g., Restrepo, Morgan, & Thompson, 2013; Thordardottir, 2015). The argument, however, should not be in what language a clinician should intervene, because for many children, the languages are necessary to communicate in their communities and home. When a child speaks a *minority* language at home, recommending that the child focus on only the *majority* language or the L2 for communication in the home will have detrimental effects on the home language, and therefore, on the child's overall communication with family and community members. Bilingual children with PLI are already at risk of language loss (Restrepo, 2003), and thus, many of them could end up with limited ability to communicate with their parents at home; moreover, their L1 is critical for cultural transmission, emotional support, and overall communication in the home, not to mention their parents' support for school. Even when no bilingual clinicians are available to provide intervention in the L1, families should not be discouraged from using their language at home, and clinicians should help them find indirect techniques and home programs to develop their L1. Ideally, bilingual intervention is available to the children (Kohnert et al., 2005).

When clinicians plan language intervention for bilingual children, they should examine whether the language skills transfer across languages, and if so, they should examine if they should treat it in only one and expect transfer, or treat in both languages to facilitate that transfer. Examining which skills transfer will ideally allow for intervention in one language to have effects in the other language. In addition, the clinician will determine which skills need language-specific intervention and thus plan the intervention to maximize gains across the two languages. For example, *narrative structure* may transfer across languages, but past tense in English and gender agreement in Spanish need to be treated in each language. Children with language disorders will need greater input to acquire regular forms and thus intervention would focus on increasing the input of these more difficult forms.

An aspect of language that shows *cross-linguistic transfer* is phonemic awareness, especially when there are similarities between languages in terms of orthography and regardless of whether the system is syllabic or alphabetic (Bialystok, Majumder, & Martin, 2003). For example, when a language is syllabic, the children's ability to manipulate and identify syllables is strengthened in all the languages. As occurs with vocabulary, when the child is not very proficient in one of the languages, the more efficient intervention might be to teach the skills in the stronger language, and the skills will often improve in the weaker language.

Other areas in which there may be *language transfer* include narrative structure and syntactic complexity. When narratives are well developed, children may transfer them readily into the L2. For example, in languages where the story is linearly organized into orientation, problem, and resolution, the child will be able to tell stories with that structure in the L2. This transfer may be even greater when there are similarities across languages (Fiestas, 2008; Squires et al., 2014). When story structure is different across languages, such as in cultures that use associative narratives, this structure is often observed in the L2. Similarly, in syntax we see transfer across languages. For example, in a study of reading comprehension in Chinese–English bilingual children, investigators found that there was cross-linguistic transfer in syntax from the L1 to the L2, especially in word order (Siu & Ho, 2015).

Vocabulary intervention is an important component in language stimulation in bilingual children. This is partly because language disorders can impact vocabulary development but also because bilingual children present with distributed vocabulary skills across languages, and vocabulary is a strong predictor of academic achievement and reading comprehension (Mancilla-Martinez, Kieffer, Biancarosa, Christodoulou, & Snow, 2011). Thus, improvements in vocabulary levels will help in these areas. However, vocabulary is an interesting issue because research indicates that there is transfer of skills between languages at the conceptual level (Kiernan & Swisher, 1990; Perozzi, 1985; Perozzi & Chavez-Sanchez, 1992), while the labels need to be learned in the language in which the concept is going to be used (Restrepo et al., 2013). The child learns a concept faster when the clinician teaches it in the L1 first, compared to when the clinician teaches it only in the L2 (Kiernan & Swisher, 1990; Perozzi, 1985).

In summary, research on assessment, intervention, and characteristics of bilingual language disorders in children is still in its early stages. Much is left to be done in terms of determining the characteristics of bilingual language disorders and which of those help us to differentiate better difference from disorder. Moreover, developing tasks, methods, and norms for different language groups may help us improve assessment accuracy, a problem that has been reported for decades. In terms of treatment, research is in its infancy, especially in relation to determining the best models of intervention when language transfer is present. Moreover, cultural factors affect performance and generalization of skills, and thus, it is best to think of the bilingual child in a larger cultural context, considering their community and its resources.

Communication Disorders in Bilingual Adults

Communication disorders in adults generally belong to one of two categories: speech-related disorders like *dysarthria* (a speech disorder due to dysfunctional motor execution resulting in uncoordinated, weak, and slow articulatory movements), *apraxia* (a speech disorder resulting from dysfunctional planning and sequencing of the motor movements necessary to produce speech), and *stuttering*, or language-related disorders such as aphasia. Language disorders presented by adults may be those carried over from childhood or those acquired as a result of brain injury, stroke or tumor, or those resulting from degenerative diseases such as Alzheimer's and Parkinson's disease. The causes and manifestations of adult communication disorders are diverse, and the varying internal and external language factors that must be considered with bilingual populations add extra layers of complexity to the discussion of assessment and treatment of this population. For the purposes of this chapter, we will review aphasia, an acquired primary language disorder, as well as two degenerative diseases, Alzheimer's disease and Parkinson's disease, that result in communication disorders. General background information, as well as information specific to the expression of language deficits, and assessment and treatment in the bilingual population related to these disorders will be described below.

What is Aphasia?

Aphasia, an impairment of the ability to produce and/or comprehend language, arises as a consequence of a focal damage to the brain, in particular in the left cerebral hemisphere (Vasić, 2006). Aphasia's most common etiologies are brain lesions due to *cerebral vascular accident* (CVA) or stroke, traumatic head injury, tumors, infections, and degenerative conditions (Ardila, 2014). Typically, lesions in the posterior frontal lobe in the left hemisphere result in non-fluent language, while lesions in the temporal and parietal lobes are associated with problems in language comprehension and word-finding.

Lesion site plays an important role in determining the pattern of deficits the individual with aphasia will experience. Although there has been extensive debate about whether multiple languages are represented in common or different neural regions, more recent developments in neuroimaging reveal that language areas for bilinguals are largely the same as for monolinguals (Abutalebi, Tettamanti, & Perani, 2009; Liu, Hu, Guo, & Peng, 2010; Paradis, 1990). However, several studies have shown that there may be differential activation *between* cerebral hemispheres and *within* the left hemisphere for each language depending on factors, such as age of acquisition (Fiebach, Friederici, Müller, von Cramon, & Hernandez, 2003; Hernandez & Li, 2007) and level of proficiency (Chee, Soon, & Lee, 2003; Halsband, Krause, Sipilä, Teräs, & Laihinen, 2002; Kotz, 2009; Perani et al., 1996).

Different language proficiency levels are associated with differences in brain region activation. In highly proficient bilinguals, L1 and L2 neural activation overlaps in the left hemisphere, while in low-proficient bilinguals an increased activation in frontal regions of the right hemisphere is observed (Ansaldo, Marcotte, Scherer, & Raboyeau, 2008). This observation is in line with studies that have shown that processing during reading of a less proficient language requires the recruitment of more extensive brain regions than for the more proficient language (Meschyan & Hernandez, 2006). Cortical areas supporting language are inversely proportional to proficiency level; therefore, a lower proficiency level requires a greater space in the brain to support it (Gomez-Ruiz, 2010; Hernandez & Meschyan, 2006; Liu et al., 2010; Xue et al., 2004). Greater activation of the low-proficient language in regions associated with cognitive control, like the prefrontal cortex, anterior cingulate cortex, and inferior parietal cortex, suggests that the individual is engaged in a monitoring process to filter out irrelevant information and inhibit inappropriate responses (Abutalebi & Green, 2007; Hernandez, Dapretto, Mazziotta, & Bookheimer, 2001). Depending on the premorbid language proficiency level, the site of the lesion can have differential effects on each language and on the ability to switch between languages.

During the discussion of the subtypes of aphasia, the reader should keep in mind that the pattern of deficits described will likely be present in both languages of the bilingual individual and that these results are based on right-handed, left hemisphere-dominant speakers. Left-handers, in some cases, may have right-lateralized language centers, resulting in quite different clinical manifestations after left hemisphere lesions. As a result, these individuals are frequently excluded from experimental studies of aphasia.

Based on the site(s) of lesion, there are two primary categories of aphasia, fluent and non-fluent. *Fluent aphasias* are so-named because they primarily affect *receptive language* abilities leaving expressive language abilities relatively intact. These aphasias can be differentiated from *non-fluent aphasias* in that the speech or language output of individuals with fluent aphasia tends to have normal rate, pitch, intonation, and rhythm (Brookshire & McNeil, 2014). The most frequently occurring fluent aphasia is *Wernicke's aphasia*, seen in about 15% of post-stroke aphasia cases (Godefroy et al., 2002). Damage in the superior temporal gyrus (Brodmann's area 22) is the classic lesion site leading to Wernicke's aphasia, although damage may extend into the inferior parietal lobe (Damasio, 2008). This subtype is characterized by fluent speech that is often semantically meaningless, contains frequent semantic and phonemic *paraphasias* (substitutions of words and sounds), and includes *neologisms* or jargon-like words (Davis, 1983; Owens, Metz, & Haas, 2000). *Conduction aphasia*, resulting from damage to the supramarginal gyrus, is fundamentally characterized by a primary deficit in repetition abilities with relatively spared fluency, although word-finding difficulties are frequently present (Damasio, 2008). *Transcortical sensory aphasia*, involving the angular gyrus and the posterior middle temporal gyrus, results in poor auditory comprehension with relatively intact repetition abilities and fluent speech (Davis, 1983; Owens et al., 2000). Finally, *anomic aphasia* is characterized by a disproportionate word-finding deficit in comparison to other symptoms, accompanied by primarily fluent speech. The lesion site can vary greatly, but generally involves the inferior temporal lobe (Damasio, 2008).

Non-fluent aphasias differ from the subtypes previously described in that the primary deficits exist in speech production with relatively spared language comprehension, and are generally a result of more anterior lesions than those causing fluent aphasias. As a group, these aphasias involve effortful and *agrammatic speech*. *Broca's aphasia* is associated with damage to the inferior frontal gyrus (Brodmann's areas 44 & 45), including the frontal operculum and possibly extending into the underlying white matter (Damasio, 2008). Individuals with Broca's aphasia produce *non-fluent speech*, often containing only content words and omitting *function words* (conjunctions, articles, prepositions), resulting in what is called *telegraphic speech*. They tend to have relatively good comprehension skills and are frequently aware of their deficits (Brookshire, 2007). *Transcortical motor aphasia* is characterized by non-fluent speech with preserved repetition abilities and is associated with damage to the left prefrontal or premotor cortices (Damasio, 2008). Finally, *global aphasia* is associated with more extensive damage to the left hemisphere language centers resulting in deficits of both expressive and receptive language skills.

Deficit and Recovery Patterns in Bilinguals

Nearly half the population of the world is bilingual or multilingual; therefore, it could be expected that half the cases of aphasia occur in bilingual people. In 2011, 27% of the population in the US, more than 60 million people, spoke a language other than English at home (Ryan, 2013). This increasing number of bilinguals has led to a rise of bilingual aphasia diagnosis, with 45,000 new cases in the US each year (Ansaldo et al., 2008). As echoed in other chapters of this volume, the study of language abilities in bilinguals (whether healthy or brain-injured) is a complex endeavor due to factors including varying definitions of bilingualism, differences in proficiency in each language, age of acquisition, *manner of acquisition*, and frequency of use of each language (Akbari, 2014; Kiran & Iakupova, 2011; Kiran, Roberts, Gitterman, Goral, & Obler, 2012; Roberts & Kiran, 2007). Factors that influence these areas, including language similarity, socioeconomic status, educational history, and relative social standing of each of the bilinguals' languages, must also be taken into account (Muñoz & Marquardt, 2003). As such, when considering the extent to which each language is affected by aphasia, one must always interpret performance after the neurological insult in terms of pre-insult functioning and in light of a detailed history of each individual's language acquisition, usage pattern, and literacy levels in each language, and the context in which each language is used and for what purposes.

There are three possible patterns of deficits among bilinguals with aphasia. In the most common pattern, the two languages are affected in a similar manner known as *parallel impairment*. In parallel impairment, an individual who is highly proficient in a first language and less proficient in an L2 would demonstrate the same pattern post-injury. For example, if an individual's speech is agrammatic and telegraphic in one language, the same would likely be true of the other language, taking into account relative premorbid proficiency. However, the structure of each of the individual's languages may play a role in how these symptoms are exhibited. Languages that are rich in morphological inflection (e.g., Spanish, German), for example, inherently provide more opportunities for noticeable morphological breakdown than less inflected languages (e.g., Mandarin, English). In terms of syntactic breakdowns, languages that rely more heavily on word order for meaning may appear more impaired than those that allow more flexibility in word order (Green, 2005; Lorenzen & Murray, 2008; Paradis, 1988).

Differential impairment exists when the two languages are impacted to different degrees when compared to premorbid abilities. This can take several forms. An individual who was previously more proficient in one language may appear equally proficient in both languages post-stroke. Alternatively, two languages that were approximately equal in terms of proficiency before brain injury may present with different proficiencies post-stroke. For example, Fabbro (2001) investigated a group of Friulian–Italian bilinguals and found that 65% were equally impaired in both languages, while 35% were differentially impaired. Similarly, Paradis (2001) found that 61% of reviewed aphasia cases exhibited parallel impairment, while 18% exhibited differential impairment. The extent to which each language is affected may differ based on the phase of recovery and the site of lesion. As Fabbro (2001) describes, during the *acute phase* (from the time of the stroke to 4 weeks post onset), the language deficits the patient experiences may be more dynamic. During the *lesion phase* (4 weeks to 4–5 months post onset), the pattern of deficits tends to be more closely associated with the site of the lesion. Finally, in the *late phase* (a few months post onset through the rest of the patient's life), deficits may be similar to those of the lesion phase or may continue to change as contralateral brain regions or unaffected regions of the same hemisphere "take over" the functions of the damaged brain regions (Fabbro, 2001).

Another possible deficit pattern is mixed or blended in which the individual blends linguistic elements from each of their languages in an uncontrolled and inappropriate way (Paradis, 1989). While healthy bilinguals may code-switch when speaking to other bilinguals, this switching is regulated by a rule system, while the mixing or blending that occurs with aphasia occurs regardless of the conversation partner and is not constrained by specific rules (Muñoz, Marquardt, & Copeland, 1999). Finally, *selective aphasia* refers to scenarios in which the brain injury affects only one of the individual's languages, while the other is left unaffected (Paradis & Goldblum, 1989). Research concerning why one language would be affected while the other is spared is ongoing. Some researchers have suggested that selective aphasia indicates that a bilingual's two languages are represented in different areas of the brain (Gomez-Tortosa, Martin, Gaviria, Charbel, & Ausman, 1995). However, Paradis' comprehensive research on bilingual aphasia suggests that the more tenable explanation is that languages are differentially inhibited, such that the activation threshold for one language becomes higher than that of the other language (Paradis, 1996).

In terms of recovery, there are six recognized patterns in bilingual aphasia. The most common of these is *parallel recovery* in which the individual's two languages recover to the same degree. This does not imply that the individual will be equally proficient in each of his languages, rather that the languages would recover according to the same pattern of strength that existed before the brain damage. *Differential recovery*, on the other hand, occurs when one language shows a steeper slope of recovery than the other when compared to premorbid abilities. *Antagonistic recovery* is seen when one language is recovered at the cost of the other. That is, that one language may be initially available yet will decline as the other language recovers. *Alternating antagonism* occurs when the above cycle repeats, causing an alternating pattern of recovery and availability of each of the two languages. *Successive recovery* refers to the recovery of one language before the other. Finally blended or mixed recovery refers to a recovery pattern in which there is involuntary mixing of the two languages during verbal expression (Paradis, 1989, 1998). These differential recovery patterns have been the subject of a large amount of research and have generated three hypotheses to explain their existence: (1) the lesion has damaged a part of the brain that only affects one language, implying that the bilingual's two languages are processed in separate brain regions (Albert & Obler, 1978); (2) the part of the brain that controls the switching between languages has been damaged; or (3) the language areas themselves are not damaged but inhibited such that the ability to access the information that is stored there is hindered (Abutalebi & Green, 2007; Paradis & Libben, 2014).

Aphasia in bilingual individuals has been shown to affect not only their language, but the cognitive processes that underlie language (Murray, 2012; Purdy, 2002). A common area in which cognitive control deficits have been observed is in the unintentional language mixing or *pathological code-switching* that occurs in some bilinguals with aphasia (Abutalebi, Della Rosa, Tettamanti, Green, & Cappa, 2009; Fabbro, Skrap, & Aglioti, 2000). This pattern of uncontrolled language mixing is theorized to be a result of deficits in the ability to inhibit unwanted cross-talk (i.e., prevent one of the languages from intruding during use of the other language; Kohnert, 2012). This inhibitory mechanism is constantly activated when typically developing bilinguals produce speech, because they must use one language at a time or carefully regulate code-switching (Green, 1998; Linck, Kroll, & Sunderman, 2009).

In a review of imaging studies pertaining to the cognitive control of language switching, Abutalebi and Green (2008) determined that the neural correlates for this switching mechanism included the anterior cingulate cortex, left prefrontal cortex, left caudate, and bilateral supramarginal gyri. When inhibition is disrupted, as is possible in bilinguals with aphasia who have damage to the previously mentioned areas, unwanted intrusions of one language into the other would be expected. As a result, some researchers have suggested that *cognitive therapy* may have a positive impact on language outcomes for bilinguals with aphasia (Coelho, 2005; Kohnert, 2004). For example, in a case study, Kohnert (2004) showed that a Spanish–English bilingual individual who received a cognitive-based training program that included no specific language training demonstrated improvements in the cognitive skills targeted as well as in Spanish and English language skills. Further exploration of the complex interaction of cognition and language in brain-injured populations is necessary to develop best practices for assessment and treatment in bilingual aphasia.

Assessment of Bilingual Aphasia

According to Ardila (2014) the assessment of an individual with aphasia should meet five fundamental goals: (1) determine if the individual's language is normal or abnormal; (2) analyze the symptoms and signs to identify underlying syndromes; (3) propose a rehabilitation procedure; (4) establish a differential diagnosis between similar conditions; and (5) propose pathologies that could be responsible for the language impairment. To reach these goals, six domains of language must be assessed: expressive language (including fluency, articulation, prosody, phonology, word selection, and grammar), language understanding, repetition, naming (external objects, body parts, colors, and actions), reading (mechanism of reading and reading comprehension), and writing (spontaneous, dictation, and copying).

The goal of the bilingual aphasia assessment is to determine the preserved and impaired communication skills in each language. This is why the assessment of bilingual aphasia should cover the same areas evaluated in a monolingual aphasia case, and additionally gather information about particular issues related to each of the languages. Age of acquisition of each language is important information because it may interact with the lesion location. Bilateral damage in large regions of the association cortex can have a bigger effect on a late acquired L2, while perisylvian left lesions are more likely to disrupt L1 (Ansaldo et al., 2008). Additionally, grammatical processing that requires more anterior temporal activation is more sensitive to L2 age of acquisition than semantic processing, which requires more posterior temporal-parietal regions activation (Neville & Mills, 1997). Therefore, differences in *syntactic processing* abilities for each language must be specified as a premorbid condition or as a result of post-aphasic language deficit.

Every bilingual aphasia assessment must include a *sociolinguistic questionnaire* focusing on the communication profile of the individual before the neurological incident. This information is very important because, in *late bilinguals* (those who acquired an L2 in adulthood), *morphosyntactic errors* due to low premorbid proficiency could be misinterpreted as consequences of a brain lesion (Ansaldo et al., 2008), given that morphosyntax is more affected by low language proficiency than semantics. Furthermore, premorbid language loss of L1 or a second or third language could be incorrectly interpreted as damage when it was, in fact, a natural process of language contact.

Fabbro (2001) describes three phases of aphasia that must be considered during the evaluation, as symptoms typically change along these phases without any intervention: (1) the acute phase generally lasts four weeks after onset. During this initial phase, several dynamic language disorders can be observed such as temporary *mutism*, relatively preserved comprehension in both languages, word-finding difficulties, and in general a more severe impairment for the less used language. (2) The lesion phase lasts for several weeks and sometimes even a few months. During this phase the language disorders can be more clearly correlated with the site and extent of the lesion. (3) The late phase begins a few months after onset and continues for the rest of the individual's life. It is during this late phase that the six different patterns of recovery described in the previous section can be observed.

Ideally, a monolingual speech-language pathologist should evaluate each language separately, using equivalent instruments that are psychometrically robust and culturally and linguistically adapted to each of the languages (Ansaldo et al., 2008). An example of an instrument developed considering language-pair specific characteristics and equivalency between languages is the *Bilingual Aphasia Test* (BAT). The BAT evaluates comprehension and production of linguistic competence and metalinguistic knowledge in various languages. It consists of three parts: Part A includes items to evaluate the individual's language history; part B is a systematic assessment that allows the clinician to compare the disorder in each of the languages the individual uses; and part C assesses the translation abilities and interference between language pairs. Part B is available in more than 60 languages, and part C in more than 150 pairs of languages. The relevance of the BAT is that the different language versions are not just translations. They are adaptations considered as culturally and linguistically equivalent tests (Paradis & Libben, 1987); however, validation is limited and thus, it is unclear how well it serves the different languages.

An important aspect of bilingual aphasia assessment is language switching. This refers to the ability to alternate between languages. In healthy bilinguals, it's under conscious control of the speaker, and depends on the environment, topic of the conversation, and the partner, so it can optimize communication (Ansaldo et al., 2008). The ability to switch languages appropriately is an important part of being bilingual and, therefore, of bilingual aphasia assessment. Language switching examination can demonstrate the individual's ability to maintain a target language with various levels of competition and control in different communication contexts and demands, which can give a clinician insight into language and executive control abilities of the individual.

Transcranial magnetic stimulation (TMS) and fMRI studies evidenced that the left dorsolateral prefrontal cortex plays a role in language switching. Hence, alternating between languages requires central executive functions' control (Hernandez et al., 2001). Individuals with lesions in the anterior portion of the cingulate gyrus and the white matter underlying the left frontal gyri showed pathological switching, where alternation between L1 and L2 occurred despite being instructed to speak in only one language and despite being aware of the switching (Hervais-Adelman, Moser-Mercer, & Golestani, 2011). Pathological switching could be a sign of bilingual aphasia or cognitive decline that causes pragmatic difficulties in communication with monolingual speakers.

Bilingual Aphasia Intervention

The first step for an effective intervention for individuals with aphasia is a comprehensive evaluation that clearly points out the specific deficits and needs of the individual. According to the American Speech and Hearing Association (ASHA), the goals of aphasia treatment include the following: (1) restoring language abilities by addressing all impaired communication modalities and focusing on training in those areas in which a person makes errors; (2) strengthening intact modalities and behaviors to support and augment communication compensating for language impairments by teaching strategies and by incorporating augmentative and alternative methods of communication if they help to improve communication; (3) training family and caregivers to effectively communicate with persons with aphasia, using communication supports and strategies in order to maximize communication competence; (4) facilitating generalization of skills and strategies in all communicative contexts; and (5) educating persons with aphasia, their families, caregivers, and other significant persons about the nature of spoken and/or written language disorders, the course of treatment, and prognosis for recovery.

Treatments for aphasia vary depending on the type of aphasia and the symptoms exhibited by the individual. *Constraint-induced language therapy* and *melodic intonation therapy* are two evidence-based treatments for increasing verbal output for individuals with non-fluent aphasias (Hurkmans et al., 2012; National Stroke Foundation, 2010). Constraint-induced language therapy consists of massed practice (2–4 hours per day) of using verbal communication while constraining the use of compensatory strategies such as writing or gesturing (Cherney, Patterson, Raymer, Frymark, & Schooling, 2008; Pulvermüller et al., 2001). Melodic intonation therapy is designed for patients with non-fluent aphasia and consists of intoning or "singing" phrases in just two pitches (higher pitch for stressed syllables and lower pitch for unstressed syllables) while the clinician taps the patient's left hand at each syllable and gradually fades support. This therapy is thought to capitalize on preserved brain function and recruit right hemisphere regions to compensate for damaged regions (Norton, Zipse, Marchina, & Schlaug, 2009). Response elaboration training and semantic feature analysis have been shown to improve word-finding abilities in individuals with aphasia (Boyle & Coelho, 1995; Chapey, 2001; Kearns, 1985). Response elaboration training focuses on shaping and expanding a patient's utterances while semantic feature analysis focuses on improving word retrieval by accessing semantically related words. A variety of treatment protocols for treating language comprehension exist. The *computer based microword treatment* (Crerar, Ellis, & Dean, 1996) is a computerized program that involves having patients organize sentences to match pictures presented or to organize pictures to match sentences presented on a computer screen. This therapy has a well-organized protocol and has been shown to improve comprehension of prepositions and verbs (Cherney & Robey, 2008). This list is by no means exhaustive, yet is a sample of evidence-based therapies for individuals with aphasia. When adapting these treatment strategies for use with a bilingual population, decisions about cueing strategies and establishing difficulty hierarchies should take into account characteristics of each language (Roberts, 2008).

A frequent question among clinicians treating bilingual individuals with aphasia is in which language(s) treatment should be provided. Although investigators have begun exploring what the best practices are for treating these individuals, there is no clear consensus in the field of which language(s) to use in treatment, for which individuals, and along which time course. There are three broad categories of treatment options for bilingual aphasia individuals: (1) monolingual (or unilingual) in which treatment is administered in the individual's first language, (2) monolingual in which treatment is administered in the individual's L2, and (3) bilingual in which the treatment is administered in both of the individual's languages.

For a long period in the history of the treatment of aphasia in bilinguals, it was considered that therapy should focus on one of the languages, especially in those cases where pathological switching was present (Chlenov, 1948; Fabbro, 2001; Wald, 1961). Typically only one language was rehabilitated under the argument that intervention in more than one language could confuse the individual with aphasia, interfering with global recovery and therefore wasting rehabilitation time. Additionally, it was believed that the benefits of intervention in a single language might extend to the other languages (Fabbro, 2001). The goal of monolingual approaches to therapy was and is to improve the language being treated but also to bring about cross-linguistic transfer. Cross-linguistic transfer refers to the phenomenon in which language skills that are treated in one language generalize to the other language without any direct treatment in that other language (Faroqi-Shah, Frymark, Mullen, & Wang, 2010).

The evidence regarding which approach is the most effective and the extent to which skills transfer between languages is mixed. Kohnert and Derr (2004) found that word-retrieval treatment provided in L2 produced cross-linguistic transfer for both *cognate* and *non-cognate* words, but only cognate words transferred when treatment was provided in L1. A recent meta-analysis by Faroqi-Shah et al. (2010) suggested that treatment in an individual's L2 improves receptive and expressive language, but evidence for cross-linguistic transfer to the untreated language was mixed. Edmonds and Kiran (2006) examined training of non-cognate words and checked for evidence of cross-linguistic transfer in three Spanish–English bilinguals. One of the individuals was a balanced bilingual and showed cross-linguistic transfer both within- and across-language transfer after a naming intervention. However, two other individuals who were more proficient in Spanish than in English did not demonstrate cross-linguistic transfer when treatment was in Spanish, their stronger language. Instead, these individuals demonstrated cross-linguistic transfer only when treated in English, their weaker language. The authors concluded that treatment for *unbalanced bilinguals* (i.e., those that are markedly more proficient in one of their two languages) might be more effective if delivered in the individual's weaker language. However, Croft, Marshall, Pring, and Hardwick (2011) found evidence of cross-linguistic transfer when treatment occurred in the individual's dominant language. Some authors suggest that cross-linguistic transfer of therapy effects are more likely to be observed in early bilinguals (i.e., those that acquired both languages as children) than in late bilinguals (i.e., those that acquired an L2 in adulthood) and that individuals with aphasia tend to demonstrate better recovery of the language that was most familiar to them prior to the neurological event, given that stronger associations in the most frequently spoken language can resist the effects of brain damage more efficiently (Ansaldo et al., 2008).

Other research suggests that intervention in one language does not transfer to other languages and may even be detrimental for those languages not being treated. A native Spanish speaker, who migrated with his family to Italy at the age of 16, presented a fluent aphasia with severe anomia (i.e., fluent speech with word-finding deficits) due to cerebral hemorrhage at the age of 56. Behavioral and neuroimaging measures were taken four weeks after the neurological event (T0), after a deficit-specific language intervention focused on picture naming conducted for six weeks (T1), and after a global language intervention that lasted 16 weeks (T2). The intervention was conducted in Italian language (L2) only. At T0 more impairment in picture naming was observed in Italian than in Spanish, but at T2 there was a greater impairment in Spanish while Italian was fully recovered. Accordingly, the naming task displayed similar brain activity for L1 and L2 during T0. At T1, there was a much more extended activation for L2 and only a slight increase in connectivity for L1. At T2, the overall progressive increase in connectivity for Italian remained, while a decrease of strength of connections was observed for Spanish (Abutalebi et al., 2009). The authors of the study concluded that reactivation of cortical areas that mediated naming only occurred for the language being trained and did not generalize for other languages. Apparently, the recovery of the treated language can "inhibit" the recovery of the non-treated language and begins a pattern of antagonistic recovery for that language.

More recently, speech-language pathologists are favoring bilingual intervention, especially in those cases of proficient bilinguals with aphasia, living in bilingual environments. Ansaldo and colleagues (2008) developed the *switch back through translation therapy approach*, which improved language control and word retrieval in one case of a Spanish–English bilingual individual. Hinckley (2003) provided bilingual therapy and saw gains in both languages; albeit these gains were more pronounced in the individual's L1. Kohnert (2004) provided cognitive therapy first in Spanish, then in English, and found improvement in both languages, but more between-language generalization for cognate than non-cognate words.

Until more conclusive data from clinical trials is available, when planning an intervention program for a bilingual individual with aphasia, the clinician must consider relevant aspects of the individual and his/her environment to determine the language or languages in which the intervention will be conducted. The decision should consider which language is preferred for the individual and his/her family, because motivational factors can influence the effectiveness of the therapy. Also, factors such as which language is most functional for the individual in their place of residence, caregivers' language, and job requirements will be key variables for the individual's wellbeing. Finally, the clinician must consider which resources are available for therapy, for example if a bilingual speech-language pathologist is available or if there is a family member who can assist and support the intervention in L2, it could be possible to conduct a rehabilitation program that covers multiple languages relevant for the individual. Translation approaches to intervention may be used in those situations to help the patient use and practice the different languages, when the clinician does not speak one of them. In general, if a patient needs and uses both languages, intervention should address both languages, and evidence indicates that bilingual intervention will improve both languages.

Degenerative Disease in Bilingual Adults

The population is getting older in almost every country in the world. The percentage of people 60 years or over has been increasing constantly, from 9.2% in 1990, to 11.7% in 2013, and is expected to be 21.1% (more than 2 billion people) in 2050 (United Nations, Department of Economic and Social Affairs, Population Division, 2013). This is why communication disorders affecting the aging population are becoming more common, and more research is being conducted to understand dementia-related language decline.

Most of the research done in this area has focused on *Alzheimer's disease* (AD), the most well-known form of dementia. The primary *linguistic deficits* identified in AD research are word retrieval, sentence comprehension, and cohesion in discourse (Kempler & Goral, 2008). Patients with AD demonstrate diminished semantic knowledge of both nouns (Chan, Butters, & Salmon, 1997; Hodges, Salmon, & Butters, 1991) and verbs (Grossman, Mickanin, Onishi, Robinson, & D'Esposito, 1997; Koenig, Thomas-Antérion, & Laurent, 1999). Some controversy has surrounded whether these language deficits result from impairments in extralinguistic factors such as attention and memory, or whether they result from a deterioration of the *semantic system*. In the early stages, word-finding difficulties may be more related to cognitive rather than linguistic deficits (Rogers, Ivanoiu, Patterson, & Hodges, 2006). Some argue that word-finding problems are the result of difficulty with effortful retrieval, because the semantic system is still intact, but accessing the information is the primary deficit (McGlinchey-Berroth, Milberg, Verfaellie, Alexander, & Kilduff, 1993; Nebes, Martin, & Horn, 1984; Ober, Shenaut, & Reed, 1995). Similarly, sentence comprehension and discourse deficits have been attributed to working memory impairment (Almor, Kempler, MacDonald, Andersen, & Tyler, 1999; Kempler, Almor, & MacDonald, 1998). However, as the disease progresses, there is increasing evidence of the deterioration of the semantic system (Aronoff et al., 2006).

During the last decade, much research has been conducted in bilingual patients with AD. Results suggest that bilingualism may serve as a protective factor against the onset of dementia-related symptoms, delaying them for as many as five years (Bialystok, Craik, & Freedman, 2007, 2010; Bialystok, Craik, Klein, & Viswanathan, 2004). Some studies controlling for variables such as age, ethnic group, level of cognitive and memory performance, and years of education, confirmed that bilingualism is a factor that modulates the behavioral expression of underlying neuropathology in AD (Gold, Johnson, & Powell, 2013; Gollan, Salmon, Montoya, & Galasko, 2011; Schweizer, Ware, Fischer, Craik, & Bialystok, 2012). These results have been associated with the concept of *cognitive reserve*. Cognitive reserve is the capacity to maintain cognitive functioning under circumstances of neuropathological damage, as the result of experience-based neural changes that are a consequence of mental activity (Bialystok, Craik, & Luk, 2012). L2 learning requires several cognitive processes, such as working memory, inductive reasoning, sound discrimination, *speech segmentation*, *task switching*, *rule learning*, and semantic memory. These processes involve extensive networks in the brain that overlap with the networks that decline with aging (Antoniou, Gunasekera, & Wong, 2013); therefore L2 learning has the potential to support and benefit cognitive reserve.

After the onset of dementia-related symptoms, studies focused on language abilities and language deficit patterns in bilinguals with AD have reported conflicting results. A group of studies concluded that the non-dominant language is more impaired than the dominant one. For example, a study with bilingual speakers of English and Afrikaans revealed that inappropriate language mixing occurred more frequently during a conversation using the non-dominant language even at early stages of AD (Friedland & Miller, 1999). Similarly, a group of caregivers of bilingual patients with dementia (31 of them with AD) reported decreased use of the non-dominant language and word intrusions from the dominant to the non-dominant language (Mendez, Perryman, Pontón, & Cummings, 1999). Meguro et al. (2003) observed that in Japanese–Portuguese bilingual patients with AD living in Brazil, there was a greater deterioration of the less used Japanese language in comparison to the Portuguese-dominant language. In contrast, Gollan, Salmon, Montoya, and da Pena (2010) designed a study to compare how AD affects Spanish–English bilinguals' ability to access picture names in their dominant and non-dominant languages. They found that the naming score that yielded the largest difference between control bilinguals and those with AD was the dominant-language naming score. Hence, the authors concluded that the non-dominant language is not particularly vulnerable to AD.

More recent studies are finding a similar level of deterioration in both languages. Costa and colleagues (2012) found that the cognitive decline associated with AD decreased the ability to name pictures in the two languages to a comparable degree. Additionally, the word translation ability between the two languages was comparable and decreased to similar extents in the two languages. The authors concluded that cognitive decline affects the two languages of a bilingual similarly, which is consistent with the notion that for proficient bilinguals, the two languages are represented within a common underlying brain network. Salvatierra, Rosselli, Acevedo, and Duara (2007) found that patients with AD did not have more difficulty in retrieving words in L2 as compared to L1. They showed a similar pattern of decline in both languages, suggesting that the semantic verbal fluency difficulties typically observed in bilingual AD patients occur regardless of the language used.

A second line of research related to bilingual patients with degenerative disease is focused on the effects of *Parkinson's disease* (PD) on language. PD is a progressive neurological movement disorder, associated with slow deterioration of subcortical structures and dopamine deficiency, and the disruption of circuits connecting the frontal lobe with the basal ganglia (Murray, 2008). In relation to language, PD patients typically have morphosyntactic processing difficulties, lexical-semantic retrieval deficits where action naming is more affected than object naming, and comprehension difficulties, especially comprehending implied information, figurative content, metaphors, or interpretation of lexical ambiguity (Murray, 2008).

In bilingual populations with PD, research has revealed that the L1 is typically more affected than the L2. Zanini et al. (2004) conducted a study to compare 12 Friulian–Italian bilingual PD patients, with 12 normal controls matched for age, sex, and years of schooling, on the performance of syntactic tasks. They found poorer performance of sentence comprehension and *grammaticality judgment tasks* (i.e., tasks in which participants are asked to read a sentence and decide if it is grammatically correct or incorrect) in the L1 (Friulian) versus L2 (Italian) in this group of PD patients. This result has been replicated in more recent studies. For example, Johari et al. (2013) found that PD patients had greater linguistic impairments in L1 than L2, and greater L1 impairments than healthy controls. This study showed that, on the sentence comprehension test, PD patients performed poorer on almost all sentence structures in L1 than in L2, and concluded that there is a general grammatical impairment for the L1 in patients with PD. In terms of language production, PD patients scored lower than normal controls in *spontaneous speech* measures, with more severe deficits in L1 than in L2. Specifically, patients with PD displayed simplified syntax, morphological and syntactic deficits particularly in the use of *closed-class words* and inflectional morphology, and made almost fifteen times more phonemic paraphasias in L1 than in L2 and four times more than normal controls in L1 (Zanini, Tavano, & Fabbro, 2010).

The cross-linguistic difference observed in L1 with respect to L2 performance in PD patients has been attributed to several aspects of PD. Some researchers emphasize the difficulty PD patients have in accessing *procedural knowledge* (the type of knowledge required to perform in a specific task, or "know-how" which is typically nonconscious) of L1, while access to the declarative knowledge (the type of knowledge expressed verbally as a fact or an argument; "know-of") more associated with L2 is more preserved (Zanini et al., 2004). Others are more focused on the dysfunctional frontal-subcortical language network (Murray, 2008; Zanini et al., 2010). Cattaneo et al. (2015) explored the role of basal ganglia network's dysfunctions and its impact on the bilingual language control system. In a language switching task, they found that PD patients were slower, made more errors, had increased switch costs, and were less accurate in L1 than in L2 as compared to controls. Researchers concluded that dysfunctions in the basal ganglia's network may lead to difficulties in the control of two languages, due to a deficient ability to select the target language and avoid cross-language interference.

The ability to maintain fluency and speak with minimal errors in more than one language decreases with advancing age. Therefore, it is expected that these effects will be exacerbated in patients with some type of dementia, and symptoms will be associated with the site of lesion. If the degenerative disease has a selective or greater effect on declarative memory, the later learned languages will be predominantly affected (e.g., AD), but if procedural memory is more affected, the L1 will present more impairment (e.g., PD; Paradis, 2008). However, more research is necessary before anything conclusive can be said about the effects of degenerative diseases on bilingual patients.

Summary and Conclusions

In summary, language disorders in bilingual children and adults provide information on how language contact alters the development and representation of the disorders. At the same time, bilingual children and adults maintain some of the language characteristics seen in the monolingual population. Bilingual children are at risk of overrepresentation in special education if there is limited input in the home language. On the other hand, bilingual children with language disorders need input in both languages to continue their development in the two languages. Language processing in bilingual children and adults presents benefits and challenges. More research is needed to examine if the benefits in typical populations extend to bilingual populations with disorders. Adult language disorders in bilingual populations, whether they are acquired or degenerative, present distinct profiles and differences from those in monolingual populations in terms of deficit patterns, recovery, and impact on the two languages. Bilingual patients are important in helping us understand how language is processed and represented in the brain, and what linguistic aspects are more vulnerable in each language and across languages and language classes. The bilingual individual has bilingual needs regardless of where they are in their lifespan, and these needs must be thoroughly assessed and considered in intervention.

List of Key Words and Concepts

Acute phase, Additive-language, Agrammatic speech, Alternating antagonism, Alzheimer's disease (AD), Anomic aphasia, Antagonistic recovery, Aphasia, Apraxia, Autism, Bilingual aphasia test (BAT), Broca's aphasia, Cerebral vascular accident (CVA), Closed-class words, Code-switching, Cognate, Cognitive etiologies, Cognitive reserve, Cognitive therapy, Communicative development inventories, Computer based microword treatment, Conceptual vocabulary, Conduction aphasia, Constraint-induced language therapy, Cross-linguistic transfer, Cross-linguistic transfer therapy, Differential impairment, Differential recovery, Down's syndrome, Dynamic assessment, Dysarthria, Elicited grammatical task, Event-related potentials (ERPs), Expressive language, Fluent aphasia, Functional magnetic resonance imaging (fMRI), Function words, Global aphasia, Global-local task, Grammaticality judgment tasks, Language loss, Language proficiency, Language transfer, Late bilinguals, Late phase, Left hemisphere, Lesion phase, Lexical processing, Linguistic deficits, MacArthur-Bates Communicative Development Inventories, Manner of acquisition, Mean length of utterance, Melodic intonation therapy, Metalinguistic skills, Mismatch negativity (MMN), Morphosyntactic errors, Mutism, Narrative structure, Neologisms, Non-cognate, Non-fluent aphasia, Non-fluent speech, P100, Parallel impairment, Parallel recovery, Paraphasias, Parkinson's disease (PD), Pathological code-switching, Phoneme discrimination, Phonological awareness, Portfolio assessment, Positive transfer, Primary language impairment (PLI), Procedural knowledge, Rapid processing, Rapid successive sounds, Receptive language, Right hemisphere, Rule learning, Selective aphasia, Semantic processing, Semantic system, Sensory etiologies, Sequential bilinguals, Simultaneous bilinguals, Sociolinguistic questionnaire, Sound discrimination, Speech segmentation, Spontaneous speech, Stuttering, Subtractive-language, Successive recovery, Switch back through translation therapy approach, Syntactic processing, Task switching, Telegraphic speech, Trail-making task, Transcortical motor aphasia, Transcortical sensory aphasia, Transcranial magnetic stimulation (TMS), Transfer therapy, Typically developing language (TD), Unbalanced bilingual, Wernicke's aphasia, word order, Working memory

Internet Sites Related to the Psycholinguistics of Bilingualism

Bilinguistics: http://bilinguistics.com/
Habla Lab: https://hablalab.wordpress.com/
Lifespan Cognition and Development Lab: http://lcad.lab.yorku.ca/
Max Planck Institute for Psycholinguistics: http://www.mpi.nl

Discussion Questions

(1) Why are bilingual children over represented in special education or as presenting language disorders?
(2) Is language in bilinguals represented differently in the brain than in monolinguals?
(3) What factors should be considered when assessing language in bilinguals after a stroke?
(4) Do bilingual children develop more slowly in language than monolingual children?
(5) Should bilingual children and adults with language disorders be treated only in one language?
(6) What is the evidence of *cross-linguistic transfer* in bilinguals? Which skills transfer and under what conditions?

Suggested Research Projects

(1) Develop an experiment that addresses how early bilingualism affects metalinguistic skills in children.
(2) Develop an intervention in a bilingual child or adult in one language, and examine whether it transfers to the other language.
(3) Take a random sample of bilingual patients with aphasia and examine their recovery patterns.
(4) Examine language inhibition in bilingual children or adults and compare to their monolingual counterparts.

Suggested Readings

Abutalebi, J., Tettamanti, M., & Perani, D. (2009). The bilingual brain: Linguistic and non-linguistic skills. *Brain and Language, 109*(2–3), 51–54.

Barrueco, S., Lopez, M., Ong, C., & Lozano, P. (2012). *Assessing Spanish–English bilingual preschoolers: A guide to best approaches and measures.* Baltimore, MD: Brookes Publishing Company.

Faroqi-Shàh, Y., Frymark, T., Mullen, R., & Wang, B. (2010). Effect of treatment for bilingual individuals with aphasia: A systematic review of the evidence. *Journal of Neurolinguistics, 23*(4), 319–341.

Goldstein, B. (Ed.). (2012). *Bilingual language development and disorders in Spanish–English speakers.* Baltimore, MD: Brooks Publishing.

Kohnert, K. (2013). *Language disorders in bilingual children and adults.* San Diego, CA: Plural Publishing Inc.

Meinzer, M., Obleser, J., Flaisch, T., Eulitz, C., & Rockstroh, B. (2007). Recovery from aphasia as a function of language therapy in an early bilingual patient demonstrated by fMRI. *Neuropsychologia, 45*, 1247–1256.

Steinhauer, K. (2014). Event-related potentials (ERPs) in second language research: A brief introduction to the technique, a selected review, and an invitation to reconsider critical periods in L2. *Applied Linguistics, 35*(4), 393–417.

Thordardottir, E. (2015). Proposed diagnostic procedures for use in bilingual and cross-linguistic contexts. In S. Armon-Lotem, J. de Jong, & N. Meir (Eds.), *Methods for assessing multilingual children: Disentangling bilingualism from language impairment* (pp. 331–358). Bristol, UK: Multilingual Matters.

References

Abutalebi, J., Della Rosa, P. A., Tettamanti, M., Green, D. W., & Cappa, S. F. (2009). Bilingual aphasia and language control: A follow-up fMRI and intrinsic connectivity study. *Brain and Language, 109*, 141–156.

Abutalebi, J., & Green, D. (2007). Bilingual language production: The neurocognition of language representation and control. *Journal of Neurolinguistics, 20*(3), 242–275.

Abutalebi, J., & Green, D. W. (2008). Control mechanisms in bilingual language production: Neural evidence from language switching studies. *Language and Cognitive Processes, 23*(4), 557–582.

Abutalebi, J., Tettamanti, M., & Perani, D. (2009). The bilingual brain: Linguistic and non-linguistic skills. *Brain and Language, 109*(2–3), 51–54.

Akbari, M. (2014). A multidimensional review of bilingual aphasia as a language disorder. *Advances in Language and Literacy Studies, 5*(2), 73–86.

Albert, M. L., & Obler, L. K. (1978). *The bilingual brain: Neuropsychological and neurolinguistic aspects of bilingualism*. New York: Academic Press.

Almor, A., Kempler, D., MacDonald, M. C., Andersen, E. S., & Tyler, L. K. (1999). Why do Alzheimer patients have difficulty with pronouns? Working memory, semantics, and reference in comprehension and production in Alzheimer's disease. *Brain and Language, 67*(3), 202–227.

Anderson, S. R. (2012). *Languages: A very short introduction*. Oxford, UK: Oxford University Press.

Ansaldo, A. I., Marcotte, K., Scherer, L., & Raboyeau, G. (2008). Language therapy and bilingual aphasia: Clinical implications of psycholinguistic and neuroimaging research. *Journal of Neurolinguistics, 21*, 539–557.

Antoniou, M., Gunasekera, G., & Wong, P. C. M. (2013). Foreign language training as cognitive therapy for age-related cognitive decline: A hypothesis for future research. *Neuroscience and Biobehavioral Reviews, 37*, 1–10.

Ardila, A. (2014). *Aphasia handbook*. Miami, FL: Florida International University. Retrieved from https://aalfredoardila.files.wordpress.com/2013/07/ardila-a-2014-aphasia-handbook-miami-fl-florida-international-university2.pdf

Aronoff, J. M., Gonnerman, L. M., Almor, A., Arunachalam, S., Kempler, D., & Andersen, E. S. (2006). Information content versus relational knowledge: Semantic deficits in patients with Alzheimer's disease. *Neuropsychologia, 44*(1), 21–35.

Barragan, B., Castilla-Earls, A., Martinez-Nieto, L., Restrepo, M. A., & Gray, S. (2017). *Performance of low-income dual language learners attending English-only schools on the CELF-4 Spanish.* Manuscript submitted for publication.

Bedore, L. M., Peña, E. D., Joyner, D., & Macken, C. (2011). Parent and teacher rating of bilingual language proficiency and language development concerns. *International Journal of Bilingual Education and Bilingualism, 14*(5), 489–511.

Bialystok, E., Craik, F. I., & Freedman, M. (2007). Bilingualism as a protection against the onset of symptoms of dementia. *Neuropsychologia, 45*(2), 459–464.

Bialystok, E., Craik, F. I. M., & Freedman, M. (2010). Delaying the onset of Alzheimer's disease. *Neurology, 75*, 1726–1729.

Bialystok, E., Craik, F. I., Klein, R., & Viswanathan, M. (2004). Bilingualism, aging, and cognitive control: Evidence from the Simon task. *Psychology and Aging, 19*(2), 290–303.

Bialystok, E., Craik, F. I. M., & Luk, G. (2012). Bilingualism: Consequences for mind and brain. *Trends in Cognitive Sciences, 16*(4), 240–249.

Bialystok, E., & Feng, X. (2005). Language proficiency and executive control in proactive interference: Evidence from monolingual and bilingual children and adults. *Brain and Language, 109*(2–3), 93–100.

Bialystok, E., Luk, G., & Kwan, E. (2005). Bilingualism, biliteracy, and learning to read: Interactions among languages and writing systems. *Scientific Studies of Reading, 9*(1), 43–61.

Bialystok, E., Majumder, S., & Martin, M. M. (2003). Developing phonological awareness: Is there a bilingual advantage? *Applied Psycholinguistics, 24*, 27–44.

Bird, E. K. R. (2009). Bilingualism and children with Down syndrome. *Perspectives on Language Learning and Education, 16*(3), 90–96.

Bird, E. K. R., Cleave, P., Trudeau, N., Thordardottir, E., Sutton, A., & Thorpe, A. (2005). The language abilities of bilingual children with Down syndrome. *American Journal of Speech-Language Pathology, 14*(3), 187–199.

Blom, E., & Paradis, J. (2013). Past tense production by English second language learners with and without language impairment. *Journal of Speech, Language, and Hearing Research, 56*(1), 281–294.

Boudreau, D. M., & Hedberg, N. L. (1999). A comparison of early literacy skills in children with specific language impairment and their typically developing peers. *American Journal of Speech-Language Pathology, 8*(3), 249–260.

Boyle, M., & Coelho, C. A. (1995). Application of semantic feature analysis as a treatment for aphasic dysnomia. *American Journal of Speech-Language Pathology, 4*(4), 94–98.

Brookshire, R. H. (2007). *Introduction to neurogenic communication disorders*. St. Louis, MO: Mosby, Elsevier.

Brookshire, R. H., & McNeil, M. R. (2014). *Introduction to neurogenic communication disorders*, (7th ed.). St Louis, MO: Elsevier Health Sciences.

Bruck, M. (1982). Language impaired children's performance in an additive bilingual education program. *Applied Psycholinguistics, 3*, 45–60.

Castilla-Earls, A. P., Restrepo, M. A., Pérez-Leroux, A. T., Gray, S., Holmes, P., Gail, D., & Chen, Z. (2015). Interactions between bilingual effects and language impairment: Exploring grammatical markers in Spanish-speaking bilingual children. *Applied Psycholinguistics, 37*(5), 1147–1173.

Cattaneo, G., Calabria, M., Marne, P., Gironell, A., Abutalebi, J., & Costa, A. (2015). The role of executive control in bilingual language production: A study with Parkinson's disease individuals. *Neuropsychologia, 66*, 99–110.

Catts, H. W. (1991). Early identification of dyslexia: Evidence from a follow-up study of speech-language impaired children. *Annals of Dyslexia, 41*, 163–177.

Chan, A. S., Butters, N., & Salmon, D. P. (1997). The deterioration of semantic networks in patients with Alzheimer's disease: A cross-sectional study. *Neuropsychologia, 35*(3), 241–248.

Chapey, R. (2001). Cognitive stimulation: Stimulation of recognition/comprehension, memory, and convergent, divergent, and evaluative thinking. In R. Chapey (Ed.), *Language intervention strategies in aphasia and related neurogenic communication disorders* (4th ed.) (pp. 397–434). Baltimore, MA: Lippincott, Williams & Wilkins.

Chee, M. W., Soon, C. S., & Lee, H. L. (2003). Common and segregated neuronal networks for different languages revealed using functional magnetic resonance adaptation. *Journal of Cognitive Neuroscience, 15*(1), 85–97.

Cherney, L. R., Patterson, J. P., Raymer, A., Frymark, T., & Schooling, T. (2008). Evidence-based systematic review: Effects of intensity of treatment and constraint-induced language therapy for individuals with stroke-induced aphasia. *Journal of Speech, Language, and Hearing Research, 51*(5), 1282–1299.

Cherney, L. R., & Robey, R. R. (2008). Aphasia treatment: Recovery, prognosis, and clinical effectiveness. In R. Chapey (Ed.), *Language intervention strategies in aphasia and related neurogenic communication disorders* (5th ed.) (pp. 186–202). Philadelphia, PA: Lippincott, Williams & Wilkins.

Chlenov, L. G. (1948/1983). On aphasia in polyglots. In M. Paradis (Ed.), *Readings on aphasia in bilinguals and polyglots* (pp. 445–454). Montreal: Didier. (Original work published 1948).

Chondrogianni, V., & Marinis, T. (2011). Differential effects of internal and external factors on the development of vocabulary, tense morphology and morpho-syntax in successive bilingual children. *Linguistic Approaches to Bilingualism, 1*(3), 318–345.

Coelho, C. (2005). Direct attention training as a treatment for reading impairment in mild aphasia. *Aphasiology*, *19*(3–5), 275–283.

Conboy, B. T., & Mills, D. L. (2006). Two languages, one developing brain: Event-related potentials to words in bilingual toddlers. *Developmental Science*, *9*, 1–12.

Core, C., Hoff, E., Rumiche, R., & Señor, M. (2013). Total and conceptual vocabulary in Spanish–English bilinguals from 22 to 30 months: Implications for assessment. *Journal of Speech, Language, and Hearing Research*, *56*(5), 1637–1649.

Costa, A., Calabria, M., Marne, P., Hernández, M., Juncadella, M., Gascón-Bayarri, J., Lleó, A., Ortiz-Gil, J., Ugas, L., Blesa, R., & Reñé, R. (2012). On the parallel deterioration of lexico-semantic processes in the bilinguals' two languages: Evidence from Alzheimer's disease. *Neuropsychologia*, *50*, 740–753.

Crerar, M. A., Ellis, A. W., & Dean, E. C. (1996). Remediation of sentence processing deficits in aphasia using a computer-based microworld. *Brain and Language*, *52*(1), 229–275.

Croft, S., Marshall, J., Pring, T., & Hardwick, M. (2011). Therapy for naming difficulties in bilingual aphasia: Which language benefits? *International Journal of Language and Communication Disorders*, *46*, 48–62.

Damasio, H. (2008). Neural basis of language disorders. In R. Chapey (Ed.), *Language intervention strategies in aphasia and related neurogenic communication disorders* (5th ed.) (pp. 20–41). Philadelphia, PA: Lippincott Williams & Wilkins.

Davis, G. A. (1983). *A survey of adult aphasia*. Englewood Cliffs, NJ: Prentice-Hall.

Dromi, E., Leonard, L. B., Adam, G., & Zadunaisky-Ehrlich, S. (1999). Verb agreement morphology in Hebrew-speaking children with specific language impairment. *Journal of Speech, Language and Hearing Research*, *42*, 1414–1431.

Eadie, P. A., Fey, M. E., Douglas, J. M., & Parsons, C. L. (2002). Profiles of grammatical morphology and sentence imitation in children with specific language impairment and Down's Syndrome. *Journal of Speech, Language, and Hearing Research*, *45*, 720–732.

Edmonds, L. A., & Kiran, S. (2006). Effect of semantic naming treatment on crosslinguistic generalization in bilingual aphasia. *Journal of Speech, Language, and Hearing Research*, *49*(4), 729–748.

Fabbro, F. (2001). The bilingual brain: Bilingual aphasia. *Brain and Language*, *79*, 201–210.

Fabbro, F., Skrap, M., & Aglioti, S. (2000). Pathological switching between languages after frontal lesions in a bilingual patient. *Journal of Neurology, Neurosurgery and Psychiatry*, *68*, 650–652.

Faroqi-Shah, Y., Frymark, T., Mullen, R., & Wang, B. (2010). Effect of treatment for bilingual individuals with aphasia: A systematic review of the evidence. *Journal of Neurolinguistics*, *23*(4), 319–341.

Fiebach, C. J., Friederici, A. D., Müller, K., von Cramon, D. Y., & Hernandez, A. E. (2003). Distinct brain representations for early and late learned words. *NeuroImage*, *19*(4), 1627–1637.

Fiestas, C. E. (2008). *The dynamic assessment of narratives: A bilingual study* (Doctoral dissertation). Retrieved from ProQuest http://search.proquest.com/docview/304474223

Friedland, D., & Miller, N. (1999). Language mixing in bilingual speakers with Alzheimer's dementia: A conversation analysis approach. *Aphasiology*, *13*(4–5), 427–444.

Friedrich, M., Weber, C., & Friederici, A. D. (2004). Electrophysiological evidence for delayed mismatch response in infants at-risk for specific language impairment. *Psychophysiology*, *41*, 772–782.

Godefroy, O., Dubois, C., Debachy, B., LeClerc, M., Kreisler, A., & Lille Stroke Program. (2002). Vascular aphasia: Main characteristics of patients hospitalized in acute stroke units. *Stroke*, *33*(3), 702–705.

Gold, B. T., Johnson, N. F., & Powell, D. K. (2013). Lifelong bilingualism contributes to cognitive reserve against white matter integrity declines in aging. *Neuropsychologia*, *51*, 2841–2846.

Gollan, T. H., Salmon, D. P., Montoya, R. I., & da Pena, E. (2010). Accessibility of the nondominant language in picture naming: A counterintuitive effect of dementia on bilingual language production. *Neuropsychologia*, *48*, 1356–1366.

Gollan, T. H., Salmon, D. P., Montoya, R. I., & Galasko, D. R. (2011). Degree of bilingualism predicts age of diagnosis of Alzheimer's disease in low-education but not in highly educated Hispanics. *Neuropsychologia*, *49*, 3826–3830.

Gomez-Ruiz, M. I. (2010). Bilingualism and the brain: Myth and reality. *Neurologia, 25*(7), 443–452.

Gomez-Tortosa, E., Martin, E. M., Gaviria, M., Charbel, F., & Ausman, J. I. (1995). Selective deficit of one language in a bilingual patient following surgery in the left perisylvian area. *Brain and Language, 48*(3), 320–325.

Green, D. W. (1998). Mental control of the bilingual lexico-semantic system. *Bilingualism: Language and Cognition, 1*(2), 67–81.

Green, D. W. (2005). The neurocognition of recovery patterns in bilingual aphasics. In J. F. Kroll & A. M. B. de Groot (Eds.), *Handbook of bilingualism: Psycholinguistic perspectives* (pp. 516–530). New York: Oxford University Press.

Grossman, M., Mickanin, J., Onishi, K., Robinson, K. M., & D'Esposito, M. (1997). Lexical acquisition in probable Alzheimer's disease. *Brain and Language, 60*(3), 443–463.

Gutierrez-Clellen, V. F., & Kreiter, J. (2003). Understanding child bilingual acquisition using parent and teacher reports. *Applied Linguistics, 24*, 267–288.

Halsband, U., Krause, B. J., Sipilä, H., Teräs, M., & Laihinen, A. (2002). PET studies on the memory processing of word pairs in bilingual Finnish–English subjects. *Behavioural Brain Research, 132*(1), 47–57.

Hernandez, A. E., Dapretto, M., Mazziotta, J., & Bookheimer, S. (2001). Language switching and language representation in Spanish–English bilinguals: An fMRI study. *NeuroImage, 14*(2), 510–520.

Hernandez, A. E., & Li, P. (2007). Age of acquisition: Its neural and computational mechanisms. *Psychological Bulletin, 133*(4), 638–650.

Hernandez, A. E., & Meschyan, G. (2006). Executive function is necessary to enhance lexical processing in a less proficient L2: Evidence from fMRI during picture naming. *Bilingualism: Language and Cognition, 9*(2), 177–188.

Hervais-Adelman, A. G., Moser-Mercer, B., & Golestani, N. (2011). Executive control of language in the bilingual brain: integrating the evidence from neuroimaging to neuropsychology. *Frontiers in Psychology, 2*, 1–8

Hinckley, J. (2003). Picture naming treatment in aphasia yields greater improvement in L1. *Brain and Language, 87*, 171–172.

Hodges, J. R., Salmon, D. P., & Butters, N. (1991). The nature of the naming deficit in Alzheimer's and Huntington's disease. *Brain, 114*(4), 1547–1558.

Hugdahl, K., Gundersen, H., Brekke, C., Thomsen, T., Rimol, L. M., Ersland, L., & Niemi, J. (2004). MRI brain activation in a Finnish family with specific language impairment compared with a normal control group. *Journal of Speech, Language, and Hearing Research, 47*, 162–173.

Hurkmans, J., De Bruijn, M., Boonstra, A. M., Jonkers, R., Bastiaanse, R., Arendzen, H., & Reinders-Messelink, H. A. (2012). Music in the treatment of neurological language and speech disorders: A systematic review. *Aphasiology, 26*(1), 1–19.

Im-Bolter, N., Johnson, J., & Pascual-Leone, J. (2006). Processing limitations in children with specific language impairment: The role of executive function. *Child Development, 77*(6), 1822–1841.

Johari, K., Ashrafi, F., Zali, A., Ashayeri, H., Fabbro, F., & Zanini, S. (2013). Grammatical deficits in bilingual Azari-Farsi patients with Parkinson's disease. *Journal of Neurolinguistics, 26*, 22–30.

Kearns, K. P. (1985). Response elaboration training for patient initiated utterances. In R. H. Brookshire (Ed.), *Clinical aphasiology* (pp. 196–204). Minneapolis, MN: BRK.

Kempler, D., Almor, A., & MacDonald, M. C. (1998). Teasing apart the contribution of memory and language impairments in Alzheimer's disease: An online study of sentence comprehension. *American Journal of Speech-Language Pathology, 7*(1), 61–67.

Kempler, D., & Goral, M. (2008). Language and dementia: Neuropsychological aspects. *Annual Review of Applied Linguistics, 28*, 73–90.

Kiernan, B., & Swisher, L. (1990). The initial learning of novel English words: Two single-subject experiments with minority language children. *Journal of Speech and Hearing Research, 33*, 707–716.

Kiran, S., & Iakupova, R. (2011). Understanding the relationship between language proficiency, language impairment and rehabilitation: Evidence from a case study. *Clinical Linguistics & Phonetics, 25*(6–7), 565–583.

Kiran, S., Roberts, P., Gitterman, M., Goral, M., & Obler, L. K. (2012). What do we know about assessing language impairment in bilingual aphasia? In M. R. Gitterman, M. Goral, & L. K. Obler (Eds.), *Aspects of multilingual aphasia* (pp. 35–51). Bristol, UK: Multilingual Matters.

Koenig, O., Thomas-Antérion, C., & Laurent, B. (1999). Procedural learning in Parkinson's disease: Intact and impaired cognitive components. *Neuropsychologia*, *37*, 1103–1109.

Kohnert, K. (2004). Cognitive and cognate-based treatments for bilingual aphasia: A case study. *Brain and Language*, *91*(3), 294–302.

Kohnert, K. (2012). Processing skills in early sequential bilinguals. In B. Goldstein (Ed.), *Bilingual language development & disorders in Spanish–English speakers* (pp. 95–112). Baltimore, MD: Brookes.

Kohnert, K., & Derr, A. (2004). Language intervention with bilingual children. In B. Goldstein (Ed.), *Bilingual language development and disorders in Spanish–English speakers* (pp. 315–343). Baltimore: Brookes.

Kohnert, K., Windsor, J., & Yim, D. (2006). Do language-based processing tasks separate children with language impairment from typical bilinguals? *Learning Disabilities Research & Practice*, *21*(1), 19–29.

Kohnert, K., Yim, D., Nett, K., Kan, P. F., & Duran, L. (2005). Intervention with linguistically diverse preschool children: A focus on developing home language(s). *Language, Speech, and Hearing Services in Schools*, *36*(3), 251–263.

Kotz, S. A. (2009). A critical review of ERP and fMRI evidence on L2 syntactic processing. *Brain and Language*, *109*(2), 68–74.

Kroll, J. F., & Bialystok, E. (2013). Understanding the consequences of bilingualism for language processing and cognition. *Journal of Cognitive Psychology*, *25*(5), 497–514.

Leonard, L. B. (1998). *Children with specific language impairment*. Cambridge, MA: MIT Press.

Leonard, L. B., Sabbadini, L., Leonard, J. S., & Volterra, V. (1987). Specific language impairment in children: A cross-linguistic study. *Brain and Language*, *32*, 233–252.

Linck, J. A., Kroll, J. F., & Sunderman, G. (2009). Losing access to the native language while immersed in a second language: Evidence for the role of inhibition in second-language learning. *Psychological Science*, *20*(12), 1507–1515.

Liu, H., Hu, Z., Guo, T., & Peng, D. (2010). Speaking words in two languages with one brain: Neural overlap and dissociation. *Brain Research*, *1316*, 75–82.

Lorenzen, B., & Murray, L. L. (2008). Bilingual aphasia: A theoretical and clinical review. *American Journal of Speech-Language Pathology*, *17*(3), 299–317.

McGlinchey-Berroth, R., Milberg, W. P., Verfaellie, M., Alexander, M., & Kilduff, P. T. (1993). Semantic processing in the neglected visual field: Evidence from a lexical decision task. *Cognitive Neuropsychology*, *10*(1), 79–108.

MacSwan, J., & Rolstad, K. (2005). Modularity and the facilitation effect: Psychological mechanisms of transfer in bilingual students. *Hispanic Journal of Behavioral Sciences*, *27*(2), 224–243.

Mancilla-Martinez, J., Kieffer, M. J., Biancarosa, G., Christodoulou, J. A., & Snow, C. E. (2011). Investigating English reading comprehension growth in adolescent language minority learners: some insights from the simple view. *Reading and Writing*, *24*(3), 339–354.

Meguro, K., L., Senaha, M., Caramelli, P., Ishizaki, J., Chubacci, R. Y. S., Meguro, M., Ambo, H., Nitrini, R., & Yamadori, A. (2003). Language deterioration in four Japanese-Portuguese bilingual patients with Alzheimer's disease: A trans-cultural study of Japanese elderly immigrants in Brazil. *Psychogeriatrics*, *3*, 63–68.

Mendez, M. F., Perryman, K. M., Pontón, M. O., & Cummings, J. L. (1999). Bilingualism and dementia. *The Journal of Neuropsychiatry and Clinical Neurosciences*, *11*, 411–412.

Meschyan, G., & Hernandez, A. E. (2006). Impact of language proficiency and orthographic transparency on bilingual word reading: An fMRI investigation. *NeuroImage*, *29*(4), 1135–1140.

Moreno, E. M., Rodríguez-Fornells, A., & Laine, M. (2008). Event-related potentials (ERPs) in the study of bilingual language processing. *Journal of Neurolinguistics*, *21*, 477–508.

Morgan, G., Restrepo, M. A., & Auza, A. (2009). Variability in the grammatical profiles of Spanish-speaking children with specific language impairment. *Hispanic Child Languages: Typical and Impaired Development, 50,* 283–302.

Morgan, G. P., Restrepo, M. A., & Auza, A. (2013). Comparison of Spanish morphology in monolingual and Spanish–English bilingual children with and without language impairment. *Bilingualism: Language and Cognition, 16*(3), 578–596.

Muñoz, M., & Marquardt, T. (2003). Picture naming and identification in bilingual speakers of Spanish and English with and without aphasia. *Aphasiology, 17*(12), 1115–1132.

Muñoz, M. L., Marquardt, T. P., & Copeland, G. (1999). A comparison of the codeswitching patterns of aphasic and neurologically normal bilingual speakers of English and Spanish. *Brain and Language, 66*(2), 249–274.

Murray, L. L. (2008). Language and Parkinson's Disease. *Annual Review of Applied Linguistics, 28,* 113–127.

Murray, L. L. (2012). Attention and other cognitive deficits in aphasia: Presence and relation to language and communication measures. *American Journal of Speech-Language Pathology, 21,* 51–64.

National Stroke Foundation. (2010). *Clinical guidelines for acute stroke management.* Melbourne, Australia: The Foundation. Available at: https://informme.org.au/guidelines/clinical-guidelines-for-stroke-management-2010

Nebes, R. D., Martin, D. C., & Horn, L. C. (1984). Sparing of semantic memory in Alzheimer's disease. *Journal of Abnormal Psychology, 93*(3), 321–330.

Neville, H., & Mills, D. L. (1997). Epigenesis of language. *Mental Retardation and Developmental Disabilities Research Reviews, 3,* 282–292.

Norton, A., Zipse, L., Marchina, S., & Schlaug, G. (2009). Melodic intonation therapy. *Annals of the New York Academy of Sciences, 1169*(1), 431–436.

Ober, B. A., Shenaut, G. K., & Reed, B. R. (1995). Assessment of associative relations in Alzheimer's disease: Evidence for preservation of semantic memory. *Aging, Neuropsychology, and Cognition, 2*(4), 254–267.

Owens, R. E., Metz, D. E., & Hass, A. (2000). *Introduction to communication disorders: A lifespan perspective.* Needham Heights: Allyn and Bacon.

Paap, K. R., & Greenberg, Z. I. (2013). There is no coherent evidence for a bilingual advantage in executive processing. *Cognitive Psychology, 66*(2), 232–258.

Paap, K. R., Johnson, H. A., & Sawi, O. (2015). Bilingual advantages in executive functioning either do not exist or are restricted to very specific and undetermined circumstances. *Cortex, 69,* 265–278.

Paap, K. R., & Sawi, O. (2014). Bilingual advantages in executive functioning: Problems in convergent validity, discriminant validity, and the identification of the theoretical constructs. *Frontiers in Psychology, 5*(962), 1–15. doi: 10.3389/fpsyg.2014.00962.

Paradis, J. (2005). Grammatical morphology in children learning English as a second language: implications of similarities with specific language impairment. *Language, Speech and Hearing Services in Schools, 36,* 172–187.

Paradis, M. (1988). Recent developments in studies of agrammatism: Their import for the assessment of bilingual aphasia. *Journal of Neurolinguistics, 3,* 127–160.

Paradis, M. (1989). La lateralización cerebral en los bilingües: ¡Basta por favor! *Investigaciones Psicológicas, 7,* 95–105.

Paradis, M. (1990). Language lateralization in bilinguals: Enough already! *Brain and Language, 39*(4), 576–586.

Paradis, M. (1996). Selective deficit in one language is not a demonstration of different anatomical representation: Comments on Gomez-Tortosa et al. (1995). *Brain and Language, 54*(1), 170–173.

Paradis, M. (1998). Language and communication in multilinguals. In B. Stemmer & H. Whitaker (Eds.), *Handbook of neurolinguistics* (pp. 417–430). San Diego, CA: Academic Press.

Paradis, M. (2001). The need for awareness of aphasia symptoms in different languages. *Journal of Neurolinguistics, 14*(2), 85–91.

Paradis, M. (2008). Bilingualism and neuropsychiatric disorders. *Journal of Neurolinguistics, 21,* 199–230.

Paradis, M., & Goldblum, M. C. (1989). Selective crossed aphasia in a trilingual aphasic patient followed by reciprocal antagonism. *Brain and Language*, *36*(1), 62–75.

Paradis, M., & Libben, G. (1987). *The assessment of bilingual aphasia*. Hillsdale, NJ: Lawrence Erlbaum Associates.

Paradis, M., & Libben, G. (2014). *The assessment of bilingual aphasia*. New York: Psychology Press.

Paradis, J., Schneider, P., & Duncan, T. S. (2013). Discriminating children with language impairment among English-language learners from diverse first-language backgrounds. *Journal of Speech, Language, and Hearing Research*, *56*(3), 971–981.

Pearson, B. Z., Fernández, S. C., & Oller, D. K. (1993). Lexical development in bilingual infants and toddlers: Comparison to monolingual norms. *Language Learning*, *43*(1), 93–120.

Peña, E., & Iglesias, A. (1992). The application of dynamic methods to language assessment: A nonbiased procedure. *The Journal of Special Education*, *26*(3), 269–280.

Perani, D., Dehaene, S., Grassi, F., Cohen, L., Cappa, S. F., Dupoux, E., Fazio, F., & Mehler, J. (1996). Brain processing of native and foreign languages. *Neuroreport*, *7*(15), 2439–2444.

Perozzi, J. A. (1985). A pilot study of language facilitation for bilingual language handicapped children: Theoretical and intervention implications. *Journal of Speech and Hearing Disorders*, *50*, 403–406.

Perozzi, J. A., & Chavez-Sanchez, M. L. (1992). The effect of instruction in L1 on receptive acquisition of L2 for bilingual children with language delay. *Language, Speech, and Hearing Services in the Schools*, *23*, 348–352.

Pihko, E., Mickos, A., Kujala, T., Pihlgren, A., Westman, M., Alku, P., & Korkman, M. (2007). Group intervention changes brain activity in bilingual language-impaired children. *Cerebral Cortex*, *17*(4), 849–858.

Pulvermüller, F., Neininger, B., Elbert, T., Mohr, B., Rockstroh, B., Koebbel, P., & Taub, E. (2001). Constraint-induced therapy of chronic aphasia after stroke. *Stroke*, *32*(7), 1621–1626.

Purdy, M. (2002). Executive function ability in persons with aphasia. *Aphasiology*, *16*(4–6), 549–557.

Restrepo, M. A. (1998). Identifiers of predominantly Spanish-speaking children with language impairment. *Journal of Speech, Language, and Hearing Research*, *41*(6), 1398–1411.

Restrepo, M. A. (2003). Spanish language skills in bilingual children with specific language impairment. In S. Montrul & F. Ordoñez (Eds.), *Linguistic Theory and Language Development in Hispanic Languages: Papers from the 5th Hispanic Linguistics Symposium and the 4th Conference on the Acquisition of Spanish and Portuguese* (pp. 365–374). Somerville, MA: Cascadilla Press.

Restrepo, M. A., Castilla, A. P., Schwanenflugel, P. J., Neuharth-Pritchett, S., Hamilton, C. E., & Arboleda, A. (2010). Effects of a supplemental Spanish oral language program on sentence length, complexity, and grammaticality in Spanish-speaking children attending English-only preschools. *Language, Speech, and Hearing Services in Schools*, *41*(1), 3–13.

Restrepo, M. A., Morgan, G. P., & Thompson, M. S. (2013). The efficacy of a vocabulary intervention for dual-language learners with language impairment. *Journal of Speech, Language, and Hearing Research*, *56*(2), 748–765.

Rice, M. L., & Wexler, K. (1996). Tense over time: The persistence of optional infinitives in English in children with SLI. In A. Stringfellow, D. Cahana-Amitay, E. Hughes, & A. Zukowski (Eds.), *Proceedings of the 20th Annual Boston University Conference on Language Development*. Somerville, MA: Cascadilla Press.

Roberts, P. M. (2008). Issues in assessment and treatment in bilingual and multicultural populations. In R. Chapey (Eds.), *Language intervention strategies in adult aphasia* (5th ed.) (pp. 245–276). Philadelphia, PA: Lippincott, Williams & Wilkins.

Roberts, P., & Kiran, S. (2007). Assessment of bilingual aphasia and bilingual anomia. In A. Ardila & E. Ramos (Eds.), *Speech and language disorders in bilinguals* (pp. 119–131). New York: Nova Science.

Rogers, T. T., Ivanoiu, A., Patterson, K., & Hodges, J. R. (2006). Semantic memory in Alzheimer's disease and the frontotemporal dementias: A longitudinal study of 236 patients. *Neuropsychology*, *20*(3), 319–335.

Ryan, C. (2013). *Language Use in the United States: 2011 American community survey reports.* Washington, DC: U.S. Census Bureau.

Salvatierra, J., Rosselli, M., Acevedo, A., & Duara, R. (2007). Verbal fluency in bilingual Spanish/ English Alzheimer's disease patients. *American Journal of Alzheimer's Disease & Other Dementias, 22*(3), 190–201.

Schweizer, T. A., Ware, J., Fischer, C. E., Craik, F. I. M., & Bialystok, E. (2012). Bilingualism as a contributor to cognitive reserve: Evidence from brain atrophy in Alzheimer's disease. *Cortex, 48,* 991–996.

Siu, C. T. S., & Ho, C. S. H. (2015). Cross-language transfer of syntactic skills and reading comprehension among young Cantonese-English bilingual students. *Reading Research Quarterly, 50*(3), 313–336.

Smyk, E., Restrepo, M. A., Gorin, J. S., & Gray, S. (2013). Development and validation of the Spanish–English Language proficiency scale (SELPS). *Language, Speech, and Hearing Services in Schools, 44*(3), 252–265.

Squires, K. E., Lugo-Neris, M. J., Peña, E. D., Bedore, L. M., Bohman, T. M., & Gillam, R. B. (2014). Story retelling by bilingual children with language impairments and typically developing controls. *International Journal of Language & Communication Disorders, 49*(1), 60–74.

Tabors, P. O. (2008). *One child, two languages: A guide for early childhood educators of children learning English as a second language.* Baltimore: Paul H. Brookes.

Thordardottir, E. (2015). Proposed diagnostic procedures for use in bilingual and cross-linguistic contexts. In S. Armon-Lotem, J. de Jong, & N. Meir (Eds.), *Assessing multilingual children: Disentangling bilingualism from language impairment* (pp. 331–358). Bristol, UK: Multilingual Matters.

Tomblin, B. J., Zhang, X., & Buckwalter, P. (1997, May). *A statistical expectation for the recovery rate of SLI from kindergarten to second grade.* Paper presented at the 18th Annual Symposium on Research in Child Language Disorders, Madison, WI.

Tomblin, J. B., Zhang, X., Buckwalter, P., & O'Brien, M. (2003). The stability of primary language disorder: Four years after kindergarten diagnosis. *Journal of Speech Language Hearing Research, 46*(6), 1283–1296.

United Nations, Department of Economic and Social Affairs, Population Division (2013). *World Population Ageing 2013.* Retrieved from ST/ESA/SER.A/348.

Vasić, N. (2006). *Pronoun comprehension in agrammatic aphasia: The structure and use of linguistic knowledge* (Vol. 140). Utrecht: LOT.

Wald, I. (1961). *Problema afazii poliglotov.* Moskova: Voprosy Kliniki I Patofiziologii Afazi.

Xue, G., Dong, Q., Jin, Z., Zhang, L., & Wang, Y. (2004). An fMRI study with semantic access in low proficiency second language learners. *NeuroReport, 15*(5), 791–796.

Zanini, S., Tavano, A., & Fabbro, F. (2010). Spontaneous language production in bilingual Parkinson's disease patients: Evidence of greater phonological, morphological and syntactic impairments in native language. *Brain and Language, 113,* 84–89.

Zanini, S., Tavano, A., Vorano, L., Schiavo, F., Gigli, G. L., Aglioti, S. M., & Fabbro, F. (2004). Greater syntactic impairments in native language in bilingual Parkinsonian patients. *Journal of Neurology, Neurosurgery, and Psychiatry, 75,* 1678–1681.

Index

References to tables are denoted by the use of **bold**. References to figures are denoted by the use of *italics*. References to notes are denoted by the use of "n."

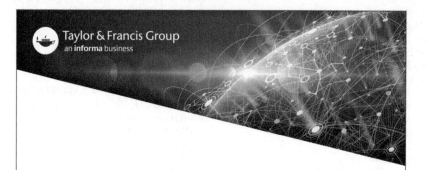